THE EASY WAY TO Good Cooking

THE EASY WAY

TO Good Cooking

By GWEN FRENCH

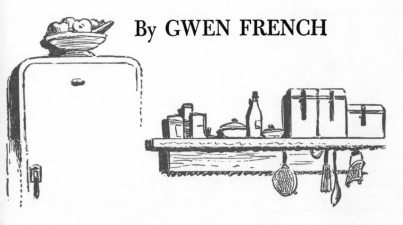

GROSSET & DUNLAP *Publishers* NEW YORK

PRINTED IN THE UNITED STATES OF AMERICA

FOR PETER . . .

Who was once a boy,

and is now a man . . .

and who urged me to write this book

Acknowledgments...

If this book pleases you ... helps you ... or inspires you in any way, join with me in the profound thanks due:

My mother, Mrs. Grace Crane Smith, that fabulous and inspiring woman of unlimited horizons, whose warm interest in home-making taught me all I know ...

My clever technical adviser, Mrs. Margaret Deeds Murphy, graduate Home Economist and one of New York's outstanding food experts, whose painstakingly thought-out suggestions have added to each chapter of this book ...

My staunch and attractive aid, Mrs. Helen S. King, of Columbia University, who has repeatedly sacrificed pleasant week ends to putting unreadable pages of my manuscript into clear and beautiful shape ...

My husband, Stuyvesant LeRoy French, who has not only supplied moral support and working equipment I needed, but that ever important "male" point of view ...

My beloved Peter, who repeatedly shooed his friends away from the house, so I might have quiet to work ...

The delightful and distinguished officers of Little, Brown and Company, whose enthusiasm, interest, and rare understanding have made a joy of work on this book ...

To all these, thanks from my heart.

G. C. F.

Preface

Gentle Reader, this is a cook book like no other cook book you've ever read. I know. I've searched for one like it. It is the book which I, as a bride and a beginning cook, wished someone had written for me.

It is a book to take the place of twenty.

A book to save time.

A book to make all cooking easy.

A book to take the hokum and mystery out of cooking.

A book to save you heartaches and headaches, burned fingers and burned cakes.

Most important, it will make you a *good* cook, *fast*.

It is *not* going to teach you everything under the sun. It will *not* include every single recipe you've ever heard of. It is not an encyclopedia.

But it *is* going to show you all the basic methods you will need for *a whole long lifetime of cooking*.

Take one chapter at a time. Make, if you wish, only *one* sample dish from each Master Recipe. When you are through all the chapters, you will find most of the mystery has disappeared from cooking. You will understand all the chief "whys and wherefores" of what you are doing; you will be "at home" on your range.

Contents

THE EASY WAY TO Good Cooking

Anybody Can Cook

Anybody. Man, woman, or child. Anybody who can read, and who longs for good flavors in food. There is no mystery, no secret, no magic about it. All cooking is based on only a few simple main rules; and despite all the volumes and volumes which would lead you to think otherwise, cooking is really not hard at all.

The whole thing is somewhat like being in a foreign country: if you don't know the main roads, it is almost impossible to get where you want to go. But once you know the few basic thoroughfares, you can reach any point with the greatest of ease.

In the land of cooking, also, there are reliable main roads. And the purpose of this book is to show them to you.

There is one highway that leads to making all yeast breads, for example. Once you feel familiar on this thoroughfare, you can branch off into the byways of coffee rings, fancy buns, fruit and nut loaves, dinner or party rolls; all these being only slight variations from the main route.

There is another main highway to roasting birds, or meat, or any flesh. Once at home on this path, you can roast anything. The variations come from the individual flavor Nature put in the flesh, plus the flavor of any seasoning you add, plus the flavor of any stuffing or gravy or sauce you add. The results will be lusciously different in taste; yet you will have had to learn only the one route.

There are similar highways that lead to gravies, to sauces, to pies, to "jelled" salads and desserts, to practically any main group of cooked foods. So instead of learning to make some isolated, individual recipe, like a chocolate cake, you are here going to discover *the main highway to cake.* And thereafter, neither chocolate cake nor any other basic sort of cake will ever be a mystery to you.

This is the speedway to cooking.

The main highways are straight, easy to follow, reliable, basically timeless. And unless earth's products change flavor, or unless chemistry stops abiding by its own laws, the basic formulas will always remain the sure, main routes to cooking success.

All else is improvisation. All the thousands of intricate "new" recipes you see in newspaper columns, magazines, and tome after tome, are merely variations, trimmings. Look underneath the trimmings and you will find the same reliable old route . . . the Master Recipe, in a new dress. A slightly different seasoning is added . . . a different stuffing . . . a little wine added to a common sauce . . . or some woman who lacks a certain ingredient substitutes another, in an emergency . . . and you have the exciting "new recipes" which often become famous (and get printed in books), but are only variations from the old main route.

Such variation is fun. It makes you feel a little like God to take a few scrappy leftovers from your refrigerator and know what to do with them to create an exciting taste treat for your family. Or to take an unexciting piece of meat or fish and dress it up into such a savory dish that it brings your family running from all parts of the house. Once familiar with the main highways, you will be able to do this. For you will know what you can safely add to a sauce, a soup, a stew, a cake batter, a biscuit dough, a dressing . . . or what you can safely leave out. You will know where you must stick to the main route, and where you can branch off for some thrilling new byway of results.

At that moment, you will know the true, creative joy of cooking; you will be a real artist. Like the great chefs, you will be able to think up your own new dresses for the old, proven combinations. And best of all, you will no longer be tied to *any* cook book; you will be able to "cook out of your head."

CHAPTER II

Let's Look at Your Kitchen

First, what have you got to cook with?

Now, of course, it is possible to cook any time, anywhere, with almost anything. Or almost nothing. With few utensils, certainly. Often without even a stove. Ask any woodsman or fisherman, who fries his "catch" over logs by a stream. Ask a beach devotee, who broils steak over driftwood.

A young girl I once knew cooked for two years in a furnished room, with only a single-burner electric plate. Yet her omelets . . . or lobster Newburg, or fried chicken, or Irish stew . . . with a green salad and a good bakery's French pastry . . . made people prefer to dine with her than go out.

So, perfect equipment is not needed. Limited utensils, limited space, limited burners for cooking, do not mean you can't cook. You can become an *excellent* cook — however limited your quarters — if you stick to menus your facilities can handle.

Begin. Begin now . . . on even a one-burner plate . . . and you'll be that much ahead. And if you have a whole modern range to use, you'll be able to try everything.

A ONE- OR TWO-BURNER PLATE

On a one- or two-burner plate (gas, oil, or electric) you can do anything you could do on the surface burners of a range. This includes all foods which are boiled, stewed, simmered, steamed, fried, French-fried, sautéed, pot-roasted, pan-broiled. For example: you can pan-broil steak, chops, liver, fish, chicken, ham steaks. You can fry chicken, fish, ham, hash, bacon. You can cook croquettes or veal cutlets; make wonderful stews, pot roasts, chicken fricassees. You can sauté liver, onions, mushrooms. You can cook eggs many ways; boil, cream, or fry vegetables; make steamed or boiled puddings, stewed fruits, boiled custards; even jam, jelly, pickles. Though some people would say it couldn't be done, a dear friend of mine dry-roasts a whole, stuffed chicken in a "Dutch oven" on top of her stove; it's delicious every time. Indeed, with only these "surface burners" you could provide a family with meals for years. The examples given above cite only a few of hundreds of dishes you can prepare on a two-burner plate.

ADD A PORTABLE OVEN

Portable ovens cost little, being simply metal boxlike affairs, with an opening in the bottom, and usually a thermometer in the door. The opening fits over one of the burners of your plate, which then heats up the oven. When through using the oven, you remove it and store it out of the way. Naturally, these portable ovens cannot be as airtight, as perfect, as the oven of an insulated range, but they are far better than none. Get one, and in it you can bake cakes, pies, quick breads; casseroles of leftovers; chicken or meat pies with crusts; potatoes; even custard. The only thing these portable ovens will not do is *broil.*

SEPARATE BROILERS

Broilers of many types (and prices) are sold in the stores, to be used only for broiling steaks, chops, fish, chicken, etc. Perhaps you'll think one worth buying. If not, your best substitute for broiling is to "pan-broil." See Chapter X.

IF YOU HAVE A COMPLETE RANGE

Let's look over your range now, so you will know what each part does. (If you already know this, skip to Utensils, page 10.)

A complete range (gas, electric, oil, wood, or coal) will have:

Surface Burners (usually 3 or 4)

These are the burners (which usually look like round openings or plates) on top of your stove. On these, you prepare all food to be boiled, stewed, simmered, steamed, fried, French-fried, sautéed, fricasseed, pot-roasted, pan-broiled. Here you boil all liquids; make soups, gravies, sauces, chowders. On these burners you do everything except *bake*, or *broil*.

There should be a removable tray or other receptacle beneath these burners, to catch drippings. Look for this tray now. Clean it frequently.

A Baking and Roasting Oven

Open your oven door, and look for a heating unit *near or underneath the floor of oven*. This is the heating unit you will use to bake cakes, pies, casseroles, bread, custard, soufflé; also to bake a ham, or a fish; or to roast a piece of meat, or bird. (Don't ask me why they say "bake" a ham, and "roast" a turkey; I'll never know. Both are done by the same heating unit, in the same oven!)

Your oven should contain one or two sliding, removable racks or shelves, on which to place food while it is cooking. It should also be equipped with a dripping pan, or a large sheet of metal protecting the lower heating unit from drippings. A heating unit clogged with juices or boiled-over food will not give good heat. If there is no dripping pan, buy a large flat pan to use for this purpose. Or you may simply line the floor of the oven with a sheet of aluminum foil. It is easier to take out a pan and wash it, or to discard a soiled piece of aluminum foil, than it is to clean a clogged burner, or scour the oven floor.

A Broiling Unit

Look for a heating unit affixed close inside the roof of some drawer or closed cooking compartment of your stove.

In some ranges, this will be found to be a separate "broiling" compartment, having no other heating unit except the unit at roof, or *above* where food is to be cooked; such compartments are called "broilers."

Sometimes a broiling drawer or compartment is found directly below the baking oven; in this case the same unit used to make heat for the baking oven above may be used to make heat for the broiling compartment beneath.

In still other ranges, there is only one closed oven space; this will have a heating unit near the roof (used for broiling) and also a heating unit near the floor of oven space (used for baking.) You may turn on both heating units at once for the purpose of *preheating* your oven quickly; but when the food is put in to cook, you *must use only one* burner: the top one for broiling; the bottom one for baking.

Remember that for broiling, heat is *above* the food; for baking, heat *below*.

A Broiling Pan. Often a range is equipped with a broad, shallow, removable pan, which slides in and out of the broiling space of the oven, fitting into grooves in the wall, and adjustable to any desired height. If you do not have one, don't worry; you can use any shallow pan large enough to hold the meat you are broiling, and place this pan on one of the adjustable oven racks.

Your broiling pan should have a shallow rack which fits inside it; this keeps the food from resting in any fat or grease which may drip from it into pan during cooking. Best are the modern-range broiling racks which are almost solid sheets of metal, containing many slots, since such a rack helps prevent grease of steaks, chops, etc. from catching fire. However, lacking one of these, you may substitute a wire mesh rack, which can be bought in any store selling kitchen wares.

Heat Control Equipment for Oven

Your oven, if modern, will have *a thermostat* (or heat control valve) which you can set to the exact degree of heat you want. A good thermostat should maintain the precise degree of heat you've set, as long as you want it.

If you have no thermostat, look for a *thermometer* set in the oven door. This does not *control* heat, but merely indicates to you what temperature the inside of the oven is attaining. By watching the thermometer, and adjusting your heat volume up or down, you can maintain a fairly even temperature for baking.

If you have neither thermostat nor thermometer, *do* go buy *a portable oven thermometer* at a hardware store. This you hang or set inside the oven. It has one disadvantage: you have to open the oven door to see what the heat inside may be; and opening the door instantly changes the heat a bit. However, this is better than cooking entirely "by guess," and will save you much money in the end.

Variations in Heat of Ovens. You will note that most written or printed recipes say (for example): "Cook 20 to 30 minutes, or until done." This is written, not because the creator of the recipe does not know how long the food would take on her own range, but because she does not know how long it will take *on yours*. Ovens . . . and indeed whole ranges . . . vary in their speed of heating up, and in their maintenance of heat. This variation may be caused by many things:

(*a*) *The type of stove.* Whether gas, electric, oil, coal, or whatever. Some ranges heat far more quickly than others.

(*b*) *Whether oven is insulated.* In modern ranges, ovens are well insulated, thus becoming hot faster and holding heat better. In older ranges, insulation may be imperfect; and some ovens have no insulation at all.

(*c*) *Whether you have a thermostat.* Without one, your oven cannot be held to as perfectly constant a heat.

(*d*) *Whether your thermostat is accurate.* Many are slightly inaccurate; if you think yours is, get the Utility Company to come and test it, and set it correctly.

(*e*) *How many foods you have in the oven at once.* If only one dish or pan of food is set in the oven, it will cook more quickly than if a number of things are being cooked at one time. This is because the heat can circulate around one dish more freely and thoroughly.

(*f*) *Wind.* If your oven is in a cold, drafty room, the wind may retard the heating of the oven, and make it harder for the oven to maintain its heat.

(g) *Variation in fuel available.* Electric current, or the supply of gas from city gas lines, may vary in intensity, often dropping to a thinner supply at rush hours, when everybody is drawing upon it, as for Thanksgiving or Christmas dinners, etc.

Don't worry, however. With a few experiments, you will soon know the mannerisms of your own range perfectly!

UTENSILS

If you have inherited an established kitchen, you're all set. But if you are a bride, you will have to buy certain essential utensils, for preparing average meals. Fancy extra equipment you can add later. We are therefore giving two lists: one for starting equipment; one for luxuries to add as you go along.

Most of the items in the "starter set" (barring the heavy saucepans and frying pans) can be bought in the five-and-dime, so don't be alarmed.

And *do* spend enough money to get heavy-quality utensils, where they are specified. Thin, cheap utensils will cost you much money in the end, in burned foods!

STARTER SET

Pots and Pans

1 coffee maker (percolator, Silex, drip pot, or whatever)
1 teapot (glass, pottery, or enamel, preferably. Metal pots may give tea a metallic flavor)
3 or 4 sturdy saucepans, with lids (cast aluminum, copper, stainless steel, preferably. Enamel pans are cheaper, but often chip, and may allow foods to burn more easily. Get a variety of sizes: ½ pint, 1 pint, 1 quart, 2 quarts)
1 "Dutch oven" with lid, and rack or trivet inside (cast aluminum)
1 roasting pan (metal or enamel, oblong or oval, with sides 1 to 3 inches deep, to catch juices. Should be big enough to hold an entire ham, turkey, or chicken). Also, metal or wire rack, to fit inside roasting pan
1 double boiler (metal, enamel, or glass)
1 7 or 8 inch skillet, or frying pan (iron, cast aluminum, or copper)

1 10 or 11 inch heavy frying pan, with lid (cast aluminum, or iron)
1 or 2 pie plates (oven glass, aluminum, tin, or enamel. Most pie recipes fill
an 8 or 9 inch pie plate. However, pie plates come in both smaller and
larger sizes)
1 8 x 8 x 2 inch square cake pan (aluminum preferably; tin is also good)
1 or 2 muffin pans (aluminum or tin; these double as pans for cup cakes;
get a size you like. The average cake or muffin recipe fills about 6 to 8 large
muffin cups, or 12 to 16 small ones)
2 8 or 9 inch layer-cake pans (aluminum or tin)
2 casserole dishes, with lids (oven glass or pottery; get one 8 or 9 inch size;
one 5 or 6 inch size)
1 set individual-size casserole dishes (oven glass or pottery)
1 set bowls, assorted sizes (glass, pottery, or aluminum. Small to large sizes
will be needed regularly for food preparation)

Tools Needed Constantly

1 metal standard measuring cup (marked for ¼, ½, ¾, ⅓, ⅔, 1 cup), for
measuring dry ingredients
1 glass standard measuring cup (marked same way) for liquids
1 set standard measuring spoons (necessary for accurate measuring of ¼, ½,
1 teaspoon; 1 tablespoon)
1 wooden board (to knead bread on; to cut vegetables and meat on)
1 fruit juicer (get the Dime Store kind first; add a fancy one later)
1 rotary eggbeater (pay the money to get a sturdy, good-quality hand beater
now, at hardware store; add an electric mixer later)
Tongs (useful for turning foods without piercing them)
1 grater *with four sides* (to permit grating of foods *in four sizes*)
1 pair kitchen scissors, with long blades
1 potato masher (mashes many other things besides potatoes)
1 spatula
1 pancake turner (doubles as egg, fish, meat, meat-patty flipper)
1 long-handled large spoon (to use when basting meat, deep-frying, etc.)
1 slotted spoon, stainless steel (to remove foods from liquids)
1 long-handled fork
1 paring knife (you'll use it constantly; get good stainless steel)
1 knife sharpener (you'll need it repeatedly)
1 long knife (cuts bread, slices meat. Get good steel)
Several large mixing spoons; at least one wooden one
1 wire whisk (good for mixing gravies, sauces)
1 pastry blender (to use for cutting shortening into dry ingredients)
Pastry cloth, if desired (to cover board, when rolling dough)
1 rolling pin (to roll biscuits, pastry. Also useful for pounding lumps out of
sugar)
Rolling-pin cover, if desired (helps keep dough from sticking to pin)
1 apple corer, with peeling slot (peels nearly all hard vegetables)
1 can opener (get the kind that doesn't leave jagged edges)
1 bottle opener

1 flour sifter (can't make light cakes, muffins without it!)
1 meat grinder (essential for making good use of many leftovers. Get one with attachments for grinding food in two or three different sizes)
1 chopping knife (a curved blade, with handle over it, for chopping raw vegetables, other foods)
1 inexpensive wooden bowl (to chop food in; can double as a wooden salad bowl)
1 colander, or large strainer
1 small strainer, fine mesh
A meat thermometer (helps in determining "doneness" of roast meat)
A deep-frying thermometer (only accurate test of hot fat, for deep-frying)
A candy thermometer (for boiled frostings, candy)
Deep-frying kettle (6 to 7 inches wide, 5 to 6 inches deep) with wire frying basket to fit inside it, if you are going to do much deep-frying

To Add Later, as Needed

Automatic toaster
Waffle iron
Electric mixer
Griddle (there are iron or cast-aluminum griddles to use over a surface burner of stove, as well as electric griddles)
A ring mold, or two (for jellied desserts, jellied salads. These come in 1 pint, 1 quart, 1½ quart sizes)
A steamed pudding mold (must have tight-fitted lid)
Individual-size metal molds (make pretty, individual molded salads or desserts)
Individual-size pie plates (very handy for making small meat pies, out of leftovers)
Individual custard cups
Cookie cutters (these come in many shapes)
1 cookie sheet, aluminum (the easiest thing to bake cookies on)
1 carving set (large knife, fork, knife sharpener; this set should last a good lifetime; invest in one of fine quality steel which will sharpen well)
1 pepper grinder (if you like freshly ground pepper)
1 or 2 pipkins, if desired (tiny, doll-size saucepans, to use for melting small amounts of butter, etc.)
Cake decorator set (metal tube, plus various attachments, for putting fancily shaped frosting on cake)
1 pressure cooker, if desired (but if you buy this, follow recipes which come from manufacturer of pressure cooker, not recipes in this book; pressure cooking requires entirely different timing)

CHAPTER III

What's in Your Pantry?

Our grandmothers had pantries . . . or at least huge grocery closets . . . or, in country houses, "lean-tos" where food stores were kept.

They needed them. There was no supermarket at the next corner, then. No home freezer, housing delicious fresh things. No chrome-trimmed modern refrigerator to hold foods dewy fresh. In your grandmother's pantry, she stored everything she would have to make a whole winter's meals: lard from the pig; flour, cereal, grains; sugar, pickles, spices, dried herbs; dried fruits and vegetables; dried, smoked, or salted meats; potatoes, apples, cheese, and a few of her own special "preserves." This was her "reservoir," the storehouse from which she made meal after meal.

Today, though most of our foods are kept under refrigeration and the "pantry" has shrunk to perhaps one small kitchen shelf, still that small space remains the "magic spot" of the kitchen. It is from that shelf (with its flour, sugar, salt, shortening, herbs, seasonings, and flavorings) that you work the magic of creating "something from nothing"; of making a small tin of fish or meat or fruit into a nourishing and beautiful dish; of whipping up a quick cake when company descends; of stretching a slim main course or dessert when Junior comes home from school with guests. Like your grandmother, you will need certain staples regularly at hand. And these are the supplies your shelf should hold, regularly:

STAPLE DRY GOODS

General purpose flour, vitamin-enriched	5 lb. bag
Cake flour (a lighter texture)	1 box
Baking powder (all recipes in this book are written for "double-acting" baking powder, as this is to-day's most popular kind. If you use any other, *double* the amount of baking powder the recipes here call for)	1 can
Baking soda	1 box
Rice (white, brown, or wild, according to your taste)	1 box
Noodles (wide, thin, or fancy shapes, as desired)	1 package
Macaroni (there are many varieties)	1 package
Sugar, granulated (for general daily use)	5 lb. bag
Sugar, confectioners' (for frostings, candy) marked "XXXX"	1 lb. box
Sugar, brown (for baking ham, baked beans, some cakes, some frostings)	1 lb. box
Sugar, powdered (to sprinkle on fresh fruit, etc.)	1 lb. box
Raisins, seedless (for desserts, hot breads, cakes)	1 box
Shelled nuts (for cakes, puddings, garnishes, muffins)	½ lb. can or jar
Coffee (get a good brand, and the right grind for your coffee maker)	1 lb.
Tea	½ lb.
Potatoes (store in cool, dry place)	5–10 lb.
Yellow onions (used in many main dishes and salads)	3 lb.
Fruit-flavored gelatine, or unflavored gelatine	1 or 2 boxes
Granulated yeast (if you like homemade bread)	1 or 2 packages

STAPLE SEASONINGS, NEEDED OFTEN

Table salt (buy iodized salt if you live where it is difficult to buy fish. This salt supplies the iodine fish would normally supply in your diet)	1 box
Black pepper (many people prefer to grind their own pepper fresh, for each occasion. If you do, buy a small pepper grinder. Otherwise, buy ground)	1 can (ground)
Paprika (a very bland red pepper with almost no taste, but pretty for garnishing. One man I know remarked that he considered paprika on food as important as lipstick on a woman)	1 can
Mustard, prepared (to spread on meats, sandwiches)	1 jar
Mustard, dry (a powder, very hot, to use in cooking)	1 box or can
Vinegar, cider (the usual vinegar for salad dressings)	1 pt.
Vinegar, tarragon (flavored with tarragon, not so sharp)	1 pt. if desired

Salad oil	1 pt. or 1 qt.
Thyme (gives good flavor to stews, soups)	1 small box
Sage (used in chicken or turkey stuffing)	1 small box
Bay leaves (laurel) (used in stews, soups)	1 small box
Dried celery leaves (dry your own in oven; good for soups, stews)	
Fresh parsley (buy or grow in garden or window box; adds both flavor and glamour to many dishes)	
Cinnamon, powdered } Nutmeg, powdered } used in spice cakes, fruit cakes, Cloves, powdered } pumpkin pie, other spicy dishes Ginger, powdered }	1 small box each
Cloves, whole (used when baking a ham, and for other dishes)	1 small box
Vanilla (needed in almost all puddings, cakes)	1 bottle
Almond extract } Maple extract } good for flavoring frostings, cakes Walnut extract }	as desired
Curry powder (makes a curry sauce for any occasion; see under white sauce, p. 249)	1 small can
Worcestershire sauce (used in gravy, soup, meat pies)	1 bottle
Bottled thick meat extract (makes hurry-up gravy)	1 bottle
Bottled gravy flavoring (adds color, flavor)	1 bottle

NOTE: For additional spices, see p. 505.

STAPLE PERISHABLE FOODS, NEEDED REGULARLY

Milk, bottled or evaporated (needed in cakes, puddings, cream pies, biscuits, bread or rolls, and for all cream soups or sauces. Evaporated milk is plain milk from which a large part of the water has been evaporated. This gives it a slightly flat taste, which is helped by adding a pinch of salt. To use evaporated milk in place of bottled milk, combine 1 part evaporated milk with an equal part of water. Evaporated milk is rich and is excellent for cream sauces or soups. It is not recommended, however, for custards or puddings in which the difference of taste would be noticeable)

Butter (or margarine)

Vegetable shortening (to use in baking, frying)

Eggs (buy fresh eggs, not storage eggs; but color of shell makes no difference in egg's value as nourishment; and a medium-sized egg contains practically as much food value as a large one)

Salad greens (there are many kinds to choose from; look in your market)

Fresh fruit, vegetables (always keep some on hand)

Mayonnaise, cooked salad dressing, French dressing (if you don't make your own)

Cheeses (to eat; to use in baking; to use in salads)

TINNED OR PACKAGED RESERVES

There are many inexpensive aids to quick meals on your grocer's shelves: delicious biscuit, muffin, cake, and pie mixes, ready-made except for adding water or milk; and gelatin desserts, to some of which you add only water; tinned meats, soups, fish, vegetables, cooked and ready to heat.

Many of these prepared, packaged foods are good to eat just as they are (once prepared per directions on package), and they make quick emergency meals. They are good to have on your shelf.

The woman of imagination, however, will do something extra with them . . . something that lifts them out of the monotonous class . . . even if it be only to add a little unexpected seasoning to the soup, or to bake the tinned hash in a pie-crust roll, or to toss together a curry or Newburg sauce for the tinned shrimp. These small touches make all the difference, and do not take long. The meal is then no longer just a meal of canned goods.

Wherever such foods are recommended in this book, directions for treating them are included.

QUICK-FROZEN FOODS

A marvelously tempting variety of quick-frozen foods now abounds, in all stores. If you have deep-freezing accommodations, try them. They are time-savers, easy to fix, and give "out-of-season" zest to menus.

Just remember this: *always read package directions carefully* before preparing food. The frozen food industry is in rapid flux; new products appear daily; new methods, also. In general, at this writing, if food is frozen raw, you may thaw it and then cook by any recipes for unfrozen food. Precooked frozen foods (such as waffles, meat pies, "French fries") usually thaw while being reheated. Frozen vegetables can be cooked without being thawed; see MR #39. To be safe, however, read the latest directions, on each package.

CHAPTER IV

How to Plan a Meal

Where do you begin?

Alice in Wonderland gave the all-time answer to this so often puzzling question. She said, "Why, begin *at the beginning,* of course!"

But what is the "beginning" of planning a meal?

I say: Begin with *the meat.*

Once you have chosen the meat, you can easily think of the vegetables, the salad, the dessert you know would taste superb with it. Naturally, you will try to choose vegetables which are in season, procurable, not too high-priced; and which will make for a "balanced" diet, vitamin-wise. (I am going to give you an easy short cut to this, in a moment.)

Don't try to visualize all your meals for a week, if you are a beginner. That will come easily, later on. Plan for one day. Think of the meat, the vegetables, the dessert you want . . . and go look for it. If what you want is not procurable, you can still change your plan at the store. If you feel completely swamped by this whole project, simply turn to the "Twenty-eight Days' Menus" at the back of this book. These will carry you through an entire month. And at the end of that time, if you want to repeat, *repeat.*

Many good meals bear repeating, so don't be dismayed. The old stand-by of steak, fried onions, salad, and apple pie could be given to most husbands once a week (budget permitting!) and they would be delighted. This is said to be the meal most American men like most. Your husband may be different. But you will soon discover what his favorite likes and dislikes are; you will soon know how to fix them just the way he likes them; and best of all, you can repeat his favorites often.

MASTER PLAN FOR A MEAL

Here is the simplest way I know to plan a meal. It takes care of both appetite appeal and vitamins.

So much has already been written about our vitamin needs in foods that you are no doubt well versed in this subject. If not, there are available many vitamin and calorie charts, such as that published by the Department of Agriculture. (*The Composition of Food, Raw, Processed and Prepared,* USDA Agricultural Handbook #8, 354. Order from Superintendent of Documents, Government Printing Office, Washington 25, D.C.)

The method of planning meals proposed below, however, covers the same needs, and is simpler.

Just plan *every* meal (even breakfast, even the contents of a lunch box) so it includes at least *one* food from *each* of the groups below:

INCLUDE:	*CHOOSE FROM:*	
1 protein	Meat, fish, fowl	
	Cheese	
	Eggs	
	Legumes	
	Nuts	
1 starch	Potatoes	
	Macaroni, noodles	
	Rice	
	Cereals or grains	
	Flour or meal	
	Anything made of flour, such as cake, pie, bread, rolls, biscuits, muffins, waffles, pancakes, fritters, doughnuts	
Fruit and/or **vegetables;** preferably both	*Red or Yellow*	*Green*
(Choose some raw, some cooked. Some red, some yellow, some green. An assortment of nature's colors insures an assortment of vitamins!)	Oranges	Green grapes
	Grapefruit	Cucumbers
	Lemons	Celery
	Pineapple	Parsley
	Peaches	Spinach
	Apricots	Lettuce

Red or Yellow	Green
Pears	Endive
Bananas	Swiss chard
Melons	Kale
Grapes, red	Beet tops
Plums	Turnip tops
Prunes	Cabbage, green
Tomatoes	Broccoli
Carrots	Any leafy vegetable
Pumpkin, squash	String beans
Beets	Lima beans
Yellow turnip	Peas
Cabbage, red	Peppers, green
Peppers, red	

A little fat
Butter, margarine
Lard, vegetable shortening used in cooking
Salad oils, or oil in mayonnaise
Edible fat on meat

A little sweet
This does not necessarily mean rich desserts or candy. There is natural sugar in most fruits, in many vegetables. Also, in most meals, some sugar is used for tea, coffee, cocoa, or in cooking

Milk
(or cream, or cheese)
Children should get 1 quart daily; adults 1 pint daily. Some of this may be got through use of milk in cooking (cream soups, sauces, puddings)

NOTE: Each person should have *1 egg per day* (if not at breakfast then in egg sauce, a pudding, custard, omelet, soufflé, or a cake containing a large number of eggs).

Each person must eat at least *one whole-grain or enriched flour product per day* (cereal, or dark bread, or foods made with vitamin-enriched flour). To get the full value of grain, however, you should eat the darker breads, made with the whole kernel.

Now the above Master Plan, as you see, gives endless choices, but it is not difficult to work out at all.

Take dinner . . . any dinner.

Choose a meat. Add a starch (probably potatoes). Add some hot vegetable; or two, if you wish, like carrots (red) and peas (green). Your salad provides raw greens, with either fruit or other vegetables to go with it; choose these in varied colors, and the more raw ones, the better, since any cooked fruit or vegetable is bound to lose a little of its vitamin value through the cooking process. Your salad dressing will doubtless provide the "fat," even if you have used no butter on bread and no fat in the cooking. Your dessert might be fruit (if you have not used fruit in the salad course). Or it might be a pudding with milk content. Or it might be crackers and cheese. Or cake. Or anything you like. Once you have provided the protein, the starch, the assorted vegetables or fruits, you may "play around" in any way you wish with the rest of the meal. Only do try not to serve too many starches, nor indeed too much of any one type of food. "Balancing" the diet means providing an *assortment*.

Look at breakfast, the favorite American breakfast:

Your oranges, or prunes, or tomato juice, provide the *fruit*. An egg and toast provide *protein* and *starch*. Butter will go on the toast, providing *fat*. *Sugar* will go in the coffee; also *milk*. It is a balanced meal. However, when a schoolboy makes his breakfast out of cereal and doughnuts, it isn't balanced at all; it is chiefly starch. He has missed the good protein content of the egg, and the important fresh vitamins of fruit.

Think of a lunch box: it usually contains sandwiches, some dessert, and some liquid to drink. The bread and butter provide *starch* and *fat*. There will also be *starch* and *sugar* in cake or pie, if you include that. You must still get in some *protein* (egg, cheese, fish, meat, fowl, or nuts) so you could make the sandwich filling egg salad, or cheese, or peanut butter, or any minced or sliced meat, chicken, or fish. If you include some lettuce or celery, you will have a *raw vegetable*. If you include a whole tomato, you have another raw vegetable, of another color. Add a raw apple, banana, peach, or plum, as a *fruit*. Do not make any lunch box all starch. And for children, the Thermos should contain *milk*, or a nourishing hot soup.

With a little thought, a little reference to the Master Plan, you will soon be able to make every meal a balanced meal. It will pay. It will save you many hours of "doctoring the sick."

HOW TO PLAN FOR TASTE

It's a funny thing, about taste. If you notice, certain foods, from time immemorial, have seemed to belong together: ham and eggs, ice cream and cake, toast and jam, pancakes and syrup.

Consider these — or any other combinations you are particularly fond of — and you will discover that the combination tickles the palate because of a *contrast* . . . either a contrast *in texture,* or a contrast *in flavor.* For contrast in texture, think of smooth ice cream in a rigid cone; soft pie filling in a crisp crust; the chewiness of meat with the yielding feel of potatoes; the brittleness of salad greens with the slickness of the dressing; the thick softness of jam with the crunchy feeling of toast. For contrast in flavors, consider the tartness of lemon pie filling against the sweetness of meringue; the saltiness of ham against the blandness of eggs; the bright tang of onions against the mellow flavor of meat.

Contrast is the secret of making any combination of foods interesting. No meal should be all made up of soft, mushy things; nor all of hard things. If you have something salty, plan something bland with it. If you have something sweet, plan something sharp, or even a little bitter, as contrast. If you have a fried chicken or fried fish dinner, include something bright and tart (fresh greens, or cole slaw, or a lemon dessert) to give a refreshing taste after the fried food. If you serve something heavy and rich (such as game, or a bird roasted with stuffing), provide a tangy sauce or jelly with it, to "cut" the heaviness of the food.

We could go on with such examples indefinitely. But you have enough now to catch the idea of the trick.

Think about it. It's a trick worth knowing. It will make you an admired wife and mother, an outstanding hostess. Because too few people use it.

CHAPTER V

Trot, Trot to Market

Now you've planned your meal, and you're off! But wait . . .
don't go without two things: (1) a marketing list; (2) a knowledge of what you're to look for when you select food.

A MARKETING LIST

Be systematic. If you're not, you'll come home without the two
or three things you may need most. Keep a pad and pencil handy
in the kitchen. Each mealtime, write down on it any staple food
you notice is running low: flour, shortening, coffee, salt. Don't
wait to restock until you find you're caught without something.
Have this list ready and waiting, when you go out to shop. Then,
at the bottom of your list, just add the things you want specifically
for dinner: (1) meat; (2) vegetables; (3) salad ingredients; (4)
dessert ingredients. Add (5) anything you may need for tomorrow's breakfast or lunch.

Even old, experienced cooks make lists. It saves time; saves
additional trips to the store; saves changing menus because you
haven't the ingredients. Make it a habit.

HOW TO SHOP FOR MEAT

Quality

Meat markets may carry AA, A, B, or even C meat. Find out
how your market is ranked. If you see no sign at your butcher's,

ask. Good quality is vital, since it indicates that animals have been inspected for health, and that meat will be wholesome, tender and flavorful.

Beef

The best beef comes from a steer. It will be firm, fine-grained, well padded with clean, white (not yellow) fat around the outer edges, and well marbled with tiny rivulets of fat running through the meat. Meat lacking in fat will lack sweetness, and will tend to dry out quickly in cooking.

Beef should not be sold (or at any rate, cooked) immediately upon slaughtering; it should be "hung" for some days (in a clean, refrigerated place, of course). This aging process may darken the meat slightly, making it nearer mahogany color than bright red, but it also breaks down the tougher fibers and tissues of the animal, thus making the meat far more tender and delicious to eat. Freezing also breaks down tough fibers, and people who own home freezers often freeze steaks, etc., before using them, to make them tender. Good beef (except "hamburger") if properly packaged and solidly frozen keeps for eight or nine months or more, in a freezer. It may begin to lose flavor after a year.

Highest-priced cuts of beef (because tenderest) come from the rib or loin section of a steer. See illustration of beef cuts (p. 25). These include prime rib roasts; rib, porterhouse, T-bone, and club steaks; sirloin, pin-bone, and hip-bone steaks. Large pieces of meat from this section of the animal make "roast beef." Steaks are broiled.

Medium-priced cuts (less tender) come from the hips and shoulders, rather fibrous parts of the animal, because he uses these parts to walk and push with. These include rump, top and bottom round, chuck, blade, and flank steaks; also arm roast or arm steak, and brisket (from the belly). If you are willing to take a chance, you may try broiling these steaks; sometimes they turn out wonderfully. They will never be as tender as the higher-priced cuts, but they are just as full of "steak flavor," and only require more chewing. If you prefer, the meat can be cut into cubes to make delicious stews, or meat pies; or it can be boned and rolled, to make pot roasts; or it can be ground to make "chopped beef."

Lowest-priced cuts (because toughest) come from the shanks (lower legs), neck, and breast. In this price group also come the short plate and short ribs, cut from the belly; the tail, good for soup; and the liver, tongue, heart, kidneys, brains. Most low-priced meats must be simmered long and gently in water, to make them tender; but with flavorful herbs and seasonings added, they make dinners a French chef would give you high praise for, and their nourishment value is as great as that of the highest-priced meats.

Never be ashamed to ask for what you want.

Veal

Veal is the flesh of baby calf, six to eight weeks old.

The flesh is nearly white, with the merest tinge of grayish pink color. The scant fat is also nearly white. Good quality and wholesomeness can be counted upon when you find the government's stamp of inspection (in purple ink), or a well-known meat packer's brand, upon the outer skin.

When buying veal cuts containing bone, allow ½ pound meat and bone together per person. If bone has been removed, allow 1 pound meat to serve 3.

Veal, like other products, is inexpensive at the time of year when it is plentiful.

Highest-priced cuts come from the leg, rib, and loin sections of the animal. From the leg come leg roasts and round roasts; from the rib or loin sections come rib roasts, crown roasts and loin roasts. All veal roasts, because they lack natural fat, should be covered with several strips of raw bacon before being put in oven, so the bacon fat may drip down over them and keep them moist while cooking. Some people like to add ½ to 1 cup water or bouillon to the roasting pan to provide additional moisture while roasting. Veal should always be roasted at slow (325°) temperature; see roasting times on p. 55; and is always served well done. If desired, you may have your roast boned by the butcher, and have an opening made to contain stuffing; stuffing greatly adds to the rather mild flavor of veal.

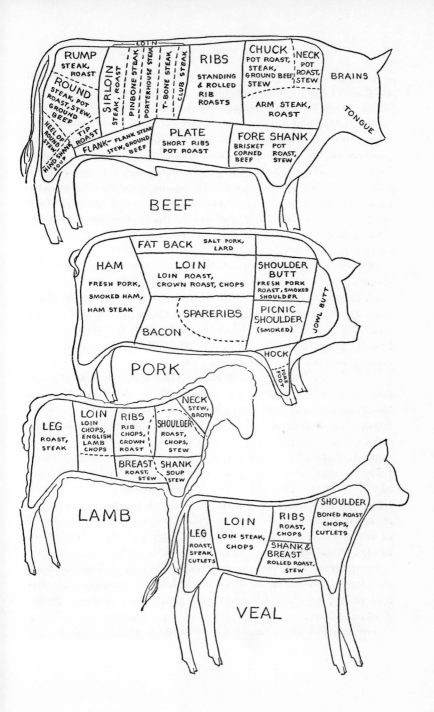

From the rib and loin sections, you may also buy rib or loin chops; and from the leg or round of veal are cut the ½-inch thick slices known as cutlets, which are all meat, no bone. Because veal is dry-meated and full of connective tissue, these chops and cutlets are never oven-broiled (a quick method which would dry them out too much), but are first seasoned and browned in a frying pan, then covered tightly to keep moisture in pan, and simmered slowly until tender. Some cooks "bread" the chops or cutlets to give them additional flavor, and add ½ cup to 1 cup tomato sauce, brown stock, sour cream, or other liquid to the pan while the meat cooks slowly, to assure moistness and increase flavor; see breaded veal cutlets, p. 138. Chops may be treated the same way.

Medium-priced cuts consist chiefly of cutlets sliced from the shoulder, not quite as tender as cutlets cut from the leg or round of veal. These are treated the same way as given above for cutlets.

Inexpensive cuts come from the breast, shoulder, and shank. Breast of veal makes a delicious oven roast if you have your butcher prepare a pocket in it, and you fill the pocket with bread stuffing or some variation, p. 59. See notes on roasts above, and follow Master Recipe in Chapter VI. Or the breast meat may be cut to 2½ inch cubes and used as the meat for veal stews, of which there can be many variations. Note that veal readily takes on the flavor of foods cooked with it, so that if you make a veal stew with onions, tomatoes, green pepper, and other tangy-tasting vegetables, you will have a tangy dish; but if you put with your veal sweet potatoes, mushrooms and peas, you will have a sweet stew; see Meat Stews, p. 120. The cooked stew meat and vegetables, if bones are removed, can be covered with biscuit or pastry crust to make veal pie; see veal pies, p. 146. Uncooked meat from breast of veal may be chopped and combined with chopped fresh pork to make meat loaf, p. 152, or to make meat cakes.

Shoulder of veal, though more bony than the leg or round, is excellent when stuffed and oven-roasted. Or you can have it boned and rolled, to make blade or arm roasts. See notes on oven-roasting above.

The shank is used chiefly for soup meat, or for making stock (see Stock Made from Bones, p. 127). The bone is rich in gelatin-forming substance which is both highly nourishing (and so often prepared for invalids), and also excellent for use in making jellied veal. Such stock indeed is used as the basic liquid for many sauces, as well as soups.

Lamb

Good quality lamb will be pinkish in color, fine-grained, with creamy, crisp-looking fat. It can be distinguished from mutton because mutton meat is dark red, its fat hard and white. Good lamb costs less per pound than good beef. It keeps up to a year in a home freezer.

Highest-priced cuts, as always, come from the rib or loin section of the lamb, including rib or loin chops, and the "crown roast" (which is a row of ribs formed into a crown shape, and roasted standing upright). In this highest-priced section, too, comes the leg of lamb, also roasted, since the animal, being a baby, still has tender legs.

Medium-priced cuts (less tender) come, as usual, from the shoulder. These include shoulder chops and Saratoga chops, to broil or pan-broil; these chops are tasty, and have more meat on them than rib or loin chops. A large section of shoulder may be stuffed and roasted, or boned and rolled for roasting. Shoulder pieces are often used for stew.

Lowest-priced cuts (least tender, and most full of bone and fat) come from neck, breast, and shanks. Breast of lamb may be rolled, boned, and stuffed, for roasting. Or it may be cut into pieces, simmered until tender, then used to make stews, curries, meat pies, delicious lamb casseroles. In this low-priced group also come lamb's kidneys, lamb's liver.

Pork

See illustration of pork cuts, p. 25.

Pork may be "fresh" (which means *unsmoked meat;* this has a pinkish-gray color); or it may be "smoked" (and the smoking process turns the meat reddish, as in smoked hams, and bacon).

Fresh Pork. Look for firm, fine-textured meat, of good pinkish-gray color. As most hogs are killed before they are a year old, none of the meat is old and tough, but naturally some parts of the animal are more tender than others. As usual, the tenderest (and highest-priced) cuts come from the rib (or loin) section of the animal. These include:

Rib chops, or loin chops. Allow 1 or 2 per person; broil, or pan-broil them.

Loin roasts. This is a section (or row) of loin chops, all attached to each other in one piece. (Allow ½ pound meat and bone per person; roast the entire piece as on page 56.)

Crown roasts. This type roast is made from two sections of loin, each bent into a semicircle, then the two put together to form a complete circle; the ribs stand up vertically, looking like points of a crown. Roast the piece intact, ribs standing upright; see page 56. (Allow about 2 ribs per person; but if roast is bigger than you can use in one meal, don't worry; you can use the remainder in many delicious dishes; see Leftovers, Chapter XVI.)

Also delicious, and a little less expensive, is the *fresh ham, or fresh shoulder,* to roast. If you want a small roast, you may buy half of a fresh ham. If you wish, you may have the butcher bone either the ham or shoulder for you, leaving a pocket into which you may loosely pack bread stuffing (p. 241), or apple stuffing. Such a roast will probably make enough meat to last a small family two or three meals, and what is left over will make other delicious dinners; see Leftovers, Chapter XVI. Roast meat as in Master Recipe #1, p. 56.

Lowest-priced cuts of pork are spareribs and hocks.

Spareribs are the lower ends of the ribs, cut off and sold separately; they are chiefly bone, but the meat on them is sweet and tasty when well cooked. Allow ⅔ pound per person when ordering. If you like them with sauerkraut, buy (for 4 people) 3 pounds spareribs, plus 1 quart or 2 pounds sauerkraut; see recipe for cooking (p. 129).

Hocks are cut from the lower foreleg, and require long (about 2¼ hours) simmering in water to make them tender. They, too, are good with sauerkraut. Allow 1 hock per person when buying. See recipe (p. 130).

Smoked Pork. Bacon. Bacon comes from the lower belly-section of a pig, and is largely fat, streaked with lean. When shopping, try to find the *leanest possible* bacon; bacon which has too much fat will shrivel up to nothing, in cooking. One half pound sliced bacon usually provides 7 or 8 slices, depending on thickness. Allow 2 or 3 slices per person when serving. Some markets sell bacon in large pieces, which you may take home and slice yourself (to any desired thickness) if you wish to do this. Some country markets also sell "bacon-ends," which are "odds-and-ends" pieces (not evenly shaped strips), but they are bacon, nonetheless, and tasty, and considerably less expensive; if you don't care about the shape of your pieces, try these.

Smoked hams. There are several cuts of smoked pork loosely classified as hams: a true ham (hind leg); also picnic shoulder, or shoulder butt (from foreleg). Hams also are sold in three conditions: cooked, or partly cooked, or uncooked. See complete information under Baked Ham (p. 132).

Internal Organs

A famous doctor once said we should discard all the flesh of our animals and eat only the organs; then we would be far better nourished and in stronger health. Remember that tongue, liver, kidneys, etc., all come in the A-plus nourishment bracket, and in the lowest price group. Have one of these dishes once a week, for health.

In buying any internal organ, look for firmness and fresh, clear, healthy color.

HOW TO SHOP FOR POULTRY

NOTE: Choose a plump bird, of clear creamy color, with meaty breast and legs. Any bird bought in the market should be delivered to you cleaned and drawn. The heart, liver, and gizzard (the only edible organs) come with the bird. Look for a bird with as few pinfeathers as possible, since you will have to remove all those still remaining, with tweezers.

Types of Chickens

Broilers. Baby chickens, weighing 1½ to 2½ pounds. Get one with as much breast as possible. Have split in half lengthwise. Allow ½ broiler per person. Broil. (See p. 73.)

Frying chickens. These are still "youngsters," and tender, weighing 2½ to 3½ pounds. Look for a meaty one. Have cut into joints for frying. Allow 1 chicken for 2 persons. Deep-fry, see p. 109, or shallow-fry, see p. 101.

Roasting chickens. These are young adults, weighing 4 to 6½ pounds. One 4 to 6 pound chicken serves about 4 people. Get a meaty (but not fatty) bird, of good creamy color. Leave bird whole. Fill cavity with stuffing (p. 241). Roast. (See Master Recipe #2, p. 61.)

Fowl. These are old birds, which require long, gentle simmering to become tender. A fricasseed chicken should serve 4 to 5 people. Usually cost less per pound than young birds. Have bird cut into joint sections. To cook: fricassee, or stew, see pp. 121, 122. This is also the bird to buy when you want a large amount of chicken meat for salad, casseroles, creamed chicken, chicken pies. One boiled fowl should yield 6 to 8 cups diced meat; see p. 122.

Other Birds

Turkey. A new, small, meaty breed weighs only 7 pounds. Others run to 30 or more pounds. Allow about 1 pound per person. Larger birds are more economical; cost less per pound. Look for meaty bird of creamy color; avoid bony, bluish birds. Stuff. Roast. (See Master Recipe #2, p. 61.)

Duck, domestic. A domestic (not wild) duck may weigh 4 to 6 pounds, but it has a large, heavy carcass of bone, and much padding of fat, so that the meat on it is not at all equivalent to the meat on a chicken of the same size. Therefore 1 duck does not usually serve more than 3, or possibly 4 people. Look for duck of good white color (not yellowish); have market help you select one with

as little excess fat as possible; have market clean and draw it. Stuff
and roast; see Master Recipe #2, p. 61.

Goose. Old geese are very tough, so choose a young one, not
over 10 to 12 pounds. A 10 pound goose serves 10 people. Look
for soft, fat, yellow feet, and pliable yellow bill. Have goose
cleaned and drawn at market. Stuff and roast; see Master Recipe
#2, p. 61.

HOW TO SHOP FOR FISH

The ancient custom of "fish on Fridays" is not merely a church
ritual; but, like many another religious ordinance, it has a reason
in health. Fish is a great source of iodine, which science considers
one of the controlling factors in the health of the thyroid and other
glands. Once a week is none too often to obtain this food element.
Fish is also a high-protein food, and a good substitute for meat.
So put fish on your menu often. Today — even inland — fresh,
frozen, and tinned fish are available in considerable variety.

When buying a whole fish, look for bright eyes, bright gills, and
firm but elastic flesh. Fresh fish will not have a strong odor. And
a fresh fish will sink when put in water.

When buying sections of a fish (such as a fillet, or fish "steak"
or a large chunk of fish) again look for firm-textured, but moist,
clean-looking flesh; and avoid fish with a strong odor.

Fish is usually bought with a definite purpose in mind; that is,
because the menu planner wants fish to broil, to bake, to fry, or
to make into fish stews or chowders. We therefore list types for
different purposes.

Fish to Oven-broil or Pan-broil

Fish steaks. These are large, crosswise slices, about ½ to 1 inch
thick, cut from large-sized fish (salmon, swordfish, haddock, halibut, tuna, cod). They are oven-broiled like steaks of beef, except
that they have to be brushed with butter or salad oil, to keep them
from drying out; see page 72. If you have no oven, you can pan-
broil them; see page 83. Allow ½ pound fish per person. Buy a
lemon, to squeeze over fish when serving.

Whole fish, split. Fish of 2 to 4 pounds, like some striped bass, bluefish, lake trout, mackerel, or whitefish, are delicious simply split in half lengthwise, cleaned, heads and tails removed, and oven-broiled, skin-side down, about 10 to 15 minutes. Have market split and clean fish for you. Allow ½ pound fish per person. Buy a lemon, to squeeze over fish when serving. Broil as on page 72.

There are also smaller (1 to 2 pound) fish which may be broiled as above, or may be cleaned the same way and pan-broiled (see page 83) if you have no oven. These include small mackerel, baby flounders (called "pan-fish"), black bass, brook trout, baby bluefish (called "snappers"). Allow ½ pound per person. Buy a lemon, to squeeze over fish when serving.

Fillets (fish flesh from which all skin and bones have been removed). Fillets of flounder, haddock, halibut, or other fish may also be broiled, though many people always fry them. Markets will fillet practically any fish for you if you ask. Or you can buy ready-prepared, or frozen fillets. If using frozen fillets, thaw them according to package directions before using. Allow only about ⅓ pound filleted fish per person, since there is no waste. To oven-broil, see page 72. To pan-broil, see page 83. Buy a lemon, to squeeze over fish when serving.

Fish to Stuff and Bake

Fish, to be big enough to hold stuffing, should be from 3 to 5 pounds; it would hardly pay to stuff a smaller fish. Also, fish used for this purpose is customarily a white-meated, rather mild-tasting type, like cod, which hasn't a highly distinctive flavor of its own. Such a bland fish, when filled with a hot, savory stuffing and topped with an egg sauce, becomes a feast to remember. Ask your market what fish are available which would suit this purpose. Have market split and clean fish (head and tail are often left on for this method of cooking, and the entire fish served intact on a platter). Allow ½ pound fish per person, and if you have fish left over, don't worry; it will make other good dishes for another day; see Chapter XVI. Stuff and bake fish as on page 245.

Fish to Fry

Fillets. Fillets of any white-meated fish (haddock, cod, perch, halibut, flounder) can be cut to serving-size pieces, then dipped in flour coating (p. 101) and pan-fried (page 88); or dipped in egg-and-crumb coating and shallow-fried (page 104). Allow ⅓ pound filleted fish per person. Buy ingredients for tartar sauce (p. 354) to serve with fried fish. If buying frozen fillets, allow time to thaw fish, according to package directions, before frying.

Whole, small fish (like smelts, fresh sardines). Allow 6 to 8 (or more) of these tiny fish per person, depending on size of fish. Fish must be split along the side and cleaned inside. Heads and tails are left on. Fish are rolled in flour coating and pan-fried (page 88) or rolled in egg-and-crumb coating and shallow-fried (page 104).

Shellfish. See types available to buy (p. 34); methods of frying (pp. 105, 111).

Fish to Poach or Boil

Fillets, or "steaks." Fillets, or crosswise steak slices (½ to 1 inch thick) cut from haddock, halibut, cod, or swordfish, are delicious if cut to serving-size pieces and poached in milk, or white wine. Allow ⅓ pound filleted fish or fish steak per person. Have available 1 or 2 cups milk, or white wine, in which to cook them. If using frozen fillets, thaw first according to package directions before cooking. To cook, see page 123.

Large, thick pieces of fish (like a 3–6 pound section of a salmon, or cod, or haddock). A large thick piece of fish of this sort is too big to fry or broil; it has to be baked or poached if left all in one piece. Poaching keeps it moister. Buy any size piece you want, allowing ½ pound per person. Dry-meated fish is best for poaching, since it will remain firm. To cook, see page 123.

Fish for Chowders

Fillets. Fillets of cod, haddock, perch, or other white-meated, non-oily fish make excellent chowder. Allow 1 pound filleted fish to make chowder for 2 or 3 persons. To make, see page 124.

Large slices of white-meated fish. If making a large quantity of chowder, it is cheaper to buy a large crosswise slice of fish and remove skin and bones yourself before using fish for chowder. Allow ½ to ¾ pound per person. See page 124.

HOW TO SHOP FOR
CRUSTACEANS (SHELLFISH)

So delicious and various are the many types of shellfish that an entire book could be written upon this group of foods alone. We can only touch upon those most popular.

Lobster

The tangiest, tenderest lobster comes from the cold waters of Maine and other New England states, and Canada. Lobsters now being flown in from Africa are not of that ilk; they lack claws (and the big claws contain some of the largest chunks of lobster meat); they are tougher, and haven't the same flavor.

All lobsters are green until cooked (when the shells turn fiery red). To enjoy lobster at its best, you should buy your lobster *alive,* and take it home and cook it at once.

If selecting your lobster from a water-filled tank, in which the creatures are swimming, choose a lively one. If selecting from a store counter filled with ice, make sure your lobster still wiggles if poked, even though he may be half numb from icing.

Small (chicken) lobsters, weighing 1, 1½, or 2 pounds, are tenderest. Over 3 pounds, the lobster is old and tough. Better buy two small ones than one large one.

To dine on boiled lobster, you take your creatures home alive, in a paper bag, and plunge them into boiling salted water. If you want broiled or baked lobster, you may have the market split the lobster in half, lengthwise, for you; but lobster should be cooked very promptly after being killed.

To make lobster salad, lobster Newburg, or creamed seafood dishes, you need *boiled* lobster meat. If you do not wish to boil a lobster yourself, many markets sell lobsters which have already been boiled. In this case, look for a lobster which is bright red of shell, and whose tail will spring back quickly if you pull it out straight; this is a sign that the lobster was alive and fresh at the time it was boiled.

Canned lobster meat (already cooked) may also be used for salads, seafood patties.

Canned "rock" lobster, though it has approximately the same flavor, is white-meated, rather than the usual pink we associate with lobster meat. It is less expensive, and makes very acceptable salad and creamed seafood dishes.

Clams

There are three kinds of clams commonly found in the United States:

Soft-shell clams, usually small, chiefly in New England waters, desirable for steaming and frying.

Hard-shell clams, found on both Atlantic and Pacific coasts, in large and small size. Large ones, "Quahogs," are generally chopped and made into chowder. Smaller ones, sometimes known as "Cherrystones" or "Little Necks," may be served raw, on the half-shell.

Razor clams, shaped something like an old-time long razor, are found on the Pacific coast, and are often used for canning.

Clams are sold in shells, removed from shells, or canned. For steamed or "clambake" clams, you must have clams in their shells. Clams sold in the shell must be alive. A tightly closed shell denotes freshness. If shell is partly open, you should be able to see the clam move when you tap the shell. A dead clam will have opened its shell and the shell stays open of its own accord. Clams in the shell are sold by quart, peck, or dozen.

Clams removed from shells are sold by pint or quart. These are ready to fry, to make fritters, or stews, chowders, without the trouble of "shucking."

Canned clams make perfectly good stews, chowders, or bisques. See quantity needed under recipe you wish to make.

Oysters

On the Atlantic seaboard, the old saying is that oysters are good only in months whose names contain an "R" (September through April). This is not quite true. Oysters are good all year; but particular markets refuse to sell oysters during the summer months, since that is when oysters spawn, and are not at their best, being flabby and of poor flavor. On the Pacific coast, however, oysters are sold all year round.

Oysters are sold in the shell (by dozen) or out of the shell (by dozen, pint, or quart). Quick-frozen oysters are also sold in many markets; these should be thawed according to directions on package, and may then be used like any raw oysters.

Large oysters are commonly called "Cape Cods," and the smaller variety "blue points"; and though not all large oysters come from Cape Cod, the market will know what you want if you give them this description. Many people prefer large oysters, for eating raw "on the half shell." Markets will open oysters for you, and deliver them on cracked ice. (Allow 6 per person.)

For frying, broiling, creaming, or making oyster casseroles or stews, buy oysters already removed from shells. (See amounts needed, under recipe you plan to make.)

Crabs

Eastern (Atlantic and Gulf) crabs usually measure 3 to 5 inches, and are known as "blue claw." Their claws are active and dangerous. To serve whole, allow 2 or 3 crabs per person. To get 2 cups crabmeat, buy 10 to 12 eastern crabs.

Western (Pacific) crabs are larger, have thicker, meatier bodies, and less dangerous claws. Allow ½ to 1 western crab per person, if serving whole. To get 2 cups crabmeat, buy 2 to 3 western crabs.

Either eastern or western crabs may be hard-shelled or soft-shelled. They are hard-shelled all year, except at a certain season when they shed their hard shells, and so for a few days become soft-shelled.

Hard-shelled crabs are dropped alive into salted boiling water (much like lobster), then the shells cracked, edible meat extracted from claws and back, and inedible parts discarded. This provides your cooked crabmeat for salad, creamed seafood dishes, or seafood cocktail, but preparing it takes some time. Therefore, markets often sell prepared crabmeat by the pound. Prepared crabmeat can also be bought tinned, or frozen.

Soft-shelled crabs, which are sold already killed and cleaned at many markets, are the ones to use for deep-frying, sautéing, etc. If you must kill and clean them yourself, this is done before cooking; see page 166.

Shrimp

A shrimp is a small, grayish-green crustacean, which when alive looks something like a tiny lobster; but before being sent to market, its head is removed, and the curled-up bodies are packed in ice, then shipped. Sold this way, they are known as "fresh" shrimp. They have parchment-thin shells, and should be firm-bodied when sold. They are sold by the pound. Though shrimp vary in size, 1 pound provides 20 to 25 shrimp, and serves 3 to 4 persons. When cooked, shrimp turn pink. Cooking and shelling them is simple; see Fresh Shrimp, page 169.

Shrimp sold in cans have already been cooked and shelled.

Before using either home-cooked or canned shrimp in salads, seafood cocktail, or creamed seafood dishes, the intestinal vein (a black line on shrimp's back) must be removed.

Scallops

What fish markets call a "scallop" is the single large muscle which opens and closes the scallop's shell; this muscle is the only edible part of the crustacean, and is all you get when buying scallops at a store.

Sea scallops are cubes about 2 inches square, or more, and are sold the year round. The little "bay scallops" found in New England waters are only about ¾ inch square. These are considered choicer, but are sold only during the "oyster months."

Frozen scallops are sold in many parts of the United States.

These should be thawed according to directions on package, and may then be used like any other raw scallops.

One pound of scallops usually serves 3 to 4 persons. Scallops are sometimes eaten raw, but most people prefer them cooked in some manner; see suggested ways, page 177.

HOW TO SHOP FOR FRUITS

Practically everyone knows fine-looking fruit at sight. A luscious bunch of grapes, a box of plump berries bursting with juice, a basket of sun-ripened fragrant peaches, needs no sign hung on it, to say "this is *it*." Your eyes and nose tell you. And I know you are not going to buy fruit with worm holes or decayed spots.

However, even smart people are sometimes fooled about oranges or grapefruit (coming home with fruit which is thick-skinned, woody, and lacking juice), or about melons (coming home with one which proves to be underripe and tasteless). To avoid such pitfalls, look up the fruit you are going to buy in Chapter XXVII, What to Do with Fruits, where helpful hints are given.

Storing. Practically all fruits (except bananas and apples) should be stored in the refrigerator, to keep them firm, fresh, and moist. Indeed, most of them keep best if stored in the covered hydrator pan of the refrigerator, thus protecting them as much as possible from air. I have known oranges to keep three weeks in such a pan. Grapes, plums, peaches, pears, indeed any juicy fruit, keep best this way. Even a box of berries keeps best if top of box is tightly covered with waxed paper or aluminum foil.

Fruits which have been cut open (such as a leftover half grapefruit, or half melon) should be tightly covered with waxed paper, to prevent air from reaching the interior of the fruit. So covered, the fruit will keep well.

Apples *may* be kept in refrigerator hydrator pan, if you wish to make them last a long while and if you like them chilled. However, apples also keep quite long in an open bin or barrel, in a cool place, and some people prefer the flavor when not chilled.

Bananas should never be stored in the refrigerator, as this robs them of much of their rich flavor; but you can help keep them from becoming overripe by enclosing them in a paper bag, or wrapping them in waxed paper, to exclude air.

HOW TO SHOP FOR VEGETABLES

Here again, even a child knows a fine, firm-looking carrot, a crisp, compact head of lettuce, a dewy-fresh lot of spinach leaves. You are not going to buy wilted, blighted produce . . . nor vegetables with bad spots; I don't need to tell you. Just remember that all hard vegetables (potatoes, turnips, beets, carrots, onions) should be really *hard* (not softened), and of clear bright color. All leafy vegetables — or stalks like celery — should be crisp, firm, sprightly, and a fresh green. All pod vegetables (peas, lima beans, string beans, snap beans) especially should be young and crisp; for when they reach the end of their seasons and become too large and too old, they are not only tough, but lacking in taste. String beans, furthermore, develop heavier and tougher strings as they get older; the same bush which produced practically "stringless" beans at the start of the season may produce beans with heavy strings, toward the end.

All green and juicy vegetables, of course, are tenderest and sweetest of flavor when young. And when fresh picked. The longer the lapse of time between picking and eating, the more the flavor will disappear. A vegetable picked from the garden, cooked, and served within an hour, will taste far superior (and cook much more rapidly) than one which was picked two or three days previously. Try, therefore, to buy at a market where vegetables are brought in fresh daily; and when fresh vegetables are hard to find, buy frozen ones; for these are frozen in garden-fresh condition as soon as picked.

The greatest difficulty about vegetables, to most beginners, is knowing how much to buy, and where to store them, for best keeping qualities. We therefore give a table for quick reference:

BUYING AND STORING
FRESH VEGETABLES

Kind of Vegetable	Amount to Buy to Serve 2	Where to Store
		(All methods below mean manner of storing IN REFRIGERATOR, unless open bin or other place is recommended)
Artichokes, French	2 artichokes	Hydrator pan
Asparagus	1 lb. (about 12 stalks)	Hydrator pan
Beets	1 lb. without leaves	Hydrator pan in warm weather, or in warm home; but these keep well in cold cellar in open bin, with cold air circulating around them
Broccoli	1½ lb.	Hydrator pan
Brussels sprouts	½ lb.	Hydrator pan, or covered with waxed paper
Cabbage	1 lb. (1 whole small cabbage or use ½ of a larger cabbage)	Hydrator pan, or covered with waxed paper
Carrots	½ lb.	Hydrator pan keeps them for months; country folk bury them in a box of sand in cold barn in winter
Cauliflower	1 small head	Hydrator pan, or completely wrapped in waxed paper
Celery	Buy 1 head; you'll have it for days, but it keeps.	Hydrator pan, or completely and firmly wrapped in waxed paper
Corn-on-cob	2 to 4 ears	Hydrator pan, or wrapped in waxed paper
Cucumber (to slice)	1 4" or 5" cucumber	Hydrator pan
Eggplant	1 small	Hydrator pan, or wrapped in waxed paper
Green peppers (to stuff)	2 huge, or 4 medium, without blemishes	Hydrator pan
Leafy greens Spinach Chard Beet tops	1 lb. to 1½ lbs. (buy the larger amount if planning to chop it fine)	Hydrator pan, or closed in paper bag, or in covered bowl

Kind of Vegetable	Amount to Buy to Serve 2	Where to Store
Lima beans	1 to 1½ lbs. in shells	Hydrator pan, or closed in paper bag, or in covered bowl
Mushrooms (to broil, or sauté)	½ lb.	Hydrator pan, or closed in paper bag, or in covered jar or bowl
Onions (to serve boiled)	¾ lb.	Keep in open bin, at room temperature
Parsnips	¾ lb.	Hydrator pan, or wrap in waxed paper
Peas	1 lb. in shells	Hydrator pan, or closed in paper bag, or covered bowl
Potatoes (to boil, mash, or fry)	1 lb.	Open bin, at room temperature
(to bake)	2 huge, or 4 medium-size	
Potatoes, Sweet	¾ lb. to 1 lb.	Hydrator pan, or wrapped in waxed paper
Squash, Summer (to mash)	1 lb.	In refrigerator
(to bake, cut in halves)	1 small squash	
Squash, Acorn (to bake, cut in halves)	1 large squash	
Squash, Winter (to mash)	1 small squash about 1½ lbs.	If squash have been thoroughly dried out after picking, they keep all winter in warm room, or at room temperature
String beans	½ lb.	Hydrator pan, or in covered bowl, or closed in bag
Tomatoes (to slice)	½ to ¾ lb.	Hydrator pan
(to stuff)	2 large, or 4 small	
(to stew)	1 lb.	
Turnips, Yellow (to mash)	1 lb.	Open bin, in cool room
Turnips, White (to boil)	1½ lbs.	Hydrator pan, or wrapped in waxed paper

BUYING AND STORING
FROZEN VEGETABLES

Amount to Buy. The size of packages varies with different brand names, but the average box serves 3. If appetites are small, it *might* serve 4.

Storing. Store in your freezer, or in the freezing compartment of your refrigerator, until cooking time.

HOW TO SHOP FOR CANNED GOODS

Canned goods are so greatly improved, in taste and quality, over what they used to be, and there is such an ever increasing variety of good things offered, that it would be foolish indeed not to experiment with these time- and work-saving products. The wise housewife keeps a good assortment on her pantry shelves; a selection of soups, tinned meats, seafood, spaghetti-with-sauce, pork and beans, all sorts of vegetables, fruits, fruit and vegetable juices, special sauces for meat.

The soups put out in cans today are so delicious that hardly anyone bothers to make soup at home any more. The cooked meats (such as tinned chicken, ham, turkey, tongue, hash, luncheon meat), and all the tinned seafoods (shrimp, lobster, tuna, salmon) are tender and well cooked, and not expensive when you consider that they contain no waste, such as fat and bone. Some of them can be used just as they are, with mere heating; all of them can be turned into other tempting and hearty homemade dishes, with a few simple additions.

The tiny boiled onions sold in glass jars are perfectly cooked, so that they are just tender, but not falling apart; and they are more even in size than a batch you could prepare at home. One brand of canned peaches I buy is as good as any peaches from my own trees which I might can in my own kitchen. Canned asparagus spears are tender and tasty for use in aspics, or for salads. We could go on, and on . . .

The point is simply that if you do not take advantage of these time-saving good foods, you have only yourself to blame; and I can assure you they are life-savers when unexpected company arrives, or when there is little time to prepare a meal, and everyone is starving.

Examine the shelves at your market, and see what is new, what you haven't tried. And when buying, remember these points:

Read labels. The labels used today are far more explicit and helpful than they used to be. They give precise weights, or amounts; tell plainly what sauce, or what type syrup, if any, is used with the solid food; whether or not the product should be diluted (and if so, how much, and with what), as with condensed soups, or concentrated fruit juices. They also often include recipes suggesting ways of converting the tinned product into another, fancier dish. Not to read the label is like reaching into a grab-bag, blindfolded. The label was put there to help.

Know your can sizes. Here is a table showing the approximate content of the sizes of cans used most regularly today:

Can Size	*Approximate Content*	*Used Chiefly for*
6 oz.	about ⅔ c.	Frozen concentrated juices
		Single-strength fruit and vegetable juices
		Shrimp, other seafood
8 oz.	about 1 c.	Ripe olives
		Fruits
		Vegetables
No. 1 (Picnic)	1¼ c. (or 10½ oz.)	Condensed soups
		Some fruits, vegetables
		Some meat, fish
No. 300	1¾ c. { 15½ oz. (dry wt.) 13½ fluid oz.	Pork and beans
		Spaghetti, macaroni
		Chili con carne
		Date-and-nut bread
		Cranberry sauce
		Clams
		Blueberries
		Pie apples
No. 303	2½ c. { 1 lb. 5 oz. (dry wt.) 1 pt. 3 fluid oz.	Most vegetables
		Apple sauce
		Fruit cocktail
		Sweet and sour cherries
		Other fruits

Can Size	Approximate Content	Used Chiefly for
No. 2	2½ c. { 1 lb. 4 oz. (dry wt.) 1 pt. 2 fluid oz.	Vegetables Fruits Fruit juices Vegetable juices, etc.
No. 2½	3½ c. { 1 lb. 13 oz. (dry wt.) 1 pt. 10 fluid oz.	Peaches, pears, plums Fruit cocktail Tomatoes Sauerkraut Pumpkin

Heating Canned Foods

It is highly important that canned and glassed vegetables be heated in their own liquor (that is, the liquid which comes with them in the can or jar). This liquid contains not only valuable vitamins which have seeped from the vegetable into the fluid during the process of canning, but also valuable flavor. The most modern, approved way of heating canned vegetables is this: drain liquid from can into a saucepan. Bring it to boiling point, and let it boil gently until reduced to about ½ its original amount. Then add the vegetable; cover pan tightly, and simmer gently about 5 minutes, or just until vegetable is well heated. If desired, add a pinch of sugar, since all nature's foods contain some natural sugar, which is apt to be lost in the cooking process. Boiling the liquid down to half volume is supposed to intensify the flavor, restoring it to that of a freshly cooked vegetable. If you are using the vegetable drained (as for salad, or in aspic), save the can or jar liquor; store it in covered jar in refrigerator, and when you get enough, use it to make a cream soup (p. 258); or add it to other soups; don't throw it out.

Storing in Opened Cans

Many people are still afraid to leave opened cans of fruit or vegetables standing in a refrigerator, for fear the food will become poisoned from the tin. All manufacturers have now changed the type of tin used, and it is now perfectly safe to leave food in tins.

HOW TO SHOP FOR FLOUR
AND OTHER STAPLES

Flour

Flour is sold in various forms, as follows:

All-purpose. This is plain, white flour, sometimes vitamin-enriched, used for all biscuits, bread, pastry, pancakes, thickening of sauces, coating of foods before frying. It can also be used for cake if sifted 4 times, to make it very light and airy, and if you use a little less flour than a recipe demanding "cake flour" calls for. For example, where 1 cup cake flour is called for, you may substitute *1 cup minus 2 tablespoons* all-purpose flour; where 2 cups cake flour is called for, substitute 1¾ cups all-purpose flour.

Self-rising flour. This is all-purpose flour to which baking powder and salt have been added, in proper amount, to use for quick breads (biscuits, muffins), pancakes, waffles. *Do not use this flour for yeast bread.*

Cake flour. This is a finer, lighter flour (nothing added) made from selected "soft" or winter wheats. It is especially milled to give delicate texture in cake. It is heartily recommended for angel or sponge cake, or indeed for any cake which you wish to make especially light and tempting.

Self-rising cake flour. This is cake flour to which leavening and salt have been added. If using this, follow recipes on package carefully, as this flour would not be appropriate for all types of cake, especially not for angel or sponge cake, nor for cakes raised with baking soda.

Whole wheat, entire wheat, and graham flours. These are three terms meaning the same thing. These flours contain all the constituents of the cleaned whole wheat grain, in natural proportions. Do not sift before measuring. Used mainly in making yeast bread and rolls; see page 232.

Rye flour. Flour made from rye grain. Do not sift before measuring. Used in making yeast bread; see page 232.

Buckwheat flour. Flour made from buckwheat grain. Do not sift before measuring. This is sometimes substituted for white flour, or used half-and-half with white flour in making pancakes or waffles.

Baking Powder

There are three types of baking powder: (1) tartrate; (2) phosphate; (3) a combination type, called "double-acting."

Tartrate baking powder begins acting quickly, at room temperature, as soon as liquid is mixed with the dry ingredients. Phosphate baking powder acts less quickly, needing the heat of stove to make it liberate its carbon dioxide. The combination (double-acting) type acts least quickly of all, releasing only about $\frac{1}{5}$ to $\frac{1}{3}$ of its carbon dioxide at room temperature, and the rest only when heat of stove acts upon it.

As 98 per cent of U.S. housewives buy double-acting baking powder, our recipes in this book are all planned for that kind. If you have bought one of the other kinds, you must *use about double the amount of baking powder* our recipes specify.

Sugar

Granulated. This is the type sugar used for general all-purpose sweetening. It is used for coffee, for cocoa, for tea; for sweetening puddings, custards, pie fillings, cakes, muffins, and other batters; also for making sugar syrups, meringues, or for boiled frostings. In our recipes, whenever the word "sugar" appears, it means granulated sugar. If another type is intended, it will be specified.

Powdered. This is merely a finer kind of granulated sugar; it is often used to sprinkle over fresh berries, or for any purpose where you want fine sugar.

Confectioners' (XXXX). This is extremely fine sugar, soft and fluffy as face powder, and because it contains practically no grit, is used for uncooked frostings. If sugar becomes lumpy, put it inside a clean paper bag or between two sheets of waxed paper and roll it firmly, with rolling pin, until fine again before using.

Brown. Brown sugar is used mainly for spicy cakes or cookies, or for glazing ham or sweet potatoes; or for combining with butter to make butterscotch syrup (used for upside-down cakes, butter-pecan buns, and so on). It is very apt to become hard and lumpy. Once a package is opened, it is best to put leftover sugar into tightly covered glass jar, to keep air from getting at it. If it becomes hard and lumpy in spite of this, turn sugar into large wooden bowl, or into closed clean paper bag, and with rolling pin, pound or roll it until fine again before using.

Brown sugar should always be firmly packed into measuring cup with back of spoon when measuring. If you don't do this, you will "short-change" yourself on the amount of sugar required in the recipe, since many air spaces will intervene between grains of sugar in the cup.

Spices

See ordinary household seasonings and spices on page 14; see list of additional herbs and their uses, page 505.

Vinegar

There are various kinds of vinegar. Buy 1 pint or 1 quart.

Cider vinegar. Made from fermented apple juice; quite "sharp."

White vinegar. Made by fermenting diluted, distilled alcohol. This is less sharp.

Malt vinegar and *tarragon vinegar* (which is malt vinegar flavored with tarragon). Very popular for salad use, and milder.

Wine vinegar. Has, as the name implies, a slightly winy taste; it is very mild, and less tangy than the others.

Probably the vinegar most commonly used for salads is cider vinegar; but there is no reason why you shouldn't experiment with others, even combining two or three kinds, to develop a flavor you like for salad dressing. You may also add herbs (see Chart, p. 505) which are suitable for salads to your vinegar, letting them stand in the bottle until vinegar has acquired the herb flavor, thus making your own brand of herb vinegar.

Salad Oils

Olive oil. This is of course made from olives, and has a pronounced taste which some people find essential to their enjoyment of salad, and other people dislike. It is expensive, because imported, but worth it if you like it. Buy a 1 pint can, to begin with.

Vegetable oils. There are many brands of vegetable oil on the market, all of which are bland-tasting, pure, and wholesome to use for salad dressing. When using these, however, you need to add to your French dressing more seasoning and more herbs, to give the dressing an interesting taste. See French dressing (p. 356) for suggestions. Buy 1 pint or 1 quart.

Shortenings and Cooking Fat

Butter. Butter of course has a delicious taste all its own, which is not duplicated by lard, or vegetable shortenings, or salad oil. If making a delicate-flavored cake or cookies, where flavor is paramount, it may be worth your while to pay the extra cost to use butter as the shortening. If you find the butter too expensive, substitute in such recipes vegetable shortening. Butter, similarly, is used for sautéing foods of very delicate taste, such as mushrooms, chicken livers, etc., because the buttery flavor adds so much to the enjoyment of the food. But in most frying or sautéing, other cooking fats may be substituted.

Butter is — to my mind — imperative on toast, on poached or soft-cooked eggs, on hot vegetables.

Butter is sold as "salted" or "sweet" (no salt added). Salted butter keeps longer, since the salt acts as a preservative, as well as giving taste. Sweet butter has an incomparable flavor — the delicate flavor of pure sweet cream, whipped until it becomes a solid; it is heavenly on hot rolls.

Butter should always be kept in refrigerator. Buy ½ or 1 pound.

Vegetable shortenings. The fine American vegetable shortenings — creamy white and light-textured, and practically tasteless — have become indispensable products in all our homes. Such shortening serves many purposes; it may be used as a substitute for butter in making cakes and cookies; it is also widely used for yeast breads and pastry (in place of the old-fashioned lard); and when melted, makes fine fat for frying chicken, croquettes, fritters, French-fried potatoes, and other deep-fried foods.

It does not need to be kept in refrigerator, unless in terrifically hot weather. I keep mine on a pantry shelf. And the large 3 pound can is an economical buy, since this is a product you will be using constantly, and it keeps almost indefinitely.

Lard. Lard comes from the fat of a pig, and has a definite flavor which adds much to some dishes. Old-timers often used it for deep-frying potatoes, and other sturdy foods; and always used it as shortening in yeast bread. Indeed it gives yeast bread that true "old-fashioned homemade" flavor. And many a gourmet would tell you that there is *no* pie crust like pie crust made with lard as the shortening; try it sometime, and see.

Most lard now sold by nationally known meat packers is homogenized and therefore does not require refrigeration; but lard bought "loose" or "in bulk" does.

Vegetable oils. Vegetable oils may be used for deep-frying, in place of lard or vegetable shortening; indeed the natives of France (where deep-frying originated) *always* use oil for deep-frying. Try it. See page 106 for method and amount needed.

Vegetable oils are sometimes substituted for other types of shortening in making pastry, and in other recipes. If trying this, however, *do not attempt to interchange salad oil for shortening in recipes in this book.* Instead, follow specific directions put out by the salad oil manufacturers; numerous such recipes appear regularly in magazine advertisements, and the method of putting recipe together is quite different.

Beef suet, bacon fat, chicken fat. All of these animal fats make excellent fats for frying different types of food. Melted beef suet gives a marvelous flavor when used for pan-frying potatoes, for example. Bacon fat is good cooking fat for browning or braising any hardy meat, or potatoes, or onions, or hash, or indeed anything which does not have too delicate a flavor. Chicken fat is sometimes used to sauté chicken giblets or mushrooms, and some people substitute it for the shortening in a cake or cookie recipe, if the recipe contains enough spice or other pronounced flavoring to disguise the slight flavor of the fat.

HOW TO SHOP FOR DAIRY PRODUCTS
Milk

Bottled Milk is sold in a number of different conditions, and any authorized dairy is obliged to label its bottles as to type milk therein. Read your labels, and know what you are buying.

There are these kinds:

Raw (sold by numerous individual farmers in local communities all over the United States). This milk is whole milk, just as it comes from the cow, and delicious; but it may be dangerous to buy unless you know the milk has been produced by healthy cows and under top sanitary conditions. Unfortunately, the farmer does not always himself know the exact state of health of the cow (unless he pays to have it examined regularly); and helpers may be careless with milk containers or conditions around the barn.

Certified. This may be "raw" milk, or it may be "pasteurized" (see below); but whichever it is, it has been produced and bottled under conditions guaranteed safe. Health of cows, dairying methods and equipment, and bottling are all regularly inspected by health officials.

Pasteurized. This is milk which has been sterilized by a method invented by Louis Pasteur, which makes the milk safe from any danger of tubercular contagion.

Homogenized. This is whole pasteurized milk which has been treated so that the cream will never separate from the rest of the milk, but is held in suspension, without need of shaking the bottle.

Vitamin D. Some milk is fortified with additional Vitamin D.

Skim milk. This is pasteurized milk which has had all the fats removed, often used in dieting. All the minerals and vitamins, however, remain.

Powdered Milk. This product (now becoming very popular because it is inexpensive, takes up little space, can be carried easily when traveling, and does not require refrigeration) is the powdered fat-free "solids" of milk, reduced to powdered form by evaporating all of the water from it. When mixed with the specified amount of cold water, it returns to the consistency of fresh fat-free (skim) milk; and is just as nourishing. Its taste compares favorably with that of fresh milk. Many housewives now use it continually, for cooking and home purposes; and as we have said, it is a perfect solution to having milk available when traveling.

Canned Milk. There are two kinds of canned milk:

Evaporated milk. This is milk from which part of the water content has been evaporated. Because of the heating process, it acquires a slightly "flat" taste, which makes it rather disappointing to use over cereals or in coffee; but it is excellent to use in many kinds of cooking. To restore it to the same consistency as bottled milk, you mix 1 part evaporated milk with 1 part water, and you may add a pinch of salt to take away the flat taste. In making sauces for vegetables, you may combine 1 part evaporated milk with 1 part water the vegetable has been cooked in; or to make sauce for a fish casserole, combine 1 part evaporated milk with the fish liquor you have available, and add water if more thinning is needed. Used in cream soups, it gives a far richer and creamier taste than plain milk would. It is something you can always have handy on the shelf, is economical, and serves in many a "pinch." Keep in refrigerator after can is opened.

Sweetened condensed. This is milk which has been condensed to a very thick, syrupy state and highly sweetened. It is used only in recipes requiring a great deal of sweetness. Once can is opened, keep it in refrigerator.

Eggs

Don't you be foolish about eggs! . . . so many people are. I know city folk who pay excessive prices to get white eggs, fearing brown ones would be of horrid quality; and I know country folk who would never cook a white egg if they could obtain a brown one; they feel brown ones are somehow more "earthy" or have more food value. However, the plain fact is that the color of the shell makes no difference; it is the interior which counts. And a big brown egg laid yesterday is just as good as a big white egg laid yesterday; both are fresh; both have similar food value and flavor.

Eggs do differ, however, in size and in degree of freshness.

Freshness. Eggs labeled "strictly fresh" are not over one week old; and they are the choicest ones for cooking in their shells, or poaching, or for use raw, as in eggnog. "Fresh" eggs may be two or more weeks old (sometimes even several months), but are still perfectly good if they have been kept in warehouses under proper refrigeration; they can be cooked in shells, or poached, or fried, or scrambled, or used in omelets, or for cakes, puddings, soufflés, meringues, and other cooking. "Storage" eggs are different; they have been laid down in water-glass, or stored in sawdust, for some time.

The reason eggs may have to be stored for some time before sale, is that the peak of egg production occurs in spring and early summer; after that chickens do not lay so prolifically, and so the supply has to be spread out, to last.

Grades and sizes. The U.S. Government classifies eggs in four grades: AA, A, B, and C. AA is the fancy or highest quality; and this is followed by the others. In country areas, however, the markings are more explicit. City stores call them "jumbo," or "extra-large" (country stands often mark them "x-large"), "large," "medium," and "pullet." (A pullet egg is one laid by a young, little-girl hen, who, bless her soul, is not adult enough yet to lay an adult-sized egg; but ounce for ounce, the egg is of just as high nutritive quality as any other.) Country stands also often sell "peewees," extra-tiny eggs. If using these, simply allow 1, 2, or 3 more eggs than the recipe calls for, enough to make up for the small size.

"Cracks." Some country stores sell "cracks" at greatly reduced price. These are perfectly good, fresh-laid eggs, but eggs which have been slightly damaged and have small cracks or other slight damage to the shell. Usually they are not cracked enough to do any harm, and if you are going to use them up within a day or two, they will keep perfectly fresh. They can often be bought

for half or a third the price of intact eggs. You will not be likely to find these at metropolitan markets, however.

Storing. All eggs should always be kept in refrigerator, in the paper cartons they come in, or in a bowl or basket which allows air to circulate around them.

CHAPTER VI

How to Cook a Roast

METHOD FOR:

Roast Beef — Rib Roast with Bones; Boned, Rolled Roasts (made from ribs, sirloin, rump, or other tender cuts)

Roast Lamb — Leg; Crown (ribs rolled into a "crown" shape, and cooked standing upright); Shoulder or Breast

Roast Veal — Leg; Loin; Shoulder or Breast

Roast Fresh Pork — Loin; Shoulder; Fresh Ham (leg); Crown (ribs rolled into crown shape)

BASIC PRINCIPLES

Roasting meat nowadays simply means seasoning it . . . placing it in a slow oven, uncovered . . . and letting dry heat circulate around it freely, from all sides, until meat is tender and done . . . which usually requires at least 2 or more hours.

And that is practically all there is to it.

A child could do it.

It is hardly even necessary to look at your roast while it cooks. In fact, many women don't; they go off to church or to play bridge while the roast cooks itself. You can do this if you have a reliable, automatic oven which you can keep fixed at a certain set temperature, and if you know the weight of your meat and so can judge quite closely when it will be done.

Old-time cooks used to make a great to-do about a roast. First it had to be put in a very hot oven, and seared rapidly all over. Then the heat was reduced to moderate; but as the meat was still

ROASTING CHART

pe of Roast	Degree of Doneness	Temperature Shown by Meat Thermometer When Meat Is Done	Approximate Roasting Time in Slow Oven (325°) (Minutes per pound)	
			Weight under 5½ Lbs.	Weight 5½ to 8 Lbs.
F				
b roast with bones	Rare	140°	27	21
	Medium	160°	34	27
	Well done	170°	41	33
ned, rolled roast, any tender beef	Rare	Same	40	31
	Medium	as	46	36
	Well done	above	52	41
B				
g with bone oned, rolled	Medium	180°	35	32
leg, shoulder	Medium	180°	45	42
rown roast	Medium	180°	35	
oin	Medium	180°	35	
uffed shoulder or breast	Medium	180°	40	
L				
g with bone	Medium	180°	45	35
oin	Medium	180°	60 (if under 4 lbs.) 40 (if 4 to 5 lbs.)	
oulder, boned, rolled	Medium	180°	42	
uffed shoulder or breast	Medium	180°	40	
SH PORK (Unsmoked. Must always be thoroughly roasted, until no pink shows in meat.)				
esh ham (leg)	Well done	190°		33 (if under 10 lbs.) 31 (if 10 to 12 lbs.)
rown roast	Well done	190°	45	40
oin	Well done	190°	38 (if under 3½ lbs.) 34 (if 3½ to 4½ lbs.) 32 (if 4½ to 6 lbs.)	
oulder, boned, rolled	Well done	190°	45	40
uffed shoulder	Well done	190°		40

cooking quite fast, and had had a good browning to begin with, it often had to be covered to keep it from drying. Water had to be added to the pan, to provide moisture until the juices started flowing. The meat had to be basted every 20 to 30 minutes with the combined juices and water. It had to be turned. It required a lot of looking at. And when done, it was very tasty, but it had shrunk a great deal, and lots of its juices and vitamins were cooked out into the pan.

Today, science has found a different method.

Repeated tests by the world's best meat producers prove that if your roast is put in a *slow* oven to start with, fatty side up . . . and if the oven is *kept* slow throughout the cooking . . . you will have a tenderer, moister, less shrunken roast, which has kept all its good juices and vitamins inside. No searing is done. No basting is necessary, for the fat on the top side of the meat keeps trickling down over it, in the slow heat, keeping the meat moist. No water needs to be added; there is no turning or basting. And because the temperature of the oven has not been so severe, your meat keeps its original size better, and does not dry out.

This latter method, therefore, is the one we recommend. And it serves for any roast.

MASTER RECIPE #1
FOR COOKING A ROAST

(1) Preheat baking oven to 325°, or "slow."

(2) While oven heats, wipe **meat** with damp cloth to clean; then rub well, on all sides, with **salt**. Add also a sprinkling of **pepper** if desired. If you have a crown roast, do not remove the tissue-thin membrane which covers it; this helps keep meat in shape.

(3) Most roasts have one side fattier than the others. Place meat, fatty side up, on a rack, in an open roasting pan. Frozen meat may first be thawed, at room temperature, before roasting. Or, as latest research proves, meat may be put into oven while still

frozen. If frozen, however, the cooking will take longer than if thawed; and oven should be hotter (400°).

If cooking a crown roast, place it on rack with points (ends of rib bones) pointing skyward; leave it in this position throughout roasting.

(4) If you like **onion** or **garlic** flavor on your meat, add this now. (Some cooks place half a raw peeled onion on top of a roast, fastening it there with skewer or toothpick, so the onion flavor may trickle over meat during cooking. Some make tiny gashes in the top (fattier) side of a leg of lamb, and insert in each gash a pin-shaped sliver of garlic).

(5) Do not cover meat. Do not add water to pan. Simply place meat in center of oven, and leave it there until done.

(6) How to know when done:

By thermometer. A roast-meat thermometer, which can be bought wherever cooking utensils are sold, is actually the only accurate guide to knowing when meat is done. Thermometer should be inserted into thickest part of meat (but not touching either fat or bone) before meat is put in oven. Meat is ready to eat when thermometer has reached temperature shown on Roasting Chart for type of roast you have, and degree of doneness you want.

By timing. Consult Roasting Chart to estimate number of hours your roast should take, for its weight, and for degree of doneness you want. As ovens vary, however, it may be necessary to make some slight adjustment in this estimate; meat may be done sooner, or take longer, so watch it during the last half hour of estimated time. Though it's not good for the roast, you may have to test it by inserting tines of a fork, to feel whether it is tender. Under-cooking is of course preferable to overcooking, since an under-cooked roast may be cooked again, after outside well-done pieces are eaten; but you can never *uncook* one which is done too much.

(7) When meat is tender, remove it from roasting pan to a warm platter; put it where it will keep warm while you make gravy, if desired.

VARIATIONS AND
ACCOMPANIMENTS—ROASTS

Roast Potatoes

Potatoes, peeled and washed, may be put in the roasting pan about 1 to 1½ hours before roast will be done. Even small potatoes will require an hour at the slow temperature being used for the meat. Place potatoes in a circle around meat, in same pan; sprinkle them with salt. To make them extra good, spoon up over them from time to time any fat or juices which have dripped into pan from meat.

Pan Gravy for Roasts

When meat is done, roasting pan will contain some liquid fat (dripped out of meat) which is more or less transparent. Under the fat will be some dark-colored meat juices, rich in savory flavor.

To make **2 cups of gravy,** pour out of roasting pan **all but 4 tablespoons** (¼ cup) **of liquid fat,** keeping remaining fat and meat juices in pan.

In a cup or bowl, mix **4 tablespoons flour,** ½ **teaspoon salt,** and ½ **cup cold water,** stirring these to a smooth, lumpless paste.

Little by little, stirring constantly, add the flour mixture to the pan juices. (If you don't stir, you'll have lumps of flour which are difficult to get out!) Add also **1 or 2 teaspoons grated raw onion** to pan.

Place roasting pan over moderate heat of a surface burner and cook, stirring, until flour has browned.

Then stir in, still mixing well, **1½ cups hot water.**

Keep cooking and stirring until mixture boils and thickens, about 5 minutes.

Taste. Gravy may need more salt for your family's liking. Or you may wish to stir in a few drops bottled **gravy flavoring,** for extra color and extra spice. Or you may wish to stir in **1 or 2 teaspoons bottled meat extract,** to give a more meaty flavor.

As soon as thickened and seasoned, gravy is ready to serve.

Stuffed Roasts

You don't want to cut "pockets" in expensive, top-quality cuts of meat (like leg of lamb and loin of pork) to hold stuffing; these prime meats are good enough without stuffing! But the more economical cuts — shoulder or breast of lamb, veal, or pork, or even a fresh ham, become doubly delectable with savory stuffing added.

Have butcher bone meat, leaving a pocket to hold stuffing. Pack into this pocket, *loosely*, **plain bread stuffing** (p. 241), or any variation desired. Close pocket by fastening skin of both sides together with skewers; or sew skin together. Season and cook your roast as under Master Recipe.

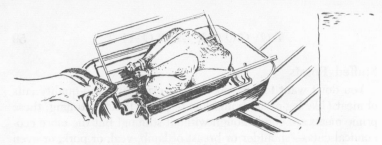

CHAPTER VII

How to Roast a Bird

METHOD FOR: *Chicken, Turkey, Domestic Duck, Goose, Giblet Gravy*

BASIC PRINCIPLES

Modern roasting of a bird merely means cleaning it, stuffing it if desired, trussing it, and placing it on uncovered roasting pan, in moderate, even-temperature oven, until done. By this modern slow-roasting process, many steps of old-fashioned roasting are eliminated; the old-time change from hot to slow oven temperature is not necessary; basting is not necessary; indeed nothing is necessary but to turn the bird over, now and again, if it seems to be browning more on one side than another. It is extremely simple.

This is a very good system, highly recommended for big birds, like roasting chicken, goose, turkey, in that the slow oven heat penetrates the bird gradually, keeping the meat moister and more succulent, and causing less shrinkage of the meat. Many experts recommend this method for all birds. However, in cooking anything, exceptions may be made (and one's brains applied) in consideration of the type of the meat. Ducks, for example, are very "fatty" birds; a somewhat hotter oven helps melt and eliminate the excess fat more handily. Tiny birds become less dry if cooked as few minutes as possible — which means in a very hot oven, or even under the broiler, the birds first having been given a protective coating of fat. Some birds (like pheasant) have such naturally dry meat that not only must they be protected with a covering of fat salt pork or bacon strips, but they must be basted frequently to keep the meat moist.

The Master Recipe given below should serve as a clear guide for the birds you will roast most often. See also Recommendations for Specific Birds, to see what special care or preparation may be needed for each individual type.

MASTER RECIPE #2
PREPARING AND ROASTING A BIRD

The main work of roasting a bird lies in *preparing* it for the roasting; that is, cleaning it, stuffing it, trussing it.

If you are a beginner, allow yourself at least an hour *before* the roasting time should commence, to make your stuffing, clean bird, stuff it, and truss it.

Frozen birds must be thawed at room temperature, before being stuffed and roasted. (And never attempt to freeze a bird with stuffing already in it.)

(1) *Clean bird.* Birds obtained from a market usually are delivered "dressed" (head, feet, and feathers removed) and "drawn" (viscera, or internal organs, removed).

The only internal organs you receive and use are the giblets: heart, liver, and gizzard. These three parts, plus the bird's neck (cut off by butcher) you set aside for making giblet gravy; you do not roast them.

In selecting your bird, it is wise to choose one as free as possible of pin feathers, for these are black and ugly, and have to be pulled out one by one with tweezers before roasting. If bird has long hairs on it, hold bird (with tongs, if desired) 3 or 4 inches above heat of surface burner, and singe off (burn off) hairs quickly. NOTE: Another way of removing both pin feathers and hairs, if these are plentiful, is to melt a cake of paraffin in a saucepan, then brush the liquid paraffin *all* over bird's body. Let it dry on. When hardened, peel it off; hairs and pin feathers come with it.

Now wipe bird clean with damp cloth, inside and outside.

Season inside of bird by sprinkling plentifully with **salt**. (Some cooks allow ½ teaspoon salt per pound of bird).

(2) *Make your stuffing.* (See plain bread stuffing (p. 241), and variations.) Notice that Master Recipe, Plain Bread Stuffing makes 2 cups of stuffing. This makes enough for a small duck, a pheasant, or several tiny birds. But for a bigger bird, you will need to multiply the entire recipe. For a 4 to 7 pound roasting chicken, you will need 4 to 6 cups stuffing. For a 10 pound turkey or goose, you will need 8 to 10 cups stuffing.

(3) *Stuff the bird.* Pack your stuffing *loosely* into body cavity of bird (stuffing expands, in cooking); and also fill crop cavity, under bird's neck. Close neck cavity by folding neck skin down neatly over the opening, on back side of bird; and using a metal skewer like a pin, pin the skin in place, fastening it to skin of back. Close the large cavity by drawing both edges of skin together as if to make a seam; then pushing a long metal skewer in and out through both layers of skin, like a pin. (Or, if preferred, you may sew the opening together, using heavy white thread and a large-eyed needle.)

(4) *Truss the bird.* Trussing has an important reason behind it. It draws legs and wings in, close to bird's body, thus preventing their sticking out into the heat of the oven, and thus drying out and burning. Also, when the entire bird is "hugged close together" the breast meat and meat at sides underneath legs are more protected, thus less apt to dry out. Lastly, but also important, a nicely trussed bird looks plumper and more enticing for serving. To truss:

Step a. Push tips of wings back, away from body, and with a slight twisting action, force them behind bird's back. This takes a little pressure, but when wings are once secured this way, they will not come loose.

Step b. Have ready a long clean string (about 1 yard long for a chicken, longer for a big turkey). Place bird on its back, in front of you. Lift both drumsticks high into air, then cross the bird's legs at bottom of leg bone (just like a lady crossing her ankles). Use the center of your long string to wrap around the crossed ankle bones, tying them securely together in crossed position, with a knot. You now have two ends of string dangling.

Step c. Carry the two ends of string down to the tail piece, or "nubbin," drawing crossed ankle bones down as close as possible to tail; then wrap both ends of string firmly around the nubbin, and tie a knot, holding the legs down. You still have two ends of string dangling.

Step d. Carry each end of string forward, toward a wing. Pass each piece of string over front of one bent wing, over wing tip, then across bird's back. Both ends of string should meet at center of bird's back. Tie securely, and tight enough to hold wings as close to bird's body as possible. Bird is now trussed.

(5) *Season the bird.* Sprinkle outside of bird all over with salt; add a light sprinkling of **pepper** if desired. Rub seasoning in with hand, so it won't fall off.

(6) *Protect bird with fat,* if needed. See under Recommendations for Specific Birds for type of bird you are cooking.

(7) *Roasting.* Place bird on rack in roasting pan, and put in oven. See roasting temperature, and time to allow, under Recommendations for type bird you are cooking.

(8) *Basting.* See under recommendations for type of bird you are cooking.

(9) *Cooking giblets for gravy.* If planning to have giblet gravy, start giblets cooking as soon as bird is in oven. Carry out steps 1, 2, 3, giblet gravy (p. 64).

(10) *Turn bird over, if needed.* Watch bird as it roasts. If browning too much on one side, turn over to another side. If toward end of roasting time, bird is becoming too brown, cover bird with sheet of brown paper or sheet of aluminum foil to protect it from heat.

(11) *When to cut trussing strings.* These should be cut (and removed) when bird is about three quarters of the way through its roasting time. The white marks left underneath strings will then brown over, in last quarter.

(12) *How to know when done.* When done, bird should be nicely browned, all over. Meat should feel very soft, when thick-

est part of drumstick is pressed between fingers. Drumstick should be easily moved, up and down. If meat of drumstick has shrunk away appreciably from lower tip of leg bone, meat was overcooked, or cooked too rapidly. If meat thermometer is used (inserted before roasting begins, in meatiest part of bird, but without touching bone or fat), temperature should read 190° when bird is done.

(13) *Before serving.* Pull out skewers, or cut sewing stitches which hold stuffing inside. Remove bird to hot platter. Combine pan juices with cooked giblets and giblet water to make giblet gravy, as below.

Giblet Gravy

(*To serve with any roast bird.*)

Step 1. Brown **giblets** (heart, liver, gizzard) in frying pan or saucepan containing **2 tablespoons butter.**

Step 2. As soon as giblets are browned all over, put them in a saucepan with **1 or 2 stalks celery, with leaves, ½ peeled onion, 1 or 2 sprigs parsley, 2 cups water, 1 teaspoon salt.**

Bring water to a boil; then cover pan; place over low heat, and simmer gently until giblets are tender. Liver becomes tender first; remove it first; heart becomes tender next; remove it; gizzard last. Giblets of a very young bird may cook tender in 35–45 minutes, but for a big old turkey, this may require 2, 3, or more hours.

Step 3. Save cooking water, but strain out the vegetable seasonings. Remove giblets to chopping bowl. Chop them to pieces the size of peas. Return them to strained cooking water.

Step 4. When roast bird is tender and ready to serve, remove it from roasting pan to hot platter. In roasting pan will be some liquid fat (transparent) and some dark meat-flavored juices. If more than **4 or 5 tablespoons liquid fat** is in pan, spoon off the excess fat.

Step 5. Now, in a cup or jar, mix **⅓ cup flour** plus **½ teaspoon salt** either with **a little cold water,** or with **a little cool liquid** giblets were cooked in, stirring to a smooth paste. Stir paste into roasting pan juices, *stirring constantly,* with wire whisk, or wooden spoon, over low heat, until smoothly blended, without lumps.

Step 6. Add chopped giblets and water they were cooked in.

Bring to boil, stirring constantly; then reduce heat and cook 1 or 2 minutes longer. If desired, season with **1 or 2 teaspoon grated onion,** plus more salt.

RECOMMENDATIONS FOR SPECIFIC BIRDS

Chicken, Turkey

Some cooks coat a **chicken** or **turkey** all over with **melted butter,** or with **vegetable shortening** or **lard,** to seal the pores, keep meat moist, and brown outside prettily. Under modern slow-tempera-ture roasting method, however, this is not necessary. Place seasoned, stuffed bird, breast-bone pointing *down,* on greased rack in open roasting pan. Roast in moderate (350°) oven, allow-ing the following roasting time (see Chart), and turning bird over to another side when one side becomes brown. If desired, you may spoon up the pan juices over the bird (baste it) every half hour or so. Keeping the breastbone pointed *down,* during first half to two thirds of the roasting time, keeps the bird's natural juices flowing toward the breast, thereby helping to keep the breast moist and succulent. Turn bird breast side up, during last part of cook-ing, to brown the breast skin nicely.

Roasting Chart for Big Birds

Bird Weighing	Minutes per Lb.
4 to 7 lbs.	25 to 30
8 to 10	20 to 25
10 to 16	18 to 20
18 to 25	15 to 18
25 to 30	15

NOTE: For a small family of 2 or 3 persons, a turkey of 10 to 12 pounds makes a great deal too much meat to use up speedily. If you have a freezer, don't worry; buy the turkey, but have butcher split it in half down the back and clean it. One half may be well wrapped and put in the freezer. The other half may be roasted, with the hollow (inner) side down on roasting pan without rack. Place the stuffing in the hollow underneath the bird. Naturally half a turkey will cook more rapidly than a whole one, since heat needn't penetrate so great a thickness. Allow proper minutes per pound of the half turkey's weight, but watch the roasting; it may cook a little faster than you expect. When ready to roast the frozen half, thaw it first at room temperature; then prepare stuffing, and roast as for first half.

Domestic Duck

(This means the usual tame duck, sold at markets; not a wild one, brought down on the wing.) One domestic duck usually weighs 4 to 6 pounds, but much of the weight is carcass, not meat. One duck therefore seldom serves over 3 or 4 people.

Whenever cooking duck, remember that it is a very fatty bird; everything you do to it should therefore be aimed at cutting some of the excess greasiness.

To stuff. Prepare about **4 cups plain bread stuffing** (p. 241), or one of the tarter variations, such as orange, apple, or apricot stuffing. Or use a "dry" type stuffing, such as cracker stuffing, peanut stuffing, or mashed potato stuffing (p. 244). Some cooks prefer not to stuff a duck at all, but to fill the cavity with **pared, cored, quartered apples, sliced oranges, celery stalks and leaves, and 2 or 3 peeled onions.** These ingredients help flavor the bird and are discarded before bird is served.

To truss. A duck's legs are very short, and the wings lie close to the body; therefore some people do not truss a duck at all. If you wish to truss it, however, draw the tips of the two legs as close together as possible, about 1 inch apart, and tie them so; then carry the same string down and wrap it around skewer which closes the stuffing cavity, tying another knot.

To roast. Many people prick tiny holes (with tines of a fork) into outer layer of duck, over back, around tail, into body, into wings, into legs, to allow excess fat to trickle out of duck rapidly while cooking. Place duck breast side up on wire rack or trivet in open roasting pan. If desired, you may roast bird in a very hot (450°) oven, allowing 12 to 15 minutes per pound. Or you may use the slow-temperature method, putting bird into a slow (325°)

oven, and allowing about 30 minutes per pound. Do not baste the bird with fat; on the contrary, pour off excess liquid fat from pan, if too much accumulates. Do not turn duck. Every 15 or 20 minutes, baste the duck with ¼ **cup orange juice**, if desired; this gives a wonderful flavor. Serve with brown rice (p. 307), and orange sauce (p. 254).

Goose

(A young goose, under 6 months old, weighing 10 pounds or less, will be tenderest; older ones are excessively fatty and tend to be tough. A 10 pound goose serves 10 people.)

To stuff. Make about **8 cups stuffing,** using apple, celery, or orange stuffing (p. 242).

To truss. If goose has very short legs, don't truss at all; otherwise truss like duck.

To roast. Goose, like duck, is improved if pricked all over body with tines of a fork, around tail, over back, into body around wings and legs; this helps fat trickle out quickly. Place goose breast side up on wire rack or trivet in open roasting pan. Place in hot (400°) oven for first 20 minutes; then reduce heat to moderate (350°) and continue cooking, allowing 25 minutes per pound. Do not baste with fat from pan. If bird creates excessive liquid fat in pan, draw out pan and pour off and discard some of the grease.

CHAPTER VIII

How to Broil a Steak

METHOD FOR: *Steaks, Chops, Meat Cakes, Ham Steak, Bacon, Liver, Fish, Chicken*

BASIC PRINCIPLES

Broiling is a quick, *"dry"* way of cooking — that is, cooking *by heated air*, without allowing food to rest in either water or fat.

It should be used only for tender meat — steaks, chops, young chicken, fish — and other tender foods which will cook quickly.

The broiler unit should be preheated to as hot a heat as can be used for the type of food you are cooking, without allowing the food to scorch.

MASTER RECIPE #3
BROILING

(1) While broiler preheats, wipe **meat,** with damp cloth, to make sure it is clean.

(2) If meat is type which might easily scorch or dry out (such as chicken, fish), brush food all over with **melted butter** or **olive oil** or **vegetable shortening,** to give the outside a protective coating.

If meat has a rim of hard fat around it (like steak), slash the fat in several places, to prevent meat from curling up in cooking.

(3) Season food: sprinkle it all over with **salt** (except ham). Sprinkle also lightly with **pepper,** if desired.

(4) Place food on broiler rack. If broiling tender food which might easily scorch or stick, such as chicken, grease the rack before putting food on it. If cooking fish, omit rack altogether, placing fish flat in greased broiling pan; fish put on a rack will stick and be hard to remove.

(5) Place broiling pan underneath preheated broiling unit, at heat specified in Recommendations for Broiling Specific Foods below.

In gas and some electric ovens, broiler heat can be adjusted by hand. If your broiler cannot be adjusted to moderate, or low, heat, then the adjustment is made by placing delicate food *farther away from the heat,* so that it will not burn.

(6) Cook food as rapidly as possible without burning it until nicely browned on top side. Then turn it; cook until nicely browned on second side. Pieces of fish only ½ inch thick, or less, do not need to be turned; heat of broiling pan cooks the under side adequately.

(7) How to tell when done. Thin pieces of meat or fish (½ inch thick) will be done as soon as browned. Thicker pieces may need longer cooking, to cook through. A 2 inch thick steak may take 10 to 15 minutes on each side; and broiled chicken usually requires 20 to 30 minutes, all told, to become tender, depending on size and thickness of chicken pieces. Refer to Broiling Chart (p. 74), for approximate time to allow for each type food.

RECOMMENDATIONS FOR BROILING SPECIFIC FOODS

Steaks

It is astonishing how many people think they cannot broil a steak. Actually it is one of the easiest things to do in all cooking, and the most rewarding. All you need, to do it well, is one bit of wisdom: *Steak must always be cooked at high heat,* to be tender. Slow cooking makes the meat "stew" instead of broil, and even a tender cut of meat may toughen if heat is not hot. So don't be timid about the amount of heat you use. Many people like a steak cooked at such intense heat that it is slightly "charred" on top.

To prepare. Slash edges of fat around outside of **steak.** Sprinkle steak well, both sides, with **salt.** Place steak on broiling rack in broiling pan. Place in preheated broiling oven, 2 inches below broiling unit if steak is 1 inch thick; 3 inches below broiling unit if steak is 2 inches thick. Cook rapidly about 5 to 7 minutes until well browned on top. Pull out the broiling pan; turn steak over with tongs; return it to broiling oven; broil until browned on second side. If steak is more than 1 inch thick, it may need a few minutes more cooking on each side; consult Broiling Chart (p. 74).

To test doneness. Since heat of different broiling ovens varies, the only way you can test doneness (until you are experienced) is to pull broiling pan out, and with sharp knife, make one cut, across the grain of the meat, into center of steak; then look inside, and see how rare or well done it is. Naturally experts frown on this method, but if you are a beginner, do it. It does no great harm; it will only let out a few drops of juice; and if you put the steak back to cook more, the cut will immediately sear closed, so no more juice comes out. Remember, you can always cook a steak *more;* but if it is done too much, you can't *un*cook it.

Occasionally, when cooking steak, the fat in the broiling pan catches fire. To avoid this, if your steak has a great deal of fat on it, you may remove broiling pan from broiling oven once or twice during the cooking and pour off the melted fat from broiler pan. If fat on the meat itself splutters a great deal, move the broiling pan a bit farther from the heat. And if steak *does* catch fire, don't be alarmed. Draw out broiling pan and douse the fire at once with quantities of salt. After fire is out, you can scrape off the excess salt and continue cooking meat. And don't be ashamed. Every good cook has, at some time, had a steak catch fire; and a slight "charring" on top of the steak is often considered delicious; it is something often found on steaks cooked over outdoor log fires or charcoal fires. Remember that steak is good lusty, hearty fare, and should be cooked lustily!

To serve. Remove steak from broiling pan to hot platter. Place a large lump of **butter** on it, letting it melt over meat. Use a sharp carving knife and cut slices *across the grain;* this makes for tender eating.

NOTE: If you have a T-bone steak, the tenderloin is a small round section of meat nestled under the smaller side of the T-bone. Tail of steak is always slightly tougher; this may be saved to use in beef and kidney pie, or in other dishes recommended under Leftovers (p. 184).

Chops

Preferably **salt** before broiling. Broil **chops** as for a steak, but with only a *moderately* hot broiler. Allow 5 to 6 minutes on each side for chops ¾ inch thick. (Exception: Do not oven-broil pork chops; they require longer, more thorough cooking. Pan-broil them; see p. 80).

Meat Cakes

Oven-broiling is recommended only for **meat cakes** which have very little fat ground in with the meat. Some types of hamburger contain so much ground fat that cakes might easily catch fire under broiler. Such meat cakes are better pan-broiled (p. 81).

As meat cakes break apart easily, do not try to place them on a rack. Instead, place in broiling pan very lightly greased (so cakes won't stick to bottom). Place pan so that top of cakes comes about 3 inches below broiler unit. Allow 2 to 4 minutes on each side for rare cakes, if cakes are ¾ inch thick (ground meat, of course, cooks more rapidly than a solid piece of steak). When turning cakes, **salt** side you are placing toward heat, if it has not already been salted.

Ham Steak

Use a center slice of **ham** which has been at least partially cooked (either by meat packer, or by you); an uncooked piece would not have time to become done in this quick method of cooking. With scissors, make several slashes through fat around the edges of the ham slice; if you omit this, ham will curl up during cooking. *Never salt ham;* it is already salty enough. If you wish, you may spread ham with **prepared mustard** before broiling. Place broiler pan so top of ham is 3 to 4 inches from it. Allow about 4 minutes on each side for a ham slice ¾ inch thick.

Bacon

Many people prefer pan-broiling **bacon** (see p. 85), but it may be broiled in oven if you watch it carefully, and take care not to have broiler too hot. Bacon burns easily; may even burn before it has cooked. Stretch bacon strips out singly, over broiling-pan rack; place pan 3 to 4 inches from a *moderately* hot broiler. Watch it; it takes only 3 to 5 minutes. When broiled on a rack, bacon needs no draining, as it is not greasy; but it may still be drained on paper towel, before serving, if you want it *extra* crisp.

Liver

Have **liver** sliced thin, for broiling — not over ¼ inch thick if possible. With sharp knife, cut out any white sinews or tendons, as these make tough eating. Wipe liver clean with damp cloth. Sprinkle liberally with **salt** and **pepper**. Place on greased rack, in broiling pan, 3 to 4 inches from heat, or where heat will be moderate (liver prefers gentle cooking!). Cook until browned on one side; turn, cook on other side. Allow about 3 minutes on each side. See Chart (p. 74). Do not overcook, or liver tends to become leathery. When done, serve at once; do not keep it standing. Serve with cooked bacon or pan-fried onions, potatoes, green vegetable.

Fish (Fish steak; fish fillets; or a whole fish, cleaned and split in half)

See Broiling Chart, page 74.

Wipe flesh of fish clean, with damp cloth or paper towel. Brush flesh with **melted butter, cooking oil,** or other bland cooking fat. Then sprinkle with **salt** and **pepper**. Place fish in lightly greased broiling pan *without rack*. If split whole fish, place skin side down. Place broiling pan 3 to 5 inches from heat, or where heat will just turn fish golden color, without burning it. Fillets may be cooked about 5–6 minutes on one side, until golden color; then turned and cooked same way on other side. If cooking *a split fish with skin,* simply *cook skin side down* until flesh is golden brown; *don't turn.* If fish seems to be drying out during cooking, add a few dots of **butter** on top of it. Remove fish to hot plate; pour over it lemon-butter sauce (p. 256); or simply dot fish with **butter** again, and serve wedges of lemon to squeeze over it.

Chicken

Have a broiler-size **chicken** dressed, drawn, cut in halves or quarters. (Save out giblets — heart, gizzard, liver; simmer as for Chicken Broth, p. 82; chop; use in omelet, or mix with mayonnaise for a sandwich or canapé spread for another day.) Wipe all chicken pieces clean with damp cloth. Singe off hairs, if any. Sprinkle pieces on all sides generously with **salt** and **pepper.** Brush all sides with **soft butter, vegetable shortening,** or **salad oil.** Place pieces, skin side down, on well-greased rack in broiling pan; chicken will stick to rack if it is not greased. Place pan in preheated, moderately hot broiling oven, 4 to 5 inches from heat. Cook chicken without turning, about 8 to 12 minutes, or until nicely golden brown on top; but look at the chicken every few minutes to see that it is not burning. If scorching, remove pan farther from heat, or reduce heat. If flesh seems to be drying too much, remove pan from oven and brush pieces again with butter or other cooking fat, then return it to oven. When browned nicely on top, turn pieces over; brush again with butter; cook similarly on second side. A broiler cut in halves will usually take 20 to 30 minutes in all to become done. Smaller pieces cook more quickly.

Remove from oven as soon as chicken is beautiful, light, golden brown; do not overcook or your chicken will lose its juiciness and become hard and dry. Well-broiled chicken is succulent, tender, and very flavorful. Delicious served with steamed rice, green peas, peach or sherry jelly. Or, if desired, add mushroom caps sautéed in butter.

BROILING CHART

Approximate *total* time for various types of meat. (This time is to be divided in half; the food cooked *half* of the total time on one side; half on the other side)

BEEF STEAKS	Thickness	Rare	Medium
Sirloin or Club	1″	10–12 min.	14–16 min.
	1½	15–16	18–20
	2	22–25	26–30
Porterhouse	1	12–15	16–18
Top Round	1½	18–20	22–25
Chuck	2	25–28	28–30
Tenderloin	1	6	8
	1½	8	10
	2	10	12
BEEF MEAT CAKES	¾	4–5	6–8
LAMB *or* MUTTON CHOPS			
Loin Chops	1		15–18
Rib Chops	1½		25–28
LAMB MEAT CAKES	¾		6–8
HAM STEAK (or slice)	¼–¾	Ready to eat	4–8
SAUSAGES			10–12
BACON			4–5
LIVER (Calf)	½		4–6
(Beef)	½		6–8
FISH			
Fillets	½–¾		Until golden brown on top, and flaky, or 6–8 min.
Whole fish, split in halves	½ to ¾		Until golden brown on flesh side, and flaky, or 8–12 min.
CHICKEN			
Broilers cut in quarters			Until golden brown and tender, on both sides, or about 20 min.
Broilers cut in halves			The same, or about 30 min.

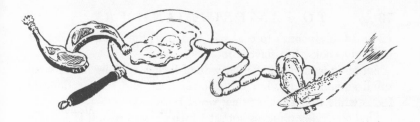

How to Pan-Broil, Pan-Fry, Sauté, or Shallow-Fry

METHOD FOR:

Pan-Broiled — Beef Steaks, Ham Steaks, Chops, Meat Cakes, Chicken, Fish, Liver, Sausages, Bacon

Pan-Fried — Apple Rings (and other fruits), Fish, Ham, Hash, Potatoes, Potato Cakes, Round Steak (country style)

Sautéed — Chicken Livers, Frogs' Legs, Kidneys, Mushrooms, Onions

Shallow-Fried — Chicken, Croquettes, Codfish Balls or Cakes, Eggplant, Tomatoes, Summer Squash, Fish, Onion Rings, Fritters, Doughnuts

Coatings for Food to be Fried

BASIC PRINCIPLES

This chapter might be called "How to Use a Frying Pan," for pan-broiling, pan-frying, sautéing, and shallow-frying are all cousins . . . all done in the same frying pan (which should be a heavy one, of cast iron or cast aluminum). The cooking differs chiefly in *the amount of fat,* and *the amount of heat* used.

Pan-broiling (a substitute for broiling in the broiler oven) is a "dry" way of cooking: that is, cooking by dry heat, with little or no fat in frying pan.

Frying is a "wet" way of cooking: cooking in enough hot fat

(2 or 3 tablespoons) to coat pan and "fry" the food. The hot fat not only cooks, but flavors food.

Sautéing is merely a gentler way of frying, cooking in the same small amount of fat, but using lower heat, and stirring delicate foods while they cook, so they won't burn.

Shallow-frying requires hot fat 1 inch deep in pan. It is actually a substitute for French-frying, and used only for types of food which might otherwise be deep-fried.

For each of these frying-pan methods, there is a Master Recipe. But as in all cooking, simple adjustments must be made for type of food you are cooking. Heat is lowered for foods which may burn easily; fat may be increased for food which might stick easily.

BASIC PRINCIPLES
FOR PAN-BROILING

Pan-broiling, remember, is a substitute for broiling in the oven. The idea is to cook food with dry heat, not with fat.

However, even if you were broiling in the oven, certain foods (like fish, chicken) would need to be lightly coated with butter or other fat, to protect meat from becoming parched and burned. So, likewise, in pan-broiling, the same types of foods (chicken, fish) need a light coating of fat in the pan, to prevent sticking or scorching.

In cases of firm red meat and chops, often no fat at all is needed. One reason for this is that such meat usually has sufficient fat or suet attached to it to prevent meat's sticking. Meat cakes, likewise, usually contain ground fat, which melts and supplies a little (sometimes too much) cooking grease.

A third group is the very fatty meats (sausage, bacon) which exude *so much* fat while cooking that the fat must be kept poured off to keep the pan anywhere near dry.

Therefore, there are variations in pan-broiling. Follow the Master Recipe for each type of meat.

MASTER RECIPE #4
PAN-BROILING

For Firm Red Meats with Fat Attached or Included

(1) Have a heavy frying pan *really hot* . . . hissing hot for steak; not quite so hot for chops. Do not grease pan.

(2) Salt the meat on side you plan to place face down in pan. Place meat in pan; sear (brown) meat rapidly on bottom side. (If meat sticks to pan, add 1 or 2 tablespoons cooking fat.)

(3) Salt upper side of meat; then turn meat over. Brown it rapidly on second side. (If necessary, add a bit more cooking fat.)

(4) When browned on both sides, reduce heat and cook usually 3 to 10 minutes longer (according to thickness) until done to taste. (Pork chops must be cooked until no pink shows inside.)

(5) If necessary to cook over 10 to 12 minutes total, *cover pan,* thus holding heat and moisture inside pan and preventing meat from becoming dried out. (This may be unorthodox, but is far better than eating dried-up meat.)

For Delicate Meats (Chicken, Fish, Liver)

(1) Heat in heavy, *moderately* hot frying pan, 2 to 3 table-spoons cooking fat, enough to cover thinly the bottom of the pan.

(2) Salt side of meat you plan to put face down in pan. Brown meat on bottom side. (If meat sticks to pan, add a bit more cooking fat.)

(3) Salt upper side of meat. Turn it over — see exception for split fish (p. 83). Brown second side. If necessary, add a trifle more fat to prevent sticking.

(4) Fish or thin liver may be done at end of browning. But for thicker pieces of meat like chicken, reduce heat; cook longer on each side, gently, until tender and done to taste inside.

(5) If necessary to cook over 10 to 12 minutes total, cover pan to prevent meat drying out.

For Very Fatty Meats (Sausage, Bacon)

(1) Start with heavy frying pan almost cool. Do not grease pan.

(2) Do not salt bacon or sausage; they have sufficient smoky taste or high seasoning already. Simply spread meat out in pan.

(3) Cook over moderate heat until browned on one side. If more than 2 tablespoons grease accumulates in pan, pour it off into a grease container; keep pan nearly dry.

(4) Turn meat over, browning second side. Again pour off excess grease if necessary.

(5) Sausage should be cooked through thoroughly, but not so long it begins to shrink. Bacon should be removed from pan before it seems quite done; it finishes crisping as it dries. See specific recommendations below.

RECOMMENDATIONS FOR PAN-BROILING SPECIFIC FOODS

Pan-Broiled Beef Steak

Consult your butcher as to best cuts to pan-broil; and also as to how much you will need, of any cut, to serve 2; amount of meat varies in different cuts, some cuts including more bone and fat than others.

For steak, always have frying pan hissing hot; slow heat will "stew" and toughen the meat. With knife, make several slashes in any fat around outer edge of steak, to prevent meat's curling. **Salt** steak well on one side. Place that side down, in ungreased pan. Brown meat rapidly on lower side. (If steak sticks to pan, add **1 or 2 tablespoons cooking fat**.) **Salt** upper side. Turn meat over. Brown second side rapidly. If steak is very thin, it may then be done. If ½ inch thick, reduce heat and cook 3 to 5 minutes longer on each side. If 1 inch thick, cook 5 to 8 minutes longer, on each side. If 1½ inches thick, cook 8 to 12 minutes longer on each side, depending on degree of doneness you like. As not only texture in steaks, but also heat supplied in stoves varies, it is absolutely impossible for anyone to give you a precise time; the only way to know whether steak meets your desires (until you know your own stove well) is to cut one slash into its center and peek inside (see *To Test Doneness* under Broiled Steak, p. 70).

When done, slide steak at once to heated platter. Put a generous lump of **butter** on top of meat; let it melt down over meat. Add **pan juices**, if desired; and if there are any. (There won't be much juice in pan if steak was properly cooked.) Always carve steak *across* the grain. This cuts the long fibers, and makes for tenderer eating. Wonderful accompaniments for steak: sautéed mushrooms (p. 95); or sautéed onions (p. 96). Or shallow-fried onion rings (p. 105). Also German-fried potatoes (p. 90); and baked stuffed tomatoes (p. 299).

Pan-Broiled Ham Steak

A 1 lb. ham steak serves 2 to 3 people. Use a crosswise slice of cooked, partly cooked, or uncooked ham, ½ to ¾ inch thick. Such a slice can be separately purchased at market; or you can have butcher cut a slice from a half ham when you buy one; one day use the slice as a steak, another day bake the remainder of the ham as on page 132.

Completely or Partly Cooked Ham (called "ready-to-eat," "tenderized," or "precooked"). Little cooking time is needed in frying pan. Rub cold frying pan with a bit of **ham fat;** then heat pan moderately. Remove any hard rind from around edge of ham. Slash with scissors the rim of fat around ham slice, in 4 or 5 places, to prevent ham's curling up while cooking. Do not salt ham; it is always salty enough. Place ham in pan; brown 3 to 4 minutes on each side. As soon as nicely browned and heated through, serve.

Uncooked Ham. First trim hard rind from outer edge of ham with sharp knife; then soak ham slice about 1 hour in lukewarm water. Drain. Dry with towel. Slash fat around edges of ham slice in 4 or 5 places, to prevent ham's curling. Rub cold frying pan with ham fat; then heat pan moderately. Do not salt ham. Place ham in pan, brown quickly on each side; then reduce heat, cover pan, and cook gently 15 to 30 minutes more, or until ham is tender when tested with fork. Don't use hot fire, or ham will toughen.

Ways to Garnish Ham Steak

Cook ham with pineapple and brown sugar. Prepare and start cooking your ham steak as above. When browned on one side, turn ham; sprinkle browned side generously with **brown sugar;** add to pan a few well-drained slices **canned pineapple.** Let pineapple brown lightly as second side of ham browns. Serve browned pineapple with ham, and pour over ham any juices in pan.

Top cooked ham with sautéed mushrooms (p. 95).

Make mustard-currant sauce. Prepare and cook your ham steak as above. When cooked, remove to warm platter. To juices left in pan, add 3 tablespoons vinegar, 1½ teaspoon prepared mustard, ½ teaspoon sugar, 1 tablespoon currant jelly. Stir well as mixture heats; pour it over ham steak.

Pan-Broiled Chops

Cook chops by method for firm meats (p. 77); having frying pan quite hot for lamb or veal chops, cooler for pork chops. Salt meat on one side; place salted side down in heated pan; brown lower side. If chops stick to pan, add **1 or 2 tablespoons cooking fat.** Salt upper side of meat; turn it over; brown second side. If lamb or veal chops are thin, they may be sufficiently cooked by end of browning. If ½ to ¾ inch thick, reduce heat and cook gently 4 to 6 minutes more on each side, depending upon thickness, until tender when tested with fork. NOTE: *Always cook pork chops until no pink shows inside.* If necessary to cook any chops over 10 to 12 minutes, *cover pan,* closing moisture inside, to prevent meat's drying out.

Pan juices. If any firm-textured meat has been properly panbroiled, fire will have been hot enough so that little juice will have escaped from meat into pan; however, what little is crusted to the pan is highly tasty. Remove chops to hot platter; loosen juice from pan by adding ¼ to ½ cup hot water, putting pan over heat and stirring rapidly, scraping bottom of pan to release juices. Pour hot juices over meat.

Thickened pan gravy. If thicker gravy is desired, after removing chops from pan as above, shake together in a small, tightly covered glass jar 2 tablespoons flour with 1 cup cold water, until thoroughly mixed. Pour this slowly into meat pan, stirring constantly and scraping bottom of pan to mix flour and water well with pan juices crusted there. Bring to boil while stirring. If desired, add ½ teaspoon grated onion, or a few drops bottled gravy seasoning, or a few drops Worcestershire sauce, to increase gravy flavor.

Pan-Broiled Meat Cakes

Beef. One half pound ground beef makes 2 medium-sized meat cakes about ¾ inch thick.

Some people like hamburgers highly seasoned. If you do, with ½ pound raw ground beef mix ½ teaspoon salt, ¼ teaspoon pepper, 1 or 2 teaspoons grated raw onion; if desired, add a few drops Worcestershire sauce. Blend well. Then shape meat into two even-sized cakes.

If you prefer meat cakes to taste like real steak, omit above seasonings; leave meat in its natural flavor. Just shape meat into cakes.

For either type cakes, follow method for firm meats (p. 77), having frying pan very hot. Salt one side of meat cakes; place salted side down on hot pan; brown rapidly. If meat sticks to pan, add 1 or 2 tablespoons cooking fat.* Salt other side of meat; turn; brown second side rapidly. If you like meat very rare, cakes will be nearly done when thoroughly browned top and bottom.

If you like meat medium or well done, after first quick browning reduce heat and cook cakes 3 to 7 minutes longer on each side, or until done to your taste.

NOTE: Rapid browning of meat over hot fire, as above, makes cakes that taste like steak — with a crisp, crusty outside, and a rarer inside. If you prefer cakes soft and well-done throughout, use only moderate heat for browning, and cook longer, gently. If you like *very* moist cakes, cover pan during last few minutes of cooking.

---

* Some meat sold as hamburger contains so much ground fat that within a few minutes after cooking is begun pan contains a good deal of liquid grease. If you don't want greasy meat cakes, pour off this excessive fat as it accumulates, leaving only 1 or 2 tablespoons in pan.

Pan juices. When meat is cooked, if only *fat* remains in pan, discard it. But if there is a little pan juice of good flavor, pour this over meat. If desired, blend a few tablespoons hot water with pan juices, and scrape pan, before pouring over meat.

Lamb. (Many stores sell lamb cakes already shaped; buy 1 or 2 per person.) Cook as for beef cakes, but using only *moderate* heat, as lamb is apt to dry out faster. If lamb cakes stick to pan, add 1 or 2 tablespoons cooking fat.

Pan-Broiled Chicken

Buy 1 broiler-size — 2 to 2½ pound — chicken for 2 people. Have butcher dress, clean it, and cut it in quarters. Wipe all meat pieces of chicken clean with damp cloth. Keep out giblets and neck; these do not make good broiling pieces. Save them to make a little Chicken Broth for next day (see below). A baby chicken this size is not apt to have pin feathers or hairs, but if it has, pull them out with tweezers. Sprinkle chicken well with **salt** and **pepper** on all sides. In moderately hot frying pan, melt **2 to 4 tablespoons vegetable shortening.** Put chicken in pan. Brown to golden color on both sides, turning as needed; add more cooking fat if chicken sticks to pan. When entirely browned, cover pan, reduce heat to low, and cook gently about 15 to 30 minutes longer, or until chicken is tender when tested with fork.

Chicken Broth Made from Giblets and Neck. Put **giblets** and **neck** in saucepan. Cover with **2 cups water.** Add **1 short branch celery with leaves, 1 sprig parsley, ½ peeled onion.** Cover. Simmer 30 to 45 minutes, or until all giblets feel tender when pricked with fork. About 15 minutes before tender, stir in ½ **teaspoon salt** (or more, if wanted). Remove celery and parsley from broth. Lift out giblets, chop them, and return them to broth. If desired, add to broth ½ **cup leftover cooked rice,** or a few **leftover cooked noodles.** Serves 2.

Chicken Pan Gravy. When broiled chicken has been lifted from frying pan, a little tasty **chicken juice** will remain in pan. If desired, stir into it ½ **to ¾ cup water** or **heavy cream,** scraping bottom of pan to loosen chicken juice. If desired, stir in also ½ teaspoon grated raw onion. Heat. Blend well. Taste; add a dash of salt, if needed. Pour over chicken.

Pan-Broiled Fish

This method is for fish steaks (salmon steaks, swordfish steaks), fish fillets (frozen or fresh), split whole fish (such as trout or mackerel split in half; head, tail and fins removed, and cleaned inside). If fish is frozen, allow 1 or 2 hours to thaw at room temperature, or according to package directions; then wipe dry before cooking.

Any crosswise slice of fish, or any small whole fish split lengthwise (provided it is not over ¾ to 1 inch thick) may be pan-broiled. Pan-broiling, however, being a quick, *dry* method of cooking, is not recommended for fish of naturally dry flesh; such fish is better poached (p. 123) or fried (p. 88). Pan-broiling is excellent for any fish which is naturally moist-meated, or rich in oils, or has a truly distinctive flavor which you do not wish to diminish or change.

Fish Steaks or Fillets. Have frying pan only moderately hot. Melt in it 2 to 3 tablespoons salad oil or vegetable shortening. Wipe all sides of fish clean with damp cloth; sprinkle fish well on all sides with salt. If cooking fillets, cut these to serving-size pieces before cooking. Using pancake turner or wide spatula, lift pieces of fish to pan. Brown lower side to rich golden color. If fish sticks to pan, add more cooking fat. When browned on lower side, gently turn fish over with spatula or pancake turner. Brown second side. When both sides are a nice rich golden brown, serve. Do not overcook; fish requires only brief cooking; its flesh should still be flaky and moist when served. Lift fish carefully to heated platter. Garnish with wedges of lemon to squeeze over fish; or with beurre noir (p. 256), or parsley butter (p. 256). Or for a weak-flavored fish, you might serve anchovy butter (p. 256).

Split Whole Fish. Have fish split, trimmed, and cleaned at market. Wipe all sides thoroughly with damp cloth. Sprinkle both skin and flesh liberally with salt. If desired, cut to serving-size pieces before cooking; or leave fish intact, in halves. Place fish, skin side down, in moderately hot frying pan containing **2 to 3 tablespoons melted cooking fat.** Cook a few minutes until skin side is nicely browned. Then reduce heat; cover pan (covering pan helps cook flesh side of fish without necessity for turning fish over; and turning it without breaking is often difficult). Cook, covered, until flesh side is flaky, but still moist. With spatula or pancake turner lift fish carefully from pan, sliding fish onto hot platter. If desired, sprinkle a dash or two of **paprika** over flesh side, to give prettier color. Garnish platter with sprigs of **parsley.** Serve with wedges of **lemon** to squeeze over fish.

Pan-Broiled Liver

Liver is often referred to on menus as "fried" or "sautéed"; but actually the method is a gentle pan-broiling. Buy **½ pound very thinly sliced beef, calf, or pork liver,** to serve 2. Try to obtain slices not over ¼ inch thick. Thicker liver becomes tough before it can cook through.

If liver has any thick, tough outer skin remaining around edges, trim this off with sharp knife. Also, with knife or scissors, remove tough stringy white tendons, if any. Prepare **flour coating** (p. 101), and dip each piece of liver in it, coating all sides; (or instead, you may simply sprinkle liver with **salt** and **pepper**).

Heat frying pan only *moderately* hot. Melt in it **2 or 3 table-spoons cooking fat** (bacon fat is tasty, for this). Place seasoned liver slices in pan — only as many as will fit in easily, without overlapping. Brown liver lightly on bottom side; if liver begins to stick to pan, add more cooking fat. Using a pancake turner, turn liver over; brown lightly on second side. Again add more cooking fat, if needed. Reduce heat, and cook 2 or 3 minutes longer on each side, just until liver feels tender (but not spongy) when pricked with fork. If red juice runs out when liver is pricked, cook liver a minute or two longer. But don't go off and leave it. Liver is done in very few minutes' cooking, and needs constant watching; for it reaches perfection at one given moment, and immediately thereafter begins to turn tough.

Have precooked, to serve with it: sautéed onions (p. 96); or shallow-fried onion rings (p. 105), or pan-broiled bacon. Also good with liver: baked or German-fried or creamed potatoes; also a leafy green vegetable, such as spinach, broccoli, brussels sprouts; or sliced fresh tomatoes on crisp water cress.

Pan-Broiled Sausages

There are 2 ways to pan-broil sausages. Both take into account the fact that sausage creates excessive fat during cooking; and that if cooked too fast, in too hot a pan, sausages will split. Try either way; choose your favorite. Remember that sausage doesn't need salting; the meat has already been highly seasoned before it is sold.

Method I. Place **link sausages or cakes of sausage meat** in cool, ungreased frying pan. Place over moderate heat. Brown meat nicely on lower side, pouring off all excess grease as it accumulates, keeping pan nearly dry. Turn meat, cook same way on other side. If link sausages, turn as needed, browning on all sides. Cooking sausage should not require over 8 to 12 minutes total time. If links still seem greasy, when browned, drain on paper towel for a minute, before serving.

Method II (for link sausages only): Place **link sausages** in cool, ungreased frying pan. Add **2 or 3 tablespoons hot water.** Cover pan. Place over moderate heat; simmer gently, about 5 minutes; simmering draws out excessive grease from sausages. Pour off all this water. Then put frying pan back over moderate to high heat, and brown sausages quickly on all sides. Serve as soon as browned.

Pan-Broiled Bacon

Allow 2 or 3 strips per person. Buy evenly sliced, good quality, *lean* bacon. Bacon which has little lean meat in it never cooks well; it just shrivels up to nothing.

Spread single strips of **bacon,** flat, side by side, in cool, ungreased frying pan. Place pan over only moderate heat (too high heat makes bacon burn in some places before it can cook in others). As heat forces bacon to bulge up, with spatula or back of fork press the bulges down, keeping entire strip in contact with pan. As excess fat develops in pan, pour it off; keep pan nearly dry. Heat will first make bacon look transparent; then fatty parts become a pale golden color. When all fat of a strip looks golden, lift bacon from pan; do not wait for the bacon to look dry. Drain it on paper towel for a minute or two before serving. Presto! . . . crisp, delicious bacon.

Cooking time is usually 7 to 15 minutes by this unhurried method; and you can't hurry bacon if you want it nicely cooked!

BASIC PRINCIPLES
FOR PAN-FRYING

Pan-frying (often just called "frying") means to cook food in a hot frying pan containing enough hot cooking fat (usually 2 to 4 tablespoons) to cover the entire bottom of the pan.

Remember that in frying it is the liquid *hot fat* (not hot air) which cooks and flavors the food. And fat must really be *hot*, before food is put in. If fat is too cool, food will (like a blotter) drink up the fat, thus becoming soggy and greasy throughout; you will have an unpleasant dish. But if fat is sizzling, it at once forms a tasty, protective crust around the outside of food, without penetrating into the interior. Properly fried food is therefore not grease-filled or indigestible.

As the frying method is a quick one, you cannot use it for large or tough pieces of raw meat, nor for large, hard-textured raw vegetables, which require longer methods of tenderizing. Raw foods, to be fried, must usually be of fairly tender texture to start with, and are usually sliced, diced, or cubed, to aid the hot fat in reaching many surfaces quickly. Of course food which has previously been cooked or canned may be quickly reheated in the frying pan.

Frying usually does not require more than 5 to 15 minutes, though if food is raw and rather hard (liked sliced or cubed raw potatoes) it will take longer, and in such case the pan may need to be covered, thus holding the steam inside, to help tenderize the food.

MASTER RECIPE #5
PAN-FRYING

(1) Clean, wash or peel food if necessary; cut it to right size; dry it, if wet.

(2) Heat, in frying pan, **2 to 4 tablespoons cooking fat** . . . enough to coat completely bottom of pan. The fat may be bacon fat, melted suet, or lard, when cooking strong-flavored foods such as meat, potatoes, onions, etc. But for delicate-flavored foods, use a bland salad oil or vegetable shortening.

(3) Season food by sprinkling with **salt** and **pepper,** before putting it into hot fat, unless food is already salty, or food is a "sweet" one, like fruit.

(4) Place food in hot fat in pan, using long-handled spoon or pancake turner. Brown food rapidly on underneath side; turn it; brown top side. If food is circular, brown all sides. Once browned and well heated through, food may be tender enough to eat. But if it is a raw, hard-textured food, like sliced raw vegetables, cover pan, reduce heat to moderate, and keep cooking until tender.

RECOMMENDATIONS FOR
PAN-FRYING SPECIFIC FOODS

Some foods commonly called "fried" on menus and in general conversation, are not actually fried at all, but sautéed, or pan-broiled, or shallow-fried, or deep-fried. In such cases, page and method are recommended.

Fried Apple Rings

As this is to be a somewhat sweet dish, do not salt **apples;** merely wash, core, and slice them into ¼ inch thick crosswise slices; you may peel them, or not. Heat **4 tablespoons butter** or **margarine** in frying pan. Add to hot shortening **2 tablespoons sugar.** Place apple slices in hot fat. Fry on each side until golden brown, and tender when tested with fork. This method gives the apples a slightly sweet "glaze." They are delectable with pork chops, ham, or sausage.

You may cook by the same method:

Drained, sliced, cooked or canned sweet potatoes.

Drained slices of canned pineapple.

Drained halves of ripe or canned pears.

Peeled bananas, sliced lengthwise.

Sliced orange sections (pits removed).

Fried Bacon

See Pan-Broiled (p. 85).

Fried Chicken

See Shallow-Fried (p. 101), or Deep-Fried (p. 109).

Fried Chicken Livers

See Sautéed (p. 93).

Fried Eggplant

See Shallow-Fried (p. 104) or Deep-Fried (p. 113).

Fried Fish

Small whole fish, like smelts, fresh sardines; or slices of larger fish (bass, flounder, cod, haddock, halibut, perch, pickerel, pike, pompano, red snapper, salmon, brook trout, whitebait, sturgeon steaks and even eels) can be pan-fried.

For small whole fish. Have fish cleaned inside. Leave heads and tails on. Roll each fish in **flour coating** (p. 101); or in **1 cup granulated corn meal** to which **1 teaspoon salt** has been added. Heat **2 to 4 tablespoons butter, olive oil,** or **vegetable shortening** in frying pan. With pancake turner, lift coated fish into pan. Brown fish on all sides. As soon as nicely browned, serve.

For slices of fish. Dip each slice in **flour coating** (p. 101); then fry in **2 to 4 tablespoons hot fat** in frying pan, just until golden brown on each side. Do not overcook, or fish becomes dry.

With any fried fish, serve tartar sauce (p. 354). Cole slaw is also good; also broiled tomato halves; creamed or mashed potatoes. See also shallow-fried fish (p. 104).

Fried Ham

Thin slices of cooked ham. Buy sliced boiled ham at store, or cut thin slices from a home-cooked ham. Rub inside of cool frying pan with ham fat, or melt 1 tablespoon bacon fat in frying pan. Heat pan only moderately. Place slices of ham in pan; brown ham quickly on each side. Serve at once. (Very good with fried eggs.)

Ham steaks. See Pan-Broiled (p. 79).

Fried Liver

See Pan-Broiled (p. 84).

Fried Potatoes

All variations below serve 2 to 3 persons.

Cottage-Fried. First boil with skins on (p. 290) **4 or 5 potatoes.** Then peel and dice. (Or, if desired, use any leftover boiled or baked potatoes, peeled and diced.) If desired, mix **1 or 2 tablespoons grated raw onion** with potatoes for added flavor. Put potatoes into hot frying pan containing **3 to 4 tablespoons hot bacon fat,** or tried-out (melted) **beef suet.** Sprinkle potatoes well with **salt.** Brown potatoes quickly on one side; turn them over and brown quickly on other side. Serve as soon as thoroughly hot.

Hashed Brown. First, boil with skins on **4 or 5 potatoes;** then peel and dice them (or you may use leftover boiled or baked potatoes, peeled and diced). Mix with cooked diced potatoes **2 tablespoons flour, ½ teaspoon salt, ⅛ teaspoon pepper, 1 tablespoon grated onion, ¼ cup light cream** (or top milk, or evaporated milk). Turn mixture into hot frying pan containing **2 or 3 tablespoons hot bacon fat,** tried-out suet, or **butter.** Fry quickly until browned on underneath side; then turn potatoes over; brown on second side. Turn heat low; cover pan; cook a few minutes longer, until well heated.

Raw-Fried. Potatoes may also be put raw into frying pan, **as** follows:

In thick slices. Peel, wash off, and dry **4 medium potatoes** for 2 to 3 people. Slice raw potatoes into large, ⅜ inch thick slices, crosswise or lengthwise. Place raw slices in hot frying pan containing **3 to 4 tablespoons bacon fat** or other cooking fat. Sprinkle potatoes with **salt**. Brown on lower side. Turn them over. Sprinkle with salt again. Brown on second side. If potatoes stick to pan, add more cooking fat. Cover pan, reduce heat, and cook 20 to 30 minutes longer, or until steam inside pan has tenderized potatoes.

German-fried. Peel, wash off, and dry **4 medium potatoes** for 2 to 3 people. Slice raw potatoes thin (in slices only ⅛ inch thick) and make slices not much larger than a 50-cent piece. Put raw slices into hot frying pan containing **2 to 3 tablespoons hot cooking fat**. Sprinkle top of potatoes with **salt**. Now add, on top of potatoes, **1 or 2 medium-sized peeled onions**, sliced thin. Cook until potatoes brown on bottom; then turn whole mixture over, blending onions in with the potatoes; salt top of potatoes again. When browned on second side, cover pan, reduce heat, and cook 20 to 30 minutes longer, until steam inside pan makes potatoes tender. These are marvelous with steak, meat cakes, liver, chops.

Fried Potato Cakes. (To make 6 cakes.) Either have available **2 cups cold leftover mashed potatoes**, or make **2 cups freshly cooked mashed potatoes** (p. 301). With seasoned mashed potatoes, mix **1 slightly beaten egg**. If desired, for extra flavoring, stir in **1 tablespoon grated raw onion**, or **1 tablespoon chopped green pepper**, or **2 tablespoons minced parsley**. Shape mixture into 6 round flat cakes about ¾ inch thick. Place cakes in hot frying pan containing **3 to 4 tablespoons melted bacon fat**, or other cooking fat. Fry rapidly until brown on lower side. Turn them over with pancake turner; fry similarly until brown on second side. Frying requires about 6 to 10 minutes. Serve hot, in place of potatoes.

Fried Shellfish

Clams, oysters, scallops and shrimps are shallow-fried or deep-fried. See Chapter XV for individual directions.

Fried Round Steak (Country Style)

To serve 2 or 3, buy **1 lb. round steak,** sliced ½ inch thick. Cut
it across the grain, into serving-size pieces. In shallow plate, mix
½ cup flour with **½ teaspoon salt.** Dip meat pieces in flour mixture, coating all sides. Melt **3 to 4 tablespoons cooking fat** in very
hot frying pan. Place pieces in pan. Brown rapidly first on one
side, then on the other. Then reduce heat, cover pan, and cook
over low heat 15 to 20 minutes.

Fried Hash

You can buy canned hash, or make your own.

Mixing your own has several advantages: (1) you can use any
variety of meat you wish (leftover cooked steak, or roast beef,
corned beef, lamb, turkey, chicken, even fish) thus utilizing odds-
and-ends in a savory fashion; (2) you can increase or decrease
the percentage of potato, in proportion to the meat, if desired;
(3) you can include as much or as little onion and other seasoning as desired; (4) economy — homemade is much less expensive. We therefore give a Master Recipe for preparing hash.

To cook either homemade or canned, begin at (5), page 92.

MASTER RECIPE #6
HASH
(Serves 2 to 3)

(Corned beef, roast beef, lamb, turkey, chicken, or fish.)
(1) Cut fine, or put through meat grinder **2 to 2½ cups** of any
one of the following:
Cooked or canned **corned beef**
Leftover cooked **lamb**
Leftover cooked **roast beef**
Leftover cooked **steak**
Leftover cooked **turkey**
Leftover cooked **chicken**
Leftover cooked **white-meated fish** (boned, and skin removed)

(When grinding up leftover roasts for hash, you can include not only tender pieces of meat, but also bits of skin, sweet tasty fat, and hardened crusty meat. When using turkey or roast chicken, if you have cooked stuffing or giblets left over, chop those in with the rest of the meat. All "trimmings" and odds-and-ends actually help give richer, more savory flavor to your hash; and none of these odds-and-ends will be tough, or even identifiable, when hash is served; you will simply have marvelous hash.)

(2) Mix with meat

1½ cups diced, peeled, cooked potatoes

These may be boiled, or even leftover baked potatoes. Some cooks prefer raw potatoes, chopped fine. These are dandy with red meat; but raw potatoes are not recommended to blend with fowl or fish, as they will not cook tender quickly enough.

(3) Season above mixture with

1 or 2 peeled raw onions, chopped or grated

½ teaspoon salt

For extra seasoning, include if desired

1 teaspoon prepared mustard
(with corned beef mixture)

½ teaspoon Worcestershire sauce
(with roast beef or steak)

½ teaspoon sage
(with turkey or chicken)

¼ cup minced parsley or 1 tablespoon
chopped green pepper (with fish)

(4) Blend entire mixture well.

(5) In large, moderately hot frying pan, heat

3 tablespoons cooking fat

(6) Turn hash into frying pan. You may now cook the hash one of two ways:

For crisp, crusty hash. Place pan over moderately high heat. Brown underneath side of hash rapidly. (If hash sticks to pan, add 1 or 2 tablespoons more cooking fat.) With pancake turner, turn hash over; brown second side rapidly. As soon as browned and thoroughly heated, serve hash. If raw potatoes have been used, however, after browning sprinkle hash with more salt, reduce heat, cover pan, and cook 15 to 20 minutes longer, until potatoes are tender.

For moist hash. Place pan of hash over only moderate heat; cover pan; cook hash gently, turning it over now and then, for about 20 to 25 minutes. Hash will be soft and moist when served; top with poached eggs if desired.

BASIC PRINCIPLES FOR SAUTÉING

Sautéing is exactly the same thing as pan-frying (cooking in 2 to 4 tablespoons hot fat — enough to coat bottom of pan), *except* for two considerations:

Sautéing is much gentler. Neither pan, nor cooking fat, should be quite so hot. Sautéing is meant for very delicate foods (like chicken livers or mushrooms) which could easily burn.

In sautéing, you stir, toss, or keep turning the food while it cooks, to prevent its sticking to pan and burning. The literal meaning of the French verb *sauter* is "to toss, to jump, to keep in motion," and this is done purely to protect food from scorching.

MASTER RECIPE #7
SAUTÉING

(1) Melt in warm frying pan **2 to 4 tablespoons butter,** or other mild cooking fat (you need a mild fat, since most foods cooked this way are delicate-flavored foods).

(2) Put **cleaned, prepared, seasoned food** into warm pan. Cook over moderate heat, stirring food, or turning it frequently, until food is nicely and lightly browned and tender throughout when tested with fork. Sautéing usually takes 5 to 20 minutes, depending on type of food.

RECOMMENDATIONS FOR
SAUTÉING SPECIFIC FOODS

Sautéed Chicken Livers

To serve sautéed chicken livers as a main course dish, order **2 to 3 chicken livers per person.**

Wash livers under running cold water; drain; cut to bite-size pieces. In moderately warm frying pan, heat **2 to 3 tablespoons butter** or other cooking fat. Put in livers. Sprinkle livers in pan with **salt**. Cook over gentle heat, stirring frequently, until livers are nicely browned all over, and tender when pierced with fork; about 5 to 6 minutes. With spoon or spatula, lift out of pan. If desired, serve on hot buttered toast. Or serve on bed of hot, cooked rice. Or combine cooked livers with hot chicken gravy, or with 1 can heated condensed undiluted cream of chicken or cream of mushroom soup, and serve this mixture on hot buttered toast, or on a bed of hot cooked rice (p. 305).

Sautéed chicken livers are also served to accompany omelet, or are sometimes chopped fine, after cooking, and folded inside an omelet.

Sautéed Frogs' Legs

Frogs' legs are small; allow **4 or 5 pairs per person.** Buy these, all cleaned, at market.

Wipe all pieces of meat clean, with damp cloth. Sprinkle meat all over with **salt**. In moderately hot frying pan, melt **3 to 4 tablespoons butter**. Add to butter **½ clove minced garlic** and **1 tablespoon minced parsley**. Put frogs' legs in pan; brown meat to light golden color on all sides, turning as needed. When all are well browned, cover pan, reduce heat, and cook a few minutes longer until flesh is tender when tried with fork. Serve like chicken; pour over frogs' legs the pan juices.

Sautéed Kidneys (Lamb)

Order **2 to 3 kidneys per person.** Market should deliver these small kidneys all cleaned of their outside layer of fat or suet, and of fibrous covering; if not, cut away this material yourself, with sharp knife.

Wipe cleaned kidneys with damp cloth. Now, with sharp knife or scissors, cut kidneys in half, so you can see white fibrous tendons inside. Cut out all tendons, leaving only tender meat. Meat may be cut to bite-size pieces. In moderately hot frying pan, melt

3 or 4 tablespoons butter; add 1 or 2 tablespoons grated raw onion. Put in pieces of kidney. Sprinkle kidneys well with **salt and pepper.** If desired, add **a few drops Worcestershire sauce** to pan. Cook kidneys over gentle to moderate heat, stirring or turning kidneys frequently, about 5 to 10 minutes, or until kidneys are browned all over and tender when pierced with fork.

Serve cooked kidneys with pan juices on hot buttered toast, garnishing with parsley; or combine hot cooked kidneys with heated undiluted condensed cream of mushroom soup and serve on bed of hot cooked rice (p. 305). Or combine hot cooked kidneys with pieces of heated leftover steak, to make beef-and-kidney stew (p. 125); or beef-and-kidney pie (p. 126).

Sautéed Mushrooms

Buy **½ pound fresh mushrooms** for 2 people.

First wash mushrooms well under cold running water (no need to peel them). Snap stems from caps; save stems to slice and cook for another day (they will keep several days if stored in covered glass jar, in refrigerator). In moderately warm frying pan, melt **2 to 3 tablespoons butter.** Put in mushroom caps, whole or sliced; if whole, place them stem side down in pan. Sprinkle mushrooms in pan with **salt.** Cook gently, without turning, 2 to 3 minutes or until browned on lower side. Then, with spatula, turn mushrooms over; cook until browned on other side. Stir frequently as needed, to keep mushrooms from sticking to pan. Cook 5 to 10 minutes, or just until mushrooms are tender when tried with fork. Do not overcook, or mushrooms will shrink. Remove from hot pan with spatula; serve on hot buttered toast; or serve to garnish broiled steak, meat cakes, or chicken.

If desired, mushrooms may be sliced before cooking, then cooked by same method as above.

Sautéed sliced mushrooms are excellent as garnish for broiled steak, or for pan-broiled liver; or to use in many sauces, or to add to creamed chicken or turkey dishes, or to use in casseroles, or meat pies.

Sautéed Onions

For 2 people, peel and slice thin 3 medium or 4 small onions.

In moderately hot frying pan, melt 2 to 3 tablespoons butter, or bacon fat, or vegetable shortening. Add sliced onions. Sprinkle onions lightly with salt. Cook over gentle heat, stirring frequently, about 5 minutes, or just until onions are golden color and tender. Never have heat high, or onions will burn black. Serve sautéed onions as garnish for broiled steak, pan-broiled liver, or meat cakes.

BASIC PRINCIPLES FOR SHALLOW-FRYING

"Shallow-frying" may seem a misnomer, when included in a chapter about frying-pan usage, for actually shallow-frying requires *deeper* hot fat in your frying pan than any other method in this chapter!

But the method is named "shallow" in contrast with its alternate method, "deep" or "French" frying (see Chapter X). Shallow-frying produces a French-fried type of food; it is simply an easier way.

Type of Food to Cook by This Method

You cannot shallow-fry large, tough pieces of food, but only foods which will tenderize quickly in the hot fat. This means you *can* shallow-fry:

Precooked mixtures — such as croquettes, or fish balls, or potato cakes, in which the ingredients have already been cooked by a previous method.

Precooked foods, or foods edible raw, dipped in batter, such as meat, seafood, or fruit fritters; or any cooked or canned meat, fish, or fruit dipped in a batter coating.

Certain meats which will tenderize easily, chiefly tender chicken; or fish fillets; or shellfish.

Batters which can be fried, such as doughnuts.

No food should be cooked by this method unless it will hold together in bubbling fat without crumbling or breaking apart.

Equipment for Shallow-Frying

Frying pan. You need a large (9-inch, 10-inch, or larger) *heavy* frying pan, which has fairly deep side walls. The heavy quality of the pan is important; a thin pan becomes too hot, and does not distribute heat evenly underneath the bubbling fat. The depth of side walls is also important; it prevents hot fat, 1 to 1½ inches deep, from boiling over the sides, when fat begins bubbling. Stores sell a type of pan made especially for shallow-frying (it is often called a "chicken fryer"); this pan meets all above specifications, and in addition has a tight-fitting lid, which is essential for frying chicken or other solid foods that take longer than "browning time" to become tender. As soon as you can buy one of these pans, do; you will use it all your life.

Turner. In addition, have a long-handled slotted spoon, or a flexible pancake turner, or tongs, to aid in turning food in the hot fat. You do not want to pierce the outer crust of food, with fork. (Piercing the crust will break this protective covering, allowing grease to seep inside.)

Frying thermometer. As soon as possible, buy a *frying thermometer*. This is the only truly *accurate* way to know how hot the fat is, before you put food into it. Fat which is *too hot* will smoke, and may boil over, starting a fire. Fat which is *not hot enough* will not brown food quickly enough; result: food which is not crisp or deliciously crusty, but soggy and underdone.

Fat for Shallow-Frying

What fat to use. For all shallow-frying, always use a mild-flavored fat; one without too distinctive a flavor. The French people use bland salad oil. Americans generally use melted vegetable shortening, or sometimes salad oil. Some old-fashioned folk like to use melted lard. Never use butter; it smokes the kitchen black. And never use a strong-flavored or salty fat, such as bacon fat, ham fat.

How much fat? You will need enough melted cooking fat in frying pan to make a depth of 1 or 1½ inches. This usually requires at least 1 quart or more of melted shortening or salad oil.

Care of fat. Fat after one using may be cooled, strained through cheesecloth or fine sieve, then stored away in covered glass jar for another occasion. Some fat will evaporate during each cooking operation; therefore a little more (new) fat must usually be added to the old, for the next occasion. Sometimes fat becomes rancid, from extreme summer heat; in this case, throw it all out, and begin with new. Also, if you have once cooked a sharp flavored food in the fat (such as onions, or fish), the fat is apt to retain that flavor, and should not again be used for more delicate foods. You may keep that fat to use again, however, for another day's onions or fish; if keeping it, put it in a separate jar, and so label it.

Temperature of fat. Much research has proven that 375° *is the ideal temperature for fat, for shallow- or deep-frying.* At this heat, fat does its work most satisfactorily, cooking food light, crisp, brown, and tender; it is neither too hot, nor too cool.

Sometimes, for precooked foods, a slightly higher temperature (385°–390°) is used, since precooked foods can be fried more rapidly.

Keep fat temperature even, while frying. Fat may be at correct temperature when you *begin* frying; but if you add cold food, that obviously will lower the fat's heat. Whenever possible, let food be at room temperature, before cooking. And after each addition of food to the fat, bring temperature back to proper degree. Then try to keep temperature steady. If fat becomes too much cooled off, food will not fry properly.

Amount of Food in Pan

In either shallow or deep frying, food should be able to "swim," or "float" in hot fat, with some space around each piece of food. Never overcrowd pan; if you do, you prevent food from frying evenly on all sides; and you may cause fat to boil over, starting a fire.

Safety Precautions

Never put into hot fat any food which has drops of moisture on it; first dry food with towel, if it is wet. Drops of water cause small explosions in hot fat, which may burn you.

Always use long-handled implements for lowering food into hot fat, or for turning food, or for removing it.

Never go away and leave hot fat over heat, even for a few minutes, even to answer phone. Fat might boil over. Pull pan off heat before leaving kitchen.

Use *moderate* heat, when heating cooking fat. High heat may cause fat to boil over, starting a fire.

If fire should ever start, at once pull pan of hot fat off heat, so it will stop bubbling. Then scatter heaps of baking soda or salt generously over fire to put it out.

But if you use proper caution, you will never have a fire.

MASTER RECIPE #8
SHALLOW-FRYING

(1) Clean, peel, wash, cut, slice, or otherwise prepare food to be fried. If food is moist, wipe it dry with towel, before cooking.

(2) Sprinkle food with **salt**, unless food is already salty, or is of sweet type (such as fruit).

(3) Dip food in **coating** (see p. 100) if needed. Most shallow- or deep-fried foods do need a coating of some kind, to help form a crisp crust.

(4) In heavy frying pan, heat **fat** of 1 or 1½ inches depth, over moderate heat, about 5 minutes, or until fat reaches correct degree: 375° for raw foods and batters; 390° for precooked foods. Test heat of fat by frying thermometer. If you have no thermometer, use this bread-cube test:

Bread-Cube Test, for Heat of Fat

375° (for raw foods) = heat of fat when a 1 inch cube of one-day-old bread will brown in it in 60 seconds.

390° (for precooked foods) = heat of fat when a 1 inch cube of one-day-old bread will brown in it in 40 seconds.

---

(5) Lower food carefully into hot fat, piece by piece, using long-handled spoon. Put in as many pieces as will not overcrowd pan; let food have room "to swim."

(6) Fry food without turning it until food is golden-brown on bottom, usually about 2 to 5 minutes. Then, using long handled spoon, or tongs, gently turn food over, taking care not to pierce or break the "crust." Fry smiliarly until golden-brown on second side.

(7) If food was precooked, it will be done when browned all over. Lift with slotted spoon from hot fat; drain on hot platter lined with paper towel. Keep in warm place, if necessary, while cooking a second lot.

(8) If food was raw and in fairly big pieces, such as chicken cut for frying, it may require more cooking after browning. Reduce heat, cover frying pan, and cook slowly until tender when tried with fork. Then lift from hot fat with slotted spoon. Drain on paper towel, before serving.

COATINGS

(For foods to be fried in shallow or deep fat)

Egg-and-Crumb

In shallow soup dish, or pie plate, have ready **1 cup fine bread or cracker crumbs**, mixed with ½ teaspoon salt. In another shallow dish, have **1 egg, slightly beaten**, mixed with **2 tablespoons cold water**. Dip food to be fried (1) in crumb mixture, or you may make the first dipping in plain flour; (2) in egg mixture; (3) in crumbs. Coat all sides of food evenly leaving no gaps.

Flour Coating

This makes a thinner, less rich crust than egg-and-crumb coating. Mix together **1 cup flour** and **1 teaspoon salt.** Dip food in flour mixture, coating all sides of food evenly. NOTE: If food is hardy enough to be shaken around without breaking, put flour mixture into paper bag; add pieces of food; close bag; shake well. This coats all pieces at once.

Batter

Beat in bowl **1 egg.** Stir into it **⅔ cup milk (or water).** Mix these liquids into **1 cup flour** blended with **¼ to ½ teaspoon salt.** (Use only ¼ teaspoon salt when coating a sweet food like fruit; but use ½ teaspoon salt for fish, meat, corn.)

RECOMMENDATIONS FOR SHALLOW-FRYING SPECIFIC FOODS

Shallow-Fried Chicken

Buy **1 frying chicken** * of 3 to 3½ pounds, to serve 2 people. Have market clean chicken, and cut it in sections for frying. Set aside giblets, neck, and wings, to make broth, as on page 82. These pieces do not make very attractive serving pieces. Wipe all other pieces of chicken clean with damp cloth. If any pin feathers are

---

* You may also use the following kinds of chicken to fry:

Frozen frying chicken. Thaw according to package directions; wipe dry; then roll pieces in **flour, egg,** and **crumbs,** as for fresh chicken, and cook same way.

Canned chicken in sections for frying. Drain chicken pieces. Roll in **flour, egg,** and **crumbs,** as for fresh chicken. Fry in hot fat same way, but only until nicely browned. As this chicken has already been cooked in canning process, it will be done when browned.

A fowl. Buy a **5 or 6 pound fowl;** have it cut in sections for fricasseeing. Wipe pieces clean with damp cloth. Remove any pin feathers with tweezer. Singe off hairs, if any. Cook by method for Boiled Chicken (p. 122), until nearly tender, about 2 to 2½ hours. Then drain chicken. Roll pieces in **flour, egg,** and **crumbs,** and fry briefly in hot fat, as for canned chicken above.

visible, pull them out with tweezers. If there are hairs on chicken, singe (burn) these off by holding one chicken piece at a time on a long-handled fork, about 1½ to 2 inches above heat of surface burner. Sprinkle chicken well with **salt.** Roll pieces in **flour,** then in **egg,** then in **crumbs,** as in egg-and-crumb coating (p. 100). Lower coated pieces into **1 to 1½ inches deep hot fat,** heated to 375°. But do not crowd pan. If frying a large number of pieces, it will save you time to have two frying pans operating at once. Fry chicken, turning as needed, until all pieces are rich, golden brown. They will still not be tender; so cook them further, by either of the following methods:

Southern Way. Reduce heat, leaving chicken in hot fat; cover frying pan; continue cooking gently another 30 to 35 minutes, or until chicken is tender. Then remove from fat; drain on paper towel.

Steaming in Oven. Remove browned chicken pieces from hot fat to a dry casserole or baking dish which has a cover. Add to dish ½ **cup chicken bouillon,** or **stock,** or plain **hot water.** Cover dish. Place in moderate (375°) oven, 30 to 35 minutes, or until tender.

Pan Gravy for Fried Chicken. After finishing frying chicken, pour from frying pan into other container all but **3 tablespoons hot fat.** To fat remaining in frying pan add **3 tablespoons flour,** ⅓ **teaspoon salt, 1 teaspoon grated onion, few grains pepper.** Stir to smooth paste. Add, stirring constantly, 1½ **cups cream,** or **top milk;** or use ¾ **cup evaporated milk** with ¾ **cup chicken broth** or **bouillon,** if you have any. Cook, stirring, over moderate heat, until gravy thickens and is smooth. Taste. It may want more salt.

Shallow-Fried Croquettes

Makes 6 to 8 croquettes. At least 2 hours before serving time, prepare your croquette mixture (p. 155). Put mixture in refrigerator to chill. One half hour before serving time, shape and coat croquettes (p. 156). Then in heavy frying pan heat **1 inch deep fat** to 390°. With long-handled spoon or pancake turner, lower croquettes, one by one, into hot fat. Do not overcrowd pan. Fry until golden brown on lower side, about 2 to 3 minutes; then with slotted spoon turn them over, being careful not to break crust or croquette. Fry similarly on other side. As soon as nicely browned all over, lift with slotted spoon from hot fat; drain on hot platter lined with paper towel. Keep first lot of croquettes in a warm place while you cook more. Before serving, stick a short branch of fresh **parsley** into one end of each croquette, and sprinkle top of each croquette with **paprika;** very pretty. If sauce is desired, have ready any variation of white sauce (p. 248) which would taste good with contents of your croquettes.

Shallow-Fried Codfish Cakes, or Balls

Serves 6. Packaged, shredded codfish is very salty and should be "freshened" in water, to remove excess saltiness, before using. Buy a package a day or so ahead of time, so you can read manufacturer's directions at leisure and can allow time for the "freshening."

After fish has been freshened, mix **1 cup codfish** with **2 cups peeled, raw potatoes** cut in small pieces; put them in deep saucepan. Cover with cold water. Boil about 20 minutes, or until potatoes are tender. Drain off all water. With potato masher, mash potato and fish mixture. Add **½ tablespoon butter, ⅛ teaspoon pepper,** and beat well with spoon. Stir in **1 beaten egg.** Cool the mixture. Then in heavy frying pan, heat **1 inch deep fat** to 385°. Using long-handled spoon, drop 1 tablespoon fish mixture at a time into hot fat, putting in as many balls as possible without crowding pan. Fry 2 to 3 minutes, until golden brown on bottom; turn them over; fry similarly until golden brown on top side. Drain on paper towel, and serve immediately. Or, if you must cook more than one lot, keep first lot in warm place until second lot is cooked. Serve hot, with ketchup if desired.

NOTE: Same mixture can be used to make delicious bite-size fish balls — wonderful morsels for cocktail parties — by dropping mixture, 1 teaspoon at a time, into hot fat.

Shallow-Fried Eggplant (or Tomatoes, or Summer Squash)

Allow **2 to 3 slices vegetable** per person. Peel eggplant or summer squash; no need to peel ripe tomatoes, just wash them. Cut any of these vegetables into ⅜ inch thick, crosswise slices. Sprinkle each slice with **salt** and **pepper;** then dip in **flour coating** (p. 101), or in **egg-and-crumb coating** (p. 100). Heat **1 inch deep fat** to 375° in heavy frying pan. With pancake turner, lower one slice of vegetable at a time into hot fat; put in as many slices as will not overcrowd pan. Fry until golden brown on one side; turn; fry until brown on second side; about 4 to 6 minutes in all. (Tomatoes cook quickly; eggplant takes longer.) Drain fried slices on paper towel; and keep first slices hot in warm place while you cook more.

Shallow-Fried Fish Fillets

Buy **½ to ¾ pound filleted fish** to serve 2. If using frozen fish, start thawing fish at room temperature about 2 hours before cooking. Before cooking, wipe fish clean, with damp cloth. Cut to serving size pieces. Sprinkle all sides of each piece with salt. Dip pieces first in **flour,** then in **egg,** then in **crumbs** (see egg-and-crumb coating, p. 100), being sure to coat evenly on all sides. Heat **1 to 1½ inches deep fat,** in heavy frying pan, to 375°. With spatula or pancake turner, lower pieces of fish, one by one, into hot fat, putting in as many pieces as will not crowd pan. Fry until golden brown on bottom side, about 2 to 4 minutes; then carefully, with pancake turner or spatula, turn fish over to brown similarly on second side. When nicely browned all over, with pancake turner lift fish from hot fat carefully, taking care not to break pieces. Drain fish on paper towel; garnish with a sprinkle of minced fresh **parsley** and **paprika** if desired. Serve hot, accompanied with tartar sauce (p. 354).

Excellent accompaniments for fried fish are creamed or mashed potatoes, cole slaw, broiled stuffed tomatoes, or any leafy green vegetable.

Shallow-Fried Shellfish (Oysters, Clams, Scallops, Shrimps)

Most shellfish are first cleaned and drained; then dipped in one of the 3 types of coating (p. 100); then lowered into 1 inch deep fat heated to 375°, and cooked about 3 to 5 minutes, or until golden brown all over. However, some shellfish must be pre-cooked; see individual instructions under each type shellfish, in Chapter XV.

Shallow-Fried Onion Rings

For 2 persons, allow 3 to 4 medium onions. Peel onions; slice them crosswise in ⅛ to ¼ inch thick slices. With fingers, push slices apart into individual rings. Soak onion rings in ⅔ cup milk for 10 to 15 minutes; then drain. Dip rings in **flour coating** (p. 101). With long-handled spoon or fork, lower rings into **1 inch deep fat,** heated to 370°. Fry 2 to 3 minutes, or just until nicely browned. Lift from hot fat with slotted spoon. Drain on paper towel. Sprinkle lightly with salt, if desired. Serve hot, with any steak, or pan-broiled liver, or pan-broiled beef cakes.

Shallow-Fried Fritters

Allow about ½ hour to make fritter batter, and to mix fritters (see p. 213). Then heat **1 inch deep fat** in heavy frying pan to 375°. Using long-handled spoon, drop fritter batter, 1 tablespoon at a time, into hot fat, putting in as many fritters as will not crowd pan. Fry 1 to 3 minutes, until nicely browned on one side; turn carefully without breaking; fry similarly on second side. As soon as browned all over, lift fritters from hot fat with slotted spoon. Drain on paper towel. If fritters contain fruit, you may sprinkle outside of fritters with **sugar,** while still warm. (Such fruit fritters can be used as accompaniment for meat, or as dessert.)

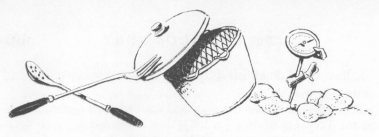

CHAPTER X

How to French-Fry

METHOD FOR: *Chicken, Fish, Shellfish, Croquettes, Potatoes, Onion Rings, Eggplant and other Vegetables*

BASIC PRINCIPLES

French- or deep-frying is a method of cooking foods in a *deep* kettle or saucepan, *one half full* of hot fat.

This is a quick method. Foods cooked this way usually require only from 3 to 6 minutes in the hot fat (though large pieces, or hard-textured pieces of food will require longer).

Because it is a quick method, only certain types of foods can be cooked this way, satisfactorily. These include:

Foods which are already partially *precooked,* such as fritters (in which the meat, fruit, or vegetable content has already been cooked or canned, and is therefore in edible condition, before frying).

Batters (like the batter that makes doughnuts, or the batters used to coat shellfish, or fritter ingredients).

Certain *vegetables,* cut thin enough, and having a texture which will tenderize quickly in deep-frying.

Tender-textured *chicken, fish, or shellfish.*

NOTE: This method cannot be used for sturdy firm-textured *meats.*

Equipment Needed

To French-fry you *must* have a *5 or 6 inch deep saucepan or kettle* which is *half filled* with liquid cooking fat. Get the 2½ or

3 quart size. The deep side walls of the saucepan are important; they help prevent the bubbling fat from boiling over the edges of the pan, onto stove, causing a fire. A *wire frying basket* which will fit into your saucepan is helpful. And you need *long-handled tools* — slotted spoon, fork, or tongs — for handling the food. You should also have a *frying thermometer*. Without this, you can never be sure of the temperature of your fat. Buy one as soon as possible. If you haven't one, test heat of fat by using the Bread-Cube Test (p. 100).

Fat for Deep Frying

Much research has proven that 375° F. is the ideal frying temperature for fat; it is neither too cool nor too hot. Too cool fat will leave your food soggy and underdone, without a nice crisp crust. Too hot fat will cause food to burn. Occasionally, for foods which are already partially precooked, fat is heated to 390°; this is because the precooked food will fry more rapidly.

What fat to use. If you do not wish to give your food a taste which does not "belong" to it, be sure to use a bland, almost taste-less fat for deep-frying. The French people (who originated this cooking method) use salad oil of bland quality, on the theory that salad oil is lighter in texture than other cooking fats, and so will produce a lighter, more delicate "crust" on the fried food. However, our modern American vegetable shortenings are also fine, light-textured, and without distinctive taste; and these make excellent liquid fat for frying. Some old-time cooks still like to use lard, for frying potatoes; but lard has a distinct "taste" which would not be good for delicate-flavored foods. Never use butter; it smokes the kitchen black; and never use a salty fat, like ham fat, or bacon fat.

Care of fat. Read paragraph of same title in Chapter IX (p. 98). Also read: *Keep fat temperature even while frying* (p. 98); and the section on safety precautions (p. 98). These rules are the same for either shallow- or deep-frying.

Never Overcrowd Pan

When deep-frying, never put into the hot fat more pieces of food than can "swim" or "float" easily in the fat, with space around each piece. If using a wire frying basket to hold the food, put in the basket only enough food to cover the bottom of basket . . . not enough to pile it with layer-upon-layer. Overcrowding not only prevents food from frying evenly on all sides, but it may cause the hot fat to boil over, starting a fire. Both for safety, and for the good flavor of your food, it is better to fry only a small amount of food at one time, keeping the first lot in a warm place, while you fry a second lot, if needed.

Coatings

Most foods, before being put into the hot fat to fry, are dipped in some sort of coating which covers the entire outside of the piece of food and enables it to form a crisp, protective crust in the hot fat. This "crust" is important. It (a) helps hold ground-up mixtures of food together; (b) helps keep tender-meated foods from drying out; and (c) has a delicious taste. When coating any food, be sure to coat it evenly on all sides, so there are no gaps; and when handling the food in hot fat, take care not to pierce or break the coating. See three types of coating, pages 100, 101.

MASTER RECIPE #9
DEEP-FRYING (FRENCH-FRYING)

(1) Clean, peel, wash, cut, slice, or otherwise prepare food to be fried. If food is moist, wipe it dry with towel before cooking. Drops of moisture cause explosions in hot fat.

(2) Sprinkle food all over with **salt**, unless food is already salty, or is of sweet type, like fruit.

(3) Coat food in **flour, egg-and-crumb,** or **batter coating**; see pp. 100, 101 for these coatings. Check recommendations for specific foods beginning on page 109, to learn which type of coating is best suited to each.

(4) Heat **cooking fat** (salad oil or vegetable shortening) — enough to fill a deep kettle (5 or 6 inches deep), 2½ to 3 quart size, *one half full.* Heat fat about 5 minutes over moderate burner, then test with frying thermometer, or make Bread-Cube Test (p. 100) to be sure fat has reached proper temperature for type food you are cooking.

(5) Lower food carefully into hot fat, using long-handled spoon or pancake turner or long tongs, so as not to splatter yourself. Put into fat only as much food as will go in easily, without crowding pan. Too much food in pan may cause fat to boil over, and will not allow enough space for hot oil to cook all sides of food evenly.

If food was cold when put into fat, it will reduce temperature of fat; therefore turn heat a little higher, to bring fat back to correct temperature.

(6) Fry food until light golden brown, on all sides. If necessary to turn food over, to brown evenly, move food with slotted spoon or tongs or pancake turner; be careful not to pierce crust by stabbing the food with a fork.

(7) Most foods are done when nicely browned. (See exception for raw chicken on page 110). Lift food from hot fat with long-handled slotted spoon; or if you used a frying basket, lift out the entire basket.

(8) Drain pieces of food on paper towel before serving. Serve hot.

RECOMMENDATIONS FOR DEEP-FRYING SPECIFIC FOODS

Chicken

There are several kinds of chicken you may fry: (*a*) a fresh-killed frying-size chicken, bought at market, cut into sections for frying; (*b*) frozen frying chicken, in sections; (*c*) chicken for frying sold in cans; (*d*) an old fowl, if it has first been boiled about 2 hours, until nearly tender. The methods of treating them differ slightly, since there is a difference in the texture of the meat.

Fresh Frying Chicken (2½ to 3½ pounds). Allow **1 chicken** to serve 2 persons, since the chicken is not large to begin with, and the only meaty pieces are the legs, and the breast and back pieces. Have butcher cut chicken into proper pieces, for you. Keep out the neck and giblets; they do not make good frying pieces; use them to make Chicken Broth for another day (see p. 82). Some people do not fry the wing pieces, either, as there is little meat on them. Wipe all chicken pieces clean with damp cloth. Dip each piece in **egg-and-crumb coating** (p. 100). Have a deep saucepan half filled with **hot fat,** heated to 375°. Carefully lower into hot fat a few pieces of chicken at a time, not overcrowding pan. Fry about 20 to 30 minutes, or until pieces are nicely browned on all sides, and tender. With slotted spoon, lift from hot fat; drain on paper towel. Place pieces on warm platter, in a slow (250°) oven; or place platter over a pan of hot water, to keep these pieces warm while you fry others, if necessary.

Frozen Frying Chicken. Thaw **chicken** according to package directions, before using. Then wipe pieces dry; coat; and cook as for fresh chicken.

Canned Chicken for Frying. Chicken sold in cans, for frying, has already been partly cooked in the canning process. It therefore needs less cooking in hot fat than a fresh chicken.

Drain all pieces; then pat dry with towel. Coat in **egg-and-crumb coating** (p. 100). Lower pieces carefully into deep saucepan half filled with **hot fat,** heated to 390°. Fry just a few minutes, until nicely browned all over. Drain on paper towel before serving.

A Fowl. Have a **5-** or **6-pound fowl** cut into fricasseeing pieces. Put all pieces in large kettle; cover with water, and cook about 2 hours by method for Boiled Chicken (p. 122). When chicken pieces are nearly tender, remove them from kettle; drain.

Select the meatier pieces, to fry. Pat them dry with towel. Coat in **egg-and-crumb coating** (p. 100), and deep-fry as for canned chicken above.

Save the pieces you do not fry (such as neck, wings, giblets). Simmer these in 2 cups of water, with seasonings, as if to make broth (p. 82); then use the cooked meat of these pieces another day to make chicken croquettes, or chicken pie, or creamed chicken in shortcake biscuits.

Fish

Small whole fish, or small sections of fish (fillets) may be deep-fried.

Fillets. If using frozen **fillets,** thaw first by package directions, and pat dry between paper towels, before preparing to cook. If fresh fillets, wipe fish with damp cloth. Cut fillets to serving-size pieces, before you go farther.

Sprinkle all pieces with **salt.** Coat in **egg-and-crumb coating** (p. 100), taking care to coat all sides evenly.

Have deep saucepan half full of **fat,** heated to 375°. Lower pieces into hot fat, with pancake turner. Fry 3 to 5 minutes, depending on size of pieces, or just until they are golden brown on all sides. With pancake turner, lift from hot fat carefully. Drain on paper towel. Garnish with dash of **paprika** and a sprig of **parsley.** Serve with tartar sauce (p. 354). Cole slaw is also much liked with fried fish. Also good: creamed or mashed potatoes; any leafy vegetable, like spinach, broccoli, sprouts; or broiled stuffed tomatoes.

Small, Whole Fish (Smelts; other small fish not over 3 or 4 inches long). Have fish split open lengthwise, head to tail, at market, and inside cleaned. Heads and tails are sometimes left on, for frying, but are cut off before eating. Have them cut off, if you prefer, at market. Roll each whole fish in **egg-and-crumb coating** (p. 100). Have deep saucepan half filled with **hot cooking fat,** heated to 375°. With long-handled instrument, or using a wire basket to hold fish, lower fish into hot fat. Fry 3 to 4 minutes, or until lightly browned all over. Lift carefully from hot fat. Drain on paper towel. Serve with tartar sauce (p. 354) and vegetables recommended for fillets.

Shellfish

Raw oysters, clams and scallops, and boiled shelled shrimp are delicious deep-fried. See individual methods for different types of shellfish in Chapter XV. The general method is to dip cleaned, drained, or otherwise prepared shellfish in **batter coating**, p. 101, or in **egg-and-crumb coating** (p. 100). Then fry in deep fat heated to 375° about 3 minutes, or just until golden brown. Drain on paper towel.

Croquettes

To make croquette mixture, shape and coat croquettes, see Master Recipe, page 155. Croquettes may be shallow-fried or deep-fried. If deep-frying, lower shaped, coated croquettes into saucepan half full of **hot fat,** heated to 390°. Fry 2 to 3 minutes, or just until nicely browned on all sides. Drain on paper towel.

Fritters

To make and fry, see Master Recipe, Fritters (p. 213).

Potatoes

Allow **1 large potato or 1½ medium-sized potatoes per person.** Peel and wash off potatoes. Cut them into lengthwise strips, ⅜ inch thick. (Or, instead, you may use a fancy potato cutter, cutting lattice shapes and so on; but in no case have potatoes more than ⅜ inch thick.) Some cooks like to let sliced raw potatoes stand in **cold water** 15 minutes to 1 hour before cooking; but this is not essential. Drain all slices; pat them dry between towels, so no drops of water will cling to them.

There are now two methods you may choose from, for cooking the potatoes, depending on preference and your circumstances. For immediate use, choose Method I.

Method I: For immediate cooking and serving. Have deep saucepan half filled with **hot cooking fat,** heated to 375°.

Potatoes do not have to be coated. Master chefs in hotels sometimes shake raw potato strips in paper bag containing ½ **cup flour** plus 2 tablespoons **paprika,** before frying potatoes. The paprika gives them a magnificent color when cooked, but such coating is not essential.

Put potato strips in wire frying basket, lowering basket into hot fat. Or, if you have no basket, lower potato strips into hot fat with long-handled spoon. Do not try to cook too many potatoes at once, or you will lower the heat of the cooking fat by adding so much cold food, and potatoes will not form a crisp crust, but remain soft and soggy. Fry about 6 to 12 minutes, or longer if necessary, just until potatoes are golden brown and tender when tested with fork. Lift them carefully from hot fat; drain on paper towel; sprinkle with **salt** while still hot. Fry more, if needed.

Method II: Boiling potatoes before frying. This is a way of partly cooking potatoes ahead of time. Early in the day, peel, wash, and cut your potatoes into strips. Put them in saucepan. Cover with **water;** add 1 teaspoon **salt;** cover pan; boil gently until *semi*-tender . . . do not cook until soft. Drain them. Store in refrigerator until a few minutes before serving time. Then heat **1 inch deep fat** in heavy frying pan, to 390°. With long-handled spoon, lower potatoes into hot fat. Fry just about 2 or 3 minutes, until golden brown and hot. Lift from hot fat with slotted spoon. Drain on paper towel. Sprinkle with **salt** while still hot.

Onion Rings

Peel medium or large raw **onions,** allowing about 1 onion per person. Slice crosswise, in ¼ inch thick slices. If slices do not separate into rings by themselves during this soaking, help them apart with your fingers. Put rings in bowl; pour on enough milk to cover them, and let stand about 10 minutes. Then drain them. Dip the rings in plain flour (no other coating). Have deep saucepan half full of **hot fat,** heated to 375°. Lower rings into hot fat. Fry 2 minutes, or just until golden color. Drain on paper towel. Sprinkle with **salt** while still hot.

Eggplant

Peel raw **eggplant.** Slice crosswise in ¼ inch thick slices. If slices are too large for an individual serving, cut them in halves, or thirds. Dip each piece in **egg-and-crumb** or **batter coating**

(p. 100). Have deep saucepan half full of **hot cooking fat,** heated to 375°. Place eggplant slices in wire frying basket, and lower basket into hot fat; or lift slices into hot fat with pancake turner or tongs. Fry 4 or 5 minutes, just until golden brown and tender. Lift from hot fat. Drain on paper towel before serving.

Cauliflower Flowerets

From a whole **cauliflower,** trim off all leaves, and excess stem. Now, with knife, cut into separate little flowerets, by cutting each cluster loose from the main stem. Wash flowerets in cold water; drain. Pat dry, with towel. Dip them in **flour, egg,** and **crumbs** (see egg-and-crumb coating, p. 100). Have deep saucepan half filled with **hot fat,** heated to 375°. Put flowerets in wire frying basket, and lower basket into hot fat; or lift flowerets into hot fat with long-handled spoon. Fry 2 to 5 minutes, until golden brown and tender. Lift out of hot fat. Drain on paper towel before serving.

Cucumbers

Peel raw **cucumber.** Cut into lengthwise strips, ¼ inch thick, like shape of French-fried potatoes. Dry the strips between towels. Dip each strip in **flour,** then in **egg,** then in **crumbs** (see egg-and-crumb coating, p. 100). Have deep saucepan half filled with **hot fat,** heated to 390°. Put cucumber strips in wire frying basket, and lower basket into hot fat; or lift strips into hot fat with pancake turner. Fry about 2 minutes, just until golden brown. Drain on paper towel.

Asparagus Tips

Drain canned or home-cooked **asparagus tips.** Dip them in **flour** coating (p. 101). Have deep saucepan half filled with **hot fat,** heated to 350°. Put asparagus tips in wire frying basket and lower basket into hot fat; or lift asparagus tips into hot fat with pancake turner. Fry about 2 minutes, or just until golden color. Lift carefully from hot fat; drain on paper towel.

Parsley

French-fried parsley is something "special," and easy. It requires no "coating." Simply wash large sprigs of **parsley;** cut off excessive stem; shake parsley dry. Then with tongs, lower parsley into deep saucepan half filled with **hot fat,** heated to 350°. Fry 1 minute. Lift from hot fat; drain on paper towel.

CHAPTER XI

How to Pot-Roast, Stew, and Fricassee

METHOD FOR: *Pot Roasts of Meat; Stews: Beef, Lamb, Veal, Chicken, Kidney, Fish; Boiled Chicken; Chicken Fricassees: "white" and "brown"; Boiled or Poached Fish; Fish Chowder; Stock made from Bones; Boiled Hams; Tongues; Spare Ribs; Pork Hocks*

BASIC PRINCIPLES

We might call this chapter: "How to Make Tough Meats Tender by Simmering in Water."

Stewing, indeed, means just that: long, slow, gentle cooking in water, in a covered kettle, until food is tender. It is the chief method used for tenderizing old chickens (fowl), and for all relatively tough cuts of meat. The long simmering is what does the tenderizing. Herbs or other seasonings added to the cooking water help make the meat delectably tasty.

This is a basic method . . . the method of *gentle* water cookery; and the one thing to remember about it is that meats must always be *simmered* (never boiled). If your water boils, the meat will only become tough.

Red meat is customarily braised (browned quickly on all surfaces, in a little hot fat) before the simmering begins; this sears the meat, helps point up its flavor, and helps close the good meat juices and vitamins inside.

Chicken may be browned before simmering, or not — depending upon whether you want the chicken to be a brown fricassee, or to remain white, for chicken salad or creamed chicken.

Fish, ham, and internal organs are not braised; just simmered. The recipes given here show the basic methods, and basic seasonings, used in these dishes the world over. Try them out, just as given here, the first time. But after you are familiar with the method, have fun; experiment. Try out different seasonings; try out different combinations of vegetables in your stews; try adding a little wine to your cooking water. There is nothing to stop you from being as creative as a French chef, and originating a version strictly your own, for which your house may become famous. Many a French restaurant, remember, has drawn patrons from halfway around the world, to savor a reliable old-time beef or lamb stew with a little wine and a few extra herbs added, or a delectable slice of poached fish with an especially well-seasoned sauce.

MASTER RECIPE #10
POT ROAST

(Serves 4 to 6)

Order

3 to 5 pounds chuck, round, or rump steak

or ask butcher what less expensive cuts of beef he has. Have meat boned, rolled, tied, to make a pot roast.

Step 1. Braising the Pot Roast. In heavy kettle or Dutch oven over burner, heat

3 to 4 tablespoons bacon fat
(or beef suet, or other cooking fat)

In hot fat, brown

2 or 3 peeled, sliced onions

Push onions aside when browned or remove them; they have done their job of flavoring the hot fat.

Salt your pot roast well, on all sides. (Some people like to coat it with **flour** on all sides also.) Now put meat in kettle containing the hot fat. Brown meat rapidly, on one side after another, over fairly high heat, until nicely seared all over.

Step 2. Simmering. To meat in kettle, add

1 to 3 cups water

(Some cooks use only 1 cup water, adding a bit more, if needed during cooking time, just to keep kettle from becoming dry.)

If you are one who likes wine cookery, you may substitute **1 cup red wine** instead of water, for cooking red meat; 1 cup white wine instead of water when cooking chicken or fish by this method.

Add with water

Group I Seasonings:

½ teaspoon salt	**1 small carrot**, if desired
¼ teaspoon pepper	**1 branch celery** with leaves
½ bay leaf, if desired	**1 sprig parsley**
1 pinch thyme, if desired	

Some prefer pot roast cooked only with salt and pepper, no additional seasonings.

To make a "spicy" pot roast, add also

Group II Seasonings:

¼ cup vinegar	**1 or 2 whole cloves**
1 tablespoon sugar	**1 pinch allspice**

Bring water to a boil; then at once reduce heat to low; cover kettle; leave meat to *simmer gently* 2 to 3½ hours, depending on size of meat. When done, meat will feel very tender, when tested with fork.

If desired to cook vegetables with the pot roast, add these to kettle *45 minutes or less* before meat will be done, depending on time of cooking required for the vegetables you are using (see Step 3).

Step 3. Adding Vegetables. You do not *need* to add any vegetables if you don't want to. Some people prefer to cook the meat all by itself, thus keeping its flavor "all meat" and unchanged. If you wish to do this, simply let meat simmer with its seasonings, until tender. Cook whatever vegetables you will have for dinner in separate pans.

On the other hand, some people like to put in the kettle with the meat such serving vegetables as potatoes, carrots, onions, perhaps others; if this is done, the meat lends flavor to the vegetables, and the vegetables to the meat; the taste of all of them becomes very savory.

If you wish to cook vegetables with the meat:

Remove from pot roast kettle, about 1 hour before meat will be done, the vegetables used for seasoning, leaving only the meat and its juice.

Peel, slice, or otherwise prepare the raw vegetables you wish to cook with meat.

Look up (see Chart, page 292, for Boiled Vegetables) the cooking time required for any vegetable you are using; for example, potatoes will require about 45 minutes, carrots about 30 minutes, small whole onions, about 25 minutes, small tender vegetables like peas, only about 10 to 15 minutes. Put into kettle first the vegetables which take longest; add later the smaller or tenderer vegetables, according to time each requires. The vegetables will simmer in the same juices with the meat (a gentler form of "boiling" the vegetables); and all should be done at the same time. Before serving, thicken the juice into gravy.

Step 4. To Thicken Gravy, When Meat Is Done. The liquid in which meat was simmered will be rich with three of the ingredients needed for gravy: meat flavor, fat, and seasonings. All you need add, to make rich gravy, is a thickening agent; and this is flour.

To make gravy:

Lift pot roast, and any vegetables cooked with it, from cooking kettle to a warm platter. Put meat and vegetables where they will keep warm. Leave meat juices in kettle, but estimate how much juice is there: that is, 1 cup or 2 cups or whatever.

Have handy a small glass jar which has a tight-fitting lid. Into the jar put (for **each cup liquid** in kettle)

2 tablespoons flour
¼ teaspoon salt

Add to jar

¼ to ½ cup cold water

Cover jar tightly with its lid; shake jar vigorously, until flour and water are thoroughly blended.

Slowly pour the flour mixture into hot juices in kettle, stirring constantly with wire whisk or wooden spoon; then, still stirring constantly, bring mixture to a boil over moderate heat, and cook until thickened, about 3 to 5 minutes.

Taste gravy. If it hasn't enough flavor to suit you, add a bit more salt, or **1 teaspoon grated raw onion,** or **a few drops bottled gravy flavoring.** If desired, add **a few drops Worcestershire sauce.**

Serve meat (and vegetables, if any) with the hot gravy.

POT ROAST VARIATIONS

Meat Stews

Stews are cooked exactly like pot roasts, except that stew meat is cut into cubes — not cooked all in one piece.

To serve 4, order **2 or 3 pounds stewing beef, lamb, or veal** (2 pounds will do if boneless meat, but get 3 pounds if it contains bones). Have meat cut into 1½- or 2-inch cubes at market.

Now follow Master Recipe, Pot Roast (p. 117); but if it is lamb you are cooking you may, if desired, omit Step 1, Braising. Simply put lamb to simmer (Step 2) with **Group I seasonings,** adding **1 or 2 peeled sliced onions,** and increasing salt to 2 teaspoons.

For all other meat stews, begin with Pot Roast, Step 1. Before putting meat into hot fat, shake all cubes of stew meat in a paper bag containing **3 tablespoons flour** and **2 teaspoons salt.** This flour coating helps sear meat quickly, sealing in the good meat juices, and giving meat a rich brown taste.

In Step 2, Simmering, increase water to enough to *cover* the meat. Add all **Group I seasonings,** but omit the salt, since you have already used 2 teaspoons salt when flouring the meat.

In Step 3, Adding Vegetables, as with Pot Roast, first remove Group I seasonings. Then peel, slice, and add to kettle the vegetables you wish to serve with stew, adding each in order of time the vegetable needs to cook. See Chart for Boiling Vegetables (p. 292). There are certain vegetables which are customarily used with certain meats, but this is not an absolute rule for all time. Sometimes you may wish to experiment, trying other kinds. So we give both the typical — and some alternate — vegetables:

For beef: Potatoes, carrots, peas; many cooks add a peeled, quartered white turnip. *Alternates:* 1 can tomatoes (or several peeled, quartered fresh tomatoes) plus sliced mushroom caps and stems, peas. Or fresh or frozen kernel corn, plus lima or string beans.

For veal: Potatoes, carrots, peas, 4 or 5 small whole onions peeled. *Alternates:* peeled sweet potatoes, instead of white, plus peas, sliced mushroom caps or stems; this makes a sweeter stew.

For lamb: Potatoes, carrots, peas. *Alternates:* peeled sweet potatoes instead of white, plus peas and sliced mushroom caps or stems. Or try it with no potatoes, but 10 tiny white whole peeled onions, plus cut string beans. (This last is extra delicious.)

In Step 4, Thickening Gravy. Follow Master Recipe, Pot Roast exactly.

Stew with Dumplings. Any stew is something to remember, if served on a wintry night with steaming herb dumplings. Try them. They are simply a variation of biscuit dough; take only 12 to 15 minutes to cook, on finished stew. See page 200.

Chicken Stew (also called **Chicken Pot Pie,** or **White Fricassee**).

Serves 4 to 6. Order a **5- or 6-pound fowl.** Have it cut in sections for fricasseeing. Wipe all sections clean with damp cloth.

Now follow Master Recipe, Pot Roast (p. 117), but omit Step 1, Braising. Just place chicken sections in kettle, and begin with Step 2, Simmering, adding to kettle enough **water to cover** chicken, and adding all **Group I** seasonings, plus **1 peeled onion,** cut in half. Increase **salt** to 2 teaspoons.

Omit Step 3. No vegetables are cooked in chicken stew.

Thicken gravy, as in Step 4. Serve hot chicken pieces and chicken gravy on hot cooked rice, or noodles, with garden peas or string beans on the side.

Or cook dumplings (p. 200) on top of finished stew to make a superb chicken pot pie.

Boiled Chicken (also called "Poached")

Order a **fowl of 6 to 8 pounds,** dressed and drawn. If you wish, you may boil it whole, but this takes quite a long time. Therefore most people have the butcher cut fowl into sections, as for fricasseeing.

In either case, follow Master Recipe, Pot Roast (p. 117), beginning with Step 2, Simmering, placing chicken in kettle and using enough water to cover. Use all **Group I** seasonings, plus **1 whole peeled onion,** cut in half; and increase **salt** to 2 teaspoons.

Omit Steps 3 and 4. As soon as chicken meat feels tender when tested with fork, chicken is done.

Remove chicken from broth (save the broth, however; it is good to drink, or can be jelled into an aspic, page 377). As soon as chicken has cooled enough to handle, you may pull off skin; remove meat from bones.

Meat may now be used for chicken salad, creamed chicken, chicken shortcakes, chicken à la King. A cooked fowl should yield 6 to 8 cups diced chicken meat.

Brown Fricassee of Chicken

Serves 4 to 6. Make just like chicken stew (white fricassee), except that you brown the **chicken pieces** before putting them to simmer.

Follow Master Recipe, Pot Roast (p. 117), beginning with Step 1, Braising, but before putting chicken pieces into **hot fat,** shake chicken in paper bag containing **3 tablespoons flour** and

2 teaspoons salt, until well coated. For cooking fat, use melted chicken fat, salad oil, or vegetable shortening instead of meat fat.

When chicken has been browned in fat, continue with Step 2, Simmering, adding to kettle enough **water** to cover all chicken, and using all **Group I seasonings, except salt.**

Omit Step 3. No vegetables are cooked with chicken fricassee. Thicken gravy as in Step 4.

Serve tender chicken pieces and gravy with hot rice or noodles, and peas, string beans, or other delicate green vegetable.

Boiled or Poached Fish

This is a method for a **large fish,** or a crosswise section of 3 to 6 pounds cut from a great cod, haddock, halibut, salmon, or other big fish. Such fish is too thick to broil or fry; it must be baked or poached. (Poaching is the name used by gourmets to signify that the fish is never *boiled hard,* but simmered very gently.)

Fish should be cleaned at market. If it is a whole fish, you may have head and tail cut off, or leave them on. If desired, you may have fish cut to serving-size slices, or leave it intact.

Wipe fish with damp cloth; sprinkle it liberally with salt. Place it on a plate which will fit inside your Dutch oven, or other cooking kettle. Wrap a square piece of clean cheesecloth around fish and platter both, holding the fish to platter; then tie the cloth into a knot at both ends so it will not come undone.

Now in kettle put enough **water** to cover fish (about 1 quart); add all **Group I seasonings,** Master Recipe, Pot Roast (p. 117), plus **1 peeled, sliced onion;** increase the salt to 2 teaspoons. For a spicy flavor, add **2 whole cloves,** plus **1 cup white wine,** if desired. Lower plate and fish into boiling, seasoned water. Simmer the fish gently, allowing 6 to 10 minutes per pound of fish, depending on whether fish is in one piece (10 minutes) or in slices (6 minutes). Don't overcook. When time is up, pour off water; lift out dish; unwrap fish; serve with egg sauce (p. 249);

celery sauce (p. 250); parsley sauce (p. 248); anchovy butter, or parsley butter (p. 256).

Poached Fillets. Fillets, or fish steaks, cut to serving-size pieces before cooking, may be poached by same method as above; but allow only 1 minute *per ounce* cooking time in the water.

Fillets or fish steaks may also be poached gently in a frying pan containing 1 to 1½ cups milk or white wine. Simmer just a few minutes, until fish is tender and flaky.

Fish Stew (or Chowder)

Serves 4. A heartening, savory main course, for a blustery night!

Buy 2 pounds filleted, white-meated fish (cod, haddock, flounder, perch, whiting). Buy also a ¼ pound piece of salt pork. Have available 1 can tomatoes, plus 4 to 5 potatoes, and 2 onions. Dice the salt pork.

To cook: Begin as in Step 1, Braising (Master Recipe, Pot Roast, p. 117) but don't braise the fish . . . only the onions. In your stew kettle, "try out" (melt, over slow heat) the diced salt pork, until you have 3 or 4 tablespoons liquid fat. Then discard the solid pieces of salt pork, keeping only the liquid. In this hot liquid fat, brown lightly the peeled, sliced onions. Then add the peeled raw potatoes, sliced about ⅜ inch thick, and the can of tomatoes (juice and pulp). Add 2 teaspoons salt, and the fish, broken into chunks about the size of small eggs. Add just barely enough water to cover all ingredients. Cover kettle, and simmer over gentle heat about 30 to 40 minutes, or until potatoes are tender. Ladle chowder out into soup plates. Delicious with pilot crackers or crusty French bread; green salad; and fruit, cheese, or a good pie for dessert.

New England Fish Chowder. If you prefer a true New England fish chowder, you will omit the tomatoes from this recipe, and change the method of cooking slightly, to this order: brown onions in melted salt pork; add sliced potatoes to kettle; add also salt, and fish; then barely cover ingredients with water; cook gently, covered, about 30 minutes until potatoes are tender.

About 5 minutes before serving, add enough **rich whole milk, top milk, light cream,** or **evaporated milk** to make chowder have the moisture you wish (about 1 to 2 cups). Heat milk or cream but do not let it boil. Adjust seasoning, before serving; after adding milk, chowder may need more salt. If desired, add also a dash of **pepper,** and a bit of minced **parsley** when serving.

Kidney Stew

(Serves 2.) Kidney stew is *called* stew and so is included here, but if you use tender lamb kidneys, which are far and away the nicest kind for this dish, the kidneys need no stewing or simmering in water; they are delicate, cook quickly, and can be sautéed. This dish is therefore *not* modeled on the Pot Roast Method. Make it as follows; and allow about ½ hour to prepare this "stew."

Buy **8 to 10 lamb's kidneys.** Allow at least 4 kidneys per person; they are small.

Clean, cut up, and cook kidneys as under sautéed kidneys (p. 94), adding **1 tablespoon grated onion** with the kidneys as they sauté. As soon as kidneys are tender (which will be in about 5 minutes), make gravy in the same pan.

To make gravy. Add and blend with cooked kidneys **3 tablespoons flour.** Stir over low heat until flour browns, and is no longer visible. Then add, gradually, stirring constantly, **1½ cup of a beef-flavored liquid.** This liquid may be any one of:

Beef stock.

Canned beef bouillon, undiluted.

Bouillon made by dissolving 2 bouillon cubes or 2 teaspoons thick bottled beef extract in 1½ cup boiling water.

Leftover steak juices, or pan juices from cooked steak, mixed with enough water to make 1½ cups total liquid.

Bring mixture to a boil, stirring constantly; add **a few drops Worcestershire sauce;** and cook until gravy thickens; about 3 to 5 minutes.

Serve hot kidneys and their gravy on a bed of hot buttered steamed white rice (p. 305); or on drained, buttered, hot noodles

(p. 310); or on hot buttered toast. Garnish with a sprinkling of minced parsley, and a dash of paprika. Very, very good.

Kidney Stew Variations

Beef and Kidney Stew

Method I. Using leftover cooked beef. This is a wonderful way to use leftover roast beef, or broiled steak, or even pot-roasted beef. Trim fat and gristle from **cooked beef;** cut meat into nice cubes, about 1 inch square. Now make kidney stew, sautéing kidneys and making gravy. Add the meat cubes to finished stew. Cover pan. Place over low heat 10 to 15 minutes, or until meat is hot. Serve. (Adding the meat of course makes a bigger stew, which will serve 3 to 4 people.)

Method II. Starting with raw beef. Buy ½ **pound boneless chuck,** or other boneless stewing beef; have it cut into 1 inch cubes. Allow 1½ hours to cook beef tender by Step 1, Braising, and Step 2, Simmering, under Master Recipe, Pot Roast (p. 117). When meat is tender, remove it from cooking water, and combine hot tender meat cubes with hot separately sautéed kidneys. Make gravy as under Kidney Stew, using water beef was cooked in as your liquid. (Adding the meat extends the kidney stew, making it serve 3 to 4 people.)

Beef and Kidney Pie.

Serves 3 to 4. This is simply **beef and kidney** stew turned into a casserole, and covered with a **biscuit crust.** After making the stew, allow about 15 minutes to make crust, and 20 to 25 minutes extra to bake the dish.

Make stew by Method I or Method II, above.

Turn mixture into baking dish or casserole which it will fill to top.

Make ½ Master Recipe, Biscuits (p. 198). Turn dough onto floured board. With floured rolling pin, shape it to circular sheet which will be big enough to cover top of pie. Lift the crust onto the pie. Crimp edges of crust to dish containing pie. With knife, cut 5 or 6 slashes in center of crust, to allow steam vents. Place pie in preheated hot (450°) oven. Bake 20 to 25 minutes, until crust is brown and done.

Stock, Broth, or Meat-and-Vegetable Soup
Made from Bones

Bones and other "trimmings" — if simmered with seasonings by the Pot Roast Method — produce a nourishing thin liquor called "stock." Stock can be used to make sauces . . . or it can be served as broth . . . or if thickened, and vegetables and scraps of meat added to it, it makes hearty meat-and-vegetable soup. So don't throw away any bones and trimmings . . . except for pork; pork is of no use for this purpose.

Begin with Step 2. Simmering (Master Recipe, Pot Roasts, p. 117). Place in large kettle **meat bones** (or chicken, turkey or duck carcass; or head, tail, backbone, other trimmings of fish). Cover bones with water. Add **Group I seasoning vegetables** given in Step 2 (Pot Roast). Bring to boil; cover kettle; turn heat low; simmer 2 to 3 hours, or until broth cooks down to less than half its original volume. (The more you cook it down, the **stronger** and more concentrated it will become.)

Strain liquor free of seasonings and bones. The clear liquor, "as is," is called *stock.*

To use as broth. Season stock with more **salt,** if needed. Add also, if desired, ½ to 1 cup cooked **noodles** or **rice,** and bits of **meat** which have cooked free from the bones.

To make hearty vegetable soup. Return strained stock to kettle; simmer in it, covered, until tender, any **peeled raw vegetables** you would like in soup: cut up potatoes, carrots, peas, limas, mushroom caps or stems, tiny onions, sliced celery, or whatever. If desired add fresh or canned tomatoes. Add any bits of **meat, fish or chicken** that came from the bones. Add cooked **rice** or **noodles** if desired. Before serving, if soup is not thick enough, thicken as in Step 4 (Pot Roast), allowing **1 tablespoon flour** per cup of liquid in the kettle; add more salt if needed.

This type of soup is marvelous on a wintry night, served with crusty French bread, green salad, and a good pie.

Stock Variations

Brown Stock (Beef). This is a doubly concentrated, highly flavored beef liquor. It is made from **beef bones, plus beef,** plus **Group I seasonings** given under Step 2 (Pot Roast) (p. 117), plus ¼ **teaspoon marjoram** . . . all cooked down until very concentrated. An easier way is to simmer for ½ hour **1 can undiluted beef bouillon** with ½ bay leaf, 1 clove, 1 pinch thyme, 1 pinch marjoram. Or combine **1 tablespoon concentrated beef extract** with 2 cups water, and simmer ½ hour with same seasonings as for bouillon.

White Stock (Veal). Usually made from a **3- or 4-pound piece of veal knuckle,** simmered with **Group I seasonings** as in Step 2 (Pot Roast). Strain.

Chicken Stock. Simmer **carcass of roast chicken,** or **bones left from broiled or fried chicken,** with **Group I seasonings** given in Step 2 (Pot Roast). Strain.

Plain Fish Stock. Simmer **head, tail, fins, backbone of fish** in **salted water** 1 hour, with **1 peeled onion** cut in quarters, **1 branch celery** with leaves, **2 sprigs parsley,** ½ **bay leaf.** Strain out bones and seasoning vegetables.

Court Bouillon. Simmer **head, tail, fins, backbone of fish** in **2 quarts water,** plus **1 cup red or white wine,** with these seasonings: 2 or 3 sprigs parsley; 1 small carrot, sliced; 1 onion stuck with 2 cloves; ½ bay leaf; 1¼ teaspoon salt, 4 peppercorns.

"Boiled" Ham

An uncooked ham will, like a pot roast, become tender if simmered long and gently in water. But note that the word is "simmered." Tests prove that hams simmered at 180°, without allowing the water to bubble, are most tender.

Any uncooked ham may be tenderized by this method, but certain types of ham must first be soaked overnight.

Soaking. All country-cured and aged hams (such as Virginia, Smithfield, Kentucky hams) — or home-cured hams — or smoked shoulders, picnics, and cottage butts — should be soaked overnight in cold water, before cooking. Hams which have already been somewhat processed (cooked) by the meat packer (called "tenderized," or "pre-cooked") do not require soaking.

Method of cooking. Scrub ham well, with stiff brush. Country cured or aged hams may have green mold on them; this does no harm; simply scrub mold off with brush and strong yellow soap; then rinse thoroughly.

Put ham in large, heavy kettle, adding enough cold water just to cover ham. You may cook ham in plain water. Or you may add to water all Group I seasonings given in Step 2, Pot Roast (p. 117), *except salt. Never use salt with ham.* Or, for variety, cook ham in part plain water, part cider. Or in part plain water, part pineapple juice. Or you may add ½ cup vinegar and ½ cup sugar to plain water.

Cover kettle and simmer ham gently (allowing about 25 minutes per pound) until tender. Cool in the cooking liquid. When cool, slit and peel off tough outer skin.

Ham is now "boiled ham" . . . ready to eat. If desired, you may now glaze it in the oven with brown sugar and cloves just like a baked ham. See Step 4, to Glaze, p. 134.

"Boiled" Tongue (Beef, Calf)

Smoked tongue should be soaked in cold water overnight before cooking. For *fresh* tongue, no soaking is needed. When ready to cook, place tongue in large kettle, as in Step 2, Master Recipe, Pot Roast (p. 117). Cover tongue with water; add 2 peeled cloves of garlic, 2 stalks of celery, 1 peeled sliced onion, 1 peeled carrot, ¼ cup vinegar, ¼ cup sugar, as seasonings. For fresh tongue, add also 1 teaspoon salt. Simmer, covered, 3½ to 4 hours or until tender. Remove from liquor. Let cool until you can handle: then peel off skin; trim off small bones at end. Slice. Serve with raisin sauce (p. 258), or mustard sauce (p. 250), or a sweet pickle relish.

Spareribs with Sauerkraut

Serves 4. Buy 3 pounds spareribs, plus 1 quart or 2 pounds

sauerkraut. Drain sauerkraut of brine. Place spareribs and drained sauerkraut together in kettle; cover with boiling water; cover kettle; simmer about 1 hour, or until meat is tender. Drain off liquor, and serve ribs and sauerkraut together.

Pork Hocks with Sauerkraut

Serves 4. Buy 4 hocks (about 3 pounds), and **2 pounds sauerkraut.** Put hocks in kettle; cover with **boiling water;** add **1 teaspoon salt, 1 bay leaf, 8 peppercorns.** Cover kettle; simmer 2¼ hours, or until meat is tender. Remove hocks from kettle, and pour off all but 2 cups liquid they cooked in. To liquid remaining in kettle, add ½ **cup minced or grated onion, 2 cored, grated apples, 1 peeled raw potato, 3 or 4 tablespoons salad oil, 2 more teaspoons salt,** and the sauerkraut. Replace hocks on top of all this mixture. Cover kettle; simmer about 30 to 40 minutes more. When done, drain the sauerkraut and serve on same platter with hocks. (This is a variation of the pot roast method, as you see.)

CHAPTER XII

How to Bake Meats and Fish

METHOD FOR: *Baked Ham, Baked Fresh Ham, Baked Fish, Baked Liver and Bacon, Baked Casseroles, Veal Cutlets, Baked Meat Ring, Main Course Shortcakes, Baked Kabobs*

BASIC PRINCIPLES

"Baking" meats actually is done in the same oven, with the same heating unit, as "roasting." Why there should be two different names for it, no one has ever vouchsafed to me. In both cases, the meat is simply placed in the oven (using heating unit near or underneath floor of oven) and the heat is kept moderate until the food is tender and done. However, inasmuch as some meats are referred to as "roasted," and some "baked," we will take up those called "baked" here.

"Baking" of meats divides itself into two general categories: (1) *baking large solid pieces of meat,* such as a ham, or a whole fish; and (2) *baking "made" dishes,* in which meat is cut to smaller pieces and blended with other ingredients.

Large pieces of meat, like a ham, are kept sufficiently moist by drippings from the fat attached to them. A fish, or chicken, which has no natural outside coating of fat, needs coating with oil, butter, drying. Casseroles, unless covered by a crust or crumb topping, are covered with lid. Any small pieces of meat are baked with a cover over the dish. Any small pieces of meat are either baked in a sauce, to keep them moist, or with liquid in the pan, or are brushed with fat, or in some way protected from drying.

This is the whole trick in baking meat: to protect the food from drying out, while allowing the moderate heat to circulate around it long enough to cook it tender all the way through. If you remember to keep your meats protected, you will always have succulent, flavorful results; if not, you will be regretful!

And now, being sufficiently warned, try any of these good things.

BAKED HAM

Before Cooking a Ham, Read These Facts

You must know two things about the kind of ham you are cooking, in order to handle its preparation properly:

(1) *Its Condition.* Hams marketed by nationally known meat packers may be sold in one of three conditions: entirely *un*cooked; *partially* cooked (called "tenderized," or "precooked"); completely *cooked* (called "ready-to-eat").

Read label on ham, or ask your butcher in which condition the ham is; your method of cooking depends on knowing this.

(2) *The Cut.* A ham (technically speaking) is the hind leg of a pig; no other part. But markets also classify as "ham" cuts taken from the pig's forequarter; the meat is similar, but sometimes a little tougher or saltier. Nonetheless, if well cooked, these smaller foreleg hams are delicious, and a good size for a small family. A few extra precautions make them sweet and tender. So know whether you have: a true "ham" (hind leg; all of it, or half of it); a "shoulder butt" (cut from front shoulder of pig); or a "picnic shoulder" (cut from upper foreleg of pig).

The entire hind leg is very large, often weighing 12 to 14 pounds or more, and though excellent for a large party, is impractical for a small family's meals. So if desired, ask butcher to sell you half a ham; he will cut the hind leg crosswise into two halves, and either half provides good tender meat.

A cooked ham is a fine thing to have in the house. It keeps almost indefinitely, and is always handy for sandwiches, or to use as cold cuts with salad, or to fry with eggs; and can be used in countless hot leftover dishes; see page 187. Even the ham bone is useful; it makes delectable split-pea soup; the recipe comes on packages of split peas.

Baking Directions for Different Type Hams

Uncooked Hams

Step 1. Soaking. If ham is a "country-cured" ham, or is a shoulder butt, or picnic shoulder, soak it at least 1 hour, or even overnight, in enough cold water to cover it; this draws out excess saltiness from meat. (This step can be omitted for hind leg hams of national meat packers.)

All "country-cured" hams (known by locality, such as Smithfield ham, Virginia Ham, Kentucky ham) are cured by a different process than national meat packers use; they therefore require long soaking — overnight — in cold water to cover. These hams are considered best when very aged; they may even be moldy. This does no harm — simply scrub off mold with stiff brush and yellow soap, before soaking ham. After soaking, proceed as for any uncooked ham, Steps 1, 3, 4.

Step 2. Baking tender. Note which is the side of ham with a thick layer of fat under the rind. Keeping this side up, slide ham inside 3 or 4 paper bags, one after another, closing each. When ham is thus thoroughly wrapped, place it, still fatty side up, on a baking pan. Center pan in slow (300°) oven. Bake 25 to 30 minutes per pound. (A 6 or 7 pound ham will require about 3 hours, to become tender.)

Step 3. Removing rind. When baked, remove pan from oven to table top; cut open the paper bags so you can get at ham, but leave bags underneath the ham to catch drippings. Now, with sharp knife, slit the tough rind lengthwise, so you can get underneath it with point of knife. With knife, loosen or cut off all hard rind, but leave a ¼ inch thick layer of the sweet white fat on ham. Discard paper bags and refuse.

Ham is now tender, hot, peeled, and ready to eat, if you wish.

Or if you wish to glaze it with brown sugar and cloves, continue to Step 4.

Step 4. To glaze. After rind is removed, with sharp knife cut a series of parallel lines through fat, about ⅜ inch apart, the lines running diagonally across ham. Now cut another set of similar parallel lines, running diagonally in the opposite direction, making a diamond-shaped crisscross pattern over all the white fat. Now press into the cut fat as much **brown sugar** as will adhere to top of ham, patting sugar on thickly. Then into each intersection of the cut fat, press **1 whole clove.** This is a slow job, but if done carefully makes a beautiful effect, good enough for a picture book. (Allow about ½ hour to do this task, the first time you try it.) When ham is all fixed with sugar and cloves, place it on a clean baking pan. Place in moderate oven (375°) for 20 to 40 minutes, until top of ham becomes golden brown and shiny, or "glazed." If desired, you may spoon pan drippings up over the ham 3 or 4 times while it glazes.

Ham may now be served hot; or may be cooled and sliced cold.

Partially Cooked Hams (called "tenderized" or "precooked"). These hams do not need soaking; but they are not tender enough to eat, for they have not been cooked enough. Prepare ham just as in Step 2, Uncooked Ham; bake at least 1 or 2 hours to finish tenderizing. Then treat as in Step 3 to remove rind; and as in Step 4 to glaze.

"Ready-to-Eat" Hams (completely cooked when sold).

These hams need no soaking; they are entirely cooked, and may be used in three ways:

(1) *To serve cold.* With sharp knife, peel off tough outer rind; slice meat, and serve.

(2) *To serve hot.* Wrap ham inside 2 or 3 paper bags; place on baking pan in slow (300°) oven, and bake 15 minutes per pound, to make thoroughly hot. Then remove from oven, and peel off rind as under Step 3, Uncooked Hams.

(3) *To serve hot and glazed.* Follow (2) above, heating ham, and peeling off tough rind. Then follow Step 4, Uncooked Hams, to glaze a ham.

NOTE: A delicious accompaniment for baked ham: allow for each person **1 or 2 drained halves of canned peach, or canned apricot,** the hollow center of each piece of fruit containing **1 teaspoon raspberry jam.**

Also good with ham: glazed sweet potatoes; or corn fritters; leafy green vegetables like broccoli, sprouts; also fried apple rings, or fried pineapple slices.

Baked Fresh Ham

This type ham requires no soaking. It is fresh pork — not smoked and not salty. It is cooked *as a roast*. Have butcher bone the meat, leaving a pocket in it for stuffing. Salt inside of pocket; pack in loosely **plain bread stuffing** (p. 241), or **apple stuffing** variation. For roasting, see page 59.

OTHER BAKED MEAT AND FISH

Baked Fish

See Stuffed Baked Fish, page 245. Omit stuffing the fish if desired, but otherwise bake fish the same way.

Baked Liver and Bacon

Buy calf's or beef liver, sliced ¼ to ½ inch thick, allowing 1 pound liver to serve 3 persons. Arrange slices of **liver** in lightly greased baking pan. Over each slice liver, arrange **2 strips uncooked bacon.** Add **½ to 1 cup hot water** to pan, to provide moisture. Bake in moderate (375°) oven 35 to 40 minutes, or until liver feels tender when tested with fork. If water completely evaporates during cooking time, add a bit more, so there is always some moisture in pan. If desired, sliced raw onions may be added to dish before baking.

Baked Pork Chops, Stuffed

See under Suggestions for Using Stuffing, page 244.

Baked Ham and Potato Casserole

Serves 3 to 4. Butter inside of a shallow, wide, ovenware casserole dish. Line bottom with **thinly sliced raw potatoes.** Over these, place a thin layer **finely sliced raw onions.** Sprinkle with **salt** and **pepper.** On top of vegetables, place one ⅜ to ½ inch thick **ham steak,** or slice from a precooked ham. On top of ham, place another layer of potatoes and onions, seasoned as above. Dot top of potatoes with **butter;** add a sprinkling of pepper. Fill casserole with **milk,** so milk comes to level of top layer of potatoes. Cover surface with fine **bread or cracker crumbs.** Bake 45 minutes to 1 hour, or until potatoes are tender. Very scrumptious. Serve with brussels sprouts, spinach, cabbage, succotash, or stewed tomatoes.

Baked Ham and Apple Casserole

Serves 3 to 4. Buy **1 ham steak** ½ inch thick (a center slice of ham); or use 6 to 8 slices leftover cooked ham. Have available **4 to 5 apples.**

In buttered wide, shallow baking dish place a layer peeled, cored, sliced tart apples (about 2 apples). Over apples, sprinkle **brown sugar** and **½ teaspoon lemon juice.** Arrange ham over apples. Top with another layer apples, more brown sugar and lemon juice. Cover dish. Bake in moderate (350°) oven about 30 minutes; then remove cover and bake 20 minutes longer.

Baked Pork Chops, Smothered in Fruit

Serves 4 to 6. You need **4 to 6 pork chops** ¾ inches thick (allowing 1 per person).

(Try this for company some time; it keeps well, even if **company** is late.)

Sprinkle chops on both sides with mixture of **½ teaspoon salt** and **½ teaspoon sage.** Then brown chops, quickly, all over, in hot frying pan. Set pan aside, keeping fat in it. Place chops in ungreased shallow baking dish. Over chops place a layer of peeled, cored, sliced **tart apples** (about 2 apples). Over apples, pour **¼ cup molasses.** Mix **¼ cup flour** with fat left in frying pan, stirring this to a paste, and gradually add 2 cups hot water, stirring over moderate heat until gravy thickens. Add to gravy 1 tablespoon vinegar, ½ teaspoon salt, ½ cup seedless raisins. Stir well, and simmer about 10 minutes. Pour gravy over chops and apples. Cover dish, and bake in a moderate (350°) oven 1 hour, or until apples are tender.

Ham Kabobs (Baked)

Serves 2. Have at hand 2 slices canned pineapple; 8 cubes cooked ham, about ¾ to 1 inch square; ¼ pound mushroom caps; 4 metal skewers.

Cut each slice of pineapple into 6 pieces, making 12 pieces in all.

Place on 1 skewer, in this order: 1 piece pineapple, 1 mushroom cap, 1 cube ham, I pineapple, 1 mushroom, 1 ham, 1 pineapple.

Fix other 3 skewers the same way.

Place skewers in shallow baking pan or dish, and over them pour a mixture of ½ cup pineapple juice, ½ teaspoon powdered ginger, 1 tablespoon lemon juice, ¼ teaspoon liquid gravy seasoning. Place pan in moderate (325°) oven, and bake 25 to 30 minutes, or until mushrooms are tender. Allow 2 skewers per person.

Baked Ham with Pineapple

Serves 3 to 4. Have at hand: 4 to 6 slices leftover cooked ham; 4 to 6 slices pineapple; brown sugar.

In bottom of oven-glass baking dish, or other shallow casserole, arrange ham slices as a solid layer. Over ham, arrange slices of pineapple (if you wish, cut the slices to make them fit in). Over pineapple, sprinkle 2 tablespoons brown sugar. If desired, add few grains powdered cloves. Bake, uncovered, in moderate (350°) oven about 20 minutes, or just until pineapple is thoroughly heated and sugar melted. This is easy, and good.

To add sweet potatoes to above. Instead of lining baking dish with ham, butter dish generously and line it with peeled cooked or canned sweet potatoes cut in halves, lengthwise. Sprinkle potatoes lightly with brown sugar, and dot with butter. On top of this, arrange ham; and on top of ham, pineapple. Cover dish, and bake longer, 30 to 45 minutes, until potatoes are well heated through.

Breaded Liver with Onion (Baked)

Serves 2. Order ¾ **pound beef liver or calf's liver**, cut in thin, even slices. Trim from liver any tough outside skin or stringy tendons. Place liver in water to cover, and simmer 5 minutes. Drain. Dip each piece, on both sides, in mixture of **1 slightly beaten egg**, mixed with **2 tablespoons lemon juice**, **½ teaspoon salt**, few grains **pepper**. Then dip each slice, both sides, in **bread crumbs**. Place pieces in well-greased baking pan or dish. Over top of each slice liver, spread grated or finely sliced **raw onion**. Dot top of liver with **butter**. Bake in moderate (375°) oven 20 to 25 minutes. If desired, add **1 cup tomato juice** to pan while liver is baking. This helps keep it moist, and gives a tomato flavor.

Breaded Veal Cutlets *

Either veal chops or cutlets may be prepared this way.

Order 1 or 2 cutlets of **veal** (slices ¼ to ½ inch thick) per person, depending on size of slices and appetite. If any skin remains on slices, trim it off. Wipe slices dry with damp cloth. Sprinkle with **salt** and **pepper**, then dip each slice in **flour** on both sides. In a shallow dish or pan, beat slightly **1 egg** combined with **1 tablespoon water**; have ready in another shallow pan about **1 cup fine bread or cracker crumbs**. Now dip each floured slice first in egg, then in crumbs, on both sides. Place slices in moderately hot frying pan containing **3 or 4 tablespoons bacon fat** (or butter, vegetable shortening, or other cooking fat); brown meat quickly on both sides. Veal will not yet be tender; and you have three choices of ways to finish the cooking:

Method 1. Remove browned slices to a casserole or baking dish which has a tight-fitting cover. Over slices, pour **½ cup to 1 cup liquid**. Use a liquid which will not only flavor the meat, but keep it moist, such as one of the following:

---

* If desired you omit "breading" (dipping in egg and crumbs); simply season and flour slices; brown quickly; continue to cook until tender, by any of the methods listed here.

(1) Part water, part highly seasoned tomato sauce. Add if desired a sliced raw onion, a slice of green pepper, a sprig of parsley, a few leaves of celery, for extra seasoning.

(2) Well-seasoned brown stock or stock substitute (see p. 128); if desired add ½ cup to 1 cup dry red wine such as claret. Or add to brown stock a pinch of garlic powder and a few drops Worcestershire sauce.

(3) Sour cream, plus 1 teaspoon paprika (this makes Wiener Schnitzel). Sour cream helps tenderize the meat, as well as flavoring it.

Cover casserole tightly. Place in slow (350°) oven; bake 35 to 40 minutes or until meat is tender.

Method 2. Instead of baking cutlets in oven, you may leave them in frying pan. Add any one of the liquids above; cover pan tightly, and simmer very gently on top of stove until meat is tender, about 35 to 45 minutes.

Method 3. If preferred, instead of adding any liquid, simply leave cutlets in frying pan; add more cooking fat as often as needed to keep chops from drying; keep pan tightly covered, and simmer over lowest heat until meat is tender, about 35 to 40 minutes.

Casseroles and Meat Loaves, Baked

See many suggestions for Casseroles, Chapter XIII, page 141. For baked meat loaf, baked chicken loaf, baked ham loaf, and baked salmon or tuna loaf, see Chapter XIV, page 151.

Baked Meat Ring in Biscuit Crust

Serves 6 to 8. This is an emergency dish, very pretty and very hearty, which can be fixed in little time when unexpected guests descend on you. It requires only biscuit dough, and a can of hash or a couple of cups of leftover, ground, cooked meat.

Make Master Recipe, Baking Powder Biscuits (p. 198).

Roll dough to oblong rectangular sheet, about 14 by 7 inches. Across center top of dough, spread 1 can hash, "as is," *or* a mixture of 2 cups leftover ground meat, 1 small peeled onion, grated, ½ teaspoon salt, dash or two of pepper, ½ teaspoon prepared mustard (optional), ¼ teaspoon **Worcestershire sauce** (optional). **¼ cup catsup** (optional), **1 raw egg** (to make mixture hold together).

Roll up sheet of dough, enclosing all meat mixture inside, so that you have a long roll shaped like a long liverwurst sausage. Bend the roll into wreath shape, and place it in a greased layer-cake pan, joining the ends of the roll together. With sharp knife, make slashes through outer edge of roll, about every 2 inches, all the way around pan. Place in preheated hot (450°) oven; bake 20 to 25 minutes, until crust is browned and done, and meat hot. Remove ring to warm serving platter. If desired, fill center of ring with hot green peas, or other vegetable. Add a tangy vegetable salad, and a dessert of fruit or ice cream. Presto . . . an ample meal.

Meat Shortcakes

Serves 6 or more. This is another quick way to extend a very *little* meat, making it serve many. Very delicious, and very party-ish-looking. All it requires is biscuit dough, leftover cooked meat, or canned meat or fish, and white sauce.

Make **Master Recipe, Baking Powder Biscuits** (p. 198), increasing shortening to 6 tablespoons.

Roll dough out about ⅔ to 1 inch thick, and cut it into 6 or 8 large biscuits. Place biscuits in greased baking pan. Bake in preheated hot (450°) oven about 20 minutes, until nicely browned and done. While biscuits bake, make **2 cups medium white sauce** (p. 248). Add to cooked, thickened sauce **2 cups ground leftover cooked meat**, or **drained, canned, flaked fish**, or **diced, cooked chicken or turkey**. Add for extra seasoning **1 teaspoon grated peeled onion**, **1 tablespoon chopped green pepper**, or **minced parsley**. When biscuits are done, split them in half horizontally. **Butter** them. Over lower halves, spoon the hot creamed meat mixture. Place top halves of biscuits over the creamed filling. Over top of biscuits, put more of the creamed meat mixture. Garnish with few dashes **paprika**; add sprigs of **parsley** to garnish platter.

CHAPTER XIII

You Can Make a Casserole

METHOD FOR: *Quick, One-Dish Dinners*

BASIC PRINCIPLES

A "casserole" (a term loosely applied today) may indeed be almost any combination of main-course foods, put together with a sauce, in a baking dish, and baked in the oven.

The number and variety is legion. Whole books have been written on this subject. Some casseroles are as simple as macaroni and cheese, baked in a sauce. Others begin with raw chicken, baking it in sauce and seasonings, and require quite long and intricate preparation. Each nation, each famous restaurant, each home, has its favorite types. To list all casseroles here would not only be impossible, but pointless. For the one most *useful* type of casserole — the sort which will become a boon to you as it has to millions of other housewives — is the type which combines a few leftovers, or handy canned goods, to make a quick main course for a hungry horde.

Being able to toss together a casserole like this is a priceless trick to have up your sleeve. It is economical, fun, easy, and most adaptable — since such a dish can be whipped together in short order if unexpected guests arrive, or can even be prepared a day in advance if you know you are going to return home only about one half hour before dinner should be on the table.

Furthermore, it is a dish which can be made sufficiently glamorous-looking to entertain the most particular people you know.

When dinner is over, you have no pots and pans waiting to be washed, and the whole of life seems gay.

Best of all, all casseroles of this type are built on one easy-to-understand, yet flexible, plan.

Try it out once, and you will make casseroles for life . . . casseroles which will vary (depending on what ingredients and trimmings you have at hand), and provide you with a huge repertoire of ever tempting dishes, each distinctively your very own.

MASTER RECIPE #11
THE "WHAT-HAVE-YOU"
CASSEROLE

(Serves 4 to 6)

NOTE: For this type of casserole, *use only foods which have been cooked or canned, or are edible raw.*

The exact amount of each ingredient may vary — depending on what you have at hand — but *total food mixture, when assembled, should equal 6 cups to serve 4 persons, or 8 cups to serve 5 or 6 persons.*

Put in large bowl:
1 to 2 cups diced cooked or canned meat
Use chicken, or ham, or turkey, or shellfish, or other cooked or canned fish; remove, of course, gristle, fat, skin, bones, and any other unattrctive bits before using the meat. Add:
1 to 2 cups drained, cooked or canned vegetable
Use any which would taste good if served as a sidedish with the meat you are using. Add:
1 to 2 cups cooked "starchy" food
Cooked, peeled, cubed potatoes; or cooked, drained noodles, rice, or spaghetti. (Starch may be omitted, but it serves to add bulk if desired.) Add:
1 to 2 cups gravy or sauce
This moistens the above ingredients. You do not want the mixture very runny, but not stiff either; about the same consistency as a creamed vegetable would be.

(If you have no leftover gravy or sauce, make **a medium white sauce** (p. 248). Or you may use a can of **undiluted condensed cream of celery soup**, or **cream of mushroom**, or **cream of chicken**. If soup seems too thick, add to it **¼ cup milk**.)

Adjust the seasoning. To heighten flavor of mixture, add, as your taste may indicate, one or more of the following:

Salt, pepper; or **celery salt;** or **chive salt**

1 or more tablespoons grated raw onion (improves almost any casserole)

1 or more tablespoons chopped parsley, or **chopped green pepper** (delicious with fish; ham)

½ to 1 teaspoon Worcestershire sauce (good with beef, liver, kidneys, pork, lamb; some like it with fish)

½ to 1 teaspoon prepared mustard (good with ham, corned beef)

¼ to ½ teaspoon sage, or **1 teaspoon poultry seasoning** (good with chicken, turkey)

Mix all ingredients well; then turn into a family-size casserole dish or individual-size dishes.

Now cover contents of casserole in some manner, so they will not become dried out in the oven. You may do one of three things:

(1) *Cover casserole with its lid,* during baking. Or

(2) *Make a crumb covering.* To do this, sprinkle over contents of casserole dish a ⅛ inch thick layer of **fine bread or cracker crumbs.** Dot top of crumbs with **8 or 10 bits of butter,** size of peas. For color, add a few dashes **paprika.** Or

(3) *Cover with* **biscuit crust** (p. 199); *or* **pastry crust** (p. 451), rolling dough about 1 inch wider than top of casserole dish. Make

slashes in crust, to allow steam vents. Place crust over casserole mixture, crimping overhanging dough to rim of casserole dish, so crust will hold in place. For color, add a few dashes of **paprika** on top of crust before baking.

However, if a casserole mixture has been stored in refrigerator, awaiting baking, you cannot at once cover it with biscuit or pastry crust, and bake it; for the contents of the casserole, thoroughly chilled as they are, would not become warm enough to eat in the short time it would take crust to bake. Therefore, when taking a casserole mixture from refrigerator, heat it until moderately warmed; take dish from oven; let dish cool off enough so you can touch it with bare hands; then fasten crust over it and bake.

To bake a Casserole: If a casserole has *pastry crust*, it must be put in *hot oven* (450°) for first 10 minutes; then heat reduced to moderate (350°) to continue cooking until crust is done, and contents thoroughly heated, or about 25 to 35 minutes more.

If casserole has *biscuit crust*, place in *hot oven* (450°), keeping heat at that point until biscuit crust is done, or about 20 minutes.

If casserole has a *crumb covering*, place dish in *moderately hot oven* (375° to 400°), and keep at that heat until crumbs are browned, and contents hot, or about 20 to 35 minutes, depending on size of dish.

If casserole is covered with a *lid*, place in *moderately hot oven* (375°) and keep at that temperature until contents are thoroughly hot, about 35 minutes.

VARIATIONS — CASSEROLES AND MEAT PIES

Meat pies and casseroles both consist of similar combinations of meat, vegetables and sauce or gravy. For meat pie, add biscuit or pastry top crust.

To make variations following, keep to method of Master Recipe #11, Casserole, page 142, using ingredients suggested for each type meat on following pages.

Beef Casseroles

Leftover broiled steak, roast beef, pot roast, beef stew meat, or canned roast beef. Combine cubed, cooked beef (1) with cooked carrots and peas, or (2) with cooked tiny onions and cut string beans, or (3) with cooked baby lima beans and corn. Include cooked potatoes, noodles, macaroni, or rice, if desired. For sauce, you may use beef gravy; or make brown gravy (p. 253); or use 1 can undiluted condensed tomato soup. Add 2 tablespoons grated raw onion. If using meat gravy or brown sauce, add ½ teaspoon Worcestershire sauce. If using tomato soup, add 2 tablespoons chopped green pepper. Top with crumb covering (p. 143), or simply cover with lid. To bake, see page 144.

Beef Pie. (1) Fill casserole with any above types of cooked beef, combined with cooked peas, carrots, small onions; beef gravy or brown gravy (p. 253); or (2) fill casserole with leftover beef stew. Cover with biscuit or herb crust (p. 199), or pastry crust (p. 451). To bake, see page 144.

Lamb Casseroles

Leftover roast lamb, cooked lamb stew meat, or any cooked lamb. Combine cubed, cooked meat (1) with cooked peas and mushroom caps, or (2) with cooked tiny white onions and cut string beans, or (3) with cooked carrots and peas. Include cooked potatoes, noodles, or rice, if desired. For sauce, use lamb gravy; or make brown gravy (p. 253); or you may substitute for sauce 1 can undiluted condensed cream of mushroom, cream of chicken, or cream of celery soup. Top with crumb covering (p. 143). To bake, see page 144.

Lamb Pie. (1) Fill casserole with leftover boned lamb stew; or (2) combine cubed cooked lamb with cooked carrots and peas; add lamb gravy, or undiluted condensed cream of mushroom soup. Top with biscuit or herb biscuit crust (p. 199), or pastry crust (p. 451). To bake, see page 144.

Veal Casseroles

Leftover cooked veal. Combine any cut-up cooked veal (1) with cooked peas, mushrooms, sweet potatoes, plus 1 can undiluted condensed cream of celery soup, or cream of mushroom soup. Or (2) combine cubed cooked veal with tiny white boiled, drained onions, cooked peas, noodles, 1 can undiluted condensed tomato soup. Top with crumb covering (p. 143). To bake, see page 144.

Veal Pie. (1) Fill casserole with leftover boned veal stew; or (2) combine cubed cooked veal with cooked peas, mushroom caps, carrots. For sauce, use 1 can undiluted condensed cream of celery soup, or veal gravy. Top with pastry crust (p. 451) or biscuit crust (p. 199). To bake, see page 144.

Pork Casseroles

Leftover roast fresh pork. Combine cut-up cooked pork, freed of bones (1) with cooked peas and mushrooms, and cooked or canned sweet potatoes, using 1 can undiluted condensed cream of chicken or cream of mushroom soup for sauce. Or (2), combine cut-up cooked pork with cooked peas, canned tomatoes, strained of juice, cooked noodles, and brown gravy or brown sauce (p. 253), adding ½ teaspoon Worcestershire sauce if desired. Top dish with crumb covering (p. 143). To bake, see page 144.

Pork Pie. Combine cut-up cooked pork with cooked peas, carrots, mushrooms; add pork gravy, or 1 can undiluted condensed cream of chicken soup. Top dish with biscuit or herb biscuit crust (p. 199), or pastry crust (p. 451). To bake, see page 144.

Ham, Tongue Casseroles

Leftover cooked ham, or tongue. Combine diced or ground cooked meat with cooked peas, mushroom caps, noodles; add 2 tablespoons grated raw onion; make 2 cups parsley white sauce (p. 248), or for sauce substitute 1 can undiluted condensed cream of celery soup. Top dish with crumb covering (p. 143). To bake, see page 144.

Or combine diced cooked ham or tongue with halves of hard-cooked eggs, a few cooked noodles and peas; 2 tablespoons grated onion, 1 teaspoon chopped green pepper; add white sauce (p. 24), curry sauce (p. 249), mustard sauce (p. 250) or cheese sauce (p. 249). Top dish with crumb covering (p. 143). To bake, see page 144.

Canned spiced ham, or luncheon meat. Cut in cubes. Combine with cooked noodles, sliced or quartered hard-cooked eggs, cooked peas if desired. Cover with deviled sauce (p. 249), or cheese sauce (p. 249), or mustard sauce (p. 250). Top dish with crumb covering (p. 143). To bake, see page 144.

Corned Beef Casserole

Canned, or home-cooked, corned beef, cut in cubes, or slices. In buttered baking dish, place a layer of thinly sliced cooked potatoes; then a layer of sliced raw onions; then a layer of boiled, drained cabbage; then a layer of cooked or canned corned beef. Cover all with mustard sauce (p. 250). Top dish with crumb covering (p. 143). To bake, see page 144.

Chicken Casserole

Leftover cooked or canned chicken. Combine cubed chicken meat (freed of bones, skin) with cooked peas, mushrooms, and chicken gravy, or use 1 can undiluted condensed cream of chicken or cream of mushroom soup instead of gravy. Leftover bits of stuffing, or chopped cooked giblets, are very good in this. If desired, add boiled white or sweet potatoes, or some cooked rice or noodles. Top dish with crumb covering (p. 143). To bake, see page 144.

Chicken Pie. Combine cut-up cooked chicken meat, cooked vegetables and add chicken gravy or sauce, as for casserole above. But omit potatoes, rice, or noodles unless these are needed to make sufficient quantity to fill pie dish The crust will provide starch enough without potatoes. If absolutely needed, use cooked noodles. Top dish with biscuit or herb biscuit crust (p. 199) or with pastry crust (p. 451). To bake, see page 144.

Turkey Casserole or Pie

Make like chicken above. Any leftover stuffing may be included in casseroles, and gives added seasoning to dish.

Fish Casseroles

Mackerel. Left-over cooked, or canned. Drain it. Cut to bite size, removing bones. Combine with cooked, drained noodles, 2 tablespoons grated raw onion, 2 tablespoons chopped parsley, 2 cups medium white sauce (p. 248). Top dish with crumb covering (p. 143). Decorate with thin strips of green pepper. To bake, see page 144.

Salmon. Leftover cooked, or canned. Drain it. Break to bite size, removing bones. Combine with sliced or quartered hardcooked eggs, cooked drained noodles, 1 teaspoon grated raw onion, 2 tablespoons chopped parsley, 2 cups medium white sauce (p. 248). Top dish with crumb covering (p. 143). To bake, see page 144.

Any White, Flaky Cooked Fish. Remove bones; break fish to bite size. Combine with thinly sliced, cooked potatoes, or cooked, drained noodles; 2 tablespoons grated raw onion, 2 tablespoons chopped green pepper; 2 tablespoons chopped parsley; 2 cups medium white sauce. If desired, sprinkle over top of dish ⅓ cup grated sharp American cheese, mixed with crumb covering. To bake, see page 144.

Tuna. Canned or home-cooked. Drain, break to bite size, removing bones. Combine with sautéed or canned mushroom caps and halves of hard-cooked eggs, in 2 cups deviled sauce (p. 249). To bake, see page 144.

Or combine drained fish with 3 slices bread, cubed, and 1 can undiluted condensed cream of celery soup. Add 1 cup drained cooked or canned cut green beans. Top dish with crumb covering, then sprinkle on 2 tablespoons grated sharp American cheese. To bake, see page 144.

Or combine tuna with cooked drained noodles, plus 1 can undiluted condensed tomato soup. Top with crumb covering, adding on top of crumbs **6 to 8 strips green pepper** and **2 tablespoons grated sharp American cheese.** To bake, see page 144.

Shrimp. Canned, or home-boiled and shelled. Drain. Remove black vein (p. 169). Combine with **cooked, drained rice, noodles, or macaroni, sliced or quartered hard-cooked eggs;** add **2 cups medium white sauce** (p. 248), or **curry sauce** (p. 249). Top dish with **crumb covering** (p. 143). To bake, see page 144.

Crab Meat. Canned, or bought cooked at fish market. Drain. Remove hard white fibers, if any. Combine with **cooked, drained noodles, peas;** add **2 cups deviled sauce** (p. 249). Top dish with **crumb covering** (p. 143). If desired, add a sprinkling of **grated sharp American cheese,** over top, before baking. To bake, see page 144.

Curry Casseroles

To curry any beef, lamb, veal, chicken, or shrimp casserole, for each cup meat gravy or sauce simply stir in **½ teaspoon curry powder** and **1 teaspoon grated raw onion,** before baking casserole.

Meatless Casseroles

Mixed Vegetables. Combine any **drained, cooked vegetables,** such as tomatoes, celery, onions, green pepper, corn kernels, lima or cut green beans, with **cheese sauce** (p. 249). Top with **crumb covering.** Or (2), combine assorted cooked or canned **drained vegetables** with **1 can undiluted condensed cream of celery, cream of mushroom,** or **cream of chicken soup,** and sprinkle top of casserole with **½ cup grated sharp American cheese.** Bake in hot (400° F.) oven about 20 minutes, or until cheese browns.

Asparagus and Egg. In oblong baking dish, arrange a row of **drained canned or home-cooked asparagus tips,** side by side. Top asparagus with a layer of **halved or sliced hard-cooked eggs.** Add sautéed or canned, drained **mushroom caps,** if desired. Cover all with **1 can undiluted condensed cream of chicken,** or **cream of mushroom soup.** Top dish with **crumb covering** (p. 143), and add a sprinkling of **grated sharp American cheese.** To bake, see page 144.

Spinach, Broccoli, or Cabbage, with Egg. In individual baking dishes, arrange a bottom layer of cooked, well-drained leafy vegetable. On top of vegetable, place 1 poached egg (p. 268) for each dish. Cover contents of each dish with cheese sauce (p. 249). Add crumb covering, over sauce, if desired. To bake, see page 144.

Gala Macaroni-and-Cheese. With cooked macaroni, combine cheese sauce (p. 249). Fold into this mixture 1/4 cup chopped green pepper, 1 tablespoon diced pimiento, 2 or 3 hard-cooked eggs, sliced. Top with crumb covering. To bake, see page 144.

Shepherd's Pie

Make any meat, chicken, or turkey casserole (see Variations under Master Recipe #11, p. 142), mixing your cooked meat with cooked vegetables, and adding a gravy or sauce to moisten. Turn mixture into family-size baking dish, or into individual pie dishes. Instead of covering dish with biscuit or pastry crust or crumbs, spread on top of contents a layer about 1/2 inch thick of well-seasoned mashed potatoes (you can use cold leftover mashed potatoes for this). Dot top of potato crust with bits of butter; add 2 or 3 dashes paprika. Bake in moderately hot (375–400°) oven, about 25–30 minutes, or until contents of dish are thoroughly heated and potato crust is a pretty golden brown.

CHAPTER XIV

You Can Make a Meat Loaf, or Croquettes

METHOD FOR:

Meat Loaf: Beef, Lamb, Veal, Ham, Chicken, Fish
Croquettes: Lamb, Ham, Fish, Shellfish, Rice, Egg

BASIC PRINCIPLES

A meat loaf and a batch of croquettes are more alike than you might think. Indeed, though the cooking of the two is different, the mixtures themselves are "near relations." Both consist of approximately 2 cups ground meat, plus tasty seasonings, to which some liquid moistening or binding ingredient is added. The meat loaf mixture is baked slowly in the oven; the croquette mixture is formed into small balls or cakes, and fried.

There is one important difference to remember. In meat loaves (since they will have long, slow baking in the oven) you may use *raw* meat; it will have time to become cooked through. In croquettes, you may *not* use raw meat, for the meat would not have time to become cooked in the few minutes it takes for frying the croquettes.

Either mixture is easy to make, and either Master Recipe given here may be altered and varied according to what you have in the house, which makes both of them highly advantageous recipes to be acquainted with.

A *meat loaf* springs to the experienced housewife's mind when she has an assortment of leftovers of meat . . . perhaps a frankfurter or two from one meal, a slice of cooked liver left from another meal, some luncheon meat or leftover ham from another . . . none of them sufficient, in itself, to do much with. All may be put through the meat grinder, however, and added to the raw hamburger which usually makes the "base" of a meat loaf, and the loaf profits in zestful taste by the subtle contributions of these differently flavored foods; and the good food is saved.

Croquettes come to mind when you have nothing much left of a roast chicken, a ham, a leg of lamb, or other roast, except a little meat clinging close to the bones. It is surprising, however, how much meat this makes, if meat is carefully cut loose from all bony sections, and put through the meat grinder; often the ground bits will amount to 2 or 3 cups. If not — if you get only 1 cup — you may add a cup of cooked peas, or cooked rice, or other solid ingredient, to make up the 2 cups of solid food required in the recipe for croquettes. Furthermore, croquettes need not be limited to being made of meat; they may be made with canned or leftover cooked fish; or they may be made with rice as the chief "solid" ingredient, or indeed with any solid food which would taste good encased in thick white sauce — this sauce being the binder for croquettes.

There is really no limit to the variety of meat loaves or croquettes you could make. We give here the two Master Recipes, plus a few well-liked variations for each. But once you see how easy they are to make, and discover how you may substitute various solids, you will create many additional versions of your own.

MASTER RECIPE #12
MEAT LOAF

(Serves 5 to 6)

A *typical* meat loaf is made *at least partially with raw meat,* the principle being that the natural fats and juices from the raw meat, during cooking, will permeate and flavor all other ingredients. These juices, plus such other liquid as is added for moistening the mixture, are absorbed and given solid form by the bread crumbs. The egg acts as binder to hold the entire mixture firmly intact.

In cases *where a meat loaf is made entirely with cooked meat* of dry texture, such as ground cooked chicken or ham, it is advisable to *substitute for the milk in this recipe a thickened sauce;* this helps both to keep the loaf moist, and to bind together the dry particles.

Put in large mixing bowl
2 to 3 cups ground meat
Buy 1½ pound ground beef for this, or buy only ¾ pound ground beef, and add enough ground leftover meat to make total of 2 to 3 cups.

Add, for high seasoning

1 peeled, grated onion
1 tablespoon or more minced green pepper
½ teaspoon salt
¼ teaspoon pepper
½ teaspoon dry mustard

2 or 3 tablespoons catsup
1 or 2 teaspoons bottled horse-radish, if desired
1 teaspoon Worcestershire sauce, if desired

Add, for body
1⅓ cup soft bread crumbs
Moisten with
½ cup milk (or broth, or gravy, or tomato juice)
Stir in, as a binder
1 raw egg
Blend mixture well. Spread evenly into lightly greased loaf pan, or square cake pan, or ovenware baking dish. Bake in moderately hot (375°) oven 1 to 1½ hours, until firm. Serve with any tomato sauce; or celery, onion, or mushroom sauce (pp. 249, 250).

RECOMMENDATIONS FOR SPECIFIC TYPES OF MEAT LOAF

(Follow Master Recipe #12, Meat Loaf, page 152, making substitutions noted below.)

Lamb or Veal Loaf

Use **ground leftover roasted lamb** or **veal,** instead of beef. Omit mustard, catsup, and horseradish; and instead of milk substitute **lamb** or **veal gravy,** or **medium white sauce** (p. 248), or **undiluted condensed cream of celery soup.**

Beef and Liver Loaf

Include any **ground cooked liver** you may have handy, as part of total meat. Increase salt to 1 teaspoon. Omit catsup and horseradish, but include **1 teaspoon Worcestershire sauce** in meat mixture.

Chicken Loaf

Substitute **diced cooked or canned chicken** for meat. You may include any **ground cooked chicken skin** or **cooked giblets** or **cooked chicken stuffing** in the meat mixture, if you have them. For seasoning, use **onion, salt, pepper,** and add **1 teaspoon poultry seasoning.** If desired, include ¼ **cup minced fresh parsley.** Omit green pepper, catsup, horseradish, Worcestershire sauce. Instead of milk, use **chicken gravy,** or **undiluted canned condensed cream of celery soup.**

Ham Loaf

Substitute **ground cooked ham** for meat. For seasoning, use **onion.** Increase green pepper to ¼ cup. Omit salt. Use **mustard.** Omit catsup, horseradish, and Worcestershire sauce. Instead of milk, use **medium white sauce** (p. 248), or **undiluted canned cream of mushroom or cream of celery soup.**

Salmon or Tuna Loaf

Substitute drained, flaked, cooked or canned **salmon or tuna fish,** for meat. In seasonings, use **onion.** Increase **green pepper** to 2 or 3 tablespoons. Add 1 teaspoon lemon juice. If desired, add 2 or 3 tablespoons minced fresh parsley. Use salt, pepper, and ¼ teaspoon prepared mustard. Omit catsup, horseradish, Worcestershire sauce. In place of milk, substitute **medium white sauce** (p. 248); or use **undiluted canned cream of mushroom or cream of celery soup.**

MASTER RECIPE #13
CROQUETTES (CHICKEN)
(Makes about 6 Croquettes)

In making croquettes, *always combine your ingredients in the proportion of 2 cups solid food to 1 cup very thick white sauce.* You may make double or triple this recipe, or half the recipe, but keep the proportion of solids-to-sauce always in this relation. This makes the proper-type mixture for frying, neither too wet nor too dry.

Many different foods may be used as the "solid" in this recipe. We are using chicken croquettes as our Master example; other variations follow.

Make in saucepan
> 1 cup **very thick white sauce** (p. 248).

To cooked sauce in pan, add
> 2 cups **diced, cooked or canned chicken meat**

For seasoning, stir into mixture:
> 1 tablespoon **grated raw onion**
> 2 tablespoons **minced fresh parsley**
> ½ teaspoon **poultry seasoning**, if desired.

Stir in, to bind mixture together
> 1 or 2 **raw eggs**

Blend well. Return saucepan to low-heated surface burner for

1 or 2 minutes, so eggs may thicken other ingredients somewhat. Then turn mixture into flat baking dish or pie plate, spreading it out so it is about 1 inch thick. Place in refrigerator 1 or 2 hours, or more, to chill. (Chilling makes the mixture firmer and easier to handle when you prepare to shape it for frying.)

To shape. About 10 or 15 minutes before time to cook, take mixture from refrigerator; cut mixture into round cakes, using a 2 inch biscuit cutter, or shape mixture into balls, or cones, with your hands.

To coat. Shaped croquettes must be rolled in **egg-and-crumb coating** (p. 100) before frying. Roll each croquette separately, in crumbs, then egg, then crumbs, taking care to coat evenly on all sides. This makes the crust which helps croquette hold together during frying.

To fry. It is easiest to shallow-fry croquettes. (See shallow-fried croquettes, p. 102.) If preferred, you may fry the croquettes in deep fat; to do this, follow Master Recipe (p. 108). In either case, drain croquettes on paper towel after they are fried.

To decorate, for serving. Old-time cooks used to call croquettes "cutlets" and try to make them look like chops by sticking a wooden skewer (to resemble a chop bone) into one end of each croquette; then decorating the wooden skewer with a fluted paper "cuff." Very elaborate, and it really doesn't prove much.

Far easier — and prettier — is to stick a sprig of fresh parsley into one end of each croquette; then sprinkle a dash of bright red paprika on center of the croquette, giving it a rosy "cheek." This is quick to do, and makes croquettes look gala enough for a company dinner.

To garnish with sauce: If you like a sauce on cooked croquettes, have ready to serve: onion sauce (p. 250); or celery sauce (p. 250); or mushroom sauce (p. 249); or plain medium white sauce (p. 248); or parsley sauce (p. 248).

RECOMMENDATIONS FOR
SPECIFIC CROQUETTES

(Follow method in Master Recipe #13, Croquettes, page 155, making substitutions noted below.)

Lamb or Veal Croquettes

Substitute **2 cups diced cooked lamb or veal,** for chicken. Omit poultry seasoning; instead use **¼ teaspoon curry powder** if desired.

Ham Croquettes

Substitute **2 cups diced cooked or canned ham,** instead of chicken. If desired, add **1 or 2 tablespoons minced green pepper.** Instead of poultry seasoning, stir in **½ teaspoon prepared mustard.** Some people like **cheese sauce** (p. 249) or **egg sauce** (p. 249) on ham croquettes.

Fish Croquettes

Substitute **2 cups any flaked white-meated cooked fish,** freed of skin and bones, instead of chicken. Omit poultry seasoning; instead use **1 or 2 tablespoons minced green pepper,** and add **1 teaspoon lemon juice.** Some people like to serve catsup or tomato sauce on fish croquettes; but try egg sauce (p. 249), or parsley sauce (p. 248).

Salmon or Tuna Fish Croquettes

When making the very thick white sauce, use **fish liquor** drained from can as part of the liquid, combining it with milk. This makes a far richer-flavored sauce to use in the croquette mixture. Instead of chicken, substitute **2 cups flaked canned fish,** freed of skin and bones . . . or, if you haven't enough fish to measure 2 cups, you can combine fish with sufficient **cooked rice,** or **cooked peas,** to make up 2 cups. Omit poultry seasoning from Master Recipe; but add **1 tablespoon minced green pepper.** Add **1 teaspoon lemon juice** with seasonings.

Lobster Croquettes

Use 2 cups flaked drained, cooked or canned lobster meat, instead of chicken. In seasonings, omit poultry seasonings; reduce onion to about ½ teaspoon; but with parsley, add 1 teaspoon lemon juice, ⅛ teaspoon prepared mustard, 1 or 2 drops Worcestershire sauce.

If sauce is desired on these superb croquettes, serve egg sauce (p. 249), or parsley sauce (p. 248). However, they are really too good to hide under any sauce.

Oyster Croquettes

Buy 1 pint fresh or frozen oysters, removed from shells. If frozen, allow 2 hours or so to thaw them, according to package directions. Drain oysters. Sauté (p. 93) oysters in frying pan containing 2 tablespoons butter, just until edges curl (about 3 minutes); then chop oysters fine. Use the chopped oysters instead of chicken. Omit poultry seasoning. With parsley, add 1 teaspoon lemon juice.

Rice and Cheese Croquettes

Make only ½ cup very thick white sauce. Add to sauce 2 cups cooked rice (this is your "solid" in place of chicken in Master Recipe). Add ½ cup grated American cheese. In seasonings, use ½ teaspoon grated raw onion, 2 tablespoons minced parsley, ¼ teaspoon salt. Omit poultry seasoning. Add ¼ teaspoon paprika. When returning pan to heat, cook gently until cheese melts. Then chill mixture as usual.

Egg Croquettes

Hard-cook, shell, and chop coarsely 7 or 8 eggs. Use these instead of chicken. For seasoning, omit onion, omit poultry seasoning; but with parsley add ¼ teaspoon paprika and ⅛ teaspoon salt. If mixture seems too moist, you may add ½ cup soft bread crumbs to thicken it, before chilling.

CHAPTER XV

What to Do with Shellfish

METHODS FOR: *Lobster, Crab, Shrimp, Clams, Oysters, Scallops, Mixed Seafood Dishes*

If you have grown up where the salt wind tugs at your hair, and the surf pounds the shores at night, and the tantalizing smell of the fishing boats is wafted in daily on the sea breeze, you will already be aching to get your hands on a fresh-caught cold-water lobster, or a mess of clams, or a catch of delicious little bay scallops and try out a good shellfish dinner. For the amazing thing about shellfish is that, treasured though they have always been, and prolific though they still are, on our shores, natives who live near the coastal supply never tire of them. On the contrary, the good wives and great restaurateurs of such regions are constantly thinking up new and more ingenious ways of preparing these delicious fish, so that they may be served more and more times.

All of which goes to prove that if you love shellfish, you just love shellfish. And if you don't, you surely have something to learn.

If you live inland, do give yourself at least a nodding acquaintance with some of the recipes in this chapter. We are not (like one cook book we have heard of) proposing 1000 ways to prepare shellfish, for we doubt that any busy woman of today would burden herself with so many methods, even for so treasured an item on the menu. What we are giving here are the very simple, reliable, basic, and most widely beloved ways of preparing the popular shellfish. With these good recipes, you will have a working repertoire for shellfish for life. And with inland markets today supplying shellfish by plane, refrigerator car, and truck, and in quick-frozen packages and cans filled within a few hours of the catch from the briny deep, no person need deny herself and her household the pleasure of these delectable dishes.

Many a famous restaurant has won its renown on nothing more.

BASIC PRINCIPLES

Shellfish differ widely; some must be alive when cooked, some not. Some are cooked in their shells; some may be removed from shells first. Some may be eaten raw; some cannot be. But there are two general rules which apply to all.

When buying, make certain that your shellfish, unless it is frozen or canned, is strictly *fresh.* Natives of coastal regions know that something of the deep sea tang disappears as the hours tick by; and that a batch of shellfish caught a couple of days ago cannot compare in flavor with that which the boats are bringing in *now,* from the sea. Try, therefore, to procure your shellfish on the very day it is received at the market, and make friends with your fish dealer, so that he will tip you off when he has something special, just in. (See Chapter V for marketing tips.)

When cooking, remember that shellfish are tender creatures, and a very few minutes suffices to cook them. Overcooking will make them tough. Oysters require only a few minutes, until their edges curl. Ten minutes usually suffices for boiling shrimps; 15 to 20 minutes for lobster or crab. When shellfish are boiled, they are boiled in salty water, as nearly as possible approximating sea water; indeed some chefs do use clean sea water for this purpose; if you live near the coast, try this sometime. No shellfish should be left standing in water, once the cooking time is over; ignore this, and you will have fish that toughens, loses flavor, and becomes waterlogged.

LIVE LOBSTER

See marketing tips for lobster (p. 34). One 2½ pound lobster yields about 2 cups cooked lobster meat.

Boiled Lobster

Have ready a large kettle of **rapidly boiling, salted water.** Add ⅓ **cup rock or table salt** for each quart of water in kettle. Kettle must be large enough so entire lobster can be submerged. Grasp your live **lobster** by its back, just behind claws, and plunge it into water head first, making sure whole body submerges. If cooking more than one, bring water again to a rapid boil before each additional lobster is put in. When all are in, cover kettle. Boil 15 minutes for chicken lobsters of 1 to 1½ pounds; 20 minutes for larger lobster. When time is up, remove lobster at once from water, placing it on drainboard, on its back, to cool. As soon as cool enough to handle, prepare meat for serving.

Inedible Parts. A lobster has three inedible parts:

The stomach, or "lady" — a small hard sac, just below lobster's head, on back.

Intestinal canal, running from stomach to tip of tail, along lobster's back. This may be black, red, or white. You may have to cut a slit in the back of body and tail meat to find it. Remove vein carefully.

Lungs (or gills), a spongy, woody substance at both sides of body, inside shell.

To Open Shell and Extract Meat. Break cooked lobster into sections, as follows:

Claws. Twist the 2 big claws from body, and the 4 pairs of smaller ones. The smaller ones contain practically no meat; save these for garnishing. Crack with hammer or nutcracker the center joint in each of the big claws; try to remove the claw meat intact, since this meat is one of the chief treasures the lobster yields.

Tail. Break tail off from body. Slit underneath side of tail, end to end, with scissors. Force shell apart. Draw out tail meat, all in one piece. Cut slit lengthwise through back of tail meat; locate and remove intestinal vein. Holding meat under running water helps wash vein out.

Body. Slit underneath side of body shell lengthwise; force apart;

then with fingers withdraw body meat, leaving stomach inside. Discard all spongy lung material.

Liver (green material) is edible and considered a delicacy; it is often used to make a sauce for the lobster, see under Baked Lobster. Coral (roe), found only in females, is also edible and considered a choice bit; it is often used as a garnish.

To Serve. Serve extracted lobster meat warm, with **melted butter.** Or chill it, and serve on crisp lettuce, garnished with **mayonnaise,** or **sauce rémoulade** (p. 359) and small lobster claws for decoration. Or use the extracted meat for lobster salad, or any dishes made with cooked lobster meat; see page 163.

Broiled or Baked Live Lobster

Allow 1 entire small lobster, or ½ big lobster, per person.

To be broiled or baked, a live lobster must be split in half, opened, and cooked as soon as possible. Splitting it is not a task to relish; have fish dealer do it for you if possible. But if you must do it yourself, grasp lobster from back, below big claws (so he will not nip you) and place him on his back. Cross the big claws, and hold them crossed in your left hand. With sharp knife in right hand, begin at lobster's mouth, and cut quickly and firmly, with one long stroke, from mouth to tip of tail. This of course kills the lobster. Now with thumbs force shell apart so that you can clean. Remove stomach and intestinal vein (see location of these under Boiled Lobster). With nutcracker or hammer, crack the big claws.

To Broil. Preheat broiling unit of oven. Place **cleaned split lobster,** shell side down, on rack in broiling pan. Sprinkle flesh with **salt, pepper;** brush with **melted butter.** (Or, you may cover meat of lobster with **buttered bread crumbs** before broiling; a crumb covering helps keep meat moister.) Place pan about 3 to 4 inches beneath broiling unit, and cook 12 minutes for a chicken (1 to 1½ pound) lobster; 15 minutes for a larger lobster. Serve hot, giving each person a small dish of melted butter to dunk the lobster meat in, and a nutcracker for claws, if needed.

To Bake. Preheat oven to very hot (450°). Meanwhile, in saucepan, cook the lobster liver with 1 tablespoon butter for 3 to 4 minutes, adding several dashes salt, few specks pepper, few drops Worcestershire sauce. Spread this mixture over flesh of split, clean, raw lobster. Place lobster, shell side down, in baking pan, and bake 15 minutes. Serve hot, with nutcracker handy for claws.

DISHES MADE WITH COOKED OR CANNED LOBSTER MEAT

Lobster Salad

See Master Recipe, Seafood Salad, page 344.

Creamed Lobster

Serves 3 to 4. Make 2 cups medium white sauce (p. 248), using as part of the liquid for sauce the liquor from lobster can, if you are using canned lobster. When sauce is cooked, heat 2 cups cooked or canned lobster meat in it. Serve over hot buttered rice, or in patty shells, or use as filling for main course shortcake biscuits; see Meat Shortcakes (p. 140).

Scalloped Lobster

Serves 3 to 4. Make 2 cups medium white sauce (p. 248), using as part of the liquid for sauce the liquor from lobster can, if you are using canned lobster. When sauce is cooked, stir in 2 cups cooked or canned lobster meat, plus 2 tablespoons minced parsley; add few drops lemon juice if desired. Turn mixture into individual ramekins, scallop shells, or a casserole. Top with bread crumbs, and dot with butter. Bake in hot (400°) oven 12 to 15 minutes, or until crumbs brown.

Lobster Coquille

Serves 4 to 6. In saucepan, combine 1 can undiluted condensed cream of mushroom soup with 1 slightly beaten egg. Add ¼ cup grated cheese. Heat until cheese melts, stirring constantly. Now stir in 1½ cups broken cooked or canned lobster meat, a 3 ounce can sliced mushrooms, and 2 tablespoons white wine (wine is optional). Turn mixture into scallop shells, or individual ramekins. Over top, sprinkle this mixture: ⅓ cup **bread crumbs** blended with ¼ cup **grated cheese**. Add a dash or two of **paprika**. Place under hot broiler about 10 to 12 minutes, until browned and bubbly, or bake in hot (400°) oven about 15 minutes, until tops brown.

NOTE: The 3 dishes above may also be made with cooked or canned shrimp, crab, clams, scallops, or mixed seafood, substituting any of these for the lobster, in the same quantity.

Lobster Thermidor

Serves 4. Put **3 cups flaked cooked or canned lobster meat** in bowl; pour ⅔ cup **sherry** over it; let stand, while you make the following white sauce: In saucepan, melt **4 tablespoons butter;** blend in **4 tablespoons flour**, stirring to smooth paste. Add gradually 1½ cups **milk**, plus ½ cup **thin cream**, stirring constantly. Cook over low heat, keeping on stirring, until sauce thickens. Then stir in ¼ teaspoon **dry mustard**, ¾ teaspoon **salt**, ¼ teaspoon **pepper**, 2 tablespoons **minced parsley**. Add 1½ cup **canned sliced mushrooms** (drained); or slice ¼ pound **fresh mushroom caps and stems**, sauté (p. 95) these in a little **butter** until tender, and add these. Add the lobster and sherry. Last, beat slightly, and stir in **2 eggs**. Cook entire mixture 1 minute more. Then turn into lobster shells, ramekins, or a casserole. Sprinkle top of mixture with **bread crumbs** blended with ⅓ cup **grated cheese**. Put under hot broiler or bake in very hot oven (450°), about 10 minutes, until crumbs brown.

Lobster Newburg

Serves 4. Make **1 to 2 cups Newburg sauce**; see page 251; add **2 cups sizable pieces of cooked or canned lobster meat** to it. Heat lobster in sauce; then serve on triangles of toast, or in patty shells, or on hot rice. Potato chips, green peas, a green salad, and ice cream make this a party luncheon or dinner. NOTE: Cooked or canned shrimp, crab, scallops, clams, or mixed cooked seafood may be substituted for the lobster in this recipe.

Lobster Bisque I

Serves 3 to 4. Made with lobster stock. Don't throw away **shells of broiled or baked lobsters.** Save all pieces of shell, including large and small claws. Put shells in kettle; cover with **water.** Add **1 tablespoon salt, ½ raw onion,** sliced, **1 branch celery with leaves, 1 bay leaf.** Cover. Simmer several hours, until stock cooks down to 2 or 3 cups and becomes strong. Strain stock, discarding shell and vegetables; add to stock **1 or 2 chicken bouillon cubes.** Now in separate saucepan, mix together to form a paste **1 tablespoon butter plus 1 tablespoon flour for each cup of stock** you have. Add stock gradually to paste, stirring constantly and cooking over low heat until thickened. Then stir in **1 cup thin cream or rich milk,** plus **1 slightly beaten egg;** cook 1 or 2 minutes more, adding **salt** if needed. Stir in **2 to 4 tablespoons sherry.** Serve hot, sprinkled with **paprika,** and garnished with a bit of **minced parsley.** This is a delicious and hearty soup.

Lobster Bisque II

Made with cooked or canned lobster meat; see Bisque, page 259. Make as many cups **thin white sauce (p. 248)** as you want cups of soup, but instead of using milk for white sauce, use **half thin cream and half chicken broth.** If using canned lobster, include **liquor** from lobster can with liquids. When sauce is thickened, stir in enough **flaked lobster meat** to give soup a real flavor. When lobster meat is well heated in soup, stir in **1 egg,** slightly beaten; add **1 or 2 tablespoons sherry.** Serve hot, garnished with **paprika** and **minced parsley.**

FRESH CRABS

See marketing tips, page 36.

In handling live crabs, never pick up a crab from the front; its claws are dangerous and lively, and the crab will have you before you have it. Take hold from back, just behind smallest leg. This is the only safe position.

Hard-Shelled Crabs

Drop live **crabs**, one by one, head first, into kettle of **boiling, salted water** (2 tablespoons salt per quart of water). Cover kettle. Boil 15 minutes. Remove crabs. Drain and cool. Break off claws and legs. Crack claws with nutcracker, and draw out meat. Break off the segment that folds under the body from rear; discard it. Now pick up crab in both hands, and insert thumbs in the opening between the two halves of the shell, forcing shell apart. Hold under running cold water to wash away all material that sticks to upper shell; and save upper shell, if desired, as a container for deviled crab meat. Discard from the creature all orange and waxy material, and spongy gills. Cut away with knife hard membranes. Pick out the tender meat from crab's back, with fork.

Meat of claws and back can now be used for crab salad, crab cocktail, creamed or deviled seafood dishes.

To Clean Soft-shelled Crabs

You can buy these already killed and cleaned at market. But if you must do it yourself, here's how: press a sharp knife point into crab, between the eyes, to kill it. With scissors, cut off head, about ½ inch behind the eyes. On each side of crab's back, you will see a tapering point. Pull up the point, folding shell back halfway; remove spongy material under it, which is the lung. Do same at other point. Remove tail or "apron" (which folds under body from rear end) and remove spongy material under it. Wash the crab thoroughly under cold running water. Crab is now ready to cook.

Boiled Soft-shelled Crabs

Allow 2 or 3 crabs per person. Drop **cleaned crabs** into **boiling salted water** (1 tablespoon salt per quart of water). Cover kettle. Boil 15 minutes. Remove crabs, drain, and serve.

Broiled Soft-shelled Crabs

Allow 2 or 3 crabs per person. Drain and clean **crabs.** In small bowl, combine **4 tablespoons melted butter, 2 tablespoons lemon juice, pinch of salt, few specks pepper.** Roll crabs in this butter mixture; then roll them lightly in **flour.** Place crabs on broiler rack. Broil under moderate heat 8 to 10 minutes, turning once. Baste with any leftover butter mixture.

Sautéed Soft-shelled Crabs

Prepare as if to broil, rolling crabs in **butter mixture and flour.** Sauté (p. 93) crabs in buttered frying pan, over moderate heat, 8 to 10 minutes, turning frequently, until golden brown on all sides.

Fried Soft-shelled Crabs

Allow 2 or 3 per person. Wipe dry the cleaned crabs. Dip them in **flour**, then in **1 slightly beaten egg** blended with **1 tablespoon water**, then in fine **bread crumbs.** Crabs are now ready to shallow-fry (p. 99) in 1½ inch deep fat, in frying pan, or to deep-fry (p. 108) in deep fat. In either case, fat should be 375°, or hot enough to brown a 1-inch cube of one-day-old bread in 60 seconds. Fry crabs about 3 to 5 minutes until golden brown on all sides, being sure fat is sufficiently hot before you put them in. When done, drain on paper towel. Serve hot with tartar sauce (p. 354) or parsley butter (p. 256).

DISHES MADE WITH COOKED
OR CANNED CRAB MEAT

Crab Meat Salad

See Master Recipe, Seafood Salad, page 344.

Deviled Crab Meat

Serves 4 to 6. Have available **1 cup cooked or canned crab meat.** In a saucepan, combine: **1 tablespoon butter, 1 tablespoon cream, ¼ teaspoon dry mustard, 1 teaspoon Worcestershire sauce, 1 tea-**

spoon grated raw onion, 1 teaspoon lemon juice, 1 tablespoon minced parsley, ½ cup hot water, ½ cup soft bread crumbs. Simmer these together about 5 minutes. Then stir in the crab meat; blend. Turn mixture into buttered shells or ramekins. Sprinkle top with **bread crumbs**. Dot with **butter**. Add a dash or two of **paprika**. Bake in moderate (375°) oven 15 to 20 minutes, or until crumbs brown. Serve hot or cold.

Crab Meat Mornay

Serves 4 to 6. Have available **1 cup cooked or canned crab meat**. Begin by making a Mornay sauce: melt **4 tablespoons butter**, stir in **4 tablespoons flour**, mixing this to a smooth paste; then gradually add, stirring continuously, **¾ cup chicken broth**, and **¾ cup milk**. Cook over low heat, stirring until thickened. Then stir in **2 egg yolks**. Add crab meat, and cook 1 or 2 minutes more. Turn mixture into buttered shells, or ramekins, and sprinkle top with **½ cup grated cheese**. Place under hot broiler, until cheese melts and top browns, about 10 to 12 minutes.

Crab Newburg

Make as for lobster Newburg (p. 164), substituting **crab meat** for lobster meat.

Scalloped Crab

Make as for scalloped lobster (p. 163), substituting **crab meat** for lobster meat.

Crab Coquille

Make as for lobster coquille (p. 163), substituting **crab meat** for lobster meat.

Crab Cakes

Serves 6. Have available **1 pound cooked or canned crab meat**. In a saucepan, melt **2 tablespoons butter**; add **2 tablespoons grated raw onion**, and cook until onion is golden. Add then the flaked crab meat and **1 cup soft bread crumbs**, **1 well-beaten egg**, **1 teaspoon** or more of prepared mustard, salt to taste, 2 tablespoons minced parsley. If too dry to shape into cakes, moisten mixture with a little milk or cream or hot water. Remove mixture from saucepan; shape into flat cakes. Sprinkle each cake lightly with flour, and fry quickly in buttered frying pan until browned on both sides; then reduce heat, and cook about 5 minutes more, so cakes can heat through. Serve with hot mayonnaise, into which you have stirred 1 or 2 teaspoons lemon juice.

FRESH SHRIMP

See marketing tips, page 37.

Boiled Fresh Shrimp

Allow 1 pound for 3 persons. Drop fresh shrimp, in their shells, into kettle of boiling salted water, using 1 tablespoon salt for each 2 quarts water. Cover. Boil until shells turn pink, about 10 minutes. Remove shrimp, drain. As soon as cool enough to handle, slip off the paper-thin shell with your fingers, freeing meat; then clean.

To clean shrimp (either home-boiled, or canned), look for black intestinal vein running entire length of shrimp, around outside curve of body. If not visible, make shallow gash with knife to find it. Pry out with knife.

DISHES MADE WITH COOKED OR CANNED SHRIMP

Fried Shrimp

For 3 to 4 persons, use 1 pound fresh shrimp, boiled, shelled, and cleaned. Or use 1 No. 1 can shrimp, drained and cleaned. Beat slightly 1 egg, adding 1 tablespoon cold water. Dip shrimp in egg, then in fine bread crumbs; then in egg, then in crumbs again. Fry coated shrimp in 1½ inch deep fat in frying pan — see Shallow-frying, page 99; or in deep fat — see Deep-frying, page 100; in either case have fat at 375°, or hot enough to brown a 1 inch one-day-old cube of bread in 60 seconds. Turn shrimp during frying if necessary, to cook to golden color on all sides. This will take 3 to 5 minutes. Drain shrimp on paper towel to remove excess grease; serve hot, with tartar sauce (p. 354).

Creamed Shrimp

Serves 3 to 4. Boil, shell, and clean **1 pound fresh shrimp, or** drain and clean **1 No. 1 can shrimp.** Make **2 cups medium white sauce** (p. 248), adding to it **½ teaspoon paprika, 1 teaspoon grated onion, ½ teaspoon prepared mustard, and 1 tablespoon minced parsley.** Heat shrimp in this sauce. Serve hot over hot buttered rice, or in patty shells, or as filling for meat shortcake biscuits (p. 140).

Curried Shrimp

Serves 3 to 4. Make as for creamed shrimp, but instead of making white sauce, make **2 cups curry sauce** (p. 249). Heat **drained, cleaned, canned or home-cooked shrimps** in this. Serve on hot rice, or on triangles of toast. If desired, **quartered hard-cooked eggs** may be combined with shrimp in the sauce before serving.

Scalloped Shrimp

Make as for scalloped lobster (p. 163), substituting **cleaned, cooked or canned shrimp** for lobster.

Shrimp Newburg

Make as for lobster Newburg (p. 164), substituting **cleaned, cooked or canned shrimp** for lobster.

Shrimp Coquille

Make as for lobster coquille (p. 163), substituting **cleaned, cooked or canned shrimp** for lobster.

Shrimp Creole

(Serves 4 to 6.) Buy a **No. 1 can Spanish Sauce,** or make it as follows: Melt **3 tablespoons butter or salad oil** in frying pan. Add

1 cup sliced peeled onions, 1 peeled clove garlic chopped fine, ½ cup diced celery; cook 10 to 15 minutes, gently, until tender. Now blend 1 tablespoon flour, 1 teaspoon salt, 1 teaspoon sugar, 1 tablespoon chili powder with 1 cup water. Add to frying pan, simmer gently 15 minutes. Now add 2 cups canned tomatoes, 2 cups cooked or canned peas (optional), 1 tablespoon vinegar. In this sauce, heat 2 cups cooked or canned cleaned shrimp. Serve on bed of hot buttered rice. (You'll need about 4 cups cooked rice; see p. 305.)

Shrimp Salad

See Master Recipe, Seafood Salad, page 344.

Shrimp-Noodle Casserole

Serves 4. Cook ½ package noodles in salted water until tender, about 10 minutes, then drain. Make 2 cups medium white sauce (p. 248). Have available 1 cup cleaned, cooked or canned shrimp, 1 cup grated American cheese, 3 or 4 shelled hard-cooked eggs. In buttered casserole, arrange alternate layers of noodles, shrimp, chopped hard-cooked eggs, cheese; repeat and end with noodles on top. Over all, pour white sauce. Sprinkle top with **bread or cracker crumbs.** Dot with butter. Bake in hot oven (400°) about 35 to 40 minutes, until crumbs brown and contents of dish are hot.

Shrimp Bisque

Make as for Lobster Bisque II (p. 165), substituting **cleaned, cooked or canned** shrimp for lobster meat.

CLAMS

See marketing tips, page 35.

Steamed Clams

Allow 1 quart live clams, in the shell (preferably soft-shell clams) per person. Scrub clams well with brush; wash in several waters; then hold tail uppermost under running water, to wash out sand. Place clams in large kettle, adding ¼ cup hot water for every 2 quarts clams. Cover kettle tightly, to hold steam in. Cook just until shells begin to open; don't overcook. Remove clams to heated soup plates. Divide any broth left in kettle into small individual cups, 1 per person. Also provide each person a small cup of melted butter.

To eat, remove clam from shell by its neck; dunk first in the clam broth, then in melted butter. Eat all except the hard black neck.

Fried Clams

Buy clams removed from shell; drain them; wipe dry. Dip clams in batter (p. 101). French-fry in deep fat heated to 375°, or hot enough to brown a 1-inch cube of one-day-old bread in 60 seconds. Fry just a few minutes, until golden color on all sides, turning if necessary. Drain on paper towel. Serve with tartar sauce (p. 354).

Clam Fritters

See page 215.

New England Clam Chowder (made with milk)

Serves 3 to 4. Buy 1 pint clams removed from shells; or a No. 1 can minced clams. In top section of double boiler, over direct moderate heat, melt a 1-inch cube of fat salt pork, diced. Cook in this fat, over low heat, for 5 minutes, 3 sliced onions, until onions turn golden color. Remove hard bits of salt pork. To onions and fat, add 2 cups peeled, diced potatoes, ½ teaspoon salt, 2 cups boiling water. Cover and cook over moderate heat until potatoes are tender. Then add chopped fresh clams with their liquor, or entire contents of can of minced clams; and heat clams thoroughly. Add 2 cups milk. Place pan over lower section of double boiler, containing hot water. Heat about 10 to 15 minutes. Serve chowder piping hot, with pilot crackers to crumble in it.

Simple, hearty; superb. Big bowls of this, with a green salad and a simple fruit dessert, make a marvelous Sunday night supper.

Manhattan Clam Chowder (made with tomatoes)

Made same as for New England clam chowder, except that with **onions,** you add ¼ **cup diced celery** and **a pinch of thyme.** Reduce potatoes to 1 cup. Instead of milk, use **2 cups canned tomatoes** or **tomato juice.** And lo, how different is the chowder! New Englanders would scarcely recognize it with a nod.

Clam Stew

Serves 3 to 4. Buy **1 pint clams** removed from shells; or **1 No. 1 can minced clams.** Melt in large saucepan **3 tablespoons butter.** Add **1 tablespoon grated raw onion.** Simmer 5 minutes. Add chopped fresh clams and their liquor, or entire contents of can of clams, and heat thoroughly. Add **2 to 3 cups milk.** Season with ½ **to 1 teaspoon salt** (taste and see). Heat thoroughly but do not boil. Serve piping hot, sprinkled with **paprika,** and garnished with a bit of minced **parsley.** Something to remember.

OYSTERS

See marketing tips, page 36.

To clean oysters removed from shells: Oysters (sold by the dozen, pint or quart, removed from shells) may have bits of shell adhering to them. They should be put in a strainer, and have cold water poured over them several times, then each oyster separately examined, with finger tips, to remove any bits of sharp shell. The entire oyster, however, is edible.

Usually you get 12 oysters in a pint, 24 in a quart.

On the Half Shell

Markets deliver oysters already opened, "on the half shell," and bedded on cracked ice. Using deep plates (like soup plates) arrange first a layer of **ice,** then **6 oysters** on top of the ice, in a circle, for each person. In center of each plate, put a small glass or cup containing **seafood cocktail sauce** (p. 358, or buy). For each plate, provide a wedge of **lemon,** to be squeezed over oysters.

To eat the oyster, sprinkle with lemon juice, then pick up from the shell, intact, with a fork, dip in sauce, and pop into the mouth, whole. If you try to bite it in half you will have a slippery time! . . . So no one does.

Broiled Oysters

Serves 2. Drain and clean **12 raw oysters,** removed from shells. Wipe dry. Dip each oyster in **melted butter,** or in **mayonnaise,** or in **lemon juice;** then roll in fine **cracker crumbs.** Place on buttered wire rack, in a broiling pan. Place pan under medium-hot broiling unit, and broil about 12 to 15 minutes, or until juices flow. Turn oysters once, during broiling. Serve with tartar sauce (p. 354).

Sautéed Oysters

Serves 2. Prepare as if to broil, but instead of putting under broiler, sauté (p. 93) oysters in a little **melted butter,** in frying pan, turning until golden on all sides.

Fried Oysters

Serves 2. Clean and drain dry **12 raw oysters,** removed from shells. Dip oysters in **lemon juice,** then in **egg-and-crumb coating** (p. 100), using oyster liquor instead of water with the beaten egg. *Or,* if preferred, simply dip in **batter** (p. 101). Deep-fry (p. 108) about 5 minutes, or until golden brown, in deep fat heated to 375°, or hot enough to brown a 1 inch cube of day-old bread in 60 seconds. Drain oysters on paper towel. Serve hot, with tartar sauce (p. 354).

Oysters with Bacon

Serves 2. Drain and clean **12 raw oysters,** removed from shells. Around each oyster wrap a **thin slice bacon;** fasten bacon with toothpick. Place wrapped oysters on rack in baking pan. Bake in very hot (450°) oven about 12 to 15 minutes, or until bacon is crisp. Try serving these for dinner with baked stuffed tomatoes and creamed or scalloped potatoes.

Oysters Casino

(Served usually as an appetizer; allow 6 oysters per person.) Order **oysters** "on the half shell." Leaving them on shells, sprinkle top of each oyster with **few drops lemon juice**, a bit of **minced green pepper, salt, pepper**; then place a 1 inch square piece of **sliced bacon** on top of each. Place oysters, in baking pan, in very hot (450°) oven; bake 12 to 15 minutes, or until bacon is crisp.

Creamed Oysters

Serves 2. Heat **12 raw oysters**, removed from shells, in the oyster liquor until edges of oysters curl. Separately, make **1 cup thick white sauce** (p. 248). Add oysters and their liquor to finished sauce and reheat. Serve on triangles of toast, or in patty shells, or on split hot baking powder biscuits (p. 198).

With Mushrooms. Sauté (p. 95) in **butter** until tender **½ pound mushrooms**, sliced thin; add these to creamed oysters. Or add **1 can sliced mushrooms**, drained.

Curried Oysters

Make as for creamed oysters, but add **1 teaspoon grated raw onion** and **½ teaspoon curry powder** to each cup of thick white sauce (p. 248).

Scalloped Oysters

Serves 4. Buy **24 raw oysters**, removed from shells. Butter a 1-quart casserole. Line it with a layer of **soft bread crumbs**. Add a layer of drained oysters. Sprinkle oysters with **salt, pepper**. Add a few dots of **butter**, size of peas. Repeat layers of crumbs and seasoned oysters, until all oysters are in dish. Top dish with layer of crumbs. Over all, pour **¼ cup oyster liquor** blended with **¼ cup cream**. Bake in hot (400°) oven 15 to 20 minutes, or until crumbs brown lightly.

Oyster Pie

Serves 4. Make Master Recipe, Pastry (p. 446), rolling **dough** to form two crusts (see page 447). Line shallow pie plate with the lower crust dough. Fill dish with **24 cleaned, drained oysters**, removed from shells. Sprinkle oysters with **salt, pepper;** dot generously with **butter**. Cover dish with top crust; fasten edges of two crusts together by crimping. Cut 5 to 6 slashes in center of top crust for steam vents. Bake pie in hot (425°) oven about 30 minutes, or until crust is golden brown and crisp.

Oyster Stew (New England Style)

Very simple, hearty, and welcoming, on a snowy night. Serves 3 to 4. Buy **24 raw oysters**, removed from shells. Drain off, but save, the oyster liquor. In saucepan, bring **1 cup oyster liquor** to a boil; simmer 5 minutes, then skim off foam. Add **2 cups heavy cream, 4 tablespoons butter, ½ teaspoon celery salt, few grains pepper**. (For a gourmet's touch, you may add also, if desired, ½ to 1 cup white wine, though this is not necessary.) In another pan, place oysters and remaining oyster liquor. Cook over low heat about 5 minutes, just until edges of oysters curl. Drain off and discard this liquid; add the oysters to creamy sauce made above. Serve hot, sprinkled with a bit of minced **parsley**, and add a dash of **paprika** for color.

For a "company" Sunday night supper, serve your oyster stew at table in a chafing dish, or in a preheated soup tureen, accompanied by a green salad, and cheese, or a simple fruit dessert.

Pilot crackers or New England hardtack should be served with oyster stew, not bread.

Chicken and Oyster Pie (A New England dish)

Serves 4. **Butter** inside of a pie plate. Put in it **12 raw oysters**, removed from shells. Sprinkle these with **salt, pepper**. Add **2 or 3 cups diced cooked chicken meat**. Over chicken, grate **1 or 2 teaspoons raw peeled onion**. Make **2 cups medium white sauce** (p. 248). Pour thickened sauce over contents of pie dish. Now make one half Master Recipe, Pastry (p. 446). Roll **dough** to form a top crust. Place crust over pie; crimp edges of crust to dish, so it will hold on. In center of crust, make 5 or 6 slashes, for steam vents. Bake pie in hot (400°) oven about 30 minutes, or until crust is golden brown and crisp. Something to remember.

Oyster Fritters
See page 215.

SCALLOPS
See marketing tips, page 37.

Deep-Fried Scallops
Serves 3 to 4. Wash **1 pound scallops**; dry between towels. If over 1 inch square, cut to bite-size pieces. In bowl, combine this mixture of seasonings to marinate scallops: **1 tablespoon lemon juice, 1 tablespoon salad oil, ¼ teaspoon salt.** Add scallops; stir until well coated; let stand in refrigerator about 1 hour, for seasoning to permeate. Then drain scallops. Now dip scallops in **egg-and-crumb coating** (p. 100), dipping them twice if you like a very "crusty" crust. Deep-fry (p. 108) in fat heated to 375° or hot enough to brown a 1 inch cube of day-old bread in 60 seconds. Turn if necessary, cooking golden brown on all sides. Drain on paper towel. Serve with strips of cooked bacon, and tartar sauce (p. 354).

Sautéed Scallops
Serves 3. Wash **1 pound scallops,** and simmer 5 minutes in hot water. Drain. Dry on paper towel. Roll in **flour coating** (p. 101), or **egg-and-crumb coating** (p. 100). Sauté (p. 93) in **butter** or **bacon fat,** turning as needed, to cook golden brown on all sides. Serve with tartar sauce (p. 354), or with wedges of lemon to squeeze over fish. Accompany with crisp strips of cooked bacon, for extra good taste.

Scalloped Scallops

Serves 3. Wash 1 pound scallops; cut to bite-size, if too large. In saucepan melt ½ cup butter, add ½ cup soft bread crumbs, plus 1 cup cracker crumbs. Now in a buttered baking dish, arrange alternate layers of the buttered crumbs and scallops, sprinkling each layer of scallops with salt and pepper. Make top layer crumbs. Over all, pour 2 cups medium white sauce (p. 248). Bake in moderate oven (375°) 20 to 25 minutes, or until top browns.

Scallops à la Newburg

Serves 3. Put 1 pound scallops in saucepan. Add 2 cups boiling water and ½ teaspoon salt; cover; cook gently 8 to 10 minutes; then drain but save liquid. Cut scallops small, if desired. Use in place of lobster, adding scallops to 2 cups Newburg sauce (p. 251, in which you have used some of the scallop water as liquid.

To Cook Scallops to Use in Seafood Cocktail or in Creamed Dishes

When scallops are to be served in some mixture in which they will have no opportunity to become cooked through, they may first be boiled gently 8 to 10 minutes in salted water if desired, though some people eat them raw.

MIXED SEAFOOD DISHES

The following recipes suggest combinations of seafood which are delicious, but actually you may substitute any seafood you have at hand, making up the same total amount of fish, provided the fish is all in edible form. When using any fish ingredient, check with list below to make sure it is edible.

Oysters (removed from shells). May be used raw, or may be cooked just a few minutes, in their own liquor, until edges curl.

Lobster meat. Must be cooked or canned.

Crab meat. Must be cooked or canned. Remove hard fibrous membranes.

Shrimp. Must be cooked or canned. Remove black vein from back, see page 169.

Scallops. Usually cooked (see p. 178). Some folk like them raw.

Fish. Flaked, cooked white fish may be used. Remove all skin and bones.

Tuna. Must be cooked or canned.

Mushrooms. Fresh mushrooms, sliced, should be sautéed (page 95) in butter until tender before adding to a cream sauce. Or you may use drained, canned, sliced mushrooms.

Seafood Cocktail

An appetizer. For each person, provide a shallow, stemmed glass or small glass cup. Line it with a crisp **lettuce leaf.** Then lightly heap in **3 to 4 tablespoons mixed seafood:** lobster, shrimp, crab meat, scallops, cooked white fish, or any combination from list above. Garnish with **1 or 2 tablespoons seafood cocktail sauce** (p. 358). Provide for each cup a **wedge of lemon,** to be squeezed over fish. Serve well chilled.

Seafood Newburg

Mix together any desired prepared **seafood,** choosing from list above. For every **2 cups prepared fish,** make **1 to 2 cups Newburg sauce** (p. 251). Heat seafood in sauce. Serve on toast triangles, or on hot rice, or from chafing dish. (Two cups fish, plus 1 cup sauce, serves 4.)

Creamed Seafood with Mushrooms

Serves 6. A noted recipe at diplomatic dinners in Washington. Dramatic served from chafing dish, or attractive in patty shells, or on triangles of toast.

First, sauté (p. 95) in **2 tablespoons butter** until tender ¼ **pound fresh mushrooms,** caps and stems, sliced. Set aside. In top of double boiler, beat **2 egg yolks;** add ¼ **teaspoon salt,** ¼ **teaspoon paprika,** ¼ **teaspoon white pepper, 1 teaspoon Worcestershire sauce, 1½ cups light cream;** blend all thoroughly and place over pan of hot water, cooking until thickened. Then add **2 dozen raw oysters**, removed from shells, **½ cup flaked cooked or canned lobster meat**, and the cooked mushrooms. Heat all in sauce. Just before serving, stir in **¼ cup sherry.**

Creamed Chicken and Seafood

Serves 6. A favorite recipe at a New York restaurant which caters to theater celebrities.

Assemble **2 cups cubed, cooked chicken meat, 1 tin crab meat.** Simmer **12 oysters** (removed from shells) in their own liquor, until edges curl. Remove black vein from **12 large cooked or canned shrimp.** Now, in frying pan, melt **2 tablespoons butter;** add to it **½ green pepper,** minced, and **6 to 8 sliced fresh mushrooms.** Sauté mushrooms about 5 to 10 minutes, or until tender. In separate saucepan, melt **2 tablespoons butter** and stir in **3 tablespoons flour, 1½ teaspoon salt, ¼ teaspoon paprika, ¼ teaspoon pepper,** making a smooth paste. Stir in slowly **2 cups cream.** Cook gently, stirring constantly, until sauce thickens. Add cooked chicken, seafood, and mushrooms to sauce; heat thoroughly; serve on toast.

CHAPTER XVI

What to Do with Leftovers

THE BASIC CHALLENGE

It is frequently charged that a European family could live for a year on what an American family discards in the same period.

This may very likely be true. For certainly, as a nation, we are wasteful. The sweep and abundant productivity of our farmlands has led us, as a people, to regard as inedible many things which a hungry nation would seize upon, to make hearty, sustaining chowders and nourishing meals. Not only do we discard outside peelings and leaves of vegetables, outside stalks of celery, bones and carcasses which still would make wonderful soups, but we do worse. We are apt to throw away perfectly good food (good even by *our* standards) just because we cannot think how to use it.

A young housewife shrugs her shoulders, and says: "What good is this half cup of pudding? This tiny scrap of meat? These few bits of vegetables? Why keep this old piece or two of dry cake?" Out it goes.

Yet this is food she (and her husband) have paid for, presumably to bring the family nourishment. Furthermore, it is very likely food the wife has worked over, to some extent, to put in its present edible form. There is still nothing wrong with it. It is not spoiled, nor sour, nor moldy, nor burned . . . there is just not enough of it to serve again "as is" at a meal, or it no longer looks quite so palatable as it did at first serving. And in this fashion an unknowing young housewife may throw away a substantial part of her year's food budget . . . just as surely as if she had taken the dollar bills and put *them* in the trash basket.

To an intelligent housekeeper this sort of waste is not only foolish; it shows lack of imagination. For any good food — even small amounts — can always be utilized in some way, and made to contribute its good nourishment and special flavor to another day's meals.

Small bits of meat and vegetables can be put to dozens of delicious uses. Dry bread makes many mouth-watering things. Dry cake acquires new glamour and flavor when moistened with a sweet sauce, or turned into frozen shortcake. That half cup of pudding can become the smooth, creamy filling to put in several scooped-out cup cakes. Leftover coffee, or fruit juice, makes gelatine. Bits of assorted leftover fruits make many refreshing desserts, or molded ginger ale fruit salad.

All you need do is acquire the habit of asking yourself: "How shall I use these bits?"

Once you begin this game, you will find it vastly exciting. For this is the Big Challenge, in running a household's food. It is also the high test of your imagination and ability, as a chef. Leftovers may be horrible; or they may be turned into the most savory, most praise-winning meals of the week. It all depends on what you do with them. And when your family exclaims: "Golly, this is good, Mom! How did you make it? Can we have it again?" you'll know you've created something.

No book, obviously, could ever list all the possible ways you might use left-overs; for this depends upon what you have, to put together, and also on the quantity of food you have available at a given time.

What we give here is *a good starting guide* . . . a list of various possibilities, for each type of leftover food. It is not by any means all-inclusive; many other possible uses will be found in chapters throughout the book, and elsewhere. But once you have become accustomed to the uses here given, you will know enough about leftovers to begin, like a true chef, making up methods of your own.

SUGGESTED USES FOR
COOKED LEFTOVERS

These lists of suggested uses for leftovers pertain, with the exception of fruit, only to foods which have been *cooked,* and left over. *Uncooked* meats and vegetables may be prepared in standard ways, found in other chapters.

MEATS, POULTRY AND FISH

Leftover Roast Beef

Slice cold. Many gourmets consider cold roast beef as delicious as hot. Serve with hot potatoes or cold potato salad (p. 340); green vegetable.

To reheat, warm as briefly as possible, in enough beef gravy to cover, in covered saucepan on surface burner, or in covered casserole placed in moderate oven (375°) about 20 minutes. *Over*cooking will remove the "roast beef" flavor, and make meat taste like "stewed" meat. If desired, cooked potatoes and vegetables may be reheated in same gravy.

Cut in bite-size chunks; use instead of steak, in beef and kidney pie (p. 126).

To curry, cut in bite-size pieces. Reheat in beef gravy, or brown gravy (p. 253), to which 2 teaspoons grated onion and ½ teaspoon curry powder have been added. Serve hot mixture over hot rice or noodles.

Heat slices in beef gravy; serve on top of buttered bread, as hot roast beef sandwich.

Cut in cubes; add cooked vegetables, gravy, and crust, to make beef pie (p. 145).

Grind last bits of meat cut from bone; combine with diced cooked potatoes, grated onion, to make beef hash (p. 91).

If only a few scraps are left, add to meat loaf (p. 152); or to any meat casserole (p. 142); or jell in catch-all luncheon mold (p. 380).

Leftover Steak

Slice cold. Cold steak is nearly as delicious as hot; makes wonderful sandwiches. Add mustard, or horseradish, or anchovy-paste, if desired, as a thinly spread garnish. Or include crisp watercress.

To reheat, slice steak, across the grain, in ½ inch thick slices; place slices flat, in covered baking dish. Add any steak juice leftover. Heat in hot oven (425°) about 10 to 15 minutes, just until slices are warm. Do not overcook. Serve slices with juice, if any, poured over them, and a small lump of butter. Add also, if desired, a bit of scraped onion juice. Serve with baked stuffed tomatoes (p. 299), crisp watercress, German-fried potatoes (p. 90).

Cut cubes; use to make beef and kidney pie (p. 126).

Grind tail end; use to make beef hash (p. 91).

Leftover Pot-roasted Beef

Slice cold; serve with mixed vegetable salad (p. 335); or stuffed tomato salad (p. 336); or with molded beet, celery, and horseradish salad (p. 374).

Slice cold; use for sandwiches; add pickle relish or grape jam to spice the meat.

Cut in bite-size pieces; reheat in beef gravy, or brown gravy (p. 253), to which you have added 1 teaspoon grated onion, ½ teaspoon curry powder. Serve on hot rice, or noodles.

Cube; add cooked vegetables, gravy, crust; make beef pie (p. 145). Or make shepherd's pie with mashed potato crust (p. 150).

Cut in bite-size pieces; combine with cooked vegetables, medium white sauce (p. 248); bake as casserole (p. 142).

Dice; combine with drained, cooked vegetables; jell in meat aspic (p. 377).

Dice or grind; combine with equal amount of medium white sauce (p. 248) or deviled sauce (p. 249); serve as the filling in meat shortcake biscuits (p. 140). (If desired, add cooked peas, to extend meat.)

Grind; make into croquettes (p. 155).

Leftover Stew (Beef, lamb, veal, or chicken)

From stew meat, remove bones and gristle. Dice the meat. Cut stew vegetables to bite size, if they are larger, or add some cooked or canned vegetables if needed. Cover with gravy, crust. Bake as meat pie (p. 144), or chicken pie (p. 147).

Remove bones and gristle from meat. Cut meat to bite size. Use stew vegetables, or add other cooked vegetables. Add cooked noodles, or mushrooms, or chopped green pepper if desired. Cover with gravy, top dish with layer of bread crumbs; dot crumbs with butter. Bake in moderate oven (375°) about 25 minutes, or until well heated. Serve as casserole.

Leftover Roast Lamb

Slice cold, for sandwiches.

Dice; reheat in lamb gravy, to which you have added 1 teaspoon grated onion, ½ teaspoon curry powder. Serve over hot rice or noodles.

Dice; cream, by combining with medium white sauce (p. 248), or onion or celery variations. Add minced parsley, or minced green pepper, or cooked peas, or cooked mushrooms, if desired. Serve on toast.

Cut to bite size; combine with lamb gravy, cooked vegetables; add crust; bake as lamb pie (p. 145).

Cut to bite size; combine with lamb gravy or medium white sauce (p. 248), cooked noodles, peas, or mushrooms. Cover with bread crumbs; dot top with butter. Bake in moderate oven (375°) about 30 minutes, as casserole.

Grind; season; make into lamb croquettes (p. 155).

Grind; season; combine with grated onion, minced green pepper, cooked potatoes, to make lamb hash (p. 91).

Cut to bite size, or grind. Combine with drained cooked vegetables, or with diced raw celery, grated onion, minced green pepper. Jell in meat or chicken aspic (p. 377).

Add to meat loaf (p. 152).

Leftover Veal

Cube; combine with cooked peas, mushrooms, tiny white onions, veal gravy or medium white sauce (p. 248); cover with biscuit crust (p. 199); bake as veal pie (p. 146).

Cube; combine with leftover chicken meat (veal tastes much the same) in chicken pie (p. 147). Or combine with diced chicken meat in à la King sauce (p. 250). Or add to chicken meat, to extend chicken salad.

Grind; make veal croquettes (p. 155).

Cube; reheat in gravy or medium white sauce to which you have added 1 teaspoon grated onion, ½ teaspoon curry powder. Serve over hot rice or noodles.

Cut to bite size; add quartered hard-cooked eggs, cooked drained peas or string beans, diced raw celery, 1 teaspoon grated onion. Jell in chicken aspic (p. 377).

Dice or cut to bite size. Use in veal casserole (p. 146).

Add to meat loaf (p. 152).

Leftover Pork

Slice cold, for sandwiches, adding grape jam, or pickle relish, or sliced fresh tomatoes.

Slice. Distribute slices in shallow baking dish containing apple stuffing (p. 242). Cover dish. Bake in moderate (375°) oven until stuffing is cooked, about 30 minutes. If desired, add hot gravy when serving.

Cube; add cooked vegetables, gravy, crust. Bake as pork pie (p. 146).

Slice; arrange slices in shallow baking dish, alternating them with slices of peeled, cored apples. Over all, sprinkle brown sugar. If desired, add a thin scattering of grated onion. Cover dish. Bake in moderate oven (375°) until apples are tender, about 30 minutes.

Grind; combine with some cooked rice; moisten all with deviled sauce (p. 249); or onion sauce (p. 250); or mushroom sauce (p. 249); or spicy tomato sauce; add cooked peas or mushroom caps, if desired; use to stuff cooked green peppers (p. 300).

Cube, or cut to bite size. Combine with gravy or medium white sauce (p. 248) cooked drained vegetables, cooked noodles if desired, to make casserole (p. 142).

Dice or grind; use with crisp raw, or drained cooked vegetables, in catch-all luncheon mold (p. 380).

Dice or grind; add to mixed vegetables used for stuffed tomato salad (p. 336).

Dice or grind; mix with cooked rice or noodles; season with 2 teaspoons grated onion, 2 to 4 tablespoons catsup. Use to fill stuffed green peppers (p. 300).

Grind; add to meat loaf (p. 152).

Leftover Ham

Need we say? . . . Slice cold, for picnics, buffet suppers, sandwiches.

Cut one ⅜ inch thick crosswise slice, or several smaller slices. Make baked ham and apple casserole (p. 136).

Cut one ⅜ inch thick crosswise slice, or several smaller slices. Make ham and potato casserole (p. 136).

Cut one ⅜ to ½ inch thick crosswise slice. Place in baking pan. Add drained slices of canned pineapple, around edge. Sprinkle ham with brown sugar. Bake in moderate (375°) oven until sugar melts and ham and pineapple are hot.

Cut thin slices; pan-fry (p. 89); serve with fried or scrambled eggs.

Cut large thin slices; roll apple stuffing (p. 242) inside each slice. Bake as ham rolls (p. 245).

Cut thin slices; combine with toasted English muffins, poached eggs, Hollandaise sauce, as eggs Benedict (p. 270).

Dice or grind; make ham croquettes (p. 155). Or make ham fritters (p. 214).

Dice or grind. Combine with equal amount of deviled sauce (p. 249). Use as filling for meat shortcake biscuits (p. 140). Or serve on toast. (Cooked or canned peas may be added, if desired; or diced green pepper.)

Dice or grind; add to any of the following:

Potato salad (p. 340)
Mixed vegetable salad (p. 335)
Vegetables used as filling for stuffed tomato salad (p. 336)
Ingredients for catch-all luncheon mold (p. 380)
Omelet (p. 278)
Meat loaf (p. 154)
Pea soup
Waffle batter (p. 216); or muffin batter (p. 210)
Grind; use to make a casserole (p. 146).
Grind; use to make soufflé (p. 282).

Leftover Sausage (Cooked)

Use in meat loaf (p. 152).
Use to make sausage stuffing (p. 188).

Leftover Bacon (Cooked)

Crumble; add to scrambled eggs (p. 273); or omelet (p. 277).

Crumble; add to tossed green salad (p. 338); or mixed vegetable salad (p. 335); or to potato salad (p. 340); or to vegetables used in stuffed tomato salad (p. 336).

Crumble; include in muffin batter (p. 210); or waffle batter (p. 216).

Crumble; add to pea soup, or cream of corn soup.

Crumble; sprinkle on top of peanut butter spread on crackers, or on small squares of toast, for canapés.

Leftover Liver

Grind; add to meat loaf (p. 152).
Grind; use in omelet (p. 278).
Grind; season with grated onion, few drops Worcestershire sauce, salt; add a small amount of meat gravy or cream, to moisten. Use as sandwich spread.

Leftover Chicken

Cube; make chicken pie (p. 147).

Cut to bite size; combine with chicken gravy, or medium white sauce (p. 248). Add cooked peas or mushrooms, if desired. Use as filling in meat shortcake biscuits (p. 140). Or serve in patty shells. Or serve on toast. Or serve over hot rice, or noodles. Or with waffles (p. 216).

Dice; add equal amount of diced raw celery, a sprinkling of salt, 1 or 2 tablespoons French dressing, enough mayonnaise to moisten. Presto: chicken salad.

Dice; make into molded chicken soufflé salad (p. 382).

Grind; make chicken croquettes (p. 155).

Grind; make chicken loaf (p. 154).

Cut to bite size; combine with raw oysters to make chicken and oyster pie (p. 176).

Dice; heat in à la King sauce (p. 250); serve on toast, or in patty shells.

Cut to bite size; use in casserole (p. 147).

Leftover Fish

Remove skin, bones, before using.

Use in fish stew (p. 124).

Use in molded fish salad (see seafood soufflé salad, p. 382).

Break into chunks. Combine in baking dish with quartered hard-cooked eggs, cooked noodles, deviled sauce (p. 249); top mixture with bread crumbs; dot crumbs with butter. Bake in moderate (375°) oven about 30 minutes, as casserole.

Flake; combine with deviled sauce (p. 249); serve on toast, or on halves of hot baking powder biscuits (p. 198).

Flake; combine with other flaked cooked or canned seafood (crab meat, shrimp, diced scallops) to make seafood cocktail (p. 179); or seafood à la Newburg (p. 179); or scalloped seafood; or seafood coquille (see NOTE, p. 164).

Flake; mix with hot or cold potato salad (p. 340); or with mixed vegetable salad (p. 335); or add to vegetables used in stuffed tomato salad (p. 336). Or use in catch-all luncheon mold (p. 380).

Flake. Mix with well-seasoned mashed potatoes; stir in 1 raw egg, ½ teaspoon grated onion. Shape into fish cakes. Dip each cake in flour, then pan-fry (like potato cakes, p. 90) or shallow-fry, as for codfish cakes (p. 103). Serve with catsup, if desired.

FRUITS AND VEGETABLES

Leftover Small Vegetables (Cooked or canned diced carrots, peas, Limas, kernel corn, cut string beans)

Drain; add diced raw celery, tomato wedges, salt, 1 or 2 table-spoons French dressing (p. 356), 1 teaspoon grated onion. If desired, add mayonnaise. Serve on crisp greens, as mixed vegetable salad.

Drain; use in jelled salads or main-course dishes, such as catch-all luncheon mold (p. 380); or vegetable salad mold (p. 374).

Drain; combine with leftover ham, fish, meat, or chicken, to make casserole (p. 142); or meat pie (p. 144).

Add vegetables and their liquor to canned vegetable soup.

Add vegetables and their liquor to beef stock (p. 128), to make hearty main-course soup.

Drain; make into creamed vegetables (p. 294); or vegetables au gratin (p. 295); or scalloped vegetables (p. 295).

Cooked peas: purée (p. 303); combine with thin white sauce (p. 248) to make cream of pea soup (p. 258).

Kernel corn: reheat in its own liquor, if any; add top milk, or cream, or thin white sauce (p. 248); add also ½ teaspoon grated onion, salt, pepper, lump of butter; add a bit of minced parsley or minced green pepper if desired. Serve as corn soup.

Or make corn fritters (p. 213).

Or use corn in meat casserole (p. 142).

Leftover Branch Vegetables (Cooked broccoli, asparagus)

Drain; alternate in shallow baking dish with halved hard-cooked eggs, or grated carrots, or slices of meat. Cover with meat aspic (p. 379). Chill until firm.

Drain; marinate in French dressing; serve on crisp greens, adding tomato wedges, or hard-cooked or deviled eggs if desired, as salad. Garnish with mayonnaise if desired.

Cook soft, and purée (p. 303). Combine with thin white sauce (p. 248), to make cream of broccoli, or cream of asparagus soup. Garnish with paprika, croutons (p. 194) if desired.

Dice; drain; add to mixed vegetable salad (p. 335). Or use in molded vegetable salad (p. 374); or in catch-all luncheon mold (p. 380).

Add to ham casserole (p. 146).

Leftover Root Vegetables (Cooked potatoes, beets, carrots, onions, turnips)

White Potatoes. (Boiled or baked, peeled)

Dice; pan-fry (p. 87) or cottage-fry (p. 89) or cream (p. 294), or scallop (p. 295) or bake au gratin (p. 295).

Cut to bite size; combine with meat, other vegetables, in meat pies (p. 144), or casseroles (p. 142).

Add to hot chowders, meat or vegetable soups.

Dice; combine with ground meat, grated onion, to make hash (p. 91).

Dice. Use in potato omelet (p. 278).

Add with other mixed vegetables, to make vegetables au gratin (p. 295); or scalloped vegetables (p. 295).

Mashed

To reheat and serve again as "mashed potatoes": place potatoes in top of double boiler, over pan of hot water. Cover. Reheat until steaming hot. Add 1 or 2 tablespoons hot milk, and beat vigorously until light. Add lump of butter; more salt, pepper, if needed.

Use as mashed potato crust on meat pie; see shepherd's pie (p. 150).

Moisten cold mashed potatoes by mixing in 1 slightly beaten egg. Add few grains salt, pepper. Shape mixture into round cakes. Pan-fry in a little hot fat, until hot and browned (see page 90); or shallow-fry like codfish cakes (p. 103).

Combine mashed potatoes with cooked, mashed, yellow turnips; blend well; reheat; add more salt, pepper if needed. Stir in a lump of butter.

Sweet Potatoes (Boiled or baked; peeled)

Cut to bite size. Add to casseroles of ham, chicken, veal, turkey; see Chapter XIII.

Slice lengthwise; arrange in shallow buttered baking dish. Over top, put a layer of marshmallows, cut in half crosswise, with cut sides down toward potatoes. Bake in moderate (375°) oven about 30 to 45 minutes, or until marshmallows become soft. Very good with ham. Some people like this dish with roast turkey, roast chicken, roast pork.

Slice potatoes crosswise, or lengthwise. Candy (see page 297).

Slice potatoes crosswise, or lengthwise. Pan-fry (p. 302).

If you have only a few scraps of sweet potato, add them to white potatoes you are pan-frying; or to hash, or to a casserole.

Beets (Cooked, peeled)

Drain; dice, julienne or slice; marinate in French dressing (p. 356). Mix with 1 or 2 teaspoons grated onion. Excellent on crisp greens.

Drain; slice, chop, or julienne; use in beet, celery, and horse-radish salad mold (p. 374).

Whole beets: Scoop out centers, making cups of the beets. Fill with potato salad (p. 340), or ham salad; or with mixed veg-etables, seasoned, and moistened with French dressing (p. 356), or mayonnaise (p. 351).

Onions (Peeled; boiled)

Purée; combine with thin white sauce (p. 248), to make cream of onion soup (p. 258).

Slice or chop; add to any casserole, Chapter XIII.

Slice or chop; add to creamed vegetables (p. 294), or scalloped vegetables (p. 295).

Dice or purée (p. 303). Combine with medium white sauce (p. 248); use as sauce for fritters (p. 213), or for meat loaf (p. 152).

Carrots (Peeled; boiled)

Drain; dice; cream (p. 294). Add cooked drained peas, in same sauce, if desired. Or combine with mixed creamed vegetables (p. 294).

Dice; add with vegetable liquor to canned vegetable soup; or add to homemade meat and vegetable soup (p. 127).

Drain; slice or dice; add to meat pies (p. 144); or casseroles (p. 142).

Drain; slice lengthwise; pan-fry (p. 302).

Use in mixed vegetable salad (p. 335). Or in vegetable salad mold (p. 374); or in catch-all luncheon mold (p. 380).

Yellow Turnips (Peeled, boiled)

Reheat, covered, in water they were cooked in, or in a little boiling water. If desired, drain, mash, season with salt, pepper, a lump of butter.

Drain; slice in $3/8$ inch thick crosswise slices; pan-fry (p. 302) in a little butter or bacon fat, until browned on both sides.

Mash leftover turnips; combine with leftover mashed potatoes. Moisten mixture with 1 or 2 tablespoons cream, or 1 slightly beaten egg. Add few grains salt, pepper, if needed. Shape into cakes. Pan-fry (like potato cakes, p. 90) in a little butter or bacon fat, until browned on both sides.

Add drained, sliced leftover turnips to peeled white potatoes you are boiling. When potatoes are tender, pour off water; mash potatoes and turnips together; season with salt, pepper; add a lump of butter.

Leftover Leafy Vegetables (Cooked spinach, chard, cabbage)

Use drained, finely chopped spinach in spinach soufflé (p. 282).

Make cream soup, by combining the chopped leafy vegetable with thin white sauce (p. 248) in which you have used some of the vegetable liquor as liquid. Add ½ teaspoon grated onion, for extra seasoning. Add a lump of butter to each cupful of soup before serving.

Chop leafy vegetable. Combine with medium white sauce (p.

248 to make creamed vegetable (p. 294). If desired, add bits of ham or corned beef or tinned luncheon meat or hard-cooked eggs, in same sauce, and serve mixture on toast.

Drain, chop; cook as vegetable au gratin (p. 295).

Drain; chop vegetable coarsely. In shallow baking dish, put some pieces of ham, or corned beef, or tinned luncheon meat. In between meat, put halves of hard-cooked eggs, and clusters of the chopped vegetable. Cover contents of dish with meat aspic (p. 377). Chill until firm. Or cover contents of dish with medium white sauce (p. 248), or mustard sauce (p. 250); top dish with layer of bread crumbs; bake in moderate (375°) oven 35 to 40 minutes, as casserole.

Fruits (fresh, cooked or canned)

See Index for additional uses, in fruit cups, fruit salads, molded fruit desserts, frozen fruit puddings, fruit shortcakes, etc.

BREAD, RICE, AND OTHER LEFTOVERS

Bread (When too dry for table use)

Make into bread stuffing (p. 241), or any bread stuffing variation.

Make into bread pudding (p. 389).

French Toast. In bowl beat 2 eggs slightly; add 1 tablespoon sugar, ¼ cup milk, ¼ teaspoon salt. Blend liquid mixture. Dip into it one piece of bread at a time, soaking bread well. Fry moistened bread in frying pan containing 2 or 3 tablespoons melted butter or hot salad oil, browning both sides of each piece of bread to golden color. Serve hot. Add, if desired, a garnish of peach or other jelly, when serving.

Milk Toast. Toast bread in toaster. While hot, spread with butter; sprinkle lightly with sugar, cinnamon. Place one or two hot pieces in soup plate. Add enough hot (not boiled) milk to cover.

Croutons (for soup). Cut bread into ½ inch cubes. Place cubes on lightly greased cookie sheet, and bake in moderate (375°)

oven until golden brown. Or fry cubes in a little butter, in frying pan, until golden brown on all sides; then drain on paper towel.

Bread Crumbs. Place bread in closed paper bag, in moderate (375°) oven, 10 to 15 minutes, or until well dried out, but not brown. With rolling pin, crush dry bread into fine crumbs. Store in covered glass jar; use as needed for coating fried foods, topping casseroles.

Leftover Cake (Too dry for serving "as is")

Remove frosting; cut cake in serving-size squares. Top with any juicy fresh fruit; or sweetened, flavored whipped cream (p. 408); or cooled soft custard (p. 385); or any cream filling (p. 441); or any desired dessert sauce (p. 405); or with ice cream. Let cake and its topping stand for 10 to 15 minutes before serving, so cake has time to become moistened.

Remove frosting; crumble cake. Use to make frozen crumb pudding (p. 404).

Remove frosting. (1) Slice cake in half, horizontally. Put layer of ice cream between halves. Place in freezer compartment of refrigerator, turned to lowest possible cold, until firm. Slice, to serve. Or (2) make frozen shortcake (p. 404).

Leftover Soups

Leftover cream soups may often be used as a sauce to pour over meat loaf, croquettes. Or they may be used as part of the sauce in making a casserole (p. 142).

Thin, clear broths may be made into aspic (p. 375). Or they may be made into heartier soups by adding cooked rice or noodles, plus leftover bits of meat and cooked vegetables.

Leftover Rice, Noodles, Macaroni

Use as the "starch" in almost any casserole (p. 142).

Add to meat, chicken, turkey, or vegetable soups, to make them heartier.

Add to curried vegetables (p. 295); or to any meat, heated in curry sauce (see curry casseroles, p. 149).

Rice may be used in rice croquettes (p. 158).

Combine with diced cooked or canned meat, chicken, fish, or ham to fill stuffed green peppers (p. 300).

Combine with enough cheese sauce (p. 249), to moisten; then bake in buttered individual molds, in moderate oven (375°) about 25 minutes, until thoroughly heated, and firm.

Leftover Crackers (Broken)

Dry out, in moderate oven (375°) just a few minutes, until crisp, but not brown. Roll into crumbs, with rolling pin. Use for topping casseroles, or coating fried foods.

Leftover Cookies (Broken)

Crumble completely. Make into frozen crumb pudding (p. 404).

Leftover Coffee

Use as iced coffee. Or make coffee gelatine (p. 371).

Leftover Tea (Brewed)

Use as iced tea. Or combine with fruit juices, to make cooling summer drink.

Leftover Fruit Juices

Use to make fruit gelatine desserts (p. 367). Or use as part of liquid to jell fruit salads (p. 373).

Combine several fruit juices with ginger ale or iced tea, to make summer drink.

CHAPTER XVII

You Can Make Biscuits

METHOD FOR: *Baking Powder Biscuits, Shortcake Biscuits, Biscuit Crusts for Pies, Casseroles, Dumplings for Stew, Fancy Biscuits, Buns Made with Biscuit Dough, Your Own Biscuit Mix, Desserts Made with Sweet Biscuit Dough*

BASIC PRINCIPLES

Biscuit dough is only flour and shortening, with salt to flavor it, baking powder to "raise" it . . . and milk to moisten.

All very simple; all things you have in the house.

The dough takes about 5 minutes to mix.

This makes plain biscuits . . . delicious, fluffy ones, if you do it right. But it makes much more. The very same dough becomes your crust for meat pies and casseroles. With a little more milk added, it makes dumplings for stew. With simple trimmings added, it makes cheese biscuits, or fruited biscuits. When spread with a filling, and rolled up like a pinwheel, it makes fancy buns. And it makes the shortcake biscuits for creamed chicken, creamed ham, or other dinner meats.

If you can make one pan of biscuits, you can make any of these good things.

There is also a second version of Biscuit Dough — made exactly the same way, but with sugar, more shortening, and an egg added — and this *rich* biscuit dough is what you use for dessert shortcakes, sweet buns, coffee rings, fruit cobblers, other desserts. It is just as easy to make.

There is only one trick to remember about biscuit making. Handle the dough *lightly*. If you want tender, feather-light biscuits, you cannot press the dough into a heavy, solid mass. When mixing the ingredients, mix lightly. Cut in the shortening lightly. When rolling or patting dough into a sheet, do *that* lightly, not with heavy strokes. When cutting out rounds, cut deftly and quickly, not with a heavy hand. If you remember this point, and keep to the proportions given in these two versions of biscuit dough, you will have flaky, tender biscuits, every time.

MASTER RECIPE #14
BAKING POWDER BISCUITS

(Makes about 14 2-inch biscuits)

Sift first; then measure
2 cups all-purpose flour
Sift same flour again, adding to it
2½ teaspoons double-acting baking powder
¾ teaspoon salt
Add, in one lump
4 tablespoons shortening
Using pastry blender, or two knives in crisscross motion, cut shortening into flour (until mixture has texture of coarse meal)
Stir in gradually just enough milk to make a *soft*—but *not sticky*—dough; about
¾ cup milk
Milk needed depends on absorbency of flour used.

Turn dough onto lightly floured board. Flour hands; shape dough lightly into a smooth mass.

To shape plain biscuits. With floured rolling pin, roll dough, with light, quick strokes, from center out, to make a circular sheet of dough ½ to ¾ inch thick. (For very thin biscuits, roll dough only ¼ inch thick. For very high biscuits roll dough 1 inch thick.) Dip in flour a biscuit cutter, or clean empty tin can, or a drinking glass, to cut out biscuits with. (Typical dinner biscuits are 2 inches wide. Tea or cocktail biscuits may be cut only 1 to 1½ inches wide; shortcake biscuits are cut 3 inches wide.) Dip cutter in flour frequently, so dough will not stick to it.

Lift out cut rounds; place them on greased baking pan. If you like *crusty* biscuits, place the rounds 1 inch apart, on baking pan. If you prefer high, soft biscuits, place rounds so they touch each other on baking pan. Gather up remnants of dough; reshape them into a ball; roll out, and cut more biscuits. Continue until all dough is used.

To bake. Place pan in *preheated hot (425°) oven,* 12 to 15 minutes, until tops of biscuits are nicely browned, and crust is dry and flaky. If biscuits have been properly and lightly mixed, and if oven was hot enough, biscuits will have just about doubled in height, when done, and the inside will be tender, light, flaky . . . never soggy.

BISCUIT VARIATIONS

Shortcake Biscuits (for Meat Shortcakes, Chicken Shortcakes)

Make Master Recipe, Biscuits, increasing shortening to 6 tablespoons if desired. (This will make "shorter" biscuits.) Cut out biscuits 3 inches in diameter. Bake as usual. When done, split biscuits in half while hot, **butter** both halves; then between halves put creamed meat, chicken, turkey, ham, seafood, or other mixture as a delicious filling; see page 140.

For dessert shortcakes, use the Sweet Biscuit Dough, Master Recipe #16 (p. 240); this has a more cakelike quality.

Biscuit Crusts (for Meat Pies, Casseroles)

Mix one half Master Recipe, Biscuits, for enough crust to cover an 8 inch casserole. If you want crusts for 4 or 5 individual casseroles, mix entire Master Recipe, Biscuits. When dough is mixed, turn it onto floured board. With floured rolling pin, lightly roll it to circular sheet about ¼ to ⅜ inch thick. Out of this sheet, cut a circular crust about 1 inch wider than top of casserole; if you can find a saucer or plate which is just a little wider than top of your casserole, place this saucer or plate on top of sheet of rolled dough, and with floured sharp knife cut around it, using saucer or plate as a guide for making a good circle. To cut crusts for individual casseroles, use smaller plate as guide, and cut as many as needed, but always making the crust a little larger than width of casserole. Now lift crust onto top of filled casserole dish. With fingers, crimp the overhanging biscuit crust firmly to the edges of the casserole dish, so crust will keep in place, and keep contents of dish entirely covered. With small sharp knife, cut in center of crust 5 or 6 slashes about 1 inch long, to allow steam vents. Place pie in preheated hot (425°) oven and bake 20 to 25 minutes, until crust is golden brown, risen, and flaky.

Since crust over casserole or meat pie usually has a liquid sauce or gravy beneath it, crust may take longer to become cooked and done than plain biscuits would.

Dumplings (for Stew)

Mix Master Recipe, Baking Powder Biscuits, but increase **milk to 1 cup.** When meat stew or chicken stew is cooked and ready to eat, drop biscuit dough, 1 teaspoon at a time, onto hot, bubbling stew, taking pains to place each spoonful of dough on a solid piece of meat or vegetable, so dough will not sink into the liquid too far. Cover kettle tightly, as soon as all spoonfuls of dough are in. Keep stew simmering 12 to 15 minutes *without peeking.* If you lift off cover of kettle before this time, dumplings will fall, and become unattractively soggy.

Herb Biscuit Dough (for Herb Biscuit Crusts for Pies and Casseroles; Herb Shortcakes; Herb Dumplings)

When mixing Master Recipe, Biscuits, add with dry ingredients: 2 to 4 tablespoons minced fresh parsley plus one of the following: ¼ teaspoon thyme, or ¼ teaspoon celery seed, or ½ to 1 teaspoon chopped fresh chives, or ¼ teaspoon curry powder, or (for chicken dishes) ½ teaspoon poultry seasoning. Continue with Master Recipe, Biscuits, as usual; for dumplings, don't forget to increase milk to 1 cup. Shape and use dough as directed for dish you wish to make.

Cheese Biscuits

Make Master Recipe, Biscuits, but when mixing dough, add with dry ingredients ½ cup grated sharp American cheese. Shape and bake as in Master Recipe.

Surprise Biscuits

Make Master Recipe, Biscuits; roll dough, cut out biscuits, and place them on greased baking pan. Before baking, press into center top of each biscuit 1 teaspoon jelly; or press in a small piece of drained canned pineapple, or ½ a cooked, pitted prune, or a piece of drained canned apricot, or fig, or peach. Bake as usual.

Orange Tea Biscuits

Mix Master Recipe, Biscuits, but with dry ingredients add 2 to 4 teaspoons grated orange rind. Roll dough; cut out biscuits; place on greased baking pan. Before baking, press into center top of each biscuit 1 lump sugar saturated in orange juice. Bake as usual.

Filled Biscuits (Put together like a sandwich)

Make Master Recipe, Biscuits, but when rolling dough, roll thin, only ¼ inch thick. Cut out rounds. Place half the rounds on greased baking sheet. In center of each of these rounds put 1 teaspoon of some filling (this may be 1 teaspoon jam; or 1 thin piece sharp cheese; or 1 teaspoon deviled ham; or 1 teaspoon thick creamed chicken, lobster, or shrimp; or 1 teaspoon liver spread; in fact any filling you like). Over each spread round, place a plain round. Press edges of top and bottom rounds firmly together, moistening edges slightly with milk, if need be, to make them stick, so filling will not come out. Bake biscuits as usual. When done, they look like plain biscuits; the filling comes as a surprise. These are terrific for cocktail parties if made bite-size (biscuits cut 1 inch wide) and filled with tangy fish, ham, or other tasty mixture.

Pigs in a Blanket (tiny cocktail sausages in biscuit covering)

Make Master Recipe, Biscuits. Turn dough onto floured board, and with floured rolling pin, roll it to oblong sheet only ¼ inch thick. Drain tiny **cocktail sausages**. From sheet of dough, using floured knife, cut out oblongs big enough so that you can completely wrap 1 sausage in each oblong. After wrapping dough around sausage, press dough together firmly, at outer edge, and at ends, so dough will not come unrolled. Place wrapped sausages on greased baking sheet. Bake in preheated hot (425°) oven 15 to 20 minutes, or until biscuit dough is golden brown and dry. Serve hot. (These always make a huge hit with men; make plenty.)

Quick Pinwheels (Fancy Buns)

Cheese Pinwheels. Make Master Recipe, Biscuits (p. 198). Turn dough onto floured board. With floured rolling pin, roll dough to oblong sheet ¼ inch thick and 10 x 14 inches wide. Spread surface of sheet of dough with ¼ **cup melted butter.** Over butter, sprinkle **½ cup grated sharp American cheese.** Now roll up dough: lift one 14 inch wide edge of the sheet of dough, and start rolling dough firmly and tightly toward opposite 14 inch edge, like jelly roll. Moisten outer edge of completed roll with **milk**, if need be, to make it stick to dough, so roll won't come unrolled. Now with sharp, floured knife, slice off from roll crosswise slices ½ to ¾ inch thick. Place slices, cut side down, on greased baking sheet. Bake as for biscuits.

Ham Pinwheels. Make just like cheese pinwheels, but instead of grated cheese, substitute a well-seasoned **ham spread.**

Cinnamon Buns. Make either Master Recipe, Baking Powder Biscuits (p. 198), or Master Recipe, Sweet Biscuit Dough (p. 204). Turn mixed dough onto floured board. With floured rolling pin, roll dough to oblong sheet ¼ inch thick and 10 x 14 inches wide. Spread surface of sheet of dough with ¼ **cup melted butter.** Over butter spread a mixture of **½ cup granulated sugar** mixed with **2 teaspoons cinnamon.** If desired, over sugar sprinkle also

¼ cup seedless raisins. Roll up dough, cut slices, and bake, as under cheese pinwheels.

Currant Buns. Make like cinnamon buns, but after spreading dough with melted butter, spread with ½ cup dried currants mixed with ¾ cup brown sugar, and ½ teaspoon cinnamon.

Honey Buns. Make like cinnamon buns, but after spreading dough with melted butter, spread with ¼ cup honey, and on top of honey sprinkle 1 teaspoon cinnamon.

Butterscotch-Pecan Buns. Make like cinnamon buns, but after spreading dough with melted butter, sprinkle on ¾ cup brown sugar (brown sugar plus butter makes butterscotch). Over brown sugar sprinkle ½ cup chopped pecan meats.

MASTER RECIPE #15
BISCUIT MIX

You can easily make your own private "biscuit mix" (just like the ones sold in packages), and have some on hand for any occasion when you wish to use biscuit dough.

To make this mix takes about 5 to 10 minutes. It provides enough mix to make three times our Master Recipe, Baking Powder Biscuits. It will serve you for three occasions when you want 12 to 14 biscuits; or six occasions when you want 6 to 7 biscuits; or will make several small lots of biscuits, plus several biscuit crusts for casseroles, or meat pies. It contains everything needed for biscuits except the milk (this cannot be added, or the mix would spoil before you used it all). It saves, repeatedly, the time required for measuring and sifting dry ingredients, measuring and cutting in shortening. It speeds every occasion when you want a biscuit dough in haste, and it will be your joy.

Stored in tightly covered canister, or in covered glass jar, this mix keeps well 3 to 4 weeks in refrigerator, or a cool, dry place. Make it once, and you will never want to be without it.

Sift, then measure

6 cups all-purpose flour

Sift flour again, adding

2 tablespoons double-acting baking powder
1 tablespoon salt

With pastry blender, or two knives in crisscross motion, cut into flour mixture

1 cup (½ pound) shortening

Cut mixture until it has texture of coarse meal. Store in covered canister or glass jar until wanted.

When biscuit dough is wanted, measure out

2 cups biscuit mix

into bowl; stir in about

½ cup milk

to make a soft dough. Turn dough onto floured board; roll, shape, and bake as for Master Recipe, Baking Powder Biscuits (p. 198). Two cups biscuit mix makes about 10 2-inch biscuits.

MASTER RECIPE #16
SWEET BISCUIT DOUGH

This dough is made just like Master Recipe, Baking Powder Biscuits, except that you add sugar and 1 egg, and increase the amount of shortening. Naturally, this makes a more cakelike dough, excellent for sweet desserts, or sweet buns, or coffee rings.

You may substitute this sweet dough for the plain dough of Master Recipe, Biscuits when making any fruit-type or sweet-filled pinwheel (p. 203).

See recipes following, for other uses.

Sift first; then measure

2 cups all-purpose flour

Sift same flour again, adding

2½ teaspoons double-acting baking powder

¾ teaspoon salt

2 to 4 tablespoons granulated sugar

With pastry blender, or two knives in crisscross motion, **cut into** dry ingredients

⅓ cup shortening

Cut in shortening until mixture has texture of coarse meal.

Then stir in

½ cup milk

1 egg, well beaten

Turn dough out onto a lightly floured board. Pat lightly into smooth ball.

SWEET BISCUIT VARIATIONS

Fruit Shortcakes

Use for strawberry, raspberry, or other fruit shortcakes, **using** entire Master Recipe to make 6 to 8 shortcakes.

With floured rolling pin, roll dough ½ inch thick; then with floured 3 inch wide cutter, cut out rounds. Place rounds on greased baking sheet. Bake in preheated hot (425°) oven 15 to 20 minutes, or until golden brown, dry and flaky on top. Remove from oven; split in half with fingers, while hot. Spread if desired with **butter.** Between halves, put **sweetened fresh berries.** Close biscuit. Over top, put more berries, and garnish with sweetened **whipped cream.**

Some new Englanders like to make one huge shortcake, to serve the entire family, instead of making individual ones. If you wish to do this, instead of cutting out biscuits, turn entire dough into greased layer cake tin; pat dough out evenly in pan; bake in hot (425°) oven 20 to 25 minutes, until golden brown on top. Remove from pan and carefully split in half horizontally. While biscuit is still hot spread inside with **butter**. Fill with **sweetened berries** or other fruit. Top with more sweetened fruit and **sweetened whipped cream**. To serve, cut in wedges, like pie. One New England man I know says he can eat nearly an entire such shortcake, whenever his wife will make one!

Fruit Cobblers

Mix ½ Master Recipe, Sweet Biscuit Dough, using the whole egg, but only half all other ingredients; this will make sufficient dough to cover a 1-quart casserole. A Cobbler has no lower crust.

Filling the dish. **Butter** the inside of a 1-quart casserole dish, having side walls 1½ to 2 inches deep. Into buttered dish, put any *one* of the following kinds of **fruit:**

1 quart picked-over fresh blueberries; or 2 cans drained blueberries.

1 quart pitted sour cherries; or 2 cans drained pitted sour cherries.

4 cups peeled, sliced fresh peaches, or 1 large can drained sliced peaches.

1 quart fresh raspberries.

4 cups peeled, cored, thinly sliced, tart apples.

Sprinkle over fruit ⅓ to ⅔ **cup granulated sugar**. (Use only ⅓ cup sugar for canned fruit, since that has already been somewhat sweetened; use ½ cup for fresh berries or peaches; use ⅔ cup for tart apples.)

On top of fruit sprinkle any **seasonings** desired—1 to 2 teaspoons lemon juice will heighten flavor of blueberries; 2 or 3 drops almond extract is marvelous with peaches or sour cherries; when using apples, add several dashes nutmeg, or cinnamon, or both.

If fruit is fresh (not canned) and of a type which will make considerable juice while cooking (such as blueberries, or juicy fresh peaches), also sprinkle over fruit thinly **2 tablespoons flour** to thicken juice as dish bakes.

Over sweetened, flavored fruit, scatter **10 to 12 bits of butter,** the size of peas.

Making the crust. Now, on floured board, with floured rolling pin, roll sweet biscuit dough to sheet ¼ inch thick, and right shape to cover top of casserole with a 1 inch overhang. Lift crust onto casserole. Crimp overhang of crust firmly to edges of casserole. In center of crust, make 5 to 6 slashes, 1 inch long, with sharp knife, to allow steam vents. Bake in preheated very hot (450°) oven 20 to 25 minutes, or until crust is risen and golden brown on top. Serve cobbler warm or cool; garnish top with whipped cream if desired.

Coffee Ring

Make entire Master Recipe, Sweet Biscuit Dough. Turn mixed dough onto floured board. With floured rolling pin, roll it to sheet ¼ inch thick and 10 x 14 inches wide (like pinwheels, page 202).

Over surface of sheet of dough, spread ¼ **cup melted butter.**

Over melted butter, spread any **sweet filling** used in making quick pinwheels (p. 202).

Now lift one 14 inch wide edge of the sheet of dough, and start rolling it firmly and tightly toward opposite 14 inch wide edge, rolling up sheet like a jelly roll. Moisten outer edge with a little milk, if needed, and press edge to roll, so roll will not come undone. Do not slice roll.

Just place roll in greased layer-cake pan, bending the roll to shape of a ring. Stretch roll with hands, if need be, to make ends meet, forming a complete circle. Moisten ends with a little milk, and press them together.

With scissors, cut slashes, 1½ inches apart, from outer edge of ring halfway to its center, all the way around ring; this helps ring spread out.

Bake ring in preheated hot (400°) oven 20 to 25 minutes, or until ring has risen and is golden brown and dry on top.

Before it cools, if desired, spread over top of it **confectioners'
icing** (p. 428).

Quick Crumb Coffee Cake

Make entire Master Recipe, Sweet Biscuit Dough, increasing
sugar to ⅓ cup and adding with sugar ¼ teaspoon mace. When
mixed, pat dough out evenly in greased 8 x 8 x 2 inch cake pan.
Now make this:

Crumb Topping. In a bowl mix 4 tablespoons soft butter, ¼
cup sugar, 2 teaspoons cinnamon, and 3 tablespoons flour. Blend
mixture well; spread it over top of dough in pan.

Bake cake in preheated hot (400°) oven, 25 to 35 minutes, or
until cake feels firm, yet springy, to touch. Delicious, served hot,
with butter to spread on it, if desired.

Dutch Apple Cake (Apple Kuchen)

Make ½ Master Recipe, Sweet Biscuit Dough, using whole
egg, but half all other ingredients. When dough is mixed, pat it
evenly into greased 8 x 8 x 2-inch baking pan.

Peel, core, and cut in even, lengthwise slices 5 or 6 tart apples.

Arrange apple slices, in a series of parallel rows, each slice
overlapping another, with sharp edge of each slice stuck down
into the dough. Arrange enough rows of apples to cover dough
entirely.

Over top of apples, sprinkle ½ cup sugar mixed with ½ teaspoon cinnamon.

Bake in hot (425°) oven about 20 minutes, then reduce heat to
moderate (350°) and continue baking until apples are tender.

CHAPTER XVIII

You Can Make Muffins

METHOD FOR: *Plain Muffins, Nut Muffins, Fruit Muffins, Bacon Muffins, Cheese Muffins, Jelly Muffins*

BASIC PRINCIPLES

Muffin batter is actually a lighter, sweeter, "shorter" kind of biscuit dough. It contains not only the biscuit ingredients (flour, baking powder, salt, shortening, milk) but adds 1 or more eggs (for flavor, and lightening of batter); and sugar (for a somewhat sweet mixture); extra shortening (for extra richness); and more liquid (so the mixture is thinner).

The main trick in making good muffins is to handle all ingredients as *quickly and lightly* as possible. Flour should be sifted before measuring, and then again, for lightness. In mixing liquid with dry ingredients, use only a few quick, light strokes . . . the fewer the better . . . beating only enough to dampen all flour, and disregarding lumps. A batter which gets the minimum of beating will make the lightest, best-textured muffins.

With one Master Recipe, you can make many kinds of muffins.

MASTER RECIPE #17
MUFFINS

(Makes 11–12 large muffins)

Sift first, then measure

2 cups flour

Sift same flour again, into large bowl, adding to it

2½ teaspoons double-acting baking powder

2 tablespoons sugar

¾ teaspoon salt

Using pastry blender, or two knives in crisscross motion, cut into flour mixture

⅓ cup shortening

(Cut in this shortening until it is hardly visible in the flour.)
In separate bowl, beat well

1 egg

Add to egg

¾ cup milk

Pour egg-milk mixture, all at once, into flour mixture. To mix, draw spoon from side of bowl toward center 15 times, turning the bowl as you do this. Then chop spoon through batter 10 times. Then stir only about 5 strokes, until all flour is dampened. Disregard lumps.

Turn batter into well-greased muffin pans, filling each muffin cup only ⅔ full of batter.

(If muffin cups are not adequately greased, muffins may stick to pans. For blueberry muffins, or other juicy fruited type, it is good to flour the pans lightly, after greasing them, for extra protection against sticking.)

Bake in preheated hot (425°) oven about 25 minutes, until muffins are risen and golden brown on top, and beginning to shrink slightly from inside edges of cups.

To remove from pans; turn pan upside down over table; muffins should slip right out. (If they stick, loosen from pan with spatula.)

To serve: keep them warm by wrapping lightly in a clean linen napkin.

MUFFIN VARIATIONS

(Follow Master Recipe #17, Muffins, page 210, making simple additions or substitutions below.)

Nut Muffins

After measuring flour, use only 1¾ cups, setting other ¼ cup aside. Increase sugar to 4 tablespoons. Mix batter. Before putting batter into greased pans, mix the saved-out ¼ cup flour with ½ cup coarsely chopped nut meats; add to batter and blend in. Bake as in Master Recipe.

Fruit Muffins

After measuring flour, use only 1¾ cups, setting other ¼ cup aside. Increase sugar to 4 tablespoons. Mix batter. Before putting batter into greased pans, mix the saved-out ¼ cup flour with the fruit — ½ cup fresh blueberries, or dried raisins, or chopped dates, or chopped drained cooked or canned prunes, apricots, or figs. Add to batter. Bake as in Master Recipe.

Bacon Muffins

Before putting batter into greased pans, stir in ½ cup crumbled, cooked bacon. Bake as in Master Recipe.

Cheese Muffins

Omit sugar. When batter is mixed, fold into it ½ to ¾ cup grated sharp American cheese. Bake as in Master Recipe.

Jelly Muffins

Put batter into greased muffin pans. Then, into center top of each muffin, press a spoonful of currant or other jelly; and bake as in Master Recipe.

CHAPTER XIX

You Can Make Fritters

METHOD FOR: *Corn Fritters, Celery Fritters, Ham Fritters, Chicken Fritters, Clam Fritters, Oyster Fritters, Fruit Fritters (Apple, Banana, Pineapple, Peach)*

BASIC PRINCIPLES

Fritters, which will bring shouts of joy from the men in your family, are simple to make, and fun.

They are made with 1 or 2 cups of (often leftover) meat, or fish, or ham, or chicken, or vegetables, or fruit, simply folded into a batter much like muffin batter, then fried in deep fat. The batter takes about 5 minutes to mix; and the deep-frying takes about 5 minutes for each group of fritters you fry.

Any solid food used in fritters (the meat, chicken, ham, corn, or whatnot) *must either have been cooked or canned* before using it, *if* it is a food which cannot ordinarily be eaten raw. The few minutes needed for cooking fritter batter would not suffice to cook raw meat, for example.

Clams and oysters, however, are used raw (since both may be eaten raw), and *fruits may be used raw if they are customarily eaten* raw.

Note that *in making fruit fritters,* sugar and shortening are added to the Master Recipe, to give fritters a richer flavor.

Fritters made in tiny size (that is, dropped into cooking fat by teaspoonful, instead of by tablespoonful) make delectable hot canapés for a party — especially seafood fritters.

Make fritters once, and you will want to make them often.

MASTER RECIPE #18
FRITTERS

(Makes 6 to 8 fritters)

In a bowl, beat until light

1 egg

Mix with egg

1 cup diced, cooked or canned meat, fish, chicken, or ham

or

1 cup diced, drained, cooked or canned vegetable

or

1 cup drained, cut-up fruit *

or

**1 cup drained, cleaned raw shellfish, if the shellfish are
of a type edible raw**

NOTE: Any 1 cup firm food as above, becomes your "solid" ingredient. See Variations following for others.

Sift into separate bowl; then measure

1 cup flour

Sift measured flour again, adding with it

1¼ teaspoons double-acting baking power

¼ teaspoon salt

Blend all above ingredients; then stir in enough milk to make a thick batter; about

¼ to ½ cup milk

Amount of milk varies because a juicy "solid" ingredient, like fruit, requires less additional liquid than a dry ingredient, like diced meat. As batter is going to be dropped by spoonful into hot fat, it must be firm enough to hold together; it should not be runny.

To cook fritters. You may shallow-fry (p. 105) or deep-fry (Chapter X) fritters. Read Master Recipe and equipment needed,

---

* If making fruit fritters, add with drained fruit and egg 2 tablespoons melted shortening; and add with dry ingredients 2 tablespoons sugar. This makes a sweeter, richer batter.

in either chapter. Hot fat should be heated to 375°, by frying thermometer, or hot enough to brown a 1 inch cube of one-day-old bread in 60 seconds. Using long-handled spoon, drop batter, 1 tablespoon at a time, into hot fat, using spatula to push batter off spoon if necessary. Cook about 5 minutes, just until golden brown on all sides. Drain on paper towel before serving. If desired, sprinkle fruit fritters with sugar, as they drain. Serve hot.

FRITTER VARIATIONS — GENERAL

(Follow Master Recipe #18, Fritters, page 213, using as your "solid" the food suggested below.)

Corn Fritters

Use **1 cup drained cooked or canned kernel corn;** increase salt to **¾ teaspoon.** Use little milk, if corn is moist. Serve with maple syrup, with ham, tongue, fried chicken.

Celery Fritters

Use **1 cup drained, cooked, sliced celery.** Increase salt to **¾ teaspoon.** Add with dry ingredients, as extra seasoning, **2 tablespoons chopped parsley,** and **2 tablespoons chopped chives** or grated raw onion. Serve celery fritters with sharp tomato sauce, or cheese sauce (p. 249).

Ham Fritters

Use **1 cup diced or ground cooked ham,** mixed with **¼ teaspoon prepared mustard.** Serve ham fritters with egg sauce (p. 249), spicy tomato sauce, or for sauce, use 1 can undiluted condensed cream of mushroom soup, heated.

Chicken Fritters

Use **1 cup diced cooked chicken,** plus **1 teaspoon grated raw onion** and **¼ teaspoon poultry seasoning.** Serve chicken fritters with chicken gravy, or for sauce, use 1 can undiluted condensed cream of chicken or cream of mushroom soup, heated.

Clam Fritters

Use 1 pint raw clams, drained, and chopped or put through meat grinder. Blend with clams, if desired, 1 tablespoon lemon juice, 1 tablespoon melted butter, 1 teaspoon grated raw onion, before adding dry ingredients. To give fritters a more pronounced clam flavor, you may use clam liquor in place of milk, if desired. Serve with celery sauce (p. 250), deviled sauce (p. 249), or mock Hollandaise sauce (p. 250).

Oyster Fritters

Make like clam fritters, substituting 1 pint raw oysters, drained, then chopped or put through meat grinder, instead of clams.

FRITTER VARIATIONS — FRUIT

(*Follow Master Recipe #18, Fritters, page 213, using any fruit below as the "solid."*)

Apple, pineapple, or peach fritters are delicious served with pork, ham, tongue . . . instead of a serving of potatoes. Or, fruit fritters may be sprinkled with sugar, while still hot, and served as a dessert.

Apple Fritters

Use 1 cup pared, cored, diced apples, blended with ¼ teaspoon nutmeg and ¼ teaspoon cinnamon.

Pineapple Fritters

Use 1 cup drained pineapple tidbits, or drained crushed pineapple.

Banana Fritters

Use 1 cup diced bananas.

Peach Fritters

Use 1 cup well-drained, diced, canned peaches, or 1 cup pared, diced fresh peaches.

CHAPTER XX

You Can Make Waffles, Griddle Cakes, Popovers

METHOD FOR: *Main-Dish or Dessert Waffles and Griddle Cakes, "No-Beat" Popovers*

BASIC PRINCIPLES

These batters are first cousins to muffin batter (Chapter XVIII) and first cousins to each other. They are all concoctions of eggs, shortening, flour, salt, and some liquid (usually milk); to some, sugar is added; to some, baking powder. All the batters are soft, and should be "light."

The *difference* between these first cousins (as between people) results only from the slightly different proportions of ingredients used . . . and from the different ways of treating them (that is, cooking them). And, as among people, those slight differences create, in the end, surprisingly and delightfully different results. So keep to the recipes here, for best results.

MASTER RECIPE #19
WAFFLES

(Makes 6 large waffles; ½ recipe is ample for 2 persons)

Sift together into bowl
    1¾ cups flour

> 3 teaspoons double-acting baking powder
> ½ teaspoon salt
> 2 teaspoons sugar

Omit sugar when making corn, cheese, or other nonsweet waffles; but use sugar for fruit waffles, and increase sugar for dessert waffles; see under Variations.

In separate bowl, with rotary beater, beat vigorously

> 2 eggs

Add to eggs

> 1¼ cups milk (for ½ recipe use ½ cup plus 2 table-spoons)
> ⅓ cup (6 tablespoons) melted butter, salad oil, or vegetable shortening

Blend dry ingredients into egg mixture, mixing only until all flour is dampened; ignore lumps.

To cook. Have waffle iron hot, but don't grease it. Some waffle irons have indicators to tell you when iron is hot enough to use; if yours has no indicator, you may use this old trick: put 1 teaspoon water inside waffle iron when turning on the current. Close the waffle iron. When there is no more steam forthcoming, iron is hot enough to use.

How much batter to use, per waffle. Great sorrow will be yours, if you let batter overflow waffle iron. Start by putting 2 *tablespoons batter* in the center of each of the 4 sections of a waffle space; if more batter is needed, to fill it out, add a little more. Batter should spread itself out between the upright points, making a thin layer. Remember, it will puff up during cooking.

When done. Waffles, when done, are puffed up, dry, and light golden brown. Lift out of iron with fork, and place on hot plate. Serve with butter and maple syrup, or with pan-broiled sausages, or cooked bacon, for breakfast. For luncheon or supper, serve with creamed ham or chicken, creamed mushrooms, or fried chicken, or baked ham.

NOTE: Never wash waffle iron. Scrape off scraps with stiff brush.

WAFFLE VARIATIONS

(Follow Master Recipe #19, Waffles, page 216, making changes as noted below.)

Blueberry Waffles

Increase sugar to 2 tablespoons. Before cooking, fold into batter 1 cup washed, well drained, fresh blueberries.

Corn Waffles

Omit sugar. Just before cooking, stir into batter 1 to 1½ cups drained canned or cooked kernels of corn. If batter is too thick to spread nicely in waffle iron, add another tablespoon or two of milk. Try corn waffles, in place of potatoes, with chicken or ham dinners; serve with maple syrup.

Cheese Waffles

Omit sugar. With milk, add 1 cup grated sharp American cheddar cheese. Serve with sausages, or serve waffles topped with creamed ham, creamed vegetables, or creamed smoked beef.

Chocolate Waffles

Melt 2 squares (2 ounces) baking chocolate over pan containing hot water; then remove from heat and cool. Mix Master Recipe, Waffles, increasing sugar to ⅓ cup. Add melted chocolate with the melted shortening. Serve chocolate waffles topped with sweetened whipped cream, rum- or brandy-flavored if desired; see page 408; or ice cream.

Ginger Waffles

Make batter for **gingerbread** (p. 420), or use packaged gingerbread mix, prepared according to package directions, as batter for waffles. Serve with sweetened whipped cream.

MASTER RECIPE #20
GRIDDLE CAKES

(Makes 15 to 18 griddle cakes, 3 inches in diameter)
Sift together into bowl

1½ cups flour
2½ teaspoons double-acting baking powder
¾ teaspoon salt
1 to 3 tablespoons sugar

(Use 1 tablespoon sugar for nonsweet griddle cakes; 3 tablespoons sugar for fruit griddle cakes.)

In separate bowl, beat well with rotary beater:

2 eggs

Add to eggs:

1¼ cups milk
3 tablespoons melted butter, salad oil, or vegetable shortening

Combine dry and liquid ingredients; beat with a few quick strokes, just until all flour is dampened; ignore lumps.

Batter may be made several hours — even a day — ahead of time, if kept stored in covered jar or other container in refrigerator.

To prepare griddle. If you have an electric griddle, read manufacturer's directions as to whether griddle should be greased, or not; some are made of highly polished material, to which batter never sticks, provided the batter itself contains the usual amount of shortening. An electric griddle is hot enough to begin cooking on when a few drops of water, sprinkled on it, dance around on the surface.

If you have a cast iron or cast aluminum griddle, meant to be used over surface burner of stove, keep heat under it only moderate. Excessive heat makes griddle cakes burn before they cook through. Such a griddle must be greased before each lot of griddle cake batter is put on it. To grease: use a brush with a handle; dip brush in **melted shortening**, and brush it lightly over entire surface of griddle.

Pouring on the batter. Batter may be poured from a pitcher, or may be ladled onto griddle by tablespoon. Allow 1 to 2 tablespoons batter per cake (cakes swell and become larger, as they cook). If batter does not form itself into a round shape, spread it to shape by using back of tablespoon.

To cook. Cook cakes, without turning, until batter has puffed up, become bubbly, and underneath side of cake is browned. Then turn cake, with pancake turner; cook other side until brown. Serve at once, with butter and maple syrup, or a favorite jelly; or, if you prefer to wait until you have several stacks of cakes, pile one on top of another, with a lump of butter between each cake, keeping them on a warm plate, in a warm place, until you have sufficient cakes cooked. Griddle cakes must be *hot* to be good.

Griddle cakes are particularly good with pan-broiled sausages, or strips of crisp bacon, or slices of fried ham.

GRIDDLE CAKE VARIATIONS

(Follow Master Recipe #20, Griddle Cakes, page 219, making changes noted below.)

Apple Griddle Cakes

Add a few dashes cinnamon with the flour. Just before cooking, fold into batter 1 cup finely chopped tart apples (peeled and cored). Very good with sausage, or pork, or ham.

Blueberry Griddle Cakes

Increase sugar to 2 tablespoons. Just before cooking, fold into batter 1 cup washed, well-drained blueberries. A heavenly summer breakfast, with syrup and butter.

Buckwheat Cakes

Omit white flour; substitute 1¼ cups unsifted buckwheat flour. Reduce sugar to 1 teaspoon. Good with sausage, bacon, ham, and of course, syrup.

Corn Griddle Cakes

Fold into batter just before cooking **1 cup canned or cooked kernel corn,** well drained. Or use only ¾ **cup white flour,** and add ¾ **cup yellow corn meal.** Serve with bacon, syrup.

MASTER RECIPE #21
"NO BEAT" POPOVERS

(Makes 6 to 8 popovers)

This is the quickest, most wonderful way to make popovers . . . and though they get none of the usual long beating, they come out light and high. Try it.

Break into a bowl

2 eggs

Add to eggs

1 cup milk
1 cup flour
½ teaspoon salt

Beat well with spoon, but quickly, and disregard lumps. Fill greased popover pans, or custard cups ¾ full. Place pans in *cold* (yes, cold) oven; and at once turn heat on, setting thermostat for 450° or very hot.

Bake 30 minutes, *without peeking.* (Opening doors may make popovers fall.)

Remove immediately from pans when done, rush to table, and enjoy!

CHAPTER XXI

You Can Make Bread and Rolls

METHOD FOR WHITE BREAD MAKES: *Raised Rolls, Parker House Rolls, Cloverleaf Rolls, Finger Rolls, Bowknots or Twists, Snails, Butterhorns or Crescents*
   With trimmings, makes: Poppy Seed Rolls, Salt Sticks
   With filling, makes: Pinwheels, Buns
   With slightly varied ingredients, makes: Currant Bread, Date Bread, Raisin Bread, or Raisin-Nut Bread, Fruit-Nut Bread, Whole Wheat Bread, Rye Bread, Bran Bread, Buns and Loaves made with Sweet Dough, Christmas Coffee Ring

Yeast dough is simple to make, and really fun. We give here only two basic doughs. One is the dough for *plain bread and rolls.* The other is *sweet dough,* made almost the same way, but used for fancy buns, fruit loaves, and coffee cakes.

Either dough is so easy to mix, many a country youngster makes it without supervision; and so can you!

Mixing either dough takes about 15 minutes. Add a few minutes more for kneading. Then you can go off and entertain yourself for an hour or so, until dough has doubled its bulk. (The yeast does this; you don't have to do anything.)

Then you come back, punch dough down, shape it into loaves or rolls or whatever, and place it in pans. Again you can go entertain yourself an hour or so, until bread doubles.

So finally you bake it — which is no trick at all, since bread is the simplest of all things to bake; it is in no danger of falling like a cake, and scarcely needs watching at all. Rolls bake in 12 to

15 minutes; loaves in 40 to 50 minutes; coffee rings in 30 to 40 minutes.

It's so easy . . . try it! I promise you, everyone will think you're terrific.

BASIC PRINCIPLES

In all yeast breads, it is the yeast which is the leavening (makes the dough rise). Otherwise, your ingredients are all very simple things: flour, salt, shortening, liquid.

Consider the yeast carefully, since it is that which makes your bread a success. Yeast is *a live plant,* which *grows* when in a proper environment. To grow, it needs sugar to feed upon; therefore even a bread which we do not consider sweet must contain some sugar. Also, to grow, yeast needs a *continuous moderate warmth* from the moment you start using it until bread is baked. The required temperature is 85° to 90° — the warmth of a good warm summer day. Remember that, from the moment you first dissolve your yeast in water. Make sure the water is *warm* (moderately warm to your finger; not hot). The liquid you add later must also be *warm* (not hot). When dough is placed to rise, bowl must be covered, and placed in a *warm* place, but never over direct heat of stove or radiator; and never in a draft. *Too much* heat will turn your dough sour, and kill the yeast. *Too cold* an environment, or drafts, chill and paralyze the yeast so it cannot rise. This sounds complicated, but it is not, really; it only means using moderately warm liquids, and finding a good nook out of drafts, in a moderately warm kitchen, to place the bowl. If the day is wintry, blizzardy, and your kitchen drafty, give the bowl extra warm covering, and place it in the warmest spot not over direct heat; and you may have to allow double the usual time for the dough to overcome the chilly air and rise to double its bulk. On a very hot summer day, dough may rise so quickly that it doubles its bulk in less than usual time. But if you help it to keep the right temperature, it will perform beautifully for you.

The only other important point is kneading. This is not hard at all, once you get the knack; if you know someone who makes bread, ask her to show you, for it is very simple. Kneading is important both to mix all ingredients thoroughly and evenly, and to press out any large air or gas bubbles formed by the growing yeast, for these large bubbles would result in bread full of holes.

Proper temperature, adequate kneading, and being sure to let the dough double in bulk in each rising are all the tricks there are to making wonderful bread; so try it.

MASTER RECIPE #22
YEAST BREAD AND ROLLS

The recipe we give here serves for *all plain white bread and rolls,* and can be adapted to making breads with dark flour. (See Variations for Dark Loaves, page 232.)

This recipe makes 2 *loaves,* 1 pound each. Or it makes *30 to 60 rolls,* depending on size of rolls. Or it will make *one 1-pound loaf, plus a good panful of rolls.* Make entire quantity of dough; it hardly pays to make less; and as noted below, you can store in refrigerator any part you do not wish to bake today.

This is a *"refrigerator dough."* This means (1) you can mix the dough, knead it, and store all of it away in your refrigerator for several days, if desired, taking it out only when you wish to shape and bake your bread and rolls; with such a recipe even a business woman can have her dough all ready ahead of time, and produce rolls during the hour or hour and a half when she is getting dinner. Or (2) you can mix the dough, knead it, store *half* in the refrigerator for another day, and prepare the second half for baking at once. Or (3) if you are going to bake the entire amount of dough right now, you can omit the extra yeast and extra sugar from the recipe, as noted therein. The extra yeast and sugar are provided only in case some part of the dough is going to be refrigerated; for once dough has been chilled, it needs both extra yeast and extra sugar to help it come to life and start rising properly.

Step 1. *Mixing dough.* Measure in measuring cup

½ **cup warm water**

Stir in

2 **packages yeast** (use only 1 package if none of dough
is to be refrigerated)

Let stand about 5 minutes, until yeast softens.

Meanwhile, in a saucepan, *scald* (do not boil, but heat just
until tiny bubbles show around edge of pan)

1½ **cups milk**

(Or substitute part milk, part water; or use part evaporated
milk, part water; or in a pinch, you can use only water. Old-
timers used water potatoes had been boiled in, as this helps keep
bread moist.)

Remove scalded milk from heat, and stir into it

2 **tablespoons lard or vegetable shortening** (lard gives
the true old-fashioned flavor)

4 **tablespoons sugar** (reduce to 2 tablespoons if none of
dough is to be refrigerated)

2 **teaspoons salt**

Cool above liquid to *lukewarm;* then mix with it the dissolved
yeast.

Pour liquid into large bowl containing

3 **cups all-purpose flour**

Stir mixture with spoon, adding as much more flour as needed
to make a firm ball of dough which leaves the sides of the bowl;
this (depending on absorbency of flour you are using) will be

2 **to 3 cups flour**

Turn dough out onto large bread board, lightly sprinkled with
flour.

Step 2. *Kneading.* Flour your hands. Shape dough into a ball.
Double ball of dough over on itself, like a folded wallet. With
heels of palms, press folded dough together; rock it together with
palms, until it sticks together. Turn dough opposite way, and fold
it double again from opposite direction; again rock it back and

forth with heels of palms until it stays together. Flour hands and board again as often as required to keep dough from sticking; and keep folding and rocking dough, from one direction, then another, until dough becomes a rather firm, shiny ball, which looks satiny and feels elastic. This takes about 6 to 8 minutes.

If planning to store any of the dough in refrigerator, now is the time to do it. Shape into a separate ball the portion you wish to store; coat ball lightly with **butter or vegetable shortening**; wrap ball tightly in waxed paper; put it in a bowl with cover; store it in refrigerator. It keeps for days. When you wish to bake it, remove dough from refrigerator, and begin with Step 4, Punching down (when dough has been refrigerated, you omit Step 3).

But for any dough you wish to bake today, continue right now to Step 3.

Step 3. First rising. Coat ball of kneaded dough lightly, all over, with **butter or vegetable shortening**. Place it in a large, well-greased bowl at least double size of dough. Cover bowl with clean towel, board, or other cover. Place in warm (85°–90°) place, out of drafts, but not over direct heat. Leave it there 1 hour or more, until dough has doubled in bulk.

Step 4. Punching down. When dough has doubled, flour your fist and punch it down hard, right into center of ball of dough in bowl. (This is fun, especially if you feel angry at someone, but its real purpose is to press out excessive air or gas bubbles from the dough.) Now turn dough out onto lightly floured board, and knead it as in Step 2 for 1 or 2 minutes, to refine texture. (If you wish to add fruit or nuts to dough, now is the time; see Fruit Loaves, p. 231. Otherwise go on to Step 5.)

Step 5. Now shape loaves or rolls. Immediately shape your punched-down dough into loaves or rolls. For loaves, see below. For rolls, see immediately thereafter. Directions for raising in pans and baking are given with each type.

WHITE LOAVES

(*Make Master Recipe #22, Yeast Bread and Rolls, p. 224, to Step 5; then shape two 1-pound loaves, as on p. 227.*)

To shape loaves. After Step 4, p. 226, Master Recipe #22, cut kneaded dough into two halves. Put one half on lightly floured board. With floured rolling pin, roll it to a sheet about 8 inches square. Now fold dough over on itself, from each of two opposite sides toward center, making something like a three-fold wallet. Knead it together in this position. Turn opposite direction, fold it again three times, always with outer edges turned into the center; knead together again. When you have done this four or five times, you will have a firm small loaf. Don't worry if it looks small for the pan; it will rise and fill it, by itself. Place your kneaded loaf in greased loaf pan; then brush over top of loaf some **soft or melted butter.** Cover pan with clean towel; place in warm (85°–90°) place, out of drafts, and not over direct heat, to rise. Do same with other half of dough, making two loaves. Let both loaves rise about 1 hour, or until doubled in bulk. Meanwhile heat baking oven to moderately hot (375°–400°).

To bake loaves. Center pans of bread in oven. Bake at 375°–400° about 40 minutes, or until loaves are nicely browned on top, and slightly withdrawn from sidewalls of pan. If oven is too hot, loaves will be done in 25 to 30 minutes; if too cool, they may take 50 minutes; but as a loaf is quite a large amount of dough, slow, thorough baking is preferable to too hot an oven, which might cook the outside rapidly but leave the inside undercooked. When loaves look done, turn them out from pan onto rack. Examine bottom of loaves; if not cooked to light golden color, put loaves back in pans (no extra greasing needed), and bake 5 or 10 minutes longer. When golden brown all over, turn loaves out of pans at once, onto wire rack. If you like a soft crust, cover loaves lightly with a clean towel, as they cool. If you like a crisp crust, let loaves cool exposed to air. Eat, and rejoice!

ROLLS — VARIATIONS

(*Make Master Recipe #22, Yeast Bread and Rolls, p. 224, to Step 5; then shape dough into any variation of rolls which follows.*)
Quantity: Half the dough of Master Recipe, Yeast Bread and

Rolls, will make 15 to 30 rolls, depending on size. Use remaining ½ dough for loaf of bread, or store in refrigerator.

NOTE: *Leftover rolls* of any type should be stored in covered tin pan, or tightly wrapped in waxed paper, to keep them from drying out. When you wish to serve them again, preheat oven to hot (425°). Place rolls in ungreased cake or pie pan, over which you can invert another pan of same size; or else enclose rolls inside a paper bag, tightly closed; place in oven about 6 to 10 minutes, or just until hot. If rolls are tightly covered during heating, they will not dry out.

Raised Rolls

To shape: There are two ways. At Step 5, Master Recipe #22 (p. 226), you may cut the dough into cubes about 1½ inches square, then roll each cube, between palms, into a small ball. Or instead, roll out your whole amount of dough into a sheet about ¾ inch thick, with floured rolling pin; then, using a floured biscuit cutter, cut out rounds about 1½ inches in diameter. In either case have ready a well-greased flat baking pan, 8 x 8 x 2, or larger if making a large quantity of rolls. Place rolls in greased pan, so they touch each other. Over top of all rolls in pan, brush about ¼ cup soft or melted butter. Then cover pan with clean towel; place in warm (85°–90°) place, out of drafts, until rolls double in bulk, or about 1 hour.

To bake raised rolls, place pan, centered, in preheated hot (425°) oven; bake 12 to 15 minutes, until rolls are golden brown on top and slightly shrunken from sidewalls of pan. Turn out of pans at once, onto rack. Serve at once, loosely enclosed in linen napkin to keep them warm.

Parker House Rolls

At Step 5 (p. 226), Master Recipe, with floured rolling pin, roll dough to sheet ⅓ inch thick. Using a floured biscuit cutter 2 inches in diameter, cut out rounds until all dough is utilized.

(Gather scraps after first cutting; shape into ball and roll out again, to cut more rounds.) With pastry brush, spread top of all rounds with **melted butter**. Now fold each round over, doubled like a wallet, butter inside. Press each roll slightly to make it stay doubled. Place rolls, either touching or ½ inch apart from each other, in greased shallow baking pan. Over tops of all rolls brush **melted butter**. Cover pan with clean towel; place in warm place, out of drafts, to rise about 1 hour or until rolls have doubled in size. Bake in preheated hot (425°) oven 12 to 15 minutes. Turn out at once onto racks.

Tip: make these rolls tiny size (cut them 1 inch in diameter), to fill, after baking, with deviled crab, or lobster, or chicken or ham salad, or cheese spread, as party canapés; and make plenty!

Cloverleaf Rolls

Muffin pans are needed for these, and your finished roll will be as big as your muffin cup. At Step 5, Master Recipe, Yeast Bread and Rolls, p. 226, with sharp knife dipped in flour cut dough to cubes about ¾ inch square. Between palms, shape each cube into a ball. Grease muffin cups. In each muffin cup, place **three** balls of dough, like a 3-leaf clover. Over top of each roll, brush **melted butter**. Cover pan with clean towel; place in warm (85°– 90°) place, out of drafts, about 1 hour, or until rolls double in bulk. Bake in preheated hot (425°) oven 12 to 15 minutes. Turn out on wire rack at once; serve hot.

Finger Rolls

At Step 5, p. 226, Master Recipe #22, with knife cut dough into 2-inch cubes. Roll one cube at a time on floured board, under palm of your hand, until dough elongates like a finger. Place rolls 1 inch apart, on greased baking sheet. Brush **melted butter** over top of rolls. Cover pan with clean towel; place in warm (85° to 90°) place, out of drafts, about 1 hour, or until rolls double in bulk. Bake in preheated hot (425°) oven 12 to 15 minutes, or until golden brown. These may be made extra-large to hold frank-furters; or may be made tiny-size to hold tasty fillings for cock-tail parties.

Bowknots, or Twists

Begin as for finger rolls, but roll each cube of dough under palm until it forms a long "rope" about ⅜ inch thick. Then tie this rope of dough into a square knot, bowknot, or any kind of fancy twisted shape you wish. Place rolls on greased baking sheet, 1 inch apart. Brush tops of rolls with **melted butter.** Cover pan; let rise until rolls double in bulk; bake as for finger rolls.

Snails

Shape as for bowknots, but roll up the elongated rope of dough in ever enlarging circles, to look like a coiled-up snail. Brush tops with **butter,** cover pan, let rise, and bake as for finger rolls.

Butterhorns, or Crescents

At Step 5, p. 226, Master Recipe, with rolling pin, roll dough to circular sheet ¼ inch thick. Brush entire surface of sheet of dough with **melted butter.** Then with sharp knife, cut circular sheet into wedges like pieces of pie, each wedge about 2 inches wide at outer edge of circle. Beginning with outside edge of each wedge, roll the wedge firmly toward the point at center; press rolled dough so it will stay together. Place each roll (point-side underneath) on greased baking sheet. If you wish them to be butterhorns, do not bend them from original rolled-up shape; but if you want them to be crescents, bend each rolled-up roll into a crescent or new moon shape before placing them on greased baking sheet. Brush tops of rolls with **soft or melted butter;** cover pan, let rolls rise 1 hour or until doubled, and bake as for finger rolls.

Poppy Seed Rolls, or Salt Sticks

At Step 5, p. 226, Master Recipe #22, shape bowknots, twists, snails, butterhorns, or crescents, as above. Place rolls on greased baking sheet. Now, in small bowl, mix **1 egg yolk** with **1 table-spoon cold water**; blend well. With pastry brush, brush this egg glaze over tops of rolls. On top of glaze, sprinkle **coarse salt or salt crystals**, or **black poppy seeds**. Cover pans; let rolls rise 1 hour or until doubled; bake as usual in hot (425°) oven 12 to 15 minutes.

Pinwheels

At Step 5, p. 226, Master Recipe, with rolling pin roll dough to oblong sheet about ¼ inch thick. Spread entire surface of sheet of dough with **melted butter**. On top of butter, you may spread any **filling** suggested under quick pinwheels (p. 202) or sweet pinwheel buns (p. 234).

After surface of dough is spread, lift one wide outer edge of oblong sheet of dough, and start rolling it firmly (like a jelly roll) toward opposite edge. Moisten last edge with milk or water on your finger tips, and press roll together so it will stay closed. Now, with sharp floured knife, cut from roll crosswise slices ¾ inch thick. Place slices, cut side down, on greased baking sheet (or if preferred, you may place each slice in a greased muffin cup). Cover pans with clean towel; allow rolls to rise in warm place until doubled in bulk. Bake in hot (425°) oven 12 to 15 minutes.

Pinwheels are a basic form of bun, and are made either with biscuit dough (p. 202) or yeast dough, and with any number of types of filling. There's nothing to prevent your inventing a filling of your own . . . now *is* there?

YEAST BREAD VARIATIONS — FRUIT LOAVES

(Make Master Recipe #22, Yeast Bread and Rolls, p. 224, following all steps through Step 4, Punching down. At that point, when kneading, and just before you shape loaves, knead into dough, for each loaf, the ingredients given below.)

Currant Bread

Knead in **½ cup dried currants** plus **¼ cup sugar.**

Raisin Bread

Knead in 1 cup seedless raisins, mixed with ¼ teaspoon cinnamon and ¼ cup sugar. Add also ½ cup coarsely chopped nutmeats if desired.

Date Bread

Knead in 1 cup pitted, chopped dates.

Fruit-Nut Bread

Knead in ¼ cup dried currants, or seedless raisins, or pitted chopped dates, plus ¼ cup chopped nutmeats (pecans are very good), plus ¼ cup candied orange peel.

To complete loaves. After fruit ingredients are kneaded into dough, shape loaf, let rise, and bake as for plain loaves (p. 226). Before loaf is quite cooled, frost if desired with confectioners' icing.

YEAST BREAD VARIATIONS— DARK-FLOUR LOAVES

When mixing Master Recipe, #22, page 224, Yeast Bread and Rolls, you can make dark loaves by substituting part dark flour for white. Making substitutions below, proceed as usual with Steps 1 to 5 of Master Recipe; then shape and bake as for plain white loaves (p. 226).

Whole Wheat Bread

Omit sugar; substitute 3 tablespoons molasses. Use only 3 cups white flour; add 3 cups whole wheat flour.

Light Rye Bread

Use brown sugar instead of white. Use only 3 cups white flour, leaving dough very soft. Let this rise once (Step 3, p. 226), until doubled. Then stir in 3 cups (about) rye flour; enough to make a stiff dough. Knead thoroughly before shaping into loaves.

Rye Bread with Caraway Seed

Make just like light rye, but reduce sugar to 1 tablespoon. After rye flour has been added, knead in ¼ to ½ cup caraway seeds.

Dark Rye Bread

Make like light rye, but use only 2 cups white flour; this will make unusually soft dough. Let this rise once until doubled (see Step 3, p. 226); then stir in 4 cups (about) rye flour. Knead thoroughly before shaping loaves.

Bran Bread

In Master Recipe, omit sugar; substitute ¼ cup molasses. Use only 4½ cups white flour. Add enough bran to make a stiff dough.

MASTER RECIPE #23
SWEET YEAST DOUGH

This yeast dough — meant for sweet buns, coffee rings, and sweet loaves — is just like Master Recipe, Yeast Bread and Rolls, except that it uses more shortening, more sugar, and adds two eggs; this gives the dough a more cake-like flavor and texture, though it is still bread. Try it once for a coffee ring or some sweet buns; see how good it is!

Like Master Recipe, Yeast Bread and Rolls, this is a *refrigerator dough;* you can store all or part of it in refrigerator until wanted (see remarks under Master Recipe # 22).

This recipe makes the same quantity of dough, also: enough for *2 loaves,* or *30 to 60 buns. One third* of the total amount of dough will make a *coffee ring;* use the rest for something else.

Step 1 Mixing dough.
Measure in measuring cup
    ½ cup warm water
Stir into water
    2 packages yeast (use only 1 package if
        none of dough is to be refrigerated)
Let stand about 5 minutes, until yeast softens.

Meanwhile, in a saucepan, scald (do not boil)
1½ cups milk
(Or substitute part milk, part water; or part evaporated milk, part water.)

Remove scalded milk from heat, and stir into it
¼ to ½ cup shortening
½ cup sugar (reduce to ⅓ cup if none
of dough is to be refrigerated)
2 teaspoons salt

Cool above liquid to *lukewarm;* then mix with it the dissolved yeast. Add also
2 well-beaten eggs
Pour liquids into large bowl containing
3 cups all-purpose flour
Stir mixture with spoon, adding as much more flour as needed to make a stiff ball of dough which leaves sides of bowl, about
2 to 3 cups more flour

Turn dough out onto lightly floured large board. Knead dough, let rise, and punch down as shown in Steps 2, 3, and 4, Master Recipe #22 (p. 225). Then to shape, follow any variation below.

SWEET DOUGH VARIATIONS

Fruited Loaves
After punching down sweet dough (Master Recipe #23), knead into dough any of the fruits suggested for fruited loaves (p. 232). Then shape dough into loaves, let rise, and bake as for any loaf (p. 227). Before loaf is quite cooled, frost with confectioners' icing if desired.

Sweet Pinwheel Buns
After punching down sweet dough (Master Recipe #23), using a floured rolling pin, roll dough to oblong sheet 10 x 14 inches wide ¼ inch thick. Spread with **melted butter**. On top of melted butter, spread any **sweet filling** suggested for quick pinwheels (p. 202),

or try any of the fillings below. After dough is spread with filling, roll sheet of dough up like jelly roll, cut off slices, place in greased pans or muffin cups; cover, let rise, and bake as for pinwheels (p. 231).

Jam Buns. Spread with marmalade or any sweet, thick jam you like. On top of jam sprinkle ¼ cup chopped nut meats, if desired.

Prune Buns. Spread with ½ cup chopped, cooked, pitted and drained prunes, mixed with 1 tablespoon grated orange peel and ¼ cup granulated sugar.

Apricot Buns. Spread with ½ cup chopped, cooked, drained, dried apricots, mixed with 1 tablespoon grated orange peel and ¼ cup granulated sugar.

Filled Coffee Rings

After punching down sweet dough (Master Recipe #23), roll out dough, spread with melted butter, then with a sweet filling, exactly as if making sweet pinwheel buns above. Roll up spread dough firmly, like jelly roll, but do not slice. Now grease a pie plate or layer cake pan. Arrange the long roll of dough like a wreath in the greased pan, stretching roll gently with your hands if necessary to make it long enough so ends join. Moisten both ends of roll slightly with milk or water, and press them together to make roll into a complete circle. Now you are going to cut slashes in the ring, to allow it to spread circular-wise, and to provide steam vents. Take scissors, and make one slash, cutting from any place on the outer edge of ring about ⅓ way in to the center of the ring (do not cut it all the way to center). About 2 inches farther along the outside edge, make another similar slash toward center. Continue until ring is slashed all the way around at 2-inch intervals. (The effect is somewhat like cutting wedges of pie, but not cutting them all the way through to center of dish.)

Cover pan with clean towel; place in warm (85°–90°) place 1 hour or more, until ring doubles in bulk.

In small bowl, beat together 1 egg yolk plus 2 tablespoons milk. Brush this glaze over top of ring before baking.

Bake in moderate (375°) oven about 45 to 55 minutes, or until crust is golden brown and ring feels springy when touched with finger tip. When done, remove to wire rack to cool. Before ring is entirely cool, mix in bowl ½ **cup confectioners' sugar, 2 teaspoons milk,** and ⅛ **teaspoon vanilla;** spread this over top of ring. If desired, you can press into top of frosting while it is still moist some nut meats, or bits of candied fruit, for extra decoration.

Christmas Coffee Ring

Make coffee ring exactly as above, using any desired filling. While frosting is still moist, press into it a holly or poinsettia design made with bits of **candied red cherries** for holly berries or flowers, and **candied citron** for leaves. Add **nuts** also if desired. Something to make the men and boys love Santa! . . . but if you once make it, I promise you, it'll become a tradition! Christmas won't be Christmas without it.

Jack Horner Buns

After punching down sweet dough (Master Recipe #23), shape dough into raised rolls; follow exactly the method given for raised rolls (p. 228). Place rolls in greased pan 1 inch apart. Then press into the center of each roll a small piece of **drained canned peach,** or **pineapple,** or **apricot,** or a **cooked drained prune,** pitted. In a bowl, mix **3 tablespoons sugar** with ½ **teaspoon cinnamon.** Put a bit of the sugar mixture over each piece of fruit. Cover pan with clean towel, let rolls rise until doubled, and bake as for raised rolls.

Orange Rolls

Make as for Jack Horner buns, but instead of fruit, press into each roll a lump of sugar soaked in orange juice. Omit the sugar-cinnamon mixture.

Hot Cross Buns

When mixing Master Recipe #23, sweet dough, add **2 teaspoons cinnamon** with the flour. Continue with all steps listed under Master Recipe #23. After punching down dough, shape like raised rolls (p. 228). Place rolls in greased pan or in greased muffin cups; cover; let rise until doubled. Now, before baking, with scissors make a shallow cross-shaped cut in top of each roll. Brush tops of rolls with 1 egg yolk mixed with 1 tablespoon water. Bake in hot (425°) oven, 12 to 15 minutes. Remove buns to wire rack, to cool. While still warm, fill in the cross-shaped cut with confectioners' icing.

CHAPTER XXII

You Can Make Stuffing

METHOD FOR: *Bread Stuffing, Giblet Stuffing, Egg-Parsley Stuffing, Orange Stuffing, Apple Stuffing, Celery Stuffing, Sausage Stuffing, Chestnut Stuffing, Oyster Stuffing, Apricot Stuffing, Mushroom Stuffing, Cracker Stuffing, Peanut Stuffing, Potato Stuffing*

BASIC PRINCIPLES

Stuffing is wonderful. Everyone loves it. It makes a few pork chops, a simple baked fish, an inexpensive shoulder roast of veal or lamb, into a dinner as savory and festive as a Thanksgiving meal; and as for the turkey — or the Sunday roast chicken — what would they be without the stuffing? The stuffing gives the high flavor, the pungent richness, to the plain, tender meat.

Yet stuffing is only bread crumbs — moistened slightly with water (or stock) — flavored with a little butter, or other tasty fat — and seasoned with a sprinkling of pungent herbs, or by adding some other flavorsome ingredient such as tart apples, oysters, or chestnuts.

Plain bread stuffing (seasoned just with onions and herbs) is so simple a child could make it; and it is good with practically any meat, fish, or fowl. Once you have made this a few times, you can easily handle any other stuffing in this chapter, all of which are little cousins of bread stuffing, and therefore easy, too. To be sure, there exist a few fancy (and seldom used) stuffings, not listed here, which you will come across in magazines and newspapers; later you may try those too. But the kinds given here are the types most people think of, when they speak of "stuffing," and these alone will provide you a proud repertoire for life.

TIPS ON STUFFING

How much to make. Our Master Recipe (p. 241), specifies *2 cups bread crumbs,* and the ingredients to go with them. *This makes 2 cups stuffing . . .* or enough to stuff 4 to 6 chops, or a medium-sized baked fish, or a duck, or to fill the pocket of a boned roast of meat. For a roast chicken of 4 to 6 pounds, however, you will need more: at least *4 to 6 cups crumbs.* For a 10 to 12 pound turkey, you will need still more: *8 to 10 cups crumbs.* For a 30 pound turkey, you may need *12 or more cups crumbs. When multiplying crumb measurement, multiply all other ingredients (except fat) in same proportion.* Fat should be increased somewhat, with each addition of crumbs, but even for the largest turkey, you would not need more than 1 cup fat in the stuffing. To add too much fat will be to make your stuffing greasy.

Type bread to use. White bread, 1 to 3 days old, is best for stuffing. It is neither too hard nor too soft, and its bland flavor makes a good base for the savory seasonings you will add to it. In an emergency you may toss in a piece or two of graham or cracked wheat bread, or even leftover rolls, if rolls are not sweet, nor too hard.

About using crust. A small proportion of bread crust may be included with the crumbs, provided crust is soft, and you flake it into small bits. But if you use too much crust, or crust which is too hard, you will have a hard-textured stuffing, not a fluffy one.

How to crumble bread. If using a whole, unsliced loaf, cut the crust from one long side; then with fork, pry out bits of bread, into a bowl. If using slices of bread, "flake" off small bits, by using thumbnail and forefinger (with clean hands, of course!); but take care not to *mat* the bread as you flake it; for if you squeeze it into tight little wads, you will have a heavy stuffing. All your crumbled bread should be airy, fluffy, when you are through flaking it.

To make stuffing dry or moist. The moisture your stuffing will have, when cooked, depends on three things: (1) how dry the bread was, to begin with; (2) how much water or other liquid you add to the crumbs; (3) how much fat you add. *For an extremely dry, crumbly stuffing,* use bread which is 3 or 4 days old. Add to it all other ingredients specified in Master Recipe, before you add water. Then sprinkle water very lightly over entire mixture, turning mixture with fork as you do so, so that no part of the mixture becomes too wet. Stop adding water when mixture is partly moist, but still crumbly. *For medium-moist stuffing,* use 1-day-old bread. Add to it all other ingredients, before adding water. Then sprinkle water over mixture, as above, turning mixture as you do so, and stopping when mixture forms slightly moist lumps. Never, *never,* add enough water to make mixture soggy, or one wet mass. Remember that once inside the meat or bird, stuffing will become even moister from the fat cooking out of the roasting meat, into the stuffing.

What fat to use. The Master Recipe calls for butter, or other melted fat. Butter, of course, always tastes perfect with bread; but if seasoning in the stuffing is going to be strong and zestful (such as herbs, onions, tart apples) it is quite permissible — even tastier — to use other fats with high flavor, such as sausage fat, bacon fat, chicken fat.

About adding onions. Some people sauté (p. 96) the sliced or chopped onion in the fat, then add both to the bread crumbs. Others do not sauté, but simply add raw onions and fat separately, leaving onions to cook during the roasting period. Sautéing the onions in fat first, however, seasons the fat, and makes it tastier.

Adding egg. Adding a raw egg, when stuffing is otherwise mixed, helps hold all ingredients together, and makes stuffing richer. It can be omitted, if you find yourself "out" of eggs; but *with* egg, it is better.

Pack stuffing loosely. If stuffing is packed too tightly into bird, meat, or fish, it will be heavy, soggy, because it has had no room to expand. Pack it in loosely, allowing a little air space in which stuffing can fluff up.

MASTER RECIPE #24
PLAIN BREAD STUFFING

(Makes 2 *cups stuffing*)

Flake into bits, in a bowl
2 cups bread crumbs
In frying pan, melt
4 tablespoons (¼ cup) butter, or other fat
Sauté in melted fat until golden color
1 medium onion, peeled and sliced
Blend onions and fat into crumbs; then add
¼ teaspoon salt
⅛ teaspoon pepper
¼ teaspoon powdered sage
or
½ teaspoon poultry seasoning
Mix well, to distribute seasonings. Then, while turning mixture over with fork, sprinkle over it
about ¼ cup hot water (or stock)
Stir in last
1 raw egg
Pack stuffing loosely into salted cavity of meat, fish, or bird. Then close opening, by holding skin of both sides together, and pushing a metal skewer through both layers as if skewer were a long pin. Or sew skin together, using strong thread or fine string, threaded through a big-eyed needle. Or insert several toothpicks across the open cut, then lace the toothpicks together with a piece of string (just like lacing a shoe).

STUFFING VARIATIONS

Giblet Stuffing
Sauté (p. 93) in a little hot fat, in frying pan, until nicely browned, the **heart, liver, gizzard** of chicken or turkey. Then cover giblets with water, and simmer until tender. Drain, and chop them. Mix chopped giblets with Master Recipe.

Egg and Parsley Stuffing

Fine with baked fish. In Master Recipe, omit onion. With season-ings, add **2 tablespoons minced parsley.** To completely mixed stuffing, add **2 cups chopped hard-cooked eggs.**

Orange Stuffing

Excellent with duck. In Master Recipe, add with seasonings **1 teaspoon grated orange rind.** Moisten stuffing with **orange juice,** instead of water. If desired, add to finished stuffing **¼ cup diced raw celery.**

Apple Stuffing

Wonderful with pork, fresh ham, duck. In Master Recipe, add **1 teaspoon sugar** plus **¼ cup chopped, tart, peeled, cored apples** for each 2 cups crumbs.

Celery Stuffing

For goose, duck. In Master Recipe, reduce onions and sage or poultry seasoning to about half the usual amount. Instead, add **¼ cup diced raw celery,** plus **¼ teaspoon celery seed,** for each 2 cups crumbs.

Sausage Stuffing

For turkey. In Master Recipe, substitute for butter an equal measurement of mashed **sausage meat** (this contributes needed fat, as well as flavor). Omit sage or poultry seasoning, as sausage is already highly seasoned. Add **2 tablespoons minced parsley** for each 2 cups crumbs, to lighten the stuffing.

Chestnut Stuffing

For turkey. Use edible "French" chestnuts, which may be bought, cooked, in cans . . . or may be purchased uncooked by the pound. If buying the uncooked kind, shake them in heavy buttered pan, over fire for 5 minutes; then shell them. Place shelled nuts in saucepan, in **boiling, salted water;** cook gently about 20 minutes, until tender when pierced with fork. Drain; then with fingertips, remove skins.

Make Master Recipe, Plain Bread Stuffing, omitting onion, sage, poultry seasoning. Add 1 cup cooked, whole chestnuts for each 2 cups crumbs. Moisten stuffing with a little turkey stock, or cream, instead of water.

Oyster Stuffing

For turkey. In Master Recipe, reduce onion to half the usual amount. Omit sage and poultry seasoning, using only **salt, pepper.** For each 2 cups crumbs, add **½ pint raw oysters,** chopped. Instead of using water to moisten, use **oyster liquor** if you have it. Add **1 teaspoon lemon juice.** If desired, add **2 tablespoons chopped parsley** to stuffing.

Apricot Stuffing

In Master Recipe, omit onion, sage, poultry seasoning . . . using only **salt, pepper.** For each 2 cups crumbs add **¼ cup diced raw celery** plus **½ cup chopped, cooked apricots.** Use apricot **juice,** instead of water, to moisten stuffing. Add few drops **lemon juice,** to cut sweetness.

Mushroom Stuffing

In Master Recipe, omit onion, sage, poultry seasoning, using only **salt, pepper.** For each 2 cups crumbs, add **1 cup sautéed** (p. 95) **sliced mushrooms.** Add **1 chopped hard-cooked egg,** if desired. Moisten stuffing with **chicken stock,** or **a little cream,** if not moist enough.

OTHER TYPES OF STUFFING

Cracker Stuffing, Apple Flavor

For duck. Cracker stuffing is a little drier than bread stuffing — therefore excellent in duck, which tends to be fatty. It is made much like bread stuffing. Put **2½ cups cracker crumbs** in fine-mesh strainer. Pour **1 cup hot water** over them, to moisten them;

then drain well. Melt ¼ cup butter; add 1 tablespoon minced onion, and the crumbs. Add ¾ teaspoon salt, ½ teaspoon sage; stir in 2 raw eggs. Blend. Fold in ¼ cup chopped tart apples (no skins or seeds).

Peanut Stuffing

For duck. To 1 cup coarse cracker crumbs, add ½ cup finely chopped peanuts. Moisten with ½ cup heavy cream. Add 2 tablespoons melted butter, few drops onion juice, salt and pepper to taste.

Potato Stuffing

For birds. Flake ⅔ cup bread crumbs. Add 1⅓ cups seasoned mashed potatoes. Mix well. Add 2 tablespoons melted butter, 2 tablespoons diced salt pork (or bacon fat), ½ grated onion. For seasoning, use ½ teaspoon salt, ½ teaspoon sage, pinch thyme. Stir in 1 raw egg. If desired, fold into stuffing ¼ cup minced parsley, for lightness. Or add chopped cooked giblets, as under Giblet stuffing.

SUGGESTIONS FOR USING STUFFING

Stuffing Any Roasted Bird

Sprinkle inside and outside of bird, well, with salt. Then pack cavity loosely with stuffing. If there is a cavity under neck of bird, fill that with stuffing, too. Some people put one type stuffing in the body, another type in the neck. Close openings as directed under Master Recipe, Plain Bread Stuffing. Roast bird as in Chapter VII.

Stuffing Double-Thick Pork Chops

Have butcher cut double-thick pork chops, slicing a pocket in the middle of each, to hold a tablespoonful or two of stuffing. Salt inside and outside of chops. Fill pockets loosely with plain bread stuffing, or apple stuffing. Fasten pockets closed with toothpicks. Place chops in ungreased baking pan, and bake in moderate

(375°) oven 1 to 1½ hours, turning chops over once, so both sides may become thoroughly cooked. Good as a turkey dinner; and very hearty. And just as good cold as hot; try taking them on a picnic supper, when you have a lot of hungry men to feed.

Stuffing Baked Fish

Any moderate-sized (3 to 7 pound) white-meated fish which does not have a great deal of taste by itself (such as cod, haddock, halibut) is given deliciously savory flavor by being baked with stuffing inside. Have market clean fish, and prepare it for stuffing. In fancy restaurants, head and tail of a baked fish are often left on; but you may have butcher cut them off, if preferred. Wipe fish, inside and out, with damp cloth. Sprinkle with salt. Fill pocket with plain bread stuffing, celery stuffing, oyster stuffing, or egg-and-parsley stuffing. Fasten fish together by sticking toothpicks vertically across opening, then lacing the toothpicks together with string. Make 3 or 4 gashes in fish's back, to prevent fish bursting from steam during cooking. Fill these gashes with bits of **butter,** or **bacon.** Place fish on oiled baking dish or pan, and brush top of fish with **salad oil.** Some cooks place a strip or two of **bacon** over top of fish, to prevent its drying out. Bake in hot oven (400°), allowing 12 minutes per pound. Serve fish with parsley sauce (p. 248); egg sauce (p. 249); celery sauce (p. 250); or any variation of Hollandaise sauce (p. 255), thinned down with a little lemon juice.

Stuffing an Inexpensive Roast of Meat, Boned

When buying a fresh ham, or a breast or shoulder roast of lamb, or veal, have butcher bone it, leaving a pocket for stuffing. Pack in loosely plain bread stuffing. Or try apple stuffing in fresh ham. Or try celery stuffing or mushroom stuffing, in lamb or veal. Close opening, and roast meat as in Chapter VI.

Stuffed Ham Rolls

For a quick, inexpensive, yet savory meat course, buy some slices of boiled ham (1 or 2 slices per person). Make plain bread stuffing, or apple, or celery stuffing, or orange stuffing; roll 1 or 2 tablespoons stuffing inside each slice ham, and fasten ham roll closed with toothpick. Place rolls in lightly buttered baking dish or pan. Place in moderate oven (350°) for 15 to 20 minutes, until stuffing is hot; and serve with egg sauce (p. 249); mushroom sauce (p. 249); or mock Hollandaise (p. 250). Garnish with stuffed olives.

CHAPTER XXIII

You Can Make a Sauce, a Gravy, a Cream Soup

METHOD FOR: *White Sauce, Parsley Sauce, Cheese Sauce, Curry Sauce, Egg Sauce, Mushroom Sauce, Deviled Sauce, Horseradish Sauce, Mustard Sauce, Onion Sauce, Mock Hollandaise Sauce, "A la King" Sauce, Newburg Sauce, Chicken Gravy, Brown Gravies, Brown Sauces, Hollandaise Sauce and Variations, Butter Sauces and other sauces for Meat and Fish, Cream Soups*

BASIC PRINCIPLES

White sauce (and all its variations), brown gravies, cream soups, are all made by the same method.

(1) You melt a few tablespoonsful of butter, or other shortening. (2) You stir in a few tablespoonsful of flour, blending to a thick, smooth paste; add salt, pepper. (3) You stir in, slowly, a liquid.

For *white* sauces, the liquid is *milk*.

For *brown* gravies, the liquid is *meat stock*, or *meat juices*.

For *cream soups*, the liquid may be *all milk or cream;* or it may be *part cream, part vegetable liquor, fish liquor, chicken liquor, or whatever you wish your soup to be flavored with.*

Only one warning is needed. To make *smooth, fine-textured* sauce, gravy, or soup, you must blend melted fat and flour until there are *no* lumps. And when adding liquid, you must add it little by little, *stirring constantly*, so no lumps form. And you *must keep* stirring constantly, until sauce thickens.

MASTER RECIPE #25
WHITE SAUCE

(Makes 1 cup sauce; for more cups, multiply entire recipe)

MEDIUM WHITE SAUCE (Proportion for creamed meats, vegetables, or as sauce)	THIN WHITE SAUCE (Proportion for cream soups)	VERY THICK WHITE SAUCE (Proportion for "binder" sauce, for croquettes, meat loaf)
Melt in saucepan, over low heat (but do not brown)		
2 tablespoons butter	1 tablespoon butter	4 tablespoons butter
Stir in, making a smooth paste		
2 tablespoons flour	1 tablespoon flour	4 tablespoons flour
Add		
¼ teaspoon salt dash of pepper	⅛ teaspoon salt dash of pepper	½ teaspoon salt dash of pepper
Stir in, little by little, blending until there are no lumps		
1 cup milk	1 cup milk	1 cup milk

Turn heat to moderate and, stirring constantly, bring sauce gradually to a boil. Then reduce heat, let sauce simmer gently about 10 minutes more, stirring as often as needed. Or put sauce in top of double boiler, over hot water, to finish cooking.

SAUCES MADE
BY VARYING MASTER RECIPE,
MEDIUM WHITE SAUCE

Ingredients or substitutions given below are for *1 cup sauce*, as in Master Recipe. For more cups, multiply.

Parsley Sauce

Add **1 to 3 tablespoons finely chopped parsley** to finished sauce. (Delicious with boiled new potatoes, boiled onions, poached fish.)

Cheese Sauce

To finished sauce, add ⅓ to ½ cup sharp American cheese, grated finely, plus ⅛ teaspoon paprika. Simmer over gentle heat, stirring, until cheese melts in. (Used for macaroni and cheese, many casseroles, or as sauce over ham, chicken, cabbage.)

Curry Sauce

With flour add ½ teaspoon curry powder, 1 teaspoon or more grated raw onion, ⅛ teaspoon paprika. Some cooks add a few flecks of grated ginger root, to make the curry "hotter." (Try quartered hard-cooked eggs, heated in this sauce, served on toast.)

Egg Sauce

For fish. Add ¼ teaspoon paprika to finished sauce, to give it rich color; then fold in 1 or 2 sliced hard-cooked eggs. Simmer until eggs are well heated.

Mushroom Sauce

When melting butter, sauté (p. 95) in it, for 3 or 4 minutes, until tender, ⅓ cup thinly sliced mushroom caps or stems. Add 1 teaspoon grated onion, if desired. Stir in flour, and complete the sauce. Substitute cream for milk, for richer sauce.

Deviled Sauce

When melting butter, sauté (p. 93) in it for 2 or 3 minutes 1 tablespoon grated raw onion. Stir in flour, and complete the sauce. Then add 1 tablespoon finely chopped parsley, 1 tablespoon finely chopped green pepper, ⅛ teaspoon paprika. If desired, add ½ teaspoon prepared mustard. Or 2 or 3 drops Worcestershire sauce. Or 2 tablespoons grated sharp cheese. (Wonderful on ham, fish, eggs; or for use in casseroles.)

Horseradish Sauce

Instead of milk, use ½ milk, ½ veal or chicken stock. Or use 1 cup milk, plus 1 teaspoon bottled meat extract. When sauce is thickened, fold in ½ teaspoon to 2 tablespoons bottled horse-radish, depending on how hot you like the horseradish flavor. Go gently with it; taste and see. If desired, add few drops lemon juice.

Mustard Sauce

When melting butter, sauté in it gently 1 teaspoon grated raw onion. Stir in flour; complete sauce. Then stir in ½ to 1 teaspoon prepared mustard, depending on how hot you want it. Go gently; taste and see. (Excellent for corned beef and cabbage casserole, or on ham.)

Onion Sauce

Simmer ½ cup peeled, thinly sliced onions, in just enough water to cover them, until onions are soft. Then force onions and their cooking liquid through a coarse sieve. In separate saucepan, make medium white sauce; if desired, you may use part milk, part veal or chicken stock, to make up the total 1 cup liquid, for the sauce. After stirring in liquid, add the sieved onions and their liquid. Cook sauce, stirring, until thick.

Celery Sauce

Make like onion sauce, substituting puréed celery and celery liquor for puréed onions and onion liquor.

WHITE SAUCES
THICKENED WITH EGGS

Mock Hollandaise Sauce

Make medium white sauce. Just before serving, stir in 2 egg yolks; then (one at a time) 6 tablespoons butter; then 1 table-spoon lemon juice.

"A la King" Sauce

For each 1½ to 2 cups seafood, turkey, or chicken, make 1 cup medium white sauce. However, instead of milk in sauce, substitute part chicken broth, part cream . . . or part fish liquor, part cream . . . making a tastier liquid. Cook sauce until thickened. Add cooked or canned chicken, turkey or seafood, and heat thoroughly. If desired, add ¼ cup sautéed or canned sliced mushrooms. Cut 8 to 10 long thin strips of canned pimiento, and 8 to 10 long thin strips green pepper; add these and let simmer until flavor blends into sauce. Just before serving, stir into sauce 1 slightly beaten egg yolk, plus 2 to 4 tablespoons sherry.

Newburg Sauce

Your sauce for lobster Newburg and seafood Newburg. To serve 3 or 4, allow 2 cups sauce, plus 2 cups drained, cooked or canned seafood, cleaned and cut to bite size. Newburg mixtures are usually served on triangles of toast, and often accompanied with green peas and potato chips.

Newburg Sauce I — Simple Newburg Sauce. (Makes 1 cup.) In top section of double boiler, placed over moderate direct heat, make Master Recipe, Thin White Sauce (p. 248), but substitute light or heavy cream, instead of milk. Cook sauce until thickened. Add 1 cup prepared seafood. Place pan over lower section of double boiler, containing 1½ inches hot water; place whole double boiler over moderate heat, and cover. Cook until seafood is thoroughly heated, about 10 to 15 minutes. Just before serving, stir in 1 egg yolk, and 2 tablespoons sherry (or 1 tablespoon sherry plus 1 tablespoon brandy). Don't leave out the liquor; it isn't Newburg sauce without sherry or brandy. Cook sauce just 1 or 2 minutes more, so egg yolk may become cooked; then serve on toast.

Newburg Sauce II. Epicures who want a very fancy Newburg sauce, made only with eggs — no flour, can make it this way: In saucepan melt 4 tablespoons butter. Sauté in this butter, for 4 or 5 minutes, 2 cups prepared lobster meat or other seafood. Add 4 tablespoons brandy; with match, set fire to brandy; let it burn until blaze goes out. Remove seafood from heat. Set over pan of hot water to keep warm. In top of a double boiler, beat 3 egg yolks, add 1 cup cream, and cook these gently over hot water, stirring constantly, until cream mixture coats a spoon. Then stir cream mixture slowly into the seafood mixture; add **salt** to taste, and serve at once. Do not cook sauce after combining lobster and cream.

GRAVIES

White Chicken Gravy

Make Master Recipe, Medium White Sauce, but use **chicken stock** as the liquid instead of milk. Or you may use **part chicken stock, part cream.**

Brown Gravies and Sauces

Once you have made a white sauce, you can make a brown one (some versions are called "sauce" and some "gravy"). The method is the same: mixing flour into fat, then stirring in a liquid.

The difference is that in making *brown* sauces, you (1) *Brown* the butter, or other fat. (2) Usually *brown* the onions in this fat before adding flour. (3) *Brown* the flour in this fat. (4) Use a *brown stock* instead of milk.

What is "Brown Stock"? "Brown stock" (in cooking schools) is literally strong *beef* stock or "double boullion," made from beef and beef bones, simmered a long time, and highly seasoned. (See how to make, page 127.)

Substitutes for brown stock. Very good hasty equivalents of brown stock, however, can be made by dissolving 1 or 2 teaspoons concentrated beef extract, or 2 or 3 bouillon cubes, in a cup of boiling water . . . and these are commodities you can always have on the shelf.

Pan drippings. Furthermore, for gravy-making purposes, brown stock can actually be *any* rich, strong-flavored, dark-colored meat juices — such as pan drippings from a roast of beef, lamb, veal, or pork; or juices from oven-broiling or pan-broiling meats. Since pan juices are strongly concentrated in flavor, you may add 1 or more cups boiling water to them, to give you the stock for making gravy.

MASTER RECIPE #26
BROWN GRAVY

(Makes 1 cup gravy)

Brown in saucepan
    2 tablespoons butter (or bacon fat, or melted meat fat)
Brown in this fat
        1 tablespoon grated raw onion
Stir in, making a smooth paste, and cooking *until brown*
        2 tablespoons flour
Add seasonings
        ¼ teaspoon salt
        few grains pepper
Stir in slowly, blending until smooth
        1 cup brown stock (p. 252)
Turn heat to moderate, and stirring constantly, bring sauce to boil. Reduce heat, and simmer, stirring as needed, until thick.

VARIATIONS OF BROWN GRAVY
(BROWN SAUCES)

Follow Master Recipe, Brown Gravy, making following additions or substitutions:

Brown Horseradish Sauce

For roast beef. Make brown gravy, using **pan drippings of** roast beef, plus **water**, as stock. When thickened, add ½ teaspoon **to 1 tablespoon bottled horseradish,** depending on how hot you want the flavor. You may also add ¼ **teaspoon Worcestershire sauce.**

Anchovy Sauce

For steak. Make brown gravy, using **beef stock or pan juices.** When thickened, add **1 or 2 teaspoons anchovy paste.**

Brown Mushroom Sauce

For lamb, veal. Melt **butter**, as for brown gravy. Omit browning onions in it; instead sauté in the butter **¼ to ½ cup sliced mushroom caps or stems**. Cook until mushrooms are brown and tender. Finish just like brown gravy, using **beef, veal, or chicken stock** as liquid.

Orange Sauce

For duck. Make brown gravy, omitting onions. Use **pan drippings** from roasting duck, plus **½ cup orange juice** and **½ cup hot water**, as stock. Before serving, stir in, if desired, **1 tablespoon grated orange rind**, or **1 or 2 tablespoons currant jelly**.

MAYONNAISE–TYPE SAUCES

Some sauces for meat, fish or vegetables are thickened not with flour but with egg yolks. Of these, mayonnaise, Béarnaise and Hollandaise are three popular examples.

Mayonnaise

Mayonnaise (p. 351) may be used cold or heated gently in top of double boiler over hot water. If desired to make it more tangy, stir in **1 tablespoon lemon juice** for **1 cup mayonnaise**.

Sauce Béarnaise

Delicious on steak, roast beef. Make a spicy vinegar mixture by simmering together in saucepan, for about 2 minutes, **2 tablespoons wine vinegar, 3 tablespoons tarragon vinegar, 1 tablespoon water, ½ peeled onion, 1 sprig parsley**. Strain seasonings out of vinegar mixture. Now, in small thick bowl, placed over pan containing hot (not boiling) water, warm **3 egg yolks**, slightly beaten. Into the egg yolks, drop by drop, pour the hot vinegar mixture, stirring constantly, until sauce begins to thicken. Then, 1 tablespoon at a time, add **4 tablespoons butter**, stirring constantly. If sauce becomes *too* thick, you may thin it with **1 or 2 tablespoons hot water**.

MASTER RECIPE #27
HOLLANDAISE SAUCE

(Makes ½ cup, serves 3 to 4)

NOTE: This is a special method — not a variation of white sauce. In top section of double boiler, put

¼ cup butter, all in one piece
2 egg yolks, slightly beaten
1 tablespoon lemon juice

Place over lower section of double boiler, which contains 1½ inches hot water. Place double boiler over low heat; do not let water *boil*. With wire whisk, stir above ingredients constantly, until all butter has melted. Then add

¼ cup butter, all in one piece

Again stir constantly, until butter has melted, and sauce becomes smooth and thickened. Remove from heat *immediately;* and serve at once.

NOTE: If Hollandaise is cooked too fast, or overcooked, it may curdle. If it curdles, beat in boiling water, a few drops at a time, just until sauce becomes smooth again; and use as little water as possible.

Hollandaise is delicious on broccoli, asparagus, poached eggs, poached fish.

HOLLANDAISE VARIATIONS

(*Follow Master Recipe #27, Hollandaise, page 255, adding ingredients as below.*)

Sauce Trianon

Add 2 tablespoons sherry just before removing from heat. Good on boiled lobster or shrimp, or on poached or baked eggs.

Sauce Henriette

Add 1 tablespoon tomato purée and 1 tablespoon chopped parsley before serving. Used for fish.

Sauce Figaro

Make the same as Sauce Henriette, adding **1 teaspoon Worcestershire sauce.** Good on cold roast beef, fish.

Sauce Mousseline

Blend in **½ cup stiffly whipped cream** just before serving.

Anchovy Hollandaise

Stir in **1 teaspoon anchovy paste** before serving.

BUTTER SAUCES

These thin sauces are made with no flour, egg, or other thickening agent. They are of course exceptions to the white sauce method.

Drawn Butter

This is actually only **melted butter,** to serve hot over fish. Melt it slowly; do not cook it.

Lemon Butter

Make drawn butter, stirring in **1 or 2 teaspoons lemon juice** for **⅓ cup melted butter.**

Beurre Noir ("Black Butter")

In saucepan, heat **⅓ cup butter** until lightly *browned,* but not black. Blend in **1 or 2 teaspoons lemon juice,** or **wine vinegar.** Serve hot, on fish.

Parsley Butter

Melt in saucepan **⅓ cup butter.** Stir in **¼ cup finely chopped parsley.** Add **few drops lemon juice.** Good on fish, brains, boiled new potatoes.

Anchovy Butter

Melt in saucepan **⅓ cup butter.** Stir in **2 teaspoons anchovy** paste; more, if desired. Add a few drops lemon juice. Marvelous on steak, or fish.

Mustard Butter

Melt in saucepan ⅓ cup butter. Stir in 1 teaspoon bottled beef extract, plus ½ teaspoon prepared mustard. For fish, ham, roast beef.

Herb Butter

Melt in saucepan ⅓ cup butter. Stir in 1 tablespoon grated onion or chopped chives, 2 tablespoons chopped parsley, plus 1 teaspoon fresh tarragon (tarragon is optional).

OTHER SAUCES FOR MEAT AND FISH

(Note that these sauces are not made according to the white sauce method.)

Almond Sauce ("Sauce Amandine")

To blanch almonds, see page 503.

Melt ⅓ cup butter in small frying pan. Sauté in it ⅓ cup blanched, slivered almonds, until nuts are light golden color. Serve hot over fish or sweetbreads.

Cranberry Sauce

Make this a day or two ahead of time. Buy 1 package (about 1 quart) fresh cranberries. Wash them in cold water; drain. In large saucepan, mix 2 cups sugar with 2 cups water; bring to boil; boil 5 minutes. Now add cranberries, whole. Boil *without stirring* about 5 minutes — or until all cranberries pop open and you see all skins have split. Remove from heat; cool in saucepan. When cooled, turn into fancy mold or a bowl; chill in refrigerator overnight or longer; sauce thickens as it chills. If cooked to just the correct second, sauce will jell firm. If it doesn't, don't worry . . . it will still be thick, tangy, delicious, and the true, old-fashioned cranberry sauce, containing skins and all.

Makes 2½ pounds sauce; serves 8 to 10 people; keeps for days.
Good with roast turkey, chicken, pork; also with baked ham.

Mint Sauce (for lamb)

Dissolve 2 tablespoons sugar in ½ cup vinegar, plus ½ cup
boiling water. Pour this mixture over ⅓ cup chopped or crushed
mint leaves (leaves must be cut or crushed to let flavor come out).
Let leaves and vinegar mixture steep ¾ hour. Strain out leaves.
Chill sauce. Or serve warm.

Raisin Sauce (for tongue, ham)

Mix together ½ cup brown sugar, ½ tablespoon flour, ¼ cup
seedless raisins, 1 teaspoon prepared mustard. Add ¼ cup vinegar mixed with 1¾ cups water. Bring to boil, then turn heat low
and cook gently, covered, until raisins are fat, and sauce is syrupy.
Serve warm on ham.

MASTER RECIPE #28
CREAM SOUP

(Serves 2 to 3)

There are so many wonderful and inexpensive canned creamed
soups in the market that we are not going to give recipes for them
all here.

However, if you can make a white sauce, you can make a cream
soup — utilizing leftover or especially purchased:

(1) Cooked or canned vegetables, and their liquor.

(2) Cooked or canned seafood, and its liquor.

(3) Cooked or canned chicken or turkey, and its broth.

Make twice the Master Recipe, Thin White Sauce, using 2
tablespoons butter, 2 tablespoons flour, ¼ teaspoon salt, but stir
in only 1 cup milk, or cream, or evaporated milk.

For remaining cup of liquid stir in one of the following as a
flavoring liquid.

1 cup liquor from cooked or canned vegetable (peas, celery, asparagus, corn, tomatoes, mushrooms, or whatever desired)

or

1 cup fish liquor from cooked or canned seafood (shrimp, lobster, clams, oysters)

or

1 cup broth from cooked or canned chicken or turkey

NOTE: If you do not have at hand an entire cup of your flavorful liquid, make up the lacking amount by adding milk.

Cook soup, stirring, until thickened; then add, if desired

½ to 1½ cups flaked, diced or puréed * cooked or canned vegetable, seafood, chicken or turkey, matching the liquor used

Heat soup thoroughly. Taste. If flavor seems flat, season with

salt

celery salt

1 teaspoon grated raw onion

1 tablespoon minced parsley

If already too salty from fish liquor, stir in a little more milk or evaporated milk; the addition of milk reduces saltiness.

CREAM SOUP VARIATION

Bisque

Make as for cream soup, but when making thin white sauce, stir in 2 cups cream. Use *not over 1 cup* vegetable, fish, or fowl liquor. Chop very fine, or purée (see above) any solid ingredient being added. Adjust seasoning. Just before serving, stir in if desired **1 raw egg,** slightly beaten, for richness. To shrimp or lobster bisque, add **1 or 2 tablespoons sherry** just before serving.

* NOTE: To purée any cooked or canned vegetable, drain it, and force the solid through a sieve.

CHAPTER XXIV

What to Do with Eggs

METHOD FOR: *Eggs Cooked in Shells, Deviled Eggs, Creamed Eggs, Poached Eggs, Fried Eggs, Scrambled Eggs, Shirred Eggs, Omelets, Soufflés, and many Variations. For other uses of eggs, see end of chapter.*

SOME DEFINITIONS

For the benefit of those who may not yet have even a nodding acquaintance with egg cookery, a few definitions:

To crack an egg. Holding egg by one end, in left hand, and holding sharp knife in right hand, give egg one sharp crack, with knife, straight across center of the shell, thus dividing egg's length in two. If crack is *sharp,* egg shell will break evenly; if crack is dull, shell will only crumble, or make a jagged break. Similarly, you may give the egg one sharp crack against sharp edge of a frying pan, or of a mixing bowl, with same result. Be sure to have handy something for the egg to slide into; it comes out fast!

To "separate" an egg. Surprisingly, this term confounds many people. (A woman I know had a foreign-born girl helping her, whom she was trying to teach to cook. The lady told the girl to get two eggs out of the refrigerator and separate them, preparatory to making a cake. The girl obediently got two eggs out of the refrigerator. She put one egg in the kitchen closet; the other on the window sill. Then she protested to the lady that she didn't see what help it had been, to separate them!)

"Separating" an egg means dividing the yolk (intact, without breaking it) from the white. This is done when preparing to make any dish which requires *egg whites only,* or *egg yolks only,* or when yolks and whites are to be separately beaten.

Eggs separate most easily when they have just come from the refrigerator and are well chilled.

To separate an egg, place a funnel with a small end over a cup. Crack one egg at a time, holding egg over the large opening of the funnel. The whole egg will slip out of the shell into the funnel, but the yolk will remain in the funnel and the white will slip through the small end of the funnel into the cup.

If you have no funnel, you can do it another way. Have two bowls in front of you. Crack egg shell cleanly in half, but tip cracked egg at once up on end, before pulling shell apart. Now pull off the top half of cracked shell. Yolk will remain in lower part of shell; egg white will spill out into one of the bowls. But not *all* the white will come out. So now tip the yolk over into the other half shell, which you hold like a cup to receive the yolk. More white will slip out. It may be necessary to slip the yolk back and forth, from one half shell to the other, several times, to get out all the white; and the trick is not to break the yolk as you do this. For if even a drop or two of yolk gets into the whites, the fat content in the yolk will prevent the whites from beating properly. When all the white has been separated, the yolk goes into the second bowl.

To beat eggs. Eggs may be beaten to different degrees, according to the use which the eggs are intended for.

To beat for scrambled eggs or custard. Whole eggs are beaten with fork, or whisk, or rotary beater, just enough to break the yolks and blend yolks with whites.

To beat for omelet. For a true French omelet, eggs are beaten as above, merely to break yolks and blend. But some cooks like to beat the eggs until lemon-colored, frothy and full of air bubbles, thus making a fluffier omelet. Some people even separate the eggs, beating whites until they stand up in soft peaks, and beating yolks until thick and lemon-colored; then combine the two.

To beat yolks separately. When this is required in a recipe, it means to beat the yolks with rotary beater until they become thick and lemon-colored, from incorporation of air bubbles. *Yolks beat best when they are at room temperature.*

To beat whites separately. When this is required in a recipe, it means to beat the whites with rotary beater (or with electric mixer at moderate to high speed) until egg whites will stand up in definite peaks, but are still moist and shiny-looking. Don't beat until they become dry, or they will collapse when cooked. *Egg whites beat best, and attain greatest volume, when they are at room temperature before being beaten.* The object of beating egg whites, at any time, is to incorporate air, and to provide an airy-light texture to other ingredients used with the eggs, as in angel food, or a soufflé, or a meringue, or a boiled frosting.

BASIC PRINCIPLES

Eggs, by whatever method cooked, should always be cooked *gently.* Cooking fast, by high heat, turns them rubbery, entirely changing the light delicate texture which is one of the charms of egg dishes. If cooking eggs in their shells, water should not be bubbling fiercely, but kept just below the boiling point. When frying, fat should not be hot enough to smoke, nor to make eggs sputter or snap while cooking. When scrambling, pan should be only warm, not very hot. When baking eggs, oven heat should be slow to moderate (not over 350°) and sometimes, for extra "insulation" the dish containing eggs is placed in a shallow pan of hot water, as when making baked custard (p. 388).

Do use as fresh country eggs as you can obtain, especially for eggs cooked in shells, poached, or scrambled eggs, where a delicate flavor is the very essence of the enjoyment. And do use butter, to scramble or fry eggs in, or to coat an omelet pan. Some people like bacon fat for frying eggs, but the combination of fresh butter and fresh eggs is one of the heavenly tastes of this world, not to be missed if you can help it.

Eggs, properly cooked, are not only easily digested, but light on the stomach; and in addition to their high protein content they contain so many other elements of nutrition that doctors now debate whether it is milk or eggs which would be the one most nearly complete food, if only one food were allowed us. So serve eggs often; learn to use them in many ways.

MASTER RECIPE #29
EGGS COOKED IN THEIR SHELLS

Eggs cooked in their shells are put into a saucepan containing enough water to more than cover eggs; and this water may be at boiling point, or may be cold, when you start the eggs cooking. The method differs, however, according to temperature of water, since eggs started in hot water will obviously cook faster. We give both methods; you take your choice.

Hot water method. If you begin your eggs cooking in water at boiling point, you will be able to gauge the doneness of the eggs by precise timing. This is therefore the better method for families who are fussy about the exact shade of hardness or softness they wish in their eggs. It has one handicap, however. Eggs cannot be taken from refrigerator in the morning and immediately lowered into boiling water without danger of the shells cracking. To get around this danger, do one of two things:

(1) Remove eggs from refrigerator early enough so they may come to room temperature before you begin cooking them; or (2) With pin or needle, prick one hole in large end of egg shell; this allows air from inside the egg to escape, and shell will not crack.

To use the hot water method, see Time Table (p. 264), for gauging doneness of eggs.

Cold water method. Unless shells are weak or defective, they do not crack when started in cold water. Place eggs in saucepan. Cover with cold water. Cover saucepan. Place over moderate heat and bring water to a real boil.

For soft-cooked eggs, remove eggs from water as soon as water has boiled.

For medium-soft eggs, leave eggs in hot water, covered, *but not over heat,* for 3 to 5 minutes more.

For hard-cooked eggs, leave eggs in hot water; keep water hot (over lowest heat) but *not boiling,* for about 25 minutes more.

TIME TABLE FOR EGGS
COOKED IN SHELLS

Type Egg	Texture of Egg	Time if Begun in Hot Water
Coddled	Entire egg soft and creamy-textured	Heat 1 qt. water; bring to hard boil; then remove from heat. At once put eggs in hot water. Let them stand in hot water (not over heating unit) 10 minutes. Crack egg, turn egg into egg cup.
Soft-cooked	Yolk very soft, white partly cooked	Heat to boiling enough water to cover eggs completely. Put eggs in water; keep water just below boiling point; take eggs out at end of 3 minutes.
Medium-cooked (1)	Yolk very soft, but white cooked	Same as soft-cooked, but take eggs out at end of 4 minutes
(2)	Yolk soft, but white cooked firm	Same as soft-cooked, but take eggs out at end of 5 minutes
(3)	Yolk partly set, white cooked firm	Same as soft-cooked, but take eggs out at end of 6 minutes
Hard-cooked	Yolk and white both cooked firm	Same as soft-cooked, but take eggs out at end of 20 minutes

To shell hard-cooked eggs. As soon as hard-cooked eggs are through cooking, pour off hot water, and run cold water over them. Cold water not only makes them easier to handle, but helps prevent discoloration of yolks. Crack egg shell into many fine cracks, by knocking egg against hard surface, like table top or porcelain sink; or by rolling egg underneath palm of hand, on a hard table top. The fine bits of shell will adhere to the skin or membrane inside the shell, and peel off easily.

Uses for hard-cooked eggs. The classic, of course, is the picnic egg, well sprinkled with salt and pepper. But hard-cooked eggs are also a basic ingredient in many attractive "made" dishes, especially suitable for luncheons and suppers. (See Master Recipes for Deviled Eggs, below, and Creamed Eggs, p. 266.)

MASTER RECIPE #30
DEVILED EGGS

Hard-cook (see Time Table, p. 264); then shell
6 eggs
Cut eggs in halves, lengthwise or crosswise; carefully remove the yolks to bowl. (Take care not to damage the whites.)

Crumble yolks fine, with tines of fork; then season them with
salt

pepper

1 teaspoon French dressing

enough **mayonnaise** or **cooked salad dressing** to make yolks into a thick paste

If you like spicy eggs, stir in also
½ teaspoon grated onion

¼ teaspoon prepared mustard

2 or 3 drops Worcestershire sauce

(If desired, stir in with yolk mixture, any *one* of following for variety: bits of ground, cooked ham, or corned beef; bits of well-drained sardines, or herring, freed of bone; bits of ground, cooked, chicken livers; bits of cooked bacon; bits of cooked or canned shrimp or lobster; ¼ teaspoon anchovy paste (go easy — this is strong and salty); cooked mushrooms, chopped fine; finely minced fresh herbs — parsley, chervil, tarragon.)

Heap well-seasoned yolk mixture back into whites. Garnish with
dash of paprika

If desired add a
pinch of minced parsley

for color. Chill before serving.

DEVILED EGG VARIATIONS

Deviled Eggs in Aspic

Make deviled eggs, as above. Arrange them in 1 inch deep dish. Over them pour **Master Recipe, Aspic,** chicken or meat flavor (p. 377). Chill in refrigerator 2 to 3 hours, or until firm. To serve cut gelatine into squares; arrange squares on crisp **lettuce;** top with **mayonnaise.** If desired, drained cooked or canned asparagus tips may be included with the prepared eggs before adding liquid aspic.

Deviled Eggs in Cheese Sauce

Make deviled eggs. Arranged them in shallow baking dish. Over top, pour **cheese sauce** (p. 249). Sprinkle top with **paprika.** Bake in moderate oven (350°) 15 to 20 minutes, until well heated.

MASTER RECIPE #31
CREAMED EGGS

Hard-cook (see Time Table, p. 264); then shell
6 eggs
Cut into halves, or quarters, or slice them.
Now make
2 cups medium white sauce (p. 248)
When sauce has cooked, add eggs; heat 10 to 15 minutes, or until eggs are thoroughly hot. Serve on triangles of toast, or on a bed of hot rice. Garnish with paprika, minced parsley.

CREAMED EGG VARIATIONS

(*Make Master Recipe #31, Creamed Eggs; treat eggs as below.*)

Creamed Eggs with Ham

When adding eggs to white sauce, add also **½ cup diced or ground cooked ham.** (Or use corned beef, or canned luncheon meat.)

Creamed Eggs with Shrimp

When adding eggs to white sauce, add also ½ cup or more whole or broken, cleaned (p. 169) shrimps, cooked or canned, drained of liquor. Delicious served on hot rice.

Creamed Eggs with Mushrooms

(1) When adding eggs to white sauce, add ½ cup sautéed or canned mushrooms, whole or sliced. Or (2), instead of white sauce, use mushroom sauce (p. 249), or use 1 can undiluted condensed cream of mushroom soup to moisten the eggs.

Creamed Eggs with Leftover Cooked White Fish

When adding eggs to white sauce, add also ½ cup or more leftover cooked white fish, flaked, plus 2 tablespoons minced parsley, 1 tablespoon minced green pepper, ½ teaspoon grated onion.

Creamed Eggs with Dried Smoked Beef

When adding eggs to white sauce, add also ½ cup or more dried smoked beef, cut to bite size.

Creamed Eggs with Chicken Livers

When adding eggs to white sauce, add also 2 or more sautéed (p. 93) chicken livers, chopped. You may also add cooked or canned mushrooms, if desired.

Creamed Egg Casseroles

Combine in baking dish 1 cup cooked rice or noodles, 1 cup cooked or canned diced ham (or shrimp, fish, chicken livers, or other tasty meat), plus 1 Master Recipe, Creamed Eggs. If desired, add 2 tablespoons minced parsley, or minced green pepper. Or add cooked peas. Top with crumbs (p. 143). Bake in moderate oven (350°) about 20 minutes, or until crumbs are browned and contents of dish hot.

Endless varieties of casseroles can be made with creamed eggs; you may put together any foods which would be good if served as a side dish with creamed eggs. For a casserole with little starch, try this: Arrange pieces of **cooked ham**, or **corned beef**, alternately with **cooked or canned asparagus tips** (drained), in a shallow casserole. Cover top with **creamed eggs**. Over creamed eggs, sprinkle a thin layer of **bread or cracker crumbs**. Dot crumbs with **butter**. Bake in moderate oven (350°) about 20 minutes, until crust is golden brown, and contents of dish hot.

Curried Eggs

Simply heat **hard-cooked eggs**, quartered or halved or sliced, in **curry sauce** (p. 249). Very good served on bed of hot rice, or in rice ring, or on hot buttered toast.

EGG SALAD

Slice or chop coarsely **several hard-cooked eggs** (allow 3 eggs for 2 persons). Add to eggs an equal amount of **finely diced crisp celery**. Season with **salt** and **pepper**. Add 1 tablespoon **French dressing**, for zest, then enough **mayonnaise or cooked salad dressing** to make egg mixture moist but not runny. Serve on **lettuce**. If garnished with tomato wedges, cold asparagus tips, and a thin slice of boiled ham or cold cooked corned beef, this makes a hearty luncheon.

For variety, try sometimes including a bit of ground chopped ham, or chicken liver, or flaked cooked fish, in your egg salad. If you do this, of course, you will not also serve meat on the side.

MASTER RECIPE #32
POACHED EGGS

A poached egg is attractive only if intact. Therefore, crack egg shells carefully, without breaking yolks. A beginner had better crack the shell close over a saucer, then slip the egg from saucer into cooking utensil, to lessen the chance of breakage.

And never, never think a poached egg is "just a poached egg." Indeed, under the knowing hands of French chefs (and good home cooks) poached eggs have unlimited kinds of appetizing fancy dress.

Nonetheless, all of these dishes are simple, once you can poach an egg; and poaching an egg is simple, too.

A simple poached egg is poached in *water* (though other liquids may be substituted, as indicated in Variations below). Put in small saucepan, or small frying pan, about ½ to 1 inch water. Have it almost boiling, but not quite. If you add a few drops of vinegar to the water, it will help the egg stay intact. Slip into the water 1 or 2 whole raw eggs, removed from shells. Keep water hot, but not bubbling, and cook about 3 minutes, or until white is well set, and yolk has a slight film of white over top. If desired, you may spoon up some of the hot water over yolk, to hasten its cooking. When egg texture pleases you, lift from water with pancake turner; place on hot buttered toast. Eat at once.

French method. The French use a deep pan of water, instead of a shallow pan, and stir the hot water into a swirling mass which leaves a hollow "well" in the center of the water. Egg is slipped into the well, and the water swirling around it keeps the egg intact. Only one egg at a time can be done by this method.

Poaching pans. Special pans are sold for poaching eggs. In these there is a compartment at bottom to hold hot water. Above this, are 2 to 4 fitted, removable cups, each one intended to hold one egg. Have water in pan simmering; put ½ teaspoon butter in each cup, then slip eggs into cups. Cover pan (this helps to cook the yolk faster); cook about 3 minutes. Remove eggs from cups with knife or spatula when they please you. Serve on hot buttered toast.

POACHED EGG VARIATIONS

Eggs Poached in Cream

Heat in small saucepan **2 tablespoons cream**, for cooking **2 eggs**. Add to cream a **pinch salt**, a **dash or two of paprika**. Slip 2 whole raw eggs into it. Keep pan moving, in rotary motion, over moderate heat, to prevent eggs sticking. When eggs are done enough to please you, lift eggs with pancake turner onto hot buttered toast, or toasted English muffins, or toasted baking powder biscuits. These are better than you think; try them.

Eggs à la Benedict

If you have a few English muffins, a few slices of ham, and some Hollandaise sauce (you can buy this, bottled), try this. Warm **Hollandaise sauce** in top of double boiler, over hot (not boiling) water. While this warms, pan-fry (p. 89) **1 slice of ham** for each egg desired. Put ham where it will keep warm. Toast **½ English muffin** for each egg desired. Then poach **eggs**, as under Master Recipe above. To assemble: on each ½ muffin, place 1 slice of ham, then 1 poached egg, then over all pour Hollandaise sauce.

Eggs à la Reine

Make **cheese sauce** (p. 249). Toast **bread.** Spread toast with **chopped sautéed mushrooms.** Top mushrooms with **hot poached egg.** Over all, pour cheese sauce.

Eggs à la Victoria

Heat **1 can condensed tomato soup,** undiluted. Fry in **butter,** in frying pan, 3 inch rounds of **bread,** until lightly browned. On each round, place **1 cooked chicken liver,** mashed. On top of liver, place **1 hot poached egg.** Pour tomato sauce (the soup) over all, and garnish with **finely chopped chives.**

Eggs Poached in Cheese Sauce

Make **1 cup cheese sauce** (p. 249) for **2 eggs.** When sauce is done, drop whole raw eggs into it, and cook gently until eggs are poached. Lift eggs onto buttered toast, or biscuits; cover with the cheese sauce.

MASTER RECIPE #33
FRIED EGGS

Whether you like fried eggs "sunny side up" or "over light" you certainly do not want them rubbery. Therefore, do remember to *avoid excess heat.* Melt butter (or bacon fat) in frying pan, over low to moderate heat. Fat should not sputter or smoke. Slip whole raw eggs from shell into hot fat. Let cook until white is set and yolk almost set. If you like "the eye closed" (as we say in my family), turn the egg over, by aid of a pancake turner, taking care not to break yolk. Leave egg just a moment, for yolk to glaze over, before serving. If you do not want to turn egg over, you may spoon up some of the hot fat over yolk, to help it finish cooking.

FRIED EGG VARIATIONS

Rocky Mountain Fried Eggs

Men living outdoors in the Rockies cook eggs this way, over campfires, and you'd have to taste them once to know how good they are. Have 2 to 4 tablespoons hot fat in frying pan. Slip whole raw eggs from shells into hot fat. Immediately tip the pan, so only one edge is close to fire, and the opposite side tilted up, two or more inches. (Obviously, you can't tip the pan so much that the eggs run out.) Begin at once basting the eggs with the hot fat, one spoonful after another. As fat keeps running off eggs, keep spooning it over them again. Do this until both whites and yolks are set. Result: lusciously thick, puffed up eggs, firm outside, soft inside. Try, and see. It's the hot fat that cooks the eggs; not the fire.

Fried Eggs with Ham or Bacon

First, pan-broil (p. 85) bacon, or pan-fry (p. 89) ham slices, before cooking the eggs. If you like the ham or bacon taste on the eggs, cook eggs in same fat, after meat is finished and has been removed to warm plate.

MASTER RECIPE #34
SCRAMBLED EGGS

Don't scrimp here. One scrambled egg is so small it can hardly be seen. Always allow 2 eggs per person, and some households add an extra egg "for the pan."

Follow these rules, and you will have light, delicate scrambled eggs.

Crack eggs into bowl. Mix yolks and whites slightly, with fork. For each egg, add 1 tablespoon cream or water,* and 1 "shake" of salt, from the salt cellar. If desired, add a few grains pepper.

Have hot (but never smoking or brown) *more* than enough butter to coat bottom of frying pan. Without enough butter, eggs will stick to pan. Besides, butter improves the taste.

Turn eggs into pan; allow whites to *begin* thickening before you start to stir. Then, with fork, stir eggs actively, scraping sides and bottom of pan frequently, and *keep* stirring. Remove pan from heat just a minute before eggs seem quite ready to eat. Heat of pan will continue cooking them, even while you get out the warm plates to put them on.

Scrambled eggs take only about 3 minutes to cook, but you can't walk off and leave them; they must have constant stirring if they are not to become hard and disagreeable in texture.

SCRAMBLED EGG VARIATIONS

For a midnight snack, for Sunday night supper, or just for fun, try adding some special tang to your scrambled eggs. Here are some suggestions, and you can think up others.

If ingredients to be added to scrambled eggs are light and delicate (such as herbs), you may combine them with the eggs before

---

* The French always use water for scrambled eggs, since it lightens the eggs without adding the taste of milk or cream. However, if you like the creamy flavor, use cream. If you like more solid-textured scrambled eggs, with distinctly separate white and yellow flakes, use neither cream, milk, nor water; just put whole eggs into buttered pan, and let eggs thicken until about half cooked before you start to scramble them.

cooking, or during cooking. If solid textured (such as ham, chicken livers) the solid food must be heated in frying pan first, before eggs are put in; otherwise solids will not have time to become heated through.

Scrambled Eggs with Bacon Bits

First, pan-broil (p. 85), drain, then chop or crumble several strips of **bacon**. Add to beaten eggs, before scrambling.

Scrambled Eggs with Anchovy

For 4 eggs, add ¼ teaspoon anchovy paste while scrambling; blend well. Or make plain scrambled eggs, then serve on hot **toast** spread with **anchovy paste**, or with strips of **anchovy filets**. Anchovy is very salty; you may wish to omit salting the eggs.

Scrambled Eggs with Sardines

For 4 eggs, drain oil from **3 to 5 small sardines**; remove tails, bones; break sardines into pieces. Heat sardines in buttered frying pan for a minute or two, before adding eggs. Scramble eggs as usual.

Scrambled Eggs with Smoked Salmon, or Kippered Herring

For 4 eggs, drain and flake **3 or 4 tablespoons fish**; break fish into bits. Heat fish a minute or two in buttered frying pan, before adding eggs. If fish is very salty, omit salt from eggs.

Scrambled Eggs with Dried Chipped Beef

For 4 eggs, break into bite-size pieces, and heat in buttered frying pan, ¼ **to ½ cup dried chipped beef**. When beef is hot, add eggs, omitting salt. Scramble eggs and beef together.

Scrambled Eggs with Ham, or Chicken Livers

For 4 eggs, heat in buttered frying pan for a minute or two ¼ **cup chopped cooked ham**, or **chopped cooked chicken livers**. If desired, add ½ teaspoon grated raw onion, and 1 teaspoon minced parsley. Then add eggs, and scramble.

Scrambled Eggs with Mushrooms

For 4 eggs, sauté in butter in frying pan ¼ cup sliced mushroom caps or stems until tender. Then add eggs, and scramble.

Scrambled Eggs with Herbs

For 4 eggs, add before or during cooking, 1 tablespoon finely minced fresh parsley, plus 1 teaspoon finely minced fresh chives. If desired, add also a pinch of minced fresh tarragon, or chervil.

Western Scrambled Eggs

In frying pan containing 2 to 3 tablespoons butter, sauté 1 medium onion, thinly sliced, until golden and tender. Add 1 small tomato, cubed in small pieces. Add 1 teaspoon finely minced green pepper. Heat these ingredients thoroughly; sprinkle with salt. Then add 4 to 6 eggs, blended with only half the usual amount of cream or water, since tomato will provide some of the total liquid. Scramble eggs as usual.

With Other Leftovers

Many other tasty foods, cooked or canned, and left over, are good in your scrambled eggs. For example: bits of kernel corn, or peas, or ground calf's, beef, or pork liver; or cut-up corned beef, or shrimp, or lobster, or mackerel. Such bits of food should not be thrown out, and they add flavor to the eggs.

MASTER RECIPE #35
SHIRRED EGGS

Baked or "shirred" eggs, as the name indicates, are baked in the oven, for about 15 to 20 minutes, and are most appealing, either in simple form, or in one of the "fancy dress" variations which have made them preferred luncheon dishes in famous Parisian restaurants. See how easy they are to fix.

For each person, use 1 shallow individual ramekin, of copper, aluminum, or oven glass or pottery. Butter each ramekin generously. In each one put **2 whole raw eggs** (yolks intact), removed from shells. Sprinkle eggs with **salt, pepper,** and a dash of **paprika;** then for each ramekin add, if desired, **2 tablespoons cream.** (Cream is not necessary; but many people like it.) Place ramekins in moderate (350°) oven, for 15 to 20 minutes, or until eggs are set. Serve at once, in the ramekins.

SHIRRED EGG VARIATIONS

Shirred Eggs with Chicken Livers

Allow **1 or 2** sautéed (p. 93) **chicken livers** per person. Cut cooked liver into small bite-size pieces. Arrange **whole raw eggs** in buttered ramekins, as above; then make a circle of liver around outer edge of eggs. Add sprinkle of **salt, pepper,** plus **2 tablespoons cream** per ramekin. Bake as in Master Recipe.

Instead of chicken livers, you may substitute ground or chopped cooked beef liver, or calf's liver.

Shirred Eggs with Ham

Allow **1 thin slice boiled ham,** or **¼ cup ground cooked ham,** per ramekin. If using sliced ham, either put the slice in bottom of ramekin, with **raw eggs** on top of it, or break slice into bite-size pieces and arrange ham in circle around raw eggs. With ground ham, ditto: either arrange ham in layer at bottom of ramekin, or arrange it in circle around raw eggs. Sprinkle eggs with **salt, pepper.** If desired, substitute **cheese sauce** (p. 249) for cream. Bake as in Master Recipe.

Shirred Eggs with Spinach

Allow **⅓ cup chopped, cooked spinach,** well drained, per ramekin. Arrange spinach in layer in bottom of buttered ramekin. Add **raw eggs, seasoning,** and either **cream or cheese sauce** (p. 249). Bake as in Master Recipe.

Eggs Baked in Cheese Sauce

Butter ramekins, then sprinkle with a layer of **bread or cracker crumbs.** Put in each ramekin **2 raw eggs.** Over eggs, put **2 or 3 tablespoons cheese sauce** (p. 249). (This sauce may be heightened in flavor by adding ¼ **teaspoon prepared mustard, few drops Worcestershire sauce, ½ teaspoon grated raw onion.**) Over sauce, sprinkle another thin layer of bread or cracker crumbs. Dot crumbs with butter, and sprinkle with **grated sharp cheese,** plus a dash of **paprika.** Bake as in Master Recipe.

Eggs Baked in Tomato Sauce

Butter ramekins. Put in each ramekin **2 raw eggs.** Over eggs, put **2 or 3 tablespoons highly seasoned tomato sauce.** Add ¼ **teaspoon grated raw onion,** for each ramekin. If desired, add also a sprinkling of **grated sharp cheese.** Bake as in Master Recipe.

Eggs Baked in Mushroom, Curry, Onion, Lobster Celery, or Deviled Sauce

First, make any one of these sauces; see Chapter XXIII. Now, put **2 to 3 tablespoons sauce** in each **buttered** ramekin. Top sauce with thin layer of **bread or cracker crumbs.** On top of crumbs, arrange **2 whole raw eggs.** Cover eggs with more sauce, then another layer of bread or cracker crumbs. Dot crumbs with butter, sprinkle with **paprika.** Bake as in Master Recipe.

MASTER RECIPE #36
PLAIN OMELET

This is the typical plain *French omelet,* firm on the outside but soft and creamy on the inside.

Crack into mixing bowl **2 eggs** per person. And for each egg, add **1 tablespoon milk or water** (the French prefer water). Add a few shakes of **salt,** from salt cellar. Beat eggs slightly with rotary beater until well blended. (Some cooks prefer to beat until eggs are frothy and light.)

Turn eggs into a large heavy frying pan, having enough hot

melted butter in pan to coat it amply. (Have butter hot, but not smoking.) Keep heat moderate. Bottom of eggs will set at once. Loosen eggs from edges of pan with spatula, then tip pan gently so that soft egg on top will run down to bottom of pan, to cook. When eggs will no longer run at all, turn up heat for just a minute to brown bottom of omelet lightly. With pancake turner, fold omelet over double, making a soft fold through the middle, and serve at once, on hot plate.

PLAIN OMELET VARIATIONS

While a plain omelet is good, an omelet with something added is better. It has more taste, more interest. And many will be the times when you will have just enough leftover meat, fish, mushrooms, or some other cooked food to fold into an omelet.

Lightweight ingredients, like herbs, may be blended with the raw eggs, and so distributed evenly throughout the omelet; or may be scattered on top of the omelet while it is cooking.

Very delicate, or soft ingredients, like jelly, or sautéed mushrooms, are usually placed within the fold of the omelet, *after* omelet is cooked, and just before it is put on plate.

Firm ingredients, like potatoes, corn, chopped ham, must be heated through, first, in frying pan, before eggs are added; otherwise the firm ingredients will not be sufficiently warm when omelet is done. Once firm ingredients are hot, eggs are poured over them, and omelet cooked as usual.

Omelet with Fine Herbs

For 4 eggs, chop very fine **1 tablespoon fresh parsley,** plus **1 teaspoon chives.** Add **½ teaspoon chervil** if desired. Add minced herbs to raw beaten eggs. Add **salt;** make omelet as usual.

Bacon Omelet

For 4 eggs, first pan-broil (p. 85) **4 to 8 slices bacon.** Drain bacon on paper towel. Break or chop into pieces. Add to raw beaten eggs; make omelet as usual.

Potato Omelet

Heat first in well-buttered frying pan **2 or 3 peeled cooked, diced potatoes** (these may be leftover baked or boiled potatoes). With potatoes, add a sprinkling of **salt, 1 tablespoon grated raw onion,** plus **1 tablespoon finely chopped fresh parsley.** When potatoes are hot, pour eggs over them. Make omelet as usual.

Kidney Omelet

For 4 eggs, first sauté in butter **2 or 3 lambs' kidneys** (p. 94), sliced, or cut in bite-size pieces. While these sauté, add to them **½ teaspoon grated raw onion, 3 or 4 drops Worcestershire sauce,** few shakes of **salt.** When kidneys are tender, set aside to keep warm. Make plain omelet. Fold hot kidneys inside just before serving. Garnish with **parsley** and **paprika.** This is superb with hot baking powder biscuits.

Chicken Liver Omelet

For 4 eggs, first sauté (p. 93) **3 or 4 raw chicken livers** until tender. (Or you may use chicken livers which have been simmered in water until tender.) Cut livers into bite-size pieces. Keep warm. Make plain omelet. Fold warm chicken livers inside just before serving. Cooked chopped beef liver or calf's liver may be substituted for chicken liver.

Ham Omelet

For 4 eggs, first heat thoroughly in buttered pan **½ to 1 cup chopped, cooked, leftover ham.** (If desired, add minced raw onion, minced green pepper, and diced cooked potatoes.) Sprinkle with **salt.** When solid ingredients are hot, add eggs; make omelet as usual.

Corn Omelet

For 4 eggs, first heat thoroughly in buttered pan **½ cup drained, cooked or canned kernel corn.** With corn, you may add **1 teaspoon grated raw onion, 1 tablespoon finely chopped green pepper** plus sprinkling of **salt** and **pepper**. When solid ingredients are hot, add eggs; make omelet as usual.

Cheese Omelet

For 4 eggs, mix ¼ cup grated **Parmesan** or **Cheddar cheese** with raw beaten eggs. Make omelet as usual, but add another sprinkling of grated cheese over omelet while it is cooking.

Onion Omelet

Wonderful with young, tender, spring onions. For 4 eggs, first sauté (p. 96) ½ cup finely sliced or coarsely chopped **tender green onions** in **2 to 3 tablespoons butter**. Use some tips of the young green shoots, too, finely sliced. When onions are cooked tender, add eggs; make omelet as usual.

Western Omelet

For 4 eggs, in saucepan sauté in **butter** (p. 96) **2 medium onions**, sliced thin; **2 medium tomatoes**, cubed fine; **1 tablespoon green pepper**, chopped fine, **salt and pepper**. Cook until tender, but not mushy. Keep warm. Make plain omelet. When ready to serve, fold in some of the onion-tomato mixture, and pour the rest over top of omelet.

Mushroom Omelet

For 4 eggs, first sauté (p. 95) in **2 to 3 tablespoons butter**, in saucepan, ½ cup or more sliced **mushroom caps or stems**. Keep warm. Make plain omelet. When ready to serve, fold mushrooms inside.

Jelly Omelet

Make plain omelet. Just before serving, place on one half the omelet **1 or 2 tablespoons jelly** (apricot, peach, currant are all good). Fold other half of omelet over jelly; serve at once before jelly melts.

Watercress Omelet

For 4 eggs, chop fine **2 to 4 tablespoons fresh, crisp watercress;** add this to raw beaten eggs. Make omelet as usual. Serve omelet garnished with branches of watercress and sliced tomatoes.

MASTER RECIPE #37
FLUFFY OMELET

This is the lightest possible omelet, made by beating egg yolks and whites separately, then folding them together. The beating in of many more air bubbles creates the additional fluffiness.

Allow **2 eggs** per person. Crack shells carefully, putting yolks in one bowl, whites in another. *Whites.* Beat with rotary beater until stiff, but not dry. *Yolks.* Add **1 tablespoon milk or water,** plus a shake of **salt** from salt cellar, for each yolk; then beat until thick and lemon-colored. Fold yolks into whites. (Some cooks also fold in **1 teaspoon baking powder,** with raw egg mixture, to help omelet stay fluffed up.)

Turn egg mixture into large heavy frying pan well coated with hot (not smoking) **butter.** (It is best to use a frying pan with metal or removable handle, as wooden handles may scorch in oven.) Cook over low heat 3 minutes. Then transfer frying pan to moderate (350°) oven, and bake 15 minutes.

Omelet is done when surface will not adhere to finger tip, or when a knife blade inserted in center comes out clean.

To fold. As this omelet will be quite firm, you may cut omelet across center with knife, but cut only partway through, leaving bottom of omelet intact. With pancake turner, turn one half over onto the other half.

Adding ingredients. Any ingredients suggested for plain omelet may also be used for fluffy omelet, and added in the same manner.

SOUFFLÉS

Soufflés are marvelously light, tempting, and when well made, simpler than most people think. For a soufflé is only a white sauce,

with any desired flavoring (for example, cheese) blended into it
. . . then separately beaten egg yolks and egg whites added. The
whole thing is baked in the oven about 30 to 45 minutes, and the
only hitch is that it *must* be eaten at once, when done; else it
will fall. When serving a soufflé, be sure you can have all the
family assembled at the same moment . . . a neat trick, if you
can do it!

We are using cheese soufflé as the Master Recipe, since all other
soufflés are made similarly, and with only slight variation.

MASTER RECIPE #38
CHEESE SOUFFLÉ

In a saucepan, melt (don't brown)
> **3 tablespoons butter**

Stir in, making a thick paste
> **4 tablespoons flour**
> **½ teaspoon salt**

Add, a little at a time, stirring constantly to avoid lumps
> **1 cup milk**

Bring this white sauce mixture to a boil, stirring constantly;
then reduce heat; cook about 2 minutes more. Fold into white
sauce
> **1 cup (¼ pound) grated or finely shaved cheese** (Amer-
> ican, Parmesan, or Swiss)

Cook until cheese is melted. Stir to blend well. Then remove
from heat; set aside to cool somewhat.

Now separate (p. 260)
> **3 eggs**
> (yolks in 1 bowl, whites in other bowl)

Beat yolks with rotary beater until thick and lemon-colored.
Stir into beaten yolks the cooled white sauce.

Wash beater, dry it; then beat whites until they stand in soft
peaks, but are still moist and glossy.

Fold yolk mixture, a little at a time, into whites; keep using fold-
over strokes, until all mixture is blended, but do not beat.

Turn mixture into buttered baking dish with straight sides (soufflé must be able to climb straight up the walls of dish). Bake in preheated hot (425°) oven 25 to 30 minutes, without opening oven door. Soufflé is done when top is nicely browned and dry, and feels firm when touched lightly with finger tip.

NOTE: This makes a soufflé crusty on outside, softer in middle. For alternate baking method, using slower oven, see under Chocolate Soufflé.

SOUFFLÉ VARIATIONS

(*Follow Master Recipe #38, Cheese Soufflé, page 281, making substitutions below.*)

Ham Soufflé

Instead of cheese, fold into white sauce **1 cup chopped or ground cooked ham.**

Salmon Soufflé

Instead of cheese, fold into white sauce **1 cup drained flaked, cooked or canned, salmon,** plus 1 teaspoon lemon juice.

NOTE: Same recipe may be used for shrimp, lobster.

Fish Soufflé

Same as salmon soufflé, but substitute **1 cup flaked, cooked white fish,** instead of salmon.

Beef Soufflé

Instead of cheese, fold into white sauce **1 cup ground or diced cooked beef.** Add to seasoning of sauce, if desired, ¼ teaspoon bottled horseradish, or few drops Worcestershire sauce, plus ½ teaspoon grated onion.

Spinach, Asparagus or Broccoli Soufflé

Instead of cheese, fold into white sauce **1½ cups finely chopped drained cooked spinach,** or **asparagus tips,** or **puréed broccoli.** Or puréed peas, celery, or onions may be used.

Chocolate Soufflé

A chocolate soufflé, being a dessert and containing sugar and melted chocolate, is a little farther from our Master Recipe, and yet the basic system is still the same. Follow directions below.

First, heat in top of double boiler, over boiling water, **1 cup milk,** adding **2 squares (2 ounces) baking chocolate, or ½ cup powdered cocoa.** Heat until chocolate melts, and can be thoroughly blended with the milk into a "chocolate-milk" mixture.

Now, as in Master Recipe, begin a white sauce, but use only **2 tablespoons butter, 3 tablespoons flour, ¼ teaspoon salt.** Add **½ cup sugar,** for sweetening. Stir in the chocolate-milk, and cook as if making white sauce, until thickened. Cool the thick chocolate sauce, and add **1 teaspoon vanilla.**

Then continue as in Master Recipe, beating **3 egg yolks** until thick. Fold cooled chocolate sauce into egg yolks. Beat **egg whites** until stiff, but not dry. Fold yolk-chocolate mixture into stiffened whites. Turn mixture into buttered baking dish.

Place baking dish in a shallow pan of warm water (to protect the delicate texture), and bake in moderate (350°) oven 50 to 60 minutes, or until center is firm when lightly touched with fingertip. Serve *at once*, from baking dish, garnished with sweetened whipped cream. Whipped cream will melt quickly on hot pudding, so should not be added until everyone is served.

OTHER USES FOR EGGS

Eggs are basic in many *sauces* (see egg sauce for fish, p. 249; mock Hollandaise sauce, p. 250; Newburg sauce, p. 251; and in *mayonnaise,* p. 351); *cooked salad dressing* (p. 354), *custards* (Chapter XXXI), *pie fillings* (see custard-type pie fillings, Chapter XXXV), *cake fillings* (Chapter XXXIV), *cakes* (Chapter XXXIII), *meringue* (p. 489), and *ice cream* (Chapter XXXII).

CHAPTER XXV

What to Do with Vegetables

METHODS FOR: *Boiled Vegetables, Creamed Vegetables, Curried Vegetables, Scalloped Vegetables, Au Gratin Vegetables, Baked Vegetables, Mashed Vegetables, Pan-fried and other Fried Vegetables (see also Chapters IX and X), Puréed Vegetables*

A WORD ABOUT VEGETABLES

Vegetables are important. Important not only for vitamins, minerals and other health essentials, but for the truly delicious variety of flavor they lend to menus, and for their eye appeal on plates.

A great chef will be as famous for his vegetables as for his meats, pastries or puddings. Indeed, you will never find him serving vegetables which are mushy, soggy, swimming in the water they were cooked in, faded in color, or so overcooked that they have lost texture and taste. Each vegetable will be sprightly, colorful, caught at the peak of its own texture and flavor; each will stand out alone, utterly distinctive and utterly delicious, appealing first to the eye, then to the palate, as a rare delight. And until you have eaten vegetables cooked with this perfection, you haven't eaten vegetables at all!

The trick of doing this is easy. Under Basic Rules for Boiling Vegetables (p. 290) you will discover how to keep them at their brightest color, their most delicious texture, and their richest taste. And until you master the trick, don't blame husband or children if they complain that they "don't like vegetables"!

Meanwhile, remember that the vegetables you assemble on a plate — and the *way* you assemble them — are also important. Every plate, at every dinner, should be tempting with color and interest. Brown meat and white potatoes may taste good, but they don't *look* exciting. Dull or monotone colors on a plate, just as in a room, or in a costume, look dreary. It is up to you to make the plate interesting. Add a bright red and a fresh green vegetable, and at once your plate comes to life. Give a pale white vegetable (mashed potatoes, creamed onions, creamed celery) a brave, bright dash of red paprika, or a sprinkling of chopped green parsley, and the food will be eaten with twice the zest. When you have *two* white foods on a platter (such as white fricassee of chicken plus rice, or fish plus mashed potatoes) take *extra* pains to plan bright, colorful vegetables and garnishes. Radishes, green pepper rings, strips of pimiento, a sprig or two of watercress, sliced stuffed olives . . . many small garnishes can add color to your plate.

Remember also that your vegetables can be arranged in a variety of ways; they need not always be heaped in whatever empty space remains on the dinner plate. Green peas, or mixed small vegetables, can be served in cups made of a scooped-out tomato or scooped-out cooked beet; the color and texture contrast is pretty and interesting. Lovely fresh green peas or string beans can be arranged in a circle, surrounding a rice ring filled with creamed chicken, shrimp, ham, or other meat. Baked potatoes can be scooped out, and the potato mixed with savory seasonings or with bits of fish, ham, or meat and stuffed back into the skins. When used in fresh or jelled salads, vegetables can be arranged in rows, circles, or other patterns of contrasting color and texture. There is no need for sameness day after day, nor for lack of interest in the appearance of your food. Watch colored photographs in women's magazines, and in advertisements, for new ideas, and you will soon find every one of your dinners is becoming colorful and appetizing.

And now — to cook the vegetables.

MASTER RECIPE #39
BOILED VEGETABLES

Here is the basic way of cooking vegetables. For though vegetables can be cooked other ways (fried, sautéed, baked, for example) you will find that this is the way you need to know constantly. All vegetables which will be served creamed, curried, scalloped, mashed, or puréed have to be boiled tender first; and many vegetables used in jellied or other salads (if they are inedible raw) must also first be boiled. If you lose the flavor and texture in the boiling, you cannot restore it by any trick later. So learn now to cook vegetables so that they retain the utmost in lovely color, full flavor, and texture. You'll always be proud of it. And it's really very simple, as you'll see!

Preparation before Boiling

Any fresh (not frozen) vegetable needs some preparation before being cooked. It needs washing, or peeling, or inedible parts removed, or strings or pods removed, or perhaps slicing. Look under the specific vegetable.

Artichokes, French. Cut off stem of each artichoke close to bottom; remove coarsest outside leaves. With scissors, cut off sharp points of all remaining leaves, leaving about ¾ inch on each leaf. Wash well under running water, and scrub with brush if leaves look dirty. Then soak ½ hour in bowl of salted cold water to draw out insects. Drain before cooking.

Asparagus. Place stalks loosely in bowl; run cool clear water over them for several minutes; cut off excess white ends; tie stalks together in a bundle with string, ready for cooking. Begin cooking with spears upright, so stalks may partially tenderize before tips are lowered into water.

Beans, Lima. Break open pod by pressing thumb against sharp edge of pod until pod pops open. Pull beans loose from pod. Rinse them with cold water. Drain.

Beans, string or snap. Break off pointed tip of bean gently, at same time pulling point down along the rounded outer side of bean pod. If there is a string, it will come off with the tip. Break off tip from opposite end of bean, pulling it toward the other side of pod; this will pull off second string if there is one. (Young beans have few if any strings, but old ones have many.) If beans are thin and young, leave whole to cook. If old and heavy, slice. Before cooking, rinse beans under cold water. Drain.

Beets. Cut off beet tops (green branches and stalks) about 1 inch from top of beet. Cut off excessive root, but leave ½ inch. Rinse beets under hot water. Do not peel. Cook beets in their skins; you can peel and slice afterward much more easily. Skin then slips off in fingers.

Beet tops. Cut off excessive red stalks, leaving green leaves. Discard any wilted or damaged leaves. Place good leaves in large dishpan; run quite hot water over them, to fill pan. Swish leaves around in water; then lift leaves, a few at a time, out of water, letting water drain from them. Empty out first water. Run fresh hot water over greens, and wash again. If very sandy or gritty, greens may need 3 or 4 such washings. If you don't get the grit and sand out now, you will have it to crunch on when you eat the greens! When finished washing, place drained greens in pan large enough for cooking them; and cook only in water which has clung to leaves.

Broccoli. Remove leaves; remove excess stem, leaving only about 3-inch stem if tender, less if not tender. Place broccoli in large pan; run cold water over it for 10 minutes, then add a tablespoon salt and let broccoli stand in cold salted water 30 minutes to draw out garden insects. Drain before cooking. If desired, you can tie broccoli into bunches, with string, before cooking.

Brussels sprouts. Remove any discolored or wilted outer leaves. Place sprouts in large bowl or pan; run cold water over them 10 minutes; then add I tablespoon salt to water and let them stand in cold salted water ½ hour to draw out garden insects. Drain before cooking.

Cabbage. Remove tough outer leaves; cut off any excess stem. Cut cabbage in half (from stem to bottom), or if preferred, cut it in a number of vertical wedges. Place under cold running water 10 minutes; then add 1 tablespoon salt and let stand in cold salted water ½ hour to draw out garden insects. Drain before cooking.

Carrots. Cut off root, if any, and stem branches. If carrots are baby-size, young and tender, you may wish to cook them whole, leaving skins on (this increases vitamin value). In this case, scrub with stiff brush under cold water; then cook. If carrots are old and tough, peel them and cut into crosswise or lengthwise slices before cooking.

Cauliflower. Remove leaves and excess stem, leaving only the flower. If desired, you can cook the flower whole; or if preferred you can separate it, with sharp knife, into a number of small flowerets. In either case, place under cold running water 10 minutes, then in cold salted water as for cabbage. Drain before cooking.

Celery. Break off some large outer branches from head of celery, saving the heart or tender center part, if desired, to eat raw. Three or 4 large branches, when sliced, should make enough cooked celery for 2 people. Scrub branches with stiff brush under running cold water to remove dirt and sand. With knife, scrape off strings from rounded outside of each branch. Remove leaves (save these to use for seasonings in soups or stews or salads). Cut very large branches in half lengthwise. Then slice all branches crosswise, into ¼-inch thick slices. Rinse off again and drain before cooking.

Corn. Pull off husks, remove all corn silk, and cut away with sharp knife any dark or defective kernels. If cooking corn on cob, it is now ready for cooking. If preferred, with sharp knife slice off kernels (2 rows at a time) into bowl or pan; then kernels are ready to cook.

Dandelion greens. Wash like beet tops.

Escarole. Wash like beet tops.

Onions. Cut off stalk, if there is one, or any shoots. Then with knife peel off dry outer skin of onion, holding onion under cold water. (If you handle onions under cold water, they will not make you cry.) For boiled onions, you should try to select onions all the same size, and preferably no bigger than a walnut; most people prefer white onions for this; allow 4 or 5 per serving.

Parsnips. Cut a thin slice off top and bottom. Peel. Cut lengthwise into quarters; cut out hard center core. If desired, slice crosswise into smaller pieces. Rinse under cold water; drain before cooking.

Peas. Press pod open, as for Lima beans. Remove peas to pan. Rinse with cold water, then drain before cooking.

Peppers. Green peppers are boiled until partly tender before being stuffed. To prepare: wash whole pepper under cold water. With sharp knife, cut circular piece out of top, around stem, removing stem and a trifle of the top around it. With tablespoon, carefully scoop out the inside core and seeds, taking care not to damage the pepper. Rinse out and drain before cooking.

Potatoes, sweet. Scrub with brush. Cook whole in skins; or peel (and slice if desired) before cooking.

Potatoes, white. Scrub potatoes with stiff brush under cold water. Small, new potatoes with very thin skins may be cooked and served whole, with skins left on. Old potatoes can also be cooked whole with skins on, if desired, and peeled after cooking water is drained off (this is the way to prepare them for use in potato salad). However, for mashed or creamed potatoes, peel potatoes and cut into cubes before cooking; the skins would be in your way later.

Pumpkin. Slice off stem and bud ends. Cut pumpkin into quarters or eighths. Peel off yellow skin. With spoon, scrape loose and discard seeds and stringy pulp. Cut firm flesh into 2- or 3-inch pieces, for cooking.

Squash, butternut (pale, tannish-orange, smooth skin). Cut crosswise slices 2 inches thick. Peel. Remove seeds and stringy pulp, then cut firm flesh into pieces. Incidentally, many New Englanders use this squash in place of pumpkin for pumpkin pie. You'd have to be very adroit to tell the difference, after pie is seasoned and baked.

Squash, summer (bright yellowish-orange color, with rough skin). If young and tender, summer squash can be cooked with skin on. Scrub squash with stiff brush under cold water. Remove stem and bud ends. Cut squash into crosswise slices 1 inch thick; then cut these slices in half again, if desired, to make smaller pieces for quick cooking. Seeds do no harm, as they are very tender; don't remove them.

Hubbard squash and *acorn squash* are not boiled, but baked.

Spinach. Prepare exactly like beet tops.

Swiss chard. Prepare exactly like beet tops.

Turnips, white or yellow. Cut off root and branch ends. Peel turnip. Cut into 2-inch pieces or smaller; rinse off and drain before cooking.

Basic Rules for Boiling Vegetables

(1) *Use the least cooking water possible.* Obviously, some small amount of water is necessary to keep your vegetable from sticking to the heated kettle, but it can be very little water indeed. When cooking leafy vegetables, add *no water* except the few drops that cling to the leaves after washing; this will presently accumulate and amount to about ½ cup water in the kettle as the vegetable cooks. For peas, Limas, or vegetables cut into small pieces, try to use no more than ½ cup water — 1 cup at most. If boiling large whole vegetables, such as whole potatoes, whole carrots, whole ears of corn, or large wedges of cabbage, you have to use enough water to cover the vegetable, or nearly cover it. But remember, the less water you can use, the less diluted your vegetable's flavor is going to be; you don't want all the good taste and vitamins to cook out into the water and be lost.

(2) *Have water boiling hard and salted before putting vegetables in it.* This is the secret of both bright color and tenderness. A vegetable dropped into rapidly boiling, salted water will become a lovely clear bright color, and tenderize much more quickly. Use ½ teaspoon salt for a small kettle, or a teaspoonful for a larger one.

(3) *Cover kettle tightly as soon as vegetables are inside.* Covering kettle keeps moisture and steam inside kettle, so that you do

not need to add more water, and so that vegetable cooks tender more quickly, without losing its savor.

(4) *Forget about soda.* Though the latest government information is that soda in the water does no harm, it often tastes and it is not necessary for keeping vegetables green, if you follow above rules. You can have lovely, bright, tender vegetables without it.

(5) *Don't overcook.* Vegetables are at their peak when a fork will go into them easily, but before they are soft and mushy. Try to keep the texture firm; the flavor is better then, too, since it has not cooked away.

(6) *Drain thoroughly before serving.* Nothing is worse than soupy spinach, or any other vegetable which *should* be firm, but appears runny. Drain well in colander, but save the liquid; when you store leftover vegetables, the liquid should be returned to the vegetable to help keep it moist and flavorful until next using.

(7) *Frozen vegetables need not be thawed before cooking.* If desired, you may bang the frozen package against side of sink or some hard surface several times, to break the package into smaller chunks for quicker cooking, but this is not necessary. As all frozen vegetables have already been blanched (bathed in boiling water 2 or 3 minutes) before packaging, they will cook tender far more quickly than raw vegetables, but the *method* of cooking is the same.

(8) *To heat canned vegetables.* Nutrition experts now advise that, when opening a can of vegetables, you pour the vegetable liquor into a saucepan, bring it to a boil, and cook until it is reduced to ½ cup. Then add the vegetable, cover pan, reduce heat to gentle, and heat until vegetable is thoroughly hot. This method is reputed to bring back more of the full natural flavor of the vegetable.

(9) *To store cooked vegetables.* Any cooked vegetables should be stored in covered container, with their own liquid added to them if there is any, and kept in refrigerator. When needed again, reheat in same liquid, or drain to use cold.

CHART FOR BOILING
VARIOUS VEGETABLES

Vegetable	Number of Minutes If Fresh	Number of Minutes If Frozen
Asparagus	25 to 30	8 to 12
Artichokes, French	About 45	(This time is counted from moment water begins to boil again after frozen vegetable is added.)
Beans, Lima	20 to 30	8 to 12
Beans, string or snap	30 to 40	8 to 12
Beets, young, whole	20 to 30	
Beets, older, whole	35 to 60	
Beet tops	20 to 30	6 to 10
Broccoli	15 to 20	6 to 10
Brussels sprouts	15 to 25	6 to 12
Cabbage, green or red, shredded, or cut in wedges	8 to 15	
Carrots, large ones, sliced, or young ones, left whole	20 to 30	
Carrots, diced	12 to 20	4 to 8
Cauliflower, head separated into flowerets	15 to 20	6 to 8
Cauliflower, whole head	25 to 30	
Celery, diced	15 to 20	
Chard, Swiss	10 to 12	
Corn, on cob	7 to 12	6 to 8
Corn, cut from cob	3 to 7	3 to 6
Dandelion greens	15 to 30	
Escarole	12 to 14	
Onions, small	20 to 30	
Parsnips, sliced	7 to 15	
Peas	15 to 25	4 to 8
Potatoes, sweet (or yams), whole	30 to 45	
Potatoes, white, medium size, whole	35 to 45	
Potatoes, white, sliced or diced	15 to 20	
Pumpkin, cut in 2½-inch chunks	20 to 25	
Spinach	10 to 15	4 to 8
Squash, butternut, in 1-inch chunks	20 to 25	
Squash, summer, cut in ½" slices	15 to 20	
Turnips, white, cut in small pieces	20 to 25	
Turnips, yellow, cut in small pieces	25 to 45	
Zucchini squash	15 to 20	

OTHER BASIC WAYS
OF SERVING VEGETABLES

Although boiling is the most common way of cooking vegetables, it is far from the *only* way.

Vegetables may be: creamed (see below), scalloped (see p. 295), curried (see p. 295), baked "au gratin" (see p. 295), used in meat pies (p. 144), used in casseroles (p. 144), added to meat or vegetable soup (p. 127), used in cold vegetable salads (p. 335), used in jellied salad molds (p. 374), jelled in aspic, with meat or hard-cooked eggs (p. 379), or puréed, then made into cream soup (p. 258).

And some may be: baked (see p. 295), mashed (see p. 300), sautéed (pp. 95–96), shallow-fried (pp. 104–105), or deep-fried (pp. 112–114).

CREAMED VEGETABLES

Any vegetable, *before being creamed, must first have been boiled* (see p. 290) *or otherwise cooked to tender condition.* (But never try to cream fried vegetables; they would be too greasy. And never use a mashed or runny vegetable; it would only make a sort of soup.)

The point to remember is that creaming will never *cook* your vegetable; it will only enclose it in a hot creamy sauce, and *reheat* the vegetable; the vegetable must be in edible form *before* being creamed.

Any firm, boiled, drained vegetable may be creamed; such as: sliced or diced cooked carrots, or peas, or both; diced or cubed cooked potatoes; whole, small, boiled, drained onions; cooked corn kernels, cut from cob; cooked lima beans; cooked succotash (lima beans and corn kernels); cooked cauliflower, cut into separate flowerets; cooked broccoli, cut to bite-size pieces; cooked asparagus, cut to bite-size pieces; cooked spinach, drained, and chopped.

MASTER RECIPE #40
CREAMED VEGETABLES

(Serves 2 or 3)

Cut to bite size
> 1½ cups drained, cooked, firm vegetable

In separate saucepan, make
> 1 cup medium white sauce (p. 248) *

If desired, add to sauce for extra flavor
> 1 teaspoon grated raw onion
> 2 tablespoons minced parsley

Add vegetables to pan of hot sauce; place over gentle heat of surface burner 15 to 25 minutes, or until vegetable is thoroughly heated.

Serve garnished with a dash of
> paprika or minced parsley

for color.

CREAMED VEGETABLE VARIATIONS

(*Follow method of Master Recipe #40, Creamed Vegetables, page 294, with changes noted below.*)

Creamed Mixed Vegetables

Instead of using 1½ cups of *one* vegetable, use 1½ cups (total) of several combined vegetables, adding **1 teaspoon grated raw onion** to heighten flavor.

Creamed Meat and Vegetables

If desired, use only ¾ cup vegetable, and add **¾ cup diced cooked or canned meat;** or use 1 cup vegetable, plus ½ cup diced cooked or canned meat (such as cooked ham, chicken, fish;

---

* When making a cup of white sauce for creamed vegetables, substitute ½ cup of water the vegetable was boiled in, plus ½ cup evaporated milk or top milk, instead of 1 cup whole milk. Using the vegetable water not only adds vitamins, but much flavor.

or coarsely chopped **hard-cooked eggs** may be used instead of meat). Combine meat and vegetables; add **1 teaspoon grated onion** to heighten flavor; serve on hot toast, or on hot steamed rice (p. 305); or as filling in main-course shortcake biscuits (p. 140).

Curried Vegetables

Make Master Recipe, Creamed Vegetables; but in making white sauce, when stirring flour into butter, add **½ teaspoon curry powder** plus **½ teaspoon prepared mustard** for each cup sauce you are preparing. Bits of leftover cooked or canned meat, or hard-cooked eggs, may be included with vegetables you are using if desired. Serve on hot rice, or noodles, or on toast.

Scalloped Vegetables

Make Master Recipe, Creamed Vegetables. Turn into buttered baking dish. Over top, sprinkle thinly and evenly **⅓ to ½ cup fine bread or cracker crumbs.** Dot top of crumbs with **8 to 10 bits of butter,** size of peas. Add, for color, **few dashes paprika.** Bake in moderate oven (375°) about 20 to 30 minutes, or until crumbs brown and sauce is bubbly.

Vegetables Baked au Gratin

Make scalloped vegetables, but when sprinkling dish with crumbs, blend with the crumbs **⅓ to ½ cup grated sharp American cheese.** Omit butter on top of crumbs. Bake in moderately hot (400°) oven, 15 to 20 minutes, or until cheese browns slightly, and sauce is bubbly.

BAKED VEGETABLES

Most baked vegetables are baked from a *raw* state, not cooked by boiling first.

Baked Acorn Squash

These are oval-shaped, green-skinned squash, with ridges in skin. Scrub squash. Cut in half lengthwise. Scoop out seeds and stringy part. In hollow where seeds were, in each piece of squash, place 1 **teaspoon butter,** 1 **teaspoon brown sugar** (or honey, or maple syrup). Place squash in buttered baking pan; cover it. Place in moderately hot oven (400°). Bake about 1 hour, or until tender.

If desired, immediately after baking squash, you may fill the scooped-out hollow with another cooked vegetable, such as hot, buttered, well-seasoned, well-drained spinach, or peas, or brussels sprouts, or tiny boiled onions.

Baked Summer Squash

Crook-necked, tender, yellow-skinned squash. One small squash serves 2 persons; a large one can be cut to serve 4. Scrub skin of **squash;** do not peel. Cut squash in half lengthwise, so each portion includes ½ the neck. Do not remove seeds; they are very tender and edible. Sprinkle inside of squash well with **salt, pepper.** Dot with **butter.** Place pieces, skin side down, in uncovered buttered baking pan or pie plate. Bake about 30 to 40 minutes, or until tender. Serve "as is." (May be mashed, if desired, for children.)

Baked White Potatoes

Idaho potatoes, or other large ones, are preferred for baking. Allow at least 1 potato per person; more if they are small ones. Scrub **potatoes** well with stiff brush, removing dirt and loose bits of skin. Some people brush skins with **fat,** but this is not at all necessary. With tines of fork, prick each potato skin in two or three places, to allow vents for steam while potato cooks. Place potatoes on rack in center of oven, heated to 375°, or moderate. Bake about 1 hour (more, if very large), or until potato feels tender when tested with fork.

Remove from oven, and if you have time before serving, place potatoes for a few minutes in brown paper bag, closing bag and keeping it in a warm place. (This is a wonderful trick, which makes potatoes deliciously tender and mealy.) Before serving, cut into center top of each potato, with knife, a 1½ in cross. Press in lower sides of potato, forcing some of the mealy inside to pop up through the opening. In center of opening, put a pat of **butter**, plus a sprinkling of **paprika**. Serve as fast as possible after opening, for they cool off.

Stuffed Baked Potato. Bake as above. When potato has finished baking, slice off the top of one flat side, taking care to keep the rest of the potato skin intact, like a cup. Scoop out the mealy potato pulp into saucepan or bowl. Mash pulp with potato masher, gradually beating in ¼ **cup** (or more, if needed) **hot milk**, until potatoes are fluffy, smooth, and creamy. Add ½ **teaspoon salt** (or more; taste and see), ⅛ **teaspoon pepper**.

If desired, add to seasoned potato pulp any one of the following, for additional flavor and interest: 2 tablespoons to ½ cup grated American cheese, 2 tablespoons minced parsley, 1 tablespoon minced chives, or grated onion, bits of cooked ham, meat, or crumbled cooked bacon, bits of anchovy, or other tangy fish.

Repack pulp into potato skins. Garnish top of each potato with **paprika**, or **minced parsley**. Return potatoes to oven, 10 to 15 minutes, to reheat.

Baked Sweet Potatoes

Scrub, prick, bake exactly as for baked white potatoes. When baked, cut open the top. Garnish with **butter, salt, paprika,** before serving.

Candied or Glazed Sweet Potatoes

Use peeled, boiled or canned **sweet potatoes.** Cut them in halves, lengthwise.

In saucepan, make this syrup to glaze or candy potatoes. Melt ¼ **cup butter** with ½ to 1 cup brown sugar. Add **few grains salt, few specks powdered cloves,** if desired. Cook about 5 minutes, until blended and syrupy.

To glaze potatoes in saucepan. Simply add potatoes to the syrup, turning them over in the syrup from time to time, and cooking gently, covered, about 20 minutes, until potatoes are well heated and shiny.

To glaze potatoes in oven. Arrange potato halves in a single layer in baking dish or frying pan having metal handle. Pour syrup over them. Place dish or pan under moderately hot broiler 10 to 15 minutes, until potatoes heat and glaze. Or place in preheated moderate oven (375°) for 30 to 40 minutes, spooning syrup over potatoes occasionally, until they are hot and glazed.

Potatoes and Onions Baked in Milk

(Wonderfully tasty with fish, liver, meat cakes, steak, ham.) For 2 to 3 persons, peel, wash, and slice in ⅛ inch thick slices **5 or 6 medium potatoes.** Also peel and slice thin, crosswise, **1 medium onion.** Now arrange in shallow baking dish (about 1½ to 2 inches deep) a layer of potatoes. Sprinkle with **salt** and **pepper.** Across these put a thin layer of onions. Repeat potatoes, salt and pepper, onions, as many times as possible, ending with potatoes on top. Now pour into dish enough **milk** to come to top of the top layer of potatoes. Add several small lumps of **butter.** Cover dish with lid. Bake, covered, in moderate (375°) oven about 30 minutes. Then uncover, and continue baking about 15 to 20 minutes more, or until potatoes feel tender when pricked with fork, and top is slightly browned. You'll repeat this dish often.

Baked Tomato Halves

(Excellent with fried or broiled fish, meat cakes, steak, ham, or liver and bacon.) Allow 1 tomato per person, choosing firm, ripe, tomatoes of matching size, and without skin blemishes. Wash **tomatoes.** Cut them crosswise, in halves. Arrange all halves, cut side up, in buttered pie plate or shallow pan. Spread cut sides lightly with **mustard;** then sprinkle lightly with **salt, pepper.** Over each sprinkle **minced parsley** and a few flecks of **grated raw onion.** Then bake in preheated moderately hot (400°) oven, about 15 minutes. Serve hot.

Alternate methods of cooking. If you like, tomatoes prepared as above may be (1) *broiled:* place prepared tomatoes in buttered baking dish; then place dish about 4 inches below preheated broiling unit for 5 to 10 minutes, or just until top of tomatoes begins to sizzle, but body of tomato is still solid, not softened. Or (2) *cooked over surface burner:* place prepared tomatoes in buttered heavy frying pan, over gentle heat of surface burner, about 15 minutes, with pan covered.

Baked Stuffed Tomatoes

(Try with steak, liver and bacon, meat cakes, or fish.) Allow 1 tomato per person, choosing firm, ripe tomatoes of matching size, and without skin blemishes. Wash **tomatoes.** Cut them in halves, crosswise. From cut side of each piece, scoop out about 1 or 2 teaspoons tomato pulp; turn this pulp into a small bowl. To pulp, add ½ cup **soft bread crumbs, 1** or 2 **teaspoons grated onion, 2 teaspoons melted butter, ¼ teaspoon salt, few specks pepper.** Blend mixture. Stuff it back into the scooped-out hollows in tomatoes. Arrange all tomato halves, stuffed side up, in buttered pie plate, or shallow pan; bake in moderately hot (400°) oven about 15 minutes, just until top is golden brown. Remove from oven before tomatoes become soft.

If using very large tomatoes, instead of filling hollow with bread-crumb stuffing above, you may stuff the hollow in each half tomato with any of the following: leftover cooked macaroni and cheese, leftover creamed vegetables,* leftover creamed ham, fish, or meat, leftover curried meat, or vegetables, or eggs, canned or home-cooked hash.

Where tomatoes are stuffed, bake in moderately hot (400°) oven about 15 minutes, just long enough to heat thoroughly.

Or, you may sprinkle the hollow in each half tomato with **salt, pepper;** then drop into it a **whole raw egg.** Bake tomatoes in moderate (375°) oven about 12 to 15 minutes, or until eggs are firm. Before serving, cover each tomato with **cheese sauce** (p. 249).

* Whenever you use a creamy, runny-type filling, sprinkle a few fine bread or cracker crumbs over top surface of filling before baking. The crumbs protect ingredients from drying out, and also help prevent filling from bubbling over the sides.

Baked Stuffed Green Peppers

You will need 1 pepper for each person. Select large, firm, blemish-free green peppers of equal size, which will stand up on end without falling over. (Test them.) Now about ½ inch below top of stem end of each pepper, slice off the entire top, so you can get a tablespoon inside pepper. With spoon, dig out white pulp and seeds, then rinse inside of pepper under cold water. Drain. Now place cleaned peppers in large saucepan; cover them with water; add **1 teaspoon salt;** cover pan. Bring water to boil over moderate heat; then simmer 5 to 10 minutes, or just until peppers *begin* to feel tender . . . not until they are soft. Remove from heat; pour off water; lift peppers out carefully, and drain them 10 to 15 minutes, upside down, so all water may run out. Then stand peppers up, side by side, in deep-walled baking dish which will hold them upright. Fill each pepper to top with any of the following types of **food mixtures:** canned or homemade cooked hash; any creamed meat, or fish, or fowl, or ham, to which you may add cooked noodles, or cooked rice, or cooked macaroni, or cooked mushrooms, or cooked vegetables; cooked spaghetti in tomato sauce (add diced cooked or canned meat, if desired); any cooked meat or vegetables in curry sauce; plain, buttered, cooked rice.

Place dish in preheated, moderate (375°) oven about 20 to 30 minutes, until peppers and their filling are thoroughly hot. Serve 1 per person.

MASHED VEGETABLES

Any vegetable, *before it can be mashed, must first be cooked tender,* which usually means boiling the vegetable in hot salted water until tender. (See Preparation and Basic Rules for Boiling Vegetables.)

Occasionally, the pulp of a baked squash or baked potato is scooped out of its shell, mashed, blended with seasonings such as salt, pepper, butter, and returned to its shell.

Mashed Potatoes

Peel, then cut into cubes or slices **4 or 5 medium potatoes,** to serve 2 or 3 people. Boil in hot salted water, in covered pan (see Basic Rules, Boiled Vegetables, p. 290) until tender. Drain. Mash the hot potatoes with potato masher until no lumps remain. Season with **salt, pepper;** add a lump of **butter,** plus **2 or 3 table- spoons hot milk** — more, if softer potatoes are desired. Beat milk in well, until potatoes are light and fluffy. If necessary to keep potatoes waiting, place pan over lowest possible heat, on asbestos pad, with lid partially covering pan, until serving; if left over high heat, they will scorch.

Mashed Pumpkin or Squash

To prepare and boil, see p. 289. To boil, see p. 290; p. 292. When tender, drain off all water. At once mash vegetable with potato masher until no lumps remain. If using as vegetable, sea- son at once with **salt, pepper,** a lump of **butter,** and serve hot. If using for pie, put mashed pumpkin or squash through sieve, to remove all lumps; then season as for Pumpkin Pie, p. 459.

Mashed Yellow Turnip

To prepare for cooking, see p. 289. To boil, see p. 290; p. 292. When tender, drain off all water. At once mash turnip with potato masher until no lumps remain. Season with **salt, pep- per,** and a lump of **butter** . . . or combine with seasoned hot mashed potatoes. Serve hot. If necessary to keep them waiting, take same precautions as for mashed potatoes so they won't burn.

PAN-FRIED VEGETABLES

Some boiled, drained vegetables may be sliced and then pan- fried in 2 or 3 tablespoons hot cooking fat until lightly browned on each side. This gives them a different taste, and adds variety to menus. Try:

Pan-Fried Carrots

Use whole, peeled, boiled **carrots,** which have been cooked in salted water until tender but not soft, then drained of water. Slice them lengthwise, in long strips about ⅜ inch thick. Place strips in frying pan containing **2 or 3 tablespoons butter** or other cooking fat. If desired, sprinkle carrots lightly with **sugar,** to give a sweet taste. Fry until browned lightly, on all sides, about 5 to 10 minutes.

Pan-Fried Parsnips

Use whole, peeled, boiled **parsnips,** which have been cooked in salted water until tender but not soft, then drained. Slice them into strips, as for pan-fried carrots, and fry same way as for carrots.

Pan-Fried Potatoes

See several ways to fry potatoes, Chapter IX (p. 89).

Pan-Fried Sweet Potatoes

Use canned **sweet potatoes,** drained; or use whole, peeled, boiled sweet potatoes which have been cooked in salted water until tender but not soft, then drained. Cut potatoes in lengthwise slices. Place slices in frying pan containing **2 or 3 tablespoons butter** (or bacon fat, or other cooking fat). Fry until lightly browned on both sides, about 5 to 10 minutes. If you prefer to glaze them (with brown sugar) see Glazed sweet potatoes (p. 297).

Pan-Fried Turnips

Either white or yellow **turnips,** peeled and boiled in salted water until tender but not soft, and then drained, may be fried. Slice them into ⅜ inch thick slices. Put slices in frying pan containing **2 to 3 tablespoons cooking fat.** Fry about 5 to 10 minutes, until lightly browned on all sides, sprinkling them lightly, once, with **salt, pepper,** as they fry.

OTHER WAYS OF COOKING
VEGETABLES

Sautéed Vegetables

Sliced raw onions, or raw mushrooms, may be sautéed (a gentler frying method). This method takes only 5 to 15 minutes; see pages 95–96.

Deep- or Shallow-Fried Vegetables

A number of raw vegetables may be cooked speedily by deep- or shallow-frying, in hot fat. In such cases, vegetables are not boiled ahead of time, but simply peeled, or washed and dried, cut to appropriate size, with seeds and other inedible parts removed before frying. Some are dipped in a coating, before frying. See: onion rings (p. 105), eggplant (p. 104), cauliflower flowerets (p. 114), cucumbers (p. 114), asparagus tips (p. 114), parsley (p. 115), white potatoes (p. 112).

Puréed Vegetables

To purée a vegetable means to boil it in salted water until tender; then to drain thoroughly, and to force the soft-cooked vegetable matter through a sieve to make the vegetable lumpless and very fine.

Puréed vegetables are often required for babies, and for invalids on soft diets.

You may purée any vegetable which can ordinarily be boiled.
Simply wash or peel and seed the vegetable, and cut to moderate or small pieces. Remove any unattractive outside leaves or skin blemishes. Then place prepared vegetable in saucepan containing ½ to 1 inch hot water plus ½ **teaspoon salt**. Cover pan. Cook over moderate heat until vegetable is tender when tried with fork. Drain. Force vegetable through a coarse sieve, or strainer, by pressing vegetable through with back of a tablespoon. Let vegetable drop into a bowl or pan underneath strainer. If desired, reheat puréed vegetable gently, and add a lump of **butter** before serving.

CHAPTER XXVI

Rice, Macaroni, Spaghetti, Noodles

METHOD FOR: *Fluffy Steamed White Rice, Rice Rings and Timbales, Brown Rice, Spanish Rice, Curried Rice, Rice Desserts, Boiled Macaroni, Spaghetti and Noodles, Noodle Rings, Macaroni and Cheese, Spaghetti with Meatballs, and many Variations*

RICE

Raw rice is sold in three lengths: long grain, medium grain, short grain. Long grain becomes fluffier and prettier when cooked. Though it costs a trifle more, it seems well worth it.

Raw rice is also sold in two "colors," as "white" or "brown" rice.

White rice means simply that the outer bran coating of each grain has been removed, thus leaving only the white inner "heart" of each kernel; and this inside white part is often artificially polished to dazzling luster, before sale, to make the rice more attractive. White rice is of course the kind to use for desserts. It is also used for the great majority of main-course dishes, especially to accompany such delicate-tasting foods as eggs, chicken, seafood, creamed foods. Its flavor is so mild that it serves as a bland and delicious "background" for other flavors.

Brown rice is rice with the outer bran coating *left on* each grain. Only a thin outside husk or skin has been removed from the kernel.

The bran coating gives the rice a brown, nutlike taste, much liked with game. The bran of course adds to the mineral and vitamin value of the rice. Brown rice must be cooked a bit longer, to become tender. Otherwise, it is cooked like white rice.

Precooked rice. If you buy the precooked white rice which is now on the market, follow recipes provided with the package rather than recipes given here. Since such rice has already been *partially* cooked, it can be used in different ways than raw rice.

MASTER RECIPE #41
FLUFFY STEAMED WHITE RICE

Quantity. 1 cup raw rice, after it expands in the cooking process, will yield *3 to 4 cups cooked rice.* This serves 3 to 4 people; or just about fills a 1 quart ring mold; or will make 4 or 5 timbales, depending on size of cups used for timbales. If you wish to cook only enough rice for 2 people, use ½ Master Recipe. On the other hand, rice keeps for days in a covered jar or bowl in refrigerator, and leftover rice can always either be reheated, or used cold, another day, as a dessert.

Measure (with measuring cup)
    1 cup uncooked rice (preferably long grain)
Turn dry rice into colander or large strainer; pick over to remove any foreign particles; hold strainer under running cold water to rinse off all grains well. Drain.

Now turn rice into 1½- to 2-quart saucepan which has a tight-fitting lid. Add to the rice grains
    2¼ cups cold water
    1 teaspoon salt
Place pan, uncovered, over direct heat; bring to boil. Let water boil 1 minute.

Remove from heat; stir rice once; then cover pan tightly. Place pan on back of a hot stove, or on an asbestos mat over your lowest burner, where rice will keep hot, *but not boil.* Leave rice there, covered tightly, 25 minutes. Then look at it. If rice is not well fluffed up and expanded to 3 or 4 times original volume, and if grains do not look fairly dry and separated from each other, cover again, and keep over low heat 5 to 10 minutes longer. When done, no water will remain in pan; rice will have absorbed it all. Each grain will be separate, tender, fluffy.

This is the easiest way to cook rice. The old-fashioned way of boiling it in large quantities of water required last-minute rinsing and reheating; a complicated method, most confusing to new cooks.

Suggestions for Foods to Accompany Rice

Cooked turkey or chicken, cut in pieces, and reheated in its own gravy.

Cooked lamb, cut up, reheated in its own gravy, or in curry white sauce (p. 249), or in curried gravy (see curry casseroles, p. 149).

Cooked chicken or turkey, cut in pieces, reheated in à la King sauce (p. 250).

Hard-cooked eggs, cut in pieces, reheated in curry white sauce (p. 249), or in mushroom sauce (p. 249), or in parsley sauce (p. 248).

Shrimps, cooked or canned, reheated in white sauce (p. 248), or curry white sauce (p. 249).

Diced cooked ham, reheated in white sauce (p. 248), or in mustard sauce (p. 250), or in deviled sauce (p. 249).

STEAMED WHITE RICE VARIATIONS

Rice Ring

For 3 to 4 people. Cook 1 cup raw rice, by Master Recipe. When cooked and still hot, stir in ¼ to ½ cup butter. Butter generously the inside of a 1 quart ring mold. Pack buttered rice into buttered mold. Place mold in a shallower pan of hot water; simmer over lowest possible heat of surface burner for 10 minutes. (This sets the ring, and also keeps rice hot.) To unmold: Remove mold from hot water. Place heated serving platter over top of mold. Invert both mold and platter simultaneously, holding them tightly together. Ring should slip out intact onto platter if mold has been adequately buttered. Lift off mold carefully, not to destroy shape of ring. Fill center of ring with any desired creamed, cooked meat, fowl, egg, or seafood combination. Or you may simply fill ring with other cooked, hot vegetables, such as peas.

Highly Seasoned Rice Ring. To give rice ring a more pungent taste, after stirring the butter into the cooked rice, you may also stir in ⅛ teaspoon garlic powder, or 1 or 2 teaspoons grated raw onion, or 1 or 2 tablespoons minced chives. If desired, add also ¼ cup minced fresh parsley, or 1 or 2 tablespoons finely shredded celery leaves; or 1 tablespoon minced green pepper; or 1 table- spoon slivered canned, drained, pimiento. Adding your own seasonings makes a Rice Ring very particularly "your own," and like no one else's.

Rice Timbales

Makes 3 to 5 timbales, depending on size of cups used. Cook **1 cup raw rice,** by Master Recipe. When cooked and still hot, stir into rice **¼ cup butter** if desired, for the buttery taste. Grease generously with butter the inside of 3 to 5 small individual metal molds, or custard cups. Pack rice in, filling cups to top. Place cups upright in shallow pan of hot water; simmer over lowest possible heat of surface burner for 10 minutes. Lift cups from hot water. Invert them, one by one, onto a heated serving platter, or onto heated dinner plates. Lift off cups, or molds, leaving mounds of rice. Garnish top of each timbale with a bit of **finely chopped parsley and a dash of paprika,** and serve in place of potatoes. (Or cover top of each timbale with cheese sauce (p. 249), mushroom sauce (p. 249), celery sauce (p. 250), onion sauce (p. 250), or with any creamed food suggested for accompanying rice.)

Brown Rice

Cook as in Master Recipe, Steamed White Rice, but cook longer; allow about 45 minutes after water has come to boil. If desired, while rice is cooking, sauté separately in frying pan (in **2 tablespoons butter**) ½ **cup peeled sliced onions,** plus ¼ **cup** sliced mushroom caps and stems. Have these tender, hot, and ready to mix with hot rice, before serving. This combination is excellent with foods of strong and pronounced flavor.

Rice Amandine (with almonds)

Serves 3 to 4. Cook 1 cup raw white rice by Master Recipe. While rice is cooking, sauté in ¼ cup butter, in frying pan, until golden color, ½ cup blanched, skinned, chopped almonds (to blanch, see page 503). When rice is done, mix with it the butter and almonds. Add ¼ cup minced parsley. Serve at once. This is delicate and delicious to serve with chicken.

Spanish Rice

Serves 3 to 4. Cook ½ cup raw white rice by Master Recipe, using only 1 cup and 2 tablespoons water, and ½ teaspoon salt. While rice is steaming, melt in large frying pan or saucepan 2 tablespoons butter. Add 1 cup thinly sliced peeled onions; simmer onions over low heat of surface burner until tender. Then add to onions 2 cups canned tomatoes, 1 teaspoon salt, 3 tablespoons diced green pepper, 1 or 2 whole cloves, ½ bay leaf, 2 teaspoons sugar. Simmer uncovered 15 minutes. Remove bay leaf and cloves; then combine all ingredients with rice. Turn into buttered 1-quart casserole. Bake in moderate (375°) oven 30 minutes, so rice may be permeated with the other flavors.

Curried Rice and Onions

Serves 3. Have available 1 cup steamed rice (this is a good way to use leftover rice). Peel and slice thin 3 or 4 medium onions. Cook onion, covered, in ½ inch boiling water to which you have added ½ teaspoon salt, about 15 to 20 minutes, or until tender; then drain. Mix with onions 2 tablespoons butter, ½ teaspoon curry powder, ¼ teaspoon salt, ½ cup top milk or cream (or evaporated milk), pinch of nutmeg or mace. Stir well. Add cooked rice, and blend. Heat thoroughly, covered, but *over very low heat*, so contents will not burn. For extra safety, you might heat this mixture in top section of double boiler, over pan of boiling water.

Rice to Be Served with Meat or Fowl

If desired, in Master Recipe, Steamed White Rice, substitute meat broth or **bouillon**, or **chicken** or **turkey stock**, in place of water. Rice, in swelling, then drinks up the flavor of the meat or fowl you plan to serve with it, and becomes more tasty.

To Reheat Left-over Cooked Rice

Put leftover **cold, cooked rice** in top section of double boiler. Place this over lower section of double boiler containing 1½ inches hot water. Place complete double boiler over medium direct heat, and keep water boiling gently 10 to 20 minutes, or until rice is thoroughly hot. Rice may then be used as if just cooked.

To Use Cold Cooked Rice as Dessert

Divide **cold cooked rice** into individual portions, in serving dishes. Garnish each serving with any desired **dessert sauce** (pp. 405–409). Or garnish with cut **fresh peaches** or other **fruit,** or **sweetened berries,** and top with **whipped cream.** Or garnish with a tablespoonful of **peach, raspberry** or **strawberry jelly,** or **jam,** or **preserves.** Or simply sprinkle cold rice with **confectioners' sugar,** add a **dash of nutmeg or cinnamon,** and serve with thick **cream.**

Rice Pudding (Baked)

Grease with **butter a** 1½ quart casserole. In a bowl, mix ¼ **cup raw, picked-over rice,** ⅓ **cup granulated sugar,** ½ **teaspoon salt, 1 quart whole milk, 1 teaspoon vanilla;** stir well to dissolve sugar; pour into casserole. Add 1 tablespoon butter and sprinkle top of mixture with **few dashes nutmeg.** Place dish in slow (325°) oven and bake 2½ to 3½ hours, as desired. At 2½ hours pudding will be soft and creamy (rather moist); if baked longer, it becomes quite firm. Stir the pudding two or three times within the first hour of baking to keep rice from settling at bottom. If desired, after the first hour of baking, you may stir in ½ **cup seedless raisins.**

Custard Rice Pudding. A richer rice pudding is made by adding 3 or 4 slightly beaten eggs with the milk, in above mixture. All other ingredients stay the same.

MACARONI, SPAGHETTI, NOODLES

These flour-paste products are all "relations" to each other, all being made of a special, high-gluten flour. Noodles usually have egg added to the paste, which gives them a yellower color. Some noodles, however, are artificially colored; see label on your package, to determine whether you are getting genuine "egg noodles," if you want these.

Of the tubular forms, macaroni is fattest; spaghetti medium-size, and vermicelli the thinnest.

Macaroni is also sold in fancy ring, fluted, or shell shapes.

Noodles are flat bands, like ribbons, and may be wide or thin.

Regardless of shape, these products, when well made, should be able to hold their shape in cooking; and should break without splintering, if you wish to break them into short lengths *before* cooking.

Many packages give cooking directions, but here is the general rule which is safe to follow for any type product of this family:

MASTER RECIPE #42
BOILED MACARONI, SPAGHETTI, NOODLES

(Serves 3 or 4)

In large kettle, bring to bubbling boil
2 quarts water
Add to boiling water
2 teaspoons salt
Add little by little, so as not to halt the boiling
4–6 ounces (about ½ package) macaroni, noodles, or spaghetti (which you have first broken into 1½–2 inch lengths if desired)
Keep water bubbling, and pan uncovered. Cook 10 to 20 min-

utes, or until tender (fish out one strand and rub it between fingers, to test tenderness).

When tender, turn contents of kettle into large colander or strainer; drain. Pour over cooked contents 1 cup boiling water, to wash away sticky starch. Drain again. Blend with

melted butter

and sprinkle with

paprika

and serve instead of potatoes. Or combine with meat and gravy or with other foods to make a casserole (see p. 142). Or use as a "bed" for cooked chicken or meat in hot gravy.

MACARONI, SPAGHETTI, AND NOODLE VARIATIONS

In all recipes below, the macaroni, noodles, or spaghetti are first *boiled* by Master Recipe #42, Macaroni, Spaghetti and Noodles, page 310, *and drained* before being used to make the dish.

Sautéed Noodles

Serves 2 to 3. Cook ½ **package noodles.** Drain. Then, in a frying pan or saucepan, melt **4 tablespoons butter.** Add drained noodles. Brown noodles lightly, until golden. Serve hot, in place of potatoes.

Noodle Ring

Serves 4 to 6. Cook 1 **package noodles.** Into hot, cooked, drained noodles, stir ¼ **cup butter.** Pack noodles into well-buttered 1½-quart ring mold. Place mold in shallower pan of hot water, and put in moderate (375°) oven 10 to 20 minutes, or until ready to serve. To unmold, lift mold from hot water; invert heated serving platter over top of ring mold; turn both mold and platter over simultaneously, holding both tightly together; noodle ring should slip out intact, if mold was sufficiently greased. Fill ring with cooked meat or fowl heated in gravy, or with any foods suggested for rice (p. 306).

If desired to make a richer noodle ring, you may mix with the cooked, drained noodles 3 egg yolks, well beaten, plus ½ cup hot milk or cream, ¼ teaspoon pepper, ½ teaspoon salt. Last, fold in 3 egg whites, beaten until they stand in soft peaks. Place mixture in well-buttered casserole; set casserole in shallow pan of hot water. Place pan or casserole in moderate (375°) oven 30 to 40 minutes, or until mixture is "set" and firm. Unmold, as for plain noodle ring.

Macaroni-and-Cheese (Baked)

Serves 3 to 4. Cook ½ package macaroni, then drain it. Then combine with other ingredients, as follows: Make double the recipe for cheese sauce (p. 249), so you will have 2 cups. Mix cooked sauce with cooked macaroni. Butter a 1½-quart casserole. Turn macaroni-and-sauce mixture into it. Bake in preheated moderately hot (400°) oven 20 to 30 minutes, until top of casserole browns.

Noodles or Macaroni with Fish (Baked)

Serves 3 to 4. Can be made with any cooked or canned white fish, mackerel, tuna, salmon, or shrimp. Cook ½ package noodles or macaroni by Master Recipe; then drain them. Make 2 cups medium white sauce (p. 248), adding 1 or 2 teaspoons grated raw onion and 1 tablespoon minced green pepper to thickened sauce. Grease with butter the inside of a 1½ quart casserole. Put in drained cooked noodles or macaroni. Stir in flaked, drained, cooked or canned fish (remove bones and skin, if any; and if using shrimps clean out the black intestinal vein before using them). Over entire contents pour the sauce. Cover top of mixture with a thin layer of fine bread or cracker crumbs. On top, scatter 8 or 10 dots of butter, size of peas. Bake uncovered in moderate (375°) oven about 30 minutes, or until crumbs brown.

Noodles or Macaroni with Meat and Gravy (Baked)

Serves 3 to 4. Cook ½ package noodles or macaroni by Master Recipe; then drain them. Grease a 1½-quart casserole with butter.

Put in it the **drained cooked noodles or macaroni.** Add **2 cups diced or cubed cooked meat** (this may be lamb, beef, pork, chicken, turkey, or ham). Over contents pour **2 cups gravy** of same flavor as your meat; or, if you lack gravy, use **2 cups white sauce** (p. 248), or use **1 can undiluted soup,** condensed cream of mushroom or cream of celery. Over top, grate **1 or 2 teaspoons peeled onion.** Cover with lid. Bake in moderate (375°) oven about 45 minutes, until thoroughly hot.

Homemade Italian Spaghetti

Serves 3 to 4. At least one hour before cooking spaghetti, make the following sauce: In saucepan, heat **2 tablespoons olive oil or salad oil.** Add **1 peeled clove garlic,** minced, plus **2 tablespoons minced peeled onion.** Sauté onion and garlic in the oil until golden brown. Then add **1 3 ounce can tomato paste,** plus **2 chopped fresh tomatoes, 2 teaspoons salt, 2 cups hot water, few grains pepper.** If desired, add a pinch of **powdered cloves,** and **½ teaspoon powdered sage.** Simmer all these ingredients together for 1½ hours, uncovered, stirring frequently. During last ½ hour of the simmering, you can cook your **spaghetti** in separate pan, as given in Master Recipe; then both will be done at about the same time. Drain cooked spaghetti; arrange a layer of it on a heated platter. Over this, pour half the sauce, and sprinkle with **grated American or Parmesan cheese.** On top place the remainder of spaghetti, and top with remainder of sauce and more grated cheese. Serve very hot.

Quick Spaghetti with Meat Balls

Serves 3. For this hurry-up dish, buy a **can of spaghetti in tomato sauce,** already cooked, and **½ pound raw ground beef.** Mix with ground meat **1 to 2 teaspoons grated raw onion, ½ teaspoon salt, few grains pepper.** If desired, add **½ teaspoon prepared mustard,** or **few drops Worcestershire sauce.** Shape the meat into small balls, the size of walnuts. Brown balls in hot frying pan, turning as fast as needed, to brown on all sides. Then add to frying pan the canned spaghetti and its tomato sauce. Cover pan; reduce heat; keep over heat until spaghetti and sauce are thoroughly hot, about 10 to 15 minutes. This is an easy dish to fix over an outdoor fire, on picnics; and children love it.

CHAPTER XXVII

What to Do with Fruits

METHOD FOR: *Fresh Fruit, Dried Fruits, Stewed Fruits, Applesauce, Baked Fruits, Fruit Cups*
For Other Uses of Fruit, See End of Chapter.

WHY FRUIT?

Anyone who has been accustomed to eating plenty of fruit, and then is suddenly deprived of it (as travelers sometimes are, in foreign lands) knows, without persuasion, that fruits do something for the human system which nothing else seems to do. A diet lacking fruits is a sorry thing; some of the litheness and lightness of living seems to disappear from the body, and a weary heaviness to take its place.

And this for good reason. Fruits *do* supply special minerals, vitamins, much-needed bulk. All citrus (and a few other) fruits — oranges, lemons, grapefruit, tangerines, cantaloupe, strawberries — supply that one essential vitamin the body cannot store up: Vitamin C, the chief preventor of deficiency diseases such as scurvy, sore gums; and this vitamin must be renewed daily, in the human body.

But aside from such vital health reasons, any wise mother will serve fruits often, just because fruits brighten and lighten a meal, making it fresh-tasting and delicious. When fresh fruits are high-priced, you can use canned, dried, or frozen fruits; and the number of ways to use them is legion. Try them not only in salads, or fruit cups; but jelled, in puddings, in pies, in cakes . . . or to garnish boiled custard, gelatine desserts, creamy puddings . . .

or to sweeten and moisten dry cake . . . or to make a fresh-tasting sauce over ice cream. In hot weather, it is not unwelcome to have some fruit in almost every meal. And remember, the more often you serve it, the clearer-skinned, brighter-eyed, and healthier your family will be.

FRESH FRUITS

Most — but not all — fruits can be eaten raw, if thoroughly ripe. Exceptions like "sour" cherries, "greening" apples, rhubarb, need cooking with sugar, to make them palatable. *Dried* fresh fruits (apricots, prunes, apples) need simmering in water, to restore moistness. Some fruits need a sprinkling of sugar. But most need nothing, if fully ripe.

To clean. Any fruit which has been handled by strangers, or exposed to flies, in a public market, should be washed (or peeled) before being eaten. Even if gathered from your own garden, fruits should be carefully "picked over," looking for possible insects, bad spots, or worms.

Apples. There are both "eating" apples, and "cooking" apples. Ask your dealer what varieties he has. Most apples of bright red or yellow color are good to eat raw. Those very "spicy" in flavor also make wonderful apples for baking, or for applesauce. Hard, green, tart apples should not be eaten raw, but make the tangiest pies and cobblers. Eating apples may be diced, sliced, cut in rings or wedges, and eaten out of the hand or used in fruit cups, salads, apple fritters.

Avocado Pears. An avocado, when fully ripe, has soft, mealy pulp, and may even be flecked with dark specks. If you object to the dark specks, serve pear before dead-ripe. Any avocado will darken (from exposure to air) within a few minutes after being opened and cut; therefore, do not prepare this fruit until time to serve. If, for any reason, prepared fruit must be kept waiting, dip it in lemon juice, or cover with waxed paper, to protect it from air as much as possible.

To open. Cut pear in half, lengthwise. Twist top half of pear off, leaving the stone in lower half. (If not using more than ½ the pear at one meal, store the half containing stone, well wrapped in waxed paper, in hydrator of refrigerator; pear keeps better if stone is left in it.) Unpeeled, the pear halves make "cups" to hold other ingredients; or peel and slice pear for salads.

Bananas. By now, thanks to the radio song, everyone knows that bananas should not be kept in a refrigerator. However, storing them in a closed paper bag helps them keep longer than if exposed to air. Buy them when yellow, tipped with green, and use them as they ripen. When dead ripe and at peak of flavor, the skins may be flecked with dark spots. This does no harm. But don't wait until they become soft. Bananas, sliced, diced, or cut in long spears, may be used in many salads; they are wonderful combined with berries or almost any fruit. Use them in all sorts of desserts: gelatine, or ice cream, on top of puddings or pudding-type pie fillings; in banana upside down cake, shortcake.

Berries. If berries come from your own land, don't wash them (washing softens them a bit, and removes some of the juicy flavor). Just pick them over carefully, removing sticks, leaves, insects, or any berries with spots. Sprinkle lightly with sugar when serving, if tart. Otherwise, wash berries in ice water.

To prepare sweet, crushed berries and juice to pour over ice cream, pudding, cake: mash berries slightly, with potato masher. Sprinkle over them several spoonfuls of sugar. Let stand, 15 to 30 minutes. Sugar draws out the juice.

Use berries in fruit cups, combined with pineapple, bananas, or peaches. Or use them in pies or cobblers. Or use them in short-cakes. Blueberries are also excellent used in waffles, pancakes, or muffins.

Cherries. Cherries, especially, are apt to harbor worms. Wash them thoroughly. Examine carefully cherries that float in water. Use only plump, firm ones with no spots. Stems may be left on, if cherries are to be eaten with the fingers. Remove stems, and squeeze out pits, before incorporating in fruit cups or salads. "Sour cherries" (a different species) are used only in cooking, for pie, cobbler, etc.

Cranberries. Use only firm, clear-red colored cranberries. They may be used raw in salads, whole or chopped. They are chopped, raw, to put into stuffing; and cooked, whole, with sugar, until skins "pop," to make cranberry sauce (p. 257).

Currants. Whether you buy red, black, or white currants, do not get overripe ones, which fall off stem. Stem, wash, and serve with a sprinkling of sugar. Currants combine well with other fruits, such as bananas, raspberries, crushed pineapple. And of course they make wonderful jelly.

Fresh Figs. Unlike dried figs, fresh ones are plump, soft, juicy. Buy only in small quantities, since they do not keep too long, even in a refrigerator. Before serving, remove outer skin or membrane with a sharp knife; then slice or leave whole. Serve with cream, if desired; no sugar.

Grapefruit. Buy grapefruit which is heavy for its size, feels thin-skinned when you pinch it, and in which you can feel juice moving (many grapefruit are thick of skin, dry and woody inside).

To separate into sections. Here's how food editors do it. Using sharp knife, slice off a straight slice about ¼ inch thick, from top of grapefruit (this slice should be deep enough to remove both outer yellow skin and white membrane coating underneath it). Cut a similar slice off bottom of grapefruit. Then peel off skin from sides by cutting with knife, spiral-fashion, around outside of grapefruit. When all skin is removed, place grapefruit on plate or cutting board. With sharp knife again (a dull one will tear the fruit!) cut one deep, long cut from outer edge of grapefruit toward the core, alongside each of the white membrane "division walls" which separate one section from another. Cut close to the division membrane, on each side of it. Do this all the way around the grapefruit. Sections can then be lifted out intact. When lifting them out, do it over a bowl, to catch any good juice which drips out.

Grapefruit sections keep well, for several days, in covered bowl or jar, in refrigerator, so if you want nice ones for a party, do them ahead of time, when you are not rushed.

To serve half grapefruit. Cut grapefruit crosswise, halfway between bud end and stem end, so that inside sections of grapefruit will be upright when fruit is open. With sharp knife, remove white pulpy core, and pits. Now slide point of knife around each section, just inside the membrane, so pulp is loosened for eating. If grapefruit is bitter, it may be sprinkled with sugar, or the core opening filled with maraschino cherry juice, or honey, or sherry.

Halves of grapefruit, prepared and sweetened as above, may be placed under moderately hot broiler for a few moments, if desired. They taste surprisingly different, hot.

Grapes. Small, seedless grapes are firm-textured, sweet, and excellent to use in salads, or fruit cups; just wash and stem them, and slice in half lengthwise. They combine pleasantly with diced apples, bananas, grapefruit sections, peaches or pineapple, diced celery, nuts.

Large firm grapes, with seeds, may be cut in half and seeded, before using in salad or fruit cup, or may be left in bunches, and served on plates, or from a bowl of fruit.

Kumquats. These are small, orange-colored fruit. Every bit of a kumquat is edible. Sliced, they may be used in fruit cups, salads.

Limes. Persian limes are green; Mexican limes quite yellow. A good juicy lime is heavy for its size. Lime juice makes cooling punches, other drinks; it makes lime gelatine; and a few drops of lime juice give brightness and refreshing tang, blended with mayonnaise for a fruit salad.

Melons. Cantaloupe. Ripeness is indicated by a strong melon "fragrance," by the network of veins of the skin standing out, by softness at stem end. If necessary to ripen hastily, place melon in very slow (250°) oven for an hour or more; then chill before serving. If you are not in a hurry, ripen it in a sunny window, or at room temperature, for one or more days.

Cut melon in half, lengthwise. Scoop out seeds and stringy portion. Then cantaloupe may be used in many ways:

Fill halves with ice cream, or frozen fruit salad, or cut fresh fruit or berries.

Or peel, cut lengthwise into half-moon-shaped slices. Place two slices, facing each other, on plate or on lettuce leaves. Fill center with cut fresh fruit or ice cream. (This makes melon serve more people.)

Or, with melon-ball cutter, cut out balls to use in fruit cups, or fruit salads.

Or serve wedges or halves of melon plain, with a sprig of mint stuck into flesh of melon. Some people like to sprinkle flesh with lemon juice, or salt, or both.

Honeydew. These are large, oval, cream-colored, smooth-skinned melons, with juicy green flesh, very sweet. Cut and clean like cantaloupe. Then:

Cut in wedges, and serve each wedge with lemon to squeeze over it, and a sprig of mint stuck in it. Some people sprinkle with salt.

Or cut melon balls, to use in salads, or fruit cups.

Honeyball. These are much like honeydew, but small, and round. Use like honeydew melon.

Watermelon. The only sure way to judge whether a watermelon is ripe is to cut into it and look inside. Because of this, and also because of their huge size, many stores sell watermelons cut in halves, or quarters. Flesh should be deep red, and seeds black, when melon is ripe. Chill melon thoroughly. Cut into serving-size wedges. With point of knife, remove as many seeds as possible, if desired; or let each person remove his own. A ripe watermelon is sweet, needs no flavoring, unless you wish to add a sprig of mint.

Chilled balls cut from watermelon are refreshing in a fruit cup, for a hot day. Combine them with berries, sliced bananas, or cut pineapple. Or combine with balls of other types of melon (green honeydew and red watermelon, decorated with a sprig of mint, are very pretty). Or use melon balls on top of a portion of lime, lemon, orange, or raspberry ice. Or pour a little ice-cold gingerale over a cup of melon balls, and garnish with a sprig of mint.

Persian. These are round, greenish-skinned melons. The flesh is much like cantaloupe. Use in the same way.

Casaba. These are large, round, yellowish melons, with deeply ridged skin, and pale, almost white, flesh. Use like honeydew melon.

Nectarines. This greenish-white fruit is a cross between peach and plum. Keep in refrigerator. Use in salads, or fruit cups.

Oranges. Select oranges which are thin-skinned, heavy for their size, and in which you can feel juice moving. The words "color added" means only that harmless vegetable coloring has been added to skins, to make them look more attractive; it does not affect juice. Russet-skinned oranges, or Valencias with a green area near stem end, are just as delicious as any others. Sweetness of juice is greatest when the orange crop has reached its peak of ripeness; oranges gathered too early, for shipping, are less sweet.

To serve orange halves. Prepare like grapefruit halves.

To obtain orange sections. Prepare like grapefruit sections.

Orange juice. Keep oranges stored in refrigerator, and do not squeeze until time to serve juice (orange juice loses some of its vitamins, if left standing long). After squeezing, seeds may be removed and pulp left in the juice, if desired; many people like it. Or put juice through strainer, to remove both seeds and pulp. If using mechanical "juicer" do not press skins too hard, or they may emit a somewhat bitter oil.

Navel oranges. These are a separate species, which have no seeds, and can be peeled and pulled apart into sections by hand, and eaten from the hand, or sliced crosswise, for use in salads, etc. They are naturally more expensive, and may often have thick skins. The skin has an open "navel" at one end. Start peeling from this point. Good navel oranges are usually juicy and full of sweet flavor.

Peaches. Ripe peaches should feel somewhat yielding to the touch (not hard), and should have a blush of pink color, or at least a ripe-looking yellow tone on the skin. When skins or flesh are green, peaches are not ripe.

Freestone peaches are most popular for eating raw. They have yellow or whitish flesh. Cling peaches are used more for canning, pies. Keep all peaches in refrigerator, in paper bag, to prevent spoiling.

Wash skins well, if leaving them on.

Peeled, sliced peaches combine well with bananas, pineapple, blueberries. Or they may be used to fill haves of melon; or on top of ice cream, or lemon ice; or to top cake, or soft puddings, or gelatine; or may be used for peach shortcake.

Peaches turn dark from exposure to air; so do not slice them until time to use.

Pears. Ripe pears, like ripe peaches, should feel slightly yielding, not hard. Many varieties have yellow or pink skin; a few varieties have green skin even when ripe. Wash skins well; serve pears whole. Or peel, cut in halves lengthwise, remove core, and fill hollows with some garnish to serve as a salad. Or peel, slice, and use in fruit cups, fruit salads, etc.

Persimmons. Never, but *never,* eat a green persimmon, or you will be sorry; it puckers your mouth for hours! When ripe, persimmons are between orange and red in color, and are soft, and very rich in flavor. Wash skins well, and chill. The entire fruit is edible. Eat with fingers or spoon or fork. Or use slices of this gay-colored fruit to garnish fruit desserts, or salads.

Pineapple. To select a ripe pineapple, find one whose leaves come out easily, if pulled. (The store won't like your pulling leaves out, but try just one, anyhow.) The pineapple should have a golden yellow undertone of color, a nice fragrance. Do not buy one which has soft spots, or blackness around "eyes" or base.

Pineapple rings. Cut crosswise slices, ¼ inch thick, through pineapple, with its skin on. Then peel off skin from each slice; remove "eyes." Cut out hard center core with knife, or a small-size biscuit cutter.

If pineapple is dead ripe, it may be sweet enough to eat "as is"; if it seems a little tart, do this: Cook in a saucepan for 10 minutes a sugar syrup made of 1 cup granulated sugar and 2 cups water. Pour this boiling syrup over the sliced, prepared pineapple, and let it stand — not over heat — until syrup cools.

Pineapple spears. Cut off topknot of leaves. Peel entire pineapple. Remove all eyes. Then cut pineapple in half lengthwise. Then cut again, so you have lengthwise quarters. Now from each quarter, remove the strip of hard core. You may now cut lengthwise strips of any length or thickness desired. To sweeten, follow same method as given for rings.

To dice pineapple. Cut smaller either spears, or rings.

Note: Never use "fresh" (only canned) pineapple in gelatine dishes. Fresh pineapple contains an enzyme which prevents gelatine from jelling.

Plums. Should be plump, juicy feeling, not hard. Wash skins, and eat raw; or they may be stewed.

Quinces. Autumn fruit, yellow to greenish-yellow in color, hard, and round. Use only for preserves, or jelly. Or may be baked. Not eaten raw.

Rhubarb. This is a plant with stalks and leaves somewhat like celery. In spring, stalks are pink; in later summer, reddish-green. Is only used cooked (p. 325), not raw. See rhubarb pie, p. 454.

Tangerines. A distant relative of the orange, but smaller, with loose, crinkly skin. Peel fruit, and use sections in salads, fruit cups.

DRIED FRUITS

In old times, dried prunes, apricots, peaches, apples and pears had to be soaked overnight, then simmered quite a time to make them tender. Today much better methods prevail in preparing these fruits for market, and the requirements for home cooking have changed. Therefore, when buying packaged dried fruits, follow directions that come with the package.

When buying dried fruit in bulk, however, cook by the safe rule below:

MASTER RECIPE #43
STEWED DRIED FRUITS

Rinse under cold water
dried fruit
Soak fruit in just enough
cold water
to cover, until fruit plumps up; 2 hours to overnight.

Leaving *same water* on fruit, simmer until fruit is tender, usually ½ to 1 hour.

When tender, add to cooking water enough
sugar
to make as sweet a liquor as you like. Stir, to dissolve sugar. Let fruit and syrup cool, or serve warm.

MASTER RECIPE #44
STEWED FRESH FRUIT

Fruits may be stewed because they are inedible raw, or because they are underripe and need sweetening, or just because someone likes them that way. In any event, stewing is a very simple matter. Any fruit which has a firm flesh (peaches, pears, apples, rhubarb, tomatoes, plums, even berries) may be stewed.

Put in condition for eating (peel, core, pit, slice, or whatever is necessary)
about 2 cups fruit
Put fruit in saucepan. Add

> ⅓ **to** ⅔ **cup sugar** (depending on
> natural tartness of fruit; see Variations, p. 325)
> ½ **to 1 cup water** (depending on
> natural juiciness of fruit; some
> fruits make so much juice that
> little water is wanted)

Cover saucepan. *Simmer* (don't boil hard) until fruit is tender. This may be 3 to 5 minutes for berries, or 20 to 40 minutes for hard-textured fruit like apples. Cool fruit in syrup.

STEWED FRESH FRUIT VARIATIONS

(Follow Master Recipe #44, Stewed Fresh Fruit, page 324, making changes noted below.)

Stewed Apples, or Hard Pears

Use about 1 cup water, ½ cup sugar.

Stewed Berries

Use ¼ to ½ cup water, and ⅓ cup sugar.

Stewed Peaches

Leave 1 or 2 pits with peaches to be cooked; it improves flavor. If peaches are juicy, use only ½ cup water; judge sugar by tartness of peaches.

Stewed Plums

Do not pit before cooking. Use 1 cup water, ⅓ cup sugar.

Stewed Rhubarb

Discard roots, leaves. Cut stalks in 1½ to 2 inch lengths. Use stalks as the "fruit." Use ⅔ cup sugar, but only ¼ cup water; rhubarb makes a good deal of juice by itself.

Stewed Tomatoes

(Literally a "fruit," though we think of them as vegetables.) Peel, or not, before stewing. Cut tomatoes into quarters, or eighths. Follow Master Recipe, Stewed Fruit, omitting sugar, or reducing it to 1 teaspoon. Use only ¼ cup water; tomatoes make much juice. Add to water ¼ teaspoon salt. If spicy seasoning is desired, add to cooking water 1 whole clove, 1 bay leaf, 1 branch celery with leaves.

Applesauce

Use 7 or 8 good-sized apples, free of spots; or more if small and spotty; cut out all spots before cooking. Peel and core apples; cut into quarters or eighths. Now, adding **½ cup water,** simmer as in Master Recipe, Stewed Fruit . . . but do not add sugar until apples are tender. When fruit is tender, mash it with potato masher if you like "chunky" applesauce, or, if you prefer smooth applesauce, force apple pulp and juice through coarse sieve or colander. Then add **⅔ to ¾ cup sugar;** cook a few minutes more, until sugar dissolves.

Spicy applesauce may be made by adding **⅛ teaspoon nutmeg,** or **cinnamon,** or **several whole cloves,** to apples as they cook, A strip of **lemon peel** may also be added, if you are one who likes lemon flavor in fruit.

BAKED FRUIT

Baked Apples

Choose **apples** free of bad spots, and matching in size. Do not peel, but wash skin well, and cut out core. Place apples on pie plate, or in shallow baking dish, with core openings standing upright. Pour into each core opening enough **granulated sugar to fill it to top.** Over top, sprinkle **several dashes nutmeg or cinnamon.** Bake in moderate oven (350°), about 35 to 50 minutes, until apples are tender. Baked apples are very good served warm, with heavy cream. Or chill them.

Baked Bananas

Use **bananas** which are not fully ripened, but are yellow with green tips. Peel them. Place them in **buttered or greased** baking dish or pie dish. Either brush them with **melted butter,** or sprinkle with **brown sugar.** Place in moderate oven (375°) and bake about 15 minutes, until tender when pricked with fork. Serve hot, as a vegetable, with ham, or chicken; or top with cooled soft custard (p. 385) or lemon sauce (p. 406) to serve as a dessert.

Baked Quinces

Peel **quinces;** core; cut in quarters or slice. Place fruit in shallow baking dish. Some people alternate thin slices of **peeled orange**

with sliced quinces. Sprinkle fruit with **brown sugar, or granulated.** Add to dish about **1 cup water.** Cover dish. Place in slow
oven (300°) and bake about 2 hours, or until tender when
pricked with fork. Good warm or cold.

FRUIT CUPS

Small quantities of several different fruits may be combined
(and their juices combined also) to make delicious fruit cups.

Fruit cups to be served as a first course should be made only
of nonsweet tangy fruits (grapefruit, oranges, tangerines, fresh
berries, seedless grapes, fresh pineapple). Very rich or sweet
fruits kill the appetite. As a dessert course, however, fruits may
be as sweet as desired.

Any fruit cup must be well chilled, to be appealing. And it
looks and tastes fresher if topped with chopped fresh mint leaves,
chopped candied ginger, or a bright red cherry for eye-appeal.

Dessert fruit cups may be given "party" flavoring by adding to
each cup 1 or 2 teaspoons sherry, or rum, or brandy.

If fruits lack sufficient juice, do one of these things:

Open and add a can of some other fruit, which will provide
juice.

Use any mixture of canned fruit juice, or nectar, with fresh
orange, or grapefruit, juice. Add few drops lemon or lime juice,
if desired.

Use part fruit juices, part ginger ale.

Use only ginger ale, letting the fruit stand in ginger ale for an
hour or more, in refrigerator, before serving.

Use part fruit juices, part white wine. Very elegant fruit cups
are made with champagne.

Instead of using any liquid, place chilled cut-up fruit over a
cupful of lemon, orange, lime, or raspberry ice. Top with a tablespoon of ginger ale if desired, and add a sprig of mint if you
have it.

OTHER FRUIT DESSERTS

Use cut fruit and berries in fruit salads (pp. 345–350) and gelatine (see Master Recipe #56, p. 361, and Master Recipe #57, p. 367).

Use cut fruit and berries on top of ice cream or ices (pp. 394–402), soft custard (p. 385), creamy pie fillings (p. 457), and dry homemade cake, store cake, or any plain cake.

Use cut fruit and berries to make fruit pies (pp. 452–456), fruit tarts (p. 456), chiffon pies (p. 461), fruit cobbler (p. 206), fruit muffins (p. 210), fruit waffles and griddlecakes (pp. 216, 219), fruit fritters (p. 213), biscuit shortcakes (p. 205), layer-cake shortcakes (p. 415), upside down cake (p. 416), and fruit sauce for desserts (see under berries, p. 317).

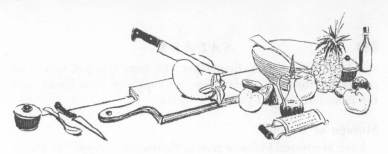

CHAPTER XXVIII

How to Make a Salad

METHOD FOR: *Vegetable Salads, Stuffed Tomato Salad, Tossed Green Salads, Chef's Salad, Cole Slaw, Potato Salads, Meat Salads, Chicken Salad, Seafood Salads, Fruit Salads*

For health, you should have salad at least once a day. In summertime, the family will like them even more often. They are refreshing.

Salads can be of endless varieties; don't always serve the same two or three kinds. Use imagination; use different types of (always crisped) greens, for variety; use all sorts of (always chilled) fruits and vegetables as garnishes or as integral part of the salad; add always some bright and decorative touch, for color. Arrange the ingredients attractively, on plate, or in bowl; a fresh, crisp appearance is a great part of the salad's appeal.

We are giving here some of the most-frequently used types of greens and other ingredients, and a few "standard" salads . . . but the fun is to make up your own, which you will readily do.

When you run out of ideas, try some of the salads in *4 Weeks Dinner Menus*, Chapter XLI. And watch the many attractive salad illustrations regularly appearing in magazines and food advertisements.

SALAD GREENS

There are many kinds; don't restrict yourself to lettuce. Try romaine, endive, chicory, escarole, watercress, spinach leaves, shredded cabbage, etc. Remember, the more types of salad you can devise, the more vitamins you are supplying your family, and the more interest you give your meals.

Storage of Greens

Keep in covered hydrator pan, or thoroughly wrapped in waxed paper, in refrigerator, until using. If uncovered, they wilt.

Preparation and Crisping of Greens

Remove outside, wilted leaves, rusty leaves, any undesirable pieces; excessive stems. Discard all these. Wash good leaves in pan of running cold water (this removes garden insects, dust, sand). Then put clean leaves in bowl of icy cold water, 10 to 30 minutes, to crisp. (If desired, you can place bowl in refrigerator for this period.) Then lift leaves from water; shake them well (the French shake them inside a clean towel) to remove every drop of water. Drops of water and salad dressing do not blend.

Greens can be washed, crisped, and dried several hours before serving time, if you wrap them in waxed paper and store in refrigerator to keep crisp until using. Or arrange in salad bowl; cover bowl with waxed paper, and store in refrigerator.

Other Preparation for Specific Greens

Lettuce

To prepare in separate leaves. First, remove undesirable outside leaves from head. Then with sharp knife, cut out from center of head the hard white core, making a cone-shaped hollow about 1 inch in diameter, where core was. Place head of lettuce in bowl, hollow-side up. Let cold water run steadily into the hollow for 3 to 5 minutes. Leaves will soon loosen and come apart, intact, without breaking. If desired to hasten the process, you can help the leaves apart with your fingers.

To prepare in wedges. First, remove undesirable outside leaves. Then with large sharp knife, cut head in half, lengthwise, through core. Now similarly cut each half into more lengthwise wedges, as many as desired. Place wedges in bowl of water, to wash; but do not leave them there too long, or leaves will begin to separate. Shake dry.

Endive. Cut off crosswise, from bottom of head of endive, a slice ¼ to ½ inch thick. Discard this. Then place head in bowl, under running cold water. Leaves will soon separate. Look at inside of each leaf to make sure it is clean; if necessary, scrub with soft brush and cold water. Endive often has much garden dirt inside the leaves. Crisp, and shake dry.

Escarole, Chicory. Break leaves off stem; wash; crisp; shake dry. See Preparation and Crisping of Greens (page 330).

Spinach Leaves. Select only young, tender leaves. Wash in several waters (spinach is often sandy); crisp; shake dry (page 330). Try combining these with 2 or 3 strips of crumbled pan-broiled bacon, a bit of crumbled blue cheese, and French dressing. Blend well.

Celery

To dice, or chop, for use in salads. Use 1 or 2 outside branches celery, if possible branches having some leaves. Scrub them under cold water, with brush, to remove clinging dirt. With sharp knife, scrape from back of each branch the "strings" (long fibers). Put cleaned celery on board, and cut fine, crosswise, with sharp knife; or cut it fine with scissors; or put it in chopping bowl and chop fine. Include a few finely shredded celery leaves whenever possible; these add much tang to a salad.

To prepare "celery hearts." (Use only the inside of a head of celery for this purpose; remove and keep outside branches to use in salad, as above.) Once outside branches have been removed, put remainder of head in bowl; wash under running cold water. Then, with sharp knife, trim off (thinly) any black matter from the "heart" (the hard white core at bottom of head), but keep the heart attached to head. Now with sharp knife, cut head in half lengthwise, starting from center of heart, and cutting right on through branches and leaves. Then, again cutting lengthwise, cut each half into two or three more long sections, each section retaining at bottom a wedge of "heart." Place celery thus cut in bowl of cold water again, to crisp. If you wish it to curl, place in bowl of cold water in refrigerator several hours, or overnight. It will keep in water, in refrigerator, several days.

Watercress. Break off unattractive leaves, and excess stems, but leave about ½ inch stem below each spray of leaves. Wash; crisp; shake dry (page 330). Watercress should be used within 1 or 2 days; it doesn't keep very long. It provides delicious contrast when used as garnish, with steak, liver, chicken, or fish; and is refreshing in salads.

VEGETABLE SALADS

A vegetable salad may be made of almost any vegetable you have at hand, provided the vegetable is edible raw — or is cooked or canned — and is not runny or mushy, but firm.

Your salad may turn out to be any one of:

A single vegetable arranged on top of greens (such as sliced tomatoes on top of watercress; or asparagus tips on lettuce).

A salad bowl in which 2 or 3 different kinds of vegetables are arranged in separate groups, or in alternating rows, on a bed of greens.

A mixture of numerous diced vegetables, well seasoned and tossed right in with chopped greens; this is called a mixed vegetable salad.

Vegetables jelled in aspic. For this type salad see pages 361–381.

Vegetables You May Use. You may use in salad:

Any vegetable which is edible raw, such as:

Celery, diced.

Green peppers, diced, or cut crosswise in rings.

Onions, peeled, then grated, or cut crosswise in rings.

Small scallions, peeled, roots cut off.

Tomatoes; peeled or not peeled (p. 336); cut in crosswise slices, or lengthwise wedges, or scooped out and used as "cups" to hold other food; see Stuffed Tomatoes (p. 336).

Cucumbers; peeled, soaked in cold water 30 minutes, sliced crosswise or lengthwise.

Cabbage; grated, or chopped fine in chopping bowl.

Carrots; grated (do not peel if young and tender-skinned).

Radishes; sliced crosswise, or cut like flowers.

In preparing any raw vegetables for salad use, remember that many vitamins are found right next to the skin; therefore leave on the skin whenever tender enough to eat.

Drained, firm, cooked or canned vegetables which have not been mashed, fried, or creamed, such as asparagus tips, string beans, Lima beans, kernel corn, beets, sliced, diced, or julienned, cauliflower flowerets, broccoli, boiled potatoes, diced or sliced.

For Taste Appeal. Whatever vegetables you plan to use, give them extra tang and "zing" by preparing them as follows:

Chill vegetables. All vegetables should be *well chilled,* before being used. Nothing is more unattractive than a luke-warm salad!

Marinate vegetables. Many vegetables (such as tomatoes, asparagus tips, cauliflower flowerets, broccoli, string beans) are far more delicious if they have first been marinated (bathed) in a small bowl of French dressing, for 10 to 30 minutes, before they are used. They may then be lifted from the dressing, drained, and arranged on greens. This is a good practice, even if you plan to garnish the salad with mayonnaise; the French dressing gives the whole salad more tang.

Add salt. To heighten the taste of your salad, lightly sprinkle vegetables with salt. There are also other salts you may use: onion salt; celery salt; chives salt; etc.

Add onion, garlic, chives. Sprinkling ½ to 1 teaspoon raw grated onion over top of a vegetable salad makes it far more tangy. Some people prefer to mix with salad 1 or 2 teaspoons finely minced chives. Others prefer to rub the inside of a wooden salad bowl with the cut surface of ½ clove garlic, letting the garlic flavor the salad when greens are put in bowl.

Herbs, for seasoning. Adding 1 or 2 tablespoons diced fresh parsley, or finely shredded celery leaves, gives surprising flavor to many vegetable salads. There are other herbs which may be added (p. 505); but of these, use only the merest pinch; too much will overpower the flavor of the vegetables.

Cheese. Crumbled blue cheese is wonderful on any vegetable salad. Or shape small balls of cottage cheese (first seasoned with salt, pepper, minced chives or grated onion) and use these as garnishes.

For Eye Appeal

Choose salad ingredients with contrasting color and texture. Lettuce and tomato has always made a popular salad, not only because tomatoes are ever present and easy to fix, but because the vivid redness and juiciness of the tomatoes contrast with the cool greenness and crispness of the lettuce. It is bright-looking; it pleases the eye, as well as the palate.

Any red-family vegetable (carrots, beets, radishes) provides this gay contrast with greens. Try to use a *bit* of red, at least, in every salad . . . even if it be only a bright dash of paprika.

With salads of *all-green* color (such as mixed greens, or asparagus tips or broccoli on lettuce), do add some contrast in color and texture either in dressing, or in garnish. Try marinated broccoli garnished with yellow mayonnaise, sprinkled with crumbled egg yolk, and topped with a dash of bright paprika. To mixed leafy greens add a sprinkling of crumbled blue cheese, or perhaps some crumbled cooked bacon, and French dressing. Some greens (Romaine, for example) are very good with Russian dressing (reddish color). Small garnishes (sliced radishes, or radish "flowers," or a strip of canned pimiento, or sliced stuffed olives, or a thin wedge of bright tomato) will bring any pale-looking salad to life.

Don't always arrange salad the same way. This means: don't always just put a heap of vegetable on top of a lettuce leaf! If using a salad bowl, you can arrange your vegetables in alternating rows, or in contrasting circles, or some other interesting pattern; watch pictures appearing constantly in food magazines, with new and interesting ideas.

You may make "cups" of cooked beets, or ripe tomatoes, to hold a stuffing of other smaller vegetables; see page 336. Or you may arrange a few canned asparagus tips to look as if they are tied together with a gay ribbon, by tucking around a "bundle" of them a thin strip of red pimiento. A "bundle" of long tender string beans may be tucked through a "hoop" of onion ring, or a green pepper ring. Do something different, and pretty.

Remember — there are no hard and fast *rules* about salads. You can put together anything you wish, so long as it is edible, will taste good, and look pretty. Sometimes you will buy special fresh vegetables (tomatoes, cucumbers, peppers) to use; other times you will use up leftover canned or home-cooked vegetables. Salad comes in the "Anything You Want Department," and depends only on your taste and imagination.

There are, however, a few well-known oft-repeated, "standard" salads, for which we now give recipes.

MASTER RECIPE #45
TANGY MIXED VEGETABLE SALAD
(Serves 2 to 3)

Peel, dice, drain, or otherwise prepare to small size, for eating

1 cup (or 1½ cups) mixed vegetables, cooked, canned,
or edible raw

Suggestions: string beans, Lima beans, kernel corn, peas, tomatoes (leave these cut in wedges if you prefer), cucumbers (peeled), celery, green pepper, carrots (either cooked, or raw and grated).

Always try to include some fresh celery; it gives tang and crispness to any mixed vegetable salad.

Assemble drained, diced, vegetables in mixing bowl; stir in for seasoning

1 to 3 teaspoons grated raw onion
sprinkling of salt
2 tablespoons French dressing

If desired, also stir in

2 or more tablespoons mayonnaise

Blend well. Turn mixture onto bed of

washed, crisped greens

Chill bowl, covered with waxed paper, about 20 minutes before serving.

Mixed Vegetable Salad with Meat, Fish or Eggs

This makes a fine main course on a hot summer night. Simply make your mixed vegetable salad by Master Recipe #45, p. 335, adding with seasoned vegetables ½ to 1 cup of any one of the following, for extra flavor and nourishment:

Ham, cooked or canned, diced; **luncheon meat,** cooked or canned, diced; **tongue,** cooked or canned, diced; leftover cooked **white-meated fish,** freed of skin and bones, and flaked; cooked **bacon,** diced; **kippered herring,** canned, broken in bits (use sparingly; very salty); **sardines,** canned, broken in bits, drained; **shrimps,** cooked or canned, cleaned of black vein (p. 169), drained; **tuna fish** or **salmon,** canned, drained, flaked; **anchovies,** canned, drained, cut up (use sparingly; very salty); **hard-cooked eggs,** quartered or sliced.

MASTER RECIPE #46
STUFFED TOMATO SALAD

You may peel or not peel tomatoes. Peeling makes tomatoes slightly easier to cut into; but leaving the skins on makes for higher nutritive value; so take your choice.

To peel whole tomatoes. There are two methods:

(1) Place tomatoes in pan, and pour boiling water over them. Leave them there a few minutes, until skins wrinkle and loosen. Lift tomatoes from hot water with fork. Pull off skins. Rechill tomatoes.

(2) Place one tomato at a time on a fork. Hold tomato over heat of surface burner, until skin cracks and splits. Skin may then be peeled off. Rechill tomatoes.

If not peeling. Wash tomatoes. Remove stem blemish, and any other blemishes, but leave skin as intact as possible.

To open tomatoes, to hold stuffing. There are three methods:

(1) With knife, cut out a small funnel-shaped piece of the tomato, from spot where stem joined it, to remove stem lump. Now cut 4, 6, or 8 wedges (depending on size of tomato) running

from top of tomato *almost* to the bottom; but leave bottom intact. Spread wedges slightly apart, like petals of a flower, and put stuffing in center.

(2) With knife, cut out quite a large funnel-shaped piece from center top of tomato, leaving tomato hollow like a cup. Save the tomato pulp you have cut out; and chop it and mix with other small vegetables you are using to stuff tomato cup.

(3) When tomatoes are scarce (or if you have tomatoes of giant size) you may cut each tomato in half, crosswise; then scoop out part of the center from each half, and stuff each half.

To make stuffing of mixed vegetables

Mix together in bowl

> **assorted leftover cooked (or canned) vegetables, well**
>> drained, cut to bite size

Add, if desired

> **tomato pulp**

you have scooped out of tomatoes.

Season mixed vegetables with

> **1 to 2 teaspoons grated onion**
> **¼ teaspoon salt**
> **few grains pepper**
> **minced parsley or minced green pepper**
> **1 or 2 tablespoons French dressing**
> **enough mayonnaise to moisten**

Put stuffing into tomatoes. Chill. Serve on

> **crisp greens**

STUFFED TOMATO SALAD VARIATIONS

(*Follow Master Recipe #46, Stuffed Tomato Salad, page 336, with changes noted below.*)

Tomatoes Stuffed with Ham Salad

Add **diced cooked ham,** or **tinned luncheon meat,** plus **½ teaspoon prepared mustard,** to your mixed vegetable stuffing.

Tomatoes Stuffed with Fish Salad

Add flaked, cooked leftover fish, or **cooked or canned seafood,** to the vegetable stuffing. Or stuff the tomatoes with **seafood salad** (p. 344).

Tomatoes Stuffed with Potato Salad

Use leftover **potato salad** in the tomato cups, instead of assorted vegetables.

MASTER RECIPE #47
TOSSED GREEN (FRENCH) SALAD

Cut in half a

clove of garlic

Rub cut side of garlic over entire inside surface of wooden salad bowl, to flavor bowl. Then discard garlic clove.

(Garlic is the seasoning always used by the French for green salad. If your family objects to garlic, omit this step. Instead add 1 or 2 teaspoons grated onion or chopped chives with salad greens.)

Wash, crisp, then shake dry in towel a mixture of crisp leafy

salad greens

(Choose two or more varieties from those listed on page 329.)

Leave greens whole, or break up into bite-size pieces. Put them in salad bowl.

(If desired, add to greens some crumbled cooked bacon, or crumbled blue cheese, or chopped fresh or dried mint leaves, or other salad herbs; p. 505.)

Sprinkle generously over greens

well-seasoned French dressing

With salad fork and spoon, toss over and over (the French say "fatigue") the salad, until all leaves are coated with dressing, on every side.

If seasoning of French dressing has been tasty enough, this is a marvelous and refreshing salad.

MASTER RECIPE #48
CHEF'S SALAD

Make tossed green salad (p. 338), but add with greens, before tossing salad

> diced celery
> tomato wedges or cubes
> diced or cubed cucumber
> onion rings
> green pepper rings, or strips,
> or any crisp, refreshing vegetable

MASTER RECIPE #49
COLE SLAW
(Serves 2 or 3)

Choose a young, tender cabbage (winter cabbage will be tougher). Cut in half, lengthwise, through core, or cut in quarters. Place cabbage in bowl. Let cold water run over it to wash it well. Drain it. Then grate, chop fine, or shred fine, until you have

> **4 cups cabbage**

Add to cabbage

> **1 whole onion, grated**
> **2 teaspoons sugar**
> **1 teaspoon salt**
> **2 tablespoons celery seed**
> **½ teaspoon prepared mustard**
> **¼ cup French dressing**

Toss well, to blend. Then stir in

> **⅓ to ½ cup mayonnaise or cooked salad dressing**

Some people add to cole slaw 1 cup finely cut celery. And for variety, some people add drained canned pineapple bits, or diced bananas, or cut-up apples, raisins, and nuts.

MASTER RECIPE #50
POTATO SALAD

(Serves 4)

If you have a real taste for food, you will never, *never* make potato salad (as so many stores and restaurants do) with *cold* potatoes. Such salad has a flat, hard, heavy feeling in the stomach, as well as a pasty feeling in the mouth.

Below is the way experts make potato salad. Try it, and you'll see the difference.

Boil whole, with skins on, in salted water, covered, until tender
5 or 6 medium potatoes
Pour off water. Leave cover off pan. Let potatoes cool a few minutes, until you can handle them. Then, holding one potato at a time on a fork, peel off skin, dropping peeled potatoes into a big bowl.

With two knives, cut in crisscross motion through hot potatoes, cutting them to bite-size pieces.

Immediately add
½ to 1 cup diced celery (including
some finely chopped celery leaves)
1 (or more) peeled, grated onion
Sprinkle mixture with
¼ teaspoon salt
¼ teaspoon sugar
Turn mixture over; sprinkle again with
¼ teaspoon salt
¼ teaspoon sugar
Over all, pour
¼ cup French dressing
Turn mixture over, so all ingredients may be coated with the dressing and seasonings. Let it stand 20 minutes, so seasonings may permeate the warm potatoes. Then add
1 cup (about) mayonnaise or cooked salad dressing

You may want more, depending on how moist you like your salad.

Taste; see if more salt is needed; individual taste differs on this.

Some people blend 2 or 3 diced hard-cooked eggs into potato salad but this is not at all necessary.

POTATO SALAD VARIATIONS

(*Follow Master Recipe #50, Potato Salad, page 340, making changes noted below.*)

Ham and Potato Salad

Add with mayonnaise 1 teaspoon prepared mustard, plus ½ to 1 cup diced cooked or canned ham; or you may substitute for ham diced canned luncheon meat, or sliced or diced cooked frankfurters.

Fish and Potato Salad

Add with mayonnaise ½ to 1 cup flaked cooked or canned fish; leftover cooked white fish, or drained cooked scallops, diced; or drained flaked kippered herring, or sardines, or other tangy fish.

Hot Potato Salad

Make Master Recipe, but with these changes: When peeling hot potatoes, place them in a baking dish. Cut them to bite size. Add celery, onion, salt, sugar. Add also ¼ cup finely chopped parsley. *Heat* your French dressing to boiling point before pouring it over the warm potatoes. (Instead of French dressing, you may combine ¼ cup bacon fat or olive oil with ¼ cup mild vinegar plus few drops lemon juice, heating this mixture before adding it to the potatoes.) Omit mayonnaise.

Turn potato mixture over several times, so all potatoes are evenly blended with dressing and seasonings. Cover baking dish. Place it in moderate oven (375°) 15 to 20 minutes, or until potatoes are again well heated. Serve hot, with hot ham or frankfurters.

SUGGESTIONS FOR QUICK, SIMPLE VEGETABLE SALADS

Washed, Crisped Drained Greens	Other Ingredients	Add for Tang	Dressing
Endive		blue cheese	French
Romaine	thin-sliced tomatoes or beets	grated onion	French
Spinach leaves		crumbled bacon crumbled blue cheese, if desired	French
Lettuce	diced, julienned, or sliced beets	grated onion or finely chopped mint	French
Watercress	thin-sliced cucumbers, tomatoes	grated onion	French
Lettuce	asparagus spears marinated in French dressing		Top with mayonnaise
Wedges of lettuce		blue cheese	Russian
Watercress, Lettuce, or Endive	young, whole string beans	grated onion blue cheese	French
Watercress	diced or thin-sliced cucumbers		Sour Cream
Lettuce or other greens	leftover mixed vegetables, marinated in French dressing	grated onion	French or mayonnaise or Russian
Lettuce	cooked, drained, broccoli, marinated in French dressing		top with mayonnaise
Lettuce	cauliflower flowerets, marinated in French dressing		top with mayonnaise

MEAT SALADS

Diced or cubed meat (never raw — but meat which has been cooked or canned) may be added to salads of various kinds, such as:

Mixed vegetable salad; see page 336.

Potato salad; see page 341.

Filling for stuffed tomatoes (p. 336).

Jelled main-course dishes. See under Aspics (p. 375).

MASTER RECIPE #51
CHICKEN SALAD

For chicken salad, you must have *cooked* (or canned) chicken meat, which has been freed of skin and bones.

You may use leftover roast chicken, or broiled chicken, or even fried chicken (provided latter is not greasy).

If preparing salad for a big party, it is best to buy a big fowl, and boil it; see Boiled Chicken (p. 122). When cooked and cooled, remove skin, bones. A fowl should provide 6 to 8 cups diced meat.

Cut meat to bite size before using, or if preferred, dice fine. The following quantity serves 2 to 3.

Put in mixing bowl
>> **1 cup cubed or diced chicken meat**

Add
>> **1 cup finely cut celery**
>> **2 or 3 finely chopped celery leaves**

Sprinkle with
>> **¼ teaspoon salt**
>> **2 tablespoons French dressing**

Mix into above
>> **⅓ cup (or more) mayonnaise**

Chill chicken mixture 15 to 30 minutes, before serving on
>> **crisp greens**

Notes for emergencies. To extend salad, if necessary, for unexpected guests, add a larger amount of chopped celery. Diced hard-cooked eggs may also be stirred in.

Salad may be made more filling by garnishing plate with quartered hard-cooked eggs and tomato wedges, when serving.

Chicken salad served in long finger rolls goes a great deal farther than if served on plates.

Chicken salad may also be served as filling in stuffed tomatoes; this makes a little go a long way.

Turkey Salad

Substitute cubed or diced cooked turkey meat for chicken in Master Recipe #51, p. 343.

MASTER RECIPE #52
SEAFOOD SALAD

(Serves 2 or 3)

This recipe makes lobster, crab meat, shrimp, tuna, or salmon salad. Or you may use leftover cooked white fish, flaked.

For *lobster.* Use leftover boiled (p. 161), or broiled (p. 162) lobster, or drained, canned lobster. Cut meat to bite size.

For *crab meat.* Buy canned crab meat; or buy crab meat already cooked and prepared at fish market. Drain.

For *shrimp.* Use home-boiled, fresh shrimp (p. 169); shell it. Or use canned shrimp. Drain off salty fish juice. Remove black vein (p. 169). Leave shrimp whole, or cut to bite size.

For *tuna or salmon.* Use canned fish; drain; flake meat or break to bite size. Or you may use home-poached or home-baked or home-broiled leftover fish.

In mixing bowl, put

> 1 cup prepared seafood, cut to bite size

Add

> 1 cup finely cut celery
> 2 or 3 finely chopped celery leaves

Sprinkle with

> ¼ teaspoon salt
> 1 or 2 tablespoons lemon juice
> *or*
> 2 tablespoons French dressing

Stir in

> ¼ cup (or more) mayonnaise

Chill 15 to 30 minutes before serving on

> crisp greens

EGG SALAD

See page 268.

FRUITS IN SALADS

There are hundreds of fruit salads . . . probably thousands. There is, in fact, no way to count them. Every day, new ones (or new versions of old ones) are born, by the mere fact that housewives are confronted with new combinations of fruit in garden or refrigerator, or are seized with new enthusiasms about how to use them.

You, too, will invent new ones. You will not always want to serve the same old fruit cocktail, or the same half of a peach or pear, for good as these fruits are, they become tiresome unless given new "dresses" and used in different ways. Instead, look about you; see what you have; let your imagination run. Set as a goal for yourself that you will never serve the same fruit salad twice in six months. Of course this will never quite work out, for you will find that you, or other members of the family, *like* certain salads so much that you *want* to repeat them. But even so, try at least to vary the salad with a new garnish, or a different flavoring, or a new arrangement of the fruit.

We give here a few general hints, to help you get started, and a chart suggesting a few easy but interesting salads.

Hints

For interest, combine large and small fruits. Not all fruits for salad need be cut to the same size. Combine long spears of pineapple, banana, or melon with small bright items like cherries, strawberries, raspberries, blueberries, sliced peaches.

When using canned halves of peach, pear, or sliced pineapple, add some interesting garnish of bright taste and different color. No need to let the salad be dull, just because it is canned fruit. (See Chart for suggestions.)

Stuff small whole fruits from which pits are removed. Prunes, dates, peeled apricots, even figs, are twice as good, split and stuffed with cheese, or with chopped fruits and nuts combined, or with any "surprise" you can dream up. Such salads are always popular.

When using fruit slices or fruit sections, arrange them in a pattern. For example, slices of three different colors (like grapefruit sections, orange sections, slices of avocado pear) would make a pretty pinwheel effect, or a flower-petal design. Or fruits of contrasting colors may be arranged in alternate rows, or in circles. Making a salad *look* pretty makes it *taste* better, too! (It literally does; one's digestive juices are stimulated.)

Accent the center of your salad with some spot of color, for eye-appeal. Use a maraschino cherry (red or green), whole, or cut like a flower. Or add a sprig of mint. Or, when using fruits not too sweet, like pear, grapefruit sections, add a strip of green pepper. If you have them, use 2 or 3 melon balls. Or a slice of peach. Or a stuffed date. Or a strip of banana. Or a fresh fig. Or a prune. Or at least add a dash of paprika.

Don't always use the same dressing. There are many varieties of dressing delicious with fruit; see Variations under Mayonnaise (p. 353), Cooked Salad Dressing (p. 356), French Dressing (p. 357). Never, never use plain thick mayonnaise or undiluted cooked salad dressing for fruit; you may thin it with 1 or 2 tablespoons lemon juice, or other fruit juice, to give it lightness and a bright taste; or thin it with cream; see page 353.

CHART
SUGGESTIONS FOR EASY
FRUIT SALADS

Fruit	Add for Flavor and Interest	Suggested Greens	Suggested Dressing
Pear halves	Chopped fresh mint leaves or Chopped candied ginger or Crumbled blue cheese or Balls of cottage cheese into which you have mixed	Watercress Lettuce Romaine	French

Fruit	Add for Flavor and Interest	Suggested Greens	Suggested Dressing
	salt, pepper, chopped chives or green pepper; or chopped olives and nuts		
	or		
	Cubes of cream cheese, with a half walnut pressed into each		
	or		
	Fill hollow with small fruit: berries, sliced bananas, or orange sections		
	or		
	Make balls of mashed banana, diced celery, chopped nutmeats, to put in hollows		
Peach halves	Crumbled blue cheese, or any cheese garnish under Pear	Lettuce Mixed Greens	French
	or		
	Fill hollows with melon balls, raspberries, sliced bananas, or grapefruit sections		
	or		
	Moisten grated cabbage, diced celery, chopped nutmeats with mayonnaise, to fill hollows		
	or		
	Sprinkle with slivered almonds		
Pineapple Spears, Slices, or Chunks	Crumbled blue cheese, or any cheese garnish under Pear	Lettuce Mixed Greens	French
	or		
	Decorate with watermelon balls, or raspberries, plus sprig of fresh mint		
	or		
	Make balls of diced green pepper, diced celery, chopped nuts, moistened with cream cheese or mayonnaise		
	or		

Fruit	Add for Flavor and Interest	Suggested Greens	Suggested Dressing
	Make balls of seedless grapes, chopped nuts, cream cheese		
	or		
	Combine with grapefruit or orange sections or sliced bananas		
Bananas Cut lengthwise in halves or quarters, like spears	Crumbled blue cheese, or any cheese garnish under Pears	Lettuce Mixed Greens	French or Mayonnaise thinned with lemon juice
	or		
	Combine with grapefruit sections, orange sections, or both; add crumbled blue cheese		
	or		
	Garnish with fresh strawberries, raspberries, sliced peaches, melon balls, or pineapple chunks		
Cut crosswise in thirds	Roll sections of banana in crushed peanuts		
Cut lengthwise in half	Spread two halves, sandwich fashion. with peanut butter or cream cheese mixed with pickle relish. Then cut banana into sections of desired length for serving		
Apples Peeled, cored, then diced	Combine with equal amount of diced celery, then stir in walnut meats, salt, mayonnaise thinned with lemon juice. (This is called Waldorf Salad)	Lettuce or Mixed Greens	Mayonnaise thinned with lemon juice
	or		
	Combine with grated raw cabbage, seedless raisins, chopped nutmeats, salt, mayonnaise thinned with lemon juice.		
	or		
	Combine with diced celery,		

Fruit	Add for Flavor and Interest	Suggested Greens	Suggested Dressing
	diced bananas or pineapple or both, moisten with mayonnaise thinned with lemon juice. Garnish with strip of green pepper, or crumbled blue cheese		
	or		
	Combine with diced peaches, diced celery or grated cabbage, crushed peanuts		
Cored, sliced crosswise, into ¼" thick slices	Some people spread with peanut butter, or pickle relish, or cheese, to use for salad; but apple rings are hard to eat with fork		
Avocado pear Cut in halves lengthwise, stone removed	Fill hollow with French dressing; add crumbled blue cheese, if desired	Watercress Lettuce Mixed Greens	French
	or		
	Fill hollow with grapefruit or orange sections; add crumbled blue cheese		
	or		
	Fill hollow with shrimp, crab meat, lobster, or other tangy salad		
Sliced	Combine in patterns with grapefruit sections, orange sections, or other refreshing fruit (avocado is rich)		
Grapefruit or Orange Sections	Combine with avocado pear	Watercress Endive Romaine Lettuce Mixed Greens	French or Mayonnaise thinned with lemon juice
	or		
	Use with spears of pineapple, banana		
	or		
	Garnish with small bright berries; melon balls		
	or		
	Sprinkle with crumbled blue cheese		
	or		
	Garnish with stuffed prunes or stuffed dates		

Fruit	Add for Flavor and Interest	Suggested Greens	Suggested Dressing
Prunes, Dates, Apricots, Figs, pitted	Stuff centers with cream or cottage cheese blended with chopped nuts; or chopped chives; or chopped olives or Fill with diced celery and chopped nuts, moistened with orange juice or Fill with a slice or a section of some other fruit	Lettuce Mixed Greens	French or Mayonnaise thinned with lemon juice
Grapes seedless; or seeded; cut in half, lengthwise	Combine with diced bananas, apples, or pineapple, plus diced celery, nuts or Use to garnish large fruits or Use in mixed fruit salad bowl	Lettuce Mixed Greens	Mayonnaise thinned with lemon juice
Berries, fresh	Use to garnish large fruits or Use in mixed fruit salad bowl		
Mixed Fruit Salad Bowl	Arrange on greens any combination of well-drained fruits, fresh or canned, of varying textures and flavors. Toss with French Fruit Salad Dressing. If desired, garnish with chopped fresh mint leaves, or crumbled blue cheese	Mixed Greens or Lettuce	French Fruit Salad Dressing or Mayonnaise
Molded Fruit Salads	See Chapter XXX		
Frozen Fruit Salad	See page 403		

CHAPTER XXIX

You Can Make Salad Dressings

METHOD FOR: *Mayonnaise, Russian Dressing, Cooked Salad Dressing, French Dressing, Fruit Salad Dressings, Sour Cream Dressing, Seafood Cocktail Sauce, Rémoulade Sauce*

READY-MADE DRESSINGS

You can buy excellent real mayonnaise, cooked creamy salad dressings, and French dressings, in the stores; and most other salad dressings are contrived by combining these basic types with special flavorings or seasonings.

However, it is fun to make your own. It is also more economical. There are times when it is easier to make your own than to race to market. So here are the recipes.

MASTER RECIPE #53
MAYONNAISE

(Makes about 1½ cups)

In real mayonnaise the oil is thickened only with eggs — never with flour, cornstarch, or other starchy ingredient.

In small bowl, combine

> 1 teaspoon salt
> 1 teaspoon dry mustard
> ¼ teaspoon paprika
> 2 egg yolks

If you like slightly sweet mayonnaise, add

1 teaspoon powdered sugar

Beat above mixture with rotary beater, thoroughly. Then **add**

1 tablespoon boiling water

Beat again. (Adding this hot water will save you many troubles.)

Add slowly, *1 tablespoon at a time, beating well after each addition*

1 cup olive or other salad oil

Finally, beat in

2 tablespoons vinegar (*or* 1 tablespoon lemon juice plus 1 tablespoon vinegar)

When well beaten, store in covered jar in refrigerator. And that's all there is to mayonnaise.

MAYONNAISE VARIATION

Modified Mayonnaise (Makes about 2½ cups.)

This is a most economical recipe, excellent in times of shortages, since it makes a larger quantity of mayonnaise from the same amount of oil and eggs as used in real mayonnaise. This recipe is partially thickened by flour. So follow directions below, rather than the Master Recipe.

Blend well in a mixing bowl 1 egg or 2 egg yolks, ¼ cup vinegar, 1¼ teaspoons salt, ½ teaspoon dry mustard, 1 teaspoon sugar, and 1 cup salad oil. In saucepan, make a paste by stirring 1 cup water into ½ cup flour. Cook paste over low heat, stirring constantly, until thick. Then stir flour paste into ingredients in bowl, beating vigorously with rotary beater until well blended and smooth. Cool. Store in refrigerator, in covered glass jar.

DRESSINGS MADE FROM MAYONNAISE

The following can be made with bought or homemade mayonnaise; or even with cooked salad dressing (p. 354).

Russian Dressing

Combine ½ cup mayonnaise with 2 tablespoons chili sauce, or ¼ cup tomato catsup. Use on mixed greens, or vegetable salads. If you like cheese, add 1 or 2 tablespoons crumbled blue or Roquefort.

Hawaiian Dressing

So-called because you combine 2 tablespoons canned pineapple juice (Hawaii's prize fruit) with ½ cup mayonnaise. Good on fruit salad.

Curry Dressing

If you like curry, try this, on fish or hard-cooked egg salads. Blend ¼ teaspoon curry powder with ½ cup mayonnaise.

Caper Dressing

For hard-cooked eggs, cold fish. Combine 1 teaspoon capers, ½ teaspoon tarragon vinegar, and if desired, a little chopped canned pimiento, with ½ cup mayonnaise.

Fruit Juice Mayonnaise Dressing

Any fruit salad tastes fruitier if you blend with the mayonnaise a little of the matching fruit juice. To ½ cup mayonnaise, add 2 tablespoons juice — canned grapefruit, pineapple, apricot, peach, or pear. If juice of fruit is very sweet, add 1 teaspoon to 1 tablespoon lemon juice, to give "zing" to the dressing.

Cream Mayonnaise Dressing

For fruit salads (either of fresh or canned fruits), whipped cream combined with the mayonnaise is delicious. Drain fruit of all but 1 tablespoon juice. Then add to fruit ⅓ cup mayonnaise combined with ⅓ cup cream, whipped — but not sweetened.

Herb Dressing

Try this on cold fish, hard-cooked eggs, luncheon meats. To

½ cup mayonnaise, add 1 tablespoon finely chopped fresh parsley, 2 teaspoons finely chopped chives. If desired, add a drop or two of Worcestershire sauce.

Cucumber Dressing

Peel and chop very fine (or grate) ⅓ medium-sized cucumber. Mix this pulp with ½ cup mayonnaise.

Anchovy Dressing

For cold roast beef, cold white fish, hard-cooked egg salads: blend ¼ teaspoon anchovy paste with ½ cup mayonnaise.

Tangy Meat Dressing

Try on cold meats. With ½ cup mayonnaise, blend ¼ teaspoon Worcestershire sauce, plus 1 teaspoon bottled horseradish, plus 1 teaspoon finely minced chives.

Cheese Mayonnaise Dressing

To ½ cup mayonnaise, add 2 tablespoons or more crumbled blue cheese. Thin dressing with a few drops lemon juice, and add a pinch of salt.

Tartar Sauce

To ½ cup mayonnaise, add 2 teaspoons grated onion, 2 teaspoons each of pickles, chopped olives, minced parsley, capers. Add 2 teaspoons mild vinegar, or lemon juice for tang. Serve with fried fish.

MASTER RECIPE #54
COOKED SALAD DRESSING

(Makes 2 cups)

Cooked salad dressing can be bought in the store, or made by this Master Recipe.

Cooked salad dressing is begun almost like a white sauce, mixing cornstarch or flour, seasonings, and milk, into a thickened sauce. After this, vinegar, eggs, and oil are added, to give a "mayonnaise" taste.

The net result is a paler, starch-thickened version of mayonnaise. It is very tasty, is used like mayonnaise, and keeps indefinitely in a covered jar in the refrigerator.

In saucepan, blend into a smooth paste
> 2 tablespoons cornstarch (or flour)
> 1 tablespoon sugar
> 2 teaspoons dry mustard
> 2 teaspoons salt
> ⅛ teaspoon pepper
> ½ teaspoon paprika
> few grains cayenne pepper
> ¼ cup milk

After paste is made, stir in
> ¾ cup milk

Cook above mixture, over low heat, stirring constantly, until it boils and thickens.

Remove from heat, and add
> 2 egg yolks, slightly beaten
> and mixed with
> ¼ cup vinegar

Gradually stir in, while beating vigorously with rotary beater
> ¾ cup salad oil

When well blended, chill. Store in refrigerator in covered glass jar.

COOKED SALAD DRESSING VARIATIONS

The following can be made with bought or homemade salad dressing:

Flavored Cooked Dressing

Cooked salad dressing can be thinned with fruit juice, or combined with whipped cream, or with catsup, or flavored in any of the same ways as mayonnaise (see p. 353).

Cole Slaw Dressing

To ½ cup cooked salad dressing, add 1 teaspoon celery seed, 1 teaspoon (or more) grated raw onion, ½ teaspoon sugar. If sharper dressing is desired, add few drops vinegar or lemon juice. Add salt to taste.

Horseradish Dressing

Add 1 teaspoon bottled horseradish to ½ cup cooked salad dressing. The flavor of the horseradish will blend in more strongly if salad dressing is hot when horseradish is added.

FRENCH DRESSING

French dressing, in purest form, is simply oil and vinegar, with enough salt and pepper to season it. In France, the custom is to use 2 parts oil for 1 part vinegar. In the United States, we seem to prefer a taste less sharp, and the popular proportion is 1 part vinegar to 3 parts oil.

Seasoning may be kept very simple, or you may put in nearly everything. Quite considerable changes in flavor can be obtained by using tarragon or wine vinegar, in place of cider vinegar; or by using lemon juice or other fruit juices, in place of vinegar.

Some people like French dressing a trifle sweet; and others like it sharp and red. We give you a Master formula and then you can do what you please with it.

MASTER RECIPE #55
FRENCH DRESSING

Put into clean, empty pint jar

> ¼ **cup vinegar** (or lemon juice)
> ¾ **cup olive** (or other salad oil)
> 1 **teaspoon salt**
> ¼ **teaspoon pepper**
> ½ **teaspoon paprika**

Put lid tightly on jar, and shake well. This is all there is to simple French dressing.

To make slightly sweet. Add ½ teaspoon sugar.

To give redder color. Add 1 teaspoon more paprika.

To make more tangy, for green salads. Add the following "taste sharpeners"; let them stand in the dressing 1 or 2 hours, before using it: 1 **peeled clove garlic** (or ½ peeled raw onion), **few dashes celery salt** (or some crumbled dried celery leaves), ¼ **teaspoon dry mustard** (or ½ teaspoon prepared mustard), 1 or 2 **strips green pepper**, 1 tablespoon minced **parsley**, and additional salt, pepper, or vinegar, to please taste.

For even spicier dressing, you may also add, with the above: **dash tabasco sauce**, or few drops Worcestershire sauce, or 1 or 2 **tablespoons catsup**, or ½ teaspoon bottled **meat extract**.

FRENCH DRESSING VARIATIONS

Fruit French Dressing

Substitute for the vinegar a tart and tasty **fruit juice**, such as lemon, or grapefruit, or orange juice. (Or you may use syrup from canned pears or peaches, if you combine with the syrup enough lemon juice to give dressing real tang.) With fruit French dressing, omit onion and herbs and all sharp or spicy ingredients listed above.

Roquefort or Blue Cheese French Dressing

Crumbled **blue cheese** may be added to any French dressing, and is delectable either on fruit or vegetable salads.

Mint French Dressing

This is excellent on a salad of greens and orange sections; or on cold pears. To Master Recipe, French Dressing, add ¼ teaspoon dry mustard, ½ teaspoon sugar, 1 teaspoon finely chopped **fresh mint leaves.** Omit onion and other "taste sharpeners."

(Fresh mint leaves from a garden may be dried out, at room temperature, until they are of crumbly consistency . . . then forced through a strainer. This produces powdered mint, which is delicious to add to fruit salads, or to use in cooking lamb, and which will keep all winter in a covered jar.)

Currant French Dressing

To ¼ cup French dressing, add a **few drops onion juice** plus 4 tablespoons **currant jelly.** Blend well; use on fruit salad.

Bought French Dressing

This is already well seasoned, but is bland enough to use on fruits, as well as on vegetables.

OTHER DRESSINGS

Sour Cream Dressing

Makes about 1 cup. If you like it, you may have it. Some people consider it delectable for cole slaw, cucumber salad, and other vegetables. Some like it on herring.

Combine in mixing bowl 1 cup thick, really *sour* cream, 2 tablespoons white vinegar, 1 dash black pepper, ¼ teaspoon salt, 1 or 2 pinches sugar, 1 tablespoon grated raw onion. Blend thoroughly, and smack your lips.

Cocktail Sauce (for cold seafood)

Makes about 1 cup. Combine in mixing bowl ½ **cup tomato catsup**, ½ **cup chili sauce**, 1 **tablespoon Worcestershire sauce**, ½ **teaspoon salt**, ½ **teaspoon dry mustard**, 1 to 3 **teaspoons horse-radish**, ¾ **teaspoon black pepper**. Blend well, and chill, before using. A lukewarm sauce is not attractive on cold fish.

Rémoulade (Mayonnaise-Type) Sauce

Makes about 1 cup. Combine in mixing bowl 1 **cup mayonnaise** (or cooked salad dressing), 1 **clove finely chopped garlic, or 2 to 3 teaspoons grated raw onion**, 1 **tablespoon capers**, 1 **table-spoon minced fresh parsley**, 1 **teaspoon minced chives**, 1 **teaspoon dry mustard**, 1 **or 2 tablespoons lemon juice**, ½ **teaspoon anchovy paste** (optional), a little **finely chopped dill** (optional), 1 **or 2 chopped, hard-cooked eggs**. Blend well. Chill before using.

This sauce is very good indeed on cold white fish or shellfish, or for fish and hard-cooked egg salads.

Simpler rémoulade-type sauce. When you are in a hurry you may make a reasonable facsimile of rémoulade sauce by blend-ing into **mayonnaise** some **grated onion, mustard, lemon juice, chopped parsley**, and a little **finely chopped pickle** and **pickle juice**, to spice the sauce. All these ingredients are things the house-wife commonly has on hand. **Hard-cooked eggs** are good, but not essential, in the sauce.

CHAPTER XXX

You Can Make a Molded
Main Course, Salad, or Dessert

METHOD FOR:

Fruit-Flavored Gelatine Mix: Molded Desserts, Molded Salads
Unflavored Gelatine: Molded Sweet Dishes, Aspics, Molded
Salads
For Other Uses of Gelatine, See End of Chapter

WHAT YOU SHOULD KNOW
ABOUT GELATINE

Gelatine is — of course — the one ingredient which jells any molded dish. (This is not so stupid to say as it may sound; I knew a bride who spent an entire year wondering what made gelatine dishes stiff, and was afraid to ask anyone!)

Gelatine, by itself, is a powdered or granulated ingredient which has practically no taste. When mixed with the proper amount of liquid, in the proper way, it stiffens it.

Gelatine is sold in *two* forms:

Fruit-flavored . . . a packaged gelatine "mix" which contains not only gelatine, but also sugar, and the flavor specified on package, such as lemon, lime, orange, raspberry, or whatever. One package jells 1 pint liquid.

Unflavored . . . sold in packages containing 4 envelopes. Each *envelope* contains enough pure gelatine to jell 1 pint liquid. This gelatine has mixed with it neither sugar nor flavoring. You can therefore use it to make a molded dish of any flavor you want — sweet, or nonsweet. It becomes a sweet dish if you mix it with sugar and any desired flavor, such as fruit, coffee, chocolate, or whatever. It becomes a nonsweet dish if you omit sugar, and mix the gelatine with a tangy-flavored meat broth, or vegetable juice, to make an aspic.

As the two types of gelatine are handled in different ways, we will take up each one separately, giving a few basic examples of dishes you can make with each. There are, of course, many more such dishes which you will come across in food columns of newspapers and magazines; and new ones are being invented every day. Those given here are meant to serve as a good "starter," to acquaint you with the methods and the possibilities for using gelatine.

Let it be said, before we go farther, that gelatine is easy and quick to fix . . . it is inexpensive . . . it stretches a little solid food a long way . . . it makes beauteous and glamorous dishes, fit for the most sophisticated guests, and yet is easily enough digested to give to a child. It is also high in protein value, and a real addition to the food value of a meal. And best of all, gelatine dishes may be prepared hours (even a day) ahead of time, and so can be ready and waiting, without fuss, at the time of the meal hour.

MASTER RECIPE #56
PLAIN FRUIT-FLAVORED GELATINE

(*Made with bought mix.*)

Quantity to use: 1 package jells 2 cups (1 pint) liquid, and makes 1 pint gelatine, or enough for 2 to 3 servings. If solid foods, such as fruits, are added, volume of finished dish will increase by 1 cup for each 1 cup added solids; in other words, 2 cups liquid gelatine, plus 2 cups solid ingredients, will fill a 1-quart mold, and serve 4 to 6 people.

Turn from package into bowl
> 1 package fruit-flavored gelatine

Heat in saucepan, until hot

2 cups water *

Pour hot water over gelatine stirring until all gelatine dissolves thoroughly.

Rinse out, under running cold water, a 1-pint mold. Drain. (This rinsing of mold is what enables gelatine to slip out intact, when jelled.)

Pour hot gelatine into mold.

Place mold in refrigerator 3 or 4 hours, or longer, until gelatine is firm (doesn't tremble, when mold is moved).

Never unmold gelatine until as near serving time as possible; it may turn soft and lose shape.

To unmold: (at serving time). Remove mold from refrigerator. Place it in a shallow pan of warm water, which will come almost all the way up outside walls of mold; but take care water doesn't get into gelatine. Leave mold in warm water just 2 or 3 minutes, until when mold is shaken slightly from side to side, gelatine appears loosened from walls of mold. At once remove mold from water. Then invert serving platter over mold; hold it there firmly; and invert both platter and mold together, at same instant. Gelatine will slip out intact. If any has melted, so that you have juice on platter, pour juice off; but this will not happen if you do not leave mold in warm water too long.

To garnish plain fruit gelatine. Garnish with sliced fresh fruit, or fresh, sweetened berries, or with sweetened whipped cream (p. 408). Many other variations may be devised, according to your taste and whim, and what you have handy. For example, orange gelatine is delicious topped with whipped cream sprinkled with shredded coconut, and a few bits of minced candied ginger. Lemon gelatine is good with sliced fresh peaches, sweetened whipped cream, and thinly slivered blanched almonds (p. 503).

* If desired to chill gelatine quickly, heat only 1 cup water; pour this over the gelatine in bowl; after gelatine is dissolved, add 1 cup *cold* water.

SIMPLE VARIATIONS OF
PLAIN FRUIT-FLAVORED GELATINE

Gelatine Containing Fruit

Serves 4. Mix Master Recipe, Plain Fruit Gelatine, any fruit flavor desired. After gelatine is mixed, rinse out under cold water a 1 quart mold, or 4 or 5 individual molds. Pour liquid gelatine into molds. Place in refrigerator until gelatine becomes as thick as unbeaten egg white. Then add any desired cut, drained, fresh or canned fruits (except fresh pineapple; never use this, as it contains an enzyme which will prevent gelatine from becoming firm). Continue chilling gelatine in refrigerator until firm. Unmold as in Master Recipe.

The reason for chilling gelatine until partly set, before adding fruits, is so that fruits will stay evenly distributed in this thicker substance. If fruits are added when gelatine is first made, some fruits rise to surface, heavier fruits sink to bottom.

Molded Fruit Salad Ring

Can be used as salad course, or dessert; serves 4. Make Master Recipe, Plain Fruit Gelatine, using 1 package lemon-flavored gelatine. Rinse out a 1-pint ring mold under cold water; drain; pour the liquid gelatine into mold. Chill until firm. Unmold. Fill center of ring with 2 cups any desired fresh fruit (such as 1 cup balls cut from honeydew melon or cantaloupe, plus 1 cup fresh hulled strawberries . . . or any other combination you like). To serve as salad: surround ring with crisped lettuce, and garnish salad with fruit-juice-mayonnaise dressing (p. 353). To serve as dessert, garnish with whipped cream.

Molded Ginger Ale Fruit Salad

Can be used as salad, or dessert; serves 4. Make Master Recipe, Plain Fruit Gelatine, using 1 package lemon- or lime-flavored gelatine, but in place of 1 cup water, substitute 1 cup (½ pint) ginger ale. Rinse out a 1-quart mold under cold water; drain. Pour into it the liquid gelatine mixture. Chill in refrigerator about 30 minutes, until thick as unbeaten egg white. Then add **2 cups drained fresh or canned fruit.** (For dessert gelatine, use sweet fruits, such as fresh berries, sliced bananas, drained canned peaches, or pears, or pineapple. For salad gelatine, use tarter fruits, such as drained grapefruit sections, plus sliced peeled avocoado pear; or drained grapefruit and orange sections.) Continue chilling until firm. After unmolding, if serving as salad, surround molded gelatine with crisped lettuce, and garnish with mayonnaise or French dressing and crumbled blue cheese. For dessert, garnish with sweetened whipped cream.

Bing Cherry Salad Mold

Serves 6 to 8. For this, you need a 2-quart mold, or 8 individual molds. Make Master Recipe, Fruit-Flavored Gelatine (p. 361), dissolving **1 package lime gelatine in 1 cup hot water;** then stir in **1 cup cold water.** Chill in refrigerator until thick as unbeaten egg white. Soften **2 3-ounce packages cream cheese** with a fork; then fold it into partly thickened lime gelatine, beating with rotary beater to blend. Rinse out mold under cold water; drain it; then put in it the lime mixture, and place in refrigerator to chill until firm. Meanwhile, make Master Recipe, Fruit-Flavored Gelatine, dissolving **1 package cherry gelatine in 1 cup hot water.** Add **1 cup juice** from a No. 2½ can Bing cherries. Add the cherries, pitted and halved. Turn cherry mixture into same mold containing the firm lime mixture. Chill until whole dish is firm. After unmolding, surround gelatine with crisped lettuce leaves. Garnish with mayonnaise, or cream mayonnaise dressing (p. 353).

Ham Soufflé Salad Mold

Serves 6. For this, you need a 1-quart mold, or 6 individual molds. Make Master Recipe, Fruit-Flavored Gelatine, dissolving **1 package lemon-flavored gelatine in 1 cup hot water.** Add **½ cup cold water, 2 tablespoons lemon juice or vinegar, ½ cup mayonnaise, ¼ teaspoon salt, dash pepper.** Beat with rotary beater until frothy; then chill in tray in freezing compartment 15 to 20 minutes, or until a layer 1 inch wide is firm around sides of tray. Then scrape gelatine from tray to a cold bowl, and beat it with rotary beater until fluffy, as quickly as possible so gelatine won't melt. Fold into beaten mixture 2 to 3 teaspoons grated raw onion, and 1 cup each of diced ham, diced celery, and cooked drained peas. Turn into 1-quart ring mold (which has been rinsed out under cold water) and chill 1 hour or more, until firm. After unmolding, surround gelatine with crisped greens. Garnish with mayonnaise if desired.

Chicken Soufflé Salad Mold

Make as above, substituting **diced cooked or canned chicken meat** for ham.

Turkey Soufflé Salad Mold

Make like chicken, but use **turkey** instead.

Tuna Fish, Shrimp, or Lobster Soufflé Salad Mold

Make like ham soufflé salad mold, but instead of ham, substitute 1 cup drained canned tuna fish, or drained cleaned shrimps, or drained canned or boiled lobster meat. Omit onion, if desired.

Meat-Vegetable Soufflé Salad Mold

Make like ham soufflé salad mold, but instead of ham, substitute **1 cup diced canned luncheon meat, or diced cooked lamb, tongue, or pork**; and instead of celery, use **1 cup drained cooked broccoli, or drained mixed cooked or canned vegetables**; or **1 cup fresh vegetables** such as sliced cucumbers, sliced radishes, grated raw cabbage, grated carrots.

Two-Tone Gelatine Whip (Dessert)

Serves 6. Make Master Recipe, Plain Fruit-Flavored Gelatine (p. 361), dissolving **1 package gelatine** (any fruit flavor) **in 1 cup hot water.** Add **1 cup cold water.** Pour 2 tablespoons this liquid gelatine mixture into each of 6 molds which have been rinsed out under cold water. Place molds in refrigerator, to chill shallow gelatine until firm. Meanwhile, also place in refrigerator, in its mixing bowl, the remainder of liquid gelatine. When gelatine in bowl has thickened to consistency of unbeaten egg whites, remove it from refrigerator; place it inside another bowl containing ice cubes, and whip gelatine with rotary beater until fluffy and thick like whipped cream. Pour this whipped gelatine over the firm gelatine in molds; continue chilling until firm. After unmolding, garnish with whipped cream if desired; or surround each mound of gelatine with fresh berries, or cut fresh fruit. Add finely chopped mint leaves with fruit, if desired.

Gelatine Cream Charlotte (Dessert)

Serves 5 to 6. Make Master Recipe, Plain Fruit-Flavored Gelatine (p. 361), dissolving **1 package orange gelatine in 1⅔ cups hot water.** Add **½ teaspoon grated lemon rind,** and **dash of salt.** Cool; then add **⅓ cup sherry.** Now put mixture in refrigerator to chill, about ½ hour, until thick as unbeaten egg white. Meanwhile, whip until thick and shiny **1 cup heavy cream.** Split **12 to 18 ladyfingers** in halves, lengthwise, and sprinkle over them a small amount of **sherry** to moisten them slightly. Arrange them upright in 5 or 6 sherbet glasses, or cups, making a fence of ladyfingers around inside of each cup. Now get partly thickened gelatine from refrigerator, and fold into it ¾ the whipped cream. Pile the blended mixture into cups, filling the centers full. Return glasses or cups to refrigerator until mixture is chilled firm. When serving, garnish with remaining whipped cream; add shelled halves of pecans, or a maraschino cherry, on top.

UNFLAVORED GELATINE

(*Flavored at home — by You*)

A box of unflavored gelatine contains several envelopes. Each *envelope* contains enough gelatine to make our Master Recipe below, stiffening 1½ to 1¾ cups liquid, making enough gelatine for 2 to 3 people.

This type gelatine, remember, has no flavoring, no sugar, included; it is all gelatine, nothing else. It will give no flavor to your mixture. The flavor of your finished gelatine dish will depend on what *liquid* you have used . . . or on what other ingredients you have added with the liquid, to give the mixture sweetness, tang, and good flavor.

To make *sweet* (dessert-type) gelatine, you combine this type of gelatine with a sweet fruit juice, or sweetened coffee, or sweet cocoa, or other sweet liquid.

To make *nonsweet* ("aspic") gelatine, you combine this type of gelatine with a nonsweet, tangy liquid, such as tasty broth, bouillon, or vegetable juice.

We will take up each type separately.

Unflavored gelatine is wonderful to have in the house. It's fun to use, and makes such an unlimited variety of dishes that we can give but a few samples of basic ones here.

MASTER RECIPE #57
SWEET (DESSERT-TYPE) GELATINE

(Made with unflavored gelatine.)

Quantity: One *envelope* unflavored gelatine stiffens 1½ to 1¾ cups liquid, producing nearly 1 pint finished gelatine, or enough to serve 2 to 3 people with good appetites.

If solid food be added, count on each cup of solids to extend gelatine dish by 1 cup; in other words, Master Recipe, Sweet Gelatine, plus 2 cups cut fruit, nearly fills a 1 quart mold, and serves 4 to 6 people generously.

WARNING. Whenever using unflavored gelatine, don't forget that *it must first be softened, 5 to 10 minutes, in ½ cup cold liquid.* Once softened, you dissolve it completely by adding *hot* liquid, and stirring well.

Step 1

Sprinkle contents of

1 envelope unflavored gelatine

into

½ cup cold liquid (fruit juice, or water,
or other liquid; see Variations)

Stir gelatine around in liquid, to dampen evenly. Then let stand 5 minutes, until gelatine softens.

Step 2

In saucepan, heat

1¼ cups additional liquid (fruit juice,
or other liquid; see Variations)

Remove hot liquid from heat; stir into it

⅛ teaspoon salt

(Increase to ½ teaspoon, if making gelatine for a salad.)

Add sweetening if needed for type liquid (see Variations)

from 2 tablespoons to ⅓ cup sugar

NOTE: When using an excessively sweet, syrupy fruit juice, remove 2 to 4 tablespoons of the hot juice, and substitute 2 to 4
tablespoons lemon juice, to cut the sweetness; and eliminate
addition of sugar altogether if desired.

Step 3

Combine hot, well-flavored liquid with the softened gelatine.
Stir until all gelatine dissolves.

Step 4

Turn liquid gelatine mixture into mold which has been rinsed
out under cold water. Chill in refrigerator 3 or 4 hours, or until
firm.

To unmold: follow directions under Master Recipe, Plain Fruit-
Flavored Gelatine (p. 362).

SWEET GELATINE VARIATIONS

(*Follow method in Master Recipe #57, Sweet — Dessert-type
— Gelatine, page 367, using ingredients below.*)

Apricot Gelatine

Canned apricot nectar, or syrup from canned apricots, makes
delicious gelatine if thinned and sharpened with a more tangy
fruit juice. It is too thick and sweet to use alone. (1) *Try grapefruit juice:* Using Master Recipe #57, soften gelatine in ½ cup
cold grapefruit juice. Heat 1 cup apricot nectar or syrup plus
¼ cup more grapefruit juice. After adding salt, taste and see if

you want sugar. Or (2) *try lemon juice*. Soften gelatine in ½ **cup cold water**. Heat 1 **cup apricot nectar or syrup**. After adding **salt**, add 2 to 4 tablespoons sugar, softened gelatine, and ¼ **cup lemon juice**.

Grapefruit Gelatine

Using Master Recipe #57, soften gelatine in ½ **cup cold canned grapefruit juice**. Heat 1¼ cups grapefruit juice, (or instead heat ¼ cup grapefruit juice plus 1 cup—½ pint—ginger ale); add **salt**, ¼ to ⅓ **cup sugar**; then the softened gelatine.

Grapefruit and Orange Gelatine

Prepare as for grapefruit, but using **canned grapefruit and orange juice** mixed.

Lemon or Lime Gelatine

These fruits are so tart that a very little fruit juice suffices to flavor a lot of water. So, using Master Recipe #57, soften gelatine in cold water. Heat 1 **cup water**. Add **salt**, ⅓ **cup sugar**, and the softened gelatine. Last, stir in ¼ **cup strained lemon or lime juice**. If using this gelatine for salad, increase salt to ½ teaspoon.

Orange Gelatine

In Master Recipe #57, soften gelatine in only ¼ **cup cold water**. Heat 1 **cup water**. Stir in salt, ¼ **cup sugar**, softened gelatine; and last, stir in ½ **cup strained orange juice**, plus 1 **tablespoon lemon juice** for tang.

Maraschino Cherry Gelatine

When you have saved up 1 **cup leftover cherry syrup**, use it for gelatine; but as it is very thick and syrupy, combine it with a liquid which will thin and sharpen it. (1) *Try grapefruit juice*. Using Master Recipe #57, soften gelatine in ½ **cup grapefruit juice**. Heat 1 **cup cherry syrup** plus ¼ **cup additional grapefruit juice**. Complete gelatine as usual. Or (2) *use lemon juice*. Using Master Recipe #57, soften gelatine in ½ **cup cold water**. Heat 1 **cup mara-**

schino cherry syrup. Add salt, softened gelatine; then stir in ¼ cup strained lemon juice. Taste. If sugar is needed, add a bit . . . about 2 tablespoons.

Peach Gelatine

Syrup from canned peaches makes delicious gelatine, but like apricot syrup is sweet and thick, and needs something to give it tang. Make by either method recommended for apricot. Or use ginger ale: Using Master Recipe #57, soften gelatine in ½ cup peach syrup. Heat 1 cup (½ pint) pale dry ginger ale. Add salt, softened gelatine; stir; then add 2 more tablespoons peach syrup plus 2 tablespoons lemon juice.

Prune Gelatine

Juice from cooked or canned prunes makes tempting gelatine if combined with something to give it zest. Using Master Recipe #57, soften gelatine in ½ cup cold prune juice. Heat 1 cup more prune juice or 1 cup pale dry ginger ale or cola. Add salt, 2 to 4 tablespoons sugar, the softened gelatine. Last, add 3 tablespoons more prune juice plus 1 tablespoon lemon juice.

Pineapple Gelatine

Never use *fresh* pineapple in gelatine. Juice from canned pineapple is excellent for gelatine if combined with grapefruit juice, or ginger ale to give it sparkle. Using Master Recipe #57, soften gelatine in ½ cup cold pineapple juice. Heat 1 cup grapefruit juice, or 1 cup (½ pint) pale dry ginger ale. Add salt, 1 or 2 tablespoons sugar if desired, and softened gelatine. Last, add 3 more tablespoons pineapple juice plus 1 tablespoon lemon juice.

Raspberry Gelatine

Bottled raspberry syrup, or crushed fresh sweetened raspberries make wonderful raspberry gelatine. It is advisable to add a little lemon juice. Using Master Recipe #57, soften gelatine in ½ cup cold water. Heat 1 cup bottled raspberry syrup, or 1 cup mashed sweetened fresh raspberries. Add salt, ¼ cup sugar, and softened gelatine. Then add 3 more tablespoons water, plus 1 tablespoon lemon juice.

Strawberry Gelatine

Make like raspberry, but using **bottled strawberry syrup,** or **crushed sweetened fresh strawberries** (hulled, of course).

Tangerine Gelatine

Make like orange, substituting **tangerine juice** for orange juice.

Grape-Ginger or Grape-Cola Gelatine

Using Master Recipe #57, soften gelatine in **½ cup cold bottled grape juice.** Heat 1 cup (½ pint) **ginger ale or cola.** Add salt, **¼ cup sugar,** the softened gelatine. Last, stir in 3 more tablespoons **grape juice** (or strained orange juice), plus 1 tablespoon lemon juice.

Coffee Gelatine

Using Master Recipe #57, soften gelatine in **½ cup cold water.** Heat 1¼ cups **strong black** (strained) **coffee.** After adding salt, stir in **⅓ cup sugar;** add softened gelatine.

Chocolate Gelatine

Using Master Recipe #57, soften gelatine in **½ cup cold water.** Meanwhile, in saucepan mix **6 tablespoons sugar** with **4 tablespoons powdered cocoa;** stir into mixture **1¼ cups hot water;** add **⅛ teaspoon salt;** cook, stirring, to make a smooth syrup, about 10 minutes. Remove from heat, and combine with softened gelatine.

WAYS OF VARYING
ABOVE DESSERT GELATINES

Fold in Fruit

To make a gelatine containing fruit, mix any fruit-flavored gelatine by Master Recipe #57. Chill liquid mixture in refrigerator

½ hour, or until thick as unbeaten egg white; then fold into gel-atine **1 or 2 cups any desired cut fresh or drained canned fruits or berries** (*except* fresh pineapple; *never* use this in gelatine, as it prevents gelatine from stiffening). Turn mixture into mold, and continue chilling until firm. Unmold onto platter. To use as salad, surround gelatine mound with crisped lettuce, and garnish with fruit-juice mayonnaise dressing, or cream-mayonnaise dress-ing (p. 353). To use as dessert, garnish with sweetened whipped cream (p. 408).

Two-Tone Whips

Make any Master Recipe #57 Variation. Turn ⅓ the liquid mixture into a 1½-pint mold, which has first been rinsed out under cold water; place mold in refrigerator until gelatine in it becomes firm, about ¾ hour. Meanwhile, also chill in refrigerator remain-ing ⅔ liquid mixture, in a large bowl. When mixture in bowl has become slightly thicker than unbeaten egg white, prepare another (larger) bowl with cracked ice, or ice cubes, in it. Get from re-frigerator the bowl containing gelatine; place this inside bowl containing ice. With rotary beater, whip gelatine in bowl until it is frothy and light colored, and about doubled in quantity. Turn whipped gelatine on top of firm gelatine in mold; continue chill-ing until entire dish is firm. After unmolding, garnish with sweetened whipped cream (p. 408).

When making coffee or chocolate two-tone whip, flavor sweet-ened whipped cream with rum instead of vanilla, if desired; very good. You may also, of course, add crumbled walnut or pecan meats, on top of the whipped cream.

"Snow" or "Sponge"

Make any Master Recipe #57 variation, but use a total of only 1½ cups liquid . . . ½ cup *cold* liquid to soften gelatine in, and 1 cup *hot* liquid. Also increase sugar by ¼ cup. When mix-ture is made, chill it in bowl in refrigerator until slightly thicker than unbeaten egg white. Then separate (p. 269) **2 eggs**; beat the 2 egg whites until they stand in soft, glossy peaks. Prepare a large bowl with cracked ice or ice cubes, in it. Get out of refrigerator the partly firm gelatine; place bowl of gelatine inside bowl containing ice; whip gelatine with rotary beater until light and frothy. Now fold whipped gelatine gently into the beaten egg whites, blending evenly. Place bowl containing egg white-gelatine mixture again in the bowl of cracked ice, and continue beating until mixture begins to hold its shape. Turn mixture into large or individual molds, and chill in refrigerator until firm.

FRUIT AND VEGETABLE MOLDED SALADS

(Follow method of Master Recipe #57, Sweet Gelatine, page 367, making changes indicated below.)

Ginger Ale Fruit Salad

Make **lemon or lime gelatine** by Master Recipe variation for either flavor (p. 369), but instead of heating water, heat 1 cup (½ pint) **ginger ale.** When liquid mixture is completed, chill in refrigerator ½ hour or until thick as unbeaten egg white. Then add **2 cups any desired cut fresh or drained canned fruit** (except fresh pineapple). Very good in this is a combination of sliced avocado pear, grapefruit and orange sections, freed of membrane and skin. Or try 1 cup melon balls (cut from cantaloupe or honeydew melon) plus 1 cup drained canned grapefruit sections. Fruits used in this type salad should have a bright, fresh, if not tart taste. If desired, stir into gelatine mixture, when adding fruit, **1 tablespoon finely chopped fresh mint leaves.**

Waldorf Salad Mold

Make **lemon gelatine,** by Master Recipe variation (p. 369) for lemon, but increasing **salt to ½ teaspoon.** When liquid mixture is completed, chill in refrigerator ½ hour or until thick as unbeaten egg white. Then fold in **½ cup diced raw apple, ½ cup diced celery, ¼ cup chopped walnut meats.** Continue chilling until firm.

Vegetable Salad Mold

Follow Master Recipe #57, p. 367, but soften gelatine in ½ cup cold water. Heat only ¾ cup water. Add to hot water ½ teaspoon salt, ¼ cup sugar, and the softened gelatine. Then stir in ¼ cup mild vinegar, plus 1 tablespoon lemon juice. Chill mixture in refrigerator until thick as unbeaten egg white. Then fold in ½ cup finely shredded cabbage, 1 cup diced celery, 2 tablespoons minced green pepper or 2 tablespoons chopped drained pimiento.

If desired, you may add with these vegetables 2 or 3 hard-cooked eggs, sliced, plus ½ cup diced cooked or canned ham, tongue, or pork. Continue chilling until mixture is firm. Unmold. Surround with crisped greens, and top with mayonnaise.

Beet, Celery, Horseradish Salad

Make gelatine with water, vinegar, and lemon juice, as under Vegetable Salad Mold. Chill in refrigerator until thick as unbeaten egg white. Then fold in 1 to 2 tablespoons bottled horseradish, 1 cup drained diced or julienned cooked beets, ½ cup diced celery. Continue chilling until firm. Unmold. Surround molded salad with crisped greens; top with mayonnaise.

Cabbage, Celery, and Pineapple Salad

Make gelatine by Master Recipe #57, p. 367, using canned pineapple juice as liquid. Soften gelatine in ½ cup pineapple juice. Heat only 1 cup pineapple juice in saucepan. Increase salt to ¼ teaspoon; use 2 tablespoons sugar; add softened gelatine. Then stir in 2 tablespoons lemon juice. Chill mixture in refrigerator ½ hour or until thick as unbeaten egg white. Then fold into gelatine ½ cup drained crushed pineapple, 1 cup finely shredded cabbage, 1 cup diced celery.

You may substitute 1 cup grated raw carrots for cabbage, if desired.

Miami Grapefruit Salad Mold

Make Master Recipe #57, p. 367, using grapefruit juice, as follows: Soften gelatine in ½ cup grapefruit juice. Heat 1¼ cups grapefruit juice. Add to hot juice ¼ teaspoon salt, ¼ cup sugar, the softened gelatine. Stir to dissolve; then chill in refrigerator until thick as unbeaten egg white. Then fold into gelatine 2 cups drained grapefruit sections, plus ¼ cup chopped pecans. Chill until firm. When unmolded, surround gelatine with crisped greens, a few bright big strawberries, more grapefruit sections, and small balls of cottage cheese. Serve with fruit-juice mayonnaise dressing, or cream-mayonnaise dressing (p. 353).

ASPICS

"Aspics" are the *nonsweet* gelatines, made by combining *unflavored gelatine* with meat broth, or chicken broth, or fish-flavored liquid, or with tomato or other vegetable juice, or sometimes just with plain water and vinegar plus lemon.

These are the gelatines used to mold main-course dishes, and salads of the nonsweet kind, such as shrimp, lobster, chicken.

If you have once made a dessert-type gelatine using unflavored gelatine, you can also make this kind. It is made the same way, but omitting sugar, and substituting a tangy — instead of a sweet — liquid.

Just be sure your liquid really has *tang*, before you combine the softened gelatine with it. Remember, the gelatine will add no flavor . . . it will only *stiffen* the mixture; so taste the hot liquid, and add any extra seasoning you wish to it, *before* you add the gelatine.

MASTER RECIPE #58
ASPIC (NONSWEET GELATINE)

Quantity: One *envelope* unflavored gelatine, combined with 1½ to 1¾ cups liquid, makes nearly 1 pint aspic (or gelatine).

If adding solids, count on size of dish increasing by 1 cup for each 1 cup solids added; in other words, Master Recipe, Aspic, plus 2 cups solid ingredients, will nearly fill a 1-quart mold, serving 4 to 6 people.

Step 1

Sprinkle contents of

1 envelope unflavored gelatine

into

½ cup cold liquid (broth, bouillon, stock, vegetable juice, or water; see under Variations)

Stir gelatine around, to dampen evenly in liquid. Then let stand 5 minutes, until gelatine softens.

Step 2

Heat in saucepan

1 cup additional liquid
(See under Variations)

Add to hot liquid

¼ teaspoon salt

(If using for hot liquid a broth not highly seasoned, you can simmer in it for a few minutes 1 bay leaf, 1 carrot, ½ onion, 1 whole clove, few drops gravy flavoring or Worcestershire sauce, if desired. Then strain. Make sure your broth or hot liquid is really *tasty*, before completing gelatine.)

Step 3

Combine hot liquid with softened gelatine. Stir well, to dissolve all gelatine. Add

lemon juice (see amounts under Variations)

(For meat aspic, add 1 tablespoon sherry with lemon juice. For a fish dish, add 2 tablespoons white wine with lemon juice.)

Step 4

Pour gelatine mixture into mold which has been rinsed out under cold water. Chill gelatine until thick as unbeaten egg white; then add

solid ingredients

Continue chilling until firm, about 2 or 3 hours.

ASPIC VARIATIONS

(*Follow method of Master Recipe #58, Aspic, page 375, using ingredients below.*)

Meat Aspic (Using meat-flavored liquid)

I. *Made with meat stock or broth.* Following Master Recipe, soften gelatine in ½ cup cold, tasty, well-seasoned, strained meat stock (or meat broth). Heat 1 cup more of same liquid. To hot liquid add ¼ teaspoon salt, 1 teaspoon onion juice (scraped from cut onion), the softened gelatine. Then stir in 1 tablespoon lemon juice. Add 1 tablespoon sherry if desired.

II. *Made with canned bouillon or bouillon cubes.* Following Master Recipe, soften gelatine in only ¼ cup cold water. Heat 1 can undiluted bouillon or consommé; or heat 1¼ cups water, dissolving in the water 3 beef bouillon cubes. To hot liquid, add same seasonings as under I, above.

III. *Made with tomato juice and bouillon cubes.* Following Master Recipe, soften gelatine in ½ cup cold water. Heat 1 cup tomato juice or V-8, dissolving in the hot juice 2 beef bouillon cubes. To hot juice, add same seasonings as under I, above.

Chicken Aspic (Using chicken-flavored liquid)

I. *Made with chicken stock or broth.* Following Master Recipe, soften gelatine in ½ cup cold, tasty, well-seasoned, strained chicken stock (or chicken broth). Heat 1 cup more of same liquid. To hot liquid add ¼ teaspoon salt, 1 teaspoon onion juice (scraped from cut onion), the softened gelatine. Stir in 1 tablespoon lemon juice.

II. *Made with canned chicken broth, or chicken bouillon cubes.* Following Master Recipe, soften gelatine in only ¼ cup cold water. Heat 1 can undiluted chicken broth; or heat 1¼ cups water, adding to the water 2 chicken bouillon cubes. Stir until dissolved. To hot liquid, add same seasonings as under I.

Tomato Aspic (Using tomato-flavored liquid)

I. *Made with tomato juice.* Using Master Recipe #58, soften gelatine in ½ cup cold tomato juice. Heat 1¼ cups tomato juice. To hot juice, add ¼ teaspoon salt, 1 teaspoon onion juice (scraped from a cut onion), few drops Worcestershire sauce (or bottled meat extract), if desired. Stir in softened gelatine. Stir in 1 table-spoon mild vinegar or lemon juice.

II. *Made with canned tomato soup.* In Master Recipe #58, soften gelatine in ½ cup cold water. Heat 1 can undiluted con-densed tomato soup, plus ¼ cup water. Add to hot liquid same seasonings as under I, above.

Plain Tart Aspic (Using water plus vinegar and lemon)

For molded vegetable salads, molded seafood. In Master Recipe #58, soften gelatine in ½ cup cold water. Heat 1 cup plain water. To hot water, add ¼ teaspoon salt; stir in the softened gelatine. Then stir in 2 to 4 tablespoons mild vinegar or lemon juice (or use 2 tablespoons vinegar, 2 tablespoons lemon juice; or for fish dishes, use 2 tablespoons lemon juice, 2 tablespoons white wine).

MANY DISHES CAN BE MADE WITH ASPIC

With the aspic variations above, you may mold practically any cooked or canned, main-course type of food you please. You may choose to mold large slices or small pieces of meat . . . or meat combined with vegetables . . . or hard-cooked eggs combined with fish . . . or chicken or seafood combined with diced celery, to make a main-course salad . . . or whatever you please. And you may use whatever flavor of aspic you please, to mold them in. The choice is yours, and the sky the limit. Just remember two rules:

1. *Mold in aspic only foods which have been cooked, canned, or are edible in raw state.* Aspic will not cook them.

2. *For amount of aspic made by Master Recipe,* plan to *use*

about two cups solid ingredients. (This may be all one kind of ingredient, or may be mixed.)

There are *two methods* of molding in aspic. You may either:

Arrange solids in a shallow dish; then pour liquid aspic over them, and chill entire dish until firm; or

Chill liquid aspic until consistency of unbeaten egg white; then stir in solids, and continue chilling until firm.

We give here a few sample dishes, all very good. After seeing how easy they are, you will make up your own.

Eggs and Asparagus, in Aspic

Hard-cook 3 or 4 eggs. Shell them. Slice them in halves, lengthwise. If desired, devil them (p. 265). Drain 1 can asparagus spears, saving the asparagus water. Arrange spears in parallel position, in shallow baking dish; here and there, between spears, place ½ egg. If desired, you may also add small slices of cooked ham, or tinned luncheon meat, or cooked or canned tongue or corned beef, distributing slices attractively among other ingredients.

Now make Meat Aspic II (p. 377), using ¼ cup cold asparagus water to soften gelatine in, instead of plain water. Pour completed liquid aspic over contents of dish. Chill in refrigerator 2 to 3 hours, or until firm.

To serve, cut in squares. Place on crisped greens; garnish with mayonnaise.

Drained cooked broccoli, or Brussels sprouts, or string beans, may be substituted for asparagus in above dish.

Shrimp-Tomato Mold

Make tomato aspic (p. 378), increasing salt to ½ teaspoon. When liquid aspic is completed, stir in, if desired, 1 teaspoon bottled horseradish. Chill aspic mixture in refrigerator about ½ hour, or until thick as unbeaten egg white. Then fold into it 1 cup cleaned boiled or canned shrimp, ¾ cup diced celery, and 2 tablespoons chopped green pepper. Turn mixture into 1 quart loaf or ring mold, rinsed out under running cold water. Chill in refrigerator 2 to 3 hours, or until firm. Unmold. Serve on crisp lettuce, with mayonnaise.

Chicken-Pineapple Mold

Make Chicken Aspic I (p. 377), but soften gelatine in ¼ **cup cold water plus ¼ cup pineapple juice** (drained from crushed pineapple used below). For hot liquid, heat 1 **can undiluted chicken broth,** or heat 1 **cup water** and dissolve 2 **chicken bouillon cubes** in it. Increase salt to ½ teaspoon. Add softened gelatine; Stir in 2 **tablespoons lemon juice.** Chill completed aspic mixture in refrigerator ½ hour or until thick as unbeaten egg white; then fold in 1½ **cups cooked or canned chicken,** cut to bite size, ½ **cup diced celery, 1 can crushed pineapple,** drained. Turn mixture into 1 quart ring or loaf mold, which has been rinsed out under cold water. Continue chilling 2 or 3 hours, or until firm. Unmold on lettuce. Garnish with **mayonnaise.**

Seafood Mold

Use lobster, crab meat, shrimp, tuna, salmon, or any flaked, cooked, white-meated fish. Clean, cut to bite size, remove bones, skin, or otherwise make ready for eating enough cooked or canned seafood to make 1 **cup seafood.** Make Plain Tart Aspic (p. 378); then chill completed aspic mixture in refrigerator ½ hour, or until thick as unbeaten egg white. Then stir in seafood prepared above, ¾ **cup diced celery, 2 tablespoons chopped parsley or green pepper,** and, if desired, 2 **or 3 diced hard-cooked eggs.** Turn mixture into 1-quart ring or loaf mold which has been rinsed out under cold water; continue chilling in refrigerator until firm, about 2 or 3 hours. When unmolded, serve with crisped **greens,** and decorate mold with **slices of cucumber** or **tomato wedges.** Garnish with **mayonnaise.**

"Catch-All" Luncheon Mold

In my household, this sort of dish is amusedly called a "Mommie dish," since it contains anything "Mommie" can find; but I notice it disappears rapidly!

Gather together **1 to 1½ cups cooked, drained vegetables** — any odds and ends you have at hand (that is, any *firm* — not runny, or mashed, or fried ones), add **¼ cup diced celery**, including some **finely chopped celery leaves;** add also **1 to 2 tablespoons grated onion, 1 tablespoon minced green pepper.** Sprinkle vegetables with **salt,** and stir to blend. Now add **½ cup any diced cooked or canned meat** you have at hand (or instead of meat you may substitute bits of leftover cooked white fish, or flaked canned tuna, or shrimp, or salmon).

If using meat, make Meat Aspic (p. 377). If using fish, make Plain Tart Aspic (p. 378). Chill completed aspic mixture in refrigerator ½ hour or until thick as unbeaten egg white. Then stir in solid ingredients above. Turn mixture into 1-quart ring or loaf mold, which has been rinsed out under cold water. Chill in refrigerator 2 or 3 hours, or until firm. When unmolded, surround with crisped **watercress or other greens;** garnish with **mayonnaise.** If desired, add wedges of tomatoes, and wedges of shelled, hard-cooked eggs, for decoration and added nourishment. Very very good . . . and the dish has the virtue of changing each time!

NOTE: If desired, you can make above dish with diced cooked or canned chicken or turkey instead of meat or fish. But if using fowl, use only delicate-tasting vegetables, such as cooked drained peas or string beans. Add celery, salt; and make Chicken Aspic (p. 377), to hold ingredients together.

MOLDED SALADS INCORPORATING MAYONNAISE

Sometimes chicken, seafood, or other foods are prepared in an aspic which has mayonnaise mixed right in with it. This naturally makes an opaque (no longer transparent) aspic, and a richer one. It is only another variation of aspic, however. You simply make a typical aspic, using far less liquid than usual (only about half). This produces a small amount of very concentrated aspic mixture. This mixture is cooled; then mayonnaise blended into it; the mayonnaise of course makes up for the amount of liquid omitted from the regular aspic formula. Examples:

Molded Chicken Soufflé Salad

Make Chicken Aspic II (p. 377), but instead of softening **gelatine** in water, soften it in ¼ **cup cold chicken broth or bouillon.** Heat ¾ **cup more chicken broth or bouillon.** To hot liquid add ½ **teaspoon salt,** ½ **teaspoon minced onion, pinch of sage** if desired. Combine hot liquid with softened gelatine; stir to dissolve, and *cool.* Then stir in ¾ **cup mayonnaise, 1 tablespoon lemon juice;** add 1 **cup diced cooked or canned chicken,** ¾ **cup diced celery, 2 tablespoons parsley,** chopped fine.

Turn mixture into 1-quart mold which has been rinsed out under cold water. Chill in refrigerator 2 or 3 hours, or until firm. When unmolded, surround with crisped **greens;** add **sliced hard-cooked eggs** and **tomato wedges** if desired. Or garnish with **sliced young cucumbers,** and **radishes** cut like roses, for color.

Molded Seafood Soufflé Salad

Makes lobster, shrimp, crab meat, tuna, or salmon salad. Clean, cut to bite size, remove bones, skin, or otherwise prepare for eating enough cooked or canned seafood to make 1 cup seafood. Now make Plain Tart Aspic (p. 378), but soften gelatine in only ¼ **cup cold water.** Heat only ½ **cup water.** To hot liquid, add ¼ **teaspoon salt,** ½ **teaspoon grated onion.** Combine hot liquid with softened gelatine; stir to dissolve; *cool* mixture. Then stir in 2 **tablespoons lemon juice,** ¾ **cup mayonnaise;** add seafood, ¾ **cup diced celery, 2 tablespoons chopped parsley or green pepper.** Turn mixture into 1 quart mold which has been rinsed out under cold water; chill in refrigerator 2 or 3 hours, or until firm. When unmolded, surround with crisped **greens;** decorate if desired with **tomato wedges, sliced hard-cooked eggs, sliced cucumber.**

MOUSSE

Mousse is another variation of aspic . . . an aspic made with a very, very *small* amount of liquid to soften the gelatine; then, after concentrated aspic mixture has cooled, whipped cream is stirred in. The whipped cream makes up for the liquid omitted in regular aspic formula. Example:

Salmon Mousse

(If desired, substitute lobster meat, crab meat, shrimp, or tuna fish, in place of the salmon.) Clean, remove bones, skin, cut to bite size, or otherwise prepare for eating, 2 cups drained cooked or canned seafood. Now make aspic by softening **1 envelope unflavored gelatine in ¼ cup cold water** plus **¼ cup vinegar.** Stir. Let stand 5 minutes, until gelatine softens. Then place this mixture over a saucepan containing boiling water, and keep stirring gelatine mixture until gelatine completely dissolves. Add **1¼ teaspoon salt, 1 teaspoon prepared mustard, 1 tablespoon sugar:** stir well. Cool. When cooled, stir in seafood, **1 tablespoon capers,** if liked; **1 cup diced celery.** Then stir in **½ cup heavy cream,** whipped stiff. Blend. Turn into 1-quart loaf or ring mold which has been rinsed out under cold water; chill in refrigerator 2 or 3 hours, or until firm. When unmolded, surround with crisped **greens,** and add decorations if desired of **tomato wedges, cucumber slices, quartered hard-cooked eggs.**

OTHER USES OF GELATINE

Gelatine is also used in pie fillings (see fruit chiffon and other chiffon pies, Chapter XXXV; and cream chiffon pie under Master Recipe, Soft Custard, Chapter XXXI). Note also Spanish cream under variations of Master Recipe, Soft Custard.

You Can Make Custards

METHOD FOR: *Soft Custards, Custard Sauce, Floating Island, Spanish Cream, Baked Custards, Bread Pudding*

BASIC PRINCIPLES

Custard is merely an eggnog mixture: egg, milk, sugar, plus flavoring. Yet this combination of ingredients lies at the base of many delicious desserts.

There are only two ways to cook custard.

(1) *Cooked on top of stove,* in double boiler, it becomes a "soft" custard — the kind used to pour over cut fruit, or to spread over fruit in some open pies; or to fill cream puffs; or to use as a sweet sauce over cake or gelatine desserts.

(2) *Baked,* the mixture becomes a "solid." It will make cups of custard, or the filling for custard pie, or with variations, it makes bread pudding, or filling for pumpkin or squash pie.

The standard custard mixture is: 1 whole egg (or 2 yolks), plus 1 to 2 tablespoons sugar, for each cup of milk. As it is the eggs, however, which thicken the mixture, it is always wise to allow a little extra amount of egg, for good measure. We have allowed for it in these recipes.

MASTER RECIPE #59
SOFT CUSTARD

Scald (do not boil)

2 cups milk

In bowl, mix together

3 eggs, slightly beaten
4 tablespoons sugar
1 pinch salt

Pour scalded milk, a little at a time, into egg mixture, stirring constantly. Then place entire mixture in top of double boiler. Place over lower section of double boiler, containing about 1½ inches hot (not boiling) water. Cook custard gently, stirring constantly, about 6–8 minutes, or until thick enough to coat a silver spoon.

Do not overcook, or custard may curdle. (If it does curdle, beat with rotary egg beater; this will restore smoothness, but make custard thinner.) Turn mixture into bowl; cool it; then stir in

½ teaspoon vanilla

Chill in refrigerator.

NOTE: Soft custard becomes thicker as it gets cold.

SOFT CUSTARD VARIATIONS

(*Follow Master Recipe #59, Soft Custard, page 385, for all these Variations.*)

Soft Custard Sauce

To pour over cut fruits, or gelatine desserts, or cake. Make Master Recipe, but using only 2 eggs. This makes the custard a little less thick. The custard may be used warm or cold as a sauce.

Soft Custard Cake Filling

To spread between layers of cake. Or you may cut out tops of cup cakes, put custard inside; recap cakes, and garnish top of each cake with whipped cream plus a sprinkling of shredded coconut. Make Master Recipe, Soft Custard; chill finished mixture in refrigerator until it becomes thick enough to use.

Banana or Peach Custard Pie

Have ready a prebaked pie shell; see page 449. Half fill it with **peeled, sliced fresh peaches, or drained canned sliced peaches, or sliced bananas.** Make Master Recipe, Soft Custard. When cooled, pour it over fruit. If desired, sprinkle top of pie with shredded coconut. Let pie stand 2 or 3 hours, so custard may thicken, before serving it.

Sherry-Custard

In Master Recipe, flavor custard with ½ **teaspoon sherry** instead of vanilla.

Tawny Custard

In Master Recipe, substitute **brown sugar** for white. Gives a quite different flavor.

Chocolate Custard

In Master Recipe, add **2 squares** (2 ounces) **baking chocolate** to milk as it scalds. Heat until chocolate melts; blend it well with milk. Finish custard as usual.

Floating Island

Make Master Recipe, Soft Custard. Chill in dessert cups. When thickened, on top of each serving place a garnish of **sweetened, flavored whipped cream** (p. 408); or make Master Recipe, Meringue (p. 489); put a heaping spoonful of **meringue** on top of each serving of custard, without cooking the meringue.

Coconut-Meringue Custard

Make Master Recipe. Chill it until thickened. Turn mixture into an ovenware baking dish. Now make Master Recipe, Meringue (p. 489), stirring into finished meringue mixture ½ **cup chopped, shredded coconut.** Spread meringue in swirly design over top of custard. Place dish in moderate oven (350°) about 15 minutes, or just until top of meringue browns a light golden color.

Cream Chiffon Pie

Prepare a prebaked pie shell; see page 449. Or instead of making and baking a pastry pie shell, you may make a crumb pie shell (p. 464), if desired. Soften **1 envelope unflavored gelatine in ¼ cup cold water.** While it softens, make Master Recipe, Soft Custard (p. 385), but with these changes: Reduce milk to 1½ cups. Instead of 3 whole eggs, use only 3 yolks. Increase sugar to ⅓ cup. When custard mixture is cooked, and still hot, stir in the softened gelatine. Cool. Stir in **1 teaspoon vanilla** (or, if preferred, you may use 1 teaspoon sherry, or rum flavoring). Chill until custard mixture is partly thickened. In a separate bowl, beat until stiff but not dry **3 egg whites,** adding to them, 1 tablespoon at a time, **4 tablespoons sugar,** and beating after each addition until smooth. Fold egg whites into custard mixture. Heap mixture into prepared pie shell. Chill pie in refrigerator several hours before serving.

Spanish Cream

Soften **1 envelope unflavored gelatine in ¼ cup cold milk** for 5 minutes. Now make Master Recipe, Soft Custard, but with these changes: Increase **milk to 2½ cups.** Instead of 3 whole eggs, use 3 yolks. Add softened gelatine to eggs. Increase sugar to ⅓ cup. When mixture has cooked, cool it; stir in **1 tablespoon sherry;** add **½ cup macaroon crumbs,** plus stiffly beaten **whites of 3 eggs.** Turn mixture into mold, rinsed out with cold water; see explanation, page 362. Chill 2 or 3 hours, or until firm. Unmold on serving platter; garnish with sweetened whipped cream (p. 408).

MASTER RECIPE #60
BAKED CUSTARD

(Makes 4 to 6 cups, depending on size,
or fills a 1-quart baking dish)

In a large bowl, beat slightly
4 whole eggs
Blend into eggs
¼ cup sugar
⅛ teaspoon salt
In a saucepan, *scald* (do not boil)
3 cups milk
Add hot milk to egg mixture; blend.

Add, for flavoring
¼ teaspoon nutmeg
½ teaspoon vanilla
(Some cooks omit vanilla.)

Pour warm custard mixture through a strainer into a quart-size baking dish, or into individual custard cups.* Place dish or cups in a shallow pan containing ½ inch warm water, to protect bottom of custard from burning. Place pan in slow oven (325° F.). Bake about 45 minutes if in cups; or about 55 minutes or more, if in large dish. You may test doneness by inserting blade of knife into center of custard; if it comes out dry, custard is "set." Don't overcook, or custard will turn watery on the bottom.

* *If planning to unmold* cups of custard onto plates, for serving, butter inside of cups before pouring liquid mixture into cups. To unmold after baking, place serving plate upside down over top of custard cup; then invert both plate and cup at same time. Custard should slip out intact.

BAKED CUSTARD VARIATIONS

(Follow Master Recipe #60, Baked Custard, page 388, making changes noted below.)

Chocolate Custard

Add **2 squares** (2 ounces) **baking chocolate** to milk as it scalds; heat until chocolate is thoroughly melted; then stir, to blend milk and chocolate well. Increase sugar to ⅓ **cup.**

Maple Custard

Omit sugar. Substitute ¾ **cup maple syrup.**

Coconut Custard

Before pouring into dish or cups, stir in ½ **to 1 cup shredded coconut.**

Caramel Custard

Caramelize (p. 565) ½ **cup sugar.** Now make Master Recipe, but add to eggs only ¼ **cup granulated sugar.** Add the caramelized sugar with the warm milk.

Rice Custard

Before pouring into dishes, stir in ½ **cup cooked rice.** If desired, add ¼ **to ½ cup seedless raisins.**

Coffee Custard

Instead of using milk, substitute 1½ **cups strong hot coffee** (strained of grounds), plus 1½ **cups scalded cream or top milk.**

Old-Fashioned Bread Pudding (Bread plus Custard)

Butter 5 or 6 slices dry bread. Sprinkle buttered side with **granulated sugar.** Place slices in a 1-quart baking dish. Now make Master Recipe, Baked Custard. Pour hot mixture over bread. If desired, add ¼ **to ½ cup seedless raisins.** Place dish in shallow pan containing ½ inch of warm water; bake as for custard.

Some people prefer bread pudding with bread *crumbled,* instead of sliced. If you do, simply omit preparing sliced bread. Begin by making Master Recipe, Baked Custard. When scalding milk, add to it **2 cups dry bread crumbs.** Let crumbs soak in milk about 10 minutes, to soften, before adding milk to egg mixture. Bake as for custard.

Custard-Type Pies

See Chapter XXXV for custard, coconut custard, pumpkin, and squash pies; all of these are made with a baked-custard-type mixture.

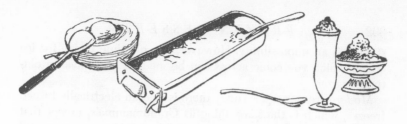

CHAPTER XXXII

You Can Make Frozen Desserts and Dessert Sauces

METHOD FOR: *Ice Cream; and suggestions for using it, Mousse, Ice, Sherbet, Frozen Fruit Salad, Frozen Puddings and Cakes, Dessert Sauces, Whipped Cream*

READ THIS BEFORE MAKING ICE CREAM

Ice cream is fun to make, and not hard — but you will come a cropper if you don't know two things:

(1) Not every ice-cream recipe can be made successfully in your refrigerator.

(2) Any ice cream (and most other frozen desserts) must be either beaten or stirred during freezing, to prevent the liquid ingredients from freezing in sharp, icy particles which are unpleasant on the tongue.

Old-fashioned method. The old-time ice-cream freezer of our grandmothers' day (and there are still many in existence) was a bucket loaded with 4 parts crushed ice to 1 part rock salt. Packed in the center of the ice and salt was a container to hold the cream. The container was equipped with a "dasher" which whipped and stirred the cream constantly, as long as the most willing slave of the family could crank the handle. Because the cream was stirred continuously, recipes could be made of different proportions of ingredients than we can use in our refrigerators, where constant stirring is an impossibility. However, any old-time recipe for ice cream which you come across can be made if you have an old-time freezer.

Modern freezers. (1) Today there is sold an electrically turned freezer, which is the same thing as Grandmamma's, except that electric current is your ever present "slavy." However, you still must have the crushed ice and rock salt. (2) Vacuum freezers are also sold. While these need no cranking, you must frequently scrape cream from edges of container, and stir contents during freezing. If using this type freezer, follow recipes provided with it. (3) There is also on the market a small freezing gadget equipped with a "dasher," which fits into ice-cube compartment of mechanical refrigerators. If you have one of these, you may make any recipe for ice cream.

Your mechanical refrigerator. Since almost every home today has a mechanical refrigerator, this is rapidly becoming the most commonly used appliance for making ice cream. And excellent ice cream can be made in it, if you use recipes specifically adapted to this purpose. Such recipes use a lower proportion of sugar to liquid; sometimes corn syrup is substituted for part of the sugar, since syrup freezes more smoothly; all ingredients are thickened and smoothed as much as possible before freezing, to avoid ice particles. For example, when eggs are the "thickener" for the ice cream, the eggs, milk, and sugar are cooked together, forming a soft thin custard; then cream is whipped stiff, and the two thickened mixtures blended together and frozen. If flour is the thickener for the ice cream, flour, sugar, salt, and milk are cooked together to form a sort of white sauce; then cream and egg whites both whipped stiff and blended with the sauce. To repeat: everything is thickened and smoothed as much as possible *before* freezing.

During freezing, albeit constant stirring is obviously impossible, it is still necessary (if you want fine-textured desserts) to scrape dessert from edges of ice-cube tray, and whip the dessert with rotary beater, or at least stir it with spoon, to break up whatever ice crystals may have formed, and to even the texture. Some cooks turn over the ice cream every 30 minutes, during freezing. Others wait until cream is about halfway frozen, then turn it out into a chilled bowl, whip it vigorously with rotary beater, and return it to ice-cube tray to freeze until solid.

If for any reason you are not going to be able to stir your ice cream, make a mousse (which needs no stirring) or buy ice cream in a store.

Time required for freezing in refrigerator. Refrigerator cold-control device should be turned to point of greatest cold, about ½ hour before dessert is put in. Leave it so until ice cream is frozen solid, which will require about 3 to 4 hours. Then turn cold-control device back to a point just slightly colder than the temperature at which you normally keep your refrigerator, where frozen dessert will not melt; and let ice cream or frozen puddings stand several hours (even 1 or 2 days) to "ripen." It is an odd fact that all frozen desserts will mellow, both in texture and flavor, and increase in goodness, upon standing. It is therefore not only forehanded, but "good cooking" to make frozen desserts well in advance.

Packaged ice cream mixes. Several specially prepared ice cream mixes are available in the market, and you can also make good ice cream using prepared packaged chocolate, vanilla, or butterscotch puddings having an arrowroot base. If using any of these, follow carefully directions that come with the package.

NOTE: Because of the growing custom of making ice cream in mechanical refrigerators, *all recipes in this book are adapted to refrigerators;* many good old-time recipes have regretfully been left out. Using the Master Recipes given here, however, you can make enough ice cream to serve your needs for life.

MASTER RECIPE #61
CUSTARD-BASE
REFRIGERATOR ICE CREAM, VANILLA

This recipe, which tastes almost like frozen eggnog, is rich and delicious, and can be varied in many ways. It makes an excellent base for the inclusion of fresh fruit or berries.

Quantity: roughly 1 ice-cube tray, or 5 to 6 servings.

In a bowl, beat slightly

> 2 eggs

Beat into eggs, little by little

> ⅓ cup sugar
> ⅛ teaspoon salt

(Instead of ⅓ cup sugar, you may use ¼ cup sugar plus ½ cup corn syrup.)

Scald

> 1 cup milk

Pour hot milk slowly into egg mixture, stirring; then turn into top of double boiler; cook over pan of hot (not boiling) water about 5 minutes, or until custard thinly coats a spoon.

Chill custard in ice-cube tray 10 to 20 minutes, or until custard is partly frozen.

While custard chills, whip stiff

> 1 cup heavy cream (½ pint)

to which you have added

> 1 teaspoon vanilla

Scrape partly frozen custard into a chilled bowl; beat with rotary beater until smooth, but not melted. Blend in whipped cream.

Immediately return mixture to ice-cube tray; freeze. Stir several times during first hour of freezing.

CUSTARD ICE-CREAM VARIATIONS

(*Follow Master Recipe #61, Custard Ice Cream, page 394, making changes as below.*)

Eggnog Ice Cream

Reduce vanilla to ½ teaspoon, and add 2 teaspoons (or more) brandy or rum-flavoring, plus ¼ teaspoon ground or powdered nutmeg. If desired, ¼ cup finely chopped maraschino cherries, or ¼ cup crumbled dry macaroons, or both, may be folded in with whipped cream.

French Vanilla Ice Cream

Instead of 2 whole eggs, use 4 yolks. Increase milk to 2 cups.

Sherry- or Rum-Flavored Ice Cream

Reduce vanilla to ½ teaspoon, and add 1 or more teaspoons sherry or rum (or rum flavoring).

Mint Ice Cream

Omit vanilla. Add instead 2 to 3 drops oil of peppermint. Before freezing, blend in 2 or 3 drops red or green food coloring, to tint cream pale pink or pale green. When serving, garnish with a fresh mint leaf and a maraschino cherry — or sprinkle with grated baking chocolate, and put 1 teaspoon rum or brandy over each serving.

Chocolate Flake Ice Cream

Add with whipped cream 1 or 2 squares (1 or 2 ounces) grated baking chocolate.

Grapenut Ice Cream

Add with whipped cream ½ cup grapenuts. Reduce vanilla to ½ teaspoon, and add few drops almond extract, or 1 teaspoon sherry, if preferred.

Bisque Ice Cream

When mixture is partly frozen, stir in ½ cup finely chopped nut meats (not salted nuts, however). Almonds, pecans, hazelnuts, Brazil nuts, are particularly good, and even better if you toast the nut meats lightly in moderate (350°) oven for about 5 minutes before chopping them.

Pistachio Ice Cream

Add ½ teaspoon almond extract with vanilla. Before freezing, blend in a few drops green food coloring to tint ice cream a delicate green. (To make pistachio bisque, fold in also ¼ cup dry, crumbled macaroons, plus ¼ cup finely chopped almonds.)

Peanut Brittle Ice Cream

Omit sugar. Instead add ¼ pound peanut brittle, pounded fine.

Macaroon Ice Cream

When adding whipped cream, fold in ½ cup dry, crumbled macaroons. Flavor with sherry, instead of vanilla.

Coffee Ice Cream

Substitute 1 cup very strong, cold, clear coffee infusion (no grounds, please!) instead of ½ cup milk.

Chocolate Ice Cream

Put with milk, to scald, 1 to 1½ squares (1–1½ ounces) baking chocolate. Whip milk and chocolate together with rotary beater, to blend well, before proceeding with recipe.

Banana Ice Cream

Omit vanilla. After ice cream is partially frozen, stir in 2 bananas, mashed, with few drops lemon juice added to the pulp, if desired.

Fresh Strawberry Ice Cream

Just before adding whipped cream, fold in ½ to 1½ cups crushed, fresh strawberries, sweetened if necessary, with 2 to 4 tablespoons confectioners' sugar. (Warning: do not add any berry juice, for excess liquid will spoil texture of ice cream.)

Red Raspberry, or Black Raspberry Ice Cream

Same as for strawberry, substituting **red raspberries, or black raspberries,** which generally need some sweetening before being used.

Fresh Peach Ice Cream

Same as for strawberry, substituting **peeled, crushed fresh peaches,** sweetened if necessary. Add **2 or 3 drops almond extract,** with the vanilla.

Pineapple Ice Cream

Use only canned. Fresh pineapple is not successful. Make like strawberry, substituting **drained canned crushed pineapple.**

Blackberry Ice Cream

Same as strawberry, substituting **fresh blackberries,** which are usually quite tart and will need some sweetening before they are used.

Maraschino Cherry Ice Cream

In Master Recipe, with whipped cream, fold in **½ cup drained, chopped maraschino cherries.** (Or use **¼ cup cherries,** plus **¼ cup crumbled dry macaroons.**)

FANCY WAYS OF USING ICE CREAM
(BOUGHT OR HOMEMADE)

Frozen Eclairs, or Cream Puffs

Have ready **1 or 2 éclair shells, or cream-puff shells,** per person (these can be bought at good bakeries), and **1 pint ice cream,** any flavor. Cut off tops of shells. Fill shells with ice cream. Replace tops. If desired, over tops put hot fudge or other sweet sauce, or whipped cream.

Cherries Jubilee with Ice Cream

Serves 4. Have ready 1 No. 2 or 2½ can pitted **Bing cherries,** 1 cup brandy or kirsch, 1½ pints vanilla ice cream. Drain cherries. Measure and heat just 1 cup cherry juice, with all the cherries added to it, bringing very slowly to a simmering point (don't boil). Add brandy or kirsch to hot cherries, just before serving. Turn cherries and juice into a glass or other serving bowl which will not be harmed by flames. Touch a match to syrup, just when serving. Liquor will blaze up for a moment or two. Serve flaming hot cherries over ice cream already arranged in dessert cups.

Quick Trick from the Liquor Cabinet

Have ready **ice cream,** in dessert cups or sherbet glasses, **1 teaspoon to 1 jigger of brandy** (or rum, or other liqueur) to pour over each serving. For worldly guests, here's how to lift simple ice cream into a memorable dessert which might be served in the most Parisian dining place. It's quick, easy, unbelievably good. Try rum over lime ice; rum or cointreau over lemon ice; rum or brandy over chocolate or mint ice cream; kirsch or rum over peach ice cream; brandy or apricot brandy over vanilla ice cream; rum or brandy over eggnog or French vanilla ice cream; peach brandy over bisque or other nut ice cream; apricot brandy over banana ice cream; sweetened, whole ripe strawberries, soaked in port wine, over vanilla ice cream; mixed, cut fresh fruits, soaked in 1 or 2 jiggers cointreau or champagne, over vanilla ice cream.

FAST, SIMPLE DESSERTS, WITH ICE CREAM (BOUGHT OR HOMEMADE)

Ice Cream Cup Cakes

Scoop out top of plain **cup cakes.** Fill center of each with **ice cream.** Put top of cup cake back on. Cover with **hot fudge or other** dessert sauce, or **whipped cream,** or **fresh fruit.**

Ice Cream Layer Cake

Between two even layers of plain **cake** (or angel cake, or sponge cake) spread a layer of any flavor **ice cream**. Top cake with **whipped cream, dessert sauce, or fresh fruit.**

Ice Cream Fruit Cups

Put a serving of **ice cream**, or your favorite-flavored ice, in each dessert cup. Over it, put **1 or 2 tablespoons fresh or frozen berries,** or fresh or frozen fruit, or drained canned fruit.

Homemade Sundaes

Put a serving of **ice cream** in each dessert cup. Top with sweetened whipped cream; then add a garnish of **nuts,** or maraschino cherry, or crumbled dry macaroons, or grated chocolate or **chocolate bits,** or shredded coconut, or fruit. Add **a tablespoon syrup or dessert sauce,** if desired. (Sundaes are easy to make, from garnishes you have at hand; and children love them. Some dessert sauces can be bought in cans.)

Ice Cream in Cantaloupe

Cut a ripe **cantaloupe** or muskmelon into halves, thirds, **or** quarters, for serving. Scoop out seeds. Fill hollow of each piece with a scoop of ice cream, or **lemon or orange ice.**

Melon Balls, Ice, and Ginger Ale

In each dessert cup, put a helping of **raspberry, orange, or lemon ice.** Add a few ball-shaped pieces cut from chilled **honeydew or watermelon.** (You can buy a melon-ball cutter in dime stores; and it is useful for cutting out potato balls, too.) Add **1 or 2 tablespoons ice-cold ginger ale.** Top with a **fresh mint leaf.** Very cool, very appealing, for hot weather.

MASTER RECIPE #62
VANILLA MOUSSE

Quantity: Roughly 1 ice-cube tray, or 5 to 6 servings

Mousse is very rich, very good, and always delights me because it doesn't have to be stirred. You mix it . . . put it in ice-cube tray . . . forget it.

Mix together in a bowl
>1 or 2 whole eggs, slightly beaten
>⅓ cup powdered sugar
>1 pinch salt

Beat above mixture with rotary beater until sugar is dissolved, and mixture thickens, like a custard.

In separate bowl, beat stiff
>1 cup heavy cream (½ pint)

Blend the two mixtures; fold in
>1 teaspoon vanilla

Freeze in ice-cube tray until firm.

MOUSSE VARIATIONS

(*Follow Master Recipe #62, Mousse, page 400, making changes below.*)

Peach Mousse

Use 1 egg. Before freezing, fold in 1 cup mashed fresh peach pulp, sweetened with 1 or 2 tablespoons confectioners' sugar if peaches are tart. Avoid adding peach juice; juice will thin mousse, and spoil texture. Add few drops almond extract.

Berry Mousse

Use 1 egg. Before freezing, fold in 1 cup mashed firm strawberries or raspberries; avoid adding juice. If much juice forms when mashing berries, pour it off, using only berry pulp, to avoid thinning mousse.

ICES

Be warned that plain water ice is very difficult to make in a mechanical refrigerator without ice crystals forming.

A sugar syrup is first cooked, and a fruit flavor added to it. Mixture is then frozen firm in ice-cube tray. It is then removed from ice cube tray to a thoroughly chilled bowl, and whipped quickly in this bowl until ice is light and creamy — but not until melted; if you don't work with alacrity, your ice will melt back to watery syrup. After whipping, the mixture is put back into ice-cube tray, and frozen firm.

MASTER RECIPE #63
WATER ICE — LEMON

Make sugar syrup by mixing together in saucepan

> 2 cups water
> ¾ cup sugar

Bring above to a boil, stirring until sugar dissolves; then cook syrup slowly 10 minutes.

Remove from heat. Add for flavoring

> ½ cup strained lemon juice
> pinch of salt

Turn mixture into ice-cube tray; freeze until firm.

Remove from ice-cube tray to thoroughly chilled bowl; and with rotary beater, beat quickly until mixture becomes light and fluffy, but not melted.

Quickly return mixture to ice-cube tray and freeze firm without further stirring.

WATER ICE VARIATIONS

Orange Ice

In Master Recipe, increase sugar to 1 cup. To cooked syrup, add ⅛ teaspoon salt, grated rind of 1 orange. *Cool* syrup. Then add 1 cup strained orange juice plus 2 tablespoons strained lemon juice. Freeze; beat in chilled bowl; freeze again, as in Master Recipe.

Raspberry Ice (Made with fresh raspberries.)

To make your syrup, crush 1 pint fresh raspberries, adding ¾ cup sugar, and ½ cup water. Slowly bring this to a boil, stirring so berries won't stick to pan and burn. Then cook slowly 5 minutes. *Cool* syrup; then add 2 tablespoons orange juice, or, if preferred, 1 teaspoon lemon juice. Freeze; beat in chilled bowl; freeze again, as in Master Recipe.

SHERBET

Sherbet is made much like an ice, except that in addition to a cooked syrup it often contains egg whites and a little thin cream.

Orange Cream Sherbet

Cook ¾ cup water with ¾ cup sugar, slowly, for 10 minutes. Add grated rind of 1 orange, and continue cooking syrup a few minutes. Strain. Add clear syrup to 1½ cups orange juice plus 1 tablespoon lemon juice. Cool. Pour into ice-cube tray, and freeze firm. Remove mixture to chilled mixing bowl, and beat until light. Have ready to add: 2 stiffly beaten egg whites, with pinch of salt added, and ½ cup chilled coffee cream, unbeaten. Combine ingredients, blend quickly, return to ice-cube tray, and freeze firm. If ingredients separate during freezing stir again in ice cube tray, with spoon.

Apricot Sherbet

Cook 1 cup apricot juice, ½ cup water, and ¼ cup sugar together, slowly, for 10 minutes. Cool. Force 1 cup apricots through sieve, then add to pulp 1½ tablespoons lemon juice, and the hot syrup. Chill. Pour into ice-cube tray, and freeze firm. Remove mixture to chilled bowl, and beat until light. Have ready 2 egg whites, stiffly beaten, with a pinch of salt, and ½ cup chilled coffee cream, unbeaten. Combine ingredients; blend quickly, and return to tray to freeze firm. If mixture separates when partly frozen, remove to chilled bowl and beat again.

MASTER RECIPE #64
FROZEN FRUIT SALAD
(Serves 6 to 8)

The following recipe (fruits frozen in a combination of whipped cream, mayonnaise, and cream cheese) is delicious for a party luncheon, Sunday dinner, or for any hot day. Many similar recipes exist. If desired, make only ½ this recipe, to try it for a small family.

When preparing frozen salads or desserts, it pays to line your pan or mold with a piece of waxed paper, long enough to stick out, over edges of pan. This helps you remove frozen food intact, later, to serve on lettuce or chilled platter.

Mix together in large bowl

> 2 3-ounce packages cream cheese
> 1 teaspoon salt
> ½ cup mayonnaise
> juice 1 lemon

Stir in

> ½ cup drained, crushed pineapple
> 2 bananas, peeled and diced
> ½ cup drained maraschino cherries, cut in halves
> ½ cup broken walnut or pecan meats

Whip, then add to above

> 1 cup heavy cream (½ pint)

Turn entire mixture into loaf pan or individual molds. Freeze until firm, about 2½ hours. Serve on

> chilled lettuce leaves

on cold plates.

EASY CHILLED PUDDINGS AND CAKES
(See page 404)

These desserts should be chilled through thoroughly, but not frozen solid.

Chilled Angel Layer Cake

Cut cold **angel cake** into 2 layers, crosswise. Between layers, spread **sweetened whipped cream** flavored with **brandy.** Over top and sides of this layer cake spread more of the same whipped cream. Sprinkle **shredded coconut** over top. Chill 2 hours in freezing compartment before serving. Cut in wedges; serve with **sweetened fresh strawberries** or **raspberries, or drained crushed pineapple.**

Frozen Crumb Pudding

Use **2 cups leftover plain cake or cookie crumbs,** without icing. (Ginger, molasses, chocolate, lemon, or vanilla cookies or cake are good.) Mix crumbs with **1 cup sweetened whipped cream,** flavored with **vanilla** or **sherry.** Add **¼ cup chopped nut meats,** and a **few chopped maraschino cherries,** if desired. Chill several hours in freezing compartment, in mold, or ice-cube tray, before serving.

Frozen Shortcake

Line ice-cube tray, or glass dish, or mold, with a **¾-inch thick layer of sponge, angel, or plain cake.** (You can use dry or stale cake for this; it will moisten during chilling.) Over cake, spread a layer of **sweetened crushed strawberries** or **raspberries,** or any **drained canned fruit,** or **sliced fresh bananas.** Over fruit, spread **1 cup sweetened whipped cream,** or **vanilla mousse.** Chill until very cold, but not until cake is frozen; about 1½ to 2 hours.

Frozen Chocolate Cookie Dessert

Have available **18 to 20 plain, un-iced chocolate cookies,** about 1½ inches in diameter. Whip **2 cups heavy cream** with **½ cup powdered sugar;** flavor cream with **vanilla,** or **rum** or **brandy** if desired. Put two cookies together with whipped cream spread between them, as a filling. Add more cream, and another cookie; keep on until you have a stack of cookies long enough to run from end to end of ice-cube tray or oblong glass dish. Place this row of cookies in the tray or dish, then make another row to place right beside it. Make as many rows as needed to fill dish, with all cookies standing on their edges. Over entire top spread a layer of whipped cream. Chill 1 to 2 hours, in freezing compartment. To serve, slice on the bias. Top with **chocolate mint or fudge sauce** (pp. 405–406).

If you omit top layer of whipped cream, you need only 1 cup whipped cream.

Try peppermint-flavored whipped cream, made by crushing ⅔ cup peppermint candy to a powdered consistency, and folding this into whipped cream, instead of using sugar. Omit vanilla or other flavoring.

WONDERFUL DESSERT SAUCES

(For ice cream, frozen puddings, cake, other desserts)

You can of course keep handy some canned or bottled chocolate syrup, marshmallow whip, and other dessert toppings. However, for something special, by way of taste, try one of these:

Bitter Chocolate Sauce

In top of double boiler, over hot water, melt **4 squares unsweetened chocolate** with **2 tablespoons butter**. When melted, stir in **2 tablespoons corn syrup, 6 tablespoons sugar, ¾ cup milk, pinch salt.** Cook, stirring constantly, for about 10 minutes. Serve warm, or cold, on ice cream, pudding, or cake. Makes about 1 cup sauce.

Hot Fudge Sauce

In top of double boiler, over hot water, melt **1 tablespoon butter** with **1 square** (1 ounce) **baking chocolate.** Blend well. Now remove top of double boiler from lower part, placing pan directly over heat. Add **⅓ cup boiling water** gradually to chocolate mixture, stirring constantly; and bring to a boil. Add **1 cup sugar,** plus **2 tablespoons white corn syrup;** stir until sugar is dissolved. Simmer 5 minutes. Then stir in **1 pinch salt,** and **½ teaspoon vanilla.**

Chocolate-Mint Sauce

Slowly melt **10 large chocolate mints,** over pan of hot water. Stir in **3 tablespoons cream.** Especially good over hot chocolate cake or coffee or vanilla ice cream.

Butterscotch Sauce

Combine in saucepan **1¼ cups brown sugar, ⅔ cup corn syrup, 4 tablespoons butter.** Cook over low heat, stirring constantly, until sugar has dissolved. Then cook until thermometer reaches 238° (see use of candy thermometer under Boiled Frostings, page 434), or cook until a small amount of syrup dropped into cold water forms a soft ball. Serve warm, or cold, over ice cream, cake, or pudding.

Lemon Sauce

In saucepan, mix **½ cup sugar** with **1 tablespoon cornstarch.** Add gradually **1 cup boiling water,** stirring constantly. Boil 5 minutes, then remove from heat; stir in **2 tablespoons butter, 1½ tablespoons lemon juice, ½ teaspoon salt,** few grains nutmeg. Very good, hot, over freshly made plain cake. And just the right tart touch for rich fruity puddings.

Orange Sauce

Separate **2 eggs** (p. 260). Mix together in saucepan: **2 egg yolks,** beaten slightly, **⅓ cup sugar, ¼ teaspoon salt, 1 tablespoon lemon juice, grated rind of ½ lemon,** plus **½ cup orange juice.** Cook over low heat, stirring constantly, until mixture thickens. Remove from heat. In separate bowl, beat stiff **2 egg whites.** Fold sauce into egg whites, stirring constantly.

Quick Brandied Fruit Sauce

Take **1 cup apricot, strawberry, or raspberry preserves;** brighten its flavor by adding **1 teaspoon to 1 tablespoon orange or lemon juice** (orange for apricot, or raspberry; lemon for strawberry);

then stir in 2 tablespoons brandy. Blend well. Just try it over vanilla, nut, or eggnog ice cream.

Custard Sauce

Make Master Recipe, Soft Custard (p. 385), increasing vanilla to 1 teaspoon. Serve warm or cold, over cake, or puddings; cold over fruit and gelatine desserts.

Hard Sauce

In a bowl, mash and work with large spoon until soft and creamy, ⅓ cup (6 tablespoons) butter. Gradually work into butter 1 cup very fine confectioners' sugar. (If sugar has become lumpy, pound lumps out, or roll sugar with rolling pin, to make fine texture, before using.) When sugar and butter are creamy and well blended, add 1 teaspoon vanilla. Chill in refrigerator until ready to serve. Hard sauce can be kept for weeks, in refrigerator, in covered glass jar. Before serving, let stand at room temperature ½ hour or so, so that sauce softens enough to bite into. Delicious on plum pudding, apple dumplings, any rich fruity dessert.

Orange Hard Sauce. Instead of vanilla, flavor with 2 teaspoons orange juice, ½ teaspoon orange extract, plus 1 tablespoon grated orange rind.

Brandy Hard Sauce. Instead of vanilla, flavor with 1 teaspoon brandy.

Marshmallow Sauce

Boil together gently in saucepan for 5 minutes, ½ cup sugar plus ¼ cup water. Cut 8 marshmallows into pieces, using wet scissors, and melt in sugar syrup. Blend well. Now beat stiff 1 egg white. Fold marshmallow mixture into egg white, and add ½ teaspoon vanilla.

Maple Sauce

Combine 1 cup maple syrup with ½ cup bottled marshmallow cream. Beat thoroughly, until well blended.

Sweetened Whipped Cream

One cup heavy cream, when whipped, amply covers entire top of a cake, or pie. If you want only a few tablespoons of whipped cream (as for garnishing individual servings of ice cream, or pudding) whip only ⅓ to ½ cup cream. Chilled cream whips more satisfactorily than cream at room temperature. Put chilled cream in cool bowl. For 1 cup cream, add **2 to 4 tablespoons powdered or confectioners' sugar,** plus ¼ **teaspoon vanilla.** Whip with rotary beater until cream will hold shape (in swirls, or in ridges), or when tracks of the beater leave definite marks in the cream. *Do not beat further,* or cream will turn to butter. Keep whipped cream in refrigerator until serving time.

Instead of vanilla, you may use ¼ **teaspoon sherry or brandy,** if desired. To make mint-flavored whipped cream, omit vanilla and add instead **1 drop oil of peppermint;** color cream with a drop of green or red food coloring if desired. To go with peaches, flavor whipped cream with a **few drops almond extract.**

Light cream, whipped. Light (or "coffee") cream may be whipped by one of 3 methods:

(1) Chill well-shaken light cream in refrigerator tray until ice crystals form in cream. Then turn cream into chilled bowl, and beat with chilled egg beater until stiff. To sweeten, for **1 cup thin cream,** use **2 teaspoons confectioners' sugar,** and flavor with ¼ **teaspoon vanilla.** Serve soon; this does not hold up as long as heavy cream.

(2) Add gelatine to cream, as follows: Soften **1 teaspoon** (⅓ **envelope**) **unflavored gelatine** in **2 tablespoons cold water,** for 5 minutes. Scald ¼ **cup thin cream,** and add gelatine mixture, stirring until gelatine dissolves. Add ¾ **cup cold thin cream,** and mix well. Chill in covered ice-cube tray about 3 hours. Remove to chilled bowl; beat 3 to 5 minutes with rotary beater, until cream is stiff. Sweeten and flavor as in (1).

(3) Add **1 3-ounce package cream cheese** to **1 cup chilled thin cream,** in a bowl, and beat together until stiff. Sweeten and flavor as in (1).

Substituting evaporated milk for cream. Undiluted evaporated milk, if chilled as in (1), Light Cream, can be whipped. Chill 1 **tall can evaporated milk** (undiluted) in ice-cube tray until ice crystals form around edges of milk. Remove to chilled bowl; whip until foamy (about 1 minute). Add **2 tablespoons lemon juice,** then continue whipping until *very* stiff (about 2 minutes longer). Sweeten with **1 tablespoon or more, powdered or confectioners' sugar.** Use like sweetened whipped cream, to top shortcakes and puddings.

NOTE: When evaporated milk does not whip stiff, it simply wasn't cold enough before beating; chill again, and beat again. Use promptly. This does not hold up as well as whipped cream.

CHAPTER XXXIII

You Can Make Cake

METHOD FOR: *Baking Powder Cakes (Cup, Layer, Square, and Loaf Varieties); Cakes Raised with Soda (Spice Cake, Gingerbread, Devil's Food); Cakes Raised with Eggs (Angel Food, Sponge Cake)*

Cake making isn't nearly so hard as you might think. In the first place, all cakes ever made come under one of three types:

(1) Cakes raised by *baking powder;*

(2) Cakes raised by an ingredient containing acid, such as *sour milk* or *molasses, plus soda;*

(3) *Cakes raised solely by air bubbles beaten into eggs.*

For each type, there is a separate set of reasons. If you understand the reasons, you can make any cake in that group. Understand all 3 sets of reasons, and you can make any cake known.

BASIC PRINCIPLES—
BAKING POWDER CAKES

This is America's favorite group of cakes. And though the number of such cakes is legion, we are giving here only one basic recipe. This recipe is not only made by the modern quick method, but it can be varied so many ways that it will provide a cake repertoire for life.

Mixing the batter takes about 10 to 12 minutes.

With only small variations, the recipe given below will make:

Cup cakes
Loaf cake
Square cake
Layer cake
Upside down cake
Cottage pudding
Boston cream pie
Chocolate cake
Marble cake
Maple cake

Spice cake
Nut cake
Date-nut cake
Orange cake
Blueberry cake
Chocolate bits cake
Gold cake
White cake
Shortcake

Ingredients. Cake is based on flour, with shortening to enrich it, sugar to sweeten, eggs for light texture and flavor, liquid to moisten, and some liquid flavoring (vanilla, almond, coffee, orange juice) to give it taste. It must have also a leavening, to make the batter rise . . . in this group of cakes, baking powder.

What baking powder does. Baking powder forms a gas which, when exposed to oven heat, pushes the tender batter up with it.

Rules for Light Cake. Follow recipe directions in all details. No leavening, however good, can raise a dead-weight batter.

1. Use cake flour; it is finer textured, makes lighter cake.

2. Sift flour *before* measuring. Unsifted, it gives you more flour than recipe calls for; weighs from $\frac{1}{4}$ to $\frac{1}{3}$ more; throws recipe out of balance. Sifting flour several times makes lighter cake.

3. Measure accurately, and *level.* Modern recipes are all made for precise level measurements; carelessly rounded spoonful or cupful throws proportions out of balance, may ruin cake.

4. Know your baking powder; read can label; there are 2 kinds. With Double-Acting, amounts specified in this book are correct; if you have Phosphate or Tartrate, use double these amounts.

5. Don't skimp on the beating. No cake can ever be lighter than the amount of air beaten in. In our "Lightning Method," beating strokes have already been reduced to the minimum. Don't reduce more. Lift batter slightly into air, with each beating stroke.

To fill pans. Always grease generously, so cake won't stick. Large pans can be greased, lined with waxed paper cut to fit bottom, then the paper greased too. For cup cakes, if you wish, you can buy Dime Store waxed paper cups, to bake in; these are set inside cup-cake pans. Fill pans only ⅔ full; cake must have room to rise. Spread batter so it is thicker at sides and in corners than in center; center will rise more than edges, and you want even cake. Jar pans against table, or cut through batter several times with knife, before baking, to eliminate any too-large air holes which would make coarse texture.

To bake. Have oven at correct heat, and steady, before putting pans in. Don't guess; use oven regulator or thermometer. Too much heat pushes cake out of shape; too little leaves it soggy inside, unrisen. Center pans in oven; heat at side walls isn't the same. Don't crowd oven; heat must have room to circulate. Don't open oven needlessly; this changes heat. Many ovens have glass windows to see through. If yours doesn't, divide total baking period into quarters; open door only at end of each quarter. By end of 1st, cake should have started rising; by 2d, should have risen more and begun browning; by 3d, should have completed rising and be browner; by last, should be done. To test for doneness, insert clean straight piece of wire, or cake tester, in center of cake. If it comes out free of moisture, it is done. Don't overbake. Cake should feel springy on top, should have shrunk slightly away from pan edges.

To remove from pans. Set hot pans on wire racks, about 5 to 10 minutes. Then invert. Cake should soon drop out of pan onto rack, of its own weight. If it doesn't, cover bottom of pan with damp towel. Steam from towel helps loosen cake. Or loosen with spatula, or dull knife. Once out of pan, turn cake right side up on wire rack; let cool, before frosting. Frosting becomes too runny if put on hot cake.

MASTER RECIPE #65
QUICK TWO-EGG CAKE

NOTE: The following recipe makes plain cake of **vanilla flavor**. Same recipe, however, with slight variations, makes many other-flavor cakes; see Other Batter Flavors, p. 417.

Have shortening *soft* (but not melted), eggs and milk at room temperature. Start oven, set at proper heat for type pan you are using (see Type Pans, below), before mixing batter.

Sift flour once, measure; then sift together into bowl
> 1¾ cups cake flour
> 1 cup sugar
> 2¼ teaspoons double-acting baking powder
> ½ teaspoon salt

Blend into dry ingredients
> ½ cup *soft* butter (or vegetable shortening)

Stir in
> ⅔ cup fresh milk (or ⅓ cup water, ⅓ cup evaporated milk)
> 1 teaspoon vanilla

Beat all together vigorously 200 strokes by hand, or 1 minute by clock with electric mixer at slow speed.

Add to batter

2 unbeaten eggs

Beat again vigorously, 200 strokes by hand, or 1 minute by clock with electric mixer at slow speed.

That's all. Batter is now ready to turn into greased pans.

Type Pans to Use for Baking

The choice of pan varies the cake. *The same batter* looks — even *tastes* — different, baked in different pans. It will make cup cakes, or a layer cake, or a square cake, or a loaf cake. Each seems a very different dessert. So choose whatever pans you wish.

To bake as cup cakes. Master Recipe, Quick 2-Egg Cake, makes the batter for 10 to 12 large cup cakes; or 18 to 25 small ones. Divide batter into generously greased cup-cake pans, filling each cup only ⅔ *full*. Center pans in moderate (375°) oven. Bake 20 to 25 minutes or until cake is light golden brown on top, springy to touch, and begins to shrink slightly from edges of pan. Cook cakes in pan, 5 to 10 minutes. Then turn out cakes, or remove from pan with spatula, and cool, right side up, on wire rack. Frost with any variation of butter frosting (p. 430) or 7-minute frosting (p. 434). Add decorations to frosting if desired, see page 443.

To bake as layer cake. Master Recipe, Quick 2-Egg Cake, makes the batter for 2 8-inch layers. Line greased layer pans with waxed paper; then grease paper too. Divide batter, putting ½ in each pan; spread it out evenly. Center pans in moderate (375°) oven. Bake 25 to 30 minutes, or until cake is light golden brown, feels springy to touch, and shrinks slightly from edges of pan. Cool layers in pans 5 to 10 minutes; then turn layers out onto wire rack. Remove waxed paper carefully from bottom of layer. Then turn layer over onto another wire rack, to cool, right side up.

Two such simple layers can be used for almost any sort of layer cake. See Layer Cake Variations (p. 415) or choose any frosting and filling from Chapter XXXIV.

To bake as square cake. Master Recipe, Quick 2-Egg Cake, makes enough batter for one 8 x 8 x 2 inch cake pan. Grease pan; line it with waxed paper; grease paper. Spread batter evenly in pan. Center pan in moderate oven (350°). Bake 35 to 50 minutes, or until cake is light golden brown, feels springy to touch, shrinks slightly from edges of pan. Cool cake in pan 5 to 10 minutes. Then turn cake out onto wire rake; remove paper carefully; turn cake over onto another rack, to cool, right side up.

When cool, frost with any frosting from Chapter XXXIV, and decorate with nuts, coconut, or any other decorations desired; see page 443. See other Square Cake Variations (p. 416).

To bake as loaf cake. Master Recipe, Quick 2-Egg Cake, makes enough batter for one 8 x 4 x 3 inch loaf pan. Grease pan; line with waxed paper; grease paper. Loaf cakes, because thick, must be baked more slowly, and longer than thinner cakes. Bake in moderate (350°) oven, about 50 minutes, or until cake feels springy, shrinks slightly from pan edges. Cool 10 minutes in pan; then turn out onto wire rack; remove paper carefully; turn cake over onto another wire rack, to cool, right side up. When cool, frost with any desired frosting from Chapter XXXIV.

LAYER CAKES MADE WITH
MASTER RECIPE,
QUICK TWO-EGG CAKE

*(Make Master Recipe #65, Quick Two-Egg Cake, page 412.
Bake as Layer Cake, page 414. Then fill and frost as below.)*

Fruit Shortcake

Between layers, spread **sweetened, drained fresh strawberries,
raspberries, or sliced peaches.** On top of cake arrange more fruit.
Top with **sweetened whipped cream.**

Quick Jelly Layer Cake (or "Washington Pie")

(Exception: Put this cake together while still warm.) Between
layers, spread **raspberry or currant jam or jelly.** On top of cake,
while still warm, simply sprinkle **powdered or confectioners' sugar**
. . . no frosting. Children love this.

Chocolate Layer Cake

Between layers and on top of cake, spread **chocolate butter
frosting** (p. 430), or **chocolate seven-minute frosting** (p. 435).
Or, for moister cake, between layers, spread **chocolate cream
filling** (p. 441), then top cake with any chocolate frosting from
Chapter XXXIV. Decorate top of cake with **nutmeats,** if desired.

Orange Layer Cake

Between layers, spread **orange cream filling** (p. 443). On top
of cake, spread **orange butter frosting** (p. 431). Sprinkle frosting
with **shredded coconut,** if desired.

Coconut Layer Cake

Make **vanilla seven-minute frosting** (p. 434). Spread ½ this
frosting between layers, and sprinkle over it **grated fresh coconut**
(or packaged shredded coconut). Use other ½ of frosting on top
of cake, again sprinkling with coconut.

Chocolate-Peppermint Layer Cake

Make **peppermint seven-minute frosting** (p. 435). Spread ½ frosting between layers; other ½ on top of cake. Decorate top of cake with **grated or flaked, bitter or semisweet chocolate.**

Boston Cream Pie

(*Exception:* Put this cake together while still warm.) Between layers, spread ½ Master Recipe, Vanilla Cream Filling, or use any flavor variation of that recipe (p. 441). Or, if preferred, make entire Master Recipe, French Cream Filling (p. 439) to spread between layers. Sprinkle top of cake, while still warm, with **powdered sugar.**

SQUARE CAKES MADE WITH MASTER RECIPE, QUICK 2-EGG CAKE

(*Make Master Recipe #65, Quick Two-Egg Cake, page 412. After batter is mixed, treat as below.*)

Upside Down Cake

In 8 x 8 x 2 inch cake pan, put **4 tablespoons butter** plus ⅓ to ½ **cup brown sugar.** Place pan in moderate (350°) oven about 10 minutes, until butter and sugar melt, forming a syrup. Then remove pan from oven. In this syrup arrange **fruit** — drained slices of canned pineapple, or drained canned halves of peaches; or sliced bananas, or drained, canned, pitted sour cherries. Over fruit, spread batter of Master Recipe, Quick 2-Egg Cake. Return pan of cake to 350° oven, baking 45 to 55 minutes. Let cake stand in pan 10 minutes after coming out of oven; then invert pan over large cake platter. Glazed fruit comes out on top. Garnish with whipped cream if desired.

Cottage Pudding

Bake Master Recipe, Quick 2-Egg Cake as square cake, p. 414. While still warm from oven, cut cake in serving-size squares. Have ready ½ recipe Master Recipe, Cream Filling (p. 441), in chocolate, butterscotch or vanilla flavor. Pour hot cream filling over warm cake squares . . . one to a person.

OTHER BATTER FLAVORS—
MASTER RECIPE, QUICK 2-EGG CAKE

To obtain cake batter of different flavors, follow Master Recipe #65, Quick Two-Egg Cake, page 412, making changes noted below.

NOTE: *All following batters may be baked in any type of pan . . . cup-cake, layer, loaf, or square pan.*
Follow baking directions for type of pan you use (p. 414).

Chocolate Cake

Melt 2 squares (2 ounces) baking chocolate in pan set over hot water and add melted chocolate to cake with milk. Bake. Try vanilla, peppermint, or chocolate seven-minute frosting (pp. 434–435). Or use maple butter frosting (p. 432).

Marble Cake

Divide completed batter into two bowls. Leave one bowl "as is." To other bowl, add 1 square (1 ounce) baking chocolate which has been melted in bowl placed over pan of boiling water. Blend well, until that batter is rich chocolate color. Now, into greased, lined square or loaf pan, put alternate spoonfuls of white and chocolate batter; the more irregular the pattern, the better. Bake cake. Use any chocolate or vanilla frosting from Chapter XXXIV.

Maple Cake

Substitute 1 teaspoon maple flavoring instead of vanilla. Add a few drops lemon juice. Bake. Use maple walnut butter frosting (p. 432).

Spice Cake (Light)

Add with dry ingredients ¼ teaspoon mace or nutmeg; ½ teaspoon cinnamon plus ⅛ teaspoon allspice. Instead of vanilla, substitute 1 teaspoon lemon juice. Bake preferably in loaf, or square pan. Use orange or lemon butter frosting (p. 431).

Nut Cake

Reserve ¼ cup flour, but mix other ingredients. Reduce vanilla to ½ teaspoon, and add ½ teaspoon maple or walnut flavoring, plus few drops lemon juice. Dredge ⅓ cup chopped nut meats in the ¼ cup flour saved out, then add to batter. Put batter in greased, lined loaf or square pan. Bake cake. Use maple, lemon, or orange butter frosting (pp. 431–432).

Date-Nut Cake

Make like nut cake, adding ⅓ cup chopped, pitted dates with nuts.

Orange Cake

Instead of milk use ⅓ cup orange juice plus ⅓ cup evaporated milk. Add 1 teaspoon grated orange rind. Instead of vanilla, use 1 teaspoon lemon juice. Bake. Use coffee or maple butter frosting (pp. 431–432).

Blueberry Cake

Save out ¼ cup flour, but mix other ingredients. Mix the ¼ cup flour with ½ to ⅔ cup well-drained fresh (not canned) blueberries. Fold blueberries into batter. Bake in greased cup-cake pans, or greased, lined, square pan. While still warm from oven, sprinkle top of cake with powdered sugar; don't frost.

Chocolate Bits Cake

Fold into batter 1 package, or about ⅔ cup, semisweet chocolate bits. Best baked in a greased, lined square or loaf pan. Top with chocolate or coffee butter frosting (p. 431).

Gold Cake (Yolks of eggs only)

Increase baking powder to 3 teaspoons, and milk to ¾ cup. Add with vanilla a few drops orange extract. Instead of 2 whole eggs, use 3 beaten egg yolks. Best baked in greased, lined, loaf or square pan. Good with orange, lemon, or coffee butter frosting (p. 431).

White Cake (White of eggs only)

Reduce baking powder to 2 teaspoons. Use only ½ cup milk. With vanilla, add few drops lemon juice. Instead of using two whole eggs, beat 3 egg whites until stiff enough to stand in peaks; then gently fold egg whites into batter; *do not beat again.* Bake in greased cup-cake pans, or greased, lined, square pan; or in greased layer pans. Use any frosting . . . rich, or simple. Fit for a bridal reception if topped with seven-minute frosting (p. 434) flavored with 1 tablespoon rum or brandy instead of vanilla, then the frosting sprinkled with grated fresh coconut.

CAKES RAISED WITH SOUR MILK
PLUS SODA

Sour milk, sour cream, or buttermilk make rich chocolate or spiced cakes. But to avoid having these milks taste sour in the cake, an alkaline (baking soda) must be added.

Sour milk and soda, when combined, form carbon dioxide gas, which provides the leavening for the cake. Therefore, in these cakes, baking powder is added only if batter is especially heavy, and then only in a small amount.

Outside the difference in leavening agent, sour-milk cakes are much like baking powder cakes. We give here three separate examples.

Spice Cake—Light

Sift cake flour, measure 2½ cups; then sift flour again into big bowl with 1 teaspoon soda, 1 teaspoon salt, 1 teaspoon ginger, ½ teaspoon allspice, ½ teaspoon powdered cloves, 1½ teaspoons cinnamon. Add 2 cups brown sugar, firmly packed. Blend in ½ cup soft shortening. Add 1 cup sour milk or buttermilk, 1 teaspoon vanilla. Beat vigorously, 200 strokes by hand, or 1 minute by electric mixer at slow speed. Add 2 unbeaten eggs. Beat again, 200 strokes by hand, or 1 minute by electric mixer at slow speed. Turn into greased loaf pan; bake in moderate oven (350°) about 50 minutes. Cool cake. Spread with orange, lemon, maple, or coffee frosting (Chapter XXXIV).

Gingerbread

Sift **cake flour**; measure 1¾ cups; then sift flour again into bowl, with ¾ teaspoon soda, 1 teaspoon salt, 2 teaspoons ginger, ½ teaspoon cinnamon, and ¼ teaspoon powdered clove. Add ½ cup brown sugar, firmly packed. Blend into above ⅓ cup soft shortening. Add ½ cup molasses, ½ cup sour milk, and ½ teaspoon vanilla. Beat 200 strokes by hand, or 1 minute by electric mixer at slow speed. Add 2 unbeaten eggs. Beat again 200 strokes by hand or 1 minute by electric mixer at slow speed. Bake in greased, lined square pan in moderate oven (350°) 35 to 45 minutes. Serve hot, topped with **plain or rum-flavored whipped cream**, if desired. Or, to serve cold, split cake horizontally into two layers, fill with **applesauce;** top cake with **whipped cream.**

Devil's Food

Melt over hot water, then set aside to cool, 2 squares (2 ounces) baking chocolate. Sift **cake flour**; measure 1½ cups; then sift flour again into bowl with 1 teaspoon soda, ½ teaspoon baking powder, and ½ teaspoon salt. Add 1¼ cups brown sugar, firmly packed. Stir in ½ cup soft shortening, 1 cup sour milk, melted chocolate (prepared above), **beaten yolks of 2 eggs**, and 1 teaspoon vanilla. Beat 300 strokes by hand, or 1½ minutes by electric beater, slow speed. In separate bowl, beat 2 egg whites until they stand in moist peaks. Gently fold them into the beaten batter, and *do not beat batter again.* Bake in greased 8-inch layer pans, or in greased, lined square pan, in moderate (350°) oven, about 35 minutes for layers, 45 minutes for square cake. Do not overbake. See chocolate cake (p. 417) and chocolate layer cake (p. 415) for frosting and filling suggestions.

CAKES RAISED BY AIR BUBBLES
BEATEN INTO EGGS

This is the **Sponge Family,** including angel food, true sponge cakes, and a few others which are the offspring of these. These cakes (1) contain no shortening at all, and (2) are raised without baking powder, without soda, without anything but air bubbles to hold the batter up while it bakes. Obviously, a good number of eggs must be used. As many bubbles as possible must be worked into them. And the batter, held up by air alone, must be handled delicately.

In angel food, *whites of eggs only are used.* They are beaten with electric or rotary beater until they stand up in soft, glossy, *moist* peaks. If egg whites become too dried out, the delicate egg-cell walls will not hold up, during baking, but will collapse.

In sponge cake, *egg yolks and whites, separately beaten,* are used; yolks are beaten well until thickened and light lemon-colored.

Eggs should be at least three days old and at room temperature to give best beating results.

For angel food and true sponge cake, *DO NOT GREASE PANS.* Batter needs the rough walls of the pans to climb up on.

When removing angel food or sponge cake from oven, invert pans on wire cake rack and let cake cool in pan at least 1 hour. If removed from pan before thoroughly cooled, cake may shrink.

This type of cake *used* to be baked at very slow heat, for as long as 1 hour. It has now been found, however, that *cake shrinks less* if baked in a moderate (375°) oven for only about 30 to 35 minutes.

MASTER RECIPE #66
ANGEL FOOD

Separate (p. 260) yolks from whites of
10 to 12 chilled eggs
putting whites into a measuring cup. (Use more eggs if necessary, until you have 1¼ cups egg whites.) Now put the whites into a very large bowl, and let come to room temperature before making cake. (Eggs at room temperature beat more satisfactorily and give more volume.)

To make cake:
Step 1
Sift first, then measure
1 cup cake flour
Add to measured flour
½ cup sugar
Sift flour and sugar together 4 times, to make airy-light. Set aside.
Step 2
Add to egg whites (when at room temperature)
¼ teaspoon salt
Beat egg whites with rotary beater, or flat wire whisk, or electric mixer at medium to high speed, until foamy. Then sprinkle into whites
1¼ teaspoons cream of tartar
Continue beating until egg whites stand up in peaks, but are still moist and glossy.

Now start adding, 1 or 2 tablespoons at a time, beating about 15 strokes after each addition
1 cup sugar
When all sugar is in, fold in with a few strokes
1 teaspoon vanilla
Step 3
If you have been using electric mixer, remove bowl from mixer now and do the rest of the mixing by hand. Sift over egg-white

mixture, ¼ cup at a time, the flour-sugar mixture already prepared. After adding each ¼ cup, fold flour mixture lightly into egg whites, using about 15 fold-over strokes, each time, and turning bowl around as you do it, to blend from all directions.

To bake:

Turn mixture into *ungreased* round 10 inch tube pan.

Bake in preheated moderate (375°) oven, 30 to 35 minutes.

Remove pan from oven. Invert pan over wire cake rack; and let cake stay in pan 1 hour, until cool.

Serve plain, or frost if desired.

ANGEL CAKE VARIATIONS

(Follow Master Recipe #66, Angel Food, page 422, with changes noted below.)

Coconut Angel Food

Before putting cake in oven, sprinkle ½ **cup finely shredded coconut** over top of batter.

Chocolate Angel Food

Instead of measuring 1 cup sifted flour, measure ¾ **cup.** Add to it ¼ cup sifted powdered cocoa.

MASTER RECIPE #67
TRUE SPONGE CAKE

Separate (p. 260) whites from yolks of
5 chilled eggs
putting whites into a very large bowl, and yolks into another bowl. Let eggs stand until they come to room temperature before making cake; they beat best at room temperature.

To mix cake:

Step 1

Sift, then measure accurately
1 cup cake flour

Add to measured flour

¼ teaspoon salt

Step 2

Also sift (but do not add to flour)

1 cup sugar

Set dry ingredients aside.

Step 3

With rotary beater, or flat wire whisk, or electric mixer at medium to high speed, beat the 5 egg whites until they stand up in soft peaks, but are still moist and glossy. Then beat in, 1 tablespoon at a time, ⅓ the sifted sugar, beating about 15 strokes after each addition. When sugar is all beaten in, set bowl aside.

Step 4

Put in front of you bowl containing 5 egg yolks. Add to yolks

1 tablespoon lemon juice (or vinegar)

With rotary beater, or flat wire whisk, or electric mixer, beat yolks until so thick beater will hardly turn. Then add

grated rind of ½ lemon

Add little by little, beating in after each addition, the remaining ⅔ cup sifted sugar.

Step 5

Now add yolk mixture, little by little, to egg whites, blending by hand, with 10 to 15 fold-over strokes after each addition, turning bowl as you do it, until all yolk mixture is blended in.

Step 6

Sift the measured flour and salt, little by little, over egg mixture, folding in lightly, by hand, after each addition, until flour is all blended in. *Do not beat.*

To bake:

Turn mixture into *ungreased* 9 inch tube pan.

Bake in preheated moderate (375°) oven 30 to 35 minutes. Remove pan from oven. Invert pan over wire cake rack; let cake cool in pan 1 hour.

VARIATIONS—TRUE SPONGE CAKE

Baby Sponge Cakes

Turn batter into ungreased muffin-tin cups or cup-cake tins. Bake in moderate (375°) oven 20 to 25 minutes. When done, invert pans over wire cake racks; let cakes stay in pans 1 hour until cool.

Chocolate Sponge Cake

In Master Recipe # 67, add 1 tablespoon vinegar (no lemon juice) to egg yolks; and add also, with vinegar, 2 squares (2 ounces) baking chocolate which has been melted in saucer over small pan of boiling water. Omit lemon rind. Complete batter as in Master Recipe. Bake in slower oven (350°) 35 to 45 minutes. When done, invert pan over wire cake rack; let cake stay in pan 1 hour until cool.

OTHER TYPE SPONGE CAKE

Hot Milk Sponge Cake

This is a different method of making sponge cake, in which fewer eggs are used. Therefore some baking powder is added.

Beat until very thick and nearly white 3 whole eggs. Add, little by little, beating constantly, 1 cup sifted granulated sugar. Add 2 teaspoons lemon juice. Sift, then measure, then sift together 3 times 1 cup cake flour plus 1 teaspoon baking powder. Fold flour, little by little, into eggs. Add, mixing quickly until batter is smooth, 6 tablespoons hot milk. Turn into greased tube pan. Bake in moderate oven (350°) about 35 minutes. Remove from oven. Invert pan over wire cake rack and *leave cake in pan about 1 hour,* or until cool.

It's Fun to Make Frostings
and Fillings

METHOD FOR:

Uncooked: Confectioners' Frosting, Butter Frosting, Fluffy
   Frosting
Cooked: Seven-Minute Frosting, Boiled Frosting and other
   Cooked Frostings
Creamy Fillings for Cakes
How to Decorate a Cake

BASIC PRINCIPLES—FROSTINGS

There are but two general kinds of frosting: cooked and uncooked.

An uncooked frosting can be mixed in two to ten minutes. We're
going to start with this type. First, simple confectioners' frosting,
which any youngster could mix. Then butter frosting, which is
nearly the same. Then "fluffy" frosting, made by blending other
ingredients into egg whites. All these are remarkably easy.

When you have made the uncooked variety once or twice, try
a cooked frosting. The easiest one is seven-minute frosting; but
none is hard, once you get the knack.

Remember these basic points about frostings:

Type of sugar. Confectioners' sugar (very fine, no grit) is used for all *uncooked* frostings.

Granulated sugar is used for *boiled* frostings, unless the flavor demands brown sugar.

Do not try to use sugar full of lumps, or you will make yourself a lot of extra trouble. Instead, put sugar on sheet of waxed paper and roll it with a dry rolling pin. This takes only a minute; saves much time in the end.

Quantity of sugar. In making frosting, *sugar* is the basic material (as flour is to bread); so, even though the sugar will melt, it still will determine the final amount of frosting you have.

Two cups sugar makes sufficient frosting for:

      (1) two 8-inch or 9-inch layers, or
      (2) top of one 9 x 13-inch cake, or
      (3) top and sides of one 8 x 8 x 2-inch cake, or
      (4) about 2 dozen cup cakes

One cup sugar makes enough frosting for:

    (1) top of one 8 or 9 inch layer cake (using something
          else for filling), or
    (2) top of one 8 x 8 x 2 inch cake, or
    (3) top and sides of one 1 lb. loaf cake, or
    (4) about 1 dozen cup cakes

One half cup sugar makes enough frosting to decorate (sparingly):

      (1) top of 1 coffee ring, or
      (2) tops of 12 to 18 sweet buns

When to spread frosting. Frostings should be spread as soon as made. Otherwise, they begin to harden. But cakes should be cooled before frosting is put on. If put on hot cake, frosting makes a seal over cake which shuts the steam inside, turning the cake's texture soggy.

Certain hot breads (hot cross buns, and raisin buns, for example) can be iced while warm, but they have a thicker crust to protect them than a cake does.

Brush any loose crumbs from your cake before spreading frosting. Otherwise, cake crumbs get mixed in it, spoiling the gloss.

How to spread frosting. Pile frosting on center top of a layer, or a square cake. Using a spatula, a knife, or the back of a mixing spoon, spread it around in a swirly, wavy design. A surface with peaks and valleys looks far more luscious than a mirror-smooth frosting. If desired, spread some of the frosting along sides of your cake.

If icing becomes too stiff to spread nicely, dip your knifeblade or spatula in hot water. This heats the blade, which then melts the frosting somewhat, making it spread more easily. Or, you can thin any *un*cooked frosting by adding more liquid.

To decorate frosting. Any decorations desired on top of frosting, such as nuts, coconut, candied fruit or grated chocolate, must be put on while frosting is still moist. Decorate frosting as soon as spread onto cake.

MASTER RECIPE #68
CONFECTIONERS' FROSTING
(UNCOOKED)

This is a thin, sweet frosting, most often used to decorate coffee rings, sweet buns, or simple cakes. It is not thick enough to serve as filling between layers.

Put in mixing bowl

1 or 2 cups confectioners' sugar

Moisten sugar by beating in, 1 tablespoon at a time until frosting is smooth, soft, and spreadable

Cream, milk, or **boiling water** (or substitute liquids given
in Variations below)

To flavor, blend in

½ teaspoon vanilla extract

If frosting becomes *too* wet (too thin to spread), simply add more confectioners' sugar.

NOTE: To make frosting stay moist — if, for instance, you are frosting your cake some time ahead of use — first moisten the sugar with 1 tablespoon light corn syrup. Then add any liquids given in recipe or Variations, to flavor the frosting.

CONFECTIONERS' FROSTING VARIATIONS

(Follow Master Recipe #68, Confectioners' Frosting, page 428, with changes below.)

Chocolate Confectioners' Frosting

(1) Melt in bowl over hot water, 2 squares (2 ounces) baking chocolate. Use this to moisten sugar. If more liquid is needed, add a bit of hot water. Or, (2) add to sugar ½ cup dry cocoa and a pinch of salt, then use hot water as liquid.

Coffee Confectioners' Frosting

Use strong coffee infusion (strained free of grounds) as liquid.

Orange Confectioners' Frosting

Use strained orange juice as liquid. Omit vanilla. Stir in 1 tablespoon grated orange rind. Add few drops lemon juice.

Lemon Confectioners' Frosting

Use 1 tablespoon strained lemon juice, plus as much hot water as needed. Omit vanilla, and stir in 1 teaspoon grated lemon rind, for tang.

Maple Confectioners' Frosting

(1) Substitute ½ teaspoon bottled maple flavoring instead of vanilla in Master Recipe. Or (2) use maple syrup as liquid, omitting vanilla.

Walnut Confectioners' Frosting

Substitute ¼ teaspoon bottled black walnut flavoring instead of vanilla.

Pineapple or Peach Confectioners' Frosting

Use juice from canned pineapple or peaches, and substitute ½ teaspoon almond extract, instead of vanilla.

Strawberry Confectioners' Frosting

(1) Use sweetened strawberry juice to moisten sugar; or (2) use water, milk or cream and substitute 1 teaspoon imitation strawberry flavoring for vanilla.

Rum Confectioners' Frosting

Substitute 1 teaspoon rum or rum flavoring for vanilla.

Brandy Confectioners' Frosting

Substitute 1 teaspoon brandy for vanilla.

Almond Confectioners' Frosting

Substitute ½ teaspoon almond extract for vanilla. Add few drops lemon juice.

MASTER RECIPE #69
BUTTER FROSTING (UNCOOKED)

Butter frosting, because it contains butter, is richer, softer, and stays moister than confectioners' frosting. Yet it is made almost the same way. Can be used as a filling between layers, as well as on top. Make full recipe to fill and frost one 2-layer cake; or to frost top and sides of an 8 x 8 x 2 inch cake; or to frost top of one 9 x 13 inch cake, or to frost about 2 to 3 dozen cup cakes.

Put in mixing bowl
4 tablespoons soft (not melted) butter
Cream with butter, blending until smooth
2 cups confectioners' sugar
Add, 1 teaspoon at a time, until mixture reaches spreading consistency

Cream or milk (or any liquid suggested in Variations below)
  Blend in, for flavoring
  ½ teaspoon vanilla extract
If frosting becomes too wet and thin, just add more confectioners' sugar.

BUTTER FROSTING VARIATIONS

(Follow Master Recipe #69, Butter Frosting, page 430, making changes below.)

Chocolate Butter Frosting

(1) Melt in bowl, over hot water, **2 squares baking chocolate.**
Now make Master Recipe, adding melted chocolate before adding cream or milk. Omit vanilla. Or (2) add **½ cup dry cocoa** with sugar, substituting **hot water** for cream or milk, and omitting vanilla.

Coffee Butter Frosting

Use **strong coffee infusion** (strained of grounds) as liquid. Omit vanilla.

Mocha Butter Frosting

Add **2 tablespoons dry cocoa** with sugar. Then use strong coffee infusion, and omit vanilla.

Orange Butter Frosting

Use **1 teaspoon lemon juice** plus as much **orange juice** as you need, to make mixture spreading consistency. Omit vanilla. Fold in, if desired, **1 tablespoon grated orange rind.**

Lemon Butter Frosting

Use **4 teaspoons lemon juice.** If more liquid is needed, add water, drop by drop. Omit vanilla. Fold in, if desired, **1 teaspoon grated lemon rind.**

Orange Coconut, or Lemon Coconut Butter Frosting

Sprinkle **shredded coconut** on top of orange or lemon butter frosting, as soon as spread.

Maple Butter Frosting

Substitute ½ **teaspoon bottled maple flavoring** instead of vanilla.

Maple Walnut Butter Frosting

Sprinkle top of maple frosting, as soon as spread, with ½ **cup chopped walnut meats.** Or arrange **halves of shelled walnuts,** in a design, on top of frosting.

Rum or Brandy Butter Frosting

Instead of vanilla, substitute **1 or 2 teaspoons rum or brandy.** Add a **dash of nutmeg.** Marvelous on cup cakes for fancy teas or receptions. Press a bit of drained maraschino cherry or shredded coconut into top of frosting, while still moist.

MASTER RECIPE #70
FLUFFY FROSTING (UNCOOKED)

Fluffy frostings are made by beating air into egg whites, or egg yolks, then blending in other ingredients. Can be used both as filling and as frosting. Make full recipe to fill and frost one 2-layer cake; or to frost top and sides of one 8 x 8 x 2 inch cake; or to frost top of one 9 x 13 inch cake; or to frost about 2 to 3 dozen cup cakes.

With rotary beater, beat until stiff
> **2 egg whites**

Very gradually, beat into egg whites
> **4 tablespoons cold water**
> **2 cups confectioners' sugar**
> **Few grains salt**

When above are thoroughly blended, fold in, for flavoring
> ½ **teaspoon vanilla extract**

FLUFFY FROSTING VARIATIONS

(Follow Master Recipe #70, Fluffy Frosting, page 432, making the substitutions below.)

Coffee Fluffy Frosting

Instead of cold water, use 4 tablespoons strong cold coffee (strained of grounds). Use only ¼ teaspoon vanilla.

Maple Fluffy Frosting

Substitute ¼ teaspoon bottled maple flavoring for vanilla.

Black Walnut Fluffy Frosting

Substitute ¼ teaspoon bottled black walnut flavoring, instead of vanilla.

Rum or Brandy Fluffy Frosting

Substitute 1 or 2 teaspoons rum or brandy, instead of vanilla.

Orange Fluffy Frosting

Substitute and beat yolks of 2 eggs (instead of whites). Instead of water, use strained orange juice. Add a few specks of salt. Omit vanilla. Fold in 1 tablespoon grated orange rind before spreading.

Chocolate Fluffy Frosting

Substitute and beat yolks of 2 eggs (instead of whites). Instead of water, use milk. Add 2 squares (2 ounces) melted baking chocolate, mixed with 1 tablespoon soft butter. If frosting becomes too thin, beat in more sugar until right consistency.

Coconut Fluffy Frosting

Shredded coconut can be sprinkled on top of vanilla, coffee, orange, rum, brandy, or maple frostings, as soon as they are spread.

Nut Fluffy Frosting

Sprinkle chopped nut meats over any desired frosting, while still moist.

COOKED FROSTINGS

There are two main types of cooked frosting:

(1) *Seven-Minute Frosting,* in which all ingredients are put into top of double boiler at once and beaten continuously for 7 minutes, or until frosting is thick.

(2) *Boiled Frostings.* Here, sugar and water are first boiled together to form a syrup; then this hot syrup is gradually beaten into the other ingredients. The only thing difficult about boiled frosting is knowing the exact moment to stop boiling the sugar syrup. If you have a candy thermometer, this is easy; the thermometer will reach 238° when syrup is at proper consistency to remove from heat. If you have no thermometer, use either of these old-time tests: When a few drops of syrup, dropped into cold water, will form a *soft ball,* syrup is ready to remove from heat. Or, syrup is cooked enough when a small amount dripped from a spoon spins a long thread.

Remember to use *granulated sugar* for all cooked frostings, unless otherwise specified.

MASTER RECIPE #71
SEVEN-MINUTE FROSTING
AND FILLING — VANILLA

This easy recipe makes a rich, moist, fluffy frosting, and makes enough extra to be used between layers as filling, too. There are many ways to vary the flavor.

Have in lower part of double boiler 1½-inch deep boiling water. Keep water boiling briskly. Place over it the top part of double boiler, in which you have placed and stirred together

    2 egg whites

    1½ cups granulated sugar

    5 tablespoons cold water

    1½ teaspoons light corn syrup (or ⅛ teaspoon cream of tartar)

Begin at once beating all ingredients with rotary beater and beat continuously for 4 to 7 minutes by the clock, or until frosting stands in peaks on the beater, keeping the water boiling underneath.

Remove frosting from boiling water. Stir in

1 teaspoon vanilla

Spread at once, for this frosting, as it cools, forms a delicate crust.

SEVEN-MINUTE FROSTING VARIATIONS

(*Follow Master Recipe #71, Seven-Minute Frosting and Filling, page 434, making changes noted below.*)

Coconut Seven-Minute Frosting

Sprinkle ½ cup shredded coconut, or grated fresh coconut, over frosting as soon as spread. Absolutely heavenly.

Peppermint Seven-Minute Frosting

Substitute 2 or 3 drops of oil of peppermint instead of vanilla. You may tint your frosting shell-pink or pale green, if desired, by blending into finished frosting a few drops of vegetable food coloring. Yummy on rich chocolate cake.

Chocolate, or Chocolate Nut, Seven-Minute Frosting

Just before spreading, fold into frosting (don't beat) 2 squares (2 ounces) melted and cooled baking chocolate. If you like, after adding chocolate, fold in ½ cup chopped walnut meats; or decorate top of frosted cake with shelled walnuts.

Orange Seven-Minute Frosting

Substitute 5 tablespoons orange juice in place of water; and 1 tablespoon grated orange rind instead of vanilla.

Marshmallow Seven-Minute Frosting

As soon as you remove frosting from heat, fold in about 15 finely cut marshmallows. Top frosted cake with **halved marshmallows,** if you wish.

Macaroon Seven-Minute Frosting

Use only ½ teaspoon vanilla, but add ¼ teaspoon almond extract. Before spreading, fold in **1 cup finely crumbled macaroons.** Very special.

Sea Foam (Brown Sugar) Seven-Minute Frosting

Substitute **1½ cups firmly packed brown sugar** instead of the granulated, and omit corn syrup. Add **few grains salt.** After spreading, sprinkle with **½ cup chopped pecans,** if desired.

Black Walnut Seven-Minute Frosting

Make brown sugar frosting, substituting **¼ teaspoon black walnut flavoring** in place of vanilla. Sprinkle spread frosting with **½ cup chopped walnut meats.**

MASTER RECIPE #72
BOILED FROSTING AND FILLING
(Made with sugar syrup)

Makes enough to use as frosting and filling, both, for a 2-layer cake.

Put in a saucepan, over moderate heat, and stir constantly until sugar is dissolved
> **2 cups granulated sugar**
> **¾ cup water**
> **few grains of salt**
> **1 tablespoon light corn syrup** (or **¼ teaspoon cream of tartar**)

When sugar has dissolved, cover saucepan, and continue to boil gently for 2 or 3 minutes. (Covering pan helps eliminate sugar crystals completely, so there will be no grit.)
Then uncover pan; boil until syrup reaches 238° by candy

thermometer, or "soft ball" stage (see under Cooked Frostings, p. 434). At this point remove pan from heat.

In a mixing bowl, beat until they stand in peaks

2 egg whites

Very gradually, 1 tablespoon at a time, beat the hot syrup into the egg whites. Keep beating with rotary beater, until frosting is thick enough to stand in peaks. Then blend in

1 teaspoon vanilla

Spread quickly, before frosting becomes too thick.

To correct a too-soft boiled frosting. If frosting does not seem stiff enough when it has been beaten and you are ready to spread it, place the bowl containing the frosting over a pan of boiling water, and place pan over heat. With a mixing spoon, "cut" through the frosting, and fold one part of frosting over onto another part; keep cutting and folding over, until mixture becomes granular at edges of bowl. Then remove bowl from hot water, and beat frosting with a spoon until it is thick enough to hold its shape. Pour at once onto cake, and spread it.

BOILED FROSTING VARIATIONS

(*Follow Master Recipe #72, Boiled Frosting and Filling, page 436, making changes noted below.*)

Coconut Frosting

Sprinkle ½ **cup shredded coconut** on top of frosting, while it is still moist.

Epicurean Frosting

Immediately after spreading frosting, while it is still moist, sprinkle on top of it **grated or curled bitter chocolate flakes** (p. 444). A gourmet's dream.

Marshmallow Frosting

While beating frosting to cool, fold in about **15 finely cut marshmallows.** Keep beating so marshmallow flavor becomes well blended into frosting. Spread on cake. Decorate top of cake with **halved marshmallows,** if you like.

Peppermint Frosting

Reduce vanilla to ¼ **teaspoon** and add **2 or 3 drops oil of peppermint.** Leave frosting white; or tint to shell-pink, or palest green, with a few drops of vegetable food coloring. Marvelous on rich chocolate cake.

Peppermint Candy Frosting

For children's parties. Make peppermint frosting. After spreading on cake, sprinkle top of frosting with some bits of **crushed peppermint candy stick.** (Crush candy sticks with a rolling pin.)

Nut Frosting

Sprinkle over frosting at once ½ **cup chopped nut meats,** or decorate top of cake with **shelled walnuts, pecans, or hazelnuts.**

Coffee, or Coffee Nut Frosting

Use **1 cup brown sugar** and **1 cup granulated sugar.** Instead of water, substitute **strong, clear coffee,** strained of grounds. Reduce vanilla to ½ teaspoon. Very special with ½ **cup chopped walnuts sprinkled on,** after spreading.

Chocolate Frosting

Add **2 squares (2 ounces) melted baking chocolate** as soon as syrup has been beaten into egg whites.

Brown Sugar Frosting

Substitute all **brown sugar,** instead of granulated.

OTHER BOILED FROSTINGS

In some boiled frostings, instead of using egg whites, butter or milk may be blended with the sugar syrup to give frosting a rich, creamy taste. Each of these recipes makes enough to frost and fill one 2-layer cake.

Fudge Frosting

Put in saucepan, and bring to boil, stirring gently until all sugar is well dissolved 1½ **cups granulated sugar, ¾ cup cold water, 1 tablespoon light corn syrup, ⅛ teaspoon salt.** Continue boiling your syrup until it reaches 238°, or will form a soft ball in water. Then remove from heat; cool to lukewarm. Meanwhile, melt **4 squares (4 ounces) baking chocolate, 4 tablespoons butter.** Blend butter-chocolate mixture into lukewarm syrup, add **1 teaspoon vanilla.** Beat frosting until thick, and right consistency to spread.

Rich Caramel Frosting

Put in saucepan, and bring to boil, stirring until sugar is well dissolved, **2 cups light brown sugar, 2 tablespoons butter,** and **½ cup hot water.** Continue boiling until syrup reaches 238°, or forms a soft ball in water. Then remove from heat, and add **1 teaspoon vanilla.** Beat until cool and thick, about 5 to 7 minutes.

THICK, CREAMY FILLINGS
FOR CAKES OR PIES

Many people, instead of using frosting as a cake filling, prefer a moist, creamy filling, thick as pudding or rich as whipped cream. So we give here two basic and easy-to-make types. When using a filling as soft and moist as these, you need only sprinkle the top of your cake with powdered sugar; it does not need frosting.

Try these fillings also in a prebaked pie shell (p. 449). They're wonderful.

MASTER RECIPE #73
"FRENCH CREAM"
(REALLY WHIPPED CREAM)
FILLING

Makes filling for one 2-layer cake. Twice this recipe fills one 8 or 9 inch prebaked pie shell. Recipe requires no cooking.

Beat with rotary beater until it begins to thicken
1 cup heavy whipping cream

Add gradually to cream, still beating

⅓ cup confectioners' sugar

When above has reached consistency of whipped cream, fold into it

1 stiffly beaten egg white

Fold in but do not beat again

½ teaspoon vanilla extract

FRENCH CREAM FILLING VARIATIONS

(Make Master Recipe #73, French Cream Filling, page 439, making changes below.)

Coconut French Cream Filling

Before spreading, fold in **½ cup shredded coconut.**

Peach French Cream Filling

Instead of vanilla, use **¼ teaspoon almond extract.** Before spreading, fold in **½ cup thoroughly drained crushed peaches** (fresh, canned, or thawed frozen ones). Delicious and delicate. You can even use this filling as topping for a square cake, and place a border of sliced peaches on top of the fluffy peach topping.

Raspberry French Cream Filling

Before spreading, fold in **½ cup crushed, thoroughly drained fresh raspberries.** If you like raspberries and cream, you'll love this.

Strawberry French Cream Filling

Before spreading, fold in **½ cup crushed, thoroughly drained fresh strawberries.** Much like strawberry shortcake effect; very good.

Fig French Cream Filling

Add **1 tablespoon sherry** at end. Before spreading, fold in **½ cup chopped table figs.** Very rich.

Brandy, or Rum, French Cream Filling

Substitute 1 teaspoon brandy or rum for vanilla.

MASTER RECIPE #74
VANILLA CREAM FILLING

This is the cooked, pudding-type filling most frequently used for Boston Cream Pie, or between cake layers. It can also be used as filling for a prebaked pie shell. Recipe makes enough to fill one 8 or 9 inch pie; for cake filling, make only half the recipe.

Mix in bowl

⅓ cup all-purpose flour (or 2 tablespoons cornstarch)
⅔ cup granulated sugar
⅛ teaspoon salt

Add, little by little, stirring to smooth paste

2 cups scalded milk

Put mixture in top part of double boiler; set over lower part, containing hot water. Cook mixture, stirring to avoid lumps, about 15 minutes, or until thick. Then add

2 slightly beaten eggs

Continue cooking 2 or 3 minutes. Cool somewhat. Then stir in

1 tablespoon butter
1 teaspoon vanilla

CREAM FILLING VARIATIONS

(*Make Master Recipe #74, Vanilla Cream Filling, page 441, making changes below.*)

Chocolate Cream Filling

Increase sugar to 1 cup. When scalding milk, add to it 2 squares (2 ounces) baking chocolate.

Banana Cream Filling

Fold in 1 banana, sliced or mashed, after adding butter.

Butterscotch Cream Filling

Use ¾ cup brown sugar and no granulated. Increase butter or other shortening to ¼ cup.

Coconut Cream Filling

Before spreading filling, fold in 1 cup shredded coconut.

Coffee Cream Filling

Instead of 2 cups milk, use 1 cup evaporated milk and 1 cup hot, strong, coffee (strained of grounds).

Mocha Cream Filling

Add ⅓ cup powdered cocoa with sugar. For liquid, use 1 cup evaporated milk; 1 cup hot strong coffee, strained of grounds.

MASTER RECIPE #75
LEMON CREAM FILLING

Lemon or orange cream filling is made with fruit juice and water, instead of milk, and requires more sugar. This makes enough soft filling to go between two layers of cake. Double the recipe, to fill 8 inch pie shell.

In top of double boiler, mix
    1 cup granulated sugar
    ¼ cup all-purpose flour (or 3 tablespoons cornstarch)
    ⅛ teaspoon salt

Add, little by little, stirring into smooth paste
                ¾ cup hot water
                ¼ cup lemon juice
Cook, stirring constantly until mixture begins to thicken. Then add, and blend in well
                1 egg, slightly beaten

Cook about 2 minutes more, until well thickened, stirring frequently to avoid lumps. Then add and mix in

3 tablespoons butter

Remove from heat. Cool. Stir in

½ teaspoon grated lemon rind

LEMON CREAM FILLING VARIATIONS

(*Make Master Recipe #75, Lemon Cream Filling, page 442, making changes below.*)

Fluffy Lemon Filling

When filling has cooled, fold in **1 cup sweetened whipped cream** (1 cup heavy cream beaten with ¼ cup confectioners' sugar). This makes a heavenly light lemon filling.

Lemon Coconut Filling

Before spreading, fold in **1 cup shredded coconut.**

Orange Filling

Use only **½ cup sugar.** Instead of lemon-flavored liquid, use **⅓ cup hot water** plus **⅔ cup orange juice,** plus 1 teaspoon lemon juice, to sharpen taste of orange. Substitute **grated orange rind** for lemon rind.

Orange Coconut Filling

Make orange filling; when cool, fold in **1 cup shredded coconut.** A dessert for the gods, on a spring night.

TO GIVE CAKES A "PARTY LOOK"

Any good cake, invitingly frosted, looks tempting . . . but it's easy to give your cake a special "party look." All it needs is a little contrasting design on top. For example:

Add a wreath of coconut. Around top edge of an orange-frosted cake, arrange a decorative wreath of shredded coconut. Every 2 inches, along the coconut wreath, place a pit-free section of fresh, peeled orange. Looks beautiful; tastes like spring.

Make a design of nuts. On top of frosting, arrange a crisscross or diagonal pattern of halves of walnuts or pecans; or for children's parties, use gumdrops.

Add a pattern of unsweetened chocolate flakes. On top of a vanilla, peppermint, or coffee-frosted cake, arrange a 2-inch wide circle, or diagonal lines, of curled bitter chocolate flakes. To make such flakes: hold sharp knife at right angles to a large bar of unsweetened (baking) chocolate; scrape knife downwards, without releasing pressure, for about 1 inch. Flakes should come out about ⅛ inch wide, 1 inch long, and slightly curled, if you do it right. Scrape the flakes over a piece of waxed paper; then you can simply lift the paper, when you have enough, and pour the flakes onto your cake without handling them.

Trim a pale-colored frosting with bitter chocolate topping. Ice a cake with vanilla or pale-green tinted peppermint frosting. When frosting has set, make this bitter chocolate topping:

Melt over hot water 2 squares (2 ounces) baking chocolate and 2 teaspoons butter. Let cool somewhat; but before mixture becomes hard, pour it from tip of spoon in a narrow wreath around edge of cake, letting chocolate drip down sides.

On square or oblong cakes, make a plaid, or crisscross design. On top of frosting, spread alternating rows (up and down, or diagonally, across cake) of two different colored trimmings; perhaps one row coconut, second row grated chocolate flakes.

For anniversaries, use tiny silver-colored beads or colored candies to spell out monograms, or number of years. Use colored candy beads to make a wedding ring design, or the letters of a monogram, or the numeral which indicates number of years being celebrated. A personal and charming touch to add to the usual array of candles.

CHAPTER XXXV

You Can Make Pies

METHOD FOR: *Never-Fail Pastry (Pie Crust), Crumb Pie Shell,
Two-Crust Pies, One-Crust Pies, Pie Shells, Tart Shells, Your
Own Pastry Mix, Fruit Pies, Cream Pies, Custard-Type Pies,
Meringue Pies, Chiffon Pies, Christmas Mince Pie, Dumplings,
Crust for Meat Pie*

BASIC PRINCIPLES

Anybody can make a pie; anybody who really wants to . . .
who will follow directions in Master Recipe, Never-Fail Pastry
. . . and who will not make her pie crust too *wet.*

Too much water has probably ruined more good pies than any
other one thing.

Pastry is only flour, salt, and shortening . . . with a very few
drops of water to make it hold together. The *shortening* (which
begins liquefying as soon as the oven heat hits it) is what actually
should provide most of the moisture throughout your pie crust.
For as this shortening continues to get hotter and hotter, in the
oven, it melts through the flour, moistening it and cooking it into
something crisp, delicate, flaky. Then during the remaining time
of baking, the pie crust dries. Result: no soggy crust, but a tender,
"short" pastry which melts in the mouth.

The first rule for pie crust is, therefore, always to *use at least*
⅓ *as much shortening as you use of flour.* This assures sufficient
shortening to make flaky, tender crust.

The *second rule* is to add the small amount of water you will need *drop by drop*, adding not one drop more than is necessary to make flour mixture barely stick together — in an almost crumbly mass.

The third — and only other important rule — is to *do lightly whatever must be done in handling* pastry. Cut in the shortening lightly (preferably with a pastry blender, or using two knives in crisscross motion, so you do not *mat* the dough with your fingers). When you roll the dough, *roll* lightly . . . with quick, light strokes of the rolling pin, rolling from center of dough, *out*. Avoid rerolling dough, any more than is necessary; additional handling and the working in of additional flour from board only toughens pastry. If you flour your rolling pin adequately, and flour the board on which you are rolling the dough as often as needed, pastry is not apt to stick, nor tear; and you will seldom need to reroll it.

Keeping these three rules in mind, you will soon make expert pastry, every time . . . and be the envy of your friends.

Pastry takes only a few minutes to mix . . . and a few minutes more to roll out and arrange in your pie plate. The remainder of the time needed to make a pie depends upon the type of filling you will use. Fruit fillings are quick to fix; pudding-type fillings take longer.

However many minutes it takes, there is no more satisfying dessert. A good pie is hearty . . . helps fill out a slim meal . . . can be prepared at leisure, in advance . . . looks mouth-watering to home-folks or guests . . . and is America's favorite dessert. You won't be happy until you can make one. And you'll find it's fun.

Get the trick of good pastry, and you can put into it any filling in this chapter.

MASTER RECIPE #76
NEVER-FAIL PASTRY (PIE CRUST)

Makes enough pastry to provide upper and lower crusts for one 8 or 9 inch pie; or for two prebaked pie shells; or for 8 to 12 tart shells.

Put into large mixing bowl

    2 cups all-purpose flour

    ¾ teaspoon salt

    ⅛ teaspoon baking powder (optional)

(NOTE: Baking powder makes pastry lighter, flakier.)

Add, in solid lump

    ⅔ cup shortening (vegetable shortening, or lard, or ½
        lard and ½ butter)

With pastry blender, or using two knives in crisscross motion, cut shortening into flour until most of the mixture is fine as coarse meal, but there still remain some lumps as large as peas.

Sprinkle on, a few drops at a time, while stirring mixture lightly with fork

    about 4 to 5 tablespoons cold water

NOTE: Add just enough water to make mixture hold together roughly, in a crumbly — not wet — mass. As different types of flour have different degrees of absorbency, water needed may vary, amounting to a little more, or a little less than 4 tablespoons.

Turn dough out onto lightly floured large board, and you are ready to shape crusts.

For Two-crust Pies

To shape lower crust. Divide dough of Master Recipe into two equal parts. Shape each half into a ball, lightly. Set one ball aside.

Flour lightly your hands, a rolling pin, and a large breadboard. Place one ball of dough in center of board. Roll dough, with rolling pin, working from center to edges, shaping a circular sheet of dough ⅛ inch thick, and 2 inches wider than diameter of top of pie plate.

(If dough sticks to board, lift it up, flour board lightly again, and turn dough over to other side. Flour rolling pin again, too. But try not to use a bit more flour than needed; adding excess flour makes pastry tough.)

When shaped, double dough over, in half, with a loose fold through the center; this makes dough easier to lift without breaking. Lift crust gently to ungreased pie plate, placing fold across middle of plate (see A, p. 448). Unfold. Dough should now fit flat against entire inside of pie plate, including walls of plate. If it doesn't quite fit, you may stretch it gently with finger tips. If it tears, you may press tear together again with moistened finger tips. Cut off any dough that overhangs edges of plate, with a sharp knife.

Plate is now ready for the filling.

To shape upper crust. Flour hands, rolling pin, large board. Put remaining ball of dough in center. Roll dough to same size as for lower crust (see p. 447). Fold pastry over double; and while doubled, with a knife, cut through both thicknesses, near the fold, a pattern of short slashes, to make steam vents through the crust.

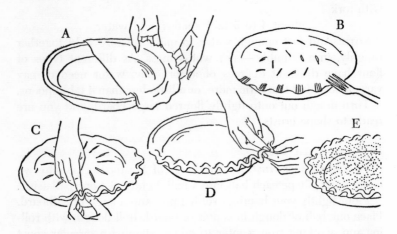

When filling has been put into plate, lift doubled upper crust onto top of filling, placing fold across center of filling. Unfold. Crust should now cover entire pie, and overhang edges of plate by about 1 inch all the way around. Tuck in overhanging dough so it goes *underneath* edge of lower crust, all the way around plate, squeezing both crusts together to seal in juices. Then either press both edges down onto rim of pie plate with tines of a fork (B); or, with fingers, press the two squeezed-together crusts into a little upright rim, or fence, running around top edge of pie plate; then "flute" the rim, with fingers (C).

To glaze a top crust. Some people like a shiny, browned, "glazed" top crust on a pie. If you wish yours glazed, do one of these things before baking pie:

Brush top crust lightly with cream or milk.

Brush top crust lightly with melted butter.

Sprinkle top crust, very sparingly, with few drops cold water. You do not want to make the crust *wet*.

To sprinkle top crust with sugar. After crust has been brushed with liquid, you may also sprinkle it lightly with granulated sugar, if desired, to make a "sweet" top crust.

For Open Pies

To shape a pie shell (a lower crust with fluted edge). Use ½ dough of Master Recipe, Pastry. Turn dough onto lightly floured board and roll out just as if making a lower crust (p. 447), but make this one a little bigger; you need enough pastry to make a fluted edge on rim of plate; so roll the crust 2½ inches wider than diameter of top of pie plate. When shaped, fold dough over double, to make it easier to lift. Lift gently to pie plate, placing fold across center of dish (A). Unfold. Pastry should now overhang edge of pie plate by about 1 inch all around. Double up this overhang, pinching two or more thicknesses of it together, to shape a little upright rim, or fence, running around top edge of pie plate; then "flute" the rim (D).

Now note the two further steps, below:

(1) *If pie shell is to be filled with liquid filling, before baking* (for example if it is to contain custard mixture, or pumpkin mixture), before putting filling into the shell, brush entire inside of pastry shell with slightly beaten raw white of egg. White of egg makes a "seal" over crust, so filling is less apt to make crust soggy.

(2) *If pie shell is to be prebaked, empty* (as for example, for a pudding-type filling which will be added later), do as follows. After pastry is shaped in pie plate, make dozens of tiny holes all over the inside of the pie shell, with tines of a fork (E). The holes prevent shell from puffing out of shape or shrinking greatly, while cooking. Bake shell in hot oven (450°) 12 to 18 minutes, or just

until pastry is golden color, dry and crisp. Cool shell in pie plate placed on a rack. Do not put in filling until shell is cool.

For Tarts

To shape tart shells. Roll out pastry to a thin, large sheet. With string or tape measure, measure outside of a muffin cup (including depth of wall on two sides, and width across bottom of cup). Now add 1 inch to this total measurement. Find a saucer or small pie plate with diameter to match this measurement. Using this saucer or plate as guide, cut out circular crusts, as many as needed. Fit each crust *inside* a right-side-up muffin cup. Use the overhang of each crust to make a fluted rim, as for large, open pie shell (see D, p. 448).

Such tart shells, made on inside of cup, may be filled with custard or pumpkin mixture, then baked. Or they may be perforated with dozens of tiny holes, made with tines of fork, to help prevent their shrinking out of shape during baking; then baked empty, and later filled with fresh-cut fruit or berries, or a pudding-type filling.

However, some people prefer to make tart shells on *outside* of a muffin cup or fancy mold. To do this, see illustration, page 450. Roll pastry to large thin sheet. Then measure diameter and walls of muffin cup, or metal mold, with string. Find a saucer or small pie plate measuring same diameter. Using this as a guide, with pastry wheel, cut out circular crusts. Fit these over *outside* (back) of inverted muffin pans or small individual molds. With tines of fork, make many small holes in each crust, before cooking. This prevents pastry from shrinking when baked without filling. Empty tart shells are baked in hot (450°) oven about 12 minutes, or until golden color and crisp.

For Pies with Top Crust Only

Deep-dish fruit pies, meat pies, casseroles, need only a top crust. Use ½ dough of Master Recipe, Pastry (p. 446). Roll and shape dough as for upper crust of a two-crust pie, making slashes in rolled dough to allow steam vents. Place crust over contents of dish. Crimp overhang of pastry to top edge of baking dish, so crust will hold in place.

"Scraps" of pastry

Collect scraps, shape lightly into a ball, wrap in waxed paper; store in refrigerator. When you wish to use pastry again, soften at room temperature.

Your Own Pastry Mix

Instead of having to mix pastry ingredients each time you want pie crust, or tarts, why not have the mix all made . . . enough of it to serve you on a number of occasions? You can mix all pastry ingredients *except the water* . . . and add the water only when you wish to roll out a crust. It's simple . . . inexpensive . . . and will save you the measuring job, when in haste.

This mix keeps for weeks if stored in covered canister or covered glass jar.

Follow Master Recipe, Pastry (p. 446), but increase measurements to **6 cups flour, 2½ teaspoons salt, ¼ teaspoon baking powder** (if desired), and **2 cups shortening**. Continue cutting mixture until it has texture of coarse meal. Store in tightly covered container until needed. When needed, measure as follows:

To use. For a 9 inch pie shell, use 1½ cups mix, sparingly sprinkled with about 2½ tablespoons water. For a 2-crust pie, use 3 cups mix, sparingly sprinkled with about 5 tablespoons water.

Turn dough onto lightly floured board, and roll to shape desired.

MASTER RECIPE #77
TWO-CRUST FRUIT PIES —

Fruit pies are easy to make . . . delicious any time of year . . . and can be made from fresh or canned fruit. What's more, all fruit pies are made on the same general plan. We will use as our "Master" example a Blueberry Pie. See Variations following, for other fruits.

BLUEBERRY PIE

This recipe makes an 8 or 9 inch pie. Have available
1 quart fresh blueberries or 2 cans blueberries
If you have only 2 to 3 cups fruit, use a smaller pie plate.

Prepare fruit. If fruit is fresh, wash and pick over, to make edible, removing poor berries, sticks, other foreign matter; drain. If canned, drain, but save juice. (See note on canned fruit, p. 454.)

Make pastry, enough for 2-crust pie, by making
entire Master Recipe, Pastry (p. 446)
Divide mixed pastry into two equal parts. Leave one part in mixing bowl. Shape other into a ball.

Make lower crust. Place ball of pastry on lightly floured board. Flour rolling pin lightly, and roll ball of pastry with quick, light strokes, rolling from center outward, shaping a circular sheet ⅛ inch thick, and 2½ inches wider in circumference than diameter of pie plate. See To Shape Lower Crust (p. 447). Double pastry over with a loose fold through center, to lift it easily. Lift it into 8 or 9 inch pie plate. Fit to plate. If pastry is too small, stretch it a little with fingers. If it breaks, dampen the break slightly with water, and press break together again with fingers. When fitted, plate is ready for filling.

Filling. Turn fruit into pastry-lined plate.

Over top of fruit, sprinkle

1 or 2 teaspoons lemon juice

⅓ to ½ cup sugar, mixed with 2 tablespoons flour or
1 tablespoon cornstarch

(Lemon juice is added to bring out the flavor of the fruit, and to give a little extra tang. If preferred, you can omit it. The flour or cornstarch is put in to thicken fruit juices which will develop in cooking.)

Over top of sugar, scatter

8 to 10 bits of butter, size of peas

Make upper crust (directions for, page 448). Shape remaining pastry into ball. Place on freshly floured board. Flour rolling pin. Roll as with lower crust, to circular sheet ⅛ inch thick and 2½ inches wider than diameter of pie plate. Double pastry over, with a loose fold through center, to make it easy to lift. Near fold, make slashes with knife, through both thicknesses, for steam vents. Lift doubled pastry onto top of pie. Unfold. Tuck edges of upper crust underneath edges of lower crust; press the two crusts together at edges, all around plate. You may press them together on edge of pie plate with tines of a fork, or "flute" the two edges with thumbs and forefingers (page 448). If edges are not firmly fastened together, juices will ooze out during cooking.

Glaze crust, if desired (see p. 449); however, this may be omitted.

To Bake. Place pie in preheated very hot (450° to 500°) oven for first 10 minutes. Then reduce heat to moderate (350°) and continue baking about 30 to 40 minutes, or until crust is golden brown, and a wee bit of fruit juice begins to ooze out through steam vent slashes. Don't cook further, or fruit will be overcooked.

To test doneness of a firm fruit, like apples, you may insert a knife blade through one of the slashes in crust. If fruit offers little resistance, it is cooked enough.

To cool. Place pie plate on rack, so air can get underneath bottom of plate. If desired, serve pie while still somewhat warm; many fruit pies are more delicious warm than cold.

NOTE ON CANNED FRUIT. Canned fruit, during processing (cooking) in its can, has already "made" its juice; it will never make much additional juice, while baking in a pie. *If you like a fairly "dry" pie* (without much juice in it), drain off canned fruit juice, using only the drained canned fruit to put in your pie; flavor the fruit as usual with lemon juice and sugar, but omit the flour or cornstarch called for in Master Recipe. *If you like juicy pie,* measure and use (with drained canned fruit) about ½ to ¾ cup of the canned juice; but in this case, to thicken the juice you are putting in, add flour or cornstarch with the sugar, as in Master Recipe. Whenever adding juice to a pie in this fashion, you must have oven extra hot, and place pie lower in oven than usual, to thicken the juice as quickly as possible; otherwise you will have soggy lower crust.

TWO-CRUST FRUIT PIE VARIATIONS

(Follow Master Recipe #77, Blueberry Pie, page 452, making changes noted below.)

Peach Pie

Instead of berries, substitute **peeled, sliced fresh peaches, or sliced canned peaches.** Instead of, or in addition to, lemon juice, sprinkle over fruit **3 or 4 drops almond flavoring;** this gives peaches a wonderful flavor.

Cherry Pie

Instead of berries, substitute **fresh, pitted sour cherries, or canned sour cherries.** As cherries are sour, use at least **½ cup sugar** in pie. Add a few drops of lemon juice or almond flavoring.

Apple Pie

Instead of berries, substitute **peeled, cored, tart apples** (greenings are best) sliced about ⅛ to ¼ inch thick; or use **1 can "pie** apples," including all juice that comes in the can. Omit lemon juice. Use ½ cup sugar, but omit flour or cornstarch. Over sweetened apples, sprinkle few dashes nutmeg or cinnamon, or a bit of each, before dotting with butter.

Prune Pie or Apricot Pie

Instead of berries substitute drained canned apricots or prunes — or, if using dried fruit, it must first be "stewed" (p. 324), to make it soft before using in pie. Use lemon juice, and only ⅓ cup sugar, as these fruits are already somewhat sweetened.

Rhubarb Pie (A great springtime favorite)

Wash 8 to 10 stalks fresh, crisp rhubarb, depending on length; remove leaves; cut stalks to 1 or 1½ inch pieces. Follow Master Recipe, but instead of berries substitute the cut fresh rhubarb pieces. Use lemon juice, and ½ to ⅔ cup sugar (rhubarb is "sour"); and include flour or cornstarch, as rhubarb makes much juice while cooking.

MASTER RECIPE #78
DEEP-DISH FRUIT PIE

This type of pie is made exactly like the fruit pies above, except: (1) there is no lower crust; (2) more fruit is used than in an ordinary pie; (3) this dessert is made in a baking dish with 1½ to 2 inch side walls, thus making a deeper pie. Such pie is a great favorite with people who like fruit better than crust.

Grease inside of a 5 to 7 inch wide baking dish, having side walls 1½ to 2 inches deep, with

butter

Put into eating condition (peel, pit, slice, pick over, drain) enough

fresh or canned fruit

of any kind customarily used for fruit pies (see Variations, p. 454), to fill dish to top. Omit canned fruit *juice;* use only fruit.

Over fruit, sprinkle

⅓ to ⅔ cup sugar (depending on tartness of fruit)
mixed with

2 tablespoons flour (or 1 tablespoon cornstarch)

Also sprinkle over fruit

lemon juice (and/or any other seasonings recommended
under Variations for fruit pies, p. 454)

Over top of fruit distribute

8 to 10 bits of butter, size of peas

Make

½ Master Recipe, Pastry (p. 446)

Roll pastry on floured board, using floured rolling pin. Shape
it into an upper crust (p. 448). When shaped, double crust over
in half, with loose fold through center. With knife, cut slashes
near fold, through both thicknesses, to make steam vents. Lift
doubled pastry onto fruit-filled dish.

With fingertips, crimp edge of pastry firmly to edge of dish,
all the way around, so no fruit juices may bubble out.

Bake as for blueberry pie (p. 453).

MASTER RECIPE #79
FRESH FRUIT OR BERRIES
IN COOKED PIE OR TART SHELLS

To make one 8 or 9 inch pie, or 3 to 4 tart shells, mix

½ dough of Master Recipe, Pastry (p. 446)

Roll dough 2½ inches wider than diameter of pie plate, fit into
plate, flute edges, making a pie shell; see page 449. Or instead,
cut dough into smaller circles, and make tart shells; see page 450.
With tines of fork, make dozens of tiny holes in unbaked shell.
Bake empty pie shell or tart shells in very hot (450°) oven about
12 minutes, or until pastry is golden color and crisp. Cool shells.

Fill cooled shells with

sweetened fruit (berries or peaches)

Top fruit if desired with

sweetened whipped cream (p. 408)

For a party, flavor the whipped cream with
sherry or rum
Luscious for a summer night.

MASTER RECIPE #80
PIES WITH PUDDING-TYPE FILLING

This recipe makes *all pudding-type pies* (except baked custard, pumpkin, or squash pies, found on page 458).

For this type pie, you need one prebaked pie shell, plus a thick, creamy filling, prepared separately.

To make one 8 or 9 inch pie, mix
½ dough of Master Recipe, Pastry (p. 446)
Roll dough 2½ inches wider than diameter of pie plate, fit into plate, flute edges, making a pie shell; see page 449. With tines of fork, make dozens of tiny holes in unbaked shell. Bake empty pie shell in very hot (450°) oven about 12 minutes, or until pastry is golden color and crisp. Cool shell.

Filling

Now prepare a cooked, thick, pudding-type filling, in saucepan. This filling may be any *one* of the following:

A packaged pudding mix (chocolate, butterscotch, vanilla, or lemon); mix by package directions. Or
Vanilla cream filling (p. 441) or any Variation. Or
Lemon cream filling (p. 443) or any Variation. Or
Soft custard (p. 385). Or
French cream filling (uncooked; p. 439) or any Variation

Turn cooked, cooled pudding or filling into cooled pie shell. For taste appeal and glamour, add some trimming, such as:

On Chocolate Pie

Arrange swirls of sweetened whipped cream (p. 408); or
Decorate with walnut or pecan meats; or
Decorate with a border of sweetened whipped cream, topped with grated bitter or semi-sweet chocolate.

On Butterscotch Pie

Decorate with halves of shelled pecans; or

Garnish with sweetened whipped cream, flavored with rum.

On Vanilla Cream Pie; or Soft Custard Filling

Over filling, sprinkle a layer of shredded coconut; or

Press into still-moist filling a "border" or other pattern of sliced fresh peaches, or drained canned peaches, or sliced bananas.

For Banana Cream Pie (see Filling, p. 441)

Garnish top of pie with sweetened whipped cream, or with shredded coconut.

For Coffee Cream Pie or Mocha Cream Pie (see Filling, p. 442)

Garnish top of pie with flaked semi-sweet chocolate; or with coarsely chopped walnut meats, or with sweetened whipped cream flavored with rum.

For Lemon or Orange Pie (see Filling, pp. 442–443)

See Meringue-Topped Pies (p. 460); or top pie with shredded coconut.

MASTER RECIPE #81
CUSTARD-TYPE PIES

Custard, coconut-custard, pumpkin, and squash pies are all relatives . . . all having fillings made of custard-type ingredients. For pumpkin or squash pies, boiled, mashed pumpkin or squash (and some special spices) are added to the custard ingredients.

For all these pies, you mix your filling, pour it into an *unbaked* pie shell; then bake shell and filling together.

For one 8 or 9 inch pie, mix

½ dough of Master Recipe, Pastry

Roll dough 2½ inches wider than diameter of pie plate; fit into plate; flute edges, making a pie shell (p. 449). Do not bake pie shell. But to keep pastry from becoming soggy when liquid filling is put in, you may now brush inside of pie shell with

raw white of egg

This "seals" over the pastry.

Now make any filling given below.

Custard Pie

In bowl, mix same ingredients as for
Master Recipe, Baked Custard (p. 388)
Turn liquid mixture into unbaked pie shell. Place pie in center
of preheated, very hot (450°) oven for 10 minutes; then reduce
heat to slow (325°) and bake 35 to 45 minutes longer, until custard
is set. Test by inserting tip of a knifeblade in center of pie. If
blade comes out dry, or practically dry, custard is done. Don't
overcook, or custard will turn watery.

Coconut Custard Pie

Make like custard pie, but add **1 cup shredded coconut** to liquid
filling before baking.

Pumpkin or Squash Pie

In mixing bowl, put
1½ cups canned or cooked mashed pumpkin or squash
(To cook and mash pumpkin or squash, see page 301.)
Add to pumpkin or squash
   ¼ teaspoon salt
   ½ teaspoon ginger
   ¼ teaspoon cinnamon
   ¼ teaspoon nutmeg
(The spices here given make a moderately spicy pie. Some families like a greater amount of spice; if you do, try adding a pinch
of powdered clove, or ⅛ teaspoon allspice, with above seasonings.
If you prefer a milder-flavored pie, omit the cinnamon, and reduce ginger to ¼ teaspoon, but use the nutmeg as is.)
Add to pumpkin mixture the custard-type ingredients
 2 eggs, slightly beaten
 ¾ cup brown sugar, firmly packed (or ½ cup granulated sugar)
 1 cup scalded light cream or top milk (or you may use
  ½ cup evaporated milk plus ½ cup whole milk,
  scalded together)

½ teaspoon vanilla

Mix all ingredients well. Turn mixture into unbaked pie shell. Bake like custard pie. Serve with wedges of American cheese, or garnish pie with sweetened whipped cream.

Pumpkin Tarts

For a party, pour pumpkin pie filling into unbaked **tart shells** made on *inside* of muffin cups (p. 450). Bake tarts like custard pie (p. 459), but watch them. They will cook faster, being smaller. Cool. Garnish with **rum-flavored sweetened whipped cream**. Very de luxe.

MASTER RECIPE #82
MERINGUE-TOPPED PIES

(For such pies as lemon meringue, orange meringue, and chocolate meringue pie.)

For one 8 or 9 inch pie, make

½ Master Recipe, Pastry (p. 446)

Roll dough 2½ inches wider than diameter of pie plate, fit it into plate, flute edges, making a pie shell; see page 449. With tines of fork, make dozens of tiny holes all over unbaked shell. Bake empty shell in very hot (450°) oven about 12 minutes, or until pastry is golden color and crisp.

Now cook (following package directions)

1 package prepared lemon pie filling; or
1 package prepared chocolate pudding mix

Or make your own

Lemon or orange cream filling (pp. 442–443)

Cool the cooked pudding or filling. Turn it into baked shell.

Now, in separate bowl, make

meringue topping for pie

(See under Master Recipe, Meringue, page 489.) Spread the meringue over entire top of pie, making it *extend to touch* (*and even overlap*) *edges of pie shell*, all around. This gives the meringue something to "hold on to," so it will not shrink during cooking.

Place pie in oven, to cook the meringue. If you like a *moist* meringue, place pie in hot (400°) oven, just a few minutes, until top of meringue browns a golden, tawny color. If you like a drier, crisper meringue, place pie in slower oven (300°) and bake slightly longer, again until top of meringue browns lightly.

Cool pie before serving.

MASTER RECIPE #83
CHIFFON PIES

Make a **crumb pie shell**, page 464. Or
Make a baked pastry shell. For one 8 or 9 inch pie, mix
½ **Master Recipe, Pastry** (p. 446)
Roll dough 2½ inches wider than diameter of pie plate, fit it into plate, flute edges, making a pie shell; see page 449. With tines of fork, make dozens of tiny holes all over unbaked shell. Bake empty pie shell in very hot (450°) oven about 12 minutes, or until pastry is golden color and crisp.

Filling. All chiffon pie fillings begin with a gelatine mixture, chilled until partly set, then blended with stiff-beaten, sweetened egg whites, for airy-light texture.

So first, you make a gelatine mixture.

There are three ways you can do this:

(1) Buy one package fruit-flavored gelatine mix. Using this, follow Chiffon Pie Filling I, p. 462.

(2) Make your own fruit-flavored gelatine mixture, if you wish a flavor (like peach, apricot, prune) not sold in packaged mixes. To do this, make gelatine by Master Recipe #57, page 367, or its variations, using only 1½ cups total liquid. Chill mixture; then proceed as for Chiffon Pie Filling I, p. 462.

(3) Certain gelatines (like lemon, coffee, cocoa) make richer filling if egg *yolks*, as well as whites, are used. To make these, follow Chiffon Pie Filling II, p. 462.

Chiffon Pie Filling I (made with Fruit-Flavored Gelatine Mix)

Empty into bowl

> 1 package fruit-flavored gelatine

Add, stirring briskly

> 1½ cups hot water

Stir until all gelatine mix has dissolved.

Place mixture in refrigerator to chill ½ hour or longer, until it is thick as unbeaten egg white.

Get ready a large bowl of cracked ice, or ice cubes.

Bring gelatine from refrigerator; place bowl containing gelatine inside the bowl of ice, and with rotary beater, beat gelatine to a froth. Return whipped gelatine at once to refrigerator.

Now, in separate bowl, beat until they stand in soft peaks

> 3 egg whites

Add to egg whites, little by little, beating to blend after each addition

> ⅓ cup sugar

Fold whipped gelatine mixture lightly and gently into egg whites, using fold-over strokes with spoon, until blended.

Turn mixture into baked pie shell or crumb crust.

Place pie in refrigerator 2 or 3 hours, or until filling is firm.

Chiffon Pie Filling II (made with Unflavored Gelatine)

Remember that when using *unflavored* gelatine, you must always first soften it in a little cold liquid, before using it to make your gelatine mixture.

For this type filling, we will use Lemon Chiffon as chief example. Coffee and Cocoa Chiffon are made similarly, with slight changes noted below.

Lemon Chiffon

Sprinkle

> 1 envelope unflavored gelatine

into

¼ cup cold water

Let stand 5 minutes until gelatine softens. Meanwhile, separate (p. 260)

3 eggs

Put into top section of a double boiler, and beat slightly the

3 egg yolks

Stir into yolks

⅓ cup sugar
½ cup lemon juice
½ teaspoon salt

Place top of double boiler over lower section, containing hot water. Cook, stirring constantly, until mixture thickens like a soft custard.

Remove from heat; stir into yolks the softened gelatine. Stir until gelatine dissolves; then add

1 teaspoon grated lemon rind

Chill mixture in refrigerator ½ hour or more, until thickened to consistency of unbeaten egg whites; then, with rotary beater, whip quickly to a froth. Return gelatine mixture at once to refrigerator.

In separate bowl, beat until they stand in moist peaks the

3 egg whites

Beat little by little into egg whites

⅓ cup sugar

Fold egg whites into gelatine mixture. Turn whole mixture into baked pie shell (p. 449), or crumb shell (p. 464). Chill pie in refrigerator 2 or 3 hours, or until filling is firm, before serving. If desired, garnish top of pie with sweetened whipped cream (p. 408).

Coffee Chiffon

Make filling just like Lemon Chiffon (preceding recipe) but instead of lemon juice, use ½ cup cold, strong coffee infusion (free of grounds). Omit lemon rind; use instead ½ teaspoon vanilla.

Cocoa Chiffon

Make like Lemon Chiffon (p. 462), but when adding sugar to yolks, add with sugar **6 tablespoons powdered cocoa**. Omit lemon juice; use instead **½ cup hot water**. Omit lemon rind.

MASTER RECIPE #84
CRUMB PIE SHELL

This type of pie shell is not cooked at all. Finely rolled crumbs are blended with melted butter and sugar (thus making them "short" and sweet) . . . then the mixture is simply patted into a layer, lining a pie plate. The pie plate is then chilled in refrigerator until the "crust" becomes firm.

Crumb shells are often used for chiffon pies, or cream pies. And some people use them to hold fresh, sweetened — but uncooked — fruit or berries. Such a crust is more "crumbly" than pastry crust.

To make crust for one 8 or 9 inch pie plate, mix together
1½ cups fine crumbs (graham cracker or gingersnap or rusk)
½ cup sugar
½ cup melted butter (or margarine)
Turn mixture into a pie plate. Pat it into an even layer, firmly, against sides and bottom of pie plate. Place pie plate in refrigerator, to chill, until crust is firm.

MASTER RECIPE #85
CHRISTMAS MINCE PIE

Mincemeat filling tastes most luscious if made at least one day (even a month) before being put in the pie. Old-fashioned folks used to keep mincemeat in their attics for a year. Many people today keep it for weeks in covered jars, in the refrigerator. The longer it stands, the more wonderfully the flavors of all the good ingredients blend. So save yourself a rush at holiday time, and make your mincemeat in advance.

The quickest, easiest way to make mince pie filling is to buy one of the excellent prepared mincemeats at your grocer's. One type comes dry, in a package, and *has to be soaked in water or fruit juice* (following package directions) *before you start using it.* You may soak mincemeat in orange, prune, grapefruit, or other fruit juice, instead of in water. The other type comes in glass jars, in moist form, ready to use. Either contains the basic ingredients of good mincemeat, and could be used to make a small pie.

For a richer, bigger, and really superb pie, however, you will put in a bowl:

1 package dry mincemeat (soaked according to directions)

or

2 or 3 cups bought moist mincemeat

Then add

1 cup peeled, cored, chopped, tart apples

½ cup seedless raisins

1 to 2 tablespoons grated orange rind

½ cup orange juice

½ cup chopped nutmeats

1 to 3 ounces (1 wineglass) brandy, whiskey, rum, or cider

More salt, if needed ⎱
More sugar if needed ⎰ Taste mixture, and see

Pinch of cinnamon (or cloves, or allspice, if desired)

These are the basic good flavorings to add. Keep tasting, keep adding, until the mixture tastes good to *you*. Yours is the family which is going to eat it.

When all ingredients are blended in large bowl, cover bowl, and store at least one night, in refrigerator, so flavors can blend.

To bake pie. Make entire

Master Recipe, Pastry (p. 446)

Roll dough to shape lower crust (p. 447). Fit crust into 9 inch pie plate. Turn mincemeat mixture into dish. Roll second half of dough to shape an upper crust (p. 448). Place slashed upper crust over pie; fold under the overhanging dough of top crust, underneath edge of lower crust. Fasten edges closed by using fork, or fluting (p. 448).

Bake in preheated hot (450°) oven 10 minutes; then reduce heat to 325°, slow, and continue baking about 35 minutes more, or until a wee bit of juice begins to ooze through slashes in crust.

Mince pie is most luscious served warm. If it has cooled and you wish to reheat it for another serving, place pie in slow (325°) oven 15 to 20 minutes, or just until heated through.

OTHER USES FOR PASTRY

Pastry Crusts for Meat Pies, or Casseroles

Half Master Recipe, Pastry (p. 446), will make a crust for the top of an 8 or 9 inch casserole or baking dish . . . or will make top crusts for 3 to 4 individual-size casseroles. See page 451, to make a "top crust," only.

Apple Dumplings

Half Master Recipe, Pastry (p. 446), will make two or three large apple dumplings . . . a hearty, delicious dessert.

Roll dough to a square or oblong sheet ⅛ inch thick. With knife, cut this sheet into square pieces about 4½ to 5 inches wide. In center of each pastry square, place 1 whole, peeled, cored, raw apple. Fill the cavity with sugar. On top of sugar, sprinkle few dashes cinnamon. Now bring corners of pastry square up over center top of apple, making the four points meet and overlap, to hold together. If necessary, moisten the points slightly with milk or water, to make them hold in place. Place dumplings on a pie plate or baking pan, and bake in hot oven (450°) for 10 minutes. Then reduce heat to slow (325°) and bake until apples are tender, about 20 to 30 minutes more. Remove from oven; let cool a few minutes; then decorate top of dumplings with a small amount of confectioners' frosting (p. 428). Serve while still warm.

CHAPTER XXXVI

Drinks "On the House"

METHOD FOR: *Coffee, Tea, Sugar Syrup, Fruit Drinks, Milk Drinks, Chocolate Drinks*

COFFEE

Coffee, a national survey shows, is our American men's favorite mealtime drink (and I do not think women lag far behind, in liking it). Yet the same survey indicates many men believe their wives *can't make* good coffee, and often go elsewhere to get it! Now this is a pretty state of affairs, indeed! For there is no mystery about making good coffee; it is no harder to make *good*, than *poor*. *You* be one who makes it clear, full-bodied, deliciously fresh and fragrant, every time. You'll never get more praise for anything, in your life!

Here are the important things to remember:

(1) Use a *good* brand; one rich in nature's best coffee flavor. Not all coffees have the same inherent strength.

(2) Buy the right *grind* for your type coffee-maker; see different methods (p. 469). Having the right grind aids in drawing out flavor from the bean.

(3) Buy coffee vacuum-sealed; or if you must buy it in paper containers, transfer the ground coffee at once to a covered canister or jar with tight-fitting lid. Open no more coffee than needed, at a time. Air steals away both fragrance and flavor from the coffee bean, leaving the coffee weak in taste and aroma. Some people

keep coffee stored in refrigerator, to help keep air from robbing it of flavor. This is an especially good idea in hot weather.

(4) When making coffee, use *enough* coffee; most people don't. Measure accurately, *allowing 2 level tablespoons coffee for each measuring cup of water*. If even this does not give you coffee of the strength you want, either (*a*) use a trifle more coffee; or (*b*) brew the coffee a bit longer; or (*c*) get a better brand.

(5) Don't try to mix methods of brewing. Stick to directions given on page 469 for whichever type coffee maker you own.

(6) Keep your coffee maker, and all its parts, clean. Wash it thoroughly, after each using. If you don't, a bitter oil will collect on all the parts, which makes the next lot of coffee taste unpleasant.

(7) Don't overcook coffee; this makes it bitter, by drawing out of the bean a bitter oil. Don't reheat it repeatedly; this also makes a bitter brew. Don't make it far in advance; no coffee improves upon standing, however good it may have been when first made.

How much coffee to make, at one time? Some experts claim a coffee maker only makes good coffee when used to full capacity (that is, to make the maximum number of cups it is capable of); but if you are given an 8-cup coffee maker for a wedding present, are you going to make 8 cups of coffee for each breakfast for two people? You will then always have at least half of it left over. And reheated coffee is never as good as fresh. So use your own judgment; make the number of cups you will use; or buy a smaller coffee maker to use just for two.

Rule for coffee proportions. The amount of brewed coffee you will have, when done, should be almost exactly equivalent to the number of cups of water you used to make it. First measure your water; then add sufficient ground coffee to give the liquid real flavor. The rule is: **1 measuring cup of water (½ pint) plus 2 level tablespoons ground coffee makes 1 very large, or 2 smaller cups, of brewed coffee.** This rule holds for any type of coffee maker.

THE FOUR DIFFERENT TYPES
OF COFFEE MAKERS

Coffee makers sold today are either (1) drip, (2) vacuum-type, (3) percolator, or (4) the old-fashioned plain coffeepot, for boiled coffee. Each method produces excellent coffee, if properly used.

People who like coffee crystal clear, free of all grounds, will prefer drip or vacuum-type coffee makers; but for complete freedom from grounds a filter cloth is needed. Some people, however, prefer the texture of percolator coffee. And many others still like good old-fashioned boiled coffee, the kind all our grandmothers used to make; this can be very good if not overcooked, and if grounds are allowed to settle before coffee is poured.

Drip Coffee Method

Description of coffee maker. Drip coffee makers may be of glass, china, metal, pottery. But they always have two sections, an upper section and a lower one, of about equal size. The floor of the upper section is always fitted with a strainer. In some coffee makers, a filter cloth is added, to hold back fine grounds.

Grind of coffee to use. Drip grind, or smaller.

To make your coffee. Have boiling *briskly,* in a teakettle or saucepan, the measured amount of water you will need for coffee (see Rule for Coffee Proportions on page 468).

Place top section of coffee maker firmly over lower section.

Into top section, measure **2 level tablespoons coffee** for each measuring cup of water you plan to use. Then pour the **briskly boiling, measured water** also into the top section. Put lid on top section. Let coffee maker stand until all liquid has dripped from upper to lower section. This usually takes 3 to 5 minutes, but depends on amount of liquid being used. (If desired, you may keep the coffee maker on an asbestos pad, over very low heat, while water drips through, to keep coffee warm; but *never let the dripping—or dripped—coffee boil*).

If coffee does not seem strong enough, after one dripping, you may pour the same liquid through the same coffee grounds a second time. Some people *always* put the water through the grounds twice.

If two drippings does not give you good strong coffee, you either have not measured the coffee accurately, or are not using a good brand.

Reheating leftover coffee is never recommended; but if you *must* reheat, *never let the coffee boil,* or it will become bitter.

Vacuum-Type Coffee Method

Description of coffee maker. Most vacuum-type coffee makers are made of glass; but some are all metal; some part metal, part glass; some part plastic. There is one type which is electric, and its cooking automatically regulated. All others must be used over a surface burner of your stove, or over an electric hot plate, and must be turned from high to low heat at the proper moment, so coffee will not boil over.

All of these coffee makers have two sections; an upper bowl, to hold the ground coffee, and a lower bowl to hold the water; there are some insignificant variations in different models. A tube connects the two parts, running from lower section to upper section. A filter cloth is provided to fit in the base of the upper section, to act as a strainer, preventing coffee grounds from dripping through into the lower bowl.

Many of these coffee makers come supplied with detailed directions for use, provided by the manufacturer. If yours has instructions, follow those carefully.

Grind of coffee to use. Drip grind; or pulverized, if stronger brew is desired.

To make your coffee. In bottom bowl of coffee maker, put the measured amount of **water** you need (see Rule for Coffee Proportions, page 468). Measure water by measuring cups. See that filter cloth is properly adjusted in upper section so no grounds can get through; then fit top bowl firmly onto lower bowl of coffee maker.

In upper bowl place the measured **coffee,** allowing 2 level tablespoons coffee for each measuring cup of water used.

Place coffee maker over moderate to high heat. Let water heat until it boils up through tube into upper bowl, where it comes in contact with the ground coffee. (A few tablespoons of water which lie below the tube will not rise; this is all right.) As soon as the water has boiled to upper bowl, turn off heat. Stir coffee well, once, in upper bowl. Let coffee maker stand over heating unit (but with heat *turned off*) until all water drips down into lower bowl again; (this usually takes 5 or 6 minutes, depending on amount of water used). Then remove top bowl containing grounds, and serve coffee at once. If necessary to reheat coffee, place lower section over *very low heat;* do not put the upper section on again.

If still stronger coffee is wanted, next time let the hot water agitate around the coffee grounds in upper bowl about 1 additional minute, before turning heat off; but take care coffee does not boil over; you will have to watch it carefully for this minute. Then turn off heat, and let it drip down as usual.

During the coffee shortage of the last war, some people made it a practice to send the water up into the upper bowl *twice,* instead of once, to obtain greater flavor from the scarce grounds; this however may produce a slightly bitter flavor.

Vacuum-type coffee — like all other coffee — is best if served very shortly after brewing; no coffee improves on standing long.

Percolator Method

Description of coffee maker. Percolator pots are made of metal, or enamel, or agate. Some are meant for use on surface burner of your stove; some are electric.

Inside, there is always a perforated container to hold the ground coffee. This container should have a cover. The container is raised on top of a long tube. Water is put into the bottom of the pot; then when pot is placed over heat, the water boils up through the tube, hits a glass inset in the lid of the coffee maker, trickles back down through the grounds in the container. This action recurs time after time, until coffee has the strength you like.

In the usual stove-type percolator (valveless), percolating action begins only when water reaches boiling point. In electric (valve-type) percolators, percolating begins within 2 or 3 minutes of turning on heat, and the water never actually boils. But either type makes good coffee.

Grind to use. Regular or drip grind. Drip grind gives more strength.

To make your coffee. Into bottom of pot, put **measured cold water** (see Rule for Coffee Proportions, page 468). Measure water by measuring cup. In perforated container, place **coffee** — 2 level tablespoons for each measuring cup of water used. Place lid on perforated container. Close coffee pot with its lid. Place pot over moderate to high heat. Counting from time when water begins perking and shows a trace of color, reduce heat somewhat and allow 7 to 10 minutes more of *gentle* perking; *do not let coffee boil too vigorously,* or it will become bitter.

Remove coffee from heat, and let pot stand a minute or two, before pouring; this allows any loose grounds to settle to bottom of pot, instead of rushing into your coffee cup.

If necessary to reheat, do it over *low heat; do not boil again.*

If you do not get proper strength from this method, "perk" coffee a minute or so longer; or try a finer grade of coffee.

Boiled Coffee

Description of coffee maker. This is the true, old-fashioned coffeepot — just a pot with cover, no gadgets included. It may be of metal, enamel, or agate.

In the old days, coffee was put loose into the pot, right along with the water, and both brought to a boil together. Nowadays, if you can find them at some hardware store, you can buy perforated aluminum coffee containers (somewhat like an oversize metal tea ball) to hold the ground coffee; but even if coffee is enclosed in these, the containers are still put right down into the pot with the water. All such pots are intended for use over surface burner of stove, or open fire.

Grind to use. Regular grind; drip grind for greater strength.

To make your coffee. Into bottom of pot measure your **ground coffee,** allowing 2 level tablespoons coffee for each measuring cup of water to be used. (See Rule for Coffee Proportions, page 468.) Add **measured cold water.** Close coffeepot with lid. Place over medium to high heat, and bring cold water to a boil. As soon as coffee has boiled 1 minute, turn off heat. Stir coffee. Keep pot standing where coffee will keep warm, for about 5 minutes, allowing water to draw flavor out of the grounds; *but do not continue boiling coffee,* or you will make the brew bitter.

If the above does not produce coffee of strength enough to suit you, allow coffee to remain over heat about 1 minute extra time; or use a better grade coffee.

Old-timers often put an empty egg shell in the coffeepot, along with the water; this was to "settle the grounds." Some people add a dash of cold water immediately after removing coffee from heat, for the same purpose. If desired, boiled coffee may be strained through fine cheesecloth before serving; but usually all grounds will have settled to bottom of pot by the time coffee has stood 5 minutes, and it is only necessary to pour carefully.

COFFEE VARIATIONS

Demitasse

When serving tiny-sized "after dinner" cups of coffee, coffee should be definitely stronger. Make it by any of the four preceding methods, but increase coffee proportion to: **3 tablespoons coffee** for **every measuring cup water** used.

Good Iced Coffee

To be truly delicious, iced coffee must be *double*-strength, since chilling somewhat reduces coffee flavor. If making it on short notice, make coffee by any of the four preceding methods, but either double the amount of coffee used, or use only half the usual amount of water. The proportion should be: **4 tablespoons coffee** for **every measuring cup water** used.

Pour hot coffee into tall glasses filled with cracked ice, or ice cubes. NOTE: If you put a silver spoon in the glass before pouring the hot coffee, glass will not crack.

Serve with **powdered sugar** and **cream, or whipped cream.**

Coffee ice-cube method. If you are preparing your iced coffee some hours before it will be served, make **coffee** of usual strength, but make two potfuls. Pour one pot cooked coffee into ice-cube trays; freeze this coffee into coffee ice cubes. Pour the other pot of cooked coffee into a pitcher, and place this in refrigerator to cool. At serving time, fill tall glasses with coffee ice cubes, then cover cubes with cool coffee. Serve with **powdered sugar,** and **cream,** or **whipped cream.**

TEA

To some people tea is a fetish; to others, a matter of no great importance. A "good" cup of tea is, in the end, *tea that suits you* . . . both in flavor and in strength.

Proportions for making tea. The amount of brewed tea you will have depends on the amount of water you use. A good general rule for tea is: **1 level teaspoon** (or 1 teabag) **tea** for **each cup water,** plus **1 level teaspoon** (or teabag) "for the pot."

Rules for Making Good Tea

(1) Keep tea in tightly covered canister, to keep it fresh until using. "Stale" tea has poor flavor.

(2) Keep teapot clean. An unwashed teapot has a strong, unpleasant taste. Wash yours after each using.

(3) Before making any tea, *preheat* the teapot, by letting it stand about 4 or 5 minutes, filled with good hot water. This is important. If pot is cold, it will chill the boiling water used for tea, and you will not only get colder tea, but tea of less flavor.

(4) While teapot becomes warm, heat in saucepan or teakettle the amount of **water** you want. Bring this water to a brisk, bubbling boil. It should be bubbling hard when poured over the tea leaves.

(5) Put **measured tea** (or tea bags) into warm, emptied teapot. (If desired, you can buy a metal tea ball to hold loose tea leaves, so as to avoid straining tea when pouring.) Pour over tea the hard-boiling water. Cover teapot.

(6) Let tea stand (not over heat) for 3 to 6 minutes, to "steep" (that is, to acquire strength and flavor). If desired to hurry it, stir the tea around in the hot water, with spoon, until of right strength.

(7) If tea becomes overly strong, you can "thin" it to normal by adding more boiling water.

(8) Don't let tea stand in the water too long, or brew will become bitter.

(9) Pour tea through strainer, if tea has been put loose into pot.

(10) To serve, add **sugar** and a **thin slice of lemon,** if desired. Or try with **milk** or **thin cream.**

TEA VARIATIONS

Iced Tea

If iced tea disappears in other homes in summer the way it does in mine, gallons must be kept on hand!

This brew has much to recommend it, however. It is quick to make; inexpensive; can be given many different flavors (by adding mint, fruit, or mixing it with other liquids); and is something which can be offered alike to young and old. It is really bracing on a hot day.

It has an extra advantage to me. Every time I make great pitchers of it, to have on hand . . . the heat wave stops. Like carrying an umbrella, to stop the rain. See if it works for you.

Quick Iced Tea. Most people want iced tea in a hurry. To do this, make your tea by the usual brewing method for hot tea (p. 474) but make it a little stronger, so the tea will withstand dilution by ice without losing all flavor.

Into teapot, measure **2 level teaspoons tea leaves** (or use 2 tea bags) for **each measuring cup boiling water** to be used. Allow one measuring cup water for each tall glass of iced tea desired. Over tea leaves, pour your separately heated, *hard-boiling* water. Let tea stand, to steep, 5 to 6 minutes. Strain. Pour into glasses filled with cracked ice, or ice cubes. (NOTE: If you put a silver spoon into glass while pouring the hot liquid, glass will not crack.) Stir, to cool quickly. See different flavorings, below:

Sweet Tea. If everyone in your family likes a sweet iced tea, add sugar to taste while tea is *still hot,* before icing. The sweetness of the sugar will much better permeate the brew *while tea is warm.* Add as much sugar as pleases your family taste. If desired, you can add a **few drops lemon juice,** or a **slice or two of lemon,** to cut too sickly sweet a flavor.

Tart, Dry Iced Tea. For those who *dislike* sweet-flavored drinks, omit sugar altogether from warm tea, or allow only about 1 teaspoon sugar for 2 people. When tea is partly cooled, stir in **1 teaspoon to 1 tablespoon strained lemon juice** (or even lime juice) for each glass of iced tea. Pour tea into glasses filled with ice cubes. Add a **sprig of fresh mint** for each glass if possible. This improves the flavor greatly. For "playboy" guests, stir in a **few drops of rum,** if you have it; this makes them think they're having a great day.

Fruity Iced Tea. Even teen-agers enjoy iced tea if it has a somewhat sweet, fruity taste. To do this, while tea is *still hot,* add **sugar** enough to make the drink sweet (judge by your own taste). Stir well. Then cool tea somewhat. Before entirely cold, add some **¼ inch thick slices of orange** and **slices of lemon.** Stir well. Add a **sprig or two of mint.** Continue chilling, in glasses or pitcher full of ice cubes. The warm liquid will have drawn out the sweet flavor of sugar, and also the fruit flavors, so that tea takes on quite a "fruity" taste. In my home, we keep pitchers of this sort of tea in the refrigerator; but every time I look, the pitchers need refilling.

SUGAR SYRUPS FOR FRUIT DRINKS

Plain Sugar Syrup

In making cool drinks it is often better to add sugar syrup than sugar; it is less gritty. Make some of this and keep it handy in your refrigerator. Mix in saucepan **2 cups granulated sugar** plus **2 cups water.** Place over heat, stirring until liquid comes to a boil. Cover. Then boil 5 minutes without stirring. Cool. Store in covered glass jar and use as needed, to combine with fruit juices.

Mint Sugar Syrup

Make just like sugar syrup (p. 476), but add **1 bunch fresh mint** to syrup while it boils. Strain out mint before storing syrup in jar.

QUICK FRUIT DRINKS

Lemonade

(For 4 people.) Squeeze **½ cup lemon juice;** strain out pits. Add **½ cup granulated sugar** or sugar syrup. Add **4 cups cold** water. Stir. Pour over ice cubes. Garnish with mint, slice of lime or orange, or a red or green maraschino cherry.

Orangeade

(For 4 people.) Squeeze **1 cup orange juice;** strain out pits. Add **2 tablespoons strained lemon juice, for tang.** Add **½ cup sugar** syrup. Add **2 cups cold** water (or if preferred, substitute club soda water). Stir well. Serve over ice cubes; garnish with sprig **of mint,** and a **slice of orange** or lemon.

Raspberry-Mint Drink

Combine **1 cup raspberry jam** with **2 cups mint sugar syrup** (see above). Heat, stirring until jam softens and blends with syrup. Cool. Add **½ cup strained lemon juice.** Then add **2 cups plain cold water** or club soda water. Stir, and pour over ice cubes. Decorate each glass with a sprig of mint. Makes 4 tall glasses.

MILK DRINKS

Hot Chocolate

This delicious drink can be made either with melted baking chocolate, or with powdered cocoa. Both chocolate and cocoa are derived from the cocoa bean, but chocolate is a little richer because it contains natural cocoa butter, which has had to be removed from the substance to produce powdered cocoa.

The trouble with many hot chocolates purchased in drugstores is chiefly that they are made *with water* as the liquid. Water gives this beverage a thin, unsatisfying taste. If possible, make yours *with milk*, especially for children, since milk is more nourishing. (If you have no milk, you can use half evaporated milk, half water.)

If hot chocolate is served only rarely in your home, you had better make it separately for each occasion; but if in fairly constant demand, you can save a lot of trouble by making chocolate syrup (p. 479), to store in your refrigerator; then any time you want hot chocolate, you simply pour into a cup a couple of tablespoons of the syrup, and add hot milk.

Hot Chocolate made with Chocolate. (For immediate serving; serves 3). Put **1 square (1 ounce) baking chocolate** plus **½ cup water** in top section of a double boiler; place this directly over moderate heat and stir constantly (chocolate will burn, if you don't) until chocolate is entirely melted and blended with the water. Now add **few grains salt**, plus **1½ tablespoons granulated sugar**, and cook gently about 4 minutes, stirring continually so chocolate will not burn and so sugar will completely dissolve. Remove from heat. Stir in gradually **1½ cups whole milk** (or ¾ cup evaporated milk plus ¾ cup water). Now place this pan over lower section of your double boiler, containing about 1½ inches hot water. Place over heat until whole chocolate mixture is hot enough to serve. *Do not let milk boil;* boiled milk changes flavor and forms a "skin" which looks unattractive. Stir, and pour into cups. Top each cup, if desired, with a whole **marshmallow** or a tablespoon **whipped cream** (p. 408).

Hot Chocolate made with Cocoa. (For immediate serving; serves 3). In top section of double boiler, combine **3 tablespoons cocoa, 3 tablespoons granulated sugar, ¾ cup water**, plus a **few grains salt**. Place pan over direct heat; stir contents until smooth, then cook, still stirring, about 2 minutes more. Remove from heat. Add **2 cups whole milk** (or 1 cup evaporated milk plus 1 cup water), and stir well to blend. Now put the pan over the lower section of double boiler, containing about 1½ inches hot water.

Place over heat. Heat mixture thoroughly (but do not let milk boil). Pour into cups. Top each cup, if desired, with a **marshmallow**, or 1 tablespoon whipped cream (p. 408).

Chocolate Syrup for Refrigerator (Made with Cocoa)

In saucepan, combine **½ cup powdered cocoa, 1 cup granulated sugar, ⅛ teaspoon salt**. Stir to mix. Then stir in just a **little hot water** (about ½ cup) to make a thick syrupy mixture. Cook gently over moderate heat about 5 minutes, stirring constantly, until sugar is completely dissolved. Cool. Pour mixture into a clean pint jar; cover and store in refrigerator. This syrup keeps a long time. When hot cocoa is wanted, pour 2 to 3 tablespoons this syrup into a cup, add hot milk, stir, and serve.

NOTE: This syrup can also be used cold as topping for ice cream, cake and puddings, or to make milk shakes, frosteds and sodas. For cold use, most people add to the cooled syrup a **few drops vanilla extract.**

Malted Milk

There are several kinds of malted milk mixtures sold in powdered form in stores. They are simple to combine with fresh milk. Follow package directions.

NOTE: Malt is very nourishing, a rich source of B vitamins; it is excellent for children, and a fine "builder-upper" for any one.

CHAPTER XXXVII

You Can Make Cookies

METHODS FOR: *Sugar Cookies (Many Flavors); Drop Cookies, Refrigerator (Sliced) Cookies, Cut-out Cookies; Decorating Cookies; Filled Cookies; Gingersnaps; Cereal Cookies; Meringues, Macaroons, Kisses; Brownies*

Some rainy afternoon, try cookies! To be sure, you can buy them . . . but homemade are better. They lend a holiday feeling to any dark day . . . to any plain cup of tea . . . to any sip of hot coffee. And they make children's eyes shine.

We give here just a few basic kinds: sugar cookies (with many possible variations); cereal cookies, gingersnaps, macaroons and meringues, brownies. You'll come across thousands more recipes in other books, in newspapers, in magazines; for everybody has a favorite cookie recipe. But those given here are the cookies most families like most, and if you try each in turn, you'll soon have a cookie repertoire to do you proud.

MASTER RECIPE #86
SUGAR COOKIES

(Makes 50 to 60 small cookies)

To mix cookies

Put in mixing bowl

½ cup soft (not melted) butter (or other shortening)

Beat into butter, one by one

1 cup sugar

1 egg
1 teaspoon vanilla
1 tablespoon milk or cream

In another bowl, sift first, then measure

1½ cups flour

Sift same flour again, adding with it

1 teaspoon double-acting baking powder
½ teaspoon salt

Mix dry ingredients into moist ingredients. Beat or stir well, to blend.

That's your cookie dough. Now there are three ways to shape the cookies; take your choice.

To shape cookies

(1) *Drop cookies.* Drop cookie dough, by teaspoonful, 1 inch apart, on lightly greased cookie sheet, using spatula to push dough off tip of spoon if necessary. (If you use a wet teaspoon, dough will come off spoon more easily.) If dough seems extremely stiff, you may thin it a little by adding 1 or 2 more tablespoons cream or milk; but the dough should be thick enough to stay put in the spot where you place it on baking sheet, without running. In baking, however, the dough will thin and spread out more, so leave room around each cookie. If you wish to decorate cookies, do it now, before baking; see page 482.

(2) *Sliced cookies.* These require firmer dough. So add to dough you have already mixed an additional ¼ cup sifted flour. Blend well. Now divide dough into two equal parts. Flour hands, and shape each half of dough into a long roll, 1½ inches in diameter. Wrap each roll firmly in waxed paper. Place both rolls in refrigerator several hours, or overnight, until roll is firm. Remove waxed paper. Then with sharp knife, slice off ⅛ inch thick slices. Place these on lightly greased baking sheet. If you wish to decorate cookies (see page 482) add decorations now, before baking.

(3) *Cut-out cookies* (cut into shapes with cookie-cutter). These cookies require firmer dough; so to dough of Master Recipe which you have already mixed, add ¼ cup additional flour; blend well. Now chill dough in refrigerator 1 hour or more, until well chilled.

(Chilled dough rolls more easily, without sticking to board; and you do not want to add any more flour than necessary in rolling, since too much flour makes cookies dry and less tender.) Flour a large board lightly; flour rolling pin. Use only ⅓ dough at one time; re-place remainder in refrigerator, to keep chilled. Roll out the first lot of dough to sheet ⅛ inch thick. Dip cookie cutter in flour; cut cookies. Dip cookie cutter in flour often enough so dough won't stick to it. When you have cut as many cookies as you have dough for, remove remnants of dough; lift cut-out cookies with spatula or pancake turner; place them on lightly greased baking sheet. If you wish to decorate them (see below) do it now, before baking. Gather up remnants of dough; reshape it into a ball; roll out again to thin sheet; cut more cookies.

To bake cookies

Place baking sheet containing cookies in preheated moderate (375°) oven about 8 to 12 minutes, or until cookies begin to turn golden color on top. Don't overcook. Cookies become crisper as they cool. Cool 10 minutes on baking sheet. Then lift cookies to wire racks to finish cooling. Store in covered cookie jar or covered tin box.

To Decorate Cookies, If Desired

For sliced or round cookies. Before baking, you may decorate top of cookies with any edible trimming which will not make cookie *wet.* Press the decoration lightly into the dough, so it will adhere. One recipe cookie dough may be divided into 4 or 5 parts, and each lot of cookies decorated differently, thus making an exciting assortment. Use any of the following, or invent decorations of your own:

Center in top	½ shelled walnut or pecan, or
of cookie:	2 or 3 semisweet chocolate bits, sold for baking purposes, or
	1 candied cherry, cut like a star, or flower, or in half, or
	½ pitted date, or
	2 or 3 bits of candied ginger, or

1 small piece well-drained canned pineapple or apricot

Or sprinkle top of cookie with: Shredded coconut (this may be dyed pink, green, or any fancy color with vegetable food color before being placed on cookie), or

Grated orange rind, or

Colored sugar beads, or

Plain granulated sugar

For birthdays: Make your husband's or child's monogram on top of cookies, with raisins

Or, with raisins, or dried seedless currants, make the figure 4 for a fourth birthday, 5 for a fifth, and so on.

For Christmas: On top of cookie, make:

A poinsettia, using candied cherry for the flower, candied citron for leaves, or

A wreath, using bits of candied cherry for holly berries, candied citron for leaves, or

A star, designed with silver or gold colored sugar beads, or

A Christmas bell, outlined in raisins or sugar beads, or bits of candied cherry

For cookies cut out in shapes. Use any decorations you please which will not make the cookie *wet* . . . and which will carry out the idea of the shape of the cookie. For example:

Star cookies: Sprinkle with gold or silver sugar beads, or with fine granulated sugar, to give the effect of "shining."

Animal shapes: Use raisins for eyes; a bit of candied cherry for mouth. For reindeer and bears, sprinkle a bit of granulated sugar over animal's back to look like snow. For sheep, press into cookie dough some shredded coconut to look like wool.

Christmas tree shapes: Decorate with bits of bright-colored candied fruit, or with colored sugar beads, to look like ornaments. Add snowy effect, if desired, by sprinkling with granulated sugar.

SUGAR COOKIES OF OTHER FLAVORS

(Follow Master Recipe #86, Sugar Cookies, page 480, making changes below.)

Master Recipe, Sugar Cookies can be altered in various small ways to make cookies of many different flavors. It is astonishing how different each flavor tastes; try it. Everyone will think you have a great repertoire!

Chocolate Cookies

Add **2 squares baking chocolate** (which you have melted in saucer over small bowl of boiling water) with milk or cream; and increase flour to **1¾ cups** for drop cookies, or to **2 cups** for sliced or cut-out cookies.

Butterscotch Cookies

Use **butter** for shortening. (You can't make butterscotch without butter!) This time, *melt* the butter in saucepan over moderate heat, adding to it **1 cup brown sugar**. Stir over heat until sugar melts. Cool this mixture. Then add milk and egg; omit white sugar and vanilla. Add dry ingredients as usual.

Maple Cookies

Substitute **maple sugar** instead of white sugar. (If maple sugar is hard, pound it in paper bag, with rolling pin, until crushed; then roll it with rolling pin, until fine.) Or make cookies as usual with white sugar, and use **½ teaspoon maple flavoring** instead of vanilla.

Nut Cookies

When dough is mixed, fold in **½ cup coarsely chopped nut meats**. Or add nutmeats to chocolate, butterscotch, or maple-flavored cookie dough. NOTE: If including nuts, it is best to make drop cookies or sliced cookies; dough containing nutmeats is difficult to roll thin, for cut-out cookies.

Chocolate Bit Cookies

Use either white or brown sugar, or half of each. When dough is mixed, fold in 1 package chocolate bits. Fold in also, if desired, ½ cup chopped nut meats. These are best made as drop cookies, since the chunky ingredients make the dough difficult to roll or slice.

Ginger Cookies

Add ½ to 1 teaspoon powdered ginger with flour. If desired, fold into mixed dough 2 tablespoons finely chopped candied ginger, also.

Lemon Cookies

Omit vanilla; substitute ½ teaspoon lemon extract. Use hot water instead of milk or cream. With flour, add 3 teaspoons grated lemon rind, if you like a strong lemon flavor.

Orange Cookies

Omit vanilla and cream, substituting 1 tablespoon strained orange juice. With flour, add grated rind from one bright-colored, blemish-free orange. Tip: decorate shaped cookies with shredded coconut before baking.

Almond Cookies

Instead of vanilla, use ½ teaspoon almond extract; add a drop or two of lemon extract. Omit milk or cream; substitute hot water. With flour, add grated rind of ½ lemon. When dough is mixed, fold in ½ cup chopped blanched almonds (p. 503). Bake as drop cookies.

Caraway Seed Cookies

When dough is mixed, stir in 1½ tablespoons caraway seeds.

Spice Cookies

Instead of vanilla, substitute ¼ teaspoon lemon extract, or few drops walnut or maple flavoring. With flour, add ½ teaspoon cinnamon, ¼ teaspoon nutmeg. When dough is mixed, if desired, stir in ½ cup seedless raisins, or chopped nutmeats. Bake as drop cookies.

Coconut Cookies

When dough is mixed fold in ⅔ cup shredded coconut. Bake as drop cookies.

Date or Fig Cookies

When dough is mixed, fold into it ½ cup finely chopped dates, or figs. If desired add also ½ cup chopped nut meats. Bake as drop cookies.

Filled Cookies

When mixing dough, add an extra ¼ cup flour. Make dough into two rolls 1½ inches in diameter (see Sliced Cookies, p. 481); chill rolls in refrigerator until firm. Then unwrap; cut off ⅛ inch thick slices. Place half the slices on lightly greased baking sheet. On top of each of these slices place 1 teaspoon jam or jelly. Cover each with a plain slice; then press upper and lower slices together with tines of fork, all the way around outer edge, holding the jam or jelly firmly inside. Place cookies on greased baking sheet. Bake in moderate (375°) oven 12 to 15 minutes, or until golden color. Cool on pans 10 to 20 minutes.

OTHER CUT-OUT COOKIES

Gingersnaps

(Makes 30 to 50, depending on cutter. These cookies are *not* made by sugar cookie recipe.) Heat ⅓ cup molasses to boiling point and pour it over 3 tablespoons shortening. Sift together 1⅛ cups flour, ⅛ teaspoon soda, ½ teaspoon salt, and 1 teaspoon powdered ginger. Mix sifted dry ingredients into molasses-shortening mixture. Chill dough in refrigerator 1 hour; then turn onto floured board. With floured rolling pin, roll dough to sheet ⅛ inch thick. Cut out cookies with floured cookie cutter, to make Christmas trees, gingerbread men, stars, or just plain rounds. Remember to do any decorating before baking — you can decorate gingerbread men by using raisins for eyes, a strip of candied citron for nose, and a bit of candied cherry for mouth. Press the fruits in place on each cookie lightly, with finger tips. Place cookies on greased baking sheet, and bake as on p. 482.

CEREAL COOKIES

Cereal cookies are wholesome and delicious, and provide a means of getting Vitamin B into youngsters who balk at eating breakfasts. Try them. They're good.

Oatmeal Cookies (Drop Cookies)

(Makes about 40 to 50 cookies.) Into 1 cup hot cooked oatmeal, melt 3 tablespoons shortening. Mix in thoroughly ½ cup molasses, 1 cup sugar, ½ cup raisins, ½ cup chopped nuts. Sift, then add to oatmeal mixture, ¾ teaspoon cinnamon, ½ teaspoon soda, and 1½ cups cake flour (or 1⅓ cups all-purpose flour). If batter is too moist to drop well, blend in another ¼ to ⅓ cup flour. Drop dough by teaspoonfuls onto well-greased cookie sheet, 1 inch apart. Bake in preheated moderate (350°) oven for 10 to 12 minutes. Then remove from baking sheet to wire rack to cool.

Crisp Oatmeal Wafers (Sliced Cookies)

(Makes 4 or 5 dozen, depending on size.) To ½ cup soft shortening, add 1 cup sugar and beat well. Stir in 2 cups uncooked rolled oats. Add ½ cup milk and ½ teaspoon vanilla, and blend in. Sift together 1½ cups cake flour (or 1⅓ cups all-purpose flour), ½ teaspoon soda, ½ teaspoon cinnamon, dash of nutmeg, and ¼ teaspoon salt. Stir into oatmeal mixture, a little at a time. Blend well. Turn dough onto lightly floured board; divide dough into two equal parts. With floured hands, shape each part into a long roll about 1½ inches in diameter. Wrap each roll firmly in waxed paper and store in refrigerator several hours, until firm. Then, with sharp, floured knife, cut off slices ⅛ inch thick. Place slices on greased cookie sheet. Bake in preheated moderate (350°) oven, about 10 minutes. When done, remove from baking sheet to wire rack to cool. Cookies become crisper during cooling.

Peanut Delights (Drop Cookies)

(Makes about 6 dozen cookies.) These cookies are made with oatmeal and cornflakes. To 1 cup soft shortening add 2 eggs. Beat until light. Then mix in 1 cup white sugar, 1 cup brown sugar, 1 cup cornflakes, 2 cups uncooked rolled oats, 1 cup chopped, salted peanuts, 1 cup chopped or whole raisins, 2 cups sifted cake flour (or 1¾ cups all-purpose flour), and 1 teaspoon soda. Blend thoroughly. Drop dough by teaspoonfuls 1 inch apart onto greased cookie sheet. Bake in preheated moderate (350°) oven 12 to 15 minutes. Remove cookies from baking sheet to wire racks to cool.

Crunchies (Drop Cookies)

(Makes about 5 dozen cookies.) These are made with cornflakes. Into ½ cup soft butter, beat 1 egg, then 2 cups brown sugar. Mix well. Add 5 cups cornflakes, 1 cup coconut, and 1 cup chopped pecans (or other nuts). Mix thoroughly. Drop dough 1 inch apart, by teaspoonfuls, onto buttered cookie sheet. Bake in preheated moderate (350°) oven about 10 minutes. Remove cookies from baking sheet to wire rack to cool.

Chocolate Surprises (Not cooked!)

(Makes about 3 dozen.) Melt ½ pound semisweet chocolate in bowl placed over saucepan of hot water, then remove from heat. While chocolate is still warm, fold into it very gently 3 cups cornflakes (or some other small-size dry breakfast cereal which needs no cooking). When all bits of cereal have been well coated with chocolate, drop mixture by teaspoonfuls onto platters or pans lined with waxed paper. Set into refrigerator to chill, until chocolate coating hardens. Children love these.

MERINGUES AND MACAROONS

A meringue mixture is only beaten whites of eggs, with granulated sugar very gradually added and beaten in, and a bit of flavoring added.

It is very simple to make. Anybody can do it who can beat with a wire whisk or rotary beater for about 4 or 5 minutes; yet it always gives the effect of being something quite tricky and elegant.

Once you know how to make this delightful concoction, you can apply its use to (a) meringue topping for a pie; (b) meringue shells, to hold fruit or ice cream; (c) "kisses"; (d) macaroons (which are meringue plus a few added ingredients).

So why not learn it right now?

MASTER RECIPE #87
MERINGUE

Master Recipe makes enough meringue for (a) topping for 1 pie; or (b) 4 to 6 meringue shells (individual servings); or (c) 6 to 8 kisses.

Remember these things, about meringue:

Eggs will separate (p. 260) best when first removed from refrigerator. But let the whites come to room temperature before beating, for best volume and finest results.

Sugar must be added little by little, and beaten in well after each addition, so that egg whites hold up. Too much weight of sugar at one time would collapse the tiny air cells beaten into the egg whites.

Meringues should be baked in a *slow* oven if you want them pleasingly dry and crisp. If you want them soft, they are baked in a moderately hot oven.

To mix meringue.

Have in large bowl, at room temperature

2 egg whites

Add

      1 pinch salt

      1 pinch cream of tartar (or ¼ teaspoon vinegar)

      ½ teaspoon vanilla (may be omitted)

Using wire whisk or rotary beater, whip egg whites until they make a *stiff foam*.

Now begin adding — 1 teaspoon at a time — and beating well after each addition

4 to 8 tablespoons sugar

(Amount of sugar depends somewhat on your taste but it is usual to use 4 to 6 tablespoons for pie topping, 6 to 8 tablespoons when making meringue shells or kisses.)

When finished beating, meringue should be stiff enough to stand up in moist, shining peaks, without losing shape. Keep beating until it does; but not until it loses its "gloss" and looks dry.

MERINGUE VARIATIONS

(*Make Master Recipe #87, Meringue, page 489, then use it to make any of the following.*)

Meringue Pie Topping

See directions under Meringue-Topped Pies (p. 460), for how to spread meringue on pie, and how to bake it.

Meringue Shells

Preheat oven to slow (275°). Grease a cookie sheet. Drop meringue mixture, by rounded tablespoonful, 2 inches apart, on cookie sheet. With back of tablespoon, swirl each mound of meringue into a round shape. Then, with back of spoon again, press a hollow into the center of each mound (the hollow should be large enough to hold your cut fruit or berries or ice cream, or whatever you plan to put into the finished shells, as filling). Place baking sheet in oven, and bake 45 to 55 minutes, until meringues are crisp and dry on surface, when tested with finger tip. Some people leave them in oven until they acquire a light golden tinge. Others remove them while they are still as near snow-white as possible. After removing from oven, let them cool on baking sheet. When cooled, they will come loose (if sheet was properly greased!) with a gentle lift with spatula or pancake turner. Handle them very gently; they crumble easily.

If making these in advance (they keep several days), do **not** store in covered tin box, but leave exposed to air, on a plate in a closet. You *want* them to keep dry.

To fill. Just before serving, fill hollow of each shell with sweetened fresh berries and whipped cream; or with cut fresh peaches and perhaps rum-flavored sweetened whipped cream; or with a scoop of ice cream, topped with grated bitter chocolate, or coconut, or chopped nuts. Very, very de luxe. And a dessert you can make well ahead of time, and simply put together at the last moment.

Kisses

Preheat oven to slow (275°). Grease a cookie or baking sheet. Drop meringue mixture, by rounded teaspoonful, 1 inch apart, on sheet. With tip of back of teaspoon, after mounds are on baking sheet, shape each mound into a pretty, swirly, round shape. Put baking sheet in oven. Bake 40 to 50 minutes, or until meringue feels dry and crisp on surface, when touched with finger tip. Let kisses cool on baking pan. Lift carefully, when cooled, with spatula. Do not store in covered tin box, but leave on open plate, in closet, exposed to air.

MACAROONS

(*To make Macaroons, follow same* **method** *as in Master Recipe #87, Meringue, page 489, but reducing eggs and adding ingredients as below.*)

Peanut Macaroons

Make Master Recipe, Meringue, but use only **1 egg white**. Omit vanilla. Beat in only **4 tablespoons sugar**. When finished beating, fold in ⅓ **cup chopped, roasted peanuts** (minus skins). Drop mixture by teaspoonfuls, 1 inch apart, on buttered baking sheet. Bake in slow (275°) oven 12 to 15 minutes, until macaroons are partly dry, and will hold their shape. Remove from baking sheet with spatula while still hot.

Coconut Macaroons

Make Master Recipe, Meringue, but use only **1 egg white**. Beat in **6 tablespoons sugar**. When finished beating, fold in **½ cup shredded coconut**. Drop mixture by teaspoonful 1 inch apart, on buttered baking sheet. Bake in slow (275°) oven 12 to 15 minutes, until they are partly dry and will hold their shape. Remove from baking sheet with spatula while still hot.

Cornflake Macaroons

Make Master Recipe, Meringue, but use only **1 egg white**. Reduce vanilla to **¼ teaspoon**. Add **¼ teaspoon almond extract**. Beat in **6 to 8 tablespoons sugar**. When finished beating, fold in **½ cup shredded coconut**, plus **1 cup cornflakes**. Drop mixture by teaspoonful, 1 inch apart, onto buttered baking sheet. Bake in preheated slow (275°) oven 12 to 15 minutes, or until partly dry and macaroons will hold their shape.

Chocolate Nut Macaroons

Make Master Recipe, Meringue, but use only **1 egg white**. Omit vanilla. Beat in **8 tablespoons sugar**. Have cool **1 square unsweetened chocolate** which you have melted in saucer or small bowl over a pan of boiling water. When finished beating meringue, stir in the cool melted chocolate; then fold in **½ cup shredded coconut**. Drop mixture by teaspoonful, 1 inch apart, on buttered baking sheet. Bake in slow (275°) oven 12 to 15 minutes, or until partly dry and macaroons will hold their shape.

BROWNIES

Chocolate-Flavor Brownies

In top of double boiler, over lower section containing boiling water, melt together **2 squares (2 ounces) baking chocolate** and **½ cup butter**. Meanwhile, in a bowl, mix and beat **2 eggs**, **1 teaspoon vanilla**, **1¼ cups brown sugar** (firmly packed). Sift; then add to egg mixture **¾ cup cake flour**, **¼ teaspoon salt**. Combine all ingredients; then stir in ½ cup chopped nut meats. Turn batter into buttered 8 x 8 x 2 inch cake pan, lined with waxed paper. Bake in slow (325°) oven about 30 minutes. Cool in pan. When cool, cut into bars or squares. Very simple. And *good*.

Butterscotch-Flavor Brownies

In saucepan, melt together, then cool ½ cup butter and 1 cup dark brown sugar (this makes butterscotch syrup). When above mixture is cool, beat into it 1 egg, ½ teaspoon vanilla, ¾ cup sifted cake flour, ½ teaspoon double-acting baking powder, ¼ teaspoon salt. If desired, fold in ½ cup nut meats, chopped. Bake as for chocolate-flavor brownies, but in moderate (350°) oven, 30 minutes. Cool in pan. Cut into bars or squares.

CHAPTER XXXVIII

You Can Make Holiday Plum
Pudding, and Fruit Cake

METHOD FOR: *The Plum Pudding of the Kings of England, Dark Fruit Cake, How to "Candy" Fruit, How to Blanch and Toast Almonds*

TO YOU, HAPPY HOLIDAYS!

Before the first Thanksgiving turkey has met his no doubt surprising end, magazines, newspapers, and radio all will be surfeiting you with so many suggestions for bought or homemade plum puddings and fruit cakes that we are not going to burden you with more, here . . . only two very choice ones.

Be warned that making any plum pudding or fruit cake is not hard, but requires a deal of preparation; there are many ingredients to be diced, chopped, or otherwise made ready for the grand mixing.

Be cheered that plum pudding or fruit cake can be (often is) made days, even weeks ahead of time, so even the busiest mother can fit its making in, somewhere. Such desserts keep beautifully; even improve with aging; indeed, in England, I was once honored by being served plum pudding which had been stored in a distinguished household's attic for eighteen years (and I must admit, I was a little loath to eat it, but it was deliciously good).

Be happy that when Thanksgiving, Christmas, or New Year's

feasts are approaching, family members can usually be cajoled into taking part in the gala preparations. Husbands have been known to shell nuts; children to chop candied fruit; aunts to measure dry ingredients, etc. If someone starts a rollicking song, or Christmas carol, others will usually chime in, even if loudly off pitch, and the boisterous chanting around the kitchen table makes memories youngsters still like to think back upon, when they have become old men and women.

So, far from regarding fruit cake or plum pudding as a "chore," let its concoction be as much fun as trimming the tree!

MASTER RECIPE #88
ROYAL PLUM PUDDING

Here is a pudding "fit for a king." It should be. It was created for royalty. It is my own adaptation of an ancient palace recipe, treasured through generations in the castles of Merrie England. Those who hand it down say it was originated for King George I. Adaptation was necessary for two reasons: (1) the original version was made in proportions sufficient to feed all the great family and hangers-on of a palace. (2) The directions called for fresh plums, which we do not easily find today at the Christmas season; and so we have here substituted prunes (dried plums), cooked to restore proper moisture and flavor. The result is the lightest, most tender, most unforgettable of plum puddings . . . truly a feast for a king.

When to make, and how long to allow. Plum pudding may be made days — even weeks — before serving, and stored in your refrigerator. It keeps indefinitely and its flavor is not at all lessened by reheating. It should of course always be served *hot.*

If you are a novice, it might be well to make your plum pudding a week or so before the holiday rush begins. It will then be all ready to reheat, and will not distract you from the other necessary tasks of getting your festive dinner.

Whenever you plan to make it, *mix the ingredients the day before you will cook the pudding.* Assemble, cut, and blend all ingredients one day; let the mixture stand 12 hours (or overnight), in a cold place (your refrigerator); then, next day, *allow 6 hours' time, to steam the pudding.* Allowing the ingredients to stand overnight before cooking greatly enriches the flavor of the pudding.

You need a mold. Any "steamed" pudding (plum pudding included) requires a mold with tight-fitting lid, so bubbling hot water used for steaming it cannot get inside, to spoil the pudding texture. Housewares stores sell a special "steamed pudding mold." This is a container which resembles a small pail, with a hollow tubular center, and tight-fitting lid which has attachments and slots to hold lid firmly to the mold. The 1½ quart size is most general for household and family use. Such a mold is a joy to have, and you will use it for many other kinds of steamed puddings, in time; so it will not be wasteful to buy one.

On the other hand, if you already have a metal melon-shaped dessert or salad mold, with a lid, you may use that (these come in 1 pint, 1 quart, and 1½ quart sizes); but with this sort of mold, which has no fastening, you must tie the lid onto the body of the mold firmly, with string, so it will not come apart during the steaming.

But even if you have no mold at all, don't let that stop you! Many a perfect plum pudding has been made in a tin can. Simply save 2 or 3 empty tin cans which have no jagged edges; wash them well; remove paper wrappers; dry cans; and have them ready to put your pudding mix in. For a lid, you will tie firmly over top of each can several layers of waxed paper, or a strong piece of buttered white or brown wrapping paper; and this will work very adequately, provided you tie the covering on securely enough so that no water can seep inside the can during the steaming process.

For Preparation of Mold, Steaming Method, see under To Cook the Pudding (p. 497). For Unmolding and Blazing (p. 498); To Store (p. 498); To Reheat (p. 499).

Now, to mix the ingredients!

This recipe makes enough for one 1½ quart mold, which will serve 10 to 15 people; and you will probably have a little of the pudding mixture left over; you can put this in a smaller mold, or tin can, and steam like the big pudding, thus having an extra dessert for another day, or for a gift to a friend.

First prepare, then combine in a very large mixing bowl
> 1 **cup cooked prunes** (measured after being drained, pitted, and cut in halves or quarters)
> 1½ **cups seedless raisins**
> 1 **cup dried currants**
> ¼ **cup candied citron,** diced
> ¼ **cup candied cherries,** diced
> ¼ **cup candied lemon peel,** diced } *
> ¼ **cup candied orange peel,** diced
> ¼ **cup blanched, toasted** (not salted) **almonds,** coarsely chopped

To above fruits and nuts, add
> 1 **cup flour** (sifted before measuring)
> 1 **cup granulated sugar**
> 1 **cup day-old bread crumbs**
> 2½ **cups** (about ½ **pound**) **finely shredded beef suet** (Remove from suet any tough fibrous tissue, using only the crisp, firm fat.)

In separate bowl, beat until frothy

4 eggs

Blend into eggs
> ⅔ **cup plus 2 tablespoons whole milk**
> 1 **wineglass brandy** (or whiskey, or sherry)

Mix liquids with fruits and dry ingredients. Place bowl, covered, in refrigerator or other cold place for 12 hours, or overnight.

To Cook the Pudding

Butter molds (p. 496) *generously,* both *inside* of mold, and *inside of the lid* or other covering. If mold is not amply greased with

---

* For the 4 candied ingredients, you may substitute 1 cup diced mixed, candied fruit, sold ready-prepared, in stores. Or, to make your own candied fruits, see page 501.

butter, pudding will not slip out easily and in perfect shape when cooked.

Turn pudding mixture into molds, filling each mold *not more than ¾ full.* This pudding becomes heavenly light if it has room for expansion. *Fasten mold closed,* securely. (See under You need a mold, page 496.)

On surface burner of stove, place a large kettle containing a wire rack and about 3 inches hot water (enough water to come about halfway up the sides of the mold, when mold is placed on rack, in kettle). Place the tightly closed mold on the rack. Cover the kettle. Bring water to a gentle boil. Keep water boiling gently 6 hours, with kettle covered all the time; add more water, if necessary, as some boils away. *At no time allow the water to boil up over the top of the mold;* water should never have a chance to get inside the pudding.

To unmold, when pudding has steamed 6 hours. Lift mold from hot water and remove lid, or covering. If serving at once, have ready a warmed serving platter. Invert platter over top of mold. Turn both over simultaneously. Pudding should slip out in perfect form.

Decorate pudding with a gay sprig of holly, if you have it.

Have ready a separate dish of hard sauce (p. 407), to pass with the pudding; this should always be served separately so the sauce will not melt from warmth of pudding before everyone can be served.

To "blaze" the pudding. When pudding is on platter, ready to serve, pour over it a jigger or two of brandy. Hold a match where you poured the brandy. It will ignite, making a handsome blue blaze which lasts only a minute. This looks fancy and festive, and also gives more brandy flavor to the pudding.

To store, instead of serving, after original cooking. Pudding may be left in its mold; allowed to cool thoroughly (if you wish, you may take off the lid of mold, to speed cooling); then may be stored in mold, tightly covered, in refrigerator or other cool place, until 2 hours before you wish to serve it.

To reheat, after storing. If you are reheating the entire pudding, again butter lid of mold and fasten it tightly. Place mold on rack in kettle containing 3 inches of water, just as for original steaming. Steam 2 hours, to make thoroughly hot.

If reheating a small amount of leftover pudding, instead of using mold, you may heat the leftover pudding in top section of double boiler. Cover top section. Place top section over lower section, which contains 2 inches of water. Place entire double boiler over surface burner, and keep water boiling gently 1 hour or so, until pudding is well heated.

MASTER RECIPE #89
GOOD, OLD-FASHIONED
DARK FRUIT CAKE

The real, old-time fruit cake consists of many kinds of dried or candied fruits, cut fine, held together in a dark batter made with flour, brown sugar, molasses, eggs, and spices.

Because of all the fruit it contains, it is a heavy batter, does not rise much, and must be baked slowly.

Because of the time needed for preparing the ingredients, you might as well make a very large fruit cake . . . or several small ones . . . at one sitting, instead of tackling the job over again several different times. Fruit cake will keep all winter, if stored according to directions following this recipe, and it is not only a gala cake for the holiday weeks, but tastes wonderful with a cup of tea any wintry afternoon. Served with a glass of sherry, muscatel, or champagne, it makes a lush offering for unexpected evening guests, any time during the cold months. In short, it is good to have in the house.

When to make. Fruit cake, like plum pudding, should be begun at least the day before cooking, so that all fruity ingredients may stand together overnight. It can, however, be cooked weeks ahead of serving, and stored until needed.

Mixing the cake. This recipe makes 6 pounds of cake; fills two

9 x 5 x 3 inch loaf pans; or fills 1 large tube pan, with a small loaf left over.

In a very large mixing bowl, combine

1 pound seedless raisins
½ pound dried currants
½ package dates, pitted and cut up into small pieces
¼ pound candied cherries, cut in halves or quarters
1 small bottle maraschino cherries, drained, and cut in
      halves or quarters
½ ounce candied orange peel, diced
½ ounce candied lemon peel, diced
⅛ pound candied pineapple, diced
¹⁄₁₆ pound candied citron, diced
½ pound broken pecan meats

Add to fruits

                ¼ cup orange juice

Cover bowl, and place in refrigerator or other cool place, over-night.

Next day, in large mixing bowl, cream until light

                ½ pound butter

Work into butter, gradually

                ¼ pound brown sugar

Blend in, little by little

                ½ cup white sugar

Beat butter-sugar mixture with spoon until light and well blended. Set aside.

In separate bowl, measure and blend

                2 cups sifted flour
                ½ teaspoon salt
                ¼ teaspoon allspice
                ¼ teaspoon powdered clove
                ¼ teaspoon nutmeg
                1½ teaspoon cinnamon
                ½ teaspoon baking soda

In another bowl, beat

6 eggs

Add eggs to butter mixture; then also add

½ cup molasses

Combine flour and spices with fruits which have stood over-night. Blend well, so fruit is coated with flour. Then blend in the egg-butter-molasses mixture. Mix the batter well, so it will hold the fruits together.

To bake fruit cake. The larger your fruit cake, the slower must be the oven, so heat will have plenty of time to work through, and cook, the thick batter. Set oven at 300°. Pans can be filled nearly to top, as fruit cake does not rise very much.

Grease loaf pans, or tube angel cake pans, or 8 x 8 x 2 square cake pans. Line them with waxed paper, or with thin light brown paper, and butter the paper after it is in the pans. Put in batter. After cake is in the oven, place a large piece of heavy brown paper over top of each pan (this helps keep cake moist). Leave paper over cake for first 35 to 45 minutes; then uncover cake. Continue baking 1½ to 2 hours more, for a large cake, or 1 to 1½ hours more, for smaller loaf, or until surface of cake feels firm but springy, when lightly touched with forefinger.

To store. Remove cake from pan, and thoroughly cool it, on rack. Then lightly wrap it in cheesecloth, or in a clean thin old linen napkin. Place cake in paper-lined tin or earthen container with lid. Sprinkle top of cake with a few drops brandy. Twice a week, sprinkle with brandy again . . . not much, just a few drops to keep cake moist and fresh. (Brandy also acts as a flavoring, and a preservative.)

YOU CAN CANDY
YOUR OWN FRUITS

Candied fruits are quite expensive to buy. If desired, you can candy your own some evening. It's fun; and they keep indefinitely.

Candied Pineapple

Put 1 or 2 slices canned pineapple in saucepan, adding enough pineapple syrup to cover. Add 1 cup granulated sugar. Bring syrup to boil, cook until sugar dissolves; then keep simmering until syrup almost evaporates. Drain pineapple slices. Sprinkle some granulated sugar on a piece of waxed paper, and dip pineapple in this sugar, on all sides, until well coated. Let pineapple dry thoroughly. Then store in covered glass jar.

Candied Cherries

Follow same method as for pineapple, but using **maraschino cherries** (red or green) and their juice, instead of pineapple.

Candied Orange Peel or Lemon Peel

After squeezing your morning fruit juice, save the nicest looking **skins** (orange or lemon). Cut skins in quarters. Remove stem or bud end. Cover skins with cold water, and cook gently until skins are tender when pierced with a fork. Drain. Now remove all white tissue from inside of skins. In saucepan, make a sugar syrup, using **2 cups granulated sugar to 1 cup water**; bring this to a boil, cook until sugar dissolves, and add the pieces of peel. Simmer gently until most of syrup is evaporated, and peel looks clear and transparent. Drain the peel. Roll peel in granulated sugar until well coated. Dry peel thoroughly, and store in covered glass jar.

Candied Citron

This is made from citron melon. If you cannot buy such a melon, you had better buy the candied citron in a store. Pare 1 citron **melon**; cut it in 6 or 8 lengthwise sections, removing all seeds. Make a sugar syrup using **2 cups sugar for 1 cup water**, and put strips of melon in this. Bring syrup to boil, cook until sugar dissolves, then simmer gently until most of syrup is evaporated, and melon looks transparent. Drain melon. Roll melon pieces in granulated sugar until well coated. Dry thoroughly, and store in covered glass jar.

YOU CAN BLANCH
AND TOAST ALMONDS

To Blanch Almonds

Place shelled nuts in a bowl, and pour **boiling water** over them. Let stand about 10 to 15 minutes, or until the thin outer skins wrinkle. Drain off water, and with fingers slip off the wrinkled skins. This part is the *"blanching."*

To Toast Almonds

Place skinned blanched almonds in shallow pan or pie plate containing **2 tablespoons melted butter** (or olive oil). Place pan in moderate (375°) oven for about 10 minutes, or just until nuts turn light golden color. Stir nuts around once or twice, so they color evenly. Remove from pan, and spread nuts on paper towel, to drain dry.

To Salt Almonds

After toasting, sprinkle nuts lightly with salt, while they are draining on the paper towel (above).

CHAPTER XXXIX

Herbs and Suggested Ways to Use Them

Herbs are powerful things. They lift a few dull, everyday ingredients into a dish which is out-of-the-ordinary, tantalizing in taste. But be warned: they should be used *with discretion*. To suffocate good natural food with seasoning is worse than not to season it at all.

Your aim should always be to make the seasoning a mere suggestion . . . a subtle overtone, so indefinite no one can guess just how you did it. This is what lifts an expert's seasoning into the realm of exciting food.

Many herbs can be grown in a kitchen garden, or even in a window box on the sill. Some may be used, fresh, as they grow. Many are dried (by being hung in a shady place until they become brittle) and then powdered (by being rolled with rolling pin, or forced through a sieve).

Dried herbs can be bought in almost any big grocery store. They are far stronger, in potency, than when fresh. Make it your rule never to use more than *one pinch* of an herb *in a dish serving 4 people.*

Certain combinations of herb seasonings are referred to by well-known names, to wit:

Fines herbes. These are basil, chervil, marjoram, thyme, rosemary, and tarragon. Any of these may be combined, finely chopped; usually 2 tablespoons or so of finely chopped parsley and 1 tablespoon chopped chives, are combined with them. The mixture is ordinarily added to the food just a minute or two before serving.

Bouquet garni. This is a bunch of assorted herbs (such as parsley, marjoram, thyme, and bay leaf) tied inside a small piece of cheesecloth, and put into the kettle with a stew, or pot roast, or other food simmering in liquid. Before serving, the "bouquet garni" is removed, intact, in its cloth. Having it in the cloth prevents the need of straining out these seasonings, at the last moment.

We give a few suggestions for the better uses of the different herbs. This does not mean you may not experiment with others.

Herb	*How Used*	*Try In*
BASIL Has a spicy, clove taste	Use chopped fresh, or dried	Tomato soup, tomato sauces, any tomato dish Vegetable juice cocktails Canned soups Add to melted butter for fish sauces (p. 256). Add to sauce for creamed or poached eggs, or hard-cooked egg sauces Use in "fines herbes" omelet Chopped meat Beef or pork pies, or beef stews The merest hint, in green or tomato salads
BAY LEAF (Actually dried laurel leaf; not really an herb, but used as one)	Use a fraction of a dried leaf, perhaps ⅓ or ½. One leaf makes a very strong flavor	In stews In pot roasts In stock In flavoring brown sauces With lentils: beans, peas
CHERVIL A lacy herb, with tender foliage, somewhat resembling parsley. Has a slightly peppery taste.	Chopped fresh, or dried	In broccoli, spinach, or other "green" soup In salads; salad dressings Add to herb butter, for fish Use with "fines herbes" in omelet, or in sauces for eggs Add to Sauce Bearnaise Add a pinch when cooking peas, tomatoes Try in potato salad

Herb	*How Used*	*Try In*
CHIVES A member of the onion family; tastes much like onion, but milder	Use tender green tops, chopped fine	Any green salad Any soup; especially potato soup Any casserole, or meat pie, or stew in which onion would be good Any white sauce for fish, eggs, vegetables Use with "fines herbes" in omelet Add to melted butter sauces for fish (p. 256). Add to aspic for jelling meats, or eggs, or vegetables
DILL A lacy, pungent herb	Chopped fine	In fish dishes In green or cucumber salads In egg dishes In some sauces
HORSERADISH Fiery, hot flavor	Roots used, chopped fine	Brown sauces for steak, roast beef A small bit, in meat loaf Mixed with sour cream, as sauce for steak, roast beef
ROSEMARY Both sweet and sharp	Chopped fresh, or dried	Often sprinkled lightly over veal, lamb, beef, pork before roasting In stews In meat-base soups In "fines herbes" combination
MARJORAM Sweet marjoram is "sweet" — but also somewhat bitter	Chopped fresh, or dried	In green salads In salad dressings In stuffings for turkey, duck In cream soups In egg, fish, or cheese dishes In stews Sprinkled over meat, before roasting Add a pinch to peas, beans, spinach, tomatoes, broccoli, cole slaw, turnips
MINT Everyone knows the taste	Chopped fresh, or dried	Sprinkle over lamb, before roasting, or use in sauce for lamb Add to fruit salads Add to cooked peas, cooked carrots Add to pea soup
OREGANO (Wild marjoram; more pungent)	Chopped fresh, or dried	In Italian dishes of all sorts: meats, soups

Herb	How Used	Try In
PARSLEY Lacy-foliaged plant; easy to grow in flower pot	Chopped fresh, preferably; or dried	Any cream soup Any white sauce Sauces for eggs, fish Casseroles Scalloped fish or vegetables Sauce for croquettes With "fines herbes" in omelet, other egg dishes In herb dumplings, or herb crust for meat pies In aspics Try French-frying whole branches to serve with steak, fish
POULTRY SEASONING (Mixed, dried herbs, with a strong flavor of sage)	Dried	Use primarily in seasoning stuffing, for poultry or pork or sometimes fish Try adding a pinch to chicken or turkey gravy Add to sauce for chicken or turkey "Leftover" dishes (such as croquettes, hash, pies)
SAGE	Chopped fresh, or dried	In stuffing for chicken, turkey, duck, goose, or pork Try a snitch in stews Try the faintest bit with salty fish Try with stewed tomatoes, string beans, cheese dishes
SAVORY Milder than sage	Chopped fresh, or dried	Add to chopped meat, meat loaf Try in stuffing In salads, salad dressings Add to cooking peas, string beans, Brussels sprouts, turnips, cabbage In stock In pot-roasted meat In potato or dried pea soup
TARRAGON Has a tangy, sharp flavor, somewhat like anise, as noted in "tarragon vinegar"	Chopped fresh, or dried	In green salads In salad dressings In Tartar sauce; other mayonnaise-type fish sauces; in Sauce Béarnaise. In egg, fish, or shellfish dishes With eggs in aspic In cream sauce used for eggs, fish With "fines herbes" combination in omelets

CHAPTER XL

How to Have Dinner Ready
on Time

The art of having a dinner all ready on time is only the art of *figuring backwards,* once you know the cooking times of different foods.

First, you plan what your dinner hour is to be. Second, you estimate (or look up in Master Recipe, or individual recipe) how long each item of your menu will require to cook. Third, you figure backwards from the dinner hour, *allowing at least ¼ to ½ hour longer than the longest item on your menu,* as a starting point for preparing dinner; for no food is ready to cook the instant you begin handling it; it requires some sort of preparation.

For Example: Program for a "Quick"-Cooking Meal

If you are going to have a meat which pan-broils in 10 to 20 minutes; a vegetable which boils in 20 to 25 minutes; baked potatoes which require about 1 hour, and even have a bought or leftover dessert all ready to use, you *still* must start to prepare dinner *about 1¼ hours before serving time.* The first quarter hour is for getting out, scrubbing and preparing potatoes, and heating oven. Once potatoes have been started, you use the interval (before it's time to cook vegetable and meat) to get out bread and butter; cream and sugar for coffee; dinner, salad, and dessert dishes; to wash salad greens, and prepare your salad; to get ready a salad dressing; to measure the coffee and water; to set your table; to arrange dessert in dishes or serving plate; and then to wash, peel, or slice the vegetable, and prepare and season meat, before cooking. All these chores take considerably more time than you expect. With these out of the way, you have the last half hour clear to devote to things which can *only* be done just before serving: that is, you cook your vegetable, and your quick-cooking meat, which may require careful watching.

Different Planning, for Long-Cooking Foods

Many foods, of course, will not fit into the "quick-meal" schedule, but must be begun in the middle of the afternoon, for a 6 P.M. dinner . . . or should be prepared in the morning.

A *gelatine dish*, for example, must be made at least by noon if it is to be jelled and firm by 6 P.M. (It *can* be made the night before.)

Most puddings need time to cook, and then to chill; they too should be made in the morning, or at least by noon. (They *can* be made the day before.)

A *cake or pie* will probably take you 2 hours to prepare and bake; and if you leave it until the last moment, it will clutter up your kitchen working space, your oven, and your mind, just when you need all your attention for meat and vegetables. Therefore, always make cake or pie ahead of time. Cake can be made in the morning. Pie crust is apt to become soggy if made too far ahead; make pie only a few hours before serving time, about midafternoon.

Ice cream or other frozen desserts can be made the night before, or a whole day before, serving; indeed, they *improve* upon standing in refrigerator. In any case, they *must* be made by morning, if to be served that night, or they will not be frozen in time.

Homemade bread or rolls. Mixing dough, allowing time for it to rise, to be shaped, and to rise again, and then baking it, will require a total of 3½ to 4 hours. If making bread for a 6 P.M. dinner, start by 2:00 or 2:15 P.M.

Salads (except jelled ones) can be made in the hour before dinner, or can be made 2 or 3 hours ahead of time, if you prefer to have that course out of the way. Washed, crisped greens and vegetables will keep very nicely in a *covered* salad bowl, in refrigerator, for 2 or 3 hours. But whenever you do it, allow 20 to 30 minutes for washing and crisping greens; for peeling, slicing or otherwise preparing your salad fruits or vegetables; for fixing a "dressing"; and for garnishing. A good salad is not usually made in 2 or 3 minutes; don't underestimate the time.

Long-cooking meats. A 6 to 8 pound oven roast (like leg of lamb, or 2-rib roast of beef) usually requires at least 2½ to 3 hours' cooking, perhaps more, depending on weight. A roasting chicken 5 to 8 pounds also requires some 2 to 3 hours' cooking. A pot roast, a fricassee of chicken, or a meat stew, also require usually 2½ to 3 hours of cooking. In addition, time must be allowed in advance to *prepare* the meat (season it, and so forth) . . . so allow ¼ hour extra. Figure the total preparation and cooking time, backward, from your dinner hour, and you will see that you must begin such dishes about midafternoon. This does not mean that you have to stay in the kitchen, watching them cook, from that time until dinner; they can be left (once well started) and you can do something else, until it's time to set table, prepare salad, dessert, make coffee and do other "last minute" things.

Last-Minute Items

Certain foods can *only* be cooked in the last 15 to 30 minutes before dinner is to be served. When you have on your menu foods of this type, it is well to prepare beforehand and get out of the way as many other dinner items as possible, thus leaving your entire attention free for the last-minute foods. Foods of this type usually require considerable "watching" while they cook. They include:

Biscuits: cooking time, 15 to 20 minutes.

Muffins: cooking time, 25 to 35 minutes.

Hot rolls: cooking time, about 12 minutes (after second rising in pan).

Waffles, griddle cakes: cooking time about 15 to 20 minutes for "a lot."

Pan-broiled foods: cooking time, usually 10 to 20 minutes; chicken, longer.

Deep or shallow-fried foods: cooking time usually 5 to 7 minutes; chicken, about 1 hour.

Pan-fried foods: cooking time, usually 10 to 30 minutes.

Sautéed foods: cooking time, usually 5 to 8 minutes.

Oven-broiled foods: cooking time, usually 10 to 25 minutes; chicken, longer.

Boiled vegetables: cooking time, usually 15 to 45 minutes.

Frozen vegetables: cooking time, usually 5 to 15 minutes.

Coffee: cooking time, usually 5 to 10 minutes.

Make a Definite Work-Plan for Your Day

Always decide right after breakfast (or even the night before) what you will have for dinner. Write down everything you need, on your marketing list.

Market as soon as possible, allowing leeway to get back home in time to prepare even long-cooking foods.

Make a list of all the dinner items, putting them in proper order according to amount of time each will take to cook, or in order in which each should be prepared to be frozen, jelled, baked, or whatever, by dinner. (Look up each item in Master Recipe, or individual recipe, if need be.)

Follow your work program faithfully.

Such a program will be particularly helpful (even sanity saving!) when preparing an elaborate Christmas or Thanksgiving dinner, or a party. It keeps your heart happy, and your nerves calm, to have a *plan*.

After a few months' cooking, you will find you begin to make such programs mentally and instinctively, without writing them down . . . you will *know* what to do first.

Don't be discouraged that you don't know it *yet;* no beginning cook ever did!

The bright day will come . . . and shortly!

The information above given is only to help you until it *does*.

CHAPTER XLI

Your First Four Weeks' Dinner Menus: A Home Cooking Course

Please Read before Trying Menus

The following twenty-eight dinner menus were planned not only to be twenty-eight tasty, "balanced," appetizing meals — but to serve as a Home Cooking Course for you.

Breakfasts were eliminated, because most families prefer to eat a set breakfast of their own choosing; see Index, for breakfast foods like bacon, eggs, coffee. Lunches were eliminated because most men are away from home at noon, either buying lunch out, or carrying a sandwich with them to work. Women, if at home, usually make a sandwich at noon, or delve in the refrigerator for "leftovers." Dinner is the main meal of the day: the meal when you learn to cook.

Because these meals were planned as a Cooking Course, certain prerequisite reading is listed for each morning (if you cannot do it in the morning, do it the night before). This reading is to serve in the place of a teacher, standing by your elbow, telling you what you are to do about each dish, and why. If you skip reading it, you will not know what you are doing, and will not have success.

Another point: Because one of the chief difficulties to beginners is the problem of getting all parts of a dinner ready for the same serving time, we are listing under each menu, an order of preparation for the dinner. Keep to this order. By the end of four weeks, you will have grasped the idea, and never have difficulty with this problem again. The order is put there simply to serve as your guide.

As to the menus themselves: Note that these begin with "simple" (so-called) dinners, the ones least complicated to prepare, and often call for store desserts or canned or quick-frozen foods, to help you expedite matters, and to leave you time to concentrate on some one or two important foods, each meal. As each day progresses, you will try another main type of food, or perhaps two, making use meanwhile of what you have learned in days before. By the end of the Four Weeks' Menus you will discover that you have prepared at least one sample food from every main branch of cooking! You will have achieved — in one month — more than many people learn in years.

Now no undertaking in a new field is ever a "breeze"; to learn, you must grasp the principles and practice them. But this program, if carried through for one month, will save you years-to-come of uncertainty, and of failures. It's worth a month's concentrated effort, isn't it, to put yourself on Easy Street.

When Four Weeks Have Been Completed

There are several ways these menus could continue to serve you . . . even for months to come.

(1) You could immediately repeat the entire Four Weeks' program, just as is, to become more adept and practiced. No one in the family could object to enjoying the same good meal again, after a four-week interval! Probably no one would even recognize that it *was* a repeat.

(2) If you prefer to broaden your repertoire, you could carry out the same general menus a second time, but *making substitutions* of foods of similar kind. For example, where a pan-broiled meat is specified, you could change it to pan-broiled fish, or liver. Similarly, where a fruit pie is called for, change it to a pudding-type pie; where a square cake is called for, try a layer cake, or

cup cakes, or an angel cake. Where a roast bird is called for, try a different breed of bird, or different-flavored stuffing, or both. In such a manner, the menus could be varied endlessly, month after month, while still serving as a marketing and planning guide.

(3) Where store products (ice cream, French dressing) are called for, in the menus, later on try making your own. After you have made ice cream a few times, try frozen pudding, etc. Each new dish . . . or each variation of a standard method . . . increases your knowledge of cooking.

Just remember one thing: Do go back and read the "Basic Principles" and "Master Recipe" for any type of dish, as often as you need to, until you know it by heart. These principles and methods were put here to help you. The sooner you know them, the sooner you can toss away cook books, be free from hunting recipes, and cook, like a great chef, "out of your head."

MENU #1: MONDAY

Pan-Broiled Lamb Chops, bought Mint Jelly, if desired
Broccoli (Frozen)
Baked Potatoes
Sliced Tomatoes and Lettuce
Store French Dressing, with crumbled Blue Cheese
Chilled Canned Fruit — Store Cookies
Coffee, Tea or Milk

A.M. **Read**

How to Pan-Broil, Chapter IX (pages 76–78); and see Chops (p. 80).

Basic Rules, Boiled Vegetables (pp. 290–291). See Chart (p. 292).

Baked Potatoes (p. 296).

Salads, Chapter XXVIII, through page 334.

Beverages: Coffee (p. 467); or Tea (p. 474).

Make marketing list including every item needed for dinner,

plus staples needed for breakfast and lunch tomorrow (if in doubt, check suggestions in Chapter V).

Go to market; store perishables in refrigerator; put in canned fruit, to chill for dinner.

Read: How to Have Dinner Ready on Time (p. 508).

P.M. Start 1½ Hours before Dinner

Carry out preparations in order given.

Heat oven. Scrub potatoes. Put potatoes in to bake.

Wash salad greens. Leave them in cold water to crisp.

Slice tomatoes. Crumble about 1 tablespoon cheese. Have dressing cool.

Set table. (Get out napkins, silver, coffee cups, cream and sugar, butter and bread if wanted, all serving plates and dishes. Put dinner plates in warming drawer of stove, or where they will become warm without being hot enough to crack.)

Shake greens dry; arrange salad in bowl. Cover bowl with waxed paper, and store in refrigerator until serving.

Turn out mint jelly onto serving dish.

Arrange chilled fruit in dessert dishes; arrange cookies on platter.

Measure coffee and water; start coffee cooking.

If desired, mix juice of ½ lemon with 2 tablespoons mayonnaise, to serve as garnish on broccoli.

Heat ½ inch water plus ½ teaspoon salt in saucepan, for broccoli. Also put heavy frying pan on moderate heat.

Put broccoli into boiling water. Salt chops on one side, and place salted side down in hot frying pan.

Turn chops as soon as browned on one side; salt second side; brown second side. Lower heat, to cook chops through.

Watch broccoli; remove from heat as soon as stalks feel tender when pricked with fork. If chops are also tender now, drain broccoli.

Get potatoes from oven; cut them open at top; place a lump of butter in each.

Serve main course. Salad, dessert, and coffee are ready when needed.

MENU #2: TUESDAY

Pan-Broiled Link Sausages
Boiled Cabbage
Mashed Potatoes
Sliced or Julienned Canned Beets, on Lettuce
French Dressing, grated onion
Lemon Gelatine with Whipped Cream
(Leftover) Cookies
Coffee, Tea or Milk

A.M. Read

Pan-Broiled Sausages (p. 85).
Basic Rules, Boiled Vegetables; Cabbage (p. 290).
Mashed Potatoes (p. 301).
Salad: For Taste Appeal (p. 333).
Gelatine (pp. 360–362). Also, To Unmold (p. 362).
Sweetened Whipped Cream (p. 408).
Make marketing list. Buy a *large* cabbage, to use for 2 days. Buy packaged gelatine mix.
Cooking: Make Gelatine; store in refrigerator.

P.M. Start 1½ Hours before Dinner

Cut head of cabbage in half lengthwise, through core; wrap ½ in waxed paper; store in refrigerator. Cut other half into 2 to 4 lengthwise wedges. Wash wedges. Let stand in cold water 15 to 20 minutes.

Peel and cut potatoes; put to cook in water to cover, plus ½ teaspoon salt.

Put drained cabbage wedges in saucepan, in water to cover, plus 1 teaspoon salt. Start cooking. (The thinner the wedges, the faster they become tender.)

Wash greens; leave in cold water, to crisp. Drain canned beets.

Get chilled cream from refrigerator; add flavoring, whip it; return bowl to refrigerator until serving time.

Get out sausages; cut links apart, to have ready for cooking.

Shake greens dry; arrange salad, grating 1 teaspoon raw onion on top of beets. Place salad in refrigerator, until serving time.

Set table (as under Menu 1).

Measure coffee in coffee maker.

As soon as potatoes feel tender when pricked with fork, drain off water; mash potatoes in saucepan; add seasoning, plus butter; *partly* cover pan; place pan back over very gentle heat, to keep warm until serving.

NOTE: If heat is not *very* low, potatoes will burn.

Test cabbage with fork; when nearly tender, place sausages in cool heavy frying pan; start cooking them.

Start coffee cooking.

As soon as sausages are done, drain cabbage thoroughly; serve main course. Salad, gelatine, whipped cream, and coffee, ready.

MENU #3: WEDNESDAY

Sautéed Chicken Livers (and Mushrooms, if desired) on Rice
String Beans (frozen)
Halves of Canned Pear, on Lettuce
Fruit French Dressing
Cheese and Crackers
Coffee, Tea or Milk

A.M. Read

How to Sauté (pp. 93–94). See Chicken Livers (p. 93); Mushrooms (p. 95). (If preferred, substitute Lambs' Kidneys, instead of Chicken Livers.)

Master Recipe, Steamed White Rice (p. 305).

Basic Rules for Boiled Vegetables (p. 290).

Fruit French Dressing (p. 357).

P.M. Start 1¼ Hours before Dinner

Wash mushrooms. Break caps from stems. Slice both stems and caps.

Cut chicken livers to good bite-size pieces. Do not cook yet.

Measure rice, salt, water; start rice cooking; as soon as it has boiled for 1 minute stir; then remove to lowest heat, keeping pan covered tightly.

Wash and crisp greens.

Open and drain canned pears. Prepare fruit French dressing. Make salad; store in refrigerator.

Arrange platter of crackers and cheese.

Set table. Warm dinner plates.

Measure coffee into coffee maker. Start coffee.

Heat ½ inch water plus ½ teaspoon salt in saucepan, for beans; put beans into boiling water; cover.

Melt 2 or 3 tablespoons butter in moderately hot frying pan, for sautéing. Add cut chicken livers and sliced mushrooms; brown lightly, stirring frequently; take care not to let burn. When browned, reduce heat.

Test beans with fork; remove from heat as soon as tender. If rice is also puffed up and done, drain beans. Spoon rice onto warm dinner plates; top rice with tender mushrooms and livers, plus pan juices; serve beans alongside.

Ready: salad, dessert, coffee.

MENU #4: THURSDAY

Pot Roast of Beef, and Thickened Gravy
Buttered Whole Carrots
Cottage Fried Potatoes
Mixed Greens
Russian Dressing
Gelatine (leftover)
Add cut fresh fruit or berries
Coffee, Tea or Milk

A.M. Read

How to Pot Roast, p. 116, through Step 4.

Basic Rules, Boiled Vegetables: Carrots (p. 290).

Cottage Fried Potatoes (p. 89).

Russian Dressing (p. 353).

Make marketing list. Don't forget any spices or seasoning you want for Pot Roast; also catsup, for Russian Dressing.

P.M. Start 2½ to 3 Hours before Dinner (depending on weight of meat)

Begin Step 1, Braising for pot roast (p. 117), browning onions in fat.

Add salted meat to kettle; brown on all sides. Turn heat low; add water and seasonings desired, as in Step 2, Pot Roast. Cover kettle; leave meat to simmer gently. You don't have to stay to watch it, if you're sure it is not bubbling. However, if you have used only 1 cup water, you must go back to see if more water is needed, every half hour or so. Don't let kettle become dry.

1¼ Hours before Dinner

Peel 6 small whole carrots, or 4 medium-size. Leave whole, or cut in halves; place in saucepan. Add ½ teaspoon salt, plus 1½ inches water. Cover pan. Boil gently.

Peel 4 to 5 medium potatoes. Dice. Put in saucepan. Cover with cold water; add ½ teaspoon salt. Cover pan; boil until tender.

Peel, slice fruit, or hull berries. Arrange over gelatine, for serving.

Wash and crisp greens. Mix Russian dressing.

Measure coffee.

Set table.

Arrange salad; put on dressing; store in refrigerator.

When potatoes are tender, drain; then start frying them in 2 or 3 tablespoons hot fat in frying pan (p. 89). Brown on both sides, then turn heat low.

Test carrots, for tenderness. When tender, drain off water, but leave carrots in saucepan; add a lump butter; let it melt, and turn carrots around in it, to butter all sides. Keep in warm place (but not cooking further) until time to serve.

Test meat. When tender, lift from kettle to warm platter. Thicken gravy, as in Step 4, Pot Roast (p. 119).

Serve sliced pot roast, with gravy over meat; serve carrots, potatoes, alongside.

Ready: Salad; gelatine with fruit; coffee.

MENU #5: FRIDAY

Broiled Salmon Steak (or Broiled Split Mackerel), Lemon Wedges
Spinach (frozen)
Parsley Creamed Potatoes
Cole Slaw (using leftover ½ raw cabbage)
Blueberry Pie
Coffee, Tea or Milk
If you have no broiling oven, pan-broil the fish (p. 83).

A.M. Read

Master Recipe, Broiling (p. 68), and Specific Recommendations for Fish (p. 72).

Cole Slaw (p. 339); list seasonings needed, for marketing.

White Sauce (p. 248); list seasonings needed, for marketing, adding 1 bunch of parsley.

Pastry (p. 445); Blueberry Pie (p. 452); list ingredients needed for marketing.

Make marketing list, including fish, spinach, lemon, plus ingredients noted from above recipes, plus staples for tomorrow.

A.M. Cooking

Make cole slaw (p. 339); store, covered, in refrigerator until dinner.

Make 1 cup medium white sauce; leave in saucepan if room is not too hot; or store, covered, in refrigerator, until night.

By 2:30 or 3 P.M.

Reread Pies, Chapter XXXV; Never-Fail Pastry, Shaping Upper and Lower Crust; Master Recipe, Blueberry Pie (p. 452).

Make Pastry. Make and bake pie. (The entire job will probably take you about 2 hours, the first time.)

1¼ Hours before Dinner

Peel, dice, and wash off 4 or 5 potatoes. Put in saucepan with water to cover, plus ½ teaspoon salt. Start them boiling gently, covered.

Wipe off fish; place on greased baking pan, ready for broiling; do not cook yet.

Set table. Warm dinner plates.

Measure coffee.

Test potatoes with fork; when tender (but not soft), drain off water; combine potatoes with white sauce made A.M.; turn mixture into top section of double boiler; place over lower section of double boiler containing 1½ inches hot water. Place over moderate heat.

Heat ½ inch water plus ½ teaspoon salt in saucepan, for spinach.

Turn on broiling oven, to preheat.

Chop fine ¼ cup parsley, stir it into creamed potato mixture; leave in double boiler, over heat.

Put spinach into boiling water; cover pan; cook over moderate heat.

Season fish; dot with butter; place in oven to broil.

Start coffee cooking.

Watch fish, so it will not burn or dry out; add more dots of butter, if needed. As soon as nicely browned and flaky, remove to warm serving platter, or dinner plates.

Drain spinach thoroughly, before serving; add lump of butter to each drained serving.

Stir parsley creamed potatoes before serving.

Serve fish, with lemon wedges to squeeze over fish; potatoes, spinach.

Ready: Cole slaw; pie; coffee.

MENU #6: SATURDAY

Sliced Pot Roast (leftover from Menu #4) and Gravy
Brussels Sprouts (frozen)
Hashed Brown Potatoes
Sliced Cucumbers on Lettuce
Sour Cream Dressing
Blueberry Pie (leftover)
Coffee, Tea or Milk

NOTE: If you have eaten all the pie, substitute fresh or canned fruit.

A.M. Read

Sour Cream Dressing (p. 357); Note ingredients for marketing list.

Pan-Fried Vegetables: Hashed Brown Potatoes (p. 89).

Boiled Frozen Vegetables; Sprouts (p. 290).

Make marketing list; add also foods needed for Menu 7, Sunday; Read Chicken Stew (p. 121); be sure you have all seasonings in Group II (p. 118).

1½ Hours before Dinner

Peel, then slice thin, crosswise, the cucumber. Put slices in bowl of cold water plus 1 teaspoon salt; leave it soaking 15 to 30 minutes.

Meanwhile, make sour cream dressing.

Wash and crisp lettuce.

Peel, dice, rinse off, then start boiling potatoes in covered saucepan, in water to cover plus ½ teaspoon salt.

Get out pot roast; cut some nice slices. Put slices plus any leftover gravy in top section of double boiler; cover. Place over lower section, containing 1½ inches hot water. Place whole double boiler over moderate heat. If desired, add 1 teaspoon grated onion, or few drops Worcestershire sauce, or 1 teaspoon bottled meat extract, to gravy, to add flavor.

Set table. Put dinner plates to warm.

Dry greens and make salad. Store in refrigerator.

Measure coffee.

Heat ½ inch water plus ½ teaspoon salt in saucepan, for sprouts. Add sprouts to boiling water; cook covered, until tender when tested with fork.

As soon as potatoes are nearly tender, when tested with fork, drain off water; heat cooking fat in frying pan; stir in other ingredients with potatoes, and start frying potatoes over moderately hot heat. Turn as soon as needed, browning both sides.

Start coffee cooking.

When potatoes and sprouts are both ready, serve on warmed plates; add hot meat slices, with gravy.

Ready: Salad, dessert, coffee.

MENU #7: SUNDAY

White Fricassee of Chicken
  Noodles
    Green Peas (frozen)
      Mixed Greens
        French Dressing
          Store Peach Ice Cream
(If desired, pour 1 teaspoon brandy, or rum, over each serving)
        Store Macaroons
          Coffee, Tea or Milk

---

3 Hours before Dinner Read:

Chicken Stew, page 121 (also called White Fricassee of Chicken), comparing the method with Pot Roast, which it much resembles. Note that you *omit* the Pot Roast Step 1, Braising, beginning for Chicken at *Step 2*.

Read also Master Recipe #42, Noodles (p. 310).

Wipe chicken pieces clean, and start them cooking as in *Step 2*. Once water has come to boil, turn heat low; leave kettle, covered, to simmer gently about 2 to 2¼ hours, or until chicken pieces feel tender when tested with fork. You do not have to stay in the kitchen to watch it. As long as there is ample water in kettle to cover chicken, and heat is very low, you can even go to church, and leave it cooking by itself.

¾ Hours before Dinner

Wash and crisp greens.

Set table. Put dinner plates and serving dishes to warm.

Make salad; store in refrigerator.

Heat large kettle of boiling, salted water for noodles (p. 310). Add noodles when water is boiling hard. Cook about 15 to 20 minutes.

Heat ½ inch water and ½ teaspoon salt in saucepan, for peas. Add peas when water is boiling hard. Remove pan from heat as soon as peas wrinkle slightly.

Measure coffee; start it cooking.

As soon as chicken pieces feel tender, lift them out to hot plate, and put where they will keep warm. Estimate how much chicken broth is left in kettle. Measure and mix together into a mixing bowl 2 tablespoons flour plus ¼ teaspoon salt for each cup broth you have in kettle; moisten this flour-salt mixture with ¼ cup or so of water, stirring flour to a smooth paste. Then slowly pour hot broth into paste, stirring constantly. Return mixture to kettle and bring to boil, stirring until thickened. If desired, you may also stir in ½ cup or more heavy cream. Taste your gravy; add more salt if needed, and 1 teaspoon grated onion.

Drain noodles in colander. Drain peas. Arrange noodles on warm plates; put chicken pieces on top; cover with chicken gravy; serve peas on side.

Ready: Salad, coffee, store ice cream (take up only at serving time, or it will melt).

MENU #8: MONDAY

Meat Pie with Pastry Crust (made from leftover Pot Roast)
Chef's Salad
Chilled Canned or Fresh Fruit
Brownies
Coffee, Tea or Milk

A.M. Read

Beef Casseroles, Beef Pie (p. 145). See To Bake a Casserole (p. 144).

Master Recipe, Chef's Salad (p. 339); note ingredients for marketing list.

Brownies (p. 492); note ingredients for marketing list.

If you do not have a few carrots and onions in the house, and some leftover cooked peas from Menu 7, buy some. Be sure you have ingredients for Pastry (p. 446); and for Brownies.

Cooking: In A.M., or *early* afternoon, make Brownies.

P.M. 2½ Hours before Dinner

Cut remaining meat of pot roast into cubes or bite-size pieces. Mix with it any leftover gravy; if you have none, make Master Recipe, Brown Gravy (p. 253), using bouillon cubes or bottled meat extract as gravy flavoring. Or instead of gravy, mix with meat 1 can condensed undiluted cream of mushroom soup.

Add to meat and gravy (or gravy substitute), any leftover peas (from Sunday Menu).

In separate saucepan, cook 1 or two large, peeled, thickly sliced carrots; 2 or 3 peeled, cubed, potatoes, and 2 to 4 tiny peeled, whole onions, all mixed together, covered with water, with 1 teaspoon salt added to water. Cook, covered, until vegetables are tender. Then drain them; combine vegetables with meat and gravy (or gravy substitute).

This combination (cooked meat, gravy, and vegetables) makes your filling for meat pie. Turn mixture into 6, 7, or 8 inch casserole, so mixture comes to top of dish.

1½ Hours before Dinner

Make ½ Master Recipe, Pastry (p. 446). On floured board, roll dough (with floured rolling pin) to shape an upper crust (p. 448), about 1¼ inches wider in diameter than top of baking dish. Fold pastry over double, with loose center fold. Cut slashes near fold, for steam vents. Place pastry over contents of dish. Crimp edges of crust to dish, firmly. Place dish in preheated very hot oven (450°) about 10 minutes, then reduce heat to moderate (350°) and bake 35 to 45 minutes more, until all contents of dish are hot.

While pie is baking, wash and crisp greens; make salad; set table; warm dinner plates. Make coffee. When pie is done, all other things should be ready too.

MENU #9: TUESDAY

Chicken à la King, on Hot Rice (using leftover chicken from Menu 7)
>String Beans (frozen)
>>Ginger Ale Fruit Salad
>>>Brownies (from Menu 8)
>>>>Coffee, Tea or Milk

A.M. Read

A la King Sauce (p. 250); note ingredients for marketing.
Ginger Ale Fruit Salad (p. 363); note ingredients for marketing.
Rice; Master Recipe, Steamed White Rice (p. 305).
Cooking: Make Ginger Ale Fruit Salad, *before noon.* Remember to rinse mold out under cold water before putting gelatine mixture in mold.

1½ Hours before Dinner

Remove leftover sections of fricasseed chicken from gravy, saving gravy for another day. Cut up into cubes enough chicken meat to make 1½ cups, removing skin and bones.

In top section of double boiler, over moderate heat, make à la king sauce. When thickened, add cubed chicken meat to it. Place top section of double boiler over lower section, containing 1½ inches hot water. Place double boiler over low heat, to keep chicken hot until serving time.

Measure rice, salt, water; start rice cooking. As soon as it has boiled 1 minute, stir; then remove to lowest heat, keeping pan covered tightly.

Wash and crisp greens.

Set table. Put dinner plates to warm.

Measure coffee.

Unmold (p. 362) ginger ale fruit salad onto serving platter; arrange crisped greens around it. Put back in refrigerator until serving time.

Heat in saucepan 1½ inches water plus ½ teaspoon salt, for beans.

When rice is nearly fully fluffed up, start beans cooking; start coffee.

When beans are tender, serve dinner. Place a helping of hot rice on each dinner plate; top it with chicken mixture. Garnish with paprika, parsley. Serve beans alongside.

Ready: Salad, coffee, brownies.

MENU #10: WEDNESDAY

Pan-Broiled Liver and Bacon
Broccoli (frozen), Hot Mayonnaise
German Fried Potatoes
Ginger Ale Fruit Salad (left over)
Square Cake, with Maple Butter Frosting
Coffee, Tea or Milk

A.M. Read

Pan-Broiled Liver (p. 84); note thinness of slices, for marketing.

Pan-Broiled Bacon (p. 85).

Cake: Read carefully: Basic Principles for Baking Powder Cakes (pp. 410–412); Master Recipe, Quick 2-Egg Cake (p. 412). To bake as Square Cake (p. 414).

Frostings; Read Basic Principles (pp. 426–428). Master Recipe, Butter Frosting (p. 430); and Maple Variation.

Note ingredients needed for cake and frosting; add to first-course foods, for marketing.

A.M. or Early Afternoon

Reread Basic Principles for Cake Making; your first cake is important, and will not be successful unless you know what you are to do. Then mix Master Recipe, Quick 2-Egg Cake. Use batter as directed under Square Cake (p. 414). Bake cake. Cool it. Make Maple Variation, Butter Frosting (p. 432). Spread frosting on. After frosting has become firm, store cake in covered tin box; it will dry out if exposed to air.

Making and baking your first cake may take about 2 hours.

1¼ Hours before Dinner

Clean and prepare liver slices, removing tendons, if any. Do not cook yet.

Set table. Put dinner plates to warm.

Prepare greens; arrange salad. Store again in refrigerator, until serving.

Peel, wash off, and slice in ⅛ inch slices, 4 or 5 medium potatoes. Place in heated frying pan, containing 2 to 3 tablespoons hot cooking fat. Add 1 peeled onion, thinly sliced. Sprinkle potatoes with salt. Cover pan, and leave cooking over moderate heat. (Turn potatoes, now and then, to prevent sticking and burning.)

Pan-broil 2 or 3 strips bacon per person (p. 85). When cooked and drained, keep in warming drawer, or other warm place (but not over direct heat) until serving.

In top of double boiler, put 2 to 3 tablespoons mayonnaise. Stir into it juice of ½ lemon. Place pan over lower section of double boiler, containing 1½ inches hot water. Place double boiler over low heat, until serving time, to heat the mayonnaise. (This makes a sort of substitute for Hollandaise Sauce.)

In saucepan, heat 1½ inches water plus ½ teaspoon salt. When boiling, add frozen broccoli. Cover pan. Cook over moderate heat.

Start coffee cooking.

Look at potatoes; if tender when pricked with fork, turn heat low.

Have heavy frying pan only moderately warm. Add 2 to 3 tablespoons bacon fat or other cooking fat. Season liver with flour, salt; place a few slices at a time in frying pan. Watch liver carefully, ignoring all else while you cook this delicate meat. Turn as soon as browned on lower side; brown on second side; turn heat low; cook a few minutes longer. The instant it is done and tender, lift pieces out, putting them on warm plate, in warm place (not over heat) while you cook more pieces if necessary.

Try broccoli with fork; when stalks are tender, remove from heat.

As soon as all liver is ready, drain broccoli; serve liver, bacon, potatoes, broccoli; over broccoli, put garnish of hot mayonnaise.

Ready: Salad, coffee, cake.

MENU #11: THURSDAY

Chicken Pie, with Pastry Crust (made from leftover Fricasseed Chicken)
> Mixed Greens
> French Dressing
> Cake (leftover from Menu 10)
If desired, add fresh or canned fruit.
> Coffee, Tea or Milk

A.M.

This is the kind of day when you can go gallivanting if you wish. Prepare the ingredients for your chicken pie in the morning, and you have nothing to do until about 1½ hours before dinner.

Re-read:

Basic Principles, Pastry (p. 445); and Master Recipe, Pastry (p. 446).

Cooking: In bowl, mix ½ all ingredients for Master Recipe, Pastry, except the water. Do not add water to pastry mixture until time to roll out the dough, just before baking pie for dinner.

Cut leftover chicken to bite-size pieces, freed of skin, bones, making about 2 cups chicken meat. Combine with 1½ to 2 cups leftover chicken gravy. If you haven't enough gravy, add to it, or substitute, undiluted canned cream of chicken, or cream of mushroom soup, or medium white sauce. Add about 1 cup combined cooked, drained peas, and sautéed or drained canned mushrooms. (If you haven't these vegetables handy, get them at market and prepare them before night.) Add also to chicken mixture 1 or 2 tablespoons grated raw onion.

1½ Hours before Dinner

Put combined chicken, vegetables and gravy (prepared in morning) into one family-sized casserole, or into individual ramekins, filling dishes to top.

Preheat oven to very hot (450°)

Complete the pastry begun in A.M., but adding water carefully. Roll out pastry dough on floured board, with floured rolling pin, shaping to make upper crust (p. 448) for 1 large, or 2 or 3 individual-size, baking dishes; cut crust 1½ inches wider in diameter than top of each baking dish. Double crusts over loosely; cut slashes near fold for steam vents; lift crusts to top of pie dishes. Crimp edges of pastry firmly to baking dish, all the way around. Place pies in oven, keeping heat very hot (450°) first 10 minutes, then reducing to moderate (350°); continue to bake 25 to 30 minutes longer.

While pie(s) bake, wash and crisp greens; prepare salad; store in refrigerator.

Set table. Put dinner plates to warm.

Arrange cake (and fruit, if using it) on dessert plates.

Measure and begin cooking coffee.

As soon as pies are nicely browned on top, and thoroughly hot, serve; the whole main course is complete in the pie.

Ready: Salad, coffee, dessert.

MENU #12: FRIDAY

Shallow-Fried Fish Fillets, Tartar Sauce
Watercress, Sliced Tomatoes
Baked Potato
Lemon Meringue Pie
Coffee, Tea or Milk

A.M. Read

How to Shallow-Fry (pp. 96–101; see Specific Recommendations for Fish, p. 104).

Egg-and-Crumb Coating (p. 100).

Jot down amount of cooking fat needed for frying, and list ingredients needed for coating of food, for marketing; also check ingredients needed for Tartar Sauce (p. 354); for Pastry (p. 446); Lemon Pie Filling (p. 460); Meringue Topping for Pie (p. 489).

Cooking: Make Tartar Sauce (p. 354); store in refrigerator until dinner.

Early Afternoon

Read Meringue-Topped Pies (p. 460). Make and bake your pie shell. Make lemon filling. Make meringue. Put pie together. Brown the meringue top, in oven. Allow yourself at least 1½ to 2 hours for this whole job, first time you do it.

1¼ Hours before Dinner

Heat oven for potatoes; scrub and prepare them; start them baking.

Wash greens; leave them to crisp.

Slice tomatoes; marinate them (p. 333) in French dressing.

Set table.

Measure coffee in coffee maker.

Wipe pieces of fish clean. Prepare crumbs in one dish, egg-mixed-with-water in another dish, to be ready for egg-and-crumb coating (p. 100).

Reread How to Shallow-Fry (p. 99), plus safety rules for shallow-frying, while waiting for potatoes to bake. It is important to know exactly what you do, and how to handle the hot cooking fat.

Coat pieces of fish in egg-and-crumb coating.

When potatoes are about tender, when tested with fork, start heating cooking fat 1 inch deep in heavy frying pan, heating it about 5 minutes over moderate heat. Then test with thermometer, or make bread-cube test (p. 100), making sure fat is at 375°.

As soon as fat is right temperature, lower fish into it carefully, using pancake turner to lift fish.

Start heat under coffee.

Watch fish; it takes only 2 or 3 minutes to brown a nice golden color on lower side. Then carefully turn it over, browning other side similarly. When golden brown all over, lift carefully from hot fat to plate lined with paper towel. Leave fish there a minute or so to drain.

While fish drains, open and season baked potatoes; put these on dinner plates. Add to plates drained watercress, topped with sliced drained tomatoes. Then put fish on plates. Add tartar sauce.

Ready also: Pie, coffee.

NOTE: Your salad this day was the watercress and tomatoes served in place of a hot vegetable. This was done to permit you to give entire last-minute attention to the shallow-frying.

MENU #13: SATURDAY

Chicken Croquettes (from leftover Chicken Fricassee)
Mashed Potatoes
Carrots and Peas, diced (frozen)
Asparagus Tips (canned) on Lettuce
French Dressing
Blue Cheese, if desired
Lemon Meringue Pie (leftover)
Coffee, Tea or Milk

If you have no more chicken, try some other kind of croquettes, so you can learn the method; see Variations under Master Recipe (p. 155).

A.M. Read

You Can Make Croquettes, Basic Principles (p. 151); Master Recipe, Chicken Croquettes (p. 155).

Jot down ingredients needed for making croquette mixture; put on marketing list. Add vegetables, salad need, for today. Also buy for Sunday. Buy *half* of a "ready-to-eat" ham, having butcher cut off a crosswise slice ½ to ¾ inch thick, to use as ham steak.

Cooking: Prepare 2 cups diced or ground chicken, for use in croquettes; you may include ¼ cup ground, cooked chicken skin, if desired. If you still haven't enough chicken, add enough cooked rice, or cooked peas, or cooked mushrooms, to make 2 cups solids, with chicken.

Make 1 cup very thick white sauce (p. 248).

Combine chicken, sauce, seasonings, egg, as in Master Recipe, Chicken Croquettes (p. 155).

Put to chill.

P.M.

Reread: How to Shallow-Fry (p. 99), through Safety Rules. See also shallow-fried croquettes (p. 102).

1½ Hours before Dinner

Peel, wash off, cut up potatoes. Put in saucepan. Cover with water. Add ½ teaspoon salt. Cover pan. Start them boiling.

Wash greens for salad; leave them to crisp. Drain canned asparagus tips; "marinate" them (p. 333) in French dressing (p. 356).

Set table. Put dinner plates to warm.

Measure coffee, for coffee maker.

Drain greens. Drain asparagus tips. Arrange tips on greens, topping with crumbled blue cheese if desired. Cover. Store in refrigerator.

Get from refrigerator croquette mixture. Shape into croquettes (p. 155). Coat in egg-and-crumb coating (p. 100), rolling each croquette in coating, covering all sides equally. Do not cook croquettes yet.

As soon as potatoes are tender, drain off water; mash them; season them (p. 301). Replace cover ¾ way over saucepan top; place pan on asbestos mat, over lowest heat, to keep potatoes warm.

Heat in another saucepan ½ inch water plus ½ teaspoon salt, for carrots and peas. As soon as water boils, put in the frozen vegetables. Cover pan; continue cooking.

Start coffee cooking.

Start heating, in heavy frying pan, 1 inch deep fat, over moderate heat; heat about 5 minutes.

Test fat in frying pan, by thermometer, or by bread-cube test (p. 100); it should be at 385° to 390°.

When fat is at proper heat, carefully lower croquettes into hot fat, with pancake turner. Watch them closely. They will only need 2 to 3 minutes on each side, to become golden brown and done. When turning them, turn carefully, not to break them. When done, lift from hot fat with pancake turner; drain on paper towel for 1 or 2 minutes before serving. Garnish croquettes, if desired, with parsley and paprika.

Serve: Croquettes, mashed potatoes, vegetable.
Ready: Salad, coffee, leftover pie.

MENU #14: SUNDAY

Ham Steak (a crosswise slice cut from ½ ham)
Glazed Sweet Potatoes (buy canned)
Brussels Sprouts (frozen)
Watercress (left from Menu #12)
Sliced Avocado Pear
French Dressing, Blue Cheese
Slices of Maple-Frosted Cake (leftover) topped with
Coffee or Maple Walnut Ice Cream
Coffee, Tea or Milk

Some families use cake up rapidly; in other homes it remains available for days. If you have no cake left, buy instead some store sponge cake; or just have dishes of ice cream topped with a dessert sauce (p. 405).

NOTE: This is a dinner which requires little time to prepare. You can get the whole dinner in ¾ hour or so.

Before starting, however, read: Pan-Broiled Ham Steak (p. 79), Glazed Sweet Potatoes (done in saucepan, page 297), Avocado Pear (p. 316).

Wash greens; put them to crisp.

Peel, then slice, ½ avocado pear. Cover sliced pear at once with waxed paper, to prevent its darkening. Store in refrigerator.

Set table. Put dinner plates to warm. Also warm a platter for ham steak.

Measure coffee, for coffee maker.

Open can of sweet potatoes. Slice them in halves lengthwise. Arrange them in saucepan, with seasonings needed; start cooking gently.

Prepare ham; if it has rind, trim this off. Cut slashes in ham fat around outside. Get out frying pan, but don't heat yet.

In saucepan, heat ½ inch water and ½ teaspoon salt, for Brussels sprouts. As soon as water boils, put sprouts in. Cover pan. Let them cook over moderate heat.

Drain greens; arrange sliced pear on top, spooning French dressing over all. Cover and store salad in refrigerator until serving.

Start coffee cooking.

Look at sweet potatoes. Turn them over, if needed.

Rub large heavy frying pan with ham fat; put over moderate heat; place slice of ham in it, without salting. Brown first on one side, then on the other; then turn fire low and cook another few minutes, until ham becomes tender and thoroughly hot.

As soon as sprouts are tender when pricked with fork, drain.

Lift ham steak to heated platter. If you have room, surround it with glazed sweet potatoes, and drained sprouts. Add garnish of 2 or 3 sprigs parsley or watercress.

Ready: Coffee, salad; cake and ice cream.

MENU #15: MONDAY

Pan-Broiled Meat Cakes
> Buttered Sliced Beets (canned)
> French-Fried Potatoes
>> Endive, with Sliced Leftover Avocado Pear, and Tomato
>> (Add crumbled blue cheese, if desired)
>>> Frozen Crumb Pudding
>>> Coffee, Tea or Milk

Even if you haven't deep-frying kettle, you may still cook these potatoes. Prepare potatoes as for any French-fried potatoes (p. 112), but shallow-fry in 1 inch deep hot fat, heated to 375°, in heavy frying pan.

A.M. Read

Frozen Crumb Pudding (p. 404). Note ingredients needed for marketing list. You can use any leftover cake or brownie crumbs for this, or buy a store box of cookies.

How to French-Fry (pp. 106–109), also, see French-Fried Potatoes (p. 112). Today, follow Method I, for these potatoes. Pan-Broiled Meat Cakes (p. 81).

By Noon

Make frozen crumb pudding. Store in refrigerator.

1¼ Hours before Dinner

Wash greens; leave them soaking, to crisp.

Slice avocado, plus 1 tomato; "marinate" them in French dressing (p. 333).

Peel, wash, and slice potatoes in ⅜ inch thick strips. Leave them soaking in cold water, while you do a few other things.

Get out ground meat; season it if desired (p. 81); shape meat cakes. Don't cook yet.

Open can of beets; turn beets and juice into saucepan. Don't cook yet.

Set table. Put dinner plates to warm.

Measure coffee, for coffee maker.

Dry greens; arrange in salad bowl, with avocado and tomatoes; if desired, add a bit of grated raw onion, or crumbled blue cheese. Cover salad bowl with waxed paper; store in refrigerator.

Drain potatoes; pat dry with towel.

Start heating oven to 250° (slow); have it ready to store potatoes in, after they are cooked, to keep them warm; for, this being your first French-frying, we are going to fry the potatoes first, and store them while you immediately afterwards pan-broil the meat.

Heat deep saucepan ½ filled with cooking fat, over moderate heat, about 5 minutes, or until fat is at 375°. Test the fat. When right temperature, lower potatoes into it; start them frying. Do not overcrowd pan. Do not go away from kitchen, leaving fat over heat. Give attention until potatoes are golden brown and tender. Lift carefully from hot fat with slotted spoon. Drain on plate lined with paper towel; sprinkle hot potatoes with salt. Place potatoes in oven, to keep warm.

Start coffee cooking.

Place pan of beets, covered, over moderate to high heat.

Heat heavy frying pan. Salt meat; start pan-broiling it; see meat cakes (p. 81).

As soon as meat cakes are browned, on both sides, turn heat low; also turn heat low under beets, until meat is done.

Drain water off beets, just before serving; add a large lump of butter to pan; turn beets around in it, to coat all sides.

Serve meat cakes, beets, potatoes. Add a sprig of parsley, for color.

Ready: Salad, coffee, dessert.

MENU #16: TUESDAY

Baked Glazed Half Ham (the ½ ham purchased for Menu #14)
Creamed Cauliflower
Glazed Sweet Potatoes (leftover)
Halves of Canned Peaches on Lettuce
Fruit-Mayonnaise Dressing
Frozen Crumb Pudding (leftover)
Coffee, Tea or Milk

A.M. Read

A Baked Ham (p. 132).

Creamed Vegetables (p. 294).

Glazed Sweet Potatoes (p. 297).

For marketing list, make note of cloves, brown sugar, to "glaze" ham. Buy a small head of of cauliflower. Add other necessities, staples.

P.M. 3 Hours before Dinner

Start oven at 300° (slow); put ham in paper bags, and start heating, allowing 15 minutes per pound; see ready-to-eat ham (p. 134). You don't have to stay and watch it.

1¼ Hours before Dinner

Prepare cauliflower. Remove all leaves, and excess stem. Wash under cold water. You may cook the head whole, or separate head into flowerets by cutting off each cluster of the head from the stem. Put cauliflower in saucepan with 1 inch hot water plus ½ teaspoon salt. Cover. Cook over moderate heat, until tender.

While cauliflower cooks, wash greens; leave them to crisp.

Slice leftover sweet potatoes lengthwise. Make syrup for glazing (p. 297); put potatoes in it, to heat.

Drain canned peaches. Set table. Put dinner plates to warm. Mix 2 tablespoons peach juice and 1 teaspoon lemon juice with ¼ cup mayonnaise, to make Fruit-Mayonnaise dressing.

Arrange dessert in dishes; store in refrigerator.

Shake greens dry; arrange salad; store in refrigerator.

Measure coffee, for coffee maker.

As soon as ham has baked 15 minutes per pound, take from oven. Follow Step (3) and Step (4) under Uncooked Hams (p. 133) to remove rind and prepare for glazing. When ham has been prepared with sugar and cloves, put in oven.

As soon as cauliflower is tender when tested with fork, drain, saving water. Make 1 cup medium white sauce (p. 248), substituting ½ cup top milk or evaporated milk, plus ½ cup cauliflower water, instead of whole milk. Taste sauce for seasoning; add more salt if needed. When sauce is thickened, add the drained cauliflower; place over asbestos mat, over lowest heat, to keep warm until ham is ready.

Start coffee cooking.

As soon as ham is well glazed, and other vegetables ready, serve. Ready also: Salad, coffee, dessert.

MENU #17: WEDNESDAY

Lamb Stew
> Sliced Canned Pineapple and Fresh Banana on Lettuce;
> Fruit Juice-Mayonnaise Dressing (p. 353).
> Cookies (Homemade)
> Coffee, Tea or Milk

This is not such an easy day as it looks. Allow yourself plenty of time to cook. You are learning to make two new things: Stew and Cookies. Both take time. A woman I know says she never hires a cook until she has tried her out on stew: if the woman can make a good stew, she can make anything. I would not hold with this, exactly; I do not think stew is difficult; but it takes time to learn what you are doing, and why, on *any* new type food.

A.M. Read

Stews (p. 120); take time to refer to Master Recipe, Pot Roast (p. 117), which you have cooked once before; refresh your mind on the system. Put stewing lamb, carrots, peas, and all stew seasonings, on marketing list.

You Can Make Cookies (p. 480) through Master Recipe, Sugar Cookies (p. 482). Today, make drop cookies; another time, try sliced or cut-out cookies, from same recipe for cookie dough. Note cookie ingredients for marketing list.

If you go to market, add salad needs, staples for tomorrow.

Early Afternoon:

Make cookies. Allow yourself 1 to 1½ hours for this.

2½ Hours before Dinner

Begin stew, starting the lamb to cook. You may either braise the pieces of lamb, as in *Step 1, Pot Roast;* or you may *omit* the braising. If omitting the braising, simply put pieces of lamb in deep kettle; add water and Group I Seasonings, as under *Step 2, Pot Roast.* Bring water to a boil; then reduce heat, covering pan, and leave lamb simmering gently. You don't have to stay and watch it.

1¼ Hours before Dinner

Peel, wash, and cut up into good-sized chunks a few large potatoes and carrots. Add these to simmering kettle of stew. If desired, peel and add also several small whole onions. Do not add peas yet. Cover kettle again, and let it continue simmering gently.

Wash salad greens; leave in water to crisp. Drain canned pineapple.

Set table. Put dinner plates to warm.

Measure coffee for coffee maker.

Dry salad greens; arrange greens and sliced fruit on salad plates; make fruit-juice mayonnaise dressing (p. 353), using a little canned pineapple juice. Garnish salad with dash or two of paprika. Store salads in refrigerator until serving.

Test stew meat, potatoes, carrots, with fork. When all seem almost tender, add shelled fresh or frozen peas; cover kettle again, and cook until peas wrinkle slightly.

Start coffee cooking.

When all stew ingredients are tender, thicken gravy, as in *Step 4, Pot Roast* (p. 119), first lifting out of kettle all meat and vegetables (with slotted spoon), then adding required flour for thickening, in accordance with amount of liquid which remains in kettle.

When gravy is thickened, put vegetables back in it, to reheat for a minute or two.

Serve Stew. Ready: Salad, coffee, cookies . . . *your own!*

MENU #18: THURSDAY

Baked Ham and Apple Casserole (from leftover cooked ham)
Succotash (frozen limas plus frozen kernel corn)
Potatoes and Onions Baked in Milk
Spinach Leaf and Bacon Salad; French Dressing
Baked Custard
Coffee, Tea or Milk

A.M. Read

Baked Ham and Apple Casserole (p. 136). Note ingredients for marketing list: brown sugar, apples, lemon.

Under Preparation of Salad Greens: Spinach Leaves (p. 331); note ingredients needed for salad.

You Can Make Custards (p. 384); skip over Soft Custard and its Variations, but read Master Recipe, Baked Custard (p. 388). Note ingredients, for marketing list.

Morning or Early Afternoon
Make baked custard; put in refrigerator to chill, until dinner.

1½ Hours before Dinner
Turn on oven to 350°, or moderate.

While oven warms, peel and slice potatoes and onions; arrange in casserole in alternate layers, sprinkled with salt; cover with milk. Put potato casserole in oven, uncovered.

In another casserole, arrange sliced ham; add peeled, cored, sliced apples; season with brown sugar, lemon juice. Cover casserole with lid, or with piece of aluminum foil. Place in oven.

Pan broil 4 strips bacon, then drain on paper towel: see page 85.

Wash and crisp tender spinach leaves in several waters; then shake dry. Put leaves in salad bowl. Add crumbled cooked bacon. Add some crumbled blue cheese if desired. Add 2 or 3 tablespoons French dressing. Cover bowl with waxed paper; store in refrigerator until serving.

Set table; put dinner plates to warm.

Measure coffee, in coffee maker.

Start coffee cooking.

Heat in 2 quart saucepan 1 inch water plus ½ teaspoon salt. As soon as water boils, add the frozen lima beans; cover saucepan and cook; and when beans begin to feel tender, add the frozen corn to same kettle. Cook, covered, about 5 minutes more, until corn is cooked, then remove pan from heat.

Test potatoes with fork; if they feel tender, and if apples in ham casserole also feel tender, serve main course.

Ready also: Salad, coffee, custard.

MENU #19: FRIDAY

Creamed (or Curried) Shrimps (buy 1 large or 2 small cans
  shrimp)
  Rice Ring
  String Beans (frozen)
    Stuffed Fresh Whole Tomatoes on Greens (allow 1
      tomato per person)
      Crackers and Cheese
        or
      a half Cantaloupe

A.M. Read

Under Boiled Fresh Shrimp (p. 169), To Clean Shrimp; note
that canned shrimps must also be cleaned this way.

Creamed Shrimp, or Curried Shrimp (whichever you wish to
make) page 170.

Master Recipe, Steamed White Rice (p. 305); and read Rice
Ring (p. 306).

Stuffed Tomato Salad (p. 336).

Note all ingredients needed, under recipes above; add string
beans, cheese or other dessert; staples.

1½ Hours before Dinner

Wash, peel (if desired), then cut open — flower-fashion — the
tomatoes.

In bowl, combine ingredients to use for stuffing tomatoes; add
seasonings, dressing. Put stuffing into tomatoes. Place tomatoes in
refrigerator, until later.

Open can of shrimps; drain off and discard juice; clean shrimps.

Measure raw rice, water, salt, and bring to boil in saucepan;
stir; then place pan, covered tightly, over lowest heat.

Make 2 cups medium white sauce (p. 248), or 2 cups curry
sauce (p. 249), in top section of double boiler, but using this pan
over direct heat. When sauce has thickened, add the cleaned
shrimps; then place pan containing shrimps and sauce over lower

section of double boiler, which has in it 1½ inches hot water. Cover. Keep over gentle to moderate heat, so shrimps may heat thoroughly in sauce.

Wash greens; shake dry; arrange on plates. Add one tomato on each plate.

Arrange dessert on plates.

Set table; put dinner plates to warm; also a platter for rice ring.

Measure coffee, for coffee maker.

As soon as rice is puffed up and done, make it into rice ring; leave ring mold in shallow pan of hot water, over lowest heat.

In saucepan, heat ½ inch water plus ½ teaspoon salt, for frozen string beans. As soon as water boils, add beans. Cover pan. Cook over moderately high heat.

Start coffee.

As soon as beans are tender, unmold rice ring onto platter. Fill center of ring with shrimps and sauce. Arrange drained beans in circle around outside of ring.

Ready: Salad, coffee, dessert.

MENU #20: SATURDAY

Broiled Steak, smothered with Sautéed Onions
Broccoli (Frozen)
Baked Potatoes
Chef's Salad Bowl
Apple Pie and Cheese
Coffee, Tea or Milk

A.M. Read

Basic Principles and Master Recipe, Broiling (p. 68), through Specific Recommendations for Steaks (p. 69).

Master Recipe, Chef's Salad (p. 339). Baked White Potatoes (p. 296).

Basic Principles and Master Recipe, Sautéing (p. 93), Sautéed Onions (p. 96).

Master Recipe, Pastry (p. 446); Two-Crust Pies (p. 447); Master Recipe #77, Fruit Pie (p. 452), Apple Variation (p. 454).

List all foods and ingredients needed for marketing. Add needs for Sunday; look up ingredients for stuffing (p. 241).

Early Afternoon

Make Master Recipe, Pastry (p. 446). Roll to shape upper and lower crusts. Peel and slice tart apples. Put pie together; bake. Cool pie on wire rack. Allow 1½ to 2 hours for the whole job, until you become more accustomed to it.

1¼ Hours before Dinner

Turn on oven, for potatoes. Scrub and prick potatoes; put them in oven to start baking.

Wash greens; leave them in water to crisp.

Peel and slice onions, for sautéing; don't cook yet.

Clean, slice, or otherwise prepare other salad ingredients.

Drain greens; arrange salad in bowl; cover with waxed paper, store in refrigerator.

Set table; put dinner plates to warm; also warm a platter for steak.

Cut some American cheese in slices or wedges, to serve with pie.

Preheat broiling unit of oven.

Heat ½ inch water plus ½ teaspoon salt in saucepan, for broccoli. When potatoes feel nearly tender, put frozen broccoli in the boiling water in saucepan; cover; leave cooking over moderate heat.

Warm a frying pan containing 2 to 3 tablespoons butter or bacon fat. Add sliced onions. Cook, stirring often, until tender.

Start coffee cooking.

Place steak in broiling pan; sprinkle top of steak well with salt; place in broiling oven, so top of steak comes 2 to 3 inches below heat of broiling unit. If fat of steak starts to splatter too much, turn broiling heat lower, or move steak farther from heat; but cook steak as rapidly as possible, allowing about 5 minutes to brown top side. As soon as well browned, turn it over; salt other side; brown second side. If steak is thin (½ to ¾ inch) it may be done, by end of browning time. If thicker, cook a few minutes more on each side.

Meanwhile, drain broccoli. Cut open tops of baked potatoes. Put a lump of butter in each potato.

When steak is done, remove it to hot platter. Cover with sautéed onions. Serve at once. Carve steak across the grain, to make tender eating.

Ready also: Salad, coffee, pie and cheese.

After Dinner Is Over

If your family has Sunday dinner at midday, read *tonight* the required information to prepare Sunday's menu; for a stuffed, roasted bird requires several hours to prepare and cook; and you'll have to start preparation early tomorrow.

Read

You Can Make Stuffing, Basic Principles (p. 238) through Master Recipe, Plain Bread Stuffing (p. 241).

How to Roast a Bird, Master Recipe for Preparing and Roasting (p. 60) through page 65.

Giblet Gravy (p. 64).

MENU #21: SUNDAY

Roast Duck, Orange Stuffing
    Brown Rice
      Green Peas (frozen)
      Giblet Gravy
        Mixed Greens
        French Dressing
          Store Ice Cream (garnished with fresh berries, or
            with 2 teaspoons rum or brandy for each portion)
           Coffee, Tea or Milk

(If you don't like duck, or can't find one to buy, prepare instead a roast chicken. Instead of orange stuffing, make Master Recipe, Plain Bread Stuffing (p. 241). Instead of Brown Rice, substitute Steamed White Rice (p. 305). Allow at least ½ to 1 hour longer to roast a chicken than to roast a duck; in other words, start earlier in the day, to prepare and stuff your chicken.)

NOTE: If you have not already done so, read about making Stuffing, and Master Method for Preparing and Roasting a Bird, as recommended at end of Menu 20. Do this early. For your first try at this job, you will need to allow yourself 3½ to 4 hours' time, to prepare, stuff, and roast your bird; and you must know how to go about it. First time, it will doubtless seem hard; next time it will seem easy.

3½ to 4 Hours before Dinner

Make Orange Variation, Plain Bread Stuffing (p. 242), for duck; or Plain Bread Stuffing, for Chicken. Leave the stuffing in a bowl until bird is ready.

Turn on oven, to moderately slow (325°).

Begin to prepare bird, at once. Follow Master Method for Preparing and Roasting Bird (p. 61), carrying out, in order, as given in book, Step 1: Cleaning the Bird; Step 2, Stuffing It; Step 3. Trussing It; Step 4, Seasoning It. (If preparing duck, see p. 66 for special additional tips on duck.)

2 Hours before Dinner (for Duck); 2½ Hours before Dinner (for Chicken)

Place prepared bird on a rack in open roasting pan.

Place pan in preheated oven, centering the bird, so heat is equal on all sides of bird.

Now relax; the worst is over. You can do other things. From now until bird has finished cooking, you need only look at it once in a while (about every 20 to 25 minutes), to see that it is not browning too much on any one side; if it is, turn it over to another side. With duck, pour off excessive grease which accumulates in pan, every ½ hour. If desired, baste the duck once or twice in first hour of cooking, with ¼ cup fresh orange juice.

While bird roasts, read Giblet Gravy (p. 64). Start giblets cooking now, so they can become tender. And read Brown Rice (p. 307); or, if roasting a chicken, reread Steamed White Rice (p. 305).

45 to 50 Minutes before Dinner

Start rice cooking; see recipe for kind of rice you are using.

Wash greens; leave in cold water, to crisp.

Set table. Put dinner dishes, and platter for bird, to warm.

Measure coffee for coffee maker.

Shake greens dry; arrange salad in bowl; cover with waxed paper; store in refrigerator.

As soon as giblets are tender when tested with fork, lift them out of cooking water (saving water); put them in chopping bowl, or on wooden board; chop them to pieces size of peas. Also remove from cooking water the parsley, celery, onion. Then return chopped giblets to cooking water. Keep on back of stove, until time to make gravy.

10 Minutes before Dinner

Start coffee cooking.

Heat ½ inch water plus ½ teaspoon salt in saucepan, for frozen peas. As soon as water boils, add frozen peas; cover pan; cook over moderate heat, about 5 minutes, or just until peas wrinkle slightly; then remove pan from heat.

Make gravy: In saucepan, mix 4 tablespoons flour, plus ½ teaspoon salt; stir in a little (¼ cup) liquid giblets were cooked in. Cook over medium heat, stirring constantly, until thick and smooth. Now lift roast bird from oven; and remove bird from roasting pan to hot platter; pour off any excess fat which may be in roasting pan, keeping only about 4 tablespoons fat. Stir this fat into flour mixture. Then stir in remainder of water used for cooking giblets, plus the chopped giblets. Cook, stirring constantly, over medium heat, until mixture boils and thickens (about 5 minutes).

If desired, add 1 teaspoon grated raw onion, to increase flavor. Taste gravy; if needed, add more salt.

Serve: Roast bird, on platter; gravy in separate gravy boat; drain rice, and put it in hot serving dish; add a lump of butter; drain and serve peas, adding a lump of butter.

Ready: Salad, coffee, ice cream.

MENU #22: MONDAY

Ham Fritters, with Maple Syrup
   Baked Squash (use Acorn, Butternut, or Summer Squash)
   Spinach (frozen)
        Rings of Green Pepper stuffed with Seasoned Cottage
           Cheese, on Lettuce
        French Dressing
              Pineapple (or Peach) Upside-Down Cake
              Coffee, Tea or Milk

Buy real maple syrup. Or you can make a good imitation, in a few minutes, in the morning, as follows: Make plain sugar syrup (p. 476). After taking syrup off heat, stir in at once 1 teaspoon (or more, if desired) bottled maple flavoring. Cool syrup before using).

A.M. Read

You Can Make Fritters (p. 212); Master Recipe, Fritters (p. 213). Note ingredients needed, for marketing list. (Use your left-over cooked ham as the meat.)

Baked Squash (pp. 295–296); select kind you wish to buy. Acorn Squash will be sweeter-tasting than the others, because of brown sugar used.

Basic Principles, Baking Powder Cakes; and Master Recipe, Quick 2-Egg Cake (pp. 410–414). Read Variation for Upside Down Cake (p. 416). Note ingredients needed, for marketing list; including cake batter ingredients, can of fruit, and brown sugar.

Add whipping cream, if desired. Add other necessities to marketing list.

Early Afternoon

Mix Quick 2-Egg Cake batter; leave batter in bowl, for the moment.

In square 8 x 8 x 2 inch cake pan melt together butter and brown sugar; add drained fruit; see Upside Down Cake (p. 416). Pour uncooked batter over top of fruit. Bake cake in moderate (350°) oven, 45 to 55 minutes. After cooling, turn cake out on platter. Do not garnish with whipped cream until serving time.

NOTE: Later, when more experienced, you can make Upside Down Cake just before dinner time, and serve it hot.

1½ Hours before Dinner

Turn on oven, to preheat for squash (see correct heat under recipe for type of squash you are cooking). While oven heats, clean and prepare squash for baking. Put squash in oven, to start baking (unless it is summer squash, which is tenderer, and requires only 30 to 40 minutes).

Wash greens; leave them in water to crisp.

Wash a whole, firm, green pepper; cut it in half, crosswise. Scoop out pulp and seeds. Into cavity, pack lightly cottage cheese seasoned with ¼ teaspoon salt, few dashes pepper, 1 teaspoon grated onion or 1 tablespoon minced fresh chives. When green pepper is all packed with cheese mixture, place pepper sideways on board, and cut off crosswise slices ⅜ inch thick. Allow 1 or 2 slices per person. Arrange slices on crisped greens; sprinkle on a dash or two of paprika; add 1 or 2 tablespoons French dressing to each salad. Store salads in refrigerator, until serving time.

Set table. Put dinner plates to warm.

Measure coffee, for coffee maker. Put maple syrup in serving pitcher.

If whipped cream is desired for cake, whip and sweeten it now. Store in refrigerator.

Dice enough cooked ham to make 1 cup. Make Master Recipe, Fritters (p. 213), using the ham as your meat.

In saucepan, heat ½ inch water plus ½ teaspoon salt. When water is boiling, add frozen spinach. Cover pan. Cook over moderate heat, until tender.

Start coffee cooking.

Meanwhile, in heavy frying pan, heat 1 inch deep cooking fat; read Master Recipe, Shallow-Frying (p. 99), if you have forgotten. Have fat at 390°. Drop fritter batter, by tablespoonful (but using a long-handled spoon) into hot fat. Fry 2 or 3 minutes just until fritters are golden brown on bottom side; turn them over carefully, without splattering yourself; fry until golden brown on second side. With slotted spoon, remove fritters from hot fat; drain on paper towel, for a minute, before serving.

While fritters drain, drain cooked spinach. Take cooked squash from oven.

Serve: Fritters, syrup, squash, spinach.

Ready: Salad, coffee, upside-down cake.

MENU #23: TUESDAY

Steak and Kidney Pie, Biscuit Crust (use leftover steak; order 6 lambs' kidneys)
> Baby Lima Beans (frozen)
> Baked Tomatoes (allow 1 tomato per person)
>> Mixed Greens
>> (add leftover green pepper rings, if any)
>> Crumbled Blue Cheese
>> French Dressing
>>> Upside Down Cake (leftover)
>>> Coffee, Tea or Milk

A.M. Read

Sautéed Lamb's Kidneys (p. 94); also Beef and Kidney Pie (p. 126). Reread: Master Recipe, Biscuits (p. 198).

Jot down required ingredients from all these recipes; add vegetables, greens, and whatever staples are needed.

1¼ Hours before Dinner

Trim off fat and suet from leftover steak; cut meat into cubes about ¾ to 1 inch square. Put the fat and suet in a frying pan, over low heat, to melt, until you have 3 or 4 tablespoons liquid fat; then discard remaining solid fat.

Clean and cut kidneys, removing hard white fibers; see sautéed kidneys (p. 94). Put cut-up kidneys into melted fat in frying pan. Sprinkle them with salt; add 1 tablespoon grated onion. Sauté kidneys about 5 minutes, or until browned on all sides and tender.

Now see under kidney stew (p. 126) To Make Gravy; add to frying pan the flour, beef-flavored liquid, Worcestershire sauce; stir and cook until thick. Add the cold steak cubes. Turn whole mixture into baking dish, or a pie plate which it will fill, to top.

Preheat oven to hot (425°).

Wash tomatoes; cut in half crosswise; season (see page 298), baked tomato halves). Arrange them, cut side up, in buttered pie plate or baking pan. Do not cook yet.

Now make ½ Master Recipe, Biscuits (p. 198). Roll dough on floured board, with floured rolling pin, to circular sheet large enough to cover top of pie. Place crust over pie. Crimp edges of crust to edges of dish. With knife, cut 5 or 6 slashes in top of crust, to allow steam vents.

Place kidney pie in hot oven; let it bake 20 to 25 minutes, or until biscuit crust is browned and done. When pie has been in oven 10 minutes, put into oven also the tomatoes.

Wash, crisp and dry greens. Arrange salad in bowl; cover bowl; store in refrigerator.

Set table. Put dinner plates to warm.

Measure coffee for coffee maker.

Start coffee cooking.

Heat ½ inch water plus ½ teaspoon salt, in saucepan. As soon as water boils, add frozen limas. Cover pan. Cook over moderate heat until limas wrinkle slightly, about 5 to 8 minutes. Remove from heat.

Serve: Pie, tomatoes, drained beans.

Ready: Salad, coffee, leftover upside-down cake.

MENU #24: WEDNESDAY

Macaroni and Cheese, with Diced Leftover Ham
 Brussels Sprouts (frozen)
  Chef's Salad
  French Dressing
   Boiled Custard, poured over Fresh Sliced Peaches,
   or drained Canned Peaches
   Coffee, Tea or Milk

A.M. Read

Master Recipe, Boiled Macaroni (p. 310). Also read: Macaroni and Cheese (Baked) (p. 312). Note ingredients for marketing list. You will add leftover ham to this dish.

Master Recipe, Soft Custard (p. 385). Note ingredients for marketing list.

Add other marketing essentials.

Morning or Early Afternoon

Make Soft Custard, Master Recipe. Store in refrigerator to chill.

1 Hour before Dinner

Cook ½ package macaroni, by Master Recipe. When tender, drain it.

Make 2 cups cheese sauce (p. 249), in separate saucepan; cook until thick.

Dice 1 cup cooked leftover ham (or put it through meat grinder).

Combine drained macaroni, cheese sauce, ham; add 1 table-spoon diced green pepper if desired. Turn mixture into buttered baking dish. Cover dish with crumb covering (p. 143) before baking.

Turn on oven to moderately hot (400°).

Place macaroni dish in oven.

Wash greens; leave in water to crisp, while you prepare other vegetables for chef's salad. Drain greens; arrange salad in bowl; season with salt, grated onion, French dressing. Cover bowl with waxed paper; store in refrigerator, until serving.

Set table; put dinner plates to warm.

Measure coffee, for coffee maker.

Arrange cut fruit in dessert cups; spoon chilled custard over top. Store in refrigerator, until serving time.

When macaroni has been in oven about 15 minutes, heat in saucepan ½ inch water plus ½ teaspoon salt. As soon as water boils, add frozen sprouts. Cover pan. Cook over moderate heat.

Start coffee cooking.

As soon as sprouts are tender, drain; take casserole of macaroni from oven; serve both.

Ready: Salad, coffee, dessert.

MENU #25: THURSDAY

Corned Beef Hash
Creamed Onions
Homemade Rolls
Watercress and Tomatoes
French Dressing
Blue Cheese
Sliced Fresh Peaches and Cream
or
Fresh Berries and Cream
or
Chilled Canned Fruit
Coffee, Tea or Milk

Buy a can of ready-made hash; or buy a can of corned beef and make your own corned beef hash by Master Recipe (p. 91); or if you have on hand leftover duck or chicken from Menu 21, you may use this as the meat in Master Recipe, Hash, instead of corned beef.

A.M.

This is a good day (without many other hard jobs) to try home-made rolls. But you must allow about 3½ hours before dinner, to do this. If you absolutely can't spare that much time, omit the roll making from the menu. But try them some other day, then.

Read

About Yeast Bread and Rolls (pp. 223–225), stopping at end of *Step 1, Mixing the Dough*. List ingredients needed, for marketing list.

Creamed Vegetables (p. 294). List ingredients for White Sauce (p. 248).

Add to marketing list other dinner foods needed; add staples, including plenty of butter to serve with hot rolls.

3½ Hours before Dinner

Mix entire dough of Master Recipe, Yeast Bread and Rolls. NOTE: Use the 2 packages yeast, and the 4 tablespoons sugar, for after this dough is kneaded, you are going to store half of it in refrigerator, for another day.

Now read, and carry out, *Step 2, Kneading* (p. 225).

When dough is well kneaded into a smooth ball, cut ball in half, making it into two balls. Grease outside surface of both balls, all over, lightly, with lard or vegetable shortening. Wrap one greased ball firmly in waxed paper; store it in covered bowl, in refrigerator, for another day.

Put second greased ball in a greased bowl at least twice its size; cover bowl; place bowl in a warm (85 to 90°) place, out of drafts, but not directly over a radiator or other heat. (Read *Step 3, First Rising*, p. 226.) Leave dough to rise, for at least an hour. You can go do something else.

Read Master Recipe, Hash (p. 91); if you have no cooked leftover potatoes handy, use this time to peel, dice, and boil 4 to 5 potatoes in salted water, until tender. Drain.

2 Hours before Dinner

Look at dough. If it has doubled in bulk, punch it down; see *Step 4* (p. 226). Then turn dough onto floured board; flour your hands, and knead it again for 1 or 2 minutes, until dough is firm and feels very elastic.

Immediately, shape rolls. Follow directions for raised rolls (p. 228); arrange them in greased baking pan; brush with butter; cover pan; place pan again in warm place (85° to 90°) for about 1 hour, or until rolls have doubled in bulk.

1¼ Hours before Dinner

Assemble and prepare all ingredients for your hash; season it; don't cook yet.

Wash greens, leave them to crisp. Slice tomatoes.

Peel 8 or more small whole onions (allow 4 or 5 per person); put them in saucepan; add water to cover, plus ½ teaspoon salt; cover pan. Boil over moderate heat about 20 to 25 minutes, just until onions are tender when tested with fork, but not until they begin to go to pieces.

While onions cook, make 2 cups Master Recipe, White Sauce (p. 248), using top section of double boiler over direct heat, as your saucepan. When sauce is cooked and thickened, remove from heat. When onions are tender, drain them; add them to pan of white sauce; place pan over lower section of double boiler, containing 1½ inches hot water. Cover. Place over moderate to low heat until serving time, to keep onions warm.

Put salad together in bowl; cover bowl; store in refrigerator.

Preheat oven to *hot* (425°).

Set table. Put dinner plates to warm.

Arrange dessert in serving dishes.

Measure coffee for coffee maker.

Heat frying pan containing 3 to 4 tablespoons cooking fat, for hash.

Now look at rolls; if they have doubled (or more) in size, remove covering you had over them; place pan in center of hot oven. Allow 12 to 15 minutes for rolls to bake (p. 228).

Meanwhile put hash into hot frying pan. Fry over brisk heat, first browning one side, then turning hash and browning second side. When browned, cover pan, if desired, and cook a few minutes longer over lower heat, just to heat thoroughly.

Start coffee cooking.

When rolls are nicely browned on top, and crust feels firm to fingertip touch, remove pan from oven. At once turn pan upside down over rack, or table top; rolls should slip out intact. If rolls should still look moist on bottom, put them back in baking pan, and return them to oven for another 2 to 3 minutes; then turn out again. Place rolls in a bread tray or basket, or other dish, lined with a clean linen towel. Fold towel loosely over top of rolls, to keep them warm.

Serve hash; onions. Put salad on table at same time; it is very good to eat with hash. And, of course, those rolls!

Ready also: Coffee, dessert.

MENU #26: FRIDAY

Fish and Noodle Casserole
>Chilled, Marinated, Cooked Broccoli on Lettuce, Russian Dressing
>>Blueberry, Raspberry, or Cherry Cobbler
>>Coffee, Tea or Milk

A.M. Read

Noodles or Macaroni with Fish (Baked) on page 312. If you like mackerel, 1 tall can mackerel is excellent (and inexpensive) in this dish. Otherwise, buy 1 tall can salmon, or a 7 ounce can tuna, or 2 small cans large-size shrimps. List ingredients needed for marketing: noodles, fish, seasonings, sauce ingredients, etc.

Master Recipe, Sweet Biscuit Dough (p. 204); Fruit Cobbler (p. 206). Note ingredients needed: fruit, sugar, biscuit dough.

List other foods and staples needed; go to market.

Cooking: Cook frozen broccoli, in covered saucepan containing ½ inch hot water plus ½ teaspoon salt, until just tender when tested with fork; don't cook until soft. Chill in covered dish refrigerator, until near dinner time.

Afternoon

About the middle of the afternoon, make fruit cobbler. Have this cooked and out of the oven before beginning to get dinner, since it requires a different temperature than the casserole, which will be in oven at dinnertime.

1¼ Hours before Dinner

Cook ½ package noodles; see Master Recipe (p. 310). Drain them; turn them into buttered baking dish which they will two-thirds fill.

Prepare fish, draining it, removing skin, bones. Break fish into bite-size chunks; mix it with noodles.

Make 2 cups medium white sauce (p. 248), using liquor from can of any fish *except shrimps,* as part of the liquid for the sauce. Add to thickened sauce 1 or 2 teaspoons grated raw onion, and 1 tablespoon minced green pepper. Pour sauce over contents of baking dish. Over sauce, sprinkle thin layer of fine bread or cracker crumbs. On top of crumbs, arrange 8 to 10 dots of butter, size of peas. Place dish in moderate (375°) oven, to bake 30 or more minutes.

While casserole bakes, drain broccoli of water; then "marinate" (p. 333) broccoli in French dressing.

Wash, crisp, and dry greens.

Set table, putting dinner plates to warm. Measure and start coffee.

Arrange marinated broccoli on greens. Mix Russian dressing (p. 353); put dressing over top of broccoli. Store salad in refrigerator until serving time.

If you wish to serve whipped cream on top of cobbler, whip

cream with sugar and flavoring now; see Sweetened Whipped Cream (p. 408). Store in refrigerator until serving time.

As soon as casserole is browned on top, and bubbly, serve. Serve salad at same time.

Ready: Coffee, cobbler.

MENU #27: SATURDAY

Link Sausages
Griddle Cakes
Maple Syrup
Waldorf Salad
Crackers and Cheese
Coffee, Tea or Milk

If you haven't a griddle, you can cook cakes in a large, heavy frying pan.

See note on maple syrup under Menu 22.

A.M. Read

Master Recipe, Griddle Cakes (p. 219). Note ingredients needed, for marketing list. Note also instructions about griddles.

Pan-Broiled Sausages (p. 85). Buy ½ pound for 2 people.

Waldorf Salad (see under Apples in Salad Chart, p. 348). One large, or 2 medium eating apples will make enough for 2 servings.

Sunday menu; add foods needed to marketing list.

¾ Hour before Dinner (This is an easy night!)

Wash greens, put them to crisp.

Peel, core, and dice apple. Crumble nuts. Mix salad ingredients, season; stir in mayonnaise. Dry lettuce; arrange your salads, on separate plates; garnish top of each with dash of paprika for color. Store in refrigerator.

Set table; put dinner plates to warm.

Measure coffee for coffee maker.

Arrange crackers and cheese on serving platter.

20 to 25 Minutes before Dinner

Break link sausages apart; put them in a frying pan; don't cook yet.

If your range does not have a "warming drawer," start oven, now, to slow (250°) so you may have a warm place to store cooked griddle cakes, while cooking more.

Mix griddle cake batter by Master Recipe (p. 219).

Heat griddle to moderately hot. At same time, melt in saucepan about 4 tablespoons vegetable shortening. Have handy a soft, clean brush which you can dip into the melted shortening, then brush over surface of griddle, to grease it. (You must grease griddle before each new lot of cakes is put on it, to cook.)

Using long-handled spoon, put onto griddle batter for first lot of cakes, allowing 1 or 2 tablespoons batter per cake; don't place them too close together; they expand and spread.

While first cakes brown on bottom side, start sausages cooking. Start coffee cooking.

As soon as cakes are browned on underneath side, and puffed and bubbly on top, turn them over, with pancake turner, allowing them to cook similarly on other side. When browned on both sides, they are done. Stack one on top of another, on warm plate, and place in warming drawer or slow oven, to keep warm while you cook more.

Look at sausages; turn if needed.

Grease griddle again; and put on another lot of cakes. Cook as for previous lot.

Watch sausages; when tender and well browned; remove them from heat before they shrink; drain them on paper towel, on a warm plate. If cakes are not ready to serve yet, store sausages in warming drawer or slow oven, until all cakes are ready.

Serve: Sausages, griddle cakes (1 stack per person), maple syrup. Serve salad at same time; apple is very good with pork.

Ready: Coffee, dessert.

MENU #28: SUNDAY

Roast Leg of Lamb, Gravy
Highly Seasoned Rice Ring
Fresh Asparagus
If asparagus is not in season, substitute another green vegetable.
Mint Jelly (if desired)
Hot Rolls (from dough in refrigerator)
Endive
Crumbled Blue Cheese
French Dressing
Coffee Ice Cream (Store)
Macaroons (Store)
Coffee, Tea or Milk

3½ to 4 Hours before Dinner

Estimate time your roast will need, to cook. If 5½ to 8 pounds, allow 30 minutes per pound. If under 5½ pounds, allow 35 minutes per pound. Add up total time, and figure backwards from dinner hour. Put roast in oven about 15 minutes before total roasting time would indicate, to allow time at end, to make gravy.

Read: Basic Principles and Master Recipe for Cooking a Roast (pp. 54–58).

Turn on oven to 325° (moderately slow). Wipe leg of lamb clean with damp cloth; season it generously, all over, with salt, rubbing salt into meat, so it will adhere. If desired, add sprinkling of pepper. If desired, insert slivers of garlic; see (4), Master Recipe, Roasting (p. 57); or fasten ½ peeled raw onion on top of roast with metal skewer, or toothpick. Place roast, fatty side up, on rack, in open roasting pan. Insert tip of a meat thermometer, if you have one, into meatiest part of roast, but not touching fat or bone.

2½ Hours before Dinner

Get out refrigerated roll dough, made under Menu 25. Flour a board; flour hands; punch down dough; see Step 4, Bread and Rolls (p. 226). Knead dough, 1 or 2 minutes. With knife or scissors, cut dough into cubes about ¾ inch square. Between palms of hands, shape each cube of dough into a ball. In separate shallow saucepan, melt 3 or 4 tablespoons butter. Grease cups of muffin pans, with vegetable shortening. Now into each greased muffin cup, fit 3 balls dough. Brush top of each roll generously with melted butter. This makes cloverleaf rolls (p. 229). Cover muffin pans with clean towel; put in warm (85° to 90°) place, until rolls double in bulk, about 1 to 1½ hours. (Refrigerated dough takes longer to rise than dough at room temperature.)

1½ Hours before Dinner

Measure out, and start cooking at once, Master Recipe, Steamed White Rice (p. 305).

Wash fresh asparagus in several waters; it is sometimes sandy. Tie bunch together, if desired, to keep it all in same direction; cut off excess tough white ends. If asparagus is very young and thin, it will cook in about 20 minutes; if older and thick of stalk, it may take 35 to 40 minutes. If possible, have ready for it a deep kettle, in which asparagus may cook *standing up* (tips up); this method cooks the heavier bottom ends of stalks first, and does not overcook the tenderer tips. Start it cooking when needed, in boiling salted water, with pan covered.

Wash endive; crisp it; arrange salad; store in refrigerator.

Put mint jelly in serving dish. Store in refrigerator until serving.

Arrange macaroons on plate; have dessert plates ready.

Measure coffee for coffee maker.

Set table; put dinner plates (also platter for roast and platter for rice ring) to warm.

As soon as rice is done, add seasonings; see highly seasoned rice ring (p. 307); pack rice into buttered ring mold; place mold in shallow pan of hot water, over lowest heat, until serving time.

As soon as roast is done (when cooking time is up, or meat thermometer registers 180°) remove roast from oven. Immediately, turn oven to very hot (450°) to heat quickly for cooking rolls.

Lift roast from roasting pan to warm platter; cover meat with waxed paper, aluminum foil, or other covering, to keep meat warm.

Make gravy (p. 58) from juices in roasting pan. When gravy has been brought to boil, reduce heat; leave it to simmer until needed.

Put rolls in oven.

Start coffee cooking. Get out carving knife and fork.

As soon as rolls begin to turn golden brown on top, unmold rice ring onto warm platter. Put gravy into serving dish, or gravy boat, with ladle. Drain asparagus; put in serving dish. Take up rolls; wrap them loosely in clean linen napkin, to keep warm at table. Serve dinner.

Ready: Salad, coffee. Take up ice cream only when time to eat it.

Glossary of Cooking Terms
and Some Odd Tips

Bake: To cook in oven, by dry heat, the hot air rising from underneath the food and circulating evenly all around it. Use heating unit near floor of oven; see page 7. This method is used for some meats (Chapter XII), and some vegetables (Chapter XXV), as well as for breads, cakes, pies, muffins, biscuits, popovers.

Baste: To spoon hot fat, or other liquid, over food while cooking it, both to keep food moist and to flavor it.

Batter: A combination of flour and other ingredients, including some liquid, beaten together into a smooth mixture moist enough to pour.

Beat: To enclose air by turning ingredients over and over, with rotary beater, electric beater, or mixing spoon. If using spoon, mixture is lifted slightly into air, with each stroke, thus folding air into mixture.

Blanch: To submerge in boiling water for a few minutes, either to loosen skins; see Blanched Almonds (p. 503), or to whiten, or to sterilize for canning.

Blaze: To pour alcoholic liquor (such as brandy) over or around food; then ignite the liquor by holding a match to it. Blaze goes out in a few seconds.

Blend: To mix ingredients until thoroughly combined.

Boil: To cook food in water hot enough to break into bubbles, on surface. (Once water has reached boiling point — 212° F. at sea level — heat may be reduced, and water reduced to very gentle boil; this cooks foods just as fast, without being too strenuous.)

Bone: To remove all bones (as from fish, meat, chicken).

Braise: To brown meat (or sometimes, vegetables) quickly, in hot fat, sealing all surfaces; then to add a small amount of liquid and cook, covered, slowly, until tender. See method under Pot Roast (p. 117).

Bread: To roll or coat food in fine bread crumbs, before cooking.

Broil: To cook rapidly, by dry heat, in oven, underneath the heating unit at roof of oven; see pages 7, 68. This method is used for meats, chicken, some fish, some vegetables. See Chapter VII. Outdoors, broiling is done by cooking on a grill over charcoal or wood fire.

Brush with Fat, or Cream: To dip pastry brush into melted shortening, cream, or whatever is specified; then brush this lightly over top of food.

Caramelize: To melt granulated sugar, very gently, in heavy frying pan, or heavy saucepan, stirring constantly, until it turns into a golden brown syrup.

Caramel Syrup: Caramelize (as above) 1 cup sugar; then add, little by little, ½ cup boiling water. Blend, and simmer 10 minutes.

Chop: To chop, in chopping bowl, or cut with sharp knife, into small bits, about size of peas. (For

speed, meat, onions, and so forth are sometimes run through meat grinder, instead of
being "chopped.")

Coat: To give food an outside "coating" or thin covering of flour, or crumbs, or meal, or other fine-
particled ingredient, as specified in recipe.

Cream: To place room-temperature shortening in a
bowl; then, with back of large mixing spoon,
work at it until shortening becomes soft and
creamy. If sugar is included in mixture, mixture must be creamed until sugar is entirely
dissolved and there is no "grit."

Cube: To cut into cubes of approximately even width,
height, depth. Stew meat is usually cut into
1½ inch cubes; meats or vegetables for casseroles, or salads, or for creamed dishes, are
usually cut to about ¾ inch cubes, or even
smaller.

Cut In: Literally "to cut" (with two knives in crisscross
motion, or with a pastry blender) a solid lump
of shortening, resting in measured flour and
other ingredients, until all shortening is cut to
fine size and all ingredients blended. (This
method is used to avoid "matting" ingredients
with finger tips.)

Dice: Same as Cube, but usually means smaller size,
cutting the solid ingredient to pieces about
size of peas.

Devil: To season highly with tangy flavorings, such
as onion, green pepper, mustard, Worcestershire sauce, perhaps vinegar, or herbs. See
Deviled Eggs (p. 265); Deviled Sauce (p.
249); Deviled Crabs (p. 167).

Dot: To arrange small bits of a substance (like
butter) at intervals, over surface of some food.

Dredge: To coat a solid but moist-surfaced food (like

berries, shellfish, some meats, some vegetables)
with flour, or other specified fine-particled
covering, before cooking. This is often done
by shaking the food in a paper bag which contains the fine-particled coating.

Dust With: To sprinkle very lightly indeed with flour,
sugar, spice, or whatever is specified.

Fillet: (*Noun*) A section of fish, meat, or chicken
from which all bones have been removed.
(*Verb*) To cut flesh of fish, meat, or chicken
from bone, and remove unpleasant skin. *Filet
Mignon.* A small round section of steak, usually 1½ inches thick, cut from the smaller end
of a fillet of beef; very tender, completely free
of skin, bones, and fat; therefore expensive.

Fold In: To add carefully to a thick mixture a more delicate air-filled mixture (such as whipped cream,
stiffly beaten white of egg), without destroy-
ing the lightness of the airy ingredient. To do
this: place air-filled ingredient on top of heavier mixture. With spoon, cut down through
both mixtures, to bottom of bowl; then bring
spoon up at one side of bowl, carrying a little
of the heavy mixture with it. Fold this bit of
heavy mixture over the light mixture. Repeat a
number of times, until both mixtures are
blended. (Never stir, or beat.)

Fricassee: To brown in hot fat; then simmer, covered, in
a liquid containing seasonings. See Fricasseed
Chicken (pp. 121–122).

Fry: To cook food in hot liquid fat, until golden
brown and tender. May be done by 4 methods:
see Deep, or French-Frying (page 108; Pan-
Frying, page 87; Sautéing, page 93; Shallow-
Frying, page 99; Chapter IX.

Grate: To rub a solid food (such as raw onion, carrot,

dry bread) against rough surface of metal "grater," until food is reduced to small particles.

Grill: See To Broil. (A "grilled" steak or chop is a broiled one.)

Grind: To put food through meat grinder, using fine, medium, or large-size blade to cut it to size needed.

Julienne: To cut food into long thin strips, like matchsticks.

Marinate: To let food soak for ½ hour or more in a liquid which will season and flavor it. Red meats and game are sometimes submerged in red wine; fish in white wine; fruits or vegetables intended for salads, in French dressing.

Mince: To chop very fine.

Pan-Broil: To cook with brisk heat, in frying pan, using little or no cooking fat. See Method, page 77, Chapter IX.

Pan-Fry: To cook in frying pan, in small amount of hot cooking fat. See Method, page 87, Chapter IX.

Parboil: Means *partially* boil; that is, boil until *partly* tender.

Pare: Another word for "peel." To remove skin, outer covering.

Poach: To cook gently in water kept *just below* boiling, so that surface of water scarcely moves at all, rather than bubbling hard. The preferred method for eggs, fish, since it does not break them apart.

Preheat: To heat oven to desired temperature *before* food is put in.

Purée: To force soft (usually boiled) fruits or vegetables through a sieve, to make a thick, smooth substance free of lumps, pits, skins.

Roast: To cook uncovered, in oven, using heating unit

beneath food. In old days, roasting was often done on a "spit" over wood or coals.

Sauté: To fry gently, in a small amount of butter or other fat, turning or stirring food frequently to prevent scorching. See Method, page 93, Chapter IX.

Scald Milk: To heat milk in saucepan until you see a fine row of tiny bubbles around edge of pan . . . but *not* until milk actually boils. Scalded milk usually makes a "skin," if left standing.

Score: To cut shallow gashes into surface, as in top of ham which is to be glazed. See page 134.

Sear: To brown in hot pan quickly, cooking all outside surfaces (usually of meat) so that none of the inner juices may thereafter seep out easily.

Shred: To cut into thin strips.

Sift: To put through fine sieve, or sifter.

Simmer: To cook in liquid *just below* boiling point. Small steam bubbles may rise to surface, but surface of water is not agitated by bubbling.

Stew: To simmer gently, covered, until tender, in water to which seasonings are often added. See under Pot Roast (p. 117).

Skewer: (*Noun*) A metal or wooden oversized "pin" used to hold together meat which has been rolled, or to close cavities filled with stuffing, etc. (*Verb*) To fasten in place, or fasten closed, with skewers.

Sliver: To cut into fine thin strips.

Stir: To mix ingredients, with a continuous circular motion of spoon, until well blended (or as long as recipe directs). This is not the same as "beating" or "whipping," since the two latter methods are intended to enfold air, whereas stirring is not.

Stock: The liquor a meat, vegetable, or fish, or

chicken, has been cooked in. This liquor usually contains savory flavor, and nutritional value. All such "stocks" resulting from your everyday cooking should be saved and used in some way, if possible . . . in sauces, aspics, or as broth or soup. See Stock, page 127.

Try Out: To cook gently, in frying pan, a piece of salt pork, or suet, or other meat fat, until the liquid fat has separated from the tissue. Liquid fat may then be used, and tissue discarded.

Whip: To beat rapidly, specifically for purpose of folding in air. Usually done today with rotary or electric beater; used to be done with wire whisk.

ODD TIPS

To Cut Sticky Foods (Marshmallows):   Use wet knife or scissors; wet implement again as often as needed. This prevents food from sticking.

To Melt Chocolate: Place squares of chocolate in saucer, over gently boiling teakettle's top opening. Or place saucer over smaller pan of simmering water. Or place chocolate in top section of double boiler, placed over pan of simmering water. It melts slowly; don't be impatient.

To Obtain Juice and Rind of Orange or Lemon: First, grate off the desired amount of rind; then squeeze out juice. It's very difficult to grate an empty rind.

To Obtain "Onion Juice":   Peel onion; cut it in half. Scrape a knife or spoon across cut surface, pressing against the onion. Juice will drip out. Save remainder of onion to use in other cooking.

To Remove Onion Smell:	Hold hands and knife under running cold water.
To Peel Onions without "Crying":	Peel them under cold water.
To Keep Peeled Potatoes from Turning Dark:	Keep them covered with water, until time to cook.
To Keep Peeled Pears, Peaches, from Turning Dark:	Submerge them in "acidulated water" (1 tablespoon lemon juice or vinegar, mixed into 1 quart water) until time to drain and serve.
To Cut Ice Cream Neatly:	Dip knife in hot water, between each cutting.
To Be Happy in Your Kitchen:	Don't expect yourself to be perfect; no cook ever will be. Just have fun.

Tables of Quick Measurements and Equivalents

The following measuring equivalents are most useful to know, particularly if one of your measuring tools is being used for some other purpose and so is not available; or if you wish to halve, double, to triple a recipe.

GENERAL EQUIVALENTS

A "dash," or pinch	equals	less than $\frac{1}{16}$ tsp.
60 drops		1 tsp.
3 tsp.	equals	1 tbsp. (or $\frac{1}{2}$ fluid oz.)
2 tbsp.		$\frac{1}{8}$ c. (or 1 fluid oz.)
4 tbsp.		$\frac{1}{4}$ c.
8 tbsp.		$\frac{1}{2}$ c.
5 tbsp. plus 1 tsp.		$\frac{1}{3}$ c.
10 tbsp. plus 2 tsp.		$\frac{2}{3}$ c.
12 tbsp.		$\frac{3}{4}$ c.
16 tbsp.		1 c.
$\frac{1}{2}$ c.	equals	1 gill
1 c.		$\frac{1}{2}$ pt.
2 c.		1 pt.
4 c.		1 qt.
4 qt.		1 gal.
8 qt. (dry measure)	equals	1 pk.
4 pk. (dry measure)		1 lb.
16 oz. (dry measure)	equals	1 lb.
4 oz.		$\frac{1}{4}$ lb.

SHORTENING IN BRICK FORM

(Butter, Lard)

1/8 lb. piece	equals	1/4 c. or	4 tbsp.
1/4 lb. "		1/2 c. or	8 tbsp.
1/2 lb. "		1 c. or	16 tbsp.
1 lb. "		2 c.	

SHORTENING SOLD IN BULK

If measuring part of a cup of shortening, the easiest way is to subtract from a total of 1 cup the amount of shortening you need for a recipe. (Let us say this is 1/3 cup). That leaves 2/3 cup. Fill measuring cup 2/3 full of water; then add, in a lump, enough shortening to bring water to a level with the 1 cup mark. This is quicker and simpler than packing shortening tightly down into cup, and later having a greasy cup to wash.

SIZES OF CANS

	Sizes of Cans	*Average Yield*
8 oz. (or "Buffet")	2 11/16" x 2 1/4"	1 cup
"Picnic" (used for soups, some meats, some fruits, or vegetables)	2 11/16" x 4"	1 1/4 c.
No. 1 (Tall can)	3 1/16" x 4 11/16"	2 c.
No. 2	3 7/16" x 4 1/2"	2 1/2 c.
No. 2 1/2	4 1/16" x 4 11/16"	3 1/2 c.
No. 3	4 1/4" x 4 7/8"	4 c.
No. 10	6 3/16" x 6 15/16"	12 c.

MISCELLANEOUS EQUIVALENTS USEFUL TO KNOW IN BUYING STAPLE GOODS

Apricots, dried	1 lb.	equals	about 3 c. uncooked
Butter, or other fat	1 lb.		2 c.
Cheese, American—to grate	1 lb.		about 4 c. grated
Cheese, cottage	1 lb.		2 c.
Cocoa, powdered, uncooked	1 lb.		4 c. powdered
Coffee, in bean, or ground	1 lb.		about 4 1/2 c. bean, or ground
Cornmeal, coarse	1 lb.		3 c.
fine	1 lb.		4 c.
Flour, all-purpose	1 lb.		4 c.
cake	1 lb.		4 1/2 c.
Macaroni, spaghetti, broken	1 lb.		about 5 c. uncooked
Oats, rolled	1 lb.		about 5 1/2 c. uncooked
Prunes, dried	1 lb.		about 2 1/2 c. uncooked

Raisins	1 lb.		about 3 c.
Rice, uncooked	1 lb.		2¼ c.
cooked	½ c.	yields	about 2 c. cooked
Sugar, brown, packed	1 lb.	equals	2¼ c.
Sugar, confectioners'	1 lb.	equals	3½ c.
Sugar, granulated	1 lb.	equals	2¼ c.

DAIRY PRODUCTS

Eggs, whites only	10–12 whites	make	1 c.
yolks only	12–14 yolks	make	1 c.
Milk, evaporated	1 small can	equals	⅔ c.
	1 tall can	equals	1¾ c.
Milk, fresh, bottled	1 qt.	equals	4 c.
Cream, light or heavy	½ pt. (liquid)	equals	1 c. (liquid)
heavy	½ pt. (liquid)	makes	2 c. (whipped)

Table of Substitutions

If, in an emergency, you find yourself lacking some one basic ingredient needed for a recipe, look below: you may find you have something else you can substitute.

For	Substitute
1 c. sifted cake flour	1 c. minus 2 tbsp. sifted all-purpose flour
1 c. sifted all-purpose flour	1 c. plus 2 tbsp. sifted cake flour
1 tsp. baking powder	¼ tsp. baking soda, plus ½ tsp. cream of tartar
1 tbsp. cornstarch (for thickening)	2 tbsp. flour
1 c. bottled milk	½ c. evaporated milk plus ½ c. water or 4 tbsp. dried milk plus 1 c. water
1 c. sweet milk	1 c. sour milk, or 1 c. buttermilk, adding to milk ½ tsp. baking soda, and omitting from recipe ½ the baking powder called for
1 c. sour milk	1 c. sweet milk, into which 1 tbsp. vinegar or lemon juice have been stirred
1 sq. unsweetened chocolate	3 tbsp. powdered cocoa. (If making frosting, or cake or cookie batter, add 1 tbsp. shortening for each 3 tbsp. cocoa; this restores to cocoa the same richness chocolate has.)
1 c. honey	¾ c. sugar, plus ¼ c. extra liquid (increasing whatever liquid your recipe calls for)
1 c. brown sugar, firmly packed	1 c. granulated sugar. (This substitution can be made when *only sweetening* is involved, such as in sweetening pumpkin pie filling, or glazing sweet potatoes. Do not substitute white for brown sugar, however, in any butterscotch-flavored recipes, nor in cake and cookie batters where brown sugar constitutes part of the dark, rich flavor.)

For	*Substitute*
¼ c. melted shortening	¼ c. bland salad oil
1 c. butter	1 c. margarine
1 c. butter or margarine * or ⅔ c. vegetable shortening	⅔ c. chicken fat. (Where chickens are plentiful, chicken fat is often substituted for other shortening to make cake, cookies, cornbread, muffins. It is excellent in batters of spicy or other pronounced flavor, but in very delicate-flavored cakes the chicken fat may "taste.")

* Butter and margarine contain a higher percentage of water than vegetable shortening. Chicken fat has a consistency nearer that of vegetable shortening.

INDEX

Index